NATURAL HISTORY
OF THE
WHITE-INYO RANGE
EASTERN CALIFORNIA

D1602895

California Natural History Guides: 55

NATURAL HISTORY
OF THE
WHITE-INYO RANGE

EASTERN CALIFORNIA

EDITED BY

Clarence A. Hall, Jr.

Director, White Mountain Research Station
University of California

University of California Press

Berkeley • Los Angeles • Oxford

CALIFORNIA NATURAL HISTORY GUIDES
Arthur C. Smith, *General Editor*

Advisory Editorial Committee:
Raymond F. Dasmann
Mary Lee Jefferds
Don MacNeill
Robert Ornduff
Robert C. Stebbins

University of California Press
Berkeley and Los Angeles, California
University of California Press, Ltd.
Oxford, England

Copyright © 1991 by
The Regents of the University of California

Library of Congress Cataloging-in-Publication Data

Natural history of the White-Inyo Range, eastern California / edited
by Clarence A. Hall, Jr.
    p.   cm. – (California natural history guides ; 55)
  Includes bibliographical references and index.
  ISBN 0-520-06895-5 (cloth). – ISBN 0-520-06896-3 (paper)
  1. Natural history–California–Inyo Mountains. 2. Natural
history–White Mountains (Calif. and Nev.) 3. Inyo Mountains
(Calif.) 4. White Mountains (Calif. and Nev.) I. Hall, Clarence A.
II. Series.
QH105.C2N39   1991
508.794'87–dc20   91-12968
                                                             CIP

Printed in the United States of America
9 8 7 6 5 4 3 2 1

The paper used in this publication meets the minimum
requirements of American National Standard
for Information Sciences—
Permanence of Paper for Printed Library Materials,
ANSI Z39.48-1984. ∞

Contributors

Archaeology

Robert L. Bettinger
Department of Anthropology
University of California, Davis

Climatology/Meteorology

Harold E. Klieforth
Desert Research Institute
Reno, Nevada

Douglas R. Powell
Department of Geography
University of California, Berkeley

Entomology

Derham Giuliani
Big Pine, California

John Smiley
University of California
Big Creek Reserve
Big Sur

Flora

Mary DeDecker
Independence, California

Timothy P. Spira
Department of Botany
Ohio State University

Geology

W. G. Ernst*
Clarence A. Hall, Jr.
Clemens A. Nelson
Department of Earth and Space Sciences
University of California, Los Angeles

Geomorphology

Deborah L. Elliott-Fisk
Department of Geography
University of California, Davis

Herpetology

J. Robert Macey
Theodore J. Papenfuss
Museum of Vertebrate Zoology
University of California, Berkeley

Ichthyology

Edwin P. Pister
State of California
Department of Fish and Game

Mammology

Hannah V. Carey
Department of Physiology
College of Medicine
Ohio State University

John D. Wehausen
Bishop, California

Ornithology

Carla Cicero
Ned K. Johnson
Museum of Vertebrate Zoology
University of California, Berkeley

Trees

Deborah L. Elliott-Fisk
Ann M. Peterson
Department of Geography
University of California, Davis

* W. G. Ernst is now at Stanford School
of Earth Sciences, Stanford University.

Contents

PART IV

ARCHAEOLOGY AND ANTHROPOLOGY   461

Preface

This guide to the natural history of the White-Inyo Range is designed to acquaint people with the anthropology, archaeology, geology, geomorphology, and meteorology of a part of eastern California and to aid in the identification of animals and plants in a region largely within Mono and Inyo counties near the California-Nevada border. Because each year more than one thousand faculty and students from universities and governmental organizations use the facilities of the University of California's White Mountain Research Station, and more than 40,000 people visit the Ancient Bristlecone Pine Forest in the White Mountains annually, it was clear to me in 1980 that there was a need for a natural history guide of the area. Experts in a variety of fields were asked to contribute to a guidebook for the White-Inyo Range; what follows is the result of their enthusiastic efforts. Those who have contributed to this guidebook wish to share with the reader and visitors to the region information that will allow for a fuller understanding and appreciation of the majesty and spirit of the beautiful White Mountains, with their local lonely areas, moonscape-like, arctic desert appearance, and dizzying heights.

The region is approximately equidistant from Los Angeles and San Francisco; east of the Sierra Nevada, the Owens Valley, and the towns of Bishop, Big Pine, Independence, and Lone Pine; and within the Inyo National Forest. The White Mountains are in the southwestern corner of the Great Basin and north of the Inyo Floristic region. This is one of the highest desert mountain ranges in North America and includes the largest expanse of rare Alpine Steppe or Tundra in the far western United States.

Special emphasis is given to the natural history of the general region north of Westgard Pass (Fig. I.1). Early researchers and inhabitants of the region either referred to both the White and Inyo mountains as simply the White Mountains or called the entire range the Inyo Mountains, with general agreement that the boundary between the White and Inyo Mountains is arbitrary. A division between the White and Inyo mountains can be made on the basis of the occurrence of alpine zones in the range. The alpine zones of the White Mountains (i.e., above 9,600 ft, or 2,930 m) extend in a narrow band roughly from Westgard Pass in the south to north of Montgomery Peak in the north. However, because the range of many animals and plants and the geology of the White Mountains are not bounded or limited by Westgard Pass, but extend south of this low pass — used by students of the area to separate the White from the Inyo mountains — we have included some of the natural history of the Inyo Mountains in the guidebook. For convenience we have referred to the region included in the guidebook as the White-Inyo Range.

The White Mountains are apparently named after White Mountain Peak, and some authorities believe that White Mountain Peak was so named either because of the long-lasting snow on the sides of the peak or because of the "white dolomite" (a calcium-magnesium carbonate rock) that they believe makes up the peak. In fact,

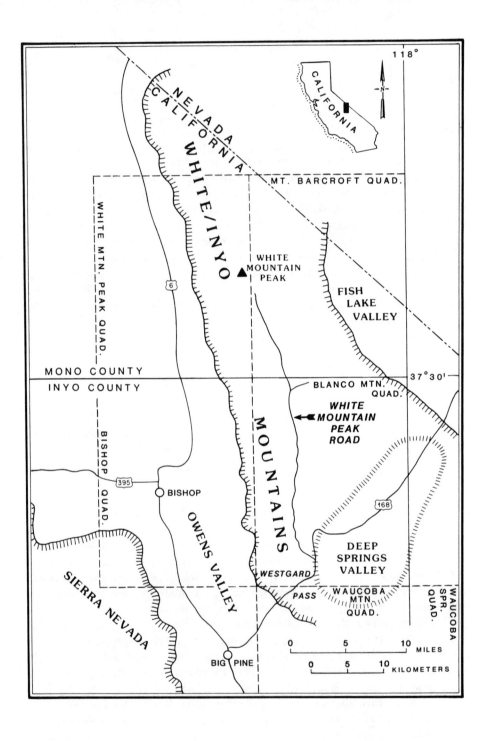

the peak consists of reddish-brown, black, and locally white metamorphosed volcanic rocks, approximately 152 million years old, and not the sedimentary rock called dolomite; the peak is not white unless covered with snow.

The term *Inyo* has been translated from Paiute as "the dwelling place of a great spirit." It seems to be a fitting translation, particularly if one considers the reverence in which the region is held by laypersons, scientists, and the regional inhabitants who know and visit the White and Inyo mountains.

Over 1,000 native species and varieties of plants have been recognized in the White Mountains, and over 34,500 native species and varieties of plants are known from the Inyo Floristic region. More than 450 of the plant species in the Inyo Floristic region do not extend into the large California Floristic Province to the west, and 200 of these do not occur elsewhere in California. The flora of the White Mountains has close affinities to that of the Great Basin region and was apparently enriched during the Pleistocene (Ice Age) with many boreal (alpine) taxa (i.e., genera, species, and varieties) from the Sierra Nevada. The Inyo Floristic region includes a rich transmontane flora and is mainly distinctive owing to the flora from the high mountain ranges. Because of the unusual nature of the flora of the White-Inyo mountains, and because it is this feature of the natural history of the region that may be of greatest interest to most visitors to the region, special emphasis has been given to it in the guidebook.

The introductory section provides a brief synopsis of some elements of the history and natural history of the White-Inyo Range. It is followed by chapters on the physical setting of the region, addressing such topics as the geology, geomorphology, and meteorology. There is a section on plant communities including two chapters on plants—one on the grasses, wildflowers, and shrubs (~ 340 taxa, of the 1078 in the region, are considered) and the other on the trees (16 taxa) of the White-Inyo Range. The chapters on animals include the insects (113 taxa), fishes (4 taxa), amphibians (8 taxa), reptiles (37 taxa), birds (85 taxa), and mammals (45 taxa) of the region. The last section of the book is a chapter on the archaeology and anthropology or human occupancy of the mountains.

Because of space limitations, it is not possible to provide information on every plant or animal known in the White-Inyo Range, so only those of common occurrence that are readily identified have been included. Each account of a plant or animal states the common name and the two-part scientific name (genus and species), which is in italics. When there is more than one common name, or if a scientific name is no longer acceptable but is well entrenched in the older literature, these additional names are included. The guidebook contains descriptions of more than 650 taxa, species, subspecies, and varieties (most of which are illustrated); distribution maps; generalized geologic maps; and selected road logs.

Acknowledgements

The Editor wishes to acknowledge the continued support of the White Mountain Research Station in developing this natural history handbook and to offer special thanks to Donna Young, Vicki Doyle-Jones, Leticia Sanchez, and Barbara Widawski for their patience and diligence during the coordination, compilation, and writing of the natural history guide over a period of several years.

The Editor and authors thank Tracey Storer, Robert Usinger, and the University of California Press for the reproduction of some figures in *Sierra Nevada Natural History*. This now-classic handbook served as a model for our volume on the natural history of the White-Inyo Range. The authors of the chapter on insects would like to thank Gordon Marsh of the Museum of Systematic Biology, University of California, Irvine, for the identification of insects and general advice; Nathan Rank for arranging and photographing the butterfly illustrations; and J. Donahue and the County Museum of Los Angeles for the loan of butterfly specimens for making photographic plates. The authors of the chapter on mammals acknowledge James Patton of the Museum of Vertebrate Zoology of the University of California, Berkeley, for his comments on the draft of the chapter, and David M. Lee for his illustrations of the mammals.

Partial financial support for the field work related to the chapters on amphibians and reptiles was provided by the Environmental Field Program, University of California at Santa Cruz, and the Wilhelm Martens Fund of the Museum of Vertebrate Zoology, University of California, Berkeley. Ben Ashworth of Independence and Richard Moss of Cinnamon Ranch, Hammil Valley, kindly allowed the authors to conduct field work on their ranches. Randy Benthin, Charles Brown, Chip Emerson, Jeramy Liu, Jay Martin, Sean Nakamura, Nancy Staub, David B. Wake, Tom Wake, and Darrell Wong assisted the authors. Derham Giuliani of Big Pine, Phil Pister of the California Department of Fish and Game in Bishop, and Lee Silvernale of Independence provided valuable information on the distribution of some of the species of amphibians and reptiles. Margaret Fusari, Harry Greene, Anne Macey, Robert I Macey, Kenneth Norris, Robert J. Trentmann, and David B. Wake provided valuable comments on the chapter.

Clarence A. Hall, Jr., Editor

Introduction

REGIONAL SETTING

The White-Inyo Range is approximately 110 mi (178 km) long and consists of mountains that rise from valleys to the east and west. The range is located at the interface of two major physiographic provinces: the Pacific-influenced Sierra-Nevada Cascade Province and the arid Basin and Range Province. The mountains at the lower elevations, near 4,000 ft (1,220 m), are dotted with Great Basin Sage, and the mountains rise to elevations of more than 14,000 ft (4,400 m) and the Alpine Steppe. The rise is an abrupt one, occurring sharply over a 12 mi (20 km) linear distance. There is close proximity to the Sierra Nevada to the west, but there are closer biologic ties with the plants and animals of the Basin and Range Province.

The White-Inyo Range expresses moderate geologic diversity (e.g., granitic rocks, basalt, metavolcanic rocks, and weakly to moderately metamorphosed sandstone, shale, limestone, and dolomite) and great topographic diversity. The range consists of complexly folded and faulted rocks, some more than 600 million years old, that lie in a triangular, fault-bounded block. The block rises abruptly on the west above the active White Mountain fault zone fronting the range, along which occurred the 1986 Chalfant Valley Earthquake. The block is more gently inclined to the east. The presence of different types of rock results in striking constrasts in landscape color and form, and the gentle rolling topography of parts of the crest of the range contrasts sharply with the steeply inclined and deeply dissected slopes.

The climate of the range is characterized by cold, dry weather. The average maximum–minimum temperature ranges are from $\sim 70°F$ (21°C) to 37°F ($\sim$ 3°C), at the base of the range near Bishop, and from 36°F (2°C) to $-26°F$ ($-32°C$) recorded at the Barcroft facilities of the White Mountain Research Station in the Alpine Zone. Precipitation averages from 4 in (10 cm) at the base of the range to 20 in (50 cm), largely as snow, along its crest. Local variation in precipitation and runoff is strongly influenced by topography. The winds at the crest of the range are persistent and frequently strong during both summer and winter. Thunder and lightning storms can be hazardous to hikers in the high country, and a hike to White Mountain Peak in a thunderstorm is strongly discouraged.

Soil quality is poor in the White-Inyo Range, and soil development is slowest in the alpine zones. The White-Inyo Range, with its high elevation and special climate, is a rare and fragile environment. Rapid changes in elevation are associated with abrupt changes in habitats and species, which enhances the area as a scientific research region. The short growing season results in limited plant productivity in a given year. As a result of the thin soil and sparse and delicate vegetation, recovery from disturbance is very slow, estimated to be more than 100 years; thus, this is an area demanding diligent preservation.

MODERN MAN IN THE WHITE MOUNTAINS

Livestock was introduced into the Owens Valley in 1861, and prospectors were working on the east side of the White Mountains the same year. There were hostilities between native Americans and American settlers during the years from 1862 to 1865. As a consequence, many immigrants and native Americans were killed, and, ultimately, more than 800 native Americans were force-marched hundreds of miles to Fort Tejon, south of Bakersfield. The stirring and interesting accounts of the history of the region by Willie Arthur Chalfant (1933, reprinted 1980) provide sobering reminders of the immoral behavior of the early settlers of the region. Little is known about the early ranching of the area, principally during the 1870s, except that at one time more than 40,000 sheep overgrazed the high meadows and plateaus of what is now the Inyo National Forest. In 1907 grazing regulations were established, and hostilities occurred, this time between angry ranchers and the U.S. Forest Service; and in 1909 the Army was called in to quell the range war. It was not until 1931 that the U.S. Forest Service achieved full control of the White Mountains. Only limited portions of the crest zone are satisfactory or usable livestock range today; however, eight range allotments currently divide the entire White Mountains among four active cattle ranches. The allotments carry only a few to approximately 300 head. The presence of livestock in the sensitive alpine zones is in conflict with those interested in the preservation of the fragile environment and scientific research.

In 1948 the U.S. Navy sought a location to test infrared sensors and chose a site at Crooked Creek; in 1949 an installation was erected. In 1950 the U.S. Navy authorized the University of California to operate the Crooked Creek facilities as a research center, and in 1978 the Navy transferred title of all facilities and equipment to the University of California's White Mountain Research Station.

White Mountain Research Station, with its principal office located in the Owens Valley near Bishop, was established in 1950 to provide laboratory facilities for any qualified research investigator wishing to utilize the high-mountain environment for his or her work, and to serve as teaching facilities for field courses conducted in the region. There are four separate laboratory sites: one in the Owens Valley; a second at Crooked Creek, at an elevation of approximately 10,000 ft (2,090 m); a third at the base of Mt. Barcroft, at an approximate elevation of 12,500 ft (3,801 m), making it the 11th highest high-altitude station in the world and the fourth highest in North America; and a fourth, the Summit Laboratory, atop White Mountain Peak, at an elevation of 14,246 ft (4,340 m). The Summit Laboratory is the fourth highest high-altitude research facility in the world and the highest in North America.

The establishment of the University of California's facilities in the area marked the beginning of two independent lines of scientific interest: (1) astronomy and astrophysics, with a need for observatory sites that could provide the best infrared telescopic seeing conditions and a minimum of atmospheric interference; and (2) biology, with the need for protection from harsh climatic conditions while studies of the ecology of the high-altitude environment and physiological processes related to reduced oxygen levels at high elevations are under way. These types of work continue today and have been augmented by other studies, such as geology, geomorphology, archaeology, dendrochronology, and a wealth of biologic studies that include predator/prey relationships, dietary studies, the cardiovascular system, speciation, plant genetics, and metabolism, among many others. Since 1950, over 750 technical papers, books, and theses have been published by those associated with White Mountain Research Station.

The panoramic views of the Sierra Nevada and the Ancient Bristlecone Pine Forest are the principal attractions for tourists, and recreational use of the White-Inyo Range is light because of lack of water. Camping is limited to the U.S. Forest Service's Grandview Campground, which is a dry camp and is thus only used by water-carrying visitors. Recreational pressures will probably continue to increase, however, and this will surely affect the White Mountains and may conflict with the concept of a wilderness area to preserve the fragile lands and animals, such as the White Mountain Bighorn Sheep. The interests of man—grazing, mining, scientific research, the local economy, preservation of endangered species, and recreation in the White Mountains—will doubtless be in conflict and represent sensitive issues; these will continue to require careful study.

The interested visitor may wish to learn more about the region and is directed to the following sources (see also references at the ends of chapters):

Cain, Ella M. 1961. *The story of early Mono County, its settlers, gold rushes, Indians, ghost towns.* Fearon Publishers, San Francisco (out of print).

Chalfant, Willie Arthur. 1933 (reprinted and revised 1980). *The story of Inyo,* Chalfant Press, Bishop.

Leadabrand, Russ. 1973. *Exploring California byways. VI. Owens Valley: Trips for a day or a week.* Ward Ritchie Press, Los Angeles.

Lloyd, Robert M. and Richard S. Mitchell. 1973. *A flora of the White Mountains, California and Nevada.* University of California Press, Berkeley.

Rinehart, Dean, Elden Vestal, Bettie E. Willard, edited by Genny Smith. 1989. *Mammoth Lakes Sierra: A handbook for roadside and trail.* Genny Smith Books, Mammoth Lakes.

Schumacher, Genny. 1969. *Deepest valley: Guide to Owens Valley and its mountains, lakes, roadsides and trails.* Wilderness Press, Berkeley (out of print, but a new edition is planned by Genny Schumacher Smith).

PART I

PHYSICAL FEATURES

1

Weather and Climate

Douglas R. Powell and Harold E. Klieforth

INTRODUCTION

The highest range of the many mountain ranges that are arranged *en echelon* in the Great Basin between the Sierra Nevada and the Wasatch Mountains is the White Mountains, situated along the California-Nevada border about 225 mi (362 km) east of the Pacific Coast. Climatically, this location is transitional between the moderating maritime influence of the Pacific Ocean and the more extreme continental influence of interior North America. The very large variation in elevation within the range, from 4,000–5,000 ft (1,200–1,500 m) at the base to 14,246 ft (4,343 m) at the summit, results in rapid and significant changes in temperature and precipitation within short horizontal distances. Any air mass reaching the White Mountains must pass over an assemblage of other ranges that vary in width and altitude. By far the most important of these mountain barriers is the equally high Sierra Nevada, lying immediately to the west, which, by inducing air to rise, clouds to form, and precipitation to fall, intercepts some of the moisture from Pacific storms in the winter half of the year. To the north, east, and south are a series of lower ranges that have lesser climatic influence. Topographically, the least impeded avenue of approach for an air mass is from the southeast, but significant movement of air from this direction is uncommon. When it does occur, normally in July or August, the result may be spectacular thunderstorms with high precipitation intensities.

ATMOSPHERIC CIRCULATION PATTERNS

Unlike other features of the physical environment, the gases that constitute the atmosphere are invisible, so that it is necessary to use indirect means to describe graphically and to map continuously changing atmospheric conditions. Atmospheric motions are complex, but when studied they are found to follow patterns. To understand the weather regimes of the White-Inyo mountains, it is helpful to recognize three principal scales of motion, each roughly an order of magnitude greater than the next.

The first and largest of these is the *synoptic scale*, so called because it is analyzed from numerous soundings, measurements, and observations made at the same time at hundreds of locations around the world. This is the scale of the familiar weather maps seen in daily newspapers and on television. These surface and upper-air charts cover horizontal distances of 100 to 2,000 mi (160 to 3,200 km) and depict such features as low- and high-pressure areas, cyclones, and anticyclones, air masses, weather fronts, and regions of precipitation. Generally, these features progress in a predictable manner,

3

and from them it is possible to produce, by computerized prediction models, future patterns of airflow, moisture, temperature, clouds, and precipitation. These are used to forecast, with varying degrees of certainty, weather conditions for a particular region for a few days following receipt of the climatic data.

The second scale of atmospheric motion, the *mesoscale*, describes airflow patterns over distances of, say, 1 to 100 mi (or 1.6 to 150 km), a range that includes many of the spectacular cloud formations and weather conditions experienced in and near the mountains of eastern California (Plates 1.1–1.8). These phenomena are closely related to the synoptic flow patterns but are controlled and shaped by major terrain features such as the Sierra Nevada and the White-Inyo Range.

The third scale, the *toposcale*, applies to weather and climatic conditions within a distance of, say, 1 mi (1.6 km) that vary in relation to prominent features shown on local (15-minute or 7.5-minute series) topographic maps. Thus, under differing synoptic and mesoscale conditions different air temperatures, wind velocities, and snow accumulations are measured, whether the location is on a mountain ridge or in a canyon, on a windward or leeward slope, or in a broad valley.

In the sections that follow we discuss the principal patterns that affect the White-Inyo Range, its inhabitants, and its visitors in each of these different scales. We begin with a survey of synoptic-scale airflow and its relation to seasonal weather.

SYNOPTIC-SCALE CIRCULATION

Weather Regimes

Figure 1.1 shows the principal airflow patterns and air-mass types or source regions that determine regional weather in different seasons of the year. The arrows indicate the directions of air movement near and above the crest of the major mountain ranges, at levels between 10,000 and 20,000 ft (3 to 6 km) above sea level. The open circles are locations from which twice-daily (near 4 A.M. and 4 P.M. PST) rawinsonde balloon ascents are made to obtain data on air temperature, humidity, and wind velocity, from which upper-air (e.g., 500 mb) weather maps are plotted and analyzed. The black circle indicates the location of the Bishop Airport, the nearest (3 mi, or 5 km) National Weather Service station to the White-Inyo Range.

The air that flows across California at any time of year is most likely to have passed over some part of the Pacific Ocean. In summer the Pacific Anticyclone (a large, slow-moving clockwise whirl of air) lies just west of California, bringing an onshore flow of cool marine air, stratus clouds, and fog to the coast and mostly clear, dry air to the Sierra and White-Inyo Range. During much of the summer the Great Basin Anticyclone develops over the warm plateau region of Nevada and Utah. When this whirl expands and shifts westward, a flow of moist maritime tropical air from the Gulf of California or the Gulf of Mexico may persist for a few days before the normally dry Pacific flow reasserts itself. Thus, during the summer season the mountainous terrain of eastern California and western Nevada is contested for by two air masses, with that from the northern or central Pacific usually prevailing.

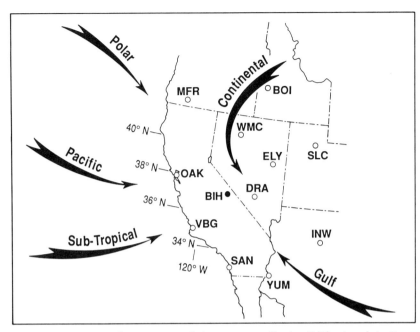

FIGURE 1.1   Major airflow patterns and air mass types affecting California and the Great Basin. Rawinsonde stations shown are:

MFR	Medford, OR	DRA	Desert Rock, NV
OAK	Oakland, CA	BOI	Boise, ID
VBG	Vandenburg AFB, CA	SLC	Salt Lake City, UT
SAN	San Diego, CA	INW	Winslow, AZ
WMC	Winnemucca, NV	YUM	Yuma, AZ
ELY	Ely, NV	BIH	Bishop, CA
			(surface observations only)

During fall, winter, and spring a series of traveling upper-air troughs (cyclonic bends with counterclockwise flow) and ridges (anticyclonic bends with clockwise flow) cross California and Nevada. Ridges and anticyclones usually bring subsiding air, few clouds, and "fair" weather, whereas the troughs and associated cyclones, low-pressure centers, and fronts bring much cloudiness and widespread precipitation. Fronts are boundaries between converging air masses from different source regions. The primary air masses affecting California are cold maritime polar air from the Gulf of Alaska and warmer, moist maritime subtropical air from lower latitudes. Occasionally there are invasions of cold continental polar air from northern Canada or the Rocky Mountains.

Seasonal Storms

Cloud formation and precipitation result primarily from ascending motion in moist air. When air rises, it expands and cools. This causes its invisible water vapor to condense, forming small cloud droplets. As the ascending motion continues, the clouds thicken and the droplets grow larger to form raindrops. If it is sufficiently below freezing (32°F, or 0°C), snow crystals form, which, when heavy enough, fall from the clouds and reach the ground as rain or snow. The precipitation that falls on the mountains each year is a result of four principal mechanisms of upward-moving air: general ascent produced by widespread horizontal convergence in cyclonic flow, more intense lifting in frontal zones, strong "orographic," or terrain-induced, lifting over the windward slopes of mountains, and thermal convective instability triggered by the ascending motion, which causes the cloud to billow upward and precipitate with greater intensity. Although heavy precipitation (40 to 80 in or 100 to 200 cm of water annually) falls on the upper western slope of the Sierra, the region immediately leeward, including the Owens Valley, the White-Inyo Range, and much of western Nevada, is in the so-called rain shadow of the Sierra and receives much less precipitation. The drying of the air results from both the loss of moisture due to precipitation on the windward slope and the adiabatic warming induced by descent over the leeward slope.

Cold fronts, moving in such a way that cold air replaces warmer air at the surface, usually approach from the northwest or the west. Before the passage of the front and its lagging upper-air trough, the airflow across the mountains is from the west or southwest, while surface winds in the valleys and basins are mild and from the south. After frontal passage the upper flow becomes northwesterly to northerly, and cold northerly to northeasterly winds sweep across the mountain ridges and along the valleys. The Sierra Nevada has a profound effect on most fronts, causing them to stall west of the crest while their northern sectors move more rapidly across Oregon and then southward over northern Nevada. Thus, many fronts converge on the Sierra Nevada and White-Inyo Range in nutcracker fashion, with the cold air reaching the leeward valleys and basins from the north before the cold air from the west can surmount the High Sierra.

When a surface low-pressure center forms in western Nevada accompanied by an upper trough that deepens excessively to form a cyclone over the region—a weather pattern known locally as a "Tonopah low"—a northeasterly to southeasterly flow often brings continental polar air or recycled maritime polar air, low clouds, and snowfall to the White-Inyo Range. When such storms involve moist Pacific air, they usually bring heavy snowfall to the region; some of the biggest snowstorms recorded in the White Mountains have occurred in such circulation patterns. Precipitation from closed cyclones over the region is most frequent in spring, resulting in a spring (April or May) precipitation maximum in much of the Great Basin, in contrast to the pronounced winter maximum in the Sierra Nevada.

On infrequent occasions, usually several years apart (e.g., January 1937, January 1949, December 1972, February 1989, and December 1990), a long northerly fetch of air may bring an invasion of true Arctic air from interior Alaska or the Yukon. These episodes bring record cold temperatures to the White-Inyo Range and adjacent valleys; at such times minimum temperatures may dip to −25°F (−31°C) or below.

Most winters include one or two episodes of "warm storms," periods of a few to several days in which very moist tropical air reaches California from the vicinity of Hawaii. In these events the freezing level may be above 10,000 ft (3,000 m), and the heavy rainfall may result in widespread flooding in much of California. It is during such storms that heavy rime icing may form on trees, structures, and power lines on high mountain ridges. This is caused by the combined effect of strong winds and supercooled clouds (composed of water droplets at air temperatures below freezing). The cloud droplets freeze on contact, building great formations of ice that grow into the direction of the wind.

Conversely, "cold storms" bring snow to low elevations, including the floor of Owen Valley and desert areas to the south and east of the White-Inyo Range. Major westerly storms that last for two or three days bring heavy accumulations of snow—a foot (30 cm) or more in the valleys, and two or three times as much at the highest elevations. Very cold storms from the northwest contain less water vapor, are of shorter duration, and usually bring only a few inches (several centimeters) of snow.

MESOSCALE PHENOMENA

Mountain Lee Waves

When a cold front approaches California from the northwest and the westerly airflow increases in speed over the Sierra crest, spectacular "stationary" clouds are usually seen over the leeward valleys. These are manifestations of a mountain lee wave, as it is known (Fig. 1.2). If the ridges and troughs of the horizontal airflow pattern are likened to the bends or meanders of a stream, the lee wave phenomena are analogous to the falls and ripples. Figure 1.3 shows a typical pattern of airflow and cloud forms in a strong lee wave. Air flowing over the Sierra Nevada plunges downward, then upward, and then downward again in a series of crests and troughs. The wavelength depends on the airflow characteristics, mainly the variation of air temperature with height (lapse rate) and the increase of wind speed with height (wind shear). The amplitude is greatest in strong waves and in cases where the vertical flow pattern is in resonance with the terrain, as, for example, when the second wave crest lies over the next mountain range downwind, such as the White-Inyo mountains, east of Owens Valley.

Updrafts and downdrafts in a strong lee wave often have speeds of 2,000 ft (600 m) per minute, sometimes exceeding 4,000 ft (1,200 m) per minute. Where the air descends, it warms, and the relative humidity decreases. The warm, dry winds, which may reach speeds of 60 mph (30 m/s) or greater at the surface, are known as foehn winds. The stratocumulus cloud deck over the Sierra Nevada is called a foehn-wall or cap cloud, and its downslope extension is known as a cloudfall. After it evaporates, the invisible moisture is cooled again in the ascending current and forms the turbulent cumuliform roll cloud. Looking at the roll cloud, an observer has the impression that it is rotating, but this is an illusion caused by the wind shear. However, below the roll cloud there is commonly a true rotor circulation, which brings easterly winds at

FIGURE 1.2   Sailplane in 4,000 ft/min (20 m/s) updraft en route to 40,000 ft (12,200 m) over Owens Valley. The view is from the towplane at 15,000 ft (4,570 m) on 18 December 1951 at 14:47 PST. The windward sides of the roll cloud and high lenticular clouds are seen in the center. At the lower right, a "cloud fall" descends the steep leeward slope of the High Sierra, and at the lower left can be seen blowing dust from Owens (dry) Lake. At about this time a Greyhound bus was blown off Highway 395 near Lone Pine.

the surface. On rare occasions a very strong lee wave will be in resonance with the terrain so that the first wave crest lies over the White-Inyo Range.

Above the roll cloud, there may be one layer or several decks of smooth, lens-shaped altocumulus clouds which appear stationary but through which the air is passing at 50–100 mph (22–45 m/s); the cloud droplets form at the windward edge and evaporate at the leeward edge. Soaring pilots make use of a mountain lee wave by flying into the wind and ascending in the updraft zone. In Figure 1.3 the dotted line shows a typical path of a sailplane: a line of flight under the roll cloud during airplane tow, release point at "x," and then a line of flight upward. Several flights above altitudes of 40,000 ft (12,000 m) have been made in lee waves by pilots equipped with oxygen to survive the low pressure (200 to 150 mb) and with warm clothing to withstand the cold temperatures ($-94°F$ or $-70°C$).

Wave clouds may appear in any month of the year, but they are most often seen in late winter and in spring. They usually reach their maximum development in

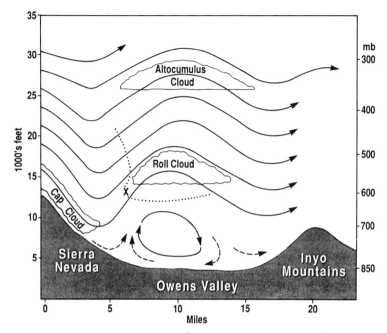

FIGURE 1.3   Vertical cross section of Sierra lee wave showing airflow pattern and cloud forms.

midafternoon and are most beautiful at sunset, when the highest clouds, at 30,000–40,000 ft (9,000–12,000 m), remain colorful long after the sunlight has left the leeward valley.

A local wind of another sort may sometimes be observed by motorists in the winter season in the Owens Valley near Olancha. During strong lee wave conditions or the passage of a cold front, a great horizontal cyclonic eddy may develop about Owens (dry) Lake; there will be a northerly (i.e., from the north) wind along the route of Highway 395 but, as evidenced by blowing dust, a southerly wind on the east side toward Keeler. When the surface flow is southerly in Owens Valley, the dust from Owens Lake may be carried far north of Bishop, lowering visibility so that the mountains are nearly obscured, and the alkali dust is sometimes tasted by pilots flying at 12,000 ft (3,600 m)! Similar phenomena occur in other arid basins of California and Nevada.

Thunderstorms

At any time from early May to early October, there may be an incursion of tropical air from the south; then thunderstorms are possible. The intense heating of the arid Southwest during the summer months creates the upper-air anticyclone and surface low-pressure area that provide the circulation necessary for the northward flow of tropical air. In eastern California and Nevada, this summer monsoon is best developed during the period from early July to late August.

At first, the moisture enters the area at the high levels, and a thundery spell is commonly heralded by the appearance of rather exotic cirrus clouds from the south quadrant. Within a day or two, if the flow persists, the air at middle and low levels is also moist, and daily thundershowers can occur. These are strongly diurnal in their development; that is, they develop as a result of the daily heating of the mountain slopes by the sun, and they decline after sunset.

The appearance of patchy, turreted altocumulus clouds at sunrise is a good indication of possible thunderstorms later in the day. Heating of the rocky mountain slopes causes the air to rise toward the crests, and soon cumulus clouds form above these upslope currents. The clouds continue to rise upward, becoming what the weather observer calls towering cumulus. Near midday their tops develop a fibrous appearance indicative of ice crystal formation, and they are said to be glaciated. Soon they develop anvil-shaped cirrus tops with streamers of ice clouds stretching downwind at those levels (30,000–40,000 ft, or 9,000–12,000 m). At this time, lightning flashes from cloud to mountain and heavy local showers of rain and, commonly, *graupel*, or pea-sized hail, fall on the crests and ridges of the ranges. By this time hikers and climbers should have taken shelter.

Later, as downdrafts of cool air predominate, the thunderstorm ceases, and as the sky brightens to the west, the clouds begin to thicken over the leeward valley, where the day-long heating has created rising thermal currents. Often at 5:00 P.M. or 6:00 P.M. PST a brief thundershower is experienced in valley locations. As the shower moves eastward and the lowering sun in the west shines on the dark cloud and rain shafts, a brilliant rainbow is visible. Finally, when the sky has cleared and stars have appeared, lightning might continue to flash in the east if a nocturnal storm continues over central Nevada.

During some summers there are numerous thunderstorms, as in 1955, 1956, 1967, 1976, 1983, and 1984; in other years there are very few. It is difficult to predict exactly where the storms will occur, as this depends on subtle differences in wind velocity, amount of moisture, rate of growth, and topography. In the morning hours, the eastern slopes of the mountains are heated, the warm currents rise, and an easterly upslope wind forms in the valleys. If the upper synoptic flow has an easterly component, the clouds will develop even more rapidly. In the afternoon, the western slopes of the mountains are heated more effectively by the sun, and, especially if aided by a westerly breeze, the cloud development intensifies there. Once the cloud has formed, latent heat is released, which increases the cloud's buoyancy and causes it to rise more vigorously. Because these storms are so localized, commonly affecting a single canyon, intense cloudbursts may cause flash floods. These commonly occur when cloud bases are below the mountain tops. Such events often go unobserved in the Inyo Mountains and remote Nevada ranges and are discovered some days or weeks later. The damage is usually greater there, though, because roads commonly follow the canyons and washes.

As a general rule, it does not rain on summer nights in the mountains, but there are exceptions. Occasionally, the remnants of tropical storms called "easterly waves" are carried northward along the Sierra and over much of Nevada. The cloudiness is general, and precipitation may be widespread, continuing at night and commonly accompanied by low clouds and fog, lightning, and thundershowers. Such episodes occurred in July 1956 and in August 1965.

TOPOSCALE EFFECTS

The hiker's pocket altimeter and the altimeter in an aircraft are merely barometers measuring atmospheric pressure and indicating the equivalent height according to average weather conditions. Pressure, which always decreases with altitude, is usually measured in millibars, as shown at the right side of Table 1.1, or in inches (or millimeters) of mercury. Some equivalent pressures and heights for average atmospheric conditions in the California-Nevada region are listed in Table 1.1. The physiological effects of increasing altitude and decreasing pressure are mainly caused by the reduced amount of oxygen and the greater effort one has to exert to get enough oxygen into the lungs. Most hikers have to become acclimated for a day or two before they can be comfortable above 10,000 ft.

TABLE 1.1   Elevation and Air Pressure in the U.S. Standard Atmosphere *(in assorted units)*

Elevation		Pressure		
(feet)	(meters)	(inches)	(millimeters)	(millibars)[a]
Sea level	Sea level	29.92	760.0	1,013.2
1,000	305	28.86	733.0	977.3
2,000	610	27.82	706.6	942.1
3,000	914	26.81	681.0	907.9
4,000	1,219	25.84	656.3	875.0
5,000	1,524	24.90	632.5	843.2
6,000	1,829	23.98	609.1	812.1
7,000	2,134	23.09	586.5	781.9
8,000	2,438	22.22	564.4	752.5
9,000	2,743	21.38	543.1	724.0
10,000	3,048	20.38	517.7	690.2
11,000	3,353	19.79	502.7	670.2
12,000	3,658	19.03	483.4	644.4
13,000	3,962	18.29	464.6	619.4
14,000	4,267	17.57	446.3	595.0

Note: In cold winter weather, pressure decreases more rapidly with altitude than in warm summer weather.

[a] In the International System of Units, pressure is measured in kilopascals (kPa), with 1 kPa = 10 mb.

At most times and places, air temperature also decreases with height because the atmosphere is mainly heated from below. The atmosphere does not absorb much of the direct radiation from the sun, but the earth's surface does and reradiates the energy at a longer wavelength, which the atmosphere absorbs mainly through two of its variable gases: water vapor and carbon dioxide. The average lapse rate (generally, the decrease of temperature with altitude) is approximately 3.6°F per 1,000 ft (6.5 °C per km). At midday in summer with strong thermal activity, the lapse rate on the slopes approaches the adiabatic value of about 5.4°F per 1,000 ft (10°C per km) of ascent. Thus, on days when the temperature is 90°F (32°C), for example, in the Owens Valley, it can be 45° to 55°F (7° to 13°C) on Mt. Whitney or White Mountain Peak (both above 14,000 ft or 4,000 m). On clear nights, on the other hand, cooler air with its greater density sinks and collects in the valleys, forming inversions in which the temperature increases with height in the lowest few hundred feet (≈ 100 m) above the ground.

Topography influences local weather and climate in many ways, examples of which will be noted throughout the following sections of this chapter.

WEATHER OBSERVATIONS AND CLIMATOLOGICAL DATA

Weather Stations

Sparseness of permanent population, little human use of the area, and inaccessibility of the terrain have led to a scarcity of reliable weather records. Students and aficionados of mountain weather and climate always bemoan the paucity of weather instruments and observers at high elevations. Figure 1.4 shows the locations and elevations for weather stations in and immediately adjacent to the White Mountains. Table 1.2 gives the average monthly and annual temperatures for these stations, and Table 1.3 lists the corresponding precipitation data. Unfortunately, there are gaps in the records from most of the stations, especially during extreme weather events when such data can be very useful. Most reliable is Bishop (see Fig. 1.4), at 4,108 ft (1,250 m) in Owens Valley to the west of the White-Inyo Range, operated by the National Weather Service since 1947. The other stations are maintained by cooperative agencies, institutions, or individuals. The only continuous records from within the mountains proper are from stations operated by the White Mountain Research Station (WMRS)—White Mountain I in the valley of Crooked Creek, at 10,150 ft (3,095 m), and White Mountain II on the east slope of Mt. Barcroft, at 12,470 ft (3,800 m). Regrettably, maintenance costs and problems have closed White Mountain II during the winter months from January 1980 to the present, and the record from White Mountain I stopped after 1977. Automated weather-recording equipment is now being installed in the White Mountains by the WMRS. Dyer, at 4,975 ft (1,517 m) in Fish Lake Valley, and Deep Springs College, at 5,225 ft (1,593 m) in Deep Springs Valley, are representative of the lowland valleys to the east and southeast of the mountains. Benton, 5,377 ft (1,640 m), and Basalt, 6,358 ft (1,940 m), to the northwest and

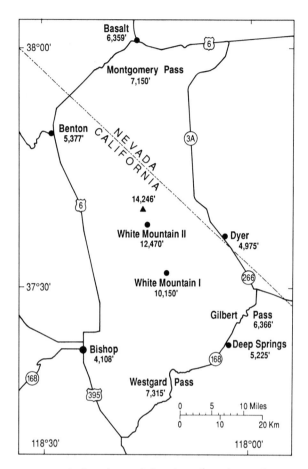

FIGURE 1.4   Locations and elevations of weather stations.

north of the mountains have incomplete records and were little used in this climatic analysis. Unless otherwise noted in the tables, the period of record is from 1956 through 1985; 30 years is generally considered by climatologists to be the minimum length of time necessary to establish meaningful averages.

Following is a summary of three important components of weather and climate in and around the White Mountains: temperature, precipitation, and wind. Data from the above-mentioned stations serve as a basis for the discussion. Monthly average temperatures are calculated by averaging the daily maximum readings for the month, averaging the daily minima, adding these two totals, and dividing by 2. In the following discussion, winter includes December, January, and February; spring March, April, and May; summer June, July, and August; and fall September, October, and November. Both authors of this chapter have many years of direct observation

TABLE 1.2 Average Monthly and Annual Temperatures and Extreme Temperatures for Stations in and near the White Mountains (*in* °F)

		Jan.	Feb.	Mar.	Apr.	May	June	July	Aug.	Sept.	Oct.	Nov.	Dec.	Annual
Bishop	Av.	37.2	42.0	46.5	53.4	61.9	70.6	76.9	74.5	67.5	57.3	45.6	38.6	56.0
4,108 ft	Max.	77	78	87	93	101	109	109	107	106	97	84	78	109
	Min.	−7	−2	9	15	23	29	40	37	26	16	5	−4	−7
Dyer	Av.	31.4	37.2	41.7	48.1	57.5	64.3	73.2	70.9	63.0	56.8	39.7	32.1	51.5
4,975 ft	Max.	69	76	82	88	95	106	104	104	102	91	78	72	106
	Min.	−21	−6	−6	8	13	20	36	31	21	5	−6	−14	−21
White Mountain I	Av.	20.2	20.6	22.1	27.1	35.8	45.8	51.7	50.3	44.2	36.2	28.1	22.6	33.7
10,150 ft	Max.	54	53	53	62	65	76	79	75	71	65	61	57	79
(1956–1977)	Min.	−21	−17	−25	−10	−12	8	22	17	6	−7	−14	−23	−25
White Mountain II	Av.	15.5	14.8	15.4	18.7	28.4	38.6	46.7	45.8	38.6	30.6	22.8	17.6	28.9
12,470 ft	Max.	47	52	46	50	59	64	72	73	60	62	50	48	73
(Winter data missing for 1981–1985)	Min.	−23	−21	−35	−30	−15	2	12	13	−8	−20	−28	−30	−35

Note: Data are from 1956–1985, unless otherwise noted.

TABLE 1.3   Average Monthly and Annual Precipitation and Extreme Monthly Precipitation for Stations in and near the White Mountains (in inches)

		Jan.	Feb.	Mar.	Apr.	May	June	July	Aug.	Sept.	Oct.	Nov.	Dec.	Annual
Bishop	Av.	1.32	0.98	0.43	0.31	0.30	0.11	0.19	0.11	0.18	0.17	0.49	1.02	5.61
4,108 ft	Max.	8.93	6.01	2.05	2.26	1.30	1.29	1.47	0.64	1.18	1.58	2.59	5.79	8.93
	Min.	0.00	0.00	0.00	0.00	0.00	0.00	0.00	0.00	0.00	0.00	0.00	0.00	0.00
Dyer	Av.	0.29	0.41	0.41	0.46	0.47	0.30	0.56	0.48	0.46	0.35	0.52	0.31	5.02
4,975 ft	Max.	2.22	2.20	1.71	2.37	2.24	2.48	2.75	3.44	2.59	2.39	3.00	1.70	3.44
	Min.	0.00	0.00	0.00	0.00	0.00	0.00	0.00	0.00	0.00	0.00	0.00	0.00	0.00
White Mountain I	Av.	1.52	1.40	1.25	1.11	1.10	0.55	1.16	1.09	0.80	0.53	0.93	1.45	12.89
10,150 ft	Max.	7.34	4.56	3.83	4.46	4.38	3.79	4.02	3.50	3.61	1.90	4.29	7.53	7.53
(1956–1977)	Min.	0.05	.T	.T	.T	.T	0.00	0.00	0.00	0.00	0.00	0.00	.T	0.00
White Mountain II	Av.	2.20	1.66	2.11	1.86	1.71	0.85	1.13	1.21	0.91	1.05	1.21	2.04	17.94
12,470 ft	Max.	6.01	4.94	6.35	6.65	6.75	4.39	4.05	4.30	3.18	3.33	3.17	8.55	8.55
(Winter data missing for 1981–1985)	Min.	.T	0.21	.T	0.00	.T	0.00	0.00	0.00	0.00	0.00	0.00	.T	0.00
Deep Springs	Av.	0.80	0.79	0.53	0.58	0.47	0.24	0.45	0.42	0.42	0.23	0.54	0.59	6.06
5,225 ft	Max.	3.49	3.43	2.05	3.80	1.46	1.77	4.16	4.86	2.72	1.42	3.46	3.68	4.86
	Min.	0.00	0.00	0.00	0.00	0.00	0.00	0.00	0.00	0.00	0.00	0.00	0.00	0.00

Notes: Data are from 1956–1985 unless otherwise noted.

.T = Trace

of weather events in the White Mountains and have used personal experience and knowledge to augment interpretation of the formal record, especially in the large portions of the range not covered by the recorded data.

Temperature

The summer visitor to Owens Valley at midday may well think the valley and the apparently barren, flat-lighted slopes of the White Mountains to the east to be under the full possession of the sun, with a forbidding aspect of heat. The same visitor to elevations above 10,000 ft (3,049 m) would likely comment—perhaps complain—about coolness, or even the cold. In July, the warmest month, average daily temperatures are 70°F (21°C) or higher on all the adjacent valley floors; the maximum daily temperature reached 109°F (43°C) at Bishop in June 1969 and July 1982, 106°F (41°C) in June 1961 at Dyer, and 104°F (40°C) at Deep Springs in June 1964. The July average is 51.7°F (10.9°C) at White Mountain I and 46.7°F (8.2°C) at White Mountain II, with maximum summer temperatures reaching 79°F (26°C) at I in July 1967, and 73°F (23°C) at II in August 1978. The decline in average July temperatures with an increase in altitude is close to the 3.6°F drop per 1,000 ft (6.5°C per km) rise in elevation regarded as the normal lapse rate throughout the world. It is a rarity for any of the summer months at either mountain station not to have one or more readings of 32°F (0°C) or below, and even the adjacent valleys have such readings in June and August. For any location on earth, trees are generally absent if the average of the warmest month is below 50°F (10°C). This critical value occurs between White Mountain I and White Mountain II; the former has trees, and the latter has none.

In January, the coldest month, the average temperature is 37.2°F (2.9°C) at Bishop, with a winter low of −7°F (−21.5°C) in January 1982. Temperatures are somewhat colder in the valleys to the east, with Dyer at 31.4°F (−0.3°C) with a winter low of −21°F (−29.5°C) in January 1962 and 1974, and Deep Springs at 30.6°F (−0.8°C), with a low of −10°F (−23.5°C) in January 1973. Fish Lake and Deep Springs Valley are colder than Owens Valley because they are at higher elevations, they are farther from the maritime influence of the Pacific Ocean, and they are more open to invasions of cold air from the north and east. At White Mountain I January is the coldest month, with an average of 20.6°F (−6.3°C) and a winter low of −25°F (−31.5°C) in March 1968. February is the coldest month at White Mountain II, with an average of 14.8°F (−9.6°C) and a winter low of −35°F (−37°C) in March 1964. In winter there is less of a decrease in monthly average temperatures with a rise in elevation than in summer. Cold air settling in the lower valleys at night from radiational cooling and downslope drainage seems to be the major reason: the temperature difference between the valleys and the slopes or highlands is less pronounced for minimum readings than for daily maxima, especially on clear nights. This phenomenon is characteristic of high mountains everywhere. At White Mountain I, located in a valley, average minima for the three coldest months

(January, February, and March) are 2°F (1°C) warmer than at White Mountain II, which is 2,320 ft (707 m) higher on a slope; average maxima for those same months are 9.5°F (5.3°C) higher. Thus, a typical early winter morning at the lower station would be just about as cold as at the higher station, but midafternoon would be noticeably warmer.

There is also a much greater variation in average monthly temperatures in winter than in other seasons at all stations and elevations. At some time during most winters, there is an invasion of continental polar or arctic air from northern Canada and Alaska, which brings below-normal temperatures. The frequency and duration of these incursions of cold air vary greatly from year to year; on rare occasions they dominate the weather for weeks. The last such major occurrence was in January and February 1949, and in January 1937 before that. In 1937, a minimum of −42°F (−41°C) was recorded in January at Fish Lake Valley; readings close to that may have occurred within the mountains. In general, the White Mountains are protected from common and prolonged cold air invasions by the many mountain ranges to the north and east.

February and March averages are lower than those for January at White Mountain II, and they are only slightly higher than January averages at White Mountain I. This is not the case at the lowland stations in the area or at most inland stations in cold-climate regions elsewhere in the United States, where January is nearly always the coldest month, with definite warming occurring in February and, particularly, March. At the two high-elevation stations March is colder than December, an anomaly for the latitude. A continous snow cover during the winter and spring could partially account for this delay in warming at high elevation, but other regions in the United States with persistent snow cover do not show this effect. It is probably the result of the frequent passage of closed low-pressure systems in late winter and spring over the White Mountain area. An analysis of 500 mb (near 18,000 ft or 5,500 m) weather maps shows that these closed lows commonly contain very cold air, which could affect the highest elevations of the White Mountains. At lower elevations the increased solar radiation from longer days and a higher angle of the sun would offset the influence of the cold air aloft. Thus, there is a pronounced lag in temperature increase in late winter and early spring at high elevation in the White Mountains. Significant warming there usually does not occur until mid-May, when the frequency and intensity of the upper-level closed lows diminish. Major cooling throughout the area generally comes in late September and October, at a slower rate at high elevation than the warming in late spring, with a marked decrease in November at all stations.

Midwinter temperatures at White Mountain I are comparable to those in central Iowa, and at White Mountain II to southern Minnesota or Anchorage, Alaska. Summer temperatures at White Mountain I are similar to those at the northern limit of trees in Alaska and Canada, and at White Mountain II to the treeless Arctic Slope of Alaska. At comparable elevations and latitudes, temperatures in the White Mountains are generally warmer in winter and cooler in summer than in Utah or Colorado, reflecting less maritime influence farther inland. From meager data and personal experience, there seem to be no significant temperature differences between the White Mountains and the Sierra Nevada at similar elevations, although the Sierra might be expected to have warmer winters and cooler summers because of closer proximity to the Pacific Ocean. It is difficult to compare climates in different mountain ranges because of topographical variations at individual recording sites—north slope, south slope, valley, orientation to prevailing winds, and other factors.

Precipitation

As discussed previously, precipitation in the White Mountain area results primarily from the passage of cyclones with associated fronts during fall, winter, and spring; from closed cyclones in late winter and spring; and from the flow of moist tropical air from the southeast to the southwest quadrant in the summer. Annual amounts vary from 5–6 in (125–150 mm) on the valley floors to 20 in (508 mm) or a little more at the highest elevations. Totals appear to increase right up to the crest of the range. The rate of increase averages about 1.5 to 2.5 in per 1,000 ft (120–205 mm per km) rise. However, this average is difficult to apply to any one portion of the range, and the increase is not linear, being higher at upper elevations. Table 1.3 gives average monthly and annual precipitation amounts for stations within the region.

From west to east in the White Mountain area, there are important differences in the seasonal distribution of precipitation. Bishop, on the west, has the typical regime of most California stations: winter wet and summer dry, with January the wettest month. White Mountain I and White Mountain II have precipitation much more evenly distributed throughout the year. At both mountain stations January is the wettest month, but only by a slight margin. There is no pronounced dry season; June is the driest month, reflecting the gap between the cyclones of winter and spring and the thunderstorms of July and August. Early fall is relatively dry, with a gradual buildup of precipitation to the winter months. Deep Springs, at the southeast edge of the White Mountains, has maximum precipitation amounts in January and February, with a minor peak in July and August, and minimum amounts in June and October. On the east margin of the White Mountains, Dyer has a slight maximum in spring and mid-summer and a minor minimum in December and January. At lower elevations, the western slope of the White Mountains is relatively open to cyclones from the west in winter, partially subject to closed cyclones from the north in the spring, and somewhat protected from thunderstorms in the summer. The eastern slope, in the double rain shadow of the Sierra Nevada and the White Mountains, is protected from winter cyclones but is more open to closed cyclones in spring and thunderstorms in summer. Upper elevations in the White Mountains are relatively open to all three types of storms and show a trimodal maximum of precipitation. Thus, the White Mountain range is truly transitional in seasonal distribution of precipitation between the winter maximum of California and the Sierra Nevada and the more even annual distribution of the eastern Great Basin and Rocky Mountains.

Yearly precipitation totals not only increase with higher elevation in the mountains but very likely are larger in the northern part of the range. There are no station records to substantiate this assertion, but the experience of many long-time residents of the area and of both writers suggests that the portion of the range from White Mountain Peak north to Boundary Peak receives more precipitation from cyclones and thunderstorms than the region south of the main peak. Occasional measurements made with a standard snow sampler at comparable elevations show greater depth and water content in the snowpack in the northern part of the range. There is also higher streamflow, more extensive former glaciation, and a less xerophytic vegetation north of White Mountain Peak. In the nearby Sierra Nevada, snow survey records show a general decrease in precipitation from north to south, reflecting a lower frequency of passing cyclones. This could also affect the White Mountains. Moreover, the crest of the Sierra Nevada is lower opposite the northern half of the White Mountains than opposite the southern half, and this may allow more moisture to reach across to the northern segment of the White Mountain Range. Still another possible effect of the Sierra Nevada is that, as previously mentioned, fronts may be retarded in crossing the massive barrier of that range, bringing in cooler air from the north and northeast, which may strengthen the fronts and increase precipitation in the northern portion of the White Mountains.

Empirical observation also indicates that the buildup of cumulonimbus clouds in summer thunderstorms is more likely to occur over specific portions of the summit upland than at random. Topographic influence on air moving into the area from characteristic directions is the probable cause. This could add a checkerboard pattern of precipitation distribution independent of more general patterns, such as the increase with elevation and from south to north. Four areas of cloud concentration are noticeable. From south to north, these are Sheep Mountain–Piute (or Paiute) Mountain, the plateau just south of White Mountain Peak, Chiatovich Flats and the area just north of the Cabin Creek–Birch Creek saddle, and the northern portion of Pellisier Flats at the head of Chiatovich Creek. Common features of the four areas are rises in elevation from south to north and broad lateral extent from west to east. Cumulonimbus clouds may form over any part of the range on any summer day, and during extensive storms all or most of the higher elevations may be cloud-covered, but initial formation and greater subsequent development more commonly occur over these four areas.

There are significant departures from normal in amounts of precipitation from month to month and year to year at all elevations in the White Mountains. Most weather stations in the United States use the calendar year in calculating annual amounts. This causes problems in much of California, with its winter-wet, summer-dry regime, and in high-mountain regions, where much of the significant precipitation falls as snow. Thus, the annual snowpack begins in the fall of one calendar year and builds to a maximum in late winter or spring of the next calendar year. Most California stations use a 1 July–30 June precipitation year to avoid this problem. An even better breakdown for the White Mountain Range is to use the water year employed by many hydrologists — 1 October–30 September. This has the advantage of including snow buildup and important July and August precipitation in one annual total, thus giving a more accurate figure of the water available for streamflow and plant growth, much of which occurs from July to September.

The following discussion uses the 1 October–30 September year to show extremes and variation from normal (see Table 1.4). Thus, the year mentioned in the table ends on 30 September and includes the precipitation from October through December of the previous year. Bishop and, by inference, the lower western slope of the range show the largest departures from normal, with the wettest year (17.28 in or 43.9 cm) in 1969 and the driest (1.68 in or 42.5 mm) in 1960. This is a range of 308% to 30% of average. Fish Lake Valley and Deep Springs Valley to the east and southeast show less variation, with both Dyer and Deep Springs ranging from about 190% to 40%. White Mountain I had maximum precipitation in 1967 (26.59 in, or 67.55 cm) and minimum in 1960 (5.57 in, or 14.15 mm), a range of 206% to 45%. At White Mountain II the high total was 33.56 in (85.35 cm) in 1967, and the low was 9.51 in (24.15 cm) in 1960, a range of 187% to 53%. It is to be expected that Bishop, with its low annual average, would have a greater variation from normal than the mountain stations, with higher averages. But Bishop also varies more than the other lowland stations. Bishop and the lower western slope of the range receive most of their rain and snow from winter cyclones, and precipitation totals reflect seasons of frequent or sporadic passage of such storms. The eastern valleys and lower slopes get relatively more moisture from spring and summer storms, and the upper elevations are more open to precipitation in all three seasons. At all stations 1967 and 1969 were very wet, and 1960 was the driest year. Unfortunately, records for the obviously wet years of 1982 and 1983 are incomplete or missing at the mountain stations; both years brought high totals to lowland stations. It is noteworthy that neither White Mountain I nor White Mountain II was very dry in 1976 and 1977, critical drought years in central California. At both stations spring and summer precipitation partially

TABLE 1.4   Extreme Annual, Monthly, and Daily Precipitation for Stations in and near the White Mountains *(in inches)*

	Annual 1 Oct.–30 Sept.	Percent of Normal	Maximum Monthly	Maximum 24-hour
Bishop 4,108 ft 1956–1985	Max. 17.28 (1969) Min. 1.68 (1960)	308 30	8.93 (Jan. 1969)	3.64 (24 Feb. 1969)
Deep Springs 5,225 ft 1956–1985	Max. 11.38 (1969) Min. 2.26 (1960)	188 37	4.86 (Aug. 1983)	2.16 (6 Dec. 1966)
White Mountain I 10,150 ft 1956–1977	Max. 26.59 (1967) Min. 5.57 (1960)	206 45	7.53 (Dec. 1966)	3.80 (6 Dec. 1966)
White Mountain II 12,470 ft 1956–1980	Max. 33.56 (1967) Min. 9.51 (1960)	187 53	8.55 (Dec. 1966)	4.40 (6 Dec. 1966)

made up for winter deficiencies. It seems probable that higher elevations in the White Mountains are less subject to either very dry or very wet years than the neighboring Sierra Nevada and Owens Valley; there is less chance that all three types of storms will be common or rare in any one precipitation year.

Extreme monthly totals at Bishop vary from 8.93 in (22.7 cm) in January 1969 to 0.00 for all months of the year. At Dyer, the extremes are 3.44 in (8.75 cm) in August 1983 and 0.00 for all months; at Deep Springs, totals vary from 4.86 in (12.35 cm) in August 1983 to 0.00 for all months. At higher elevation, White Mountain I shows a maximum of 7.53 in (19.1 cm) in December 1966 and a minimum of no rainfall or a trace for all months but January; White Mountain II shows a high at 8.55 in (21.7 cm) for December 1966 and a low of no rainfall or a trace for all months but February. However, summer thunderstorms at high elevation have certainly exceeded these monthly totals. In part of July 1955, one of the authors (D. R. Powell) measured over 11 in (28.0 cm) in a standard rain gauge at Chiatovich Flats, between 10,000 ft (3,050 m) and 11,000 ft (3,350 m), 8.48 in (21.55 cm) of which fell in 2 1/2 hours on July 23. This is the greatest 24-hour total yet recorded in the White Mountains, although it probably has been approached or exceeded during other summer thunderstorms in the range. At the two mountain stations, maximum summer 24-hour totals are about 2 in (50 mm). It is evident that neither station has yet been in the direct path of the most intense thunderstorms. White Mountain II has a winter high 24-hour sum of 4.40 in (11.2 cm) on 6 December 1966, and White Mountain I recorded 3.80 in (9.65 cm) on the same date. Dyer and Deep Springs each show about 2 in (50 mm) for the maximum daily total for any season; Bishop has received more than 3 in (7.6 cm) in each of the three winter months, from Pacific cyclones.

Snowfall

At elevations above 10,000 ft (3,050 m), over 80% of the mean annual precipitation falls as snow. On the valley floors, from 15 to 25% of the average precipitation is snow, with wide fluctuations from year to year in the snow-to-rain ratio. Regardless of the temperature of air masses moving onto land, rainfall is rare from November through April at White Mountain I and practically nonexistent from October through May at White Mountain II. Moreover, snow has been recorded, usually in amounts of less than 6 in (15 cm), in all of the warmest months from June through September at White Mountain II (see Table 1.5 for a summary of snowfall).

Average annual snowfall is low at the base of the mountains, with 9 in (23 cm) at Bishop, 12 in (30 cm) at Dyer, and 15 in (38 cm) at Deep Springs. It builds to 106 in (270 cm) at White Mountain I and 164 in (417 cm) at White Mountain II. As discussed earlier, annual totals are very likely higher at upper elevations north of White Mountain Peak. Maximum seasonal snowfall amounts have been 50–60 in (125–150 cm) at Bishop and Deep Springs, and a little less at Dyer, with low average precipitation in winter. Bishop has had a few seasons with no snowfall; the other lowland stations have had at least 1 in (2.5 cm) or more of snow in all years of

TABLE 1.5 Snowfall for Stations in and near the White Mountains (*in inches*)

	Average Annual 1 Oct.–30 Sept.	Maximum Annual 1 Oct.–30 Sept.	Maximum Monthly	Maximum 24-hour	Maximum Recorded Depth
Bishop 4,108 ft 1956–1985	9	59 (1969)	32 (Feb. 1969)	18 (24 Jan. 1969)[a]	
Deep Springs 5,225 ft 1956–1985	15	54 (1969)	23 (Jan. 1969)	20 (24 Jan. 1969)	
White Mountain I 10,150 ft 1956–1977	106	170 (1969)	76 (Dec. 1966)	38 (6 Dec. 1966)	94 (Mar. 1969)
White Mountain II 12,470 ft 1956–1980	164	238 (1969)	86 (Dec. 1966)	44 (6 Dec. 1966)	123 (Mar. 1969)

[a]Data from National Oceanic and Atmospheric Administration (1950–1990); however, D. Powell measured 36 inches of snow at this site on this date.

record. At higher elevations measurable snowfall certainly occurs every year. Seasonal totals, 1 October to 30 September, range from 170 in (432 cm) in 1969 to 48.5 in (123 cm) in 1960 at White Mountain I, and from 238 in (605 cm) in 1969 to 83 in (211 cm) in 1960, at White Mountain II. Maximum monthly falls are 76 in (193 cm) at White Mountain I, e.g., in January 1969, and 86 in (218 cm) at White Mountain II in December 1966. Maximum 24-hour totals are 38 in (97 cm) at I and 44 in (36.37 cm) at II, both on 6 December 1966. At White Mountain II, 76 in (193 cm) of snow fell on the two days 5–6 December. Daily accumulations of 10–24 in (25–60 cm) are not infrequent at higher elevation. These are impressive figures for any location in the world, though exceeded in the nearby Sierra Nevada, and winter travelers in the White Mountains should be aware of the difficulty and danger of being out in such intense snowstorms, commonly accompanied by high winds. Where snow has been measured for water equivalent in both stations, or elsewhere at high elevations, a ratio of about 10 in (25 cm) of snow, as it falls, to 1 in (2.5 cm) of water is common. In lieu of actual measurements of melted snow, a ratio of 10-to-1 (snow depth to water equivalent) has been used in the records from all stations. A 10% density is occasionally too high, but less commonly too low, for snowfall at the two mountain stations.

Continuous snow cover at elevations above 10,000 ft (3,050 m) usually begins in late October or mid-November but can begin as early as the end of September and as late as February. Disappearance of snow cover usually occurs in May or June at White Mountain I, and in June or July at White Mountain II. Average duration of snow cover is about 160 days at the lower station and 210 days at the higher locations, but there is great variation from year to year, with a range at White Mountain II of 292 days in 1973 to 54 days in 1964. Snow depths at upper elevations generally increase until March or April, and occasionally May. Maximum recorded depth at White Mountain I is 94 in (239 cm), in March 1969, and 123 in (312 cm) at White Mountain II, in the same month. A measurement of 144 in (366 cm) was made with a snow sampler at Chiatovich Flats, at 10,600 ft (3,230 m), in March 1967. It is difficult to measure accurately such parameters as snowfall, snow cover, and snow depth; significant differences can occur in short horizontal distances. Much depends on the location and exposure of the site, the instruments used, the times of observation, and the knowledge, persistence, and hardiness of the observer. It is commonly difficult to differentiate snow that has fallen directly from the sky and that subsequently removed or deposited by wind. Thus, the figures used here should be taken as approximations.

At the base of the mountains snowfall is much lower than above 10,000 ft (3,050 m), but individual storms can still bring impressive 24-hour totals. All of the lowland stations have had daily accumulations up to 20 in (60 cm). Snow cover in the lowlands is discontinuous, with durations rarely longer than six weeks. There is notably rapid disappearance of snow cover on the western slopes of the range, facing Owens Valley, up to elevations of 8,000–9,000 ft (2,440–2,745 m), even following major snowfalls. This slope faces a high angle of the sun during the relatively warm temperatures of afternoon. As expected, snow cover lasts longer on north- and east-facing slopes than on south- or west-facing ones—often many weeks longer. In late spring and early summer, the snowline is distinctly lower and the cover more continuous in the mountains as viewed from Fish Lake Valley in the east than from Owens Valley in the west.

Precise measurements are nonexistent, but it is obvious that some snow is removed from its site of original fall on the extensive summit upland to slopes and canyons adjacent to the plateau. Because prevailing winds generally have a westerly component, the wind-blown snow is generally deposited on eastern slopes, although occasionally the direction is reversed, especially in conjunction with northeast winds following the passage of storms or with closed cyclones in late winter and spring. Quite probably, the sites of deepest snow accumulation in the White Mountains are at the heads of the major canyons on the east side of the range. Maximum Pleistocene glaciation occurred in these canyons, the heads of which are now steep-walled, east- or northeast-facing cirques—favorable locations for the accumulation and retention of snow. A conspicuous sight from Fish Lake Valley is a discontinuous, but commonly prominent, line of snow cornices at the edge of the summit plateau, commonly lasting through the summer months and sometimes well into fall or until the next season's snowpack begins. A worthwhile addition to the knowledge of the White-Inyo Range climate would be the acquisition of reliable data on how much snow is moved by wind and deposited either east or west of the summit upland. It may well be less than visual inspection, perhaps affected by the discomfort and poor visibility caused by fine blowing snow, indicates. Sporadic measurements of wind-blown snow in the Sierra Nevada in similar terrain do not substantiate the notion of a significant increase in snowpack in leeward sites, except in localized areas.

Wind

Wind is even more difficult to measure accurately than snow. Instruments are commonly of doubtful accuracy, and there are wide fluctuations in speed and even direction in short periods of time at any one location, and across very short horizontal distances. Topography obviously exerts a major influence on wind speed and direction. Wind data, somewhat incomplete, exist for the two mountain stations, and there is a more complete and accurate record at Bishop.

Direction is easier to measure than speed. At both mountain stations, for about two-thirds of the year the prevailing direction (from which the air is moving) is westerly—northwest, southwest, and west. East is the least common, although the northeast can be of importance in some years. At Bishop prevailing directions are northerly and southerly, reflecting the topographical influence of Owens Valley. Fish Lake Valley and Deep Springs Valley very likely have the same regime as Owens Valley.

Maximum wind velocities have approached or exceeded 100 mph (45 m/s) at both mountain stations. The strongest winds usually come in the winter, from west to south in association with storm fronts, or from west to north after frontal passage. Monthly average maximum speeds are about 30 mph (13.5 m/s) during the winter at White Mountain II and near 20 mph (9 m/s) in the summer; averages are about 5 mph (2.5 m/s) less in all seasons at White Mountain I. At Bishop average speeds are much less than at high elevation, but a peak gust of 75 mph (33.5 m/s) was recorded in August 1976. In general, maximum velocities in the lowlands occur in winter and early spring. Experience indicates that Fish Lake Valley and the eastern slopes of the White Mountains have the highest velocities of the lowland areas.

The intensity, frequency, and duration of high-velocity winds in the White Mountains do not seem extraordinary for a mountain range of its height and latitude. However, an extensive portion of the range above treeline has no shelter from wind. The most notable aspect of wind at higher elevations is not high velocity, although that may occur, but rather the constancy of moderate wind, with a conspicuous lack of calm, even in summer. Significant results of wind are the redistribution of snow, poor visibility from blowing snow, and the wind chill factor. At 10°F (−12°C), a wind speed of 30 mph (13.5 m/s) is calculated to have roughly the same effect on humans as an equivalent temperature of −33°F (−36°C) without wind.

Wind also significantly affects snow texture. At upper elevations the snow surface is seldom smooth or powdery but is generally hard-packed, ridged, and of unequal depth, with patches of bare ground present even in wet years, because of frequent wind action. The snow is commonly packed and ridged as it strikes the ground; most snowstorms occur with moderate to high wind velocities. Despite increasing attention in recent years to the White Mountains as an area for cross-country skiing and winter snow camping, snow conditions in the range are not particularly favorable for such activities. Added to the adverse surface texture is the problem that, in many years, the amount of snow accumulation is insufficient to cover ground irregularities adequately.

Climate Hazards

The traveler or resident in the White Mountains should be aware of troublesome or possibly hazardous weather and climatic conditions that can occur. Snowstorms, sometimes heavy and often accompanied by moderate to high winds, can happen from fall through spring, and even in summer. These may bring poor visibility and drifting snow, which can make vehicular, foot, or air travel difficult or dangerous. From October through May, temperatures well below freezing make frostbite a problem if adequate clothing is not worn. The wind chill factor commonly has the effect on humans of lowering the effective temperature 20 to 40°F (10 to 22°C).

June through September is the thunderstorm season, which can bring flash floods in canyons, such as the Narrows below Westgard Pass, and common lightning strokes. Anyone who has experienced a major thunderstorm above treeline in the White Mountains with little or no protection available is acutely aware of danger from lightning.

At any elevation, but particularly above 10,000 ft (3,048 m), solar radiation—especially ultraviolet—may be intense, resulting all too quickly in painful sunburn and chapped lips. Water is not readily available throughout most of the range, particularly along the road to the two mountain stations, and dehydration due to the wind and low humidity can be a problem.

Travelers into the White Mountains—by foot, ski, road vehicle, or helicopter—are strongly advised to check weather reports before entering the range. San Francisco, Los Angeles, Reno, and Salt Lake City are major forecast centers, and the National Weather Service station at Bishop can be contacted during daylight hours for briefing on local conditions. Mountain weather is notorious for rapidly developing adverse events, but knowledge of seasonal patterns, empirical observation of cloud sequences, and current information from forecast offices can do much to reduce potential hazards.

REFERENCES

Goodridge, James D. 1981. *California rainfall summary, monthly total precipitation, 1849–1980*. California Dept. of Water Resources.

Holmboe, J., and H. Klieforth. 1957. *Investigations of mountain lee waves and the air flow over the Sierra Nevada, final report*. Contract AF 19 (604)–708. Meteorology Department, University of California, Los Angeles.

Houghton, J. 1969. *Characteristics of rainfall in the Great Basin*. Desert Research Institute, University of Nevada System, Reno.

Houghton, J., C. Sakamoto, and R. Gifford. 1975. *Nevada's weather and climate*. Nevada Bureau of Mines and Geology, University of Nevada, Reno.

National Oceanic and Atmospheric Administration. Climatological data (1950–1990): California, vols. 54–94; Nevada, vols. 65–105 (monthly and daily tabulations and annual summary). NOAA, National Climate Center.

Neiburger, Morris, James G. Edinger, and William D. Bonner. 1982. *Understanding our atmospheric environment*, 2d ed. W. H. Freeman, San Francisco, p. 453.

Powell, Douglas. 1963. Physical geography of the White Mountains, California-Nevada. M.A. thesis, Geography Department, University of California, Berkeley.

White Mountain Research Station. Unpublished observations from White Mountain Research Station weather recording sites I and II. White Mountain Research Station, Bishop, Calif.

2

Geomorphology

Deborah L. Elliott-Fisk

Geomorphology is the scientific study of landforms. This discipline, which has traditionally been a part of both geography and geology, focuses on (1) describing the various landforms that make up the earth's natural landscape, (2) determining the processes that have shaped these landforms, and (3) reconstructing the environments in which these features formed. Because of its high diversity of bedrock types, large elevational gradient, and geologic history, the White-Inyo Range possesses a diverse suite of landforms.

What is a landform? It is simply a part of the landscape that has a distinctive shape or morphology, a unit that can be delineated either qualitatively by visual means in the field or quantitatively through an analysis of morphology, composition, and relative position on the landscape. Hills, valleys, mountain peaks, dunes, and floodplains are all landforms. Landforms in the White-Inyo Range are listed by their origin in Table 2.1.

It is easiest to think of a landform as being a function of process, materials, and time (Gregory, 1978). The three external processes shaping landforms are (1) weathering, (2) erosion, and (3) deposition. These three processes will each be discussed briefly.

WEATHERING

Weathering is the chemical decomposition and mechanical disintegration of rock materials. We can think of this as the wearing away of earth materials through time. Different weathering processes have relative degrees of importance in different environments and are partially functions of climate. Many mechanical weathering processes require temperature and moisture fluctuations. These changes exert a mechanical stress on the rock (such as frost wedging), which causes it to disintegrate along joint planes or between individual mineral grains (Fig. 2.1). Chemical weathering, like all chemical processes, is a function of temperature. With the presence of water, at higher temperatures chemical weathering will take place more rapidly.

Thus, we see different types and rates of weathering of particular rock types (such as granite) in low-, middle-, and high-elevation climates of the White-Inyo Range. Weathering rates in the range have been quantified by Denis Marchand (1968, 1970, 1971, and 1974) in his studies of weathering and soil development at Sage Hen Flat and the Cottonwood Basin. He estimated that weathering and accompanying erosion (removal of weathered materials) of 0.3 to 1.2 in (1 to 3 cm) of material occur in 1,000

TABLE 2.1 Landforms of the White-Inyo Range

	Glacial	Periglacial[a]	Mass Wasting (Gravity)	Fluvial	Aeolian	Anthropogenic
Erosional	Cirque	Frost wedges	Slide scar	Entrenched stream	Abrasion marks	Mines
	U-shaped valley	Disintegrated rocks	Avalanche chute	Stream channel	Polished rocks	Earth mounds
	Polished rocks	Slump scars	Rock creep	Drainage net		
	Abrasion marks	Monadnock	Soil creep	Meander scar		
	Arete		Slump scar	Arroyo		
	Col		Rock fall			
	Glacial staircase					
	Hanging valley					
	Roche moutonnee					
Depositional	?	Rock glacier	?	Alluvial terrace	Sand dune	Rock rings, walls, and houses (prehistoric and historic)
	Lateral moraine	Felsenmeer	Debris flow	Floodplain	Silt deposit	
	Recessional moraine	Patterned ground	Mudflow	Alluvial fan		
	Ground moraine	Gelifluction lobe	Colluvial fan	Point bar		
	Outwash (valley train)	Rock terrace	Talus cone/apron	Midchannel bar		
	Till sheet		Protalus rampart	Flood deposit		
	?		Avalanche deposit	Debris dam		

[a]This is really a mix of landforms created as a consequence of frost action (a weathering process).

FIGURE 2.1   Weathering of granitic rocks may result in the formation of angular fragments along joint planes or rounded forms with pressure release. Here a combination of mechanical and chemical weathering processes has resulted in the formation of a very large weathering pit (note person lying in it for scale) in Mt. Barcroft Granodiorite below White Mountain Peak. Felsenmeer surrounds this unusual boulder.

years. In conjunction with this, Valmore LaMarche (1968) has measured weathering and erosion on slopes inhabited by Bristlecone Pine (*Pinus longaeva*). Tree roots are exposed through time as material is removed around them. Using dendrochronology (tree-ring dating), LaMarche was able to quantify the amount of material removed for a given unit of time. Elliott-Fisk (1987) has investigated the weathering of glacial till boulders deposited by a series of glaciers over time; her results show that weathering is slow but progressive in the White Mountains. All of these researchers have shown that weathering is a relatively slow process in the dry climate of the White Mountains. Because precipitation (available moisture) increases with altitude (to the crest), weathering may be thought to be more rapid at higher elevations, but it must be remembered that temperature decreases with altitude as well, and frost and ice are weathering agents.

It may prove fruitful to look at the relative degree of soil development as an indication of weathering along an altitudinal gradient through the range. Soils form as the result of weathering and the decomposition of organic matter and are functions of climate, organisms, parent material, relief, and time (Jenny, 1941). Thus, one must try to hold these factors constant to assess the relative importance of climate (or altitude) to soil formation and weathering. It is possible to find the same geologic formation (for example, a particular granitic pluton) at different altitudes in the range. The relief, or slope position, can also be held constant. If we can determine that the surface of the landscape has not been exposed to disturbance through various erosional or depositional agents, time can also be held constant. However, it has been difficult to locate a sequence of landforms of the same age that span the range's entire elevational gradient. Elliott-Fisk (1987) has studied soils formed on glacial deposits of different ages (i.e., allowing time to vary) and shown that soils do progressively develop through time. It is also difficult to hold the organisms, especially the vegetation, constant as one goes up an altitudinal gradient. Sagebrush (*Artemisia* spp.) communities span virtually all altitudes of the range, but, as their productivity varies, they do not allow soil development to be evaluated only as a function of climate.

EROSION

Erosion, the second geomorphic process, is the removal of weathered material from a slope. In order for material to be removed from a slope, its initial inertia must be overcome by the mass and momentum of the erosional agent. Erosional agents include running water (streams, rivers, sheetflow, soil water, and groundwater), glacier ice, ground ice, waves, tides and currents, wind, gravity, and organisms (especially humans). Geomorphic agents are linked to climate because some of them occur only in particular climatic settings, and their relative importance varies with the climate of an area. Waves, tides, and currents are obviously limited to water bodies, and gravity is common to all slopes, regardless of climatic setting. However, running water, glacier ice, ground ice, wind, and organisms (to some degree) vary with climate. All of these terrestrial geomorphic agents have operated in the White-Inyo Range during recent geologic time.

It is possible to reconstruct climatic events of the recent or distant past by studying landforms. Beaty (1963, 1968, 1970, and 1974) has worked for many years on determining the role that debris flows play in the development of alluvial fans flanking the White Mountains (Fig. 2.2). Debris flows are triggered by intense summer thunderstorms or very rapid snowmelt, where a large amount of weathered material is catastrophically eroded, transported down valley, and deposited at the valley floor on the alluvial fan. Debris flows and other deposits that result from flooding can be devastating on the landscape below, especially if it is inhabited, so these events are regarded as natural hazards. By mapping and dating debris flows, one may be able to calculate the periodicity of the events (with changes in frequency and magnitude of the flows an indication of climatic change) and use this information to estimate the probability of their recurrence.

Another erosional agent that has left its mark on the eastern slope of the White Mountains is the glacier (Fig. 2.3). A glacier is a moving body of ice; ice actually flows through a glacier much as water slowly flows down a stream channel. The moving ice can erode and transport materials, later depositing them down gradient (e.g., down valley). A series of valley glaciers formed south to north from Wyman Creek to Trail Creek along the eastern slope of the White Mountains, on high plateaus along the crest, and in the upper reaches of a few of the western drainages (Elliott-

FIGURE 2.2   Several alluvial fans are visible here fronting the western mountain escarpment below White Mountain Peak. The largest fan to the left center is that of Lone Tree Canyon. A light-colored, recent debris flow extends down the center of the fan. Dark, irrigated fields of alfalfa are seen just beyond the foreground of the Bishop Tuff Volcanic Tableland.

Fisk, 1987). Studies of glacial landforms (Elliott-Fisk, 1987; Elliott-Fisk and Dorn, 1987; Swanson et al., 1988) show at least six stages of Quaternary glaciation that correlate with the glaciations of the Sierra Nevada and also provide more detailed information on the glacial history of the region. One can reconstruct climate during these glacial events using several techniques, perhaps most directly by mapping the glacial deposits, reconstructing the glacier that deposited them, and then determining the climatic conditions necessary to form such a glacier.

DEPOSITION

After the materials are transported by the erosional agent, they are eventually deposited at a new location. Deposition is the third geomorphic process. These depositional materials commonly form distinct landforms that are attributed to a particular geomorphic agent. These landforms can then be identified as fluvial (running water), glacial (glacier), colluvial (gravity), periglacial (ground ice), aeolian (wind), marine (waves, tides, and currents), or biological (organisms) in origin. They too can then yield climatic information, as these depositional agents vary with climate.

FIGURE 2.3   The upper part of the South Fork of Perry Aiken Creek's drainage basin was once occupied by coalescing cirque and valley glaciers. Linear or lobate deposits seen along the valley bottom in the center of the photo are glacial moraines (depositional landforms). Initial work suggests that these moraines are from three glaciations that occurred during the past 200,000 years. A small rock glacier is visible above the uppermost moraine, along with several avalanche/talus chutes and fans.

Depositional landforms commonly can be identified by their distinctive shapes, but landforms deposited many years ago may have been worn down by weathering processes and lost their once-distinct appearance. It is still possible to identify these landforms as to their depositional agent based on knowledge of how various geo- morphic agents shape and sort materials. Table 2.2 lists the characteristic shapes and degrees of sorting of sediments by various agents. This table serves as a guide to identifying depositional landforms in the White-Inyo Range. It can be seen from this chart that glacial clasts (particles) are commonly subangular and poorly sorted, in contrast to fluvial clasts, which are rounded and well sorted. (These differences are due to the densities and velocities of the fluids [agents], among other factors.) Thus, if we find a deposit with no characteristic morphology on a ridgetop, valley floor, or intermediate slope, we can commonly identify its agent of deposition. Early Qua- ternary high-altitude ridgetop (interfluve) deposits on Cottonwood Plateau (Fig. 2.4) and Chiatovich Flats (Fig. 2.5) have been identified as glacial in origin by sediment analyses, as surface expression of glacial landforms is lacking.

TABLE 2.2   Characteristics of Sediments

Geomorphic Agent	Clast Shape[a]	Degree of Sorting
Gravity (mass wasting)	Angular	Poorly sorted
Frost action[b] (periglacial)	Angular to round	Poorly to well sorted
Glacier (glacial)	Subangular	Very poorly (fill) to moderately sorted (outwash)
Running water (fluvial)	Round	Well sorted
Wind (aeolian)	Faceted (more or less)	Very well sorted
Waves	Disc (flattened)	Well sorted

[a] Clast shape is a function not only of the transporting geomorphic agent, but to some degree of the original nature of the rock material.

[b] Frost action is a weathering process. Its products are very much a function of rock type, as well as the intensity of freeze–thaw and the amount of moisture present.

FIGURE 2.4   Glacial erratics are present on high plateaus or interfluves between valley bottoms in the White Mountains. Here, erratics of the Barcroft Granodiorite rest on a highly weathered surface of Reed Dolomite on the Cottonwood Plateau. It is believed that these and other glacial features indicate the former presence of an ice cap in the range in the mid- to early Quaternary time (Elliott-Fisk, 1987).

Geomorphologists have long been interested in the presence of apparent high-altitude planation surfaces at crestal and mid-elevation positions in many mountain ranges (see Fig. 2.5). These surfaces are commonly present on fault-block mountains and have been hypothesized to have been eroded in valley floor positions, then uplifted with the range. They are typically mantled with depositional material. It is possible to identify multiple planation surfaces at several distinct elevations in a particular mountain range. If these surfaces were formed at valley bottom locations, determination of their time of formation could shed light on rates of tectonic activity for a range (e.g., when was the range uplifted?) (Curry, 1984). However, many workers believe that these high-altitude surfaces were simply eroded in place by various agents, especially frost action (ground ice); as such, they have been referred to as cryoplanation surfaces. A third group of scientists believe that these surfaces were very likely the result of both past lower-elevation and present higher-elevation processes.

High-altitude erosion surfaces are distinct in the White Mountains. The best example is Pellisier Flats, which extends from an elevation of 12,400 ft (3,775 m), near Mt. Hogue at the south, to 13,400 ft (4,080 m) at The Jumpoff, just south

FIGURE 2.5   Several high-altitude planation surfaces are visible looking north along the east side of the White Mountains. In the foreground is Perry Aiken Flat (10,460–11,880 ft, 3,190–3,620 m elevation), mantled with various periglacial landforms (such as gelifluction lobes). The valley just to the north is glaciated Leidy Creek Canyon, with the headwaters of Cabin Creek (surrounded by stands of dark Lodgepole Pine) imposed upon Chiatovich Flats just beyond. Indian Creek cirque is to the north of Chiatovich Flats, with Pellisier Flats seen as the range crest along the top of the photo. These high-altitude surfaces are exposed to primarily periglacial geomorphic processes today, although glacial ice and running water played an important role in shaping these surfaces in the past.

of Boundary and Montgomery peaks to the north. What appears to be an extremely flat surface from distant positions to the west or east of the range is actually a gently rolling surface with small, residual bedrock outcrops (inselbergs, tors, and monadnocks) (Fig. 2.6). The surface is mantled with frost-shattered debris and is presently a periglacial landscape. Both active and relict patterned ground occur here (Mitchell, LaMarche, and Lloyd, 1966; Elliott-Fisk, 1987; Mahacek-King et al., 1987) and dominate the surficial geology of other high plateaus in the range.

Ongoing research focuses on how extensively these plateaus were covered with glacial ice, which requires either the formation of an ice cap, under present topographic constraints, or the presence of valley glaciers prior to tectonic uplift and an episode of major stream incision (valley formation). Many of the high plateau surfaces are mantled by glacial deposits that have been somewhat reworked by frost action and fluvial processes (Elliott-Fisk, 1987). Chiatovich Flats (10,200–11,600 ft, or 3,130–3,560 m, elevation) and the Cottonwood Plateau (11,200–12,000 ft, or 3,435–3,680 m, elevation) are the best examples. Other surfaces are mantled by rock glaciers (such as the North Fork Perry Aiken Creek, Fig. 2.7) and felsenmeer (i.e., frost-shattered boulder fields; see Figs. 2.1 and 2.6).

Geomorphologists have long debated whether felsenmeer indicates the absence of glaciation. This is a difficult question because our knowledge of high-altitude weather-

FIGURE 2.6   Erosional remnants (tors, inselbergs, and monadnocks) are present along the range crest and on interfluves surrounded by weathering debris. Here, at 12,680 ft (3,865 m) elevation on the plateau above Barcroft, a large inselberg is seen. The bedrock here is Mt. Barcroft Granodiorite. Areas such as this were favored by early native Americans as summer home sites and parts of game drives.

FIGURE 2.7   Rock glaciers occur at high altitudes in the range east of the crest in formerly glaciated canyons. The aspect of many of these rock glaciers is north to northeast, where snow can accumulate and be retained into the summer. The largest rock glacier in the range is in the north branch of the North Fork Perry Aiken Creek, pictured here. Rock glaciers such as this show movement, although inactive (relict) ones persist for some time at these high altitudes.

ing rates is poor. The thin ice cover of a cold-based glacier (frozen to the surface) may allow the preservation of felsenmeer. The plateau between Mt. Barcroft and White Mountain Peak apparently had such an ice cover in the past, as large, frost-shattered blocks on the plateau above the cirques of the North and South Forks of McAfee Creek show surface polish and abrasion, indicating that this area was in the zone of accumulation of a former glacier (Elliott-Fisk, 1987). The same or an adjacent glacier may have deposited the granodiorite erratics on the dolomite surface of the Cottonwood Plateau to the south (see Fig. 2.4). If the time of formation of these glaciers can be deduced, the rate of high-altitude weathering since its disintegration can be calculated.

The tectonic activity of the earth can be characterized as an internal geomorphic process. Displaced, faulted, and warped landforms attest to local tectonic activity. Good examples of these exist along the western and eastern escarpments of the White-Inyo Range in the form of displaced alluvial fan (Fig. 2.8) and lake bed materials.

Alluvial fans are triangular or cone-shaped masses of debris at the base of a mountain front (see Fig. 2.2). Deposition of alluvial and colluvial material results when the lower gradient and wider channel of the valley floor are encountered as the material is transported down the mountain flanks. The velocity of the fluid drops, causing

FIGURE 2.8   Raised alluvial fan materials (fanglomerates) are seen here along the south flank of Black Canyon on the western slope of the White Mountains. The white layer between these deposits is Bishop Tuff (including lapilli-size particles), which was deposited about 0.79 Ma. This deposit signifies tectonic uplift of this region.

the deposition of these materials. Streams spread out as distributaries at this point, instead of coming together in the form of tributaries to a main stream channel, as they do in the drainage basin above.

As one ascends the stream canyons at the apex (head) of these alluvial fans, older fan materials (fanglomerates) may be seen perched on the walls many meters above the present fan surface (as along Indian Creek, Milner Creek, and Black Canyon). It is also possible to find an older fan apex at a higher elevation back in the mountain front (as at Jeffrey Mine Canyon on the west slope of the White Mountains). If these materials can be dated, the amount of tectonic uplift can be calculated. Unfortunately, these deposits are difficult to date, as they are usually beyond the age range of radiocarbon or lack organic materials necessary for radiocarbon dating. However, along Black Canyon in the southwestern White Mountains (see Fig. 2.8), a volcanic deposit is interbedded with fanglomerate. This material is tephra (air-filled lapilli and ash) from the catastrophic eruption of the Long Valley caldera and is referred to as the Bishop Tuff (volcanic ash) (Bateman, 1965). It has been dated by uranium fission and other techniques, with the best estimate of its age currently at 0.79 Ma (millions of years before present). This deposit is present in Black Canyon 490 ft (150 m) above the valley floor, attesting to 7.6 in (19 cm) of uplift per 1,000 years.

Near the Westgard Pass road at the Waucoba Embayment of the western front of the White-Inyo Range, a series of lake beds (the Waucoba Lake beds) is exposed.

Walcott (1897) speculated that these lake deposits have been uplifted 3,300 ft (1,000 m) above the valley floor. Although intensive studies of these deposits have not yet been conducted, their age is estimated at 3 million years, suggesting an uplift rate of 13 in (33 cm) per 1,000 years.

The relatively slow tectonic uplift of the range may not seem important in reference to our short lifetimes, but some tectonic activity, generating earthquakes and displacement along fault lines, can be abrupt. Escarpments along fault lines cutting through alluvial fans suggest rapid vertical displacements of several meters. Further research needs to focus on dating this tectonic activity, which can be accomplished through studies of soil formation on the fans. The presence of ash from the Mono and Inyo craters interbedded with uplifted fan sequences and other deposits (Fig. 2.9) suggests tectonic disturbance in the last 5,000 years (Mahacek-King et al., 1987; Mahacek-King et al., 1988). It is now well known that the entire region is tectonically, and hence geomorphically, very active, as has been shown by intensive studies in the Long Valley caldera region and along the White Mountains fault zone, and by historical records of earthquake occurrence. It is believed by some workers (Curry, 1984) that this tectonic activity is accompanied by volcanism and basin formation and is migrating north from the Owens Valley (which witnessed a catastrophic eruption about 790,000 ka (thousands of years before the present) to the Mono Basin (which is still volcanically active) and the Bridgeport basin. This may be related to major plate rifting along the axis of the Gulf of California and to crustal extension.

A wide variety of materials is available for landform generation in the White-Inyo Range. All three basic rock classes (igneous, metamorphic, and sedimentary) are present and range from Precambrian to Quaternary in age (see Chapter 3). The mineralogy and petrology of these rocks vary, with some more susceptible to jointing, chemical weathering, and other processes. Thus, some types of landforms tend to be associated with distinct rock formations. For example, the Campito Formation (especially the Andrews Mountain Member), a sandstone or quartzite, is very susceptible to frost action, resulting in the formation of angular felsenmeer seen as stone stripes on slopes along White Mountain Road. Bateman (1965) contrasts this with the Montenegro Member shale, which forms slabs and breaks down rapidly to clay-rich soils. Differences in patterned ground derived from metamorphic and granitic materials are apparent at high elevations.

The White-Inyo Range is largely lacking in organic-rich deposits and landforms, in the form of either peat or fossilized organic remains. This is most likely due to the present aridity of the range and the lack of topographic depressions along the steep mountain flanks. Organic-rich deposits may compose distinct landforms, but they possess other advantages in that they are a superb source of material for the study of fossil plant and animal communities and for dating of geomorphic events (see Fig. 2.9). Recently, turf and earth hummocks have been found in the Alpine Zone of Pellisier Flats and register geomorphic change with the deposition of volcanic tephra and changing hydrology of the site (Mahacek-King et al., 1987). The arid climates of the range have allowed woodrat middens to be preserved in a diversity

FIGURE 2.9   Organic-rich deposits are occasionally found
along stream terraces, primarily on the east side of the range.
The study of sediments, soil, and fossils in this stratigraphic
section (stream cut) yields valuable information on the late
Holocene (past 3,000 years) behavior of Crooked Creek. The
two light layers to the left of the shovel are volcanic ash
from the Mono and Inyo craters and serve as valuable time-
stratigraphic markers.

of environments. Analysis of plant macrofossils from these middens is providing
valuable information on the late Quaternary geologic and climatic history of the
range (Jennings, 1988; Jennings et al., 1989).

Reference has been made throughout this section to the role of time in the control
of landform development. If we think of the White-Inyo Range as a dynamic mountain system that is continuing to evolve, we can ask not only what landforms are
developing now, but which ones were formed in the past, when they were formed,
and what this tells us about the evolution of the range.

The geologic evolution of the range is discussed in Chapter 3 of this book. However, in a general sense, it can be stated that all landforms visible today are the

products of late Cenozoic processes. We can imagine many of the high peaks (such as White Mountain Peak) forming over millions of years through weathering and erosion. It is very likely that the peak was always exposed to the subaerial environment, perhaps a nunatak above a hypothetical White Mountain ice cap. Other landforms are more recent, forming with the glaciation of the range or by recent fluvial activity.

REFERENCES

Bateman, P. C. 1965. *Geology and tungsten mineralization of the Bishop District California*. U.S. Geological Survey Professional Paper 470.

Beaty, C. B. 1963. Origin of alluvial fans, White Mountains, California and Nevada. *Annals, Association of American Geographers* 53:516–535.

Beaty, C. B. 1968. *Sequential study of desert flooding in the White Mountains of California and Nevada*. Technical Report 68-31-ES. U.S. Army Natick Laboratories, Natick, Mass., January.

Beaty, C. B. 1970. Age and estimated rate of accumulation of an alluvial fan, White Mountains, California, U.S.A. *American Journal of Science* 268:50–77.

Beaty, C. B. 1974. Debris flows, alluvial fans, and a revitalized catastrophism. *Zeitschrift für Geomorphologie*, N.F. Suppl. Bd. 21:39–51.

Curry, R. R. 1984. Mountain summit glacial tills and their tectonic implications, eastern Sierra Nevada, California. *Abstracts, Annual Meeting of the Geological Society of America*, Reno, Nevada, p. 481.

Elliott-Fisk, D. L. 1987. Glacial geomorphology of the White Mountains, California and Nevada: Establishment of a glacial chronology. *Physical Geography* 8:299–323.

Elliott-Fisk, D. L., and R. I. Dorn. 1987. Pleistocene glaciation of the White Mountains, CA-NV, and correlation with the Sierra Nevada. *Geological Society of America, 1987 Annual Meeting, Abstracts with Programs*, p. 655.

Gregory, K. J. 1978. A physical geography equation. *National Geographer* 12:137–141.

Jennings, S. 1988. Late Quaternary vegetation change in the White Mountain region. In C. A. Hall, Jr. and V. Doyle-Jones (eds.). *Plant biology of eastern California*. Natural History of the White-Inyo Range, symposium vol. 2, pp. 139–147. University of California, Los Angeles.

Jennings, S. A., D. L. Elliott-Fisk, T. W. Swanson, and R. I. Dorn. 1989. A late-Pleistocene chronology of the White Mountains, CA-NV. *Association of American Geographers Program Abstracts, Baltimore*. Washington, D.C.

Jenny, H. 1941. *Factors of soil formation*. McGraw-Hill, New York.

LaMarche, V. C., Jr. 1968. *Rates of slope degradation as determined from botanical evidence, White Mountains, California*. U.S. Geological Survey Professional Paper 325-I, pp. 341–377.

Mahacek-King, V. L., J. A. Onken, D. L. Elliott-Fisk, and R. L. Bettinger. 1987. Quaternary silicic tephras in the White Mountains, CA-NV: Depositional environments and geomorphic history. *Geological Society of America, Annual Meeting, Abstracts with Programs*, p. 756.

Mahacek-King, V. L., D. L. Elliott-Fisk, T. E. Gill, and T. A. Cahill. 1988. Elemental analysis by PIXE applied to tephrochronology of the White Mountains, California-Nevada. *Geological Society of America, Abstracts with Programs*, vol. 20, no. 7, p. A54.

Marchand, D. E. 1968. Chemical weathering, soil formation, geobotanical correlations in a portion of the White Mountains, Mono and Inyo Counties, California. Ph.D. thesis, University of California, Berkeley.

Marchand, D. E. 1970. Soil contamination in the White Mountains, eastern California. *Geological Society of America, Bulletin* 81:2497–2505.

Marchand, D. E. 1971. Rates and modes of denudation, White Mountains, eastern California. *American Journal of Science* 270:109–135.

Marchand, D. E. 1974. *Chemical weathering, soil development, and geochemical fractionation in a part of the White Mountains, Mono and Inyo Counties, California.* U.S. Geological Survey Professional Paper 352-J.

Mitchell, R. S., V. C. LaMarche, and R. M. Lloyd. 1966. Alpine vegetation and active frost features of Pellisier Flats, White Mountains, California. *American Midland Naturalist* 75:516–525.

Swanson, T. W., D. L. Elliott-Fisk, R. I. Dorn, and F. M. Phillips. 1988. Quaternary glaciation of the Chiatovich Creek Basin, White Mountains, CA-NV: A multiple dating approach. *Geological Society of American, Abstracts with Programs*, vol. 20, no. 7, p. A209.

Walcott, C. D. 1897. The post-Pleistocene elevation of the Inyo Range, and the lake beds of Waucobi Embayment, Inyo County, California. *Journal of Geology* 5:340–348.

3

Geologic History
of the White-Inyo Range

Clemens A. Nelson, Clarence A. Hall, Jr., and W. G. Ernst

INTRODUCTION AND GENERAL HISTORY

The White-Inyo Range (Fig. 3.1), representing the westernmost range of the Basin and Range structural province, extends for 110 mi (175 km) from Montgomery Pass south-southeastward to Malpais Mesa opposite Owens Lake. Its maximum width, east of Bishop, is approximately 22 mi (35 km). The terminological separation of White from Inyo mountains is placed along the Westgard–Cedar Flat–Deep Springs Valley Road, a division that has no particular topographic or geologic significance. As is typical of the ranges of the province, it is bounded, generally on both sides, by normal faults of large-magnitude slip. The northern part of the range is mainly an easterly tilted block marked by an impressive escarpment from the Owens-Chalfant-Hamill valleys on the west, at 4,300 ft (1,310 m), to the crest of the range at White Mountain Peak, 14,246 ft (4,342 m). The southern, Inyo Mountains, part of the range has been tilted slightly to the west, with its maximum relief from Saline Valley at 1,100 ft (353 m) on the east to the range crest at Mt. Inyo, 11,107 ft (3,385 m).

Rocks in the White-Inyo Range span the time from the late Precambrian (700 Ma [Ma, millions of years ago]) to the Holocene, or Recent (i.e., last 10,000 years). Figure 3.2 is a simplified geologic timetable showing major time units and millions of years before the present (Ma) for the beginning of each, and the time spans of mountain building episodes (orogenies) referred to in the text. All periods of the Paleozoic (570–225 Ma), Mesozoic (225–65 Ma) and Cenozoic (65 Ma to the present) are represented, some incompletely. Rocks from the late Precambrian to the end of the Devonian Period (345 Ma) are entirely of sedimentary origin, having been deposited as sand, shale, dolomite, and limestone along the western edge of the North American continent by stream systems flowing westward into a marine basin called the Cordilleran geosyncline (Fig. 3.3). The total accumulation of uppermost Precambrian through Lower Jurassic surficial deposits in the geosyncline exceeded 4.5 mi (7 km) in thickness in the White-Inyo region. Beginning in Mississippian time, about 345 million years ago, the sedimentation pattern changed in response to elevated lands lying to the north and possibly west, resulting in the accumulation of coarse-grained sands and conglomerate, reflecting higher-energy stream systems. This pulse of uplift has been considered by some geologists as the result of the first of several collisions of the North American lithospheric plate and an ancient Pacific plate; the inferred plate collision is held responsible for the Antler orogeny, or time

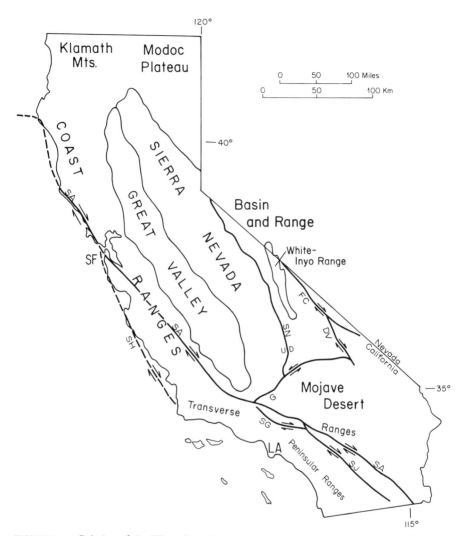

FIGURE 3.1   Relation of the White-Inyo Range to major physiographic and structural features of California. Faults: SA—San Andreas, SN—Sierra Nevada, G—Garlock, SG—San Gabriel, SJ—San Jacinto, FC—Furnace Creek, DV—Death Valley, SH—San Gregorio–Hosgri; other abbreviations: SF—San Francisco, LA—Los Angeles. Arrows show relative horizontal slip on faults. U, D indicate relative vertical slip on faults.

of mountain building. The Pennsylvanian and Permian (320–225 Ma) were times of renewed deposition of limestone, reflecting a return to conditions of quiet carbonate bank formation.

This lull was again succeeded by extensive tectonic activity, apparently resulting from a second plate collision, the Sonoma orogeny (230–220 Ma). This event, as in

Era	Period	Ma	Orogeny
Cenozoic	Quaternary	1.8	
	Tertiary	65.0	
Mesozoic	Cretaceous	136.0	
	Jurassic	195.0	} NEVADAN
	Triassic	225.0	} SONOMA
Paleozoic	Permian	280.0	
	Pennsylvanian	320.0	
	Mississippian	345.0	
	Devonian	395.0	} ANTLER
	Silurian	435.0	
	Ordovician	500.0	
	Cambrian	570.0	
Precambrian			

FIGURE 3.2   Geologic timetable showing millions of years before the present (Ma) and the approximate time span of orogenies mentioned in text.

the Sierra Nevada to the west, resulted in extensive volcanism in a marine environment, the products of which are exposed as interlayered lava flows, ash beds, and continental sedimentary rocks in the southern Inyo Mountains and in the northern White Mountains.

In both the White-Inyo Range and the Sierra Nevada, surficial volcanism and its deep-seated counterpart, igneous intrusion, continued intermittently until approximately 155 million years ago as a consequence of the most intense orogeny to affect the region, the Nevadan (see Fig. 3.2). This complex episode, the result of terrane

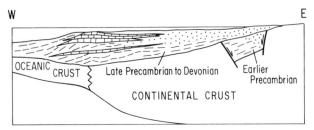

FIGURE 3.3   Schematic cross section of the western margin of North America during late Precambrian (700 Ma) to Devonian time (345 Ma), illustrating the mode of sediment accumulation in the Cordilleran geosyncline. Sediment transport direction was dominantly from east to west.

accretion (plate collision) and amalgamation of far-traveled subcontinental fragments outboard of the North American plate and large-scale subduction of an ancient Pacific plate beneath the North American plate, produced major compressional deformation, metamorphism, and the emplacement of numerous coarse-grained intrusive bodies, termed plutons. The latest Mesozoic (90–75 Ma) was a time of renewed plutonic activity, represented by cross-cutting granitic intrusive rocks that transect the earlier-formed deformational structures. The physical conditions inferred to have attended crystallization of the metamorphic minerals associated with the intrusive rocks document the presence of a volcanic-plutonic arc marking the western margin of the North American continent throughout Mesozoic time (Fig. 3.4).

The early and middle Cenozoic Era was a time of large-scale uplift and extensive erosion; no sedimentary record of this time has been left in the White-Inyo Range. A major erosion surface truncates all previously formed rocks, including the deep-seated granitic plutons, which had solidified at depths of perhaps 6 mi (10 km) or more. Beginning approximately 10 million years ago, the range experienced the outpourings of extensive fragmental volcanic ejecta (volcanic tuff) and basaltic lava flows. Remnants of this episode can be seen in the volcanic rocks that mantle the northeast corner of the White Mountains at Montgomery Pass and east, in the table-like flows extending from the Cottonwood Basin (SE of Mt. Barcroft) to the north end of Deep Springs Valley, in the large expanse of volcanic rocks covering the saddle area between Eureka and Saline valleys on the east flank of the Inyo Mountains, and in the Malpais Mesa at the south end of the Inyo Mountains.

The latest Cenozoic was a time of renewed uplift along Basin and Range normal faults flanking the range, and transcurrent motion along the Furnace Creek fault zone at the margin of the White Mountains and Fish Lake Valley. Both styles of faulting reflect a major episode of crustal extension that was initiated in the Basin and Range Province approximately 15 million years ago. That this style of deformation continues to the present in the White-Inyo region is attested to by such events as the Chalfant earthquakes of July 1986, which measured up to 5.5 on the Richter scale.

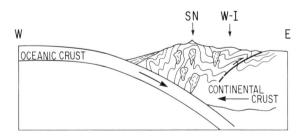

FIGURE 3.4   Schematic cross section of the western margin of North America during the convergent episode of the Nevadan orogeny, illustrating the development of compressional fold and fault structures and the generation of granitic bodies (SN — Sierra Nevada, W-I — White-Inyo Range).

An additional result of the uplift in latest Cenozoic time was the onset of Quaternary glaciation, which affected the area east and north of Mt. Barcroft and White Mountain Peak. This was followed by further uplift and the development of extensive aprons of alluvial deposits at the western and eastern margins of the range.

THE CENTRAL WHITE-INYO RANGE

The area of principal interest for this guide extends from directly north of White Mountain Peak south to approximately 37°00' N. lat., a distance of 47 mi (75 km). All of this area has been mapped geologically at a scale of 1:62,500 or 1:24,000 (Fig. 3.5), and a more detailed discussion of its sedimentary, deformational, and igneous history is possible. This is also the area covered by the enclosed geologic map and by the principal and subsidiary road logs included at the end of this chapter.

The central White-Inyo Range exposes the best stratigraphic sections of the uppermost Precambrian to middle Paleozoic strata in the range. The basal part of the section (Fig. 3.6) contains the Precambrian-Cambrian transition. The Lower Cambrian portion of this section, the Waucoban Series, is regarded as the North American-type succession for rocks of this age. It contains the oldest trilobite faunas in the Americas, abundant archeocyathans (primitive reef-forming animals), numerous crisscrossing tracks and trails of primitive molluscs and arthropods, and molluscan body fossils (*Wyattia* and others), now regarded as marking the beginning of the Paleozoic Era. This section of strata and its fossils illustrate a remarkable explosion of life at the Precambrian-Cambrian boundary, in which "explosion" all invertebrate phyla are represented. These fossil representatives occur in the limited span extending from the upper Wyman Formation (animal tracks and trails), through the Reed and Deep Spring formations (primitive molluscs and fossil animal trails), to the Campito and Poleta formations (trilobites). This succession represents a group of rocks deposited in largely tidal and subtidal environments, as well as reefal and off-reef carbonate bank and shoal environments. The terrigenous strata are largely shale-siltstone and quartzite deposited on the shallow continental shelf of the time. It has been speculated that one could have walked across the early Paleozoic sea in the White-Inyo region in water only chest-deep. The strata contain abundant shallow water indicators, such as sedimentary rocks with cross-bedding, current and wave ripple marks, mud cracks, and very highly bioturbated beds.

The geologic structure of the area from 37°00' N. lat. north to just south of Mt. Barcroft is relatively simple: the range is largely anticlinal. North of Westgard Pass, the White Mountains are principally a gently south-plunging, asymmetrical anticlinorium (east flank nearly vertical) exposing the oldest stratigraphic unit, the Wyman Formation, in the core. The central, relatively simple structure (Fig. 3.7), is modified on both the west and east sides by more complex, closely appressed sets of compressional structures. The Inyo Mountains are dominated by a more open and nearly horizontal anticline with a southeast trend, also exposing the Wyman Formation at its core and similarly modified on its flanks by folds as well as faults.

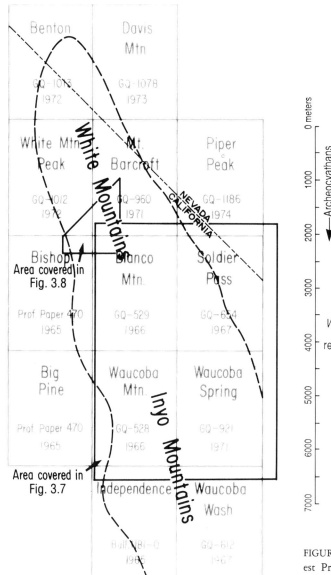

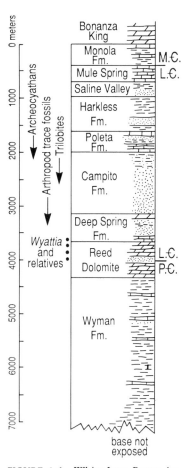

FIGURE 3.5 Index map of published geologic maps of the U.S. Geological Survey, scale 1:62,500 (see references).

FIGURE 3.6 White-Inyo Range latest Precambrian to Middle Cambrian stratigraphic section, showing distribution of key faunal elements of the Precambrian-Cambrian transition.

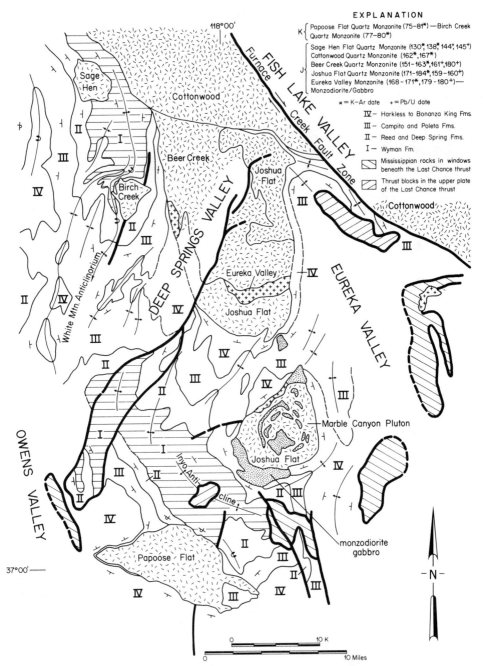

FIGURE 3.7 Generalized geologic map of the central portion of the White-Inyo Range showing distribution, structural position, and radiometric dates of Jurassic (J) and Cretaceous (K) plutons.

Lying between the Inyo anticline and the White Mountain anticlinorium is a structural downwarp containing many closely spaced anticlinal and synclinal folds and associated faults, along the western side of Deep Springs Valley. These are the famed Poleta folds, an area used for instructional purposes by many academic departments of geology.

The Inyo Mountains, and areas to the southeast, expose structures interpreted as the consequence of extreme compression: a system of low-angle reverse faults—extensive, gently inclined surfaces across which old rocks have been thrust from beneath, onto and over younger rocks. In the Inyo Mountains, this fault system has been termed the Last Chance thrust, along which Precambrian and lower Paleozoic rocks have been juxtaposed above rocks of middle and late Paleozoic age. In its northernmost exposures, the fault is inclined to the north, suggesting that the northern Inyo Range and a part of the White Mountains may lie entirely above the Last Chance thrust.

A roughly similar interpretation can be made for the area of the White Mountains north of Mt. Barcroft. Even though this part of the range has been invaded by many Mesozoic intrusive bodies (to be discussed later), the gross distribution of the pre-intrusive strata suggests that the lower to middle Mesozoic core of the range has been overthrust by Paleozoic and Precambrian strata, which appear to lie structurally above, along the northwest, north, and northeast flanks of the range.

Dating the many structural features of the White-Inyo Range is difficult because of the large temporal gap between the deformed and undeformed strata. Many of the structures are truncated by one or more of the Mesozoic intrusive bodies. Consequently, the major folding and thrust faulting can be regarded as pre-intrusive (pre-Nevadan), generally before 180 Ma, possibly consequences of the Antler ($\approx$350–340 Ma) and/or the Sonoma ($\approx$230–220 Ma) mountain building episodes (see Fig. 3.2).

The uppermost Precambrian to middle Mesozoic strata of the central White-Inyo Range are essentially "swimming" in a sea of middle to late Mesozoic intrusive rocks. The plutons have disrupted pre-intrusive structures, have metamorphosed the sedimentary strata to slate, schist, and quartzite, and in some cases have strongly deformed and stretched sedimentary layers. The plutons have been radiometrically dated and range in age from 180 to 75 Ma.

The plutons of the range exhibit a variety of emplacement mechanisms. This is well illustrated by the several bodies in the southern White Mountains and the northern Inyo Mountains (see Fig. 3.7). The oldest, the Marble Canyon composite pluton and the Eureka Valley and Joshua Flat plutons, are Jurassic in age. They have invaded the axial portion of major synclinal (downwarp) and basinal structures to the east and northeast of the White Mountain and Inyo anticlines, respectively. They are in part discordant to the original sedimentary layering but have principally shouldered aside their host rocks and locally thinned them to approximately 40% of the initial thicknesses.

The slightly younger Jurassic Beer Creek and Cottonwood plutons occupy the same synclinal downwarp but are more broadly discordant, as they cut across the eastern limb of the White Mountain anticlinorium. The youngest Jurassic pluton, the Sage

Hen Flat (145 Ma), is unique among the White-Inyo intrusive rocks in that it has not significantly deformed its host rocks. It has passively invaded the west flank of the White Mountain anticlinorium, apparently by a process of magmatic stoping: blocks of the overlying host rocks were fractured and, because of their greater density, sank into the magma chamber, allowing the molten granitic column to rise buoyantly.

Cretaceous intrusive activity in this area is represented by the Birch Creek and Papoose Flat plutons, each of which attained its present structural position by a process of forcible injection. Both appear to have initially invaded their host rocks along pre-intrusive faults (see Fig. 3.7). The Birch Creek Pluton occupies the east flank of the central portion of the White Mountain anticlinorium. During emplacement, it deflected to the northwest and overturned the central anticlinal structure and the strata of the east flank. The Papoose Flat Pluton was emplaced within the southwest limb of the Inyo anticline, drastically disrupting the southeast trend of the structure, producing a pronounced westward bulge and overturning the strata along its northeast border. Accompanying the bulging, the sedimentary succession at the contact with the pluton was in places stretched and thinned to less than 10% of initial thicknesses, an extreme example of forcible emplacement and accompanying attenuation of wall rocks.

North of the area of Fig. 3.7, Jurassic plutonism is represented by the Barcroft Pluton (see enclosed geologic map). The pluton transects the White Mountain anticlinorium, diverting the western limb of the structure from its regional northward trend to the northeast, parallel to the southeast border of the intrusive (Fig. 3.8). Alternatively, this change in trend could be related to reverse movement along the Marmot thrust, a south-dipping fault within the Precambrian-Cambrian rocks directly south of the Barcroft Pluton. It has also been suggested that the pluton was emplaced along a steeply inclined structural discontinuity along which the Paleozoic rocks of the southern block had been uplifted or overthrust into contact with the Mesozoic rocks of the northern block.

The White Mountain anticlinorium with its N–S trend is thought by some to have developed during the Sonoma orogeny of latest Paleozoic to early Mesozoic age. The Cottonwood Pluton (Fig. 3.8) intruded preexisting folds in the Precambrian and Cambrian sequence and is apparently responsible for the overturning of the east limb of the anticlinorium.

The dominant minor fold axes in the Wyman and Deep Spring formations are approximately N–S and are nearly horizontal. Exposure of the Wyman and Deep Spring formations in the northeast part of Fig. 3.8 and south of the Marmot thrust are more highly deformed than in the southern part of the area depicted in Fig. 3.8. The dominant trends of minor fold axes in this more deformed area are N30°E. These folds are interpreted to be a result of deformation associated with the Marmot thrust and postdate the folds with N–S trends. An alternative interpretation is that the more highly deformed Wyman and Deep Spring formations in this area are related to emplacement of the Barcroft Pluton, and that the Marmot thrust follows the preexisting structural grain or was reactivated during intrusion of the granodiorite pluton.

Folds with NE–SW or E–W trends in the Poleta Formation (see Fig. 3.8) north of the Marmot thrust are associated with the emplacement of the Barcroft Pluton. Metamorphic minerals (tremolite, scapolite, and diopside) in the Wyman Formation of this area and south of the surface trace of the Marmot thrust could reflect either the close proximity of the Barcroft Pluton at depth or, less likely, metamorphism that occurred during movement along the Marmot thrust. Thinning of the Reed Dolomite and the Deep Spring Formation in the northeast part of the area and above the Wyman-cored anticline or dome, as depicted in Fig. 3.8, suggests either: regional upwarping during deposition of the Reed and Deep Spring formations; thinning related to deformation associated with the White Mountain anticlinorium, along whose trend the dome in the Wyman Formation lies; or attenuation owing to the proximity of the Barcroft and Cottonwood plutons in a manner similar to that proposed for the Papoose Flat Pluton. Hence, folding or upwarping within the study area could have first occurred during the Cambrian or late Precambrian, and again during the Antler and/or Sonoma orogenies, or perhaps partly during the Nevadan tectonic events.

Plutons of Cretaceous age (90–75 Ma) in the region to the east and northeast of Mt. Barcroft and White Mountain Peak are represented by the Indian Garden Creek and McAfee Creek granitic bodies, which occupy large areas on the east slope of the White Mountains (see enclosed geologic map). The Indian Garden Creek Pluton is entirely within and discordant to the Cottonwood Pluton. The McAfee Creek Pluton intrudes Precambrian strata, the Cottonwood Pluton, and the Barcroft Pluton.

Recrystallization (metamorphism) of the Precambrian, Paleozoic, and Mesozoic strata of the White-Inyo Range took place repeatedly in response to the periods of heating and deformation just described. The early metamorphic mineral assemblages were overprinted and were partly to completely replaced by other assemblages produced by the younger thermal events. The rocks are typified by a regional development of greenschist facies minerals; common phases in recrystallized, stratified rocks include quartz, albite, microcline, white mica, chlorite, biotite, epidote, and magnetite. Thermal annealing reflects more intense baking occasioned by the emplacement of plutons of various ages; many, but not all, have produced distinct metamorphic aureoles or halos in the surrounding strata, indicated by the localized formation of new, higher-temperature minerals such as garnet, cordierite, tremolite, tourmaline, fluorite, scapolite, andalusite, sillimanite, and calcic plagioclase.

In the central White-Inyo Range, the record of the early to middle Cenozoic (65–15 Ma) is missing. During this time, broad regional uplift resulted in the unroofing of the range, exposing the deep-seated granitic bodies. Erosional products of the uplift and resulting denudation were probably shed chiefly westward, across what is now the Sierra Nevada (then low-lying), to the Cenozoic seaway in the region of the present San Joaquin Valley. With the development of crustal extension beginning about 15 million years ago, erosional debris was transported to adjacent down-dropped basins such as the Owens, Fish Lake, Eureka, and Saline valleys.

The character of the erosional surface produced by this long period of denudation is well illustrated in the area of Cottonwood Basin, southeast of Mt. Barcroft. From there to east of the north end of Deep Springs Valley, Miocene volcanic tuff and

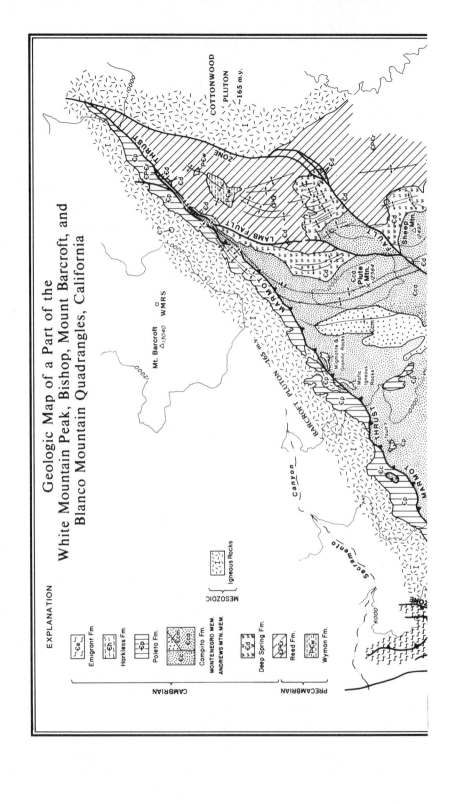

Geologic Map of a Part of the
White Mountain Peak, Bishop, Mount Barcroft, and
Blanco Mountain Quadrangles, California

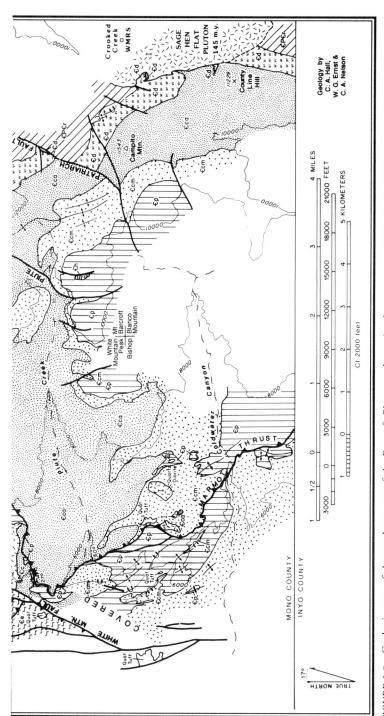

FIGURE 3.8   Geologic map of the southern part of the Barcroft Pluton and associated structures.

overlying basaltic flows (10 Ma) lie upon a generally smooth surface planed across the Jurassic plutonic rocks of the range. This erosional surface and its basaltic cover was uplifted and tilted, mainly to the east, as shown by its elevation of 11,800 ft (3,595 m), 2.5 mi east of Mt. Barcroft on the northwest, to 5,500 ft (1,675 m) in Deep Springs Valley, from where it has been uplifted along a marginal fault to an elevation of 7,700 ft (2,350 m) east of the valley at Piper Mountain.

The development of Deep Springs Valley is typical of the late Cenozoic history of the region. The valley lies wholly within the range and trends northeastward across the regional structural grain. It is marked by a major fault system along its eastern margin, as illustrated by the steep escarpment, with a relief of 2,400 ft (730 m), east of the valley, and numerous small fault scarps, which attest to the recency of uplift. Geophysical data suggest that structural relief between the granitic rocks on the east side of the valley to the granite surface below the valley fill is as much as 5,000 ft (1,520 m) and that the alluvial fill beneath Deep Springs Lake on the east side of the valley is approximately 2,600 ft (790 m) thick.

An additional aspect of the crustal extension that the region has experienced is illustrated by the fault system that marks the margin between the northeast flank of the White Mountains and Fish Lake Valley. This is the Furnace Creek fault, which extends from Death Valley to its termination at the northwest end of Fish Lake Valley. It is a major transcurrent fault, along which the White Mountain block has been moved, principally horizontally, northwestward perhaps as much as 13 mi (20 km) relative to rocks on the northeast side of the fault.

As discussed previously, uplift during the late Cenozoic resulted in elevations sufficiently high to support small valley glaciers during Quaternary time. Small cirque basins and glacial moraines occupy the upper reaches of Leidy, Perry Aiken, McAfee, and Cottonwood creeks on the east slope of the White Mountains.

A major, relatively recent geological event, the extrusion of the Bishop Tuff from the Long Valley caldera east of Mammoth Lakes, had a marginal effect on the White Mountains. The event, which took place 700,000 years ago, was a huge volcanic explosion that resulted in the outpouring of pumice and ash amounting to more than 144 cu mi (600 cu km) and the collapse of the base of the caldera to below sea level. The volcanic tuff resulting from this eruption mantles or underlies much of northern Owens Valley and most of Chalfant and Hamill valleys, and it occurs interbedded with alluvial materials flanking the west slope of the White Mountains and in several canyons, notably Black Canyon, southeast of Bishop.

That uplift and associated volcanism has continued to the present is suggested by the presence of the very recent scarps along the range margins, especially marked along the east side of Deep Springs Valley (Road Log C), by a series of young volcanic cinder cones on the west side of the Inyo Mountains southeast of Big Pine, and by the historic earthquakes of the general eastern Sierra Nevada–Owens Valley region. This region has had a long and diverse geologic history, and geologic activity continues to the present day.

Road Logs A, B, C

Clemens A. Nelson
with botanical additions
by Mary DeDecker and James Morefield

In the following road logs, figures in the left column are distances between points of interest with comments; figures in the next column (in parentheses) represent cumulative mileage.

Frequent reference is made to clock directions to various features, such as prominent peaks (e.g., Mt. Tom is at 11:00). The clock is oriented with noon straight ahead.

For each road log, reference is made to appropriate U.S. Geological Survey 15-min-topographic quadrangle maps showing road networks.

ROAD LOG A

Owens Valley Laboratory (OVL) to Barcroft Station of White Mountain Research Station (WMRS) and return (Bishop, Big Pine, Waucoba Mountain, Blanco Mountain, and Mt. Barcroft 15-min quandrangles).

0.0   (0.0)   Depart OVL, note odometer at gate, turn left, and proceed on East Line Street to Bishop. The high pyramidal peak ahead is Mt. Tom (13,652 ft). Its crest exposes brown metasedimentary rocks of Paleozoic age, which extend north to Pine Creek Canyon; here these rocks contain the ores of the Pine Creek Tungsten Mine. Farther north, the prominent steep-faced ridge is the Wheeler Crest. South of Mt. Tom, the flat-topped feature is Basin Mountain. The Sierran front from Bishop northward is marked by a major fault escarpment along which the Sierra Nevada has been uplifted in relation to the Owens Valley.

3.6   (3.6)   Intersection of East Line Street and U.S. Highway 395. Turn left.

At the south end of Bishop, the eastern front of the Sierra has changed significantly. This portion, called the Coyote Warp, is that part of the Sierran front extending from Bishop Canyon some 15 mi south to Big Pine Canyon, which has experienced bending or warping. This is in sharp contrast to the steep fault scarp faces of the eastern Sierran front both south and north of the Coyote Warp. This interpretation is supported by well data in the Owens Valley that indicate that, at this latitude, the alluvial fill of the valley varies from nearly zero on the west to several thousand feet beneath the east edge of the valley.

5.5   (9.1)   Collins Road. Marble Canyon is at 9:00 in the White Mountains. The Precambrian-Cambrian section exposed on both sides of the canyon

55

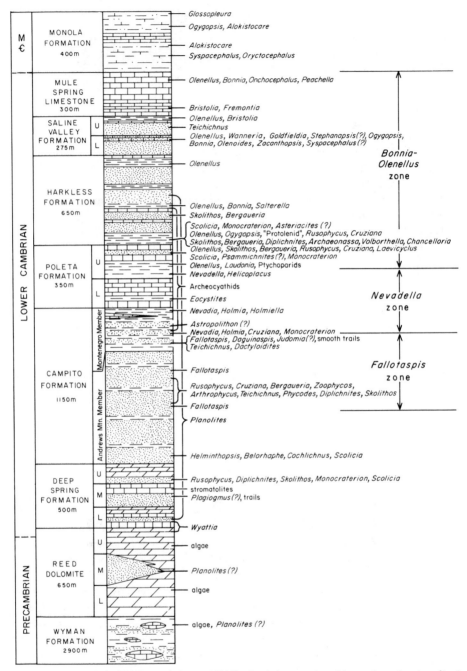

FIGURE 3.9 White-Inyo Precambrian to Middle Cambrian stratigraphic section, showing distribution of trilobite faunas, archeocyathans, trace fossils, and *Wyattia*. Abrreviations: M-€—Middle Cambrian.

is obscure in the morning light; it can be seen in better detail on the return leg.

1.7   (10.8)   Keough's Hot Spring Road. The hot springs, at 3:00, are located along a bounding fault at the front of the Sierra. Even in the area of the Coyote Warp, frontal faulting is of local significance.

5.5   (16.3)   Reynolds Road on right. Crater Mountain, a Pleistocene volcano, is at 1:30; the rugged profile of the Sierran Palisades Crest, south of the Coyote Warp, is visible from 2:00 to 3:00.

Beyond Reynolds Road, from 10:00 to 11:00, are the Waucobi embayment (the large recess in the front of the White-Inyo Range), the Pleistocene Waucobi Lake beds (white), and the Caltech radio telescopes on the floor of the valley.

1.3   (17.6)   Turn left onto Westgard Pass–Bristlecone Road (State Highway 168). Bristlecone Pine forest display on right.

1.4   (19.0)   Owens River.

From this point to just before the gate on the Mt. Barcroft road, we will be passing through a structurally complicated succession (7,000 m, 23,000 ft) of Precambrian to lower Middle Cambrian strata, illustrated in Fig. 3.9. The Lower Cambrian portion of this section, the Waucoban Series, is regarded as the North American–type succession for rocks of this age. It contains the oldest trilobite fauna in the Americas, as well as scattered primitive molluscan forms (*Wyattia*) and abundant tracks and trails.

The White-Inyo succession represents a largely tidal and subtidal group of rocks, together with reefal and off-reef carbonate bank deposits. The terrigenous strata are largely shale-siltstone and quartzite deposited off (west of) the Cambrian continental edge. It has been speculated that one could have walked across the Early Cambrian sea in the White-Inyo region and been in water no more than chest-deep. In other words, the strata have abundant shallow water indicators, such as crossbedding, ripple marks, mud cracks, and very highly bioturbated beds.

0.7   (19.7)   *STOP* (A-1), just before Death Valley–Waucoba Road (on the right). Turn and face west for an excellent view of the Sierran front. Mt. Sill, (14,162 ft) is at 12:00, Birch Mountain (13,665 ft) at 11:10, Split Mountain (14,051 ft) at 11:00, Mt. Tinemaha (12,561 ft) at 10:45, and Mt. Williamson (14,384 ft) at 10:00 in the distance. The Coyote Warp is to the northwest between 12:00 and 2:45. The Palisade Glacier lies below Mt. Sill.

At this locality is an example of the Greasewood Scrub Community, which covers much of the valley floor. Dominant plants are *Sarcobatus vermiculatus* and *Atriplex* species. These can tolerate the combination of heavy soils, varying degrees of alkalinity, and intense summer heat. They depend on groundwater rather than precipitation.

The structure of the White-Inyo Range is largely anticlinal, which can be seen readily by examination of the several U.S. Geological Survey quadrangle maps of the area. In a similar portrayal, this gross structure is shown in Fig. 3.7 and the enclosed geologic map.

The White Mountains are principally a south-plunging, asymmetrical anticline (east flank nearly vertical) exposing the Wyman Formation, a succession of argillites, phyllitic siltstone, and limestone at its core. The Inyo Range has a southeast trend, is a more open and nearly horizontal anticline, and also has the Wyman Formation at its core. Each of these structures has numerous subsidiary folds superimposed on it, is highly modified by faulting, and is moderately to severely affected by Mesozoic intrusive rocks. At several places in the Inyo Range and in areas to the southeast, structural windows, with late Paleozoic shales and limestones, are exposed. These rocks are overthrust by the Precambrian-Cambrian strata along the Last Chance thrust fault. Dating of the structural features of the White-Inyo Range is difficult because of the large temporal gap between the deformed and undeformed strata. Some have expressed the view that deformational episodes representing the Antler orogeny (late Devonian to early Mississippian time), the Sonoma orogeny (late Permian to early Triassic time), and the Nevadan (largely Jurassic in age) are involved. Timing of the Last Chance thrust can be bracketed between late Paleozoic (the age of the rocks in the structural windows) and Jurassic (the age of diorite that intrudes the thrust fault).

Road Log B (p. 64), to Papoose Flat, begins at the junction of the Westgard Road and the Waucoba Road. Mileage figures begin at zero.

Continue on Westgard Road.

2.4   (22.1)   The exposures on the right are mixed gravels and lake bed deposits of the Waucobi embayment.

1.1   (23.2)   5,000 ft elevation sign.

1.0   (24.2)   The first bedrock exposures (on right) are brown quartzite and blue-gray limestone of the Poleta Formation; the dark-gray rocks capping the hill are shales and siltstones of the Harkless Formation.

Just beyond (farther up the road) are exposures of limestone of the basal Poleta Formation, which extends as a light-colored band up the slope on the left side of the canyon. It is capped by the very dark-gray shales of the middle Poleta. The beds at road level, stratigraphically beneath the basal Poleta, are shales and sandstones of the Campito Formation.

1.1   (25.3)   Toll House Spring. This site marks the location of a former toll house at which tribute was extracted (one dollar per wagon load) from ranchers traveling between the Owens Valley and Fish Lake Valley to the northeast. The road was originally built as a private road, hence the toll. A spring issues from along a fault in the small gulley on the north side of the canyon just west of the site.

                   6,000 ft elevation sign.

                   Up the Westgard Road, all exposures are of the Andrews Mountain Member of the Campito Formation. This member contains the earliest of the Cambrian trilobites. These rocks are especially well exposed in the first "narrows" farther up the canyon.

1.9   (27.2)   First "narrows," cut in Campito sandstone.

0.8   (28.0)   7,000 ft elevation sign. Entering second "narrows" through exposures of the basal member of the Poleta Formation, an archeocyathan-bearing limestone. Beyond are less-exposed shales and minor limestone beds of the middle Poleta.

                   Here you see plants that commonly occur on limestone, along with others that are largely restricted to rocky places. These include the Heermann Buckwheats (*Eriogonum heermannii* ssp. *argense* and ssp. *humilius*), two brickellias (*Brickellia microphylla* and *B. oblongifolia*), Heath Daisy (*Leucelene ericoides*), and the showy Giant Four-o'clock (*Mirabilis multiflora* var. *pubescens*).

0.5   (28.5)   Third "narrows." Another exposure of basal Poleta limestone, just before Cedar Flat, with nary a cedar tree to be seen. You have entered a typical Pinyon-juniper Woodland Plant Community. Pinyon Pine (*Pinus monophylla*) and Utah Juniper (*Juniperus osteosperma*) are the dominant species. The juniper will gradually drop out as the elevation increases. Exposures on the right (east) side of Cedar Flat are basal Poleta limestone.

0.8   (29.3)   *STOP* (A-2). Park on right side of road for a view of some of the features of the White Mountains. In the middle distance at 12:00, the rather flat but rugged exposures of light rocks are the Birch Creek Pluton; at 11:00 is a fault block of white Reed Dolomite, with Deep Spring Formation and dark Campito sandstone on the skyline.

0.7   (30.0)   White Mountain Road. Turn left.

                   Road Log C (p. 70) to Deep Springs Valley begins at the junction of Westgard Road and White Mountain Road. Mileage figures begin at zero.

0.4   (30.4)   Bristlecone Forest Service kiosk.

0.8   (31.2)   Small "narrows" is cut in basal Poleta limestone.

More limestone plants at a higher elevation. Squaw Apple (*Peraphyllum ramosissimum*) is seen at the road junction just below the narrows and on the wash bank to the right. The endemic Westgard Penstemon (*Penstemon scapioides*) provides groundcover on the left of the narrows, and a large Mojave Mound Cactus (*Echinocereus triglochidiatus* var. *mohavensis*) may be seen high on the rocks to the right. Immediately to the right of the road, one of the large boulders in the alluvial deposits contains archeocyathans from the Poleta Formation.

1.0 (32.2) At 9:00 at the crest of the Sierra Nevada, one has a good view of the Palisade Glacier, the largest glacier in the Sierra Nevada, and, farther to the right, Coyote Flat, from which the Coyote Warp gets its name.

1.8 (34.0) 8,000 ft elevation sign.

0.7 (34.7) Outcrop on left of gray shale and buff limestone of the middle Poleta Formation.

0.4 (35.1) Entrance to Grandview Campground on left.

0.5 (35.6) The somber gray hills in this vicinity are Campito Formation.

0.9 (36.5) Mt. Tom, in the Sierra west of Bishop, is at 9:00.

0.2 (36.7) View of Deep Springs Lake at 3:00.

0.8 (37.5) *STOP* (A-3). Sierra View. An opportunity to view peaks in the Sierra Nevada and the Inyo Mountains and to take a short stroll to view Mt. Whitney.

0.7 (38.2) On the canyon wall opposite (9:00) is an exposure of the contact between the Deep Spring and Campito (dark) formations. You have entered the Bristlecone-Limber Pine Forest. If you are in a botanical mood and wish to learn how to quickly distinguish Bristlecone Pine and Limber Pine: the Bristlecone Pine needles are darker green, are distributed evenly along the branchlets, and look rather like a foxtail or bottlebrush; the Limber Pine needles are a lighter green and are clustered at the ends of the branchlets. Bristlecone Pine branches are fairly regular, closely set, short, and symmetrical on young trees, whereas Limber Pine branches are notably irregular, with some very long.

1.1 (39.3) Reed Flat on left and ahead. The flat lies along the trend of the Deep Spring Formation, parts of which are exposed ahead—the red-brown quartzite and immediately underlying light-gray limestone. The light cream-colored beds are Reed Dolomite. The Campito sandstone crops out on the left to the west.

In June and July delicate Silver Lupine (*Lupinus argenteus* var. *tenellus*) may make the slopes blue, or Clokey Paintbrush (*Castilleja martinii* var. *clokeyi*) color them red in the vicinity of Reed Flat. Numerous other wildflowers occur among them.

0.5   (39.8)   Turn right to enter Schulman Grove. *STOP* (A-4). Depending on the time, spend either a short or moderate length of time here in the Bristlecone Pine forest. The best stands of the Bristlecone Pine are on soils developed on the Reed Dolomite. They do quite well on the limestone of the Deep Spring Formation, and not at all well on the sandstone of the Campito Formation.

Return to White Mountain Road.

0.3   (40.1)   Turn right and continue north.

0.9   (41.0)   The next valley north of Reed Flat is also along the trend of the Deep Spring Formation. The Reed–Deep Spring contact is near the top (left) of the cream-colored rocks; the Campito Formation occupies the west side of the valley.

0.5   (41.5)   Coldwater Spring at 3:00.

0.7   (42.2)   At saddle on road, Blanco Mountain (11,278 ft), underlain by Reed Dolomite, is the sharp pyramidal peak at 2:00; radio relay station at 9:00.

0.8   (43.0)   Silver Canyon–Wyman Canyon roads. The high scenic route provides an excellent opportunity to observe and compare the Bristlecone Pine and Limber Pine in all stages of growth.

0.6   (43.6)   Gray-blue limestone on left is basal Poleta Formation. Beyond, and for the next three miles, one travels within the upper, shaley part of the Campito Formation (Montenegro Member).

3.0   (46.6)   Junction with Wyman Canyon road (on right). On the lower road, just before it meets the north intersection with the scenic route, are good populations of Silver Moss (*Lupinus breweri* var. *bryoides*) and Mono Clover (*Trifolium andersonii* ssp. *monoense*). The latter is mostly restricted to the White Mountains. The bushy Palmer Lupine (*Lupinus palmeri*) may be found blooming long after flowers of the delicate Silver Lupine are gone.

Continue northward. County Line Hill on right; tree-covered hills at 11:00–12:00 are Poleta Formation; the treeless, soft-weathering hills and valley to the west are underlain by shales of the next overlying unit, the Harkless Formation.

Ahead are three sharp black peaks, each underlain by Campito sandstone: Campito Mountain (11,543 ft) at 12:00, Sheep Mountain (12,497 ft) lies beyond and to the left at 11:45, and Paiute Mountain (12,564 ft) is at 11:30.

0.6   (47.2)   Inyo-Mono County Line.

2.0   (49.2)   Turn right to Crooked Creek Station.

Here, in Campito Meadow, are a good variety of meadow plants, including Meadow Arnica (*Arnica chamissonis*), Yellow-cress (*Rorippa curvipes*), Toad Lily (*Montia chamissoi*), Meadow Mimulus (*Mimulus primuloides*), and various meadow grasses.

0.4   (49.6)   Rough-weathering rocks here are granitic intrusive rocks of the Sage Hen Flat Pluton. In this vicinity, it is principally in contact with the Deep Spring Formation.

0.6   (50.2)   Take right fork at sign to station.

0.3   (50.5)   Crooked Creek Station (White Mountain Research Station). *STOP* (A-5).

Return to White Mountain Road.

1.2   (51.7)   Rejoin White Mountain Road. Turn right. The road for the next 6 mi is along the trend of the Deep Spring Formation, largely covered by scree from the Campito Formation on the ridges to the west.

0.9   (52.6)   At pass on road. Contact (poorly exposed) of Deep Spring and Campito (on left). Campito Mountain to west. The skyline peak, just to the right of Sheep Mountain, at 12:00, is underlain by Deep Spring carbonate rocks; the tree-covered ridges ahead and to right are underlain by Reed Dolomite.

1.6   (54.2)   Patriarch Grove Road. Visit the Patriarch Grove on the return trip.

0.9   (55.1)   Reed Dolomite on right. Across the main canyon to the east are exposures of Tertiary basalt. These lava flows lie above a major erosional surface or uncomformity, here cut across the granitic rocks of the Cottonwood Pluton.

0.3   (55.4)   Road summit. *STOP* (A-6). White Mountain Peak (14,246 ft) is at 11:00. Rocks in foreground and on right are Reed Dolomite; somber, rough-weathering rocks beyond Reed are intrusive granitic rocks of the Barcroft Pluton.

2.7   (58.1)   Lamb Camp on left. At pass just beyond, an excellent view of the Barcroft Pluton. The regional trend (NNW) of the Reed–Deep Spring–Campito rocks has been significantly modified by the intrusion of the Barcroft Pluton. The beds have been severely deformed so that they parallel the NE trend of the south contact of the pluton.

Some favorite White Mountain species occur in the shallow drainage channels. These include Shooting Star (*Dodecatheon redolens*), Duran Alumroot (*Heuchera duranii*), and the Miniature Alpine Androsace (*Androsace septentrionalis* var. *subumbellata*).

Locked gate to Barcroft Station, Nello Pace Laboratory, White Mountain Research Station (WMRS) facilities. Foot traffic beyond this point.

0.5	(58.6)	Barcroft Gate. Here the road passes from the ancient metasedimentary terrain to the relatively young granitic rocks of the pluton.
1.9	(60.5)	Nello Pace Laboratory (WMRS). *STOP* (A-7).

If the weather is clear, from the Barcroft station there are excellent views: to the east, the basalt-Cottonwood granitic rocks unconformity, and beyond, the Silver Peak Range; to the southeast, the Last Chance Range and the Eureka Valley sand dunes; to the south, Paiute and Sheep Mountains, and in the distance, Blanco Mountain and Waucoba Mountain.

Return south on White Mountain Road.

1.9	(62.4)	Barcroft gate.

In the alpine meadows to the east are the endemic White Mountain Ivesia (*Ivesia lycopodioides* ssp. *scandalis*) and Alpine Gentian (*Gentiana newberryi*), along with other hardy alpine perennials.

1.1	(63.5)	At small saddle along road, the small ridge to the right is an outcrop of a dike probably related to the main body of the Barcroft Pluton.
2.3	(65.8)	At road summit, a good view at 12:00 of Sage Hen Flat and Blanco Mountain beyond; the Last Chance Range and Eureka Valley dunes lie in the distance at 10:00 to 11:00.
1.0	(66.8)	Patriarch Grove Road. Turn left.
1.0	(67.8)	Patriarch Grove. *STOP* (A-8). The rocks all about are Reed Dolomite. In addition to the Bristlecone Pine, an excellent view to the northeast of the basalt-Cottonwood granitic rocks unconformity, and several north-northeast-trending faults along each of which the basalt-granite contact has been down-dropped on the west side.

Rocky outcrops above Patriarch Grove. An assortment of low tundra plants including Erect-pod Oxytropis (*Oxytropis parryi*), Limestone Aster (*Haplopappus acaulis*), and Clokey Daisy (*Erigeron clokeyi*). Above the cliffs one finds the mustards, Lemmon Rock-cress (*Arabis lemmonii* var. *depauperata*), and minute tufts of White Mountain Draba (*Draba oligosperma*).

Return to White Mountain Road.

1.0	(68.8)	White Mountain Road. Turn left.
2.5	(71.3)	Turn left to Crooked Creek Station. *STOP* (A-5).

Return to White Mountain Road.

2.5	(73.8)	White Mountain Road. Turn left.
8.9	(82.7)	Schulman Grove Road.
2.3	(85.0)	Sierra View. *STOP* (A-3). A good place to view a continuous stratigraphic section exposed on the south side of Deep Springs Valley.

From right to left on the ridge above the valley are the following formations: Wyman (brown); Reed and Deep Spring (buff striped) units; Campito (black); Poleta (gray-brown-white stripes); Harkless (brown); and at the major saddle directly above green valley floor is the contact of the Joshua Flat Pluton and the Paleozoic section.

Continue south on White Mountain Road.

7.5   (92.5)   Westgard Pass Road. Turn right.

9.4   (101.9)   Approaching Big Pine, two prominent fault scarps created during the 1872 Owens Valley earthquake cut across the east face of Crater Mountain, here seen to the southwest at 10:00.

2.9   (104.8)   Highway 395. Turn right.

7.5   (112.3)   At 3:00, on the west face of the White Mountains below Black Mountain (9,083 ft), are two exposures of a part of the Paleozoic stratigraphic section. The prominent canyon is Marble Canyon. South of the canyon, the formations from the foot of the range upward are: Reed (light-brown nonbedded rocks); Deep Spring (striped buff beds); Campito (black). The same section is exposed on the north side of the canyon, but higher on the range, above soft-weathering old alluvial fan gravels; farther to the north, the tree-covered rocks above the Campito Formation are Poleta limestone.

6.5   (118.8)   East Line Street, Bishop. Turn right.

3.6   (122.4)   Owens Valley Laboratory.

End of Road Log A.

ROAD LOG B

Owens Valley to Papoose Flat (Big Pine and Waucoba Mountain 15-min quadrangles).
    For travel to Papoose Flat, either a 4 × 4 vehicle or one with extra-low gear is essential. Log begins at intersection of Waucoba Road and Westgard Pass Road.

0.0   (0.0)   Turn right at fork, onto Waucoba Road.

The two areas of trees to left of the highway are along springs that mark the trace of the frontal fault along which the Inyo Range has been uplifted relative to the Owens Valley.

In morning light, a small fault scarp can be seen cutting the apex of the young alluvial fan, just to the right of the Waucoba Road where the road turns left to enter Waucoba Canyon.

Approaching the entrance to Waucoba Canyon, granitic rocks (largely diorite) of probable Jurassic age crop out in the hills on left from 1.4 to 2.0 mi from the road fork.

2.9   (2.9)   Plio-Pleistocene Waucobi Lake beds on left. A volcanic ash in the lake bed succession has been dated at 2.3 Ma. The lake beds have a general westward inclination of approximately 7° illustrating a recent westward tilting of the range.

0.8   (3.7)   Outcrops of limestone and siltstone of the Monola Formation (Middle Cambrian) on both sides of road.

For the next 2 mi, the rocks exposed on both sides of the road are Quaternary gravels lying above the Waucobi Lake beds.

2.3   (6.0)   On the left is a monoclinal fold in the Waucobi Lake beds. This fold is at the southeast end of one of the many recent normal faults that cut the Waucobi embayment.

0.1   (6.1)   Outcrop of Reed Dolomite on right side of road. At 9:00, exposure of Waucobi Lake beds overlain by Quaternary gravels.

0.3   (6.4)   On the right, at upper part of gravel road leading up small gulley, are exposures of the Wyman Formation, the oldest rock unit present in the White-Inyo Range.

For the next mile, rocks on both sides of road are Quaternary gravels.

1.0   (7.4)   On the right, a buttress unconformity with the coarse Quaternary gravels deposited against the eroded edges of Wyman siltstone.

0.8   (8.2)   *STOP* (B-1). Devils Gate. This is a water gap, produced by the super-position of a Waucobi Canyon stream from a former higher level when the bedrock here was buried in the old alluvial gravels.

The highly folded and faulted quartzites and sandy dolomites here are within the Reed Dolomite. Beyond Devils Gate to the east, you will note that the gradient of the canyon is considerably gentler. The gate is a knickpoint that has provided a local base level for the erosional lowering of the canyon above this point.

1.0   (9.2)   Road to Harkless Flat on right.

3.2   (12.4)   Turn right onto dirt road.

0.2   (12.6)   Road fork. Take right fork onto Hines Road. The odd structure on the right is a "quail guzzler," a device to provide a watering hole for small desert fowl.

2.0   (14.6)   *STOP* (B-2)—to view the stratigraphic section exposed on Hines Ridge to the north.

The buff carbonate directly to the north is basal Reed Dolomite; gray-brown strata to right are Wyman siltstones; brown band to left of buff carbonate is the unit exposed in Devils Gate; the cream-colored dolomite to the left is upper Reed; overlying beds, up to the top of the thin band of light-colored carbonate, are Deep Spring Formation; this is overlain by dark gray Campito sandstones.

The high peak at 11:00 (the road is 12:00) is Andrews Mountain (9,460 ft), from which the lower member of the Campito Formation gets its name; the jagged rocks on the skyline at 11:30 are quartzites within the Harkless Formation. Proceed up the Hines Road.

Shortly, the road turns left and drops into a gulley. The trees here are predominantly Pinyon Pine and a few scattered juniper.

0.9   (15.5)   The "narrows" here exposes a section from the middle Deep Spring to the base of the Campito.

1.0   (16.5)   The next "narrows" is cut in limestone of the basal Poleta.

0.1   (16.6)   STOP (B-3), just before the steep rise, to prepare for the assault on a set of switchbacks. The road is steep and rough and must be traveled with a bit of abandon (though carefully, of course). Turn left at fork.

The switchback road exposes (poorly) units from the middle Poleta to middle Harkless Formation; just ahead, the road passes over exposures of the upper Poleta, which here is about 50 ft thick. Compare this figure with that for the same units at Papoose Flat.

After the first switchback, the high peak on the right is White Mountain Peak (14,246 ft).

At the second switchback, exposures straight ahead are quartzites of the Harkless Formation.

1.2   (17.8)   STOP (B-4), just beyond the road summit, to view Sierran peaks. At 1:30 is Split Mountain (14,051 ft); at 11:00 is the blunt north face of Mt. Williamson (14,384 ft); the ramplike peak to the right of Williamson is Mt. Tyndall (14,018 ft); the ramplike peak to the south of Williamson is Mt. Whitney (14,495 ft).

Exposures to the left of the road are shales of the upper Harkless Formation lying above the quartzites.

Proceed down the slope to the west.

0.3   (18.1)   Just before the sharp left turn at the base of the slope is a good view, at 2:00–3:00 across Owens Valley, of the Coyote Warp; Bishop is the green area in the distance, and the front of the Volcanic Tableland and the Benton Range are beyond. Wheeler Crest lies beyond the Coyote Warp.

As you proceed south toward Papoose Flat, observe how the rocks exposed in the rounded hills to the left become progressively shinier (if the sun angle is right). This is a result of increased metamorphic grade as you approach the Papoose Flat Pluton.

For the next 2 1/2 mi, the road passes through poorly exposed shales and siltstones of the Saline Valley Formation.

1.4 (19.5)   After the sharp left turn, the gray-blue bluff on the right at 2:00–3:00 is the Mule Spring Limestone, the youngest of the early Cambrian rocks in the White-Inyo Range.

From this point south, until the next broad curve to the right, the road follows the general south-southeast strike of the bedding north of the Papoose Flat Pluton.

2.0 (21.5)   As the road begins to swing west, it follows the westerly trend of the beds produced by the westward bulge of the Papoose Flat Pluton.

0.2 (21.7)   Road fork; Papoose Flat to the left. Proceed straight ahead beyond fork.

0.5 (22.2)   Turn left at saddle and proceed southwest along road to crest of ridge.

0.2 (22.4)   *STOP* (B-5) at ridge crest. Rocks on ridge are metaquartzite of the Harkless Formation.

See Fig. 3.10.

Across Owens Valley, from north to south: Coyote Warp at 3:00; Crater Mountain at 2:30; Perlite quarry (white) at 1:30; Red Mountain at 1:00; on the Sierran crest, just south of Red Mountain, the prominent horizontal stripe is a metamorphic rock septum between a lower yellow-buff granite and a dark-colored granodiorite; Big Pine volcanic field at 12:00 (across Owens Valley); volcanic rocks at base of Inyo Mountains at 12:00.

From this point, a short distance down the slope to the south is the contact between the highly foliated, feldspar-rich Papoose Flat Pluton and the Poleta Formation (here, very poorly exposed). The Poleta contact rocks are better exposed along the south border of the pluton two stops ahead.

The foliation (layering) of the pluton is expressed by the alignment of both large feldspar crystals and smaller grains of quartz and biotite mica, and by numerous dikes of aplite (fine-grained granite) that have been reoriented during intrusion from an earlier random pattern to parallelism with the mineral foliation and the bedding of the metasedimentary rocks above the contact.

Return to vehicle, return to saddle, turn right.

0.4 (22.8)   Road fork (road to right is washed out). Rocks exposed a short distance down the road are andalusite-biotite schist, the metamorphic equivalent of the upper Harkless shales.

Proceed east to main road fork.

0.3 (23.1)   Road fork. Turn right and proceed southwest across Papoose Flat.

0.1 (23.2)   The prominent exposure at 9:00 is the highly foliated upper part of the Papoose Flat Pluton.

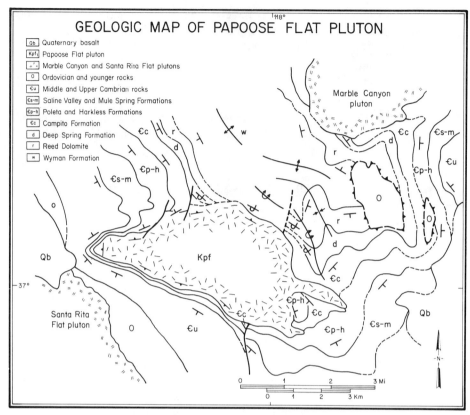

GEOLOGIC MAP OF PAPOOSE FLAT PLUTON

Qb Quaternary basalt
Kpf Papoose Flat pluton
Marble Canyon and Santa Rita Flat plutons
O Ordovician and younger rocks
Єu Middle and Upper Cambrian rocks
Єs-m Saline Valley and Mule Spring Formations
Єp-h Poleta and Harkless Formations
Єc Campito Formation
d Deep Spring Formation
r Reed Dolomite
w Wyman Formation

FIGURE 3.10 Generalized geologic map of Papoose Flat Pluton, illustrating position of pluton on southwest flank of the Inyo Mountain anticline.

1.2 (24.4)   At the west end of the flat, the west-dipping foliation in the pluton is shown by numerous aplite dikes. Stay on main road.

0.2 (24.6)   Take right fork (Badger Flat Road); shortly the road turns left and climbs the ridge, more or less paralleling the trend of metasedimentary units just south of the pluton contact. You have crossed the axis of the Papoose Flat anticline, and the folation in the plutonic rocks and in the metasedimentary units are parallel and dip to the south.

Proceed along Badger Flat Road through several switchbacks and sharp curves.

0.9 (25.5)   After road drops into small gulley, turn right and *STOP* (B-6) adjacent to large juniper 50 yd ahead.

The light grey rocks on the ridge SW of the parking area are dolomite beds of the Bonanza King Formation (Middle Cambrian).

The tree species in this part of the Papoose Flat area are Pinyon Pine, juniper, and Mountain Mahogany. On the higher ridges to the east and southeast are stands of Limber Pine and Bristlecone Pine.

From the parking area, take walking trail N15°E for approximately 250 yd to the contact between the Papoose Flat Pluton and the Poleta Formation. At this place, the southwesterly dipping foliation of the plutonic rocks and their abundant large feldspar crystals are excellently exposed. The metasedimentary section adjacent to the pluton is of greatest interest, however.

The rocks above the pluton (the contact is covered by slope wash) here are black schist and calc-silicate boudins (sausage-shaped bodies), probably equivalent to much of the middle Poleta Formation elsewhere. Boudins (sausage-shaped rock segments) are common at many places at and near the contact, and attest to the flattening and attenuation these rocks have undergone. Next above is 3.25 ft of metaquartzite, which is equivalent to approximately 115 ft of sandstone of upper middle Poleta Formation in the Deep Springs Valley area. The overlying 4.25 ft buff-blue-buff highly foliated marble here is the metamorphic equivalent of the uppermost Poleta, elsewhere approximately 125 ft in thickness.

The overlying Harkless Formation regionally comprises (from base to top) basal black shale, vitreous quartzite, and buff-brown shale. Here, as can be seen by making a short south traverse to the crest of the ridge, the equivalents of the Harkless Formation are basal fine-grained black schist, brown metaquartzite, and coarse-grained brown biotite schist. Each of the stratigraphic units has retained its integrity, even though stretched and thinned to less than 10% of its original stratigraphic thickness. This was accomplished by the forcible injection of the Papoose Flat Pluton, which can be seen in Fig. 3.10 and on the geologic map in the pocket to have disrupted the regional southeast trend of the west flank of the Inyo anticline several miles westward.

At the end of the short traverse, by looking S10°W, can be see the offset pluton-metasedimentary rock contact, illustrating one of the many left-lateral faults that cut the pluton-Poleta contact.

To the east, the rounded skyline peak is Waucoba Mountain (11,123 ft).

Return to vehicle and go back on same road. The road to the right continues on to Badger Flat, and eventually to Independence and the Owens Valley, via Mazourka Canyon, but it is very rough.

0.2 (25.7)   Exposures adjacent (on the right) to the road are highly foliated blue-gray marble, the metamorphic equivalent of the Mule Spring Limestone.

In this vicinity, the slabby red-brown float fragments are metasiltstones of the Monola Formation (basal Middle Cambrian), which lies between the Mule Spring Limestone and the overlying Bonanza King Dolomite.

0.2   (25.9)   A short distance down the road to the right is an abandoned flagstone quarry in the metaquartzite of the middle Harkless Formation.

0.7   (26.6)   STOP (B-7), at west end of Papoose Flat, at junction with road to east, to view the Wyman overturn at 3:00. The pluton contact is at the major saddle on the skyline. Rocks to the left (north) of the saddle are overturned carbonates (buff-gray) and siltstones (brown) of the Wyman Formation. This overturning represents a northeast-directed blister produced by the injection of the pluton.

End of Road Log B

ROAD LOG C

Cedar Flat to Deep Springs Valley (Blanco Mountain and Soldier Pass 15-min quandrangles).

0.0   (0.0)   White Mountain Road and Westgard Road. Proceed north on Westgard Road.

0.9   (0.9)   Westgard Pass, elevation 7,271 ft. From here the road descends through Payson Canyon. From the north end of Cedar Flat, just ahead, all the rocks exposed in the canyon, except for a small dike 2 1/2 mi ahead, are Campito Formation. The road traverses around the nose of the south-plunging White Mountain anticline (see Fig. 3.7).

Pinyon-juniper Woodland dominates the local vegetation, with a dense understory of sagebrush. Bitterbrush and Rabbitbrush are also scattered in the area. A number of weedy species were probably first introduced to the White Mountains along the road margins in this area.

1.2   (2.1)   Elevation 7,000 ft.

0.3   (2.4)   Canyon on left is Mollie Gibson Canyon. A jeep road leads up this canyon and provides rough access to the northwest corner of the Birch Creek Pluton (see Fig. 3.7).

The tall shrubs preferring the wash of Payson Canyon are Rabbitbrush (*Chrysothamnus nauseosus*). You are now in transition from Pinyon-juniper Woodland to Desert Scrub communities.

1.0   (3.4)   As you approach the sharp curve to the left, dead ahead is an outcrop of jointed gray dike rock, which occurs along a northeast-trending fault valley. The dike rock stands out against the darker-colored Campito sandstone.

The steep, fractured sandstone canyon walls below harbor a number of petrophytes, rock-loving plants that require the extra moisture channeled through crevices and, commonly, the shelter from direct radiation. Locally, these include the Cliff Goldenbush (*Ericameria cuneata*), Desert Snowberry (*Symphoricarpos longiflorus*), Plateau Gooseberry (*Ribes velutinum*), Rock Mustard (*Halimolobos diffusa*), and Rock Parsley (*Pteryxia petraea*).

1.8 (5.2) *STOP* (C-1), at crest of small rise just beyond the mouth of Payson Canyon, for a good view of Deep Springs Valley. On the skyline of the ridge to the south, the formations exposed are from the Wyman (red-brown), Reed–Deep Spring (buff-colored layered units), and Campito (dark gray); the two narrow, light bands separated by the dark band at 2:00 are the Poleta Formation; immediately to the left at the notch on the skyline and above the right-hand edge of Deep Springs Lake is the contact of the Cambrian section with the Joshua Flat Monzonite. At 1:00 is the contact of the Joshua Flat granitic body (dark) and the younger Beer Creek Quartz Monzonite (light). Ahead at 11:30 is Soldier Pass at the far side of Deep Springs Valley.

Beyond Deep Springs dry lake, at the foot of the range, a large alluvial fan is developed at the mouth of the major canyon. In morning light, a large fault scarp can be seen at the foot of the fan, and a smaller scarp is visible at the apex of the fan.

Outward from the lake, several distinctly colored bands of vegetation can be discerned. These represent distinct plant communities whose compositions are determined by soil salt concentrations, particle size, and proximity of the water table the lake represents. The most frequently encountered species away from surface water is Black Greasewood (*Sarcobatus vermiculatus*). This dominates in the broad, outermost green band that merges with the general desert vegetation away from the lake.

1.5 (6.7) *STOP* (C-2), just beyond the 38-mi Inyo Co. sign, and walk south to the edge of the terrace surface. Good desert pavement can be observed on the terrace. From here, with the highway as 12:00, the view from 8:45 to 10:00 shows the Birch Creek Pluton (on the left), and the Wyman, Reed, Deep Spring, and Campito (dark gray) formations.

The isolated hill at 11:00, known locally as "The Elephant," is a block containing east-dipping upper Deep Spring and Campito formations far out of structural position; it is probably a large landslide block that has moved south from about 10:00, where these rocks are in normal structural position.

Nearby vegetation is typical of coarse upper-desert alluvial fans derived in part from calcareous rocks. The dominant plant in such situations is usually a low scrub with thick spines, *Menodora spinescens*. Many other species are usually present as well, locally including Spiny Hopsage (*Grayia spinosa*), Shadscale (*Atriplex confertifolia*) and Cooper Goldenbush (*Ericameria cooperi*). Shadscale can also become dominant in these situations.

Looking south across the large wash, you can see excellent exposures of a part of the Poleta folds, a set of closely spaced, northeast-trending, alternating anticlines and synclines. In this view, you can see (from right to left) a sharp anticline, a major syncline, a faulted broad gentle anticline, and a steep-limbed syncline. The rocks exposed in this view range from the middle Poleta Formation to the basal Harkless Formation, the latter exposed in the core of the eastern syncline.

Return to vehicle and proceed east into Deep Springs Valley.

1.2   (7.9)   As you pass the south edge of the isolated hill on the left of the road, immediately to the left is a small terrace 10–15 ft above the road. This is a beach terrace of Pleistocene Deep Springs Lake at an elevation of 5,200 ft. The lake was somewhat higher than this, as it drained eastward through Soldier Pass (directly ahead, across the valley) into Eureka Valley.

0.6   (8.5)   At the "cattle" road sign, look to 9:00 for a view of the contact of the Cambrian metasedimentary rocks and the Eureka Valley Monzonite (Fig. 3.7). The rocks adjacent to the pluton are largely metamorphosed carbonates, including marble and calc-silicates, of the Mule Spring and Monola formations.

As you travel across Deep Springs Valley, look to 3:00–4:00 to view the faceted spurs along the fault scarp on the east side of the valley. If the light is right, you can see very fresh minor scarps at the base of the mountain.

0.9   (9.4)   *STOP* (C-3), just after broad turn to left. Straight ahead is a concentration of trees at Deep Springs College. The high peak directly above is Piper Mountain (7,703 ft), capped by late Tertiary basalt. To the left of Piper Mountain (Chocolate Mountain), the basalt has been faulted down 400 ft. From there it has been faulted down again to the floor of the northeast end of Deep Springs Valley. These down-faulted blocks of basalt are called lauderbacks.

To the east at 2:30, the dark exposures at the foot of the range and within the Beer Creek Quartz Monzonite (see Fig. 3.7), are diorite masses representing the oldest plutonic rocks of the White-Inyo Range (180 Ma).

4.1   (13.5)   Turn right to Deep Springs College. The college, founded in 1917, combines diverse, rigorous academic studies, ranch and administrative labor, and democratic self-government, and is largely run by the students. The student body is presently all male and numbers about 25. A brochure, available at the entrance to the campus, gives further details.

Pass through the campus, turning right at the southeast edge of the campus.

1.2   (14.7)   Turn left through two gates and proceed south along the east face of the range. Along this route are numerous very fresh fault scarps, generally 5–20 ft high. The are very young geologically, but precisely how young is not known.

1.2   (15.9)   Exposures of rounded, spheroidal weathering boulders at 9:00 are Beer Creek Pluton (Fig. 3.7).

1.5   (17.4)   At 9:00 is an excellent example of a small fault scarp at the foot of range.

Between here and the gate ahead, we pass from the pale-colored desert scrub vegetation to bright-green greasewood vegetation as the surface drops toward the local water table. On higher, sandier ground in this community are stands of Big Sagebrush and Rabbitbrush, and among the Greasewood are commonly Shadscale and Inkweed (*Suaeda torreyana*, another salt-tolerant phreatophyte).

3.5   (20.9)   Gate. Rocks at range front at 9:00 are Joshua Flat Monzonite.

0.6   (21.5)   Turn right at stone corral.

0.1   (21.6)   Pass through gate on left.

0.1   (21.7)   *STOP* (C-4) in meadow beyond gate. Walk to east end of meadow, cross creek to south, and take trail about 200 yd to the small knob to right side of trail.

From this knob, several fault features can be observed: sag ponds, scarps, and a prominent graben. If you examine the distribution of debris material to the west of the graben (you are standing on the scarp bounding the west side of the graben), you can see that the graben faults have cut across the upper (apex) part of a long debris flow. The rocks in the flow are typical Joshua Flat Monzonite boulders.

Looking to the southwest, you can see that the fault marking the east side of Deep Springs Valley swings to the southwest. It forms the south edge of the valley and then passes southwestward into the bedrock of the range, at the major change in slope on the skyline ridge, where it marks the contact between the Wyman Formation on the south and the Deep Spring Formation on the north.

Looking across Deep Springs Valley to the west, you can see the Poleta folds area. The surface of the fold area is generally flat and slopes gently toward the valley. If you follow the surface northward, you can see that it extends across the highway, where it truncates the dark rocks of the Campito Formation. This surface is an exhumed stream cut surface called a pediment.

Return to vehicle and go back along east side of valley.

End of Road Log C.

REFERENCES

Bateman, P. C. 1965. Geology and tungsten mineralization of the Bishop District, California. U.S. Geological Society Professional Paper 470.

Ernst, W. G., and C. A. Hall. 1987. Geology of the Mount Barcroft–Blanco Mountain area, eastern California. Geological Society of America Map and Chart Series. Map MCH066.

Hanson, R. B. 1986. Geology of Mesozoic metavolcanic and metasedimentary rocks, northern White Mountains, California. Ph.D. dissertation, University of California, Los Angeles.

Oakeshott, G. B. 1978. *California's changing landscapes: A guide to the geology of the state.* McGraw-Hill, New York.

Rinehart, C. D., and W. C. Smith. 1982. *Earthquakes and young volcanoes, along the eastern Sierra Nevada.* Genny Smith, Palo Alto, Calif.

Ross, D. C. 1965. Geology of the Independence quadrangle, Inyo County, California. U.S. Geological Survey Bull. 1181-O.

Sharp, R. P. 1976. *Geology field guide to southern California,* rev. ed. Kendall Hunt, Dubuque, Iowa.

Smith, Genny, ed. 1978. *Deepest valley: Guide to Owens Valley.* Wm. Kaufman, Los Altos, Calif.

U.S. GEOLOGICAL SURVEY GEOLOGIC MAPS

Crowder, D. F., P. T. Robinson, and D. L. Harris. 1972. Geologic map of the Benton quadrangle, Mono County, California, and Esmeralda and Mineral Counties, Nevada. U.S. Geological Survey Map GQ-1013.

Crowder, D. F., and M. F. Sheridan. 1972. Geologic map of the White Mountain peak quandrangle, Mono County, California. U.S. Geological Survey Map GQ-1012.

Krauskopf, K. B. 1971. Geologic map of the Mt. Barcroft Quandrangle, California-Nevada. U.S. Geological Survey Map GQ-960.

McKee, E. H., and C. A. Nelson. 1967. Geologic map of Soldier Pass quandrangle, California and Nevada. U.S. Geological Survey Map GQ-654.

Nelson, C. A. 1966. Geologic map of the Waucoba Mtn. quadrangle, Inyo County, California. U.S. Geological Survey Map GQ-528.

Nelson, C. A. 1966. Geologic map of the Blanco Mtn. quadrangle, Inyo and Mono Counties, California. U.S. Geological Survey Map GQ-529.

Nelson, C. A. 1971. Geologic map of the Waucoba Spring Quadrangle, Inyo County, California. U.S. Geological Survey Map GQ-921.

Robinson, P. T., and D. F. Crowder. 1973. Geologic map of the Davis Mountain quadrangle, Esmeralda and Mineral Counties, Nevada, and Mono County, California. U.S. Geological Survey Map GQ-1078.

Ross, D. C. 1967. Geologic map of Waucoba Wash quadrangle. U.S. Geological Survey Map GQ-612.

Stewart, J. H., P. T. Robinson, J. P. Albers, and D. F. Crowder. 1974. Geologic map of the Piper Peak quadrangle, Nevada-California. U.S. Geological Survey Map GQ-1186.

PART II

PLANTS

4

Plant Zones

Timothy P. Spira

DESERT SCRUB ZONE (4,000–6,500 ft, 1,219–1,981 m)

A shrub-dominant vegetation covers the valley floors and mountainsides of the White-Inyo Range up to elevations of approximately 6,500 ft (1,980 m) (Fig. 4.1). The vegetation is remarkably uniform in appearance, even though many different species are present. The dominant shrubs are generally less than 3 ft (0.9 m) tall, grayish, small-leaved, and small-flowered.

The most common species is Shadscale (*Atriplex confertifolia*), an erect, stiffly branched, spiny shrub with round, crowded deciduous leaves that resemble fish scales. Shadscale commonly occurs on heavy alkaline (pH 8–10) and saline soils locally underlain with a hardpan. At higher elevations, sagebrush (*Artemisia* spp.) becomes dominant. Other important shrubs include Creosote Bush (*Larrea tridentata*), Nevada Ephedra (*Ephedra nevadensis*), Rabbitbrush (*Chrysothamnus nauseosus*), and Spiny Hopsage (*Grayia spinosa*).

At least seven species of sagebrush (*Artemisia*) occur in the White-Inyo Range. These aromatic shrubs or herbs with lobed silvery gray-green leaves form a dominant part of the vegetation from the desert floor to the alpine desert. In the Desert Scrub zone, both Bud Sagebrush (*Artemisia spinescens*) and Basin Sagebrush (*A. tridentata*) are common.

The primary factor preventing tree growth in the Desert Scrub vegetation is the small amount of rainfall (less than 10 in, or 25.4 cm per year). The stress imposed by scanty precipitation is intensified by high summer and low winter temperatures, strong winds, and shallow soils. The wide spacing between shrubs probably reflects intense root competition for soil moisture or a phenomenon known as allelopathy, whereby plants produce chemical substances that inhibit the growth of other plants.

Perennial and annual herbs commonly occur in open areas between shrubs. Among the more conspicuous perennial herbs are penstemons (*Penstemon* ssp.), the Large White Evening Primrose (*Oenothera caespitosa* ssp. *marginata*), Wishbone Bush (*Mirabilis bigelovii*), and various grasses. Showy displays by annuals such as Little Blazing Star (*Mentzelia albicaulis*), Wilcox Woolly Star (*Eriastrum sparsiflorum* var. *wilcoxii*), and Chia (*Salvia columbariae*) are restricted to favorably moist years.

The vegetation of washes and springs differs dramatically from that of surrounding areas. For example, trees such as Black Cottonwood (*Populus trichocarpa*) and Yellow Willow (*Salix lutea*) occur in areas where there is a permanent source of water.

Plant zones are based on Mooney's treatment in Lloyd, R. M., and R. S. Mitchell 1973. *A flora of the White Mountains, California and Nevada*. University of California Press, Los Angeles.

FIGURE 4.1   Desert Scrub. Loosely scattered shrubs in foothills of the White-Inyo Range.

PINYON-JUNIPER WOODLAND ZONE
(6,500–9,500 ft, 1,981–2,896 m)

The vegetation of the Pinyon-Juniper Woodland zone (Fig. 4.2) derives its name from codominant trees, the Pinyon Pine (*Pinus monophylla*) and the Utah Juniper (*Juniperus osteosperma*). From a distance, these two tree species look very similar. Up close, however, they are easily distinguished, as Pinyon Pines have gray-green needle-like leaves and woody seed-bearing cones, whereas junipers have yellow-green scale-like leaves and fruitlike berries.

Like many trees in arid environments, Pinyon Pines and Utah Junipers grow slowly. Mature trees are rarely more than 20 ft (6.1 m) tall, and because trees tend to be widely spaced, this community is called a woodland rather than a forest.

Pinyon Pines commonly occur on shallow-soiled, rocky hillsides and mesas, where their deep-spreading roots probe for underground water. Utah Junipers occur on a variety of substrates, including rocky and deep alluvial soils. In moister areas, such as north-facing slopes, trees are taller and more crowded, and the vegetation resembles a dwarfed forest rather than a woodland. In drier areas, trees are commonly absent, and shrubs form the dominant cover.

Important shrubs in the Pinyon-Juniper Woodland include broom and Great Basin Sagebrush (*Artemisia nova* and *A. tridentata*), Bitterbrush (*Purshia tridentata* and *P.*

FIGURE 4.2   Pinyon-Juniper Woodland. Sagebrush (*Artemisia* sp.) is the shrubby vegetation in the foreground, with Pinyon Pine (*Pinus monophylla*) and Utah Juniper (*Juniperus osteosperma*) in the background.

glandulosa), Green Ephedra (*Ephedra viridis*), and Curly Rabbitbrush (*Chrysothamnus viscidiflorus* ssp. *viscidiflorus*). In late summer and fall, the golden flowers and silver gray-green foliage of Curly Rabbitbrush is particularly striking along roadsides in both the Pinyon Woodland and Desert Scrub zones.

SUBALPINE ZONE
(9,500–11,500 ft, 2,896–3,505 m)

The Subalpine Zone (Fig. 4.3) consists of a patchy mosaic of sagebrush and open forest. The discontinuous nature of this vegetation is due largely to differing soil type. On sandstone and granitic soils, sagebrush (*Artemisia* spp.) is dominant. Where the soil is white, indicating a dolomite substrate, Bristlecone Pine (*Pinus longaeva*) predominates.

Limber Pine (*Pinus flexilis*) occurs with Bristlecone Pine or forms pure stands. Other conifers, such as Lodgepole Pines (*Pinus murrayana*) and Ponderosa Pine (*P. ponderosa*), are rare.

Forests of Quaking Aspen (*Populus tremuloides*) occur in moist areas, particularly on the east side of the range. On dry slopes at lower elevations, pure stands of Mountain Mahogany (*Cercocarpus ledifolius*) are common.

One of the most striking features of the White-Inyo Range is the gnarled, beautifully sculptured Bristlecone Pines. These trees are known to live up to 5,000 years and are commonly considered to be the world's oldest living organisms. Some of the trees that are alive today were young plants when the great pyramids of Egypt were constructed and were mature trees at the time of Christ.

Many of the oldest known Bristlecone Pines grow in the Schulman Grove of the White Mountains at an elevation of about 10,000 ft (3,050 m). Here one can take a self-guided nature trail to Pine Alpha, a 4,300-year-old tree that continues to produce fertile seeds. Pine Alpha derives its name from the first letter of the Greek alphabet because it was the first Bristlecone Pine determined to be more than 4,000 years old. The oldest known living tree, aptly named the Methuselah, is still growing vigorously in the Schulman Grove after more than 4,600 years. One older tree, estimated to be approximately 5,000 years old, grew on Wheeler Peak in Nevada before it was accidentally felled.

Many of the older Bristlecone Pines consist of one or two leafy branches with a narrow strip of living bark running through an otherwise dead trunk. Pine Alpha, for example, has a trunk nearly 4 ft (1.2 m) in diameter with only a 10 in (25 cm)–wide strip of living tissue. Hence, only a small amount of living tissue is necessary to keep a Bristlecone Pine alive.

FIGURE 4.3   Subalpine. Note sharp transition in vegetation due to edaphic (soil) factors. The sagebrush (*Artemisia* sp.) vegetation in the foreground is on sandstone, and the Bristlecone–Limber Pine (*Pinus longaeva–P. flexilis*) forest in the background is on dolomite.

Bristlecone Pines grow slowly, commonly less than 1 in (2.54 cm) in diameter every 100 years. The wood of these slow-growing trees is very dense and highly resinous and is therefore relatively resistant to the insect, fungal, and bacterial organisms that attack most other trees. The extremely dry air also helps prevent rotting. Because of their unusually slow decomposition rate, Bristlecone Pines can remain standing long after they have died, and fallen trees thousands of years old dot the landscape.

The oldest Bristlecone Pines commonly grow in the harshest areas — low-elevation, south-facing slopes with thin dolomitic soils. On these extremely dry, nutrient-poor sites, Bristlecone Pines grow especially slowly. Trees growing in more favorable areas do not live as long because their more rapid growth results in a less dense, less resinous wood that is more susceptible to disease and decay. Therefore, the harsh environment and slow growth rate of Bristlecone Pines actually contribute to their remarkable longevity.

ALPINE ZONE
(11,500–14,246 ft, 3,505–4,342 m)

The vegetation above treeline is referred to as alpine (Fig. 4.4). In the White-Inyo Range, treeline generally occurs at elevations above 11,500 ft (3,505 m). In many

FIGURE 4.4   Alpine. Photo taken on Sheep Mountain at an elevation of 11,600 ft (3,536 m). Note the lack of trees at this elevation. White Mountain Peak (14,246 ft, 4,342 m) is in background. Light areas on right represent moonscape-like dolomite barrens.

respects, the Alpine Zone in the White-Inyo Range resembles a high-elevation desert: solar radiation is intense, wind speeds are high, and evaporative water loss is severe. Since precipitation occurs primarily as winter snow, the only water available during the summer growing season is from melting snow and occasional summer storms. Other factors limiting plant growth in the summer are low temperatures, occasional frosts, and a short growing season.

Among the most distinctive areas of the White-Inyo Alpine Zone are the dolomite barrens. Viewed from a distance, the white landscape and apparent lack of vegetation give one the impression of a moonscape. Up close, however, small, loosely scattered plants are visible. Among these are Dwarf Paintbrush (*Castilleja nana*), Cushion Phlox (*Phlox condensata*), Raspberry Buckwheat (*Eriogonum gracilipes*), and Blue Flax (*Linum lewisii*).

On granite substrates above 12,000 ft (3,658 m), Alpine Fell-fields are common. The plant cover on these rock-strewn fields and slopes is fairly dense, sometimes covering all of the available soil surface. Important species include Mono Clover (*Trifolium andersonii* ssp. *monoense*), Fell-field Buckwheat (*Erigonum ovalifolium* var. *nivale*), Whorlflower (*Penstemon heterodoxus*), and numerous grasses and sedges. Two of the more common grasses, Junegrass (*Koeleria macrantha*) and Squirreltail Grass (*Sitanion hystrix*), extend down into the Pinyon Woodland zone.

Dwarf Sagebrush (*Artemisia arbuscula*) is widely distributed on dry, sandy soils. On talus slopes, the rocky substrate is unstable, and the soil is poorly developed; hence, the vegetation is quite sparse. Interestingly, three of the more conspicuous species present on talus slopes are restricted to elevations higher than 13,000 ft (3,962 m). These high alpine species are White Mountain Sky Pilot (*Polemonium chartaceum*), Alpine Daisy (*Erigeron vagus*), and Broad-podded Parrya (*Anelsonia eurycarpa*).

The lower precipitation in the White-Inyo Range relative to the nearby Sierra Nevada results in a more open, less luxuriant vegetation. However, in areas of the White-Inyo Range where streams and ponds provide a source of water throughout the summer season, the vegetation can be relatively lush. In moist alpine areas, grasses and sedges predominate, particularly Tufted Hairgrass (*Deschampsia caespitosa*) and Alpine Sedge (*Carex subnigricans*). Meadow species with showy flowers that form colorful displays include Little Elephant's Head (*Pedicularis attolens*), Meadow Mimulus (*Mimulus primuloides* var. *primuloides*), and Alpine Gentian (*Gentiana newberryi*).

A conspicuous feature of alpine plants is their prostrate growth form. By growing close to the ground, these plants gain shelter from potentially damaging winds. Plants with tightly interwoven clumps of leaves and a hemispherical shape are called cushion plants. Examples include Fell-field Buckwheat (*Eriogonum ovalifolium* var. *nivale*) and Cushion Phlox (*Phlox condensata*). Similar to cushion plants, but with greater lateral growth, are mat-forming species such as Mono Clover (*Trifolium andersonii* ssp. *monoense*) and Whorlflower (*Penstemon heterodoxus*). The close-knit foliage of these species counters cold nighttime temperatures by trapping daytime heat. For example, the interior of a cushion plant may be as much as 20°F (6.7°C) warmer than the surrounding air. Rosette plants, such as Alpine Gentian (*Gentiana newberryi*) and Dwarf Lewisia (*Lewisia pygmaea* ssp. *pygmaea*), represent a third prostrate growth form. These plants have leaves that lie flat on the ground and receive direct sunlight as well as the added heat from the ground below.

Alpine plants tend to have well-developed root and/or rhizome systems. In fact, most alpine species have more of their biomass underground than aboveground. Along with absorbing water and nutrients from the soil, a primary function of the underground portion is food storage, particularly during the long winter season, when plants are dormant. Following snowmelt in late spring or summer, stored food reserves are used to initiate rapid vegetative growth. Because flower buds are generally produced one or more years prior to flowering, open flowers are commonly present shortly after vegetative growth is initiated each year.

For a number of reasons, sexual reproduction in alpine plants occurs infrequently. Flowers may fail to produce fruits and seeds due to limited resources, lack of pollination, or insufficient time prior to the onset of winter conditions. Low germination rates and high seedling mortality may further limit reproductive success. However, the ability of many alpine species to reproduce vegetatively and to persist for many years, once successfully established, may partially compensate for infrequent reproduction by seed.

REPRESENTATIVE SPECIES OF MAJOR PLANT ZONES

Desert Scrub Zone (4,000–6,500 ft, 1,219–1,981 m)

	COMMON NAME	SCIENTIFIC NAME	FAMILY
Trees	Joshua Tree	*Yucca brevifolia*	Agavaceae
Shrubs	Shockley Goldenhead	*Acamptopappus shockleyi*	Asteraceae
	Burro-bush	*Ambrosia dumosa*	Asteraceae
	Bud Sagebrush	*Artemisia spinescens*	Asteraceae
	Great Basin Sagebrush	*Atremisia tridentata*	Asteraceae
	Rabbitbrush	*Chrysothamnus nauseosus*	Asteraceae
	Brittlebush	*Encelia virginensis* ssp. *actonii*	Asteraceae
	Cooper Goldenbush	*Ericameria cooperi*	Asteraceae
	Shadscale	*Atriplex confertifolia*	Chenopodiaceae
	Hopsage	*Grayia spinosa*	Chenopodiaceae
	Nevada Ephedra	*Ephedra nevadensis*	Ephedraceae
	Indigo bush	*Psorothamnus arborescens* var. *minutifolius*	Fabaceae
	Spiny Menodora	*Menodora spinescens*	Oleaceae
	Desert Almond	*Prunus fasciculata*	Rosaceae
	Desert Mountain Penstemon	*Penstemon fruticiformis*	Scrophulariaceae
	Creosote Bush	*Larrea tridentata*	Zygophyllaceae
Herbs	Desert Milk-aster	*Stephanomeria pauciflora*	Asteraceae
	Nevada Viguiera	*Viguiera multiflora* var. *nevadensis*	Asteraceae
	Mojave Aster	*Xylorhiza tortifolia*	Asteraceae
	Fragrant Forget-me-not	*Cryptantha utahensis*	Boraginaceae

Bush Peppergrass	*Lepidium fremontii*	Brassicaceae
Prince's Plume	*Stanleya elata*	Brassicaceae
Beavertail	*Opuntia basilaris*	Cactaceae
Purple Phacelia	*Phacelia crenulata*	Hydrophyllaceae
Chia	*Salvia columbariae*	Lamiaceae
Little Blazing Star	*Mentzelia albicaulis*	Loasaceae
Apricot Mallow	*Sphaeralcea ambigua*	Malvaceae
Wishbone Bush	*Mirabilis bigelovii* var. *retrorsa*	Nyctaginaceae
Tall Bottle-washer	*Camissonia boothii* ssp. *desertorum*	Onagraceae
Large White Evening Primrose	*Oenothera caespitosa* ssp. *marginata*	Onagraceae
Prickly Poppy	*Argemone munita* ssp. *rotundata*	Papaveraceae
James Galleta	*Hilaria jamesii*	Poaceae
Wilcox Woolly Star	*Eriastrum sparsiflorum* var. *wilcoxii*	Polemoniaceae
Showy Gilia	*Gilia cana* ssp. *triceps*	Polemoniaceae
Desert Trumpet	*Eriogonum inflatum*	Polygonaceae

Pinyon-Juniper Woodland Zone (6,500–9,500 ft, 1,981–2,896 m)

	COMMON NAME	SCIENTIFIC NAME	FAMILY
Trees	Utah Juniper	*Juniperus osteosperma*	Cupressaceae
	Pinyon Pine	*Pinus monophylla*	Pinaceae
Shrubs	Broom Sagebrush	*Artemisia nova*	Asteraceae
	Great Basin Sagebrush	*Artemisia tridentata*	Asteraceae
	Curly Rabbitbrush	*Chrysothamnus viscidiflorus* ssp. *viscidiflorus*	Asteraceae
	Gray Horsebrush	*Tetradymia canescens*	Asteraceae
	Green Ephedra	*Ephedra viridis*	Ephedraceae
	Fern Bush	*Chamaebatiaria millefolium*	Rosaceae
	Desert Bitterbrush	*Purshia glandulosa*	Rosaceae
	Bitterbrush	*Purshia tridentata*	Rosaceae
	Plateau Gooseberry	*Ribes velutinum* var. *glanduliferum*	Saxifragaceae
Herbs	Inyo Onion	*Allium atrorubens* var. *inyonis*	Amaryllidaceae
	Douglas Pincushion	*Chaenactis douglasii*	Asteraceae
	Gold Buttons	*Erigeron aphanactis*	Asteraceae
	Basin Senecio	*Senecio multilobatus*	Asteraceae
	Golden Forget-me-not	*Cryptantha confertiflora*	Boraginaceae
	Woolly Caulanthus	*Caulanthus crassicaulis*	Brassicaceae
	Wallflower	*Erysimum capitatum*	Brassicaceae
	Pinyon Streptanthus	*Streptanthus cordatus*	Brassicaceae
	Mojave Prickly Pear	*Opuntia erinacea* var. *erinacea*	Cactaceae
	Fendler Spurge	*Chamaesyce fendleri*	Euphorbiaceae
	Limestone Lupine	*Lupinus argenteus* var. *tenellus*	Fabaceae
	Palmer Lupine	*Lupinus palmeri*	Fabaceae
	Death Valley Phacelia	*Phacelia vallis-mortae*	Hydrophyllaceae
	Blazing Star	*Mentzelia laevicaulis*	Loasaceae

Apricot Mallow	*Sphaeralcea ambigua*	Malvaceae
Large White Evening Primrose	*Oenothera caespitosa* ssp. *marginata*	Onagraceae
Prickly Poppy	*Argemone munita* ssp. *rotundata*	Papaveraceae
Needle and Thread	*Stipa comata*	Poaceae
Wilcox Woolly Star	*Eriastrum sparsiflorum* var. *wilcoxii*	Polemoniaceae
Stansbury Phlox	*Phlox longifolia* var. *Stansburyi*	Polemoniaceae
Mat Buckwheat	*Eriogonum caespitosum*	Polygonaceae
Clokey Paintbrush	*Castilleja martinii* var. *clokeyi*	Scrophulariaceae
Heller Bird's-beak	*Cordylanthus kingii* ssp. *helleri*	Scrophulariaceae
Scarlet Penstemon	*Penstemon rostiflorus*	Scrophulariaceae
Westgard Penstemon	*Penstemon scapoides*	Scrophulariaceae

Subalpine Zone (9,500–11,500 ft, 2,896–3,505 m)

	COMMON NAME	SCIENTIFIC NAME	FAMILY
Trees	Limber Pine	*Pinus flexilis*	Pinaceae
	Bristlecone Pine	*Pinus longaeva*	Pinaceae
	Quaking Aspen	*Populus tremuloides*	Salicaceae
Shrubs	Dwarf Sagebrush	*Artemisia arbuscula*	Asteraceae
	Broom Sagebrush	*Artemisia nova*	Asteraceae
	Great Basin Sagebrush	*Artemisia tridentata*	Asteraceae
	Curly Rabbitbrush	*Chrysothamnus viscidiflorus* ssp. *viscidiflorus*	Asteraceae
	Clokey Blue Sage	*Salvia dorrii* var. *clokeyi*	Lamiaceae
	Mountain Mahogany	*Cercocarpus ledifolius*	Rosaceae
	Fern Bush	*Chamaebatiaria millefolium*	Rosaceae
	Cream Bush	*Holodiscus dumosus* var. *glabrescens*	Rosaceae
	Wax Currant	*Ribes cereum*	Saxifragaceae
Herbs	Clokey Daisy	*Erigeron clokeyi*	Asteraceae
	Gray Goldenflower	*Hymenoxys cooperi* var. *canescens*	Asteraceae
	Basin Senecio	*Senecio multilobatus*	Asteraceae
	Beadpod	*Lesquerella kingii* ssp. *kingii*	Brassicaceae
	Prickly Sandwort	*Arenaria aculeata*	Caryophyllaceae
	Little Gray Milk-vetch	*Astragalus calycosus*	Fabaceae
	Dolomite Milk-vetch	*Astragalus kentrophyta* var. *implexus*	Fabaceae
	Limestone Lupine	*Lupinus argenteus* var. *tenellus*	Fabaceae
	Palmer Lupine	*Lupinus palmeri*	Fabaceae
	Limestone Evening Primrose	*Oenothera caespitosa* ssp. *crinita*	Onagraceae
	Cushion Phlox	*Phlox condensata*	Polemoniaceae
	Raspberry Buckwheat	*Eriogonum gracilipes*	Polygonaceae
	Limber Pine Buckwheat	*Eriogonum rupinum*	Polygonaceae
	Shooting Star	*Dodecatheon redolens*	Primulaceae
	Clokey Paintbrush	*Castilleja martinii* var. *clokeyi*	Scrophulariaceae
	Showy Penstemon	*Penstemon speciosus*	Scrophulariaceae

Alpine Zone (11,500–14,246 ft, 3,505–4,342 m)

	COMMON NAME	SCIENTIFIC NAME	FAMILY
Shrubs	Dwarf Sagebrush	*Artemisia arbuscula*	Asteraceae
	Wax Currant	*Ribes cereum*	Saxifragaceae
Herbs	Alpine Daisy	*Erigeron vagus*	Asteraceae
	Alpine Gold	*Hulsea algida*	Asteraceae
	Lemmon Rock Cress	*Arabis lemmonii* var. *lemmonii*	Brassicaceae
	White Mountain Draba	*Draba oligosperma*	Brassicaceae
	Alpine Sandwort	*Arenaria kingii* ssp. *compacta*	Caryophyllaceae
	Mono Clover	*Trifolium andersonii* ssp. *monoense*	Fabaceae
	Alpine Gentian	*Gentiana newberryi*	Gentianaceae
	Blue Flax	*Linum lewisii*	Linaceae
	Prickly Phlox	*Leptodactylon pungens*	Polemoniaceae
	Cushion Phlox	*Phlox condensata*	Polemoniaceae
	White Mountain Sky Pilot	*Polemonium chartaceum*	Polemoniaceae
	Raspberry Buckwheat	*Eriogonum gracilipes*	Polygonaceae
	Fell-field Buckwheat	*Eriogonum ovalifolium* var. *nivale*	Polygonaceae
	Dwarf Lewisia	*Lewisia pygmaea* ssp. *pygmaea*	Portulacaceae
	Snow Buttercup	*Ranunculus eschscholtzii* var. *oxynotus*	Ranunculaceae
	White Mountain Ivesia	*Ivesia lycopodioides* ssp. *scandularis*	Rosaceae
	Brewer Cinquefoil	*Potentilla breweri*	Rosaceae
	Dwarf Paintbrush	*Castilleja nana*	Scrophulariaceae
	Meadow Mimulus	*Mimulus primuloides* var. *primuloides*	Scrophulariaceae
	Little Elephant's Head	*Pedicularis attolens*	Scrophulariaceae
	Whorlflower Penstemon	*Penstemon heterodoxus*	Scrophulariaceae

REFERENCES

Barbour, M. G., and J. Major (eds). 1988. *Terrestrial vegetation of California,* 2d ed. John Wiley & Sons, New York.

Lloyd, R. M., and R. S. Mitchell. 1973. *A flora of the White Mountains, California, and Nevada.* University of California Press, Los Angeles.

Munz, P. A. 1968. *A California flora.* University of California Press, Los Angeles.

Ornduff, R. 1974. *An introduction to California plant life.* University of California Press, Los Angeles.

Zwinger, A. H., and B. E. Willard. 1972. *Land above the trees: A guide to American alpine tundra.* Harper & Row, San Francisco.

5

Trees

Deborah L. Elliott-Fisk and Ann M. Peterson

A tree is a woody plant 6 ft (2 m) or more in height with a single main stem (trunk). However, some tree species may take on a shrub growth form under environmental stress. We typically envision trees composing a forest, which has a relatively closed canopy such that little direct sunlight reaches the forest floor. In the White-Inyo Range, true forests are rare, as low amounts of precipitation prohibit forest development. Instead, there are open woodlands of scattered trees, with the ground (vegetation) cover also discontinuous. For this reason, it is correct to refer to tree communities in the range as woodlands; riparian and aspen forests are the only exception to this rule.

Traveling to higher elevations in the range (e.g., by driving up Westgard Pass and the White Mountain Road), one passes through a series of vegetation zones, where plant communities and their associated species each occupy a particular elevational belt. Riparian woodlands and forests are seen along streams at lower elevations (Fig. 5.1), and Pinyon or Pinyon-juniper Woodland inhabit most sites between 6,500 and 9,500 ft (2,000 and 2,900 m). Above this, instead of the montane forest/woodland of Red and White Fir (*Abies magnifice* and *A. concolor*), various pines, Western Juniper (*Juniperus occidentalis*), and Mountain Hemlock (*Tsuga mertensiana*) so characteristic of the nearby Sierra Nevada, is a shrubland dominated by Great Basin Sagebrush. This treeless zone extends up to the subalpine Bristlecone-Limber Pine Woodland, and locally to the Alpine Tundra Zone, depending on the type of rock the plants are growing on.

The absence of a montane forest/woodland is a consequence of the range's floristic history and its setting in the rain shadow of the Sierra Nevada. Beginning in mid-Tertiary time (approximately 25 million years ago), western North America experienced a cooling and drying trend, which forced more mesic species coastward. As mountain building activity further restricted the movement of moisture-laden air masses from the Pacific Ocean inland, much of the Great Basin woodland disappeared. However, some mesic species were able to persist in high-elevation habitats where soils or microclimates were favorable (Fig. 5.2). Thus, most tree stands in the White-Inyo Range are relicts of the more extensive woodlands and possibly forests that once inhabited the area (Elliott-Fisk, 1986).

A number of different types of evidence support this hypothesis. Several tree species that form extensive forests in the Sierra Nevada and Rocky Mountains exist only as patches (relict stands) of trees on special substrates in the White-Inyo Range (Fig. 5.3). The soils that develop on these substrates possess either a higher water-holding capacity or more favorable nutrient status, or both. Thus, Ponderosa Pine (*Pinus ponderosa*), Jeffrey Pine (*Pinus jeffreyi*), Lodgepole Pine (*Pinus murrayana*), Western Juniper

FIGURE 5.1 Riparian forest along Silver Canyon at an elevation of 6,790 ft (2,070 m). This community is dominated by Water Birch, Arroyo Willow, and Narrowleaf Willow. Sagebrush Scrub covers the upper slopes.

FIGURE 5.2 Ponderosa Pine on north-facing colluvial slope in Lone Tree Creek canyon at 7,000 ft (2,135 m). Trees are anchored on rocky outcrops along this steep, talus-covered slope. Growth rings show that the trees have been injured many times by rockfalls.

FIGURE 5.3   Isolated stand of Lodgepole Pine, with a few Limber Pine on south-facing slopes, at Cabin Creek, elevation 10,000 ft (3,050 m). These trees are on a deposit of early Quaternary alluvium and outwash, where a well-developed soil with a high water-holding capacity has formed. Sagebrush Scrub is present on the adjacent, drier colluvial slopes.

(*Juniperus occidentalis*), Quaking Aspen (*Populus tremuloides*), Narrowleaf Cottonwood (*Populus angustifolia*), and Water Birch (*Betula occidentalis*) still have small populations existing in the range.

Although the Bristlecone-Limber Pine Woodland occurs on several different substrates (including Reed Dolomite, sandstone of the Campito Formation, and Barcroft Granodiorite), it too is commonly edaphically and/or competitively restricted to particular lithologies. Wright and Mooney (1965) have documented the dominance of Bristlecone Pine (*Pinus longaeva*) on dolomite (Fig. 5.4); such trees are able to tolerate the poor nutrient and water status of these soils. In contrast, Limber Pine (*Pinus flexilis*) is more abundant on granitic soils. Although these two species are not as restricted as those listed in the preceding paragraph, it is very likely that they too were more widespread in the past and have been edaphically restricted in range due to low precipitation.

The irregular distribution of riparian communities is not as well understood, although it is probably related to changes in surface and subsurface hydrology. Upper

FIGURE 5.4 In the southern half of the White Mountains, Bristlecone Pine Woodlands are best developed on the light-colored Reed Dolomite, with Sagebrush Scrub inhabiting the darker Campito sandstone. The stand shown here occurs along White Mountain Road between Campito and Sheep mountains in the Ancient Bristlecone Pine Area, elevation approximately 10,650 ft (3,250 m).

valleys commonly possess a deep mantle of weathered, coarse debris, usually of glacial origin. Water percolates rapidly into this regolith, eventually forced to the surface down valley as the groundwater table rises. Most commonly, riparian trees are present just below the point where water first appears at the surface in the stream channel, but this is not always the case. Ranching practices may have played a role in the eradication of some of these communities (Peterson and Elliott-Fisk, 1988).

The marginal nature of the environment for tree existence is also attested to by the presence of hybrids and genetic dwarfs. Although Quaking Aspens occur as large trees in moist settings in the White Mountains, they also occur as (genetic) dwarfs at scattered high-elevation (treeline) sites (Fig. 5.5). Dwarf Aspens also occur at other alpine treeline locations in the mountain ranges of western North America. The intermediate appearance of some individuals in the Yellow-Jeffrey Pine stand at Jeffrey Mine Canyon suggests that *Pinus ponderosa* × *P. jeffreyi* hybrids may be present here. Juniper hybrids (*Juniperus occidentalis* × *J. osteosperma*) are also present in the White-Inyo Range (Vasek, 1966). Because hybrids more commonly occur where stressful climatic conditions shorten the flowering season, possibly resulting in overlapping pollen shed and fertilization for two species whose flowering periods may not normally be time-synchronous, it is not unusual that hybrids occur in the White-Inyo Range.

FIGURE 5.5   At the alpine rockfall along McAfee Creek, elevation 10,800 ft (3,290 m), an extensive stand of Dwarf Aspens occurs. These individuals range from 3 to 6 ft (1 to 2 m) in height. Photo taken in early July, before the trees had fully leafed out. In the valley immediately below, nondwarfed aspens are widespread on both the valley walls and along the creek itself.

Although many of the tree species of the White-Inyo Range have interesting ecological adaptations and distributional patterns (Lloyd and Mitchell, 1973), it is the Bristlecone Pine (Fig. 5.6) that has generated the most scientific interest. This species is the longest-lived plant documented, with some individuals in the White Mountains reaching ages of 4,500 years or more. It is interesting to note that the oldest trees are not the largest, healthiest-appearing individuals, but instead are somewhat shortened trees with spike (dead) tops and incomplete bark (strip growth). These old trees occur on marginal, dry sites, and their growth is very slow, as evidenced by narrow tree-ring widths. Because the wood of the Bristlecone Pine is very dense and resinous, it is resistant to decay, with fallen or even upright dead individuals persisting on the landscape for thousands of years.

The presence of both long-lived individuals and dead tree remnants has allowed dendrochronologists, such as E. Schulman, C. W. Ferguson, and V. C. LaMarche, Jr., of the Laboratory of Tree-Ring Research at the University of Arizona, to construct long tree-ring series. As tree growth is primarily a function of climate, these chronologies can be used to reconstruct climate changes. C. W. Ferguson has constructed a Bristlecone Pine chronology that spans approximately the last 8,700 years. This chronology and others have many scientific applications; for example, the rate of production of

FIGURE 5.6 Bristlecone Pines are the oldest living individual organisms known, with some attaining ages over 4,500 years. The individuals shown here in the Patriarch Grove, elevation 11,200 ft (3,415 m), exhibit partial die-back and strip-bark growth, with exposed wood weathering into beautiful patterns and colors.

radiocarbon (isotope C^{14}) in the atmosphere has been determined by its extraction from Bristlecone Pine wood (tree-ring) samples, which has allowed scientists to calibrate radiocarbon dates for this period. LaMarche (1973) has determined that the elevation of the upper Bristlecone Pine limit (treeline) has decreased in postglacial time, due to a general cooling. Dead trees above the current alpine treeline may be seen on Sheep Mountain above Patriarch Grove.

The remainder of this chapter lists and describes the tree species that occur in the White-Inyo Range.

PINACEAE (Pine Family)

Pinyon Pine, *Pinus monophylla* Torr. & Frém. (Fig. 5.7*a*) 10–33 ft (3–10 m) in height; locally multiple-stemmed above base; bark gray to dark brown (as tree ages), with narrow, flat ridges and thin scales; one needle per fascicle, rigid, incurved, sharp, gray-green, 1–1.6 in (2.5–4 cm) long; male catkins 0.2 in (5–6 mm) long; female cones initially sticky, bright green, concentrated on upper branches, 2–4 in (5–10 cm) in length, broadly spherical to globose, opening widely after seeds ripen,

FIGURE 5.7   (*a*) Pinyon Pine. (*b*) Ponderosa Pine. (*c*) Jeffrey Pine. (*d*) Lodgepole Pine. (*e*) Limber Pine.

turning shiny russet brown, scales thickening at outer edge; large seeds to 0.8 in (20 mm) in length with short wings, dispersed in autumn.

Distribution.   Common in Pinyon-juniper Woodland on all aspects and topography from 5,900 to 9,500 ft (1,800 to 2,900 m) throughout range; well-developed stands may be seen along the Westgard Pass Road in the Cedar Flat area and on the White Mountain Road on the way to Sierra Vista.

Pinyon Pines are the dominant trees in all of the lower woodlands of the Great Basin, Mojave Desert, and Colorado Plateau. The Two-needled Pinyon (*Pinus edulis* Engelm.) occasionally hybridizes with the Single-needled Pinyon (*P. monophylla*) where their ranges overlap. Single-needled Pinyon Pine has a wide range of environmental tolerance and can persist on severe sites, where individuals may live to be at least several hundred years old, displaying erratic growth patterns. It may occur in association with various juniper and pine species in the White-Inyo Range, including Bristlecone Pine on granitic substrates.

The seeds (commonly referred to as nuts) of the Pinyon Pine tree have been not only a valuable food resource for native American populations but are collected by various birds and rodents. In fact, animals are a valuable dispersal agent for the tree's seeds. For an excellent treatment of the tree's ecology and use, see Lanner and Lanner (1981).

Ponderosa (Yellow) Pine, *Pinus ponderosa* Dougl. ex P. & C. Lawson. (Fig. 5.7*b*) 30–80 ft (10–25 m) in height; typically straight trunk; crown occasionally conical to spreading with spike tops on older trees; bark thick (up to 4 in [10 cm] on oldest trees), yellow-brown to pink with broad plates and shallow furrows, inner surface yellow, resinous odor; young green branchlets, turning brown with age; three needles per fascicle, yellow-green, 4.5–7 in (12–18 cm) long, tufted, rows of stomates largely indistinguishable; male catkins 1 in (2–3 cm) long, clustered; female cones terminal to subterminal, typically 2.8–5 in (7–13 cm) in length, outturned prickles on needle scales, young cones green, yellow-brown to russett brown with age, oval; seeds about 0.2 in (5–6 mm) in length with long, narrow wings.

Distribution. Rare, occurring in isolated relict patches on west slope of the White Mountains from 6,800 to 7,550 ft (2,085 to 2,300 m) in Lone Tree Creek and Jeffrey Mine Canyon; best developed on north-facing slopes.

Although Ponderosa Pine is perhaps the most common and widespread conifer in the western United States, its distribution in the White-Inyo Range is very restricted, most likely as a consequence of aridity, because the range is situated in the rain shadow of the Sierra Nevada. The isolated stands on the west slope of the White Mountains could represent relicts from a montane forest that might have existed in the range prior to major uplift of the Sierra Nevada.

Trees in the Ponderosa Pine stands occur on steep slopes and are widely spaced, attesting to the severe competition for water. Single-needled Pinyon Pine and Jeffrey Pine, other xerophytic conifers, occur as associates.

Jeffrey Pine, *Pinus jeffreyi* Grev. & Balf. (Fig. 5.7*c*) 30–80 ft (10–25 m) in height; thick, straight trunk; crown spreading but symmetrical, branches widely spaced, thickening with age; bark thick, reddish brown (darker than Ponderosa Pine), deep furrows with typically narrow plates, inner surface pink to brown, vanilla odor; three needles per fascicle, blue-green, 4.5–7 in (12–18 cm) long, visible rows of stomates; male catkins 1 in (2–3 cm) long; female cones subterminal, 4.5–6 in (12–15 cm) in length, inturned prickles on needle scales, young cones purple, turning russet brown when ripe, long oval; seeds 3–4.5 in (8–12 cm) long, with wings 1 in (2–3 cm) in length.

Distribution. Rare, known only from Jeffrey Mine Canyon, although individuals may also be present in nearby canyons along the western slope of the White Mountains; elevational range 6,775–7,710 ft (2,065–2,350 m); best developed on perched alluvial fan deposits.

Jeffrey Pine is commonly the dominant and largest tree in the lower montane forest of the eastern Sierra Nevada. The Jeffrey Pine community of the western White Mountains is probably a relict of a former montane forest in the range (as may be the case for Ponderosa Pine). The stand at the apex of the Jeffrey Mine Canyon alluvial fan is composed of individuals of all ages, with the oldest perhaps 600 to 800 years old. Trees are widely spaced (forming an open woodland), as seen elsewhere in more arid parts of their range.

A few *Pinus ponderosa* × *P. jeffreyi* hybrids appear to be present here, although confirmation is not yet complete. The two species do hybridize elsewhere in California (Haller, 1962).

Lodgepole Pine, *Pinus murrayana* Grev. & Balf.   (Fig. 5.7*d*) 50–80 ft (15–25 m) in height; trunk straight, widening at base; open crown with heavy branching, particularly with age (and the concurrent development of a spiked top); bark relatively thin with small, thin scales, light gray-brown; two needles per fascicle, bright green, 1.2–2 in (3–5 cm) long, densely clothing branches; male catkins to 0.3 in (8 mm) in length; female cones clustered, commonly subterminal, ovoid, semiserotinous, 1.2–2 in (3–5 cm) long, slender (semi–deciduous) prickles, purple-green when young, turning clay-brown when ripe; seeds to 0.2 in (4 mm) in length with long wings.

Distribution.   Although Lodgepole Pine has been reported from several sites in the White Mountains (Lloyd and Mitchell, 1973), it has been collected (verified) only from Cabin Creek and adjacent Chiatovich Flats and the Middle Creek cirque. The well-developed stand along Cabin Creek occurs at about 10,000 ft (3,050 m) on early Quaternary alluvial and outwash deposits derived from metavolcanic material. Scattered, rare individuals may occur elsewhere on both the western and eastern slopes of the White Mountains.

Lodgepole Pine has a wide range throughout the mountains of western North America, occurring even near the Arctic treeline in the Yukon Territory. The taxon has now, however, been divided into separate species (which were originally all classified as *Pinus contorta* Dougl.), with *Pinus murrayana* largely restricted to the Pacific coastal region.

Although Lodgepole Pine has a wide tolerance range, commonly occurring from the upper to lower montane treelines and in wet as well as dry sites, its existence in the White Mountains is very marginal. As with Ponderosa and Jeffrey pines, Lodgepole Pine is probably relictual in nature. Soil moisture retention is greater on these older alluvial and glacially derived soils—a possible explanation for the restriction of the main population to the Cabin Creek site. The trees here are some of the most massive in California and may be up to 1,000 years in age.

Limber Pine, *Pinus flexilis* James.   (Fig. 5.7*e*) 30–50 (rarely 65) ft (10–15 [rarely 20] m) in height; trunk straight to contorted with age and increasing environmental severity, wide at base; symmetrical to broadening crown with age; young trees with silvery gray, smooth bark, turning into broken plates with thin scales with age; five needles per fascicle, dark green, stiff and erect, with visible rows of stomates, 1–2.8 in (2.5–7 cm) long, in dense tufts at ends of branches; male catkins red, up to 0.4 in (1 cm) long; female cones subcylindric, 4–7 in (10–18 cm) long, without prickles, scales thickened and incurved, green to yellow-brown when ripe; seeds dark brown, about 0.4 in (1 cm) long with narrow wings.

Distribution. Most commonly present as a codominant with *Pinus longaeva*, forming a subalpine woodland between 10,000 and 11,500 ft (3,050 and 3,500 m), although individuals extend down to 6,850 ft (2,085 m) in isolated canyons (such as Lone Tree Creek) and thus can occur in association with most of the other tree species in the range. Several vigorous stands occur along White Mountain Road between the Schulman and Patriarch groves.

Limber Pine is perhaps the most widely distributed tree in the White-Inyo Range. It grows on all substrates and is especially important in forming the subalpine woodland on granitic soils, although *Pinus longaeva* commonly forms the alpine treeline proper. Although the species prefers mesic sites, it occurs in xeric habitats, where it reaches its maximum age. Though not as long-lived as *Pinus longaeva*, the species displays basically the same growth pattern (as it too is a five-needled pine) and so is similar dendrochronologically.

The relatively large seeds of Limber Pine are a food resource for birds and small mammals; they may have also been used by native Americans inhabiting high summer camps in the White Mountains.

Bristlecone Pine, *Pinus longaeva* D. K. Bailey. Typically 15–50 ft (5–15 m) in height; trunk commonly thick and contorted or split, but straight when young; very stressed trees may have large, spreading crowns almost shrubby in appearance; old trees commonly spike-topped, with strip-bark growth; relatively thin, reddish to dark brown bark with flat, irregular ridges; five needles per fascicle, slender, 1–1.5 in (2.5–3.5 cm) long, with characteristic bristle-like appearance on branches; male catkins about 0.4 in (1 cm) long, red-purple; female cones ovoid, dark purple to brown when ripe, 2.8–3.5 in (7–9 cm) long, slender, incurved prickles; seeds about 0.3 in (8 mm) long, with wings up to twice the length of seeds, light brown.

Distribution. Common in the subalpine from 10,000 to 11,650 ft (3,050 to 3,550 m), occasionally extending down to 8,500 ft (2,600 m), forming a mixed Pinyon Pine–Bristlecone Pine Woodland. Best developed and dominant on dolomite and limestone, especially along the southern half of the White Mountain summit surface. Occurs on outcrops of Reed Dolomite along White Mountain Road in and between Schulman and Patriarch groves.

The White Mountains are better known for their Bristlecone Pines than for any other natural feature. The science of dendrochronology (tree-ring dating) has advanced through work on the White Mountains' Bristlecone Pines (Ferguson, 1968, 1970). Trees over 4,500 years old have been dated, with their growth-ring sequences matched to those of dead individuals whose existence overlapped in time. To date, a yearly chronology has been developed to 6,700 B.C., giving a detailed record of postglacial climatic change and radiocarbon fluctuation in the atmosphere (Ferguson and Graybill, 1983). The Bristlecone Pine tree-ring chronology is an extremely important dating tool for natural scientists (Suess, 1970).

As one walks through the Bristlecone Pine Woodlands, many fallen, dead individuals are seen (which is not unusual for any forest/woodland where fire frequency is low). Perhaps it is more surprising to see these same types of specimens outside of the distribution of the living trees. Scientists have used dead Bristlecone and Limber pines to infer shifts in the upper and lower treelines (LaMarche, 1973). This is another valuable tool for the reconstruction of climatic (environmental) change.

CUPRESSACEAE (Cypress Family)

Utah Juniper, *Juniperus osteosperma* **(Torr.) Little.** (Fig. 5.8*a*). Small tree, usually 6–20 ft (2–6 m) in height, although larger individuals occur; usually one stem at base, dividing to four to eight stems above 3 ft (1 m); gray-brown bark, weathering ash white; leaves mostly in threes (ternate), with "hidden" glands (imbedded in mesophyll with overlying layers obscuring their presence), 0.1 in (2–3 mm) long; male cones 0.1–0.2 in (3.5–4.5 mm) long; female cones ("berries") 0.3–0.4 in (7–9 mm) long, red to reddish brown, with sweet, dry pulp; seeds 0.04 in (1 mm) long usually one per cone with four cotyledons per embryo; usually monoecious.

Distribution. An important codominant of the Pinyon-juniper Woodland (here and in the Great Basin as a whole), Utah Juniper ranges from 6,850 to 10,335 ft (2,085 to 3,150 m) and is occasionally associated with Limber and Bristlecone pines. Well developed on alluvium, as at junction of Westgard Pass and White Mountain roads (Cedar Flats).

Juniper trees of short stature and shrublike appearance are commonly seen in lower montane woodlands in western North America. Although the species vary geographi-

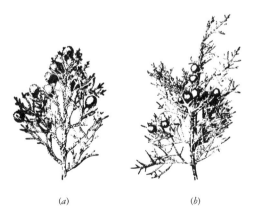

(*a*)   (*b*)

FIGURE 5.8   (*a*) Utah Juniper. (*b*) Western Juniper.

cally (with *J. scopulorum* Sarg. in the Rocky Mountains, *J. monosperma* (Engelm.) Sarg. throughout the southern Rocky Mountains and the Southwest, *J. california* (California Juniper) common along the California desert margins, etc.), the physiognomy of the vegetation is similar, with the understory as open in appearance as the tree canopy.

Although Utah Juniper appears to prefer deep alluvial soils in the White-Inyo Range, it occurs on rocky volcanic outcrops, on steep slopes covered by colluvial deposits, and on most other substrates. Changes in its geographical range over the last several thousand years have been documented using plant macrofossils from woodrat middens (Elliot-Fisk, 1986; Jennings, 1988).

Western (Sierra) Juniper, *Juniperus occidentalis* Hook ssp. *australis* Vasek. (Fig. 5.8*b*) 15–50 ft (5–15 m) in height, locally contorted or depressed (stunted); one well-defined trunk; reddish brown to brown, shreddy bark; spreading branches; leaves mostly ternate (in threes), gray-green, each with a conspicuous gland that secretes a whitish, sticky substance, 0.1 in (3 mm) long; male cones ca. 0.15 in (3.5–4 mm) long; female cones ("berries") ca. 0.3 in (7–8 mm) long, blue-black at maturity, with resinous pulp; seeds ca. 0.2 in (5–6 mm) long, one or, more commonly, two per cone, with two to three cotyledons per embryo; primarily dioecious.

Distribution.   Rare in the White-Inyo Range, with individuals reported between 9,050 and 10,570 ft (2,760 and 3,220 m) at the upper Pinyon-juniper and lower Bristlecone-Limber pines woodland transition in the central eastern canyons of the White Mountains (east Cottonwood and Crooked Creek areas) and the upper eastern slopes of the Inyo Mountains (Seephole Trail Springs and New York Butte).

Western Juniper is a spectacular tree commonly seen on rocky outcrops in the montane forest of the Sierra Nevada, especially on granitic substrates. Although its geographical range in the White-Inyo Range is not well documented, a large stand of several hundred trees exists in the eastern Cottonwood Creek drainage on glacially sculpted and jointed quartz monzonite outcrops (Elliott-Fisk, 1986; Elliott-Fisk and Ryerson, 1988; Jennings et al., 1988). One problem hindering its identification is its possible hybridization with Utah Juniper. Trees of apparently hybrid origin occur at the head of San Lucas Canyon in the Inyo Mountains and at the northern end of the White Mountains (Vasek, 1966).

BETULACEAE (Birch Family)

Water Birch, *Betula occidentalis* Hook.   (Fig. 5.9) 10–30 ft (3–9 m) in height; bark glossy, reddish brown, smooth, not separating into thin layers; twigs rough; leaves round-ovate, 0.8–1.6 in (2–4 cm) long, rounded at the base, acute at the apex, margins sharply serrate (uncommonly doubly serrate) except near the base, glabrous, dull green above, glandular, dotted, light green beneath; petioles 0.2–0.4 in (5–10 mm) long; monoecious, catkins 0.8–1.6 in (2–4 cm) long.

Distribution.   Forming scattered stands, some thick, in riparian areas and springs throughout the range from 6,500 to 8,500 ft (1,675 to 2,600 m) on the east side of

FIGURE 5.9   Water Birch.

the range along South Fork Perry Aiken Creek (7,610–8,530 ft [2,320– 2,600 m]) and Wyman Canyon (7,400 ft [2,255 m] and below) and on the west side of the range along Silver Canyon (6,800 ft [2,075 m]).

Water Birch is a common tree species throughout the White Mountains and occurs predominantly in the Pinyon-juniper Woodland zone (6,500–9,500 ft [1,980–2,895 m]). This tree forms thick stands in riparian areas and is intermixed with willows, aspen, and cottonwood. Water Birch stands are best developed on the east side of the range (Peterson and Elliott-Fisk, 1988).

Water Birch is a common species in the Great Basin–Rocky Mountain vegetation complex. According to Lloyd and Mitchell (1973), this species once had a wider range and has become restricted to higher elevations and riparian areas.

SALICACEAE (Willow Family)

Black Cottonwood, *Populus trichocarpa* T. & G.   (Fig. 5.10*a*) 40–100 ft (12–30 m) in height; trunk 1–3 ft (0.3–1 m) in diameter; grayish, smooth bark that is furrowed with age; branches spread to form a broad, open crown; leaves ovate, 1.5–3 in (4–8 cm) long (less commonly longer), truncate or cordate at the base, acute at the apex, margins finely serrate, shiny dark green above, paler and glaucous beneath; petioles rounded, 0.6–1.6 in (1.5–4 cm) long; dioecious, male and female catkins rare, 1.5–3 in (4–8 cm) long.

Distribution.   Sporadic in the range, occurring mostly near streams, springs, or meadows from 4,900 to 8,850 ft (1,500 to 2,700 m). This species forms part of the riparian community in Wyman Canyon (7,610 ft [2,320 m]), Queen Canyon (7,200–8,300 ft [2,195–2,530 m]), and at Toll House Springs (5,970 ft [1,820 m]).

Black Cottonwood is the largest of the American poplars. It commonly occurs as part of the riparian community in both the desert scrub and pinyon-juniper vegetation zones in the White Mountains. Black Cottonwood is able to capture, use, and store great quantities of water from streams, springs, and the groundwater table. It is commonly intermixed with various willows (*Salix* spp.). Black Cottonwood is very shade-intolerant, and an individual must occupy a dominant position to thrive.

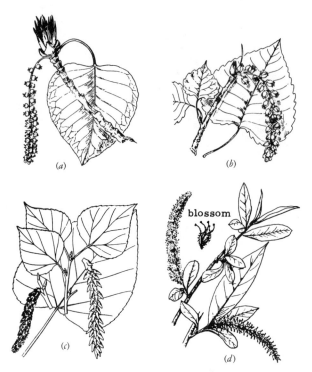

FIGURE 5.10 (*a*) Black Cottonwood. (*b*) Fremont Cottonwood.
(*c*) Quaking Aspen. (*d*) Willow.

Male and female flowers are present on separate trees. Female flowers form hanging clusters that are covered with cottony hairs. When the seeds are released, they are scattered by the wind and form small, white drifts in sheltered places, hence the name *cottonwood*.

Fremont Cottonwood, *Populus fremontii* **Wats.** (Fig. 5.10*b*) 40–100 ft (12–30 m) in height; bark whitish gray, roughly cracked; branches spreading, forming a broad, open crown; twigs stout; leaves deltoid, 1–3 in (3–8 cm) long, 1.5–3.5 in (4–9 cm) wide, truncate to cordate at the base, sharply pointed at the apex, margins crenate, yellowish green and glossy above, paler beneath; petioles flattened, 1.5–3 in (4–8 cm) long; dioecious, catkins dense, 2–4 in (5–10 cm) long, female catkins loosely flowered; seeds with long white hairs.

Distribution. Spotty along creeks and streams from 5,580 to 7,875 ft (1,700 to 2,400 m), forming part of the riparian community along Wyman Canyon (6,990 ft [2,130 m]), Silver Canyon (6,800 ft [2,075 m]), and Montgomery Canyon (7,790–8,010 ft [2,375–2,440 m]).

Fremont Cottonwood was named for John C. Fremont. He discovered this large arid-land cottonwood in 1844 on an expedition to Nevada and California. Typically a southwestern species, it occurs in a few scattered locations in the White Mountains. Fremont Cottonwood occurs in the riparian community at Wyman and Indian canyons, on the east side of the White Mountains, and at Silver, Lone Tree, and Montgomery canyons, on the west side of the range (Peterson and Elliott-Fisk, 1988).

Fremont Cottonwood has been widely planted as an ornamental tree in the West. Whether this species is native or was introduced to the White Mountains is unclear. The distribution of Fremont Cottonwood is very patchy, and the number of individuals at each location is small.

Narrowleaf Cottonwood, *Populus angustifolia* James.   30–60 ft (10–20 m) in height; grayish bark; narrow crown; slender twigs; leaves mostly lanceolate, 1.5–3 in (4–8 cm) long, 0.4–1.2 in (1–3 cm) wide, rounded at the base, somewhat acuminate at the apex, margins coarsely serrate, light green and glabrous; dioecious.

Distribution.   Rare; moist habitats; known only from two sites in the range—at Wyman Canyon (7,020–8,200 ft [2,140–2,500 m]) and Queen Canyon (8,300 ft [2,530 m]).

Narrowleaf Cottonwood is common in much of the Rocky Mountain region. Isolated sites in California define the western edge of this species' distribution.

Quaking Aspen, *Populus tremuloides* Michx.   (Fig. 5.10*c*) 10–50 ft (3–20 m) in height; straight trunk; smooth, greenish-white bark (darkening at base with age); slender twigs that commonly droop; leaves round-ovate, 1–2 in (2.5–5 cm) long and about as wide, broadly rounded to cordate at the base, sharply pointed at the apex, margins crenate or serrulate to almost entire, glabrous and green above, paler beneath; petioles flattened, 1–2.5 in (2.5–6 cm) in length; flowers rare, dioecious, male catkins 1.5–2.5 in (4–6 cm) long, female catkins 2–4 in (5–10 cm) long; tiny seeds (2 million/pound), brown with white hairs.

Distribution.   Occurs predominantly in the Subalpine Zone from 9,025 to 10,825 ft (2,750 to 3,300 m) in rocky areas and moist locations along streams or at the edges of meadows. Major stands occur on the east side of the range on the South Fork McAfee Creek (10,825 ft [3,300 m] and below), Crooked Creek (9,850 ft [3,000 m]), and Indian Creek (8,850 ft [2,700 m]).

Quaking Aspen forests are one of the most productive communities in the White Mountains. Major stands are located on the eastern slopes of the range. This species does not inhabit a distinct zone, as in some parts of the Great Basin region; instead it has a patchy distribution. It is possible that Quaking Aspen was previously more extensive in the range and that these are relict stands (Peterson and Elliott-Fisk, 1988).

Even though an aspen stand can produce millions of seeds annually, reproduction— or, more properly, stand growth and maintenance—is predominantly vegetative. New trees arise from a common root system; groves of these trees are referred to as clones. All of the trees that make up an individual clone are genetically identical.

Quaking Aspen is intolerant of both shade and competition from conifers. There-fore, this taxon does not occur intermixed with coniferous woodlands in the White-Inyo Range, but only in disjunct stands. Quaking Aspen is best developed on moist soils derived from colluvium or glacial till.

Dwarf Quaking Aspen trees occur in two localized exposed sites at the head of Silver Canyon (10,400 ft [3,170 m]) and on the slopes surrounding the South Fork McAfee Creek (10,800 ft [3,292 m]). These trees are considered to be genetic dwarfs. According to Strain (1964), Dwarf Aspen exist in a more severe environment than nondwarfs. Dwarf Aspen take on a recognizably different growth form and typically have short trunks with many low branches, giving the tree a shrublike appearance. The leaves of Dwarf Aspen are somewhat larger than those of nondwarfs.

Willows, *Salix* L. spp. (Fig. 5.10*d*) May attain height of 10–20 ft (3–6 m); bark light in color, on older trees fissured and darker; commonly multistemmed above base; twigs slender, yellow to reddish; leaves long, simple, mostly narrow, pinnately veined, and alternately arranged; petioles short; dioecious, catkins distinct, yellow to green; seeds tiny (2–3 million/pound) with small tufts of hair.

Distribution. Common in riparian areas throughout the range, 4,500–10,000 ft (1,375–3,050 m). *Salix exigua* rarely occurs in nonriparian sites.

Willows line creeks and streams throughout the White Mountains. Eight species are known to exist in the range. The most common include *Salix exigua, S. lasiolepis,* and *S. lutea,* which occur from 4,500–10,000 ft (1,370–3,050 m). The other species have a more sporadic distribution and include *S. geyeriana, S. laevigata, S. lasiandra, S. pseudocordata,* and *S. orestera* (Peterson, 1986; Peterson and Elliott-Fisk, 1988).

Willows commonly have multiple, branching trunks and take on either a tree or a shrub form. Of the 175 species native to North America, only 30 attain tree size. Willows are commonly associated with Quaking Aspen, Water Birch, and cottonwoods in the White-Inyo Range and locally form an impenetrable wall of vegetation.

Although willows are an easily recognizable element of the riparian community, the identification of individual species can be a difficult task. Male and female flowers occur on separate plants, and both are needed to make a correct identification.

Willows are intolerant of shade and dry soils. Germination rates are low, but many seeds are produced by each plant. The seeds have fine, cottonlike hairs, which aid in their dispersal by wind. Because this species is riparian, seeds are also transported by water.

ACERACEAE (Maple Family)

Mountain Maple, *Acer glabrum* Torr. var. *diffusum* (Greene) Smiley. (Fig. 5.11) Shrub to small tree 6–20 ft (2–6 m) in height; twigs whitish gray; leaves simple, palmately lobed; leaf blades 0.6–1 in (1.5–2 cm) long, 0.5–1.1 in (1.2–2.8 cm) wide, with few blunt teeth on lobes; peduncle plus pedicel 0.4–0.8 in (1–2 cm) long; fruit a samara, three to six pairs, 0.8–1.2 in (2–3 cm) long.

samara

FIGURE 5.11   Mountain Maple.

Distribution.   Rare in White-Inyo Range; on rocky slopes between 8,000 and 9,000 ft (2,440 and 2,750 m). Collected from Birch Creek (8,400 ft [2,560 m]), Wyman Creek (8,600 ft [2,620 m]), and Cottonwood Creek (8,700 ft [2,650 m]) drainages.

Mountain Maple prefers moist, shaded habitats near streams and springs or under a canopy. It is the smallest of the Great Basin maples. This variety also grows in the Panamint Mountains and along the eastern Sierra Nevada. It is a favorite deer browse (Lanner, 1984).

Box Elder, *Acer negundo* **L. ssp.** *californicum* **(Torr. & Gray) Wesmael.**   Tree 20–65 ft (6–20 m) in height with broad, rounded crown; twigs slender, pubescent, greenish; leaves pinnately trifoliate, three to five lobes, ovate, 2–4.8 in (5–12 cm) long, coarsely serrate, densely pubescent beneath; flowers unisexual, greenish; pedicels filiform; four to five stamens; samara straw-colored when mature, finely pubescent, 1–1.2 in long.

Distribution.   Rare in the White-Inyo Range. Lowland and riparian tree, often introduced. Present at old Roachville town site along Cottonwood Creek at 5,800 ft (1,770 m).

Box Elder occurs throughout North America, but its distribution is patchy, especially in eastern California and the Great Basin. This tree has been widely planted for shade in semi-arid regions. The sap of this tree has been collected as a source of syrup (Lanner, 1984).

SIMARUBACEAE (Quassia Family)

Tree of Heaven, *Ailanthus altissima* **(Mill.) Swingle.**   Spreading tree up to 50 ft (15 m) in height; bark thin, gray, rough; branchlets stout, hairy; leaves odd-pinnately compound, 12–24 in (30–60 cm) long, 11–25-foliate; leaflets lanceolate to oblong, 2.8–6 in (7–15 cm) long, with 2–4 teeth near base; fruit a samara, 1.2–2 in (3–5 cm) long, reddish.

Distribution.   Introduced at Toll House Springs along Westgard Pass Road at 5,970 ft (1,820 m).

The Tree of Heaven, a native of southeastern Asia, has become naturalized in California as the result of extensive planting by Chinese miners in the mid- and late 1800s. The tree is moderately drought-resistant and rapid-growing, quickly producing shade in areas that native trees cannot readily colonize. The male flowers are unpleasant-smelling, and suckers may spread the species to sites where it is not wanted.

ULMACEAE (Elm Family)

Smooth-leaved Elm, *Ulmus carpinifolia* **Gleditsch.**   Tree to 65 ft (20 m) in height; branchlets juicy, terete, subglabrous; leaves simply or doubly serrate, with axillary tufts beneath, 2– 3 in (5–8 cm) long; flowers in fascicles (cymes), appearing before the leaves; fruit an elliptic samara, cuneate at the base.

Distribution.   Introduced at Toll House Springs along Westgard Pass Road at 5,970 ft (1,820 m).

The Smooth-leaved Elm, a native of Europe, was introduced to North America after it was discovered to be highly resistant to Dutch Elm disease. This species has been widely planted across the United States, becoming naturalized (as an escapee) in some areas.

KEY TO TREES

A. Seeds produced in cones or berries
   B. Female cones woody; leaves needle-like
      C. Needles one per fascicle   *Pinus monophylla*
      CC. Needles more than one per fascicle
         D. Needles two per fascicle   *Pinus murrayana*
       DD. Needles more than two
           per fascicle
           E. Needles three per fascicle
              F. Inner surface of bark pink to brown,
                 vanilla odor   *Pinus jeffreyi*
              FF. Inner surface of bark yellow,
                 resinous odor   *Pinus ponderosa*
         EE. Needles five per fascicle
           F. Cones with slender, incurved prickles;
             needles with bristle-like appearance
             on branchlets   *Pinus longaeva*
           FF. Cones unarmed, needles in dense
             tufts at end of branchlets   *Pinus flexilis*
  BB. Female cones berries; leaves flattened, ternate

      C. Bark gray-brown, weathering ash white;
          leaves with hidden glands;
          berries with sweet, dry pulp   *Juniperus osteosperma*
    CC. Bark shreddy, reddish to brown;
          leaves with conspicuous glands;
          berries with resinous pulp   *Juniperus occidentalis*
AA. Seeds not produced in cones or berries,
    but in ripened ovaries
    B. Carpellate (female) flowers with a true perianth   *Ailanthus altissima*
  BB. Carpellate (female) flowers
      without an apparent perianth
      C. Leaves pinnately compound; fruit a samara   *Acer negundo*
                                              ssp. *californicum*

      CC. Leaves simple
        D. Flowers in fascicles; fruit a samara
          E. Leaves palmately lobed   *Acer glabrum*
                                    var. *diffusum*
         EE. Leaves simply or doubly serrate   *Ulmus carpinifolia*
       DD. Flowers borne in catkins;
          fruit a nutlet or capsule
          E. Trees monoecious   *Betula occidentalis*
        EE. Trees dioecious
            F. Leaves ovate lanceolate to deltoid,
             stamens six or more,
             buds with many scales
             G. Petioles flattened or laterally
                compressed
                H. Leaves yellowish green, alike
                   on both sides, coarsely
                   crenate-dentate   *Populus fremontii*
               HH. Leaves green above,
                   paler beneath,
                   crenate or serrulate
                   to almost entire   *Populus tremuloides*
             GG. Petioles terete
                H. Leaves dark green above,
                   paler and glaucous beneath,
                   finely serrate; common   *Populus trichocarpa*
               HH. Leaves light green on both
                   surfaces, glabrous, coarsely
                   serrate; rare   *Populus angustifolia*
          FF. Leaves lanceolate to oblanceolate,
             stamens two to six buds with
             a single scale

G. Mature leaves glabrous or
glaucous beneath
  H. Leaves entire or nearly entire
    I. Leaves 0.6–1.6 in
    (1.5–4 cm) wide,
    yellowish green above   *Salix lutea*
    II. Leaves 0.4–0.8 in
    (1–2 cm) wide,
    dark green above   *Salix lasiolepis*
  HH. Leaves serrulate to
glandular serrulate
    I. Catkin scales dark brown   *Salix pseudocordata*
    II. Catkins scales yellow
      J. Stamens two, twigs
      yellowish to brownish   *Salix lutea*
      JJ. Stamens four to six
      twigs reddish to
      brownish
        K. Leaves dark green
        and shiny above   *Salix lasiandra*
        KK. Leaves light green
        above, paler beneath   *Salix laevigata*
GG. Mature leaves pubescent or hairy
beneath
  H. Leaves linear, less than 0.4 in
  (1 cm) wide   *Salix exigua*
  HH. Leaves oblanceolate to
elliptic-oblong, 0.2–0.8 in
(0.6–2 cm) wide
    I. Capsules glabrous   *Salix lasiolepis*
    II. Capsules pubescent to
minutely pubescent
      J. Scales yellow with
      reddish tips   *Salix geyeriana*
      JJ. Scales dark brown   *Salix orestera*

REFERENCES

Elliott-Fisk, D. L. 1986. Relict tree populations in the White Mountains. In C. A. Hall, Jr. and Young (eds.) *Natural history of the White-Inyo Range, eastern California and western Nevada, and high altitude Physiology.* University of California, White Mountain Research Station Symposium, August 23–25, 1985, Vol. 1, pp. 64–67. University of California, Los Angeles.

Elliott-Fisk, D. L., and A. D. Ryerson. 1988. The dendroecological potential of east-central California. In C. A. Hall, Jr. and V. Doyle-Jones (eds.). *Plant biology of eastern California.* Natural

History of the White-Inyo Range, symposium vol. 2, pp. 212–222. University of California, Los Angeles.

Ferguson, C. W. 1968. Bristlecone Pine: Science and esthetics. *Science* 159(3817):839–846.

Ferguson, C. W. 1970. Dendrochronology of Bristlecone Pine, *Pinus aristata*: Establishment of a 7,484-year chronology in the White Mountains of eastern central California, U.S.A. In I. V. Olsson (ed.). *Radiocarbon variations and absolute chronology*, Nobel symposium 12, pp. 237–259. John Wiley & Sons, New York.

Ferguson, C. W., and D. A. Graybill. 1983. Dendrochronology of Bristlecone Pine: A progress report. *Radiocarbon* 25:287–288.

Haller, J. R. 1962. Variation and hybridization in Ponderosa and Jeffrey pines. *University of California Publications in Botany* 34: 123–166.

Jennings, S. 1988. Late Quaternary vegetation change in the White Mountain region. In C. A. Hall, Jr. and V. Doyle-Jones (eds.). *Plant biology of eastern California*. Natural History of the White-Inyo Range, symposium vol. 2, pp. 139–147. University of California, Los Angeles.

Jennings, S., D. L. Elliott-Fisk, J. Watkins, and M. Winter. 1988. Dynamics of *Juniperus* populations in the White Mountains, CA-NV. *Association of American Geographers Program and Abstracts*, Phoenix, p. 88. Washington, D.C.

LaMarche, V. C., Jr. 1973. Holocene climatic variations inferred from treeline fluctuations in the White Mountains, California. *Quaternary Research* 3:632–660.

Lanner, R. M. 1984. *Trees of the Great Basin: A natural history*. University of Nevada Press, Reno.

Lanner, R. M., and H. Lanner. 1981. *The Piñon Pine, a natural and cultural history*. University of Nevada Press, Reno.

Lloyd, R. M., and R. S. Mitchell. 1973. *A flora of the White Mountains, California and Nevada*. University of California Press, Berkeley.

Peterson, A. M. 1986. The distribution and ecology of deciduous trees in the White Mountains, California-Nevada. M.A. thesis, University of California, Davis.

Peterson, A. M., and D. L. Elliott-Fisk. 1988. The distribution and ecology of deciduous trees in the White Mountains. In C. A. Hall, Jr., and V. Doyle-Jones (eds.). *Plant biology of eastern California*. Natural History of the White-Inyo Range, symposium vol. 2, pp. 59–68. University of California, Los Angeles.

Strain, B. 1964. Physiological and morphological variability of local Quaking Aspen clones. Ph.D. dissertation, University of California, Los Angeles.

Suess, H. E. 1970. Bristlecone Pine calibration of the radiocarbon time scale, 5200 B.C. to the present. In I. U. Olsson, (ed.). *Radiocarbon variations and absolute chronology*, Nobel symposium 12, pp. 303–311. John Wiley & Sons, New York.

Vasek, F. 1966. The distribution and taxonomy of three western junipers. *Brittonia* 18:350–372.

Wright, R. D., and H. A. Mooney. 1965. Substrate-oriented distribution of Bristlecone Pine in the White Mountains of California. *American Midland Naturalist* 73:257–284.

6

Shrubs and Flowering Plants

Mary DeDecker

Although this chapter focuses on wildflowers, it also includes ferns, Ephedraceae (Ephedra Family), and Equisetaceae (Horsetail Family), which are not flowering plants.

Flowers have easily recognized parts (Fig. 6.1): a corolla subtended by a calyx, an ovary and a stigma (female), and anthers, which furnish pollen (male). The corolla may be tubular, cupped, or divided into separate petals. The calyx also varies in form and may be divided into separate sepals. After fertilization, when the pollen reaches the ovary, the latter develops into the fruit.

Most flowers are perfect: that is, they contain both ovaries and stamens. Some plants, however, carry those parts in separate flowers (monoecious), and others have them on entirely separate plants (dioecious). But even perfect flowers may be irregular in form. It is the irregular flower forms and apparent exceptions to the rules that make classification a challenge.

The plants herein are grouped alphabetically by family, the members of which have certain common features. Within each family, plants are listed alphabetically by their scientific names. Any given plant is known worldwide by its scientific name. The capitalized first part is the generic name, which is similar to a surname. A genus may have one species or many; the species name uncapitalized, follows the genus. Species are commonly divided into varieties or subspecies. When the scientific name, on the basis of recent studies, has been changed, we show the former name as a synonym within parentheses. The names or abbreviations of names, following the italicized scientific name, refer to the author or authors who first published the description of the species.

One or more common names follow the scientific name. A plant may have several common names, some of only local use. Although they are easier and more fun to use, these names do not have formal standing and are not sufficiently accepted to be considered authoritive; they may be considered nicknames. The use of scientific names avoids confusion.

This limited book does not permit the description of the complete flora of the White-Inyo Range. An attempt has been made to arrive at a reasonable balance between those species common enough to attract attention and those unusual enough to be of special interest. The flower color is indicated for most species. Distribution is in both the White and Inyo mountains unless otherwise indicated.

Abbreviations of authors' names follows those used by Munz and Keck (1970, pp. 1551–1576).

KEY TO THE NONFLOWERING PLANTS

A. Plants that reproduce by spores
    B. Spores borne on the back of leaves;   Ferns
        mostly small, leafy plants
    BB. Spores in terminal conelike parts;   Equisetaceae
        stems hollow, finely fluted; plants leafless
AA. Plants that reproduce by seeds in small cones
    B. Broomlike shrubs, appearing leafless   Ephedraceae

AGAVACEAE (Agave Family)

Yucca brevifolia Engelm. Joshua Tree. (Plate 6.1) Erect, commonly single-stemmed trees, 10–40 ft (3.3–13 m) tall, usually branching well above the ground in an erratically spreading pattern. Leaves are clustered at the ends of the branches, resembling bristly rosettes. The blades are rigid, up to 14 in (3.5 dm) long, tapering to a stiff spine. Inflorescences are very dense terminal clusters, 8–10 in (2–2.4 dm) long, set in rosettes of leaflike bracts. The crowded flowers are roundish or elongated. The petal-like tepals are oblong, 1 1/2–2 1/2 in (4–6.5 cm) long, fleshy and waxen. Mature seed capsules are broad, 2–3 1/2 in (5–7.8 cm) long, dry and spongy. *Flower:* Greenish white to cream.

Distribution. The dominant plant on certain dry slopes and flats, but more commonly widely scattered; mostly in the Inyo Mountains; Desert Scrub to Pinyon-juniper Woodland, up to 7,000 ft (2,134 m).

APIACEAE (UMBELLIFERAE) (Parsley Family)

Flowers are fine, usually in umbels with branches of the inflorescence spreading umbrella-like, but some individuals congested in heads. The main stems are commonly hollow and the leaves much divided. The dry fruit separates into two flattish parts when mature, these usually ribbed and/or winged. This family contains many food plants such as parsley, carrots, and parsnips, and some indigenous species were commonly used by the native peoples. Several species are deadly poisonous, however, so no native plant should be even tasted.

Angelica lineariloba Gray. Tall Angelica, Sierra Soda-straw. (Plate 6.2) A stout perennial 2–5 ft (6–15 dm) tall. Leaves are 4–14 in (1–1.5 cm) in length with long, linear segments. Flowers are in large, rounded umbels, 4–6 in across. *Flower:* Whitish.

Distribution. Rare; moist places, streamsides or roadsides; Pinyon-juniper Woodland, White Mountains, 7,500–9,500 ft (2,287–2,896 m).

FLOWERS

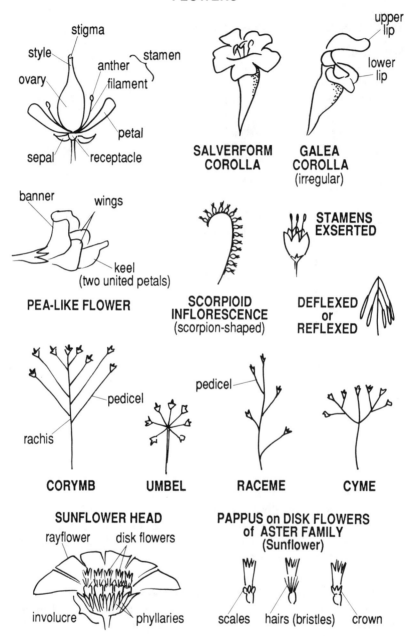

FIGURE 6.1 A guide to plant part designations.

LEAVES

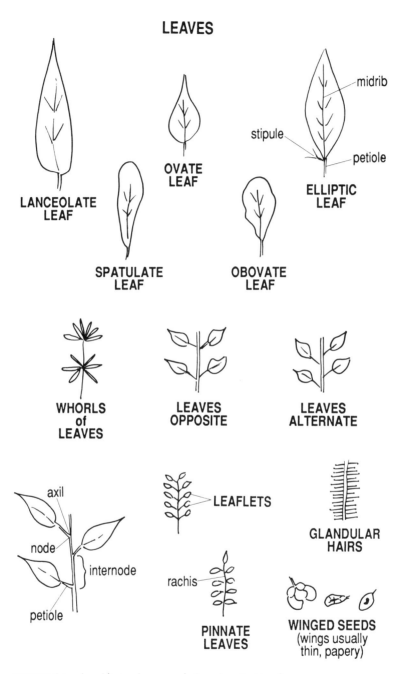

FIGURE 6.1   A guide to plant part designations (*continued*).

Cymopterus aboriginum Jones. White Cymopterus, Indian Parsley.   (Plate 6.3) A stemless perennial from a rootstock covered with the persistent bases of old leaf stems. Leaf blades 1–4 in (2.5–10 cm) long, naked, with 3 to 10 spreading rays. Fruit winged on all sides. *Flower:* White.

Distribution.   Rocky places, especially on dolomite; Desert Scrub and Pinyon-juniper Woodland, 5,500–9,000 ft (1,677–2,744 m).

Lomatium foeniculaceum (Nutt.) Coult. & Rose. ssp. *inyoense* (Mathias & Constance) Theobald. Inyo Mountain Parsley. *(Lomatium inyoense)*   (Plate 6.4) A very small, stemless perennial with leaf blades tufted at ground level, their stems below the surface. The blades are $1/2$–1 in (13–25 mm) long, finely divided, grayish, some purple-tinged. Flowering stems are mostly $1 1/2$–3 in (4–8 cm) long, naked, commonly turned to one side rather than erect, usually with only one ray developed. Fruit is narrowly winged on the edges. This is the smallest parsley in the range. *Flower:* Whitish to pale yellow.

Distribution.   Mostly in the Bristlecone Pine Forest in the Inyo Mountains, but there are some occurrences in the White Mountains; Subalpine Zone, 9,400–11,000 ft (2,866–3,354 m).

Ssp. *fimbriatum* Theobald. White Mountain Parsley. *(Lomatium macdougallii* Coult. & Rose) Much like ssp. *inyoense* but a larger, sturdier plant with less of the stems underground. Rays of the inflorescence are longer, and 2 to 14 are well developed. *Flower:* Pale yellow.
    Distribution.   Rocky slopes and flats; mostly in the White Mountains; Desert Scrub to Subalpine Zone, 5,700–10,500 ft (1,738–3,201 m).

Lomatium mohavense (Coult. & Rose) Coult. & Rose. Mojave Parsley.   (Plate 6.5) A grayish perennial with much the same growth habit as *L. foeniculaceum* but much larger and coarser. Leaf blades are triangular in outline, mostly $1 1/2$–$2 1/2$ in (4–6.4 cm) long and much divided, on stems about the same length. Flowering stems are 4–12 in (1–3 cm) tall, with rounded umbels 3–4 in broad. Mature fruit is roundish, pale-veined, and narrowly winged on the edges. *Flower:* Yellow, purple, or deep maroon.

Distribution.   Dry slopes; Desert Scrub to Pinyon-juniper Woodland, up to 8,500 ft (2,591 m).

Pteryxia petraea (Jones) Coult. & Rose. Rock Pteryxia.   A perennial from a deep root, the slender stems 6–16 in (1.5–4 dm) high. Leaf blades are pale green, 1–6 in (2.5–15 cm) long, narrowly oblong in outline, much divided, and fernlike, as the species name implies. The ultimate segments are extremely fine, scalelike on threadlike divisions. Lower stems are covered with the persistent bases of old leaf stems. The inflorescence is rather slender and open, with unequal rays up to 2 in (5 cm) long. Flowers are minute. The fruit is ovoid to oblong, flattened, and winged on the edges, about ¼ inch (6 mm) long. *Flower:* Yellow.

Distribution.   Rocky canyon walls; Pinyon-juniper Woodland, 6,000–8,800 ft (1,829–2,683 m).

ASTERACEAE (COMPOSITAE) (Sunflower Family)

This is the largest family represented. It includes shrubs as well as perennial herbs and dainty annuals. Flowers are borne in a head enclosed in a cuplike or cylindrical involucre made up of phyllaries (bracts). In the sunflower, for example, the center is composed of numerous tubular flowers, known as disk flowers, which vary from one to many. Ray flowers also vary in size and number, or may be entirely lacking. Flowers may be perfect, with both female and male parts, or may possess only one or the other. The ovary matures as a single fruit (achene), usually bearing a persistent pappus at the apex. The pappus may be: composed of fine bristles (plain or feathery), composed of scales, merely a ring, or lacking. The Chicory tribe of this family has only ray flowers. The strap-shaped "petals," known as ligules, are five-toothed at the apex.

Acamptopappus shockleyi Gray. **Shockley Goldenhead.**   (Plate 6.6) A small, rounded shrub 6–18 in (1.5–4.5 dm) high. Its white-barked, woody branches become spinescent. The small leaves are mostly spatulate, tapering to the base, ¼–⅝ in (6–16 mm) long. The comparatively large flower heads tend to be spherical, about 1 in broad, with rays about ½ in (13 mm) long. The rounded phyllaries have tissuelike fringed borders. Achenes are plump with white, furry coats, and a pappus of white bristles. *Flower:* Golden yellow.

Distribution.   Dry, rocky flats and washes; Desert Scrub, up to 6,500 ft (1,982 m).

Ambrosia dumosa (Gray) Payne. **Burro-bush, Bur Sage.** *(Franseria dumosa)*   (Plate 6.7) A small, intricately branched shrub, 8–24 in (2–6 dm) high, with spinescent branches. The slender stems are leafy throughout, the leaves ½-1 inch (12–25 mm) long, grayish, and divided into short, rounded lobes. Flower heads are borne spikelike on the upper 2–3 in (5–8 cm) of the stems. The male and female flowers are borne on the same spikes. The heads are about ½ in (13 mm) broad, lacking rays, and the fruit is a spiny bur about the same size. *Flower:* Dull yellowish.

Distribution.   A dominant shrub on desert slopes, commonly occurs with Creosote Bush or Shadscale; Desert Scrub, up to 5,000 ft (1,524 m).

Anisocoma acaulis Torr. & Gray. **Scale Bud.**   (Plate 6.8) An annual with naked stems 2–8 in (5–20 cm) high. Leaves are 1¼–2 in (3–5 cm) long, toothed, and arranged in a basal rosette. Each stem bears a single head an inch or more across. This plant is in the Chicory tribe, so the flowers all have strap-shaped rays. The characteristic phyllaries have dark midribs and broad, papery margins. They are graduated in length, scalelike. *Flower:* Pale yellow.

Distribution.   Limited, in sandy washes; Desert Scrub, below 7,000 ft (2,134 m).

Antennaria microphylla **Rydb. Rosy Everlasting Flowers, Pussytoes.** *(Antennaria rosea)*   (Plate 6.9) A mat-forming perennial with whitish foliage. Flowering stems are 2–8 in (5–20 cm) high, with heads terminally clustered. The leaves, about 1 in (2.5 cm) long, are broadest toward the apex. Staminate and pistillate flowers are on different plants; the pistillate heads are about ¼ in (6 mm) long, lacking rays. The abundant pappus of fine, white bristles and the dry, transparent phyllaries are the chief attractions of this plant. *Flower:* Bright white to rosy tinged.

Distribution.   Somewhat moist places; Desert Scrub to Alpine Zone, 6,000–12,200 ft (1,829–3,720 m).

Other species of *Antennaria* in the range are similar but are smaller and less attractive. One that is more unusual is *A. dimorpha:*

Antennaria dimorpha **(Nutt.) Torr. & Gray. Dwarf Everlasting.**   A perennial that forms dense gray-green mats. Stems are hardly an inch (2.5 cm) long, with the single heads fairly buried in the leaves. *Flower:* Phyllaries brownish.

Distribution.   Rare; open places in the Pinyon-juniper Woodland and Bristlecone Forest; Inyo Mountains; 8,200–10,500 ft (2,755–3,201 m).

Artemisia tridentata **Nutt. Big Sagebrush, Great Basin Sagebrush.**   A large, silvery-gray shrub, usually 2–6 ft (1.6–2 m) tall, but grows to a height of 15 ft (5 m) in favorable sites. Trunks have shreddy bark and are 3–4 in (7–10 cm) or more in diameter. Leaves are ½–1½ in (13–40 mm) long, wedge-shaped, usually with three blunt teeth at the apex, although those on the upper branches may lack teeth. Flowering stems rise above the leafy branches 6–16 in (1.5–4 dm) and are heavily laden with the small flowers. *Flower:* Inconspicuous; the general color of the inflorescence is gray.

Distribution.   A dominant plant on dryish slopes and flats and in canyons where soil is deep and loamy; mostly at or below middle elevations but may occur in Desert Scrub to Subalpine Zone, up to nearly 11,000 ft (3,354 m).

Similar but smaller species of sagebrush are *A. arbuscula* and *A. nova:*

Artemisia arbuscula **Nutt. Dwarf Sagebrush.**   Usually less than 1½ ft (0.5 m) high, with flowering stems rising above the leafy branches. Leaves are similar but shorter than for *A. tridentata.* Flower heads are short and plump, with five to nine flowers, and branches of the inflorescence are short and somewhat spreading. *Flower:* Phyllaries grayish.

Distribution.   Exposed slopes and flats; Subalpine and Alpine zones, up to 12,000 ft (3,658 m).

Artemisia nova A. Nels. Broom Sagebrush. *(Artemisia arbuscula* Nutt. ssp. *nova* [A. Nels.] Ward)   Similar to Dwarf Sagebrush, but the branches of the inflorescence are very slender and angled upward close to the stem. Heads are narrow, with three to five flowers. When dry, the stems are a warm tan color rather than gray and reveal their broomlike growth habit. *Flower:* Phyllaries smooth and greenish yellow, gray only at the base.

Distribution.   Common on slopes and flats of limestone areas; Desert Scrub to Alpine Zone, 5,500–12,500 ft (1,677–3,811 m).

Brickellia arguta Robbins. Pungent Brickellbush.   A small, much-branched shrub, 8–16 in (2–4 dm) high. Branches are rather brittle, usually densely leafy. Leaves are bright green, ovate and tapering to a sharp point, and usually sharply toothed, up to $3/4$ in (2 cm) long. Each flowering stem carries a single head, $1/2$ in (13 mm) or more long. Outer phyllaries are broad, shaped like miniature leaves, up to $1/2$ in (13 mm) long, and sharply tapering; the inner phyllaries are narrower. Disk flowers do not exceed the abundant, pale bristles of the pappus in length, and ray flowers are lacking. *Flower:* Whitish to pink, but hidden in the pappus.

Distribution.   Rocky canyon walls; Inyo Mountains; Desert Scrub Zone, 3,500–5,000 ft (1,067–1,524 m).

Brickellia oblongifolia Nutt. var. *linifolia* D.C. Eat. Pinyon Brickellia.   (Plate 6.10) A bushy perennial from a woody base. The numerous stems are 8–15 in (2–3.5 dm) high and leafy throughout, each bearing a single head. Leaves are pale green, elliptic to ovate, mostly less than 1 in (2.5 cm) long. Flower heads are about $1/2$ in long, with striate phyllaries and only disk flowers. *Flower:* Whitish.

Distribution.   Limited, in rocky places; mostly but not always in the Pinyon-juniper Woodland, 5,000–8,500 ft (1,524–2,591 m).

Calycoseris parryi Gray. Yellow Tack-stem.   (Plate 6.11) An annual with stems simple or branching, 4–12 in (1–3 dm) high. Leaves have linear lobes and are mostly on the lower portion of the plant. Stems have dark, tack-shaped glands. Typical of the Chicory tribe, the flower heads have strap-shaped rays. *Flower:* Yellow, commonly tipped with red.

Distribution.   Limited, on desert flats or slopes; Desert Scrub Zone, up to 6,500 ft (1,982 m).

Calycoseris wrightii Gray. White Tack-stem.   Similar to *C. parryi* but has pale tack-shaped glands. *Flower:* White, tipped with rose.

Distribution.   Inyo Mountains; Desert Scrub Zone, up to 5,500 ft (1,677 m).

Chaenactis carphoclinia Gray. **Pebble Pincushion.**   (Plate 6.12) A slender, much-branched annual, 4–14 in (1–3.5 dm) high, with green foliage. The leaves, mostly near the base, are up to 2 in long but are divided into very slender segments and appear dainty. The flower heads, up to 1/2 in (13 mm) long, are terminal on the short upper branches. There are no ray flowers, but the disk flowers are full and attractive. The pappus consists of scales. *Flower:* White.

Distribution.   Lower canyons and washes; Desert Scrub Zone, below 5,500 ft (1,677 m).

Chaenactis douglasii (Hook.) **Hook & Arn. Douglas Pincushion.**   Erect biennial or short-lived perennial, 8–20 in (2–5 dm) high. Stems commonly reddish and usually branching, thinly woolly. Leaves are loosely white-woolly when young, with four to eight pairs of finely divided segments. The first growth is a most attractive rosette of leaves, and these remain as the basal leaves of mature plants, with a few reduced leaves on the stems. Heads are 1/2–3/4 in (13–20 mm) long, the tubular disk flowers are longer than the involucre, and the anthers protrude like pins in a pincushion. There are no ray flowers. The pappus consists of 10 tissuelike scales. *Flower:* Whitish to pinkish.

Distribution.   Widespread; open, gravelly places; Desert Scrub to Subalpine Zone, 6,000–10,500 ft (1,829–3,201 m).

Chrysothamnus viscidiflorus (Hook.) **Nutt. ssp.** *viscidiflorus.* **Curly Rabbitbrush.** (Plate 6.13) A small evergreen shrub with white bark and brittle twigs, usually 4–24 in (3.5–6 dm) high. Typical leaves are bright green, 3/4–2 in (2–5 cm) long, and about 3/16 in (5 mm) wide, conspicuously twisted. There is considerable variation, however. Flowers are in small terminal clusters, with each head narrow and about 1/4 in (6 mm) high. Phyllaries in the rabbitbrushes are lined up in vertical ranks. Rays are lacking. *Flower:* Yellow.

Distribution.   Common and widespread; Desert Scrub to Subalpine Zone, 5,700–11,000 ft (1,738–3,354 m).

Other subspecies at somewhat the same elevation are:

Ssp. *axillaris* (Keck) **L.C. Anderson. Fine-leaved Rabbitbrush.**   Leaves very narrow; flower heads somewhat turbinate.

Ssp. *puberulus* **D.C. Eat. Hall & Clements. Pinyon Rabbitbrush.**   Leaves grayish with fine hairs; stems very slender.

Cirsium nidulum (Jones) **Petr. Red Thistle.**   (Plate 6.14) An erect, spiny perennial with stems up to 36 in (1 m) tall. Leaves are somewhat white-woolly, 8–16 in (1–4 dm) long, wavy margined and deeply lobed, with long, yellow spines. Heads are twice as long as wide; they have a layered appearance, with the pappus exceeding the phyllaries, the rose-red disk flowers exceeding the pappus, and the anther tubes protruding above the flowers. This is truly a handsome thistle, and the only reddish one in the range. *Flower:* Rose red to red-purple.

Distribution.   Rocky places; limestone areas; Pinyon-juniper Woodland to Subalpine Zone, 6,400–11,000 ft (1,951–3,354 m).

Crepis intermedia Gray. **Hawksbeard.**   (Plate 6.15) An erect perennial herb with branching stems, 12–24 in (3–6 dm) high. Leaves are grayish, irregularly cut and toothed, 6–16 in (15–40 cm) long at the base, reduced upward. The many flowering heads have slender involucres and the strap-shaped petals of the Chicory tribe. *Flower:* Yellow.

Distribution.   Relatively common; Desert Scrub to Subalpine Zone 5,600–10,500 ft (1,707–3,201 m).

Encelia virginensis A. **Nels.** ssp. *actonii* (Elmer) **Keck. Bush Sunflower, Brittlebush.**   (Plate 6.16) A low, rounded shrub, 1–3 ft (3–9 dm) high, with flowering stems rising above the leafy branches. Leaves are broadly ovate, gray-green, and 1–1 1/2 in (2.5–4 cm) long. Each stem bears a single head, about 1 1/2 in (4 cm) broad, with generous rays. *Flower:* Yellow.

Distribution.   Commonly abundant along roadways and washes of the Inyo Mountains and the southern part of the White Mountains; Desert Scrub, below 6,000 ft (1,829 m).

Ericameria cooperi (Gray) **Hall. Cooper Goldenbush.** (*Haplopappus cooperi* [Gray] Hall)   A small, green shrub, 9–24 in (2.2–6 dm) high, densely clothed with linear leaves up to 1/2 in (13 mm) long. Bundles of smaller leaves grow at the base of the primary ones, and these persist on the lower stems after the others have fallen. The inflorescence is flat-topped. Individual heads are barely 1/4 in (6 mm) long, with all disk flowers except for some with one or two rays. They bloom in the spring. *Flower:* Bright yellow.

Distribution.   Common on desert slopes; Desert Scrub, below 6,500 ft (1,982 m).

Ericameria cuneata (Gray) **McClatchie. Cliff Goldenbush.** (*Haplopappus cuneatus*) A small, compact green shrub, 4–20 in (1–4.8 dm) high. Leaves are crowded, very glandular, wedge-shaped to roundish, rather thick, 1/4–3/4 in (6–20 mm) long. Flower heads are in compact cymes. Involucres are very narrow, with phyllaries in four to six series. There are few, if any, ray flowers. *Flower:* Yellow.

Distribution.   Widespread; on cliffs; Desert Scrub to Pinyon-juniper Woodland, 5,000–8,800 ft (1,524–2,683 m).

Erigeron aphanactis (Gray) Greene. Gold Buttons. (Plate 6.17) A tufted perennial from a branching root crown, with flowering stems 3–10 in (7–24 cm) high. Basal leaves are 1–3 in (2.5–7.7 cm) long, widest toward the apex, narrowing to a long petiole. Leaves on the stem are much reduced. The foliage throughout is clothed with fine, spreading hairs. The heads, usually single, are rounded, 1/4–3/8 in (6–10 mm) high, lacking ray flowers. *Flower:* Yellow.

Distribution.   Common in open places throughout the range; Desert Scrub and Pinyon-juniper Woodland, 5,000–9,500 ft (1,524–2,896 m).

Erigeron argentatus Gray. Nevada Daisy. (Plate 6.18) A densely tufted, silvery green perennial with flowering stems 4–16 in (1–4 dm) high. Leaves are narrowly linear or slightly broadened toward the end, 2–3 in (5–8 cm) long, mostly crowded at the base. The stems have a few reduced leaves, and each carries a single head. These are large and showy, about 1 1/2 in (4 dm) across. *Flower:* Disk yellow; rays lavender to lilac, or paler.

Distribution.   Desert Scrub or Pinyon-juniper Woodland, 6,000–8,500 ft (1,829–2,591 m).

Erigeron clokeyi Cronq. Clokey Daisy.   (Plate 6.19) A tufted perennial with slender flowering stems 2–6 in high. The woody taproot branches below the surface and is densely clothed with the persistent stems of old leaves. Foliage is grayish with spreading, curved hairs. Leaves are linear, broader in their upper portion, tufted at the base, and well developed on the stems. Flower heads are terminal, 3/4–1 in (2–2.5 cm) across, including the petals, and fairly showy. *Flower:* Disk flowers yellow; rays mostly purple, but may be pink or bluish.

Distribution.   Relatively common; dwarfed at high elevations; Pinyon-juniper Woodland to Alpine Zone, 8,000–12,500 ft (2,439–3,811 m).

Erigeron compositus Pursh var. *glabratus* Macoun. Cut-leaf Daisy.   (Plate 6.20) A perennial 2–6 in (5–15 cm) high, from a branching root crown. Leaves are mostly in a dense basal tuft, cushionlike. They are dissected two or three times into linear lobes. The involucres, about 1/4 in (6 mm) high, have thin, slender phyllaries, often purple-tinged. Rays are fine and numerous, or sometimes lacking. *Flower:* Disk flowers yellow; rays white, pink, or bluish.

Distribution.   Rocky places and meadow borders; White Mountains; Subalpine and Alpine zones, 9,500–14,000 ft (2,896–4,268 m).

Note: Var. *discoideus* is a more compact form that occurs over much of the same range.

Gutierrezia microcephala (DC.) Gray. Threadleaf, Yellow-green Matchweed.   A small yellow-green shrub with very slender branches and tiny flower heads. It is much branched above, strongly resinous, and 12–24 in (3–6 dm) high. Leaves are well distributed but sparse, almost threadlike, and up to 2 in (5 cm) long. Flower heads are closely clustered, fairly covering the bush, and are only ⅛ in long and very narrow, each with only one or two disk and ray flowers. *Flower:* Yellow.

Distribution.   Common in desert canyons and on open slopes; Desert Scrub to Pinyon-juniper Woodland, 3,500–7,000 ft (1,067–2,134 m).

Hulsea algida Gray. **Alpine Gold.**   (Plate 6.21) A strongly glandular perennial from a branching rootstock. Leaves are 1½–5 in (4–12 cm) long, green, narrowly oblong to elliptic, usually toothed, and in basal tufts as well as on the stems. Flowering stems are 6–10 in (1.5–2.4 dm) tall, each bearing a single head 1½–2 in (4–5 cm) broad, including petals. The phyllaries are conspicuously glandular and also white-woolly. *Flower:* Yellow.

Distribution.   Rocky places; White Mountains; Subalpine and Alpine zones, 10,000–14,230 ft (3,049–4,338 m).

Hulsea vestita Gray ssp. *inyoensis* (Keck) Wilken. **Inyo Gold, Inyo Hulsea.** (Plate 6.22) A perennial clump with single or branching flower stems 10–18 in (24–48 cm) tall. Leaves are mostly basal, 2–3 in (5–8 cm) long, spatulate, and irregularly toothed, with those on the stems reduced and usually elliptic. Although green and glandular, they are loosely woolly when young. Flower heads are large and showy, 1½ to 2½ in (4–6.4 cm) across, including petals. *Flower:* Yellow.

Distribution.   Rare, calls for protection; loose shale slopes; Inyo Mountains; Desert Scrub, approximately 6,500 ft (1,982 m).

Hymenopappus filifolius Hook. var. *nanus* (Rydb.) Turner. **Inyo Cutleaf.**   A grayish biennial or perennial 6–18 in high. The leaves, 1–3 in (2.5–8 cm) long, are densely and evenly tufted at the base and are twice divided into linear lobes. Flower heads are terminal on branches of nearly naked stems. The elliptic phyllaries, ¼ in (6 mm) long, have pale tissuelike margins. There are no ray flowers. This plant strongly resembles *Hymenoxys,* but the latter has rays. *Flower:* Light yellow.

Distribution.   Dry places; Desert Scrub to Subalpine Zone 5,500–10,200 ft (1,677–3,109 m).

Hymenoxys cooperi (Gray) Cockerell var. *canescens* (D.C. Eat.) Parker. **Gray Goldenflower.**   (Plate 6.23) A biennial or perennial with erect, commonly reddish stems, 2–10 in (5–24 cm) tall. Leaves are gray-canescent, ½–2 in (13–50 mm) long, divided into three to five linear lobes, densely tufted at the base and on the lower stems. Above the middle the stems branch and bear a showy display of terminal heads, each about 1¼ in (3 cm) across, including rays. *Flower:* Yellow.

Distribution.   Open places; Pinyon-juniper Woodland to Alpine Zone, 7,500–12,000 ft (2,287–3,658 m).

Layia glandulosa (Hook.) **Hook & Arn. White Tidy-tips.** (Plate 6.24) An annual, 4–12 in (1–3 dm) high, with simple or branched stems. Leaves are somewhat hairy; those at the base are toothed or lobed, and those on the stem have plain edges. Involucres are about 1/4 in (6 mm) high. The rays are broad with toothed ends. Although they are commonly called "daisies," they are not in the same tribe as the Erigerons. *Flower:* Disk flowers yellow, rays white.

Distribution.   Sandy or gravelly places; Desert Scrub and Pinyon-juniper Woodland, 5,000–8,500 ft (1,524–2,591 m).

Leucelene ericoides (Torr.) **Greene. Heath Daisy.** (Plate 6.25) A tufted, heathlike perennial from a deep running rootstock. Leaves are 1/4–3/8 in (6–10 mm) long, narrow and crowded, and quite gray. The leafy stems, 2–6 in (5–16 cm) high, are topped by daisylike flower heads 1/2–3/4 in (13–20 mm) broad. *Flower:* Disk flowers yellow, rays white to pink.

Distribution.   Dry limestone areas, possibly restricted to dolomite; Desert Scrub and Pinyon-juniper Woodland, 5,500–9,000 ft (1,677–2,744 m).

Machaeranthera canescens (Pursh) **Gray. Sticky Aster.**   A biennial or short-lived perennial 8–24 in (2–6 dm) high. The stem is rigidly erect, usually racemosely branched in the upper portion. The leaves are oblanceolate and grayish with a fine, velvety surface; they are prickle-toothed on the edges. Those toward the base are 2–3 in (5–8 cm) long, on petioles equaling the blade. Leaves on the stem are gradually reduced upward. Flower heads, about 1/2 in (13 mm) high, are terminal, each with 6 to 10 series of phyllaries, their tips curved outward. Rays are 1/4 in (6 mm) long or more. *Flower:* Disk flowers yellow, rays bluish purple.

Distribution.   Common but not abundant; Desert Scrub to Subalpine Zone, 5,000–10,300 ft (1,524–3,104 m).

Machaeranthera shastensis **Gray var.** *montana* (Greene) **Gong & Keck. Shasta Aster.**   Similar to *M. canescens* but only 2–8 in (5–20 cm) high. Leaves are more likely to be basal. They are spatulate, and the teeth are only weakly prickle-pointed. Branches of the inflorescence are short and close. The heads are smaller, with only two to five series of phyllaries. *Flower:* Same as *M. canescens*.

Distribution.   Apparently limited to limestone areas; Pinyon-juniper Woodland and Subalpine Zone, 9,000–10,500 ft (2,744–3,201 m).

Perityle inyoensis (Ferris) **Powell. Inyo Perityle.** *(Laphamia inyoensis)*   A perennial in dense, leafy clumps 5–10 in (12–27 cm) high. Foliage is green and clothed with soft hairs. Leaves are broadly ovate and evenly toothed, 1/4–1/2 in (6–12 mm) long. Heads are 1/4 in (6 mm) long, with disk flowers only. *Flower:* Yellow.

Distribution.   Crevices in cliffs or rocky places; Inyo Mountains; Desert Scrub and Pinyon-juniper Woodland, 5,900–8,500 ft (1,798–2,591 m).

Perityle megalocephala (Watson) J.F. Macbr. Tall Perityle. (*Laphamia megalocephala* Watson)   A green perennial, somewhat woody at the base, with stems 12–22 in (3–5.4 cm) long. The leaves are so small and remote that the long, slender, tangled stems appear to be almost leafless. Leaves are ovate and minute, up to 3/8 in (1 cm) long. Heads are about 1/4 in (6 mm) long, lacking ray flowers. This species is variable and confusing. There may be more than one variety of it represented here. *Flower:* Yellow.

Distribution.   Cliffs and rock crevices throughout the range; Desert Scrub and Pinyon-juniper Woodland, 5,000–8,500 ft (1,524–2,591 m).

Petradoria discoidea L.C. Anderson. Rock Goldenrod. (*Chrysothamnus gramineus* Hall)   A perennial with many slender stems, 10–24 in (2.7–6 dm) high, from a woody base. Leaves are stiff, narrowly lanceolate, 1–2 1/2 in (2.5–6 cm) long, and alternate on the stem, grasslike. Heads are narrow and in small, terminal clusters. Involucres are narrow and up to 1/2 in (6 mm) long, with four to six series of broad, stiff phyllaries, which are blunt and prickle-tipped. There are only a few disk flowers, well protruded, along with a pappus of dull-gold bristles. Ray flowers are lacking. *Flower:* Pale yellow.

Distribution.   Uncommon; rocky limestone slopes or canyons; Inyo Mountains; Pinyon-juniper Woodland to Subalpine Zone, 7,500–9,500 ft (2,287–2,896 m).

Senecio canus Hook. Rock Senecio.   (Plate 6.26) A perennial with stems 3–12 in (7–30 cm) high from a branching root crown. Leaves are light gray, mostly tufted at the base, with those on the stem reduced. The blades are ovate with rounded ends, mostly 1/2–1 in (13–25 mm) long, on longer petioles. Heads are in terminal clusters, each with five to eight rays. Each head with rays measures about 3/4 in (2 cm) across. The pappus is gleaming white. *Flower:* Yellow.

Distribution.   Open, rocky places; Pinyon-juniper Woodland and Subalpine Zone, 7,500–11,000 ft (2,287–3,354 m).

Senecio douglasii DC. var. *monoensis* (Greene) Jepson. Mono Senecio.   (Plate 6.27) A bushy perennial, 12–36 in (3–9 dm) high, with a somewhat woody base. In open places it is erect and rounded, but where it is protected it may sprawl in an irregular form. The foliage is green, with the leaves divided into very narrow linear segments. The stems branch above and are topped by numerous showy flower heads. The senecios commonly have small outer bracts at the base of the phyllaries, and these quite obvious in this plant. Flower heads are about 1 in (2.5 cm) across, including rays. *Flower:* Yellow.

Distribution.   Dry canyons; below Desert Scrub and Pinyon-juniper Woodland, 7,500 ft (2,287 m).

Senecio multilobatus Torr. & Gray. Basin Senecio.   (Plate 6.28) A perennial with erect stems 6–15 in (1.5–3.6 dm) high. The attractive green foliage is densely tufted at the base. Leaves are 1–3 in (2.5–7.7 cm) long, including petioles, and are deeply cut into irregular lobes and toothed. The stems have a few leaves, and many flower heads are clustered above on very slender branches. Outer bracts of the involucres are poorly developed or lacking. Flower heads are 1/4 in (6 mm) high with about eight rays. *Flower:* Yellow.

Distribution.   Common; White Mountains; Desert Scrub to Subalpine Zone, 5,600–10,500 ft (1,707–3,201 m).

Solidago multiradiata Ait. Alpine Goldenrod.   (Plate 6.29) A perennial herb from a branching root crown, with stems 2–12 in (5–30 cm) high. Leaves, mostly 1–2 in (2.5–5 cm) long, are oblanceolate or spatulate, tapering to the stems. Although tufted at the base, the stems are fairly leafy too. Heads are in dense terminal clusters and each about 3/16 in (5 mm) long, with very small rays. *Flower:* Yellow.

Distribution.   Open, rocky places; White Mountains; Pinyon-juniper Woodland to Alpine Zone, 9,000–13,000 ft (2,744–3,963 m).

Stephanomeria pauciflora (Torr.) Nutt. Desert Milk-aster.   (Plate 6.30) An intricately branched, bushy perennial, 12–18 in (3.0–4.5 dm) high, with a woody base. Basal leaves are 1–3 in long and deeply divided, but those on the stem are commonly reduced to scales. The plant appears to be a tangle of leafless branches with flowers of the Chicory tribe. The phyllaries have several short outer bracts at the base. The common name comes from the milky juice in the plant. *Flower:* Pink or paler.

Distribution.   Common in Desert Scrub, up to 6,000 ft (1,829 m).

Stephanomeria spinosa (Nutt.) Tomb. Wool Cache Plant, Thorny Skeleton Plant. *(Lygodesmia spinosa)*   (Plate 6.31) A perennial with rigid, spiny branches, 6–16 in (1.5–4 dm) high. It carries a tuft of woolly fibers at the base of the stem. There are some linear leaves below, but those above are reduced to mere scales, so the plant appears as a leafless, rounded little bush. The flower heads, scattered throughout, are only three- to five-flowered, similar to the Milk-aster. *Flower:* Rose to pink.

Distribution.   Common on dry slopes; Desert Scrub and Pinyon-juniper Woodland, 5,000–9,500 ft (1,524–2,896 m).

Tetradymia canescens DC. Gray Horsebrush.   (Plate 6.32) A somewhat straggly shrub, 4–15 in (10–36 cm) high, with pale gray foliage. Leaves are linear, up to 3/4 in (2 cm) long and fairly dense on the stems. Flower heads are in terminal clusters. Each head has four disk flowers enclosed in four or five rigid, keeled phyllaries 1/4 in (6 mm) long. *Flower:* Yellow.

Distribution.   Common on dry slopes; Pinyon-juniper Woodland to Subalpine Zone, 7,000–10,500 ft (2,134–3,201 m).

Note: There are other species of *Tetradymia,* common at lower elevations. All are larger, more rigid shrubs. All but one have needle-like spines on the branches.

Townsendia scapigera **D.C. Eat. Ground Daisy.**   (Plate 6.33) A small perennial with spatulate leaves tufted on the branches of a slender root crown. The entire plant is rarely more than 1 in (2.5 cm) high. The daisylike flower heads, 1/2–1 in (13–25 mm) across, barely exceed the leaves. A shining white pappus shows through the flowers. It is a charming little plant. *Flower:* Pink or lavender to almost white.

Distribution.   Infrequent; Pinyon-juniper Woodland to Subalpine Zone, 8,800–10,200 ft (2,683–3,110 m).

Viguiera multiflora **(Nutt.) Blake var.** *nevadensis* **(A. Nels.) Blake. Nevada Viguiera.**   (Plate 6.34) A perennial with erect, slender stems 10–18 in (2.4–4.5 dm) high. Leaves are narrowly lanceolate, 3/4–2 in (2–5 cm) long, with those on the stems opposite. Heads are showy, about 1 in (2.5 cm) broad, including rays. *Flower:* Rich yellow.

Distribution.   Roadsides and canyons; Desert Scrub and Pinyon-juniper Woodland, 5,500–8,000 ft (1,677–2,439 m).

Xylorhiza tortifolia **(Gray) Greene. Mojave Aster.** *(Machaeranthera tortifolia)*   (Plate 6.35) A bushy perennial, 10–28 in (2.4–7 dm) high. Leaves are linear to oblong, the wavy edges prickle-toothed, 1–3 in (2.5–8 cm) long. The lower part of the plant, to about halfway up the stems, is quite leafy. The heads are large and showy, up to 2 in (5 cm) across, including rays. They are general favorites of desert visitors. *Flower:* Disk flowers yellow, rays blue-violet to lavender or paler.

Distribution.   Dry, rocky places; Desert Scrub, below 6,000 ft (1,829 m).

BORAGINACEAE (Borage Family)

A large family represented here by annual or perennial herbs, many of them small and inconspicuous. A large percentage are gray with appressed hairs; some are bristly with spreading hairs also, especially around the inflorescence. Flowers have tubular corollas with five rounded lobes spreading from the throat, and many species have a ring or raised crest at the throat. The blooms of some are arranged on one side of a scorpioid stem. The fruit is composed of one to four hard nutlets at the base of the style.

Amsinckia tessellata Gray. Fiddleneck.   (Plate 6.36) An annual, bristly with stiff hairs, the stems erect, 8–24 in (2–6 dm) high. Leaves are bright green, linear to lanceolate, and 1–3 in (2.5–7.7 cm) long. Flowers are in scorpioid spikes. The corolla tube is up to ¹/₂ in (13 mm) long. Nutlets are irregularly roughened. *Flower:* Yellow or orange-yellow.

Distribution.   Abundant, weedy in disturbed places; Desert Scrub to Pinyon-juniper Woodland, below 7,500 ft (2,287 m).

Cryptantha cinera (Greene) Cronq. var. *abortiva* (Greene) Cronq. Bow-nut Forget-me-not.   *(Cryptantha Jamesii* var. *abortiva)* A sprawling perennial with stems 2–6 in (5–15 cm) long. Foliage is pale gray-green with fine, appressed hairs; the leaves are narrow, 1 ¹/₂–4 in (4–10 cm) long. Flowering stems hardly exceed the leaves. The corolla tube is less than ¹/₄ in (6 mm) long, and the spreading lobes about that broad. The one to four nutlets are smooth and shining. Although the plant is not showy, it has a prominent place in the high mountain flora. *Flower:* White.

Distribution.   Open places in mountain scrub; Pinyon-juniper Woodland and Subalpine Zone, 8,000–11,700 ft (2,439–3,567 m).

Cryptantha confertiflora (Greene) Payson. Golden Forget-me-not.   (Plate 6.37) Perennial with stems 6–20 in (15–48 cm) tall from a branching root crown. Leaves are linear, 1–4 in (2.5–10 cm) long, gray-green, with appressed hairs. They are mostly tufted on branches of the root crown, but the stems are somewhat leafy too. The plant becomes somewhat bristly with spreading hairs in the upper portion. The corolla is about ¹/₂ in (13 mm) long, with broadly spreading lobes. The inflorescence is in terminal clusters, with lesser clusters or single flowers at the leaf nodes below. The multiple stems are generous with flowers and make showy displays. *Flower:* Yellow to pale yellow.

Distribution.   Widespread but rarely plentiful; common on limestone but not limited to it; Desert Scrub and Pinyon-juniper Woodland, 4,000–9,500 ft (1,220–2,896 m).

Cryptantha flavoculata (A. Nels.) Payson. Sulphur-throated Forget-me-not. (Plate 6.38) A perennial with stems 4–12 in (1–3 dm) high. Leaves are somewhat spatulate, with the broad upper portion narrowing to the base, 1–2 in (2.5–5 cm), rarely 4 in (10 cm), long in all. They are densely tufted on the root crown and so even that they appear cropped. Foliage is dull gray-green with appressed hairs; the upper stems and inflorescence have spreading hairs also. Flowers are clustered on the upper part of the stems, similar to *C. confertiflora* but more compact. The corolla tube is ¹/₄–³/₈ in (6–10 mm) long, its lobes spreading about the same width. Nutlets are rough and much exceeded by the long style. This species varies in size, becoming truly dwarfed—as little as 1 in (2.5 cm) high—at its upper elevations. *Flower:* White with yellow crests at throat.

Distribution.   Widespread; commonly abundant in limestone areas; Desert Scrub to Subalpine Zone, 6,200–10,400 ft (1,090–3,171 m).

Cryptantha pterocarya (Torr.) Greene. Wing-nut Forget-me-not.   (Plate 6.39) An erect annual, 4–20 in (1–5 dm) tall, with linear, mostly basal leaves. The stems branch above into two or three scorpioid spikes. Although the corolla is minute, the calyx is fat. In the typical variety three of the four nutlets have broad, white, fringed wings. There is another variety with all the nutlets wing-margined, and still another in which the wings are narrow and knifelike. These are uncommon, however. *Flower:* White.

Distribution.   Common; Desert Scrub to Pinyon-juniper Woodland, 3,500–7,000 ft (1,067–2,139 m).

Cryptantha roosiorum Munz. Roos Forget-me-not.   (Plate 6.40) A rare miniature perennial only about 1 in (2.5 cm) high. It resembles the dwarf form of *C. flavoculata* but is more compact. Its appressed hairs are silkier and the spreading hairs of the inflorescence softer. Leaves are relatively broad, and the flowering stems hardly exceed them. The corolla tubes are very short, and their spreading lobes angle upward with edges curled outward. This tufted miniature looks like a jeweled brooch. *Flower:* White with deep yellow crests at the throat.

Distribution.   Extremely rare; open places in Bristlecone Pine forests; Inyo Mountains; Subalpine Zone, 9,500–10,500 ft (2,896–3,201 m). Known populations should have full protection, and any new populations should be reported.

Cryptantha utahensis (Gray) Greene. Fragrant Forget-me-not.   (Plate 6.41) A slender annual, 4–12 in (1–3 dm) high. Leaves are narrow, 1–2 in (2.5–5 cm) long, with a silky coat of fine, appressed hairs. The corolla is exquisite in detail, although little more than 1/8 in (3 mm) long and broad. Flowers are abundant enough to show up well and have a spicy fragrance. The one or two nutlets are shining, with sharp, knifelike edges. This species lacks the spreading hairs of most cryptanthas, so it appears sleek and trim in comparison. *Flower:* White.

Distribution.   Common, locally abundant; Desert Scrub to Pinyon-juniper Woodland, 3,500–7,500 ft (1,067–2,287 m).

Note: There are many more annual cryptanthas in the range, all with small, white flowers. Although characteristics vary, it is necessary to have mature nutlets to determine the species.

Cryptantha virginensis (Jones) Payson. Virgin Valley Cryptantha.   (Plate 6.42) A sturdy biennial or short-lived perennial, 4–6 in (10–15 cm) long, spatulate, and densely tufted on the stout taproot. They are gray-green with fine, tangled hairs, along with coarse, spreading hairs set in blisterlike swellings. Flowering stems bear short, scorpioid branches of blooms along their entire length, these subtended by leaflike bracts. Single stems are common, but some plants have many. Flowers are broader than they are long and abundant enough to be showy. Nutlets are ridged on the back. *Flower:* White, fragrant.

Distribution.   Common, especially in Pinyon-juniper Woodland, less common in Desert Scrub, 4,500–8,500 ft (1,372–2,591 m).

Hackelia brevicula (Jepson) Gentry. White Mountain Forget-me-not.   A perennial 8–30 in (2–7 dm) high. Basal leaves are well developed, 2 1/2–6 in (6.3–15 cm) long, the narrowly elliptic blade tapering to a petiole of about the same length. Leaves on the stem are gradually reduced upward. Branches of the inflorescence angle outward. The corolla is salverform, about 1/4 in (6 mm) across. *Flower:* Light blue.

Distribution.   Moist to dryish places; White Mountains; Pinyon-juniper Woodland to Subalpine Zone, 8,000–9,500 ft (2,439–2,896 m).

Hackelia floribunda (Lehm.) Johnston. Tall Hackelia.   A robust biennial or short-lived perennial, 12–48 in (3–12 dm) tall, the lower stem spreading-hairy. Basal leaves are not as well developed as those on the stem and soon wither. Stem leaves are lance-elliptic, gradually reduced upward. The inflorescence is strict, its branches ascending at narrow angles. The corolla is salverform, the lobes hardly 1/4 in (6 mm) across, slightly smaller than *H. brevicula*. *Flower:* Blue with a yellow eye.

Distribution.   Moist places; White Mountains; Pinyon-juniper Woodland and Subalpine Zone, 8,400–10,000 ft (2,561–3,049 m).

Lappula redowskii Hornem. Greene. Stick-seed.   An erect annual, 6–14 in (15–35 cm) high, the stems with soft, spreading hairs. Leaves are narrowly spatulate to linear and green, with hairs spreading from small, blisterlike bases. Those in a small tuft at the base are 1/2–1 in (13–25 cm) long, and those on the leafy stems are 1–2 in (2.5–5 cm) long. Flowers, subtended by green bracts, are distributed along the upper branches. The corollas are very small and inconspicuous, but the fruit demands attention. The nutlets have barbed prickles, which readily cling to any convenient object. *Flower:* Blue or dull yellowish.

Distribution.   Common; roadsides and open places; Desert Scrub to Subalpine Zone, 6,000–10,000 ft (1,829–3,049 m).

BRASSICACEAE (CRUCIFERAE) (Mustard Family)

Mostly annual or perennial herbs, locally shrubby plants. Some have glaucous foliage, as in the cabbage group. Flowers are usually small and arranged in terminal spikes or racemes. There are four sepals, and four petals spreading in the form of a cross—hence the name *Cruciferae*. Ovaries are usually two-celled pods (capsules), each with a thin partition between the outer walls (valves). When pods are mature, the valves separate, allowing the seeds to fall. It is not unusual to find only the tissuelike partitions left on the stem. Mature pods are more important than the flowers in identification. The long, narrow form is called a silique and the short form a silicle—not much longer than wide.

This is a large family that includes the cultivated cabbage, broccoli, radish, and mustard.

Arabis holboellii Hornem. **Holboell Rock Cress.**   (Plate 6.43) An erect perennial or biennial with one or several stems 6–30 in (1.5–7.3 dm) high. The lower stems are clothed with closely set leaves. Plants are grayish green and densely coated with fine, branched hairs. Basal leaves are oblanceolate or slender spatulate, narrowing to a slender stem, 1/2–2 in (1.3–5 cm) long in all. Those on the stem are linear to arrow-shaped and eared at the base except in the following varieties. Siliques are up to 3 in (7.5 cm) long. *Flower:* Petals white to pink. There are three varieties of this species:

Var. *pendulocarpa* (A. Nels.) **Rollins.**   The stems are only 4–8 in (1–2 dm) tall, and the stem leaves lack ears at the base. Siliques hang downward.

Distribution.   May be limited to limestone; Pinyon-juniper Woodland to Alpine Zone, 9,000–12,100 ft (2,744–3,689 m).

Var. *pinetorum* **Tides.**   The branched hairs are coarser in this variety. Siliques are commonly curved, arching downward.

Distribution.   Apparently restricted to areas of granitic and volcanic rock; Pinyon-juniper Woodland and Subalpine Zone, 7,500–10,000 ft (2,287–3,049 m).

Var. *retrofracta* (Graham) **Rydb.**   This variety tends to have sturdy lower stems. Siliques are straight, on pedicels that abruptly bend downward so that they hang close to the stem.

Distribution.   May not tolerate limestone soil; Desert Scrub to Subalpine Zone, 5,900–11,000 ft (1,799–3,353 m).

Arabis inyoensis Rollins. **Inyo Rock Cress.**   Perennial with slender stems, 8–12 in (2–3 dm) long, from a branching root crown. The leaves are about 1 in long, narrowly spatulate or oblanceolate, coated with fine, branched hairs, and tufted at the base. Siliques are mostly 1 1/2–2 in (4–5 cm) long, ascending or spreading on pedicels 1/4–1/2 in (6–13 mm) long. *Flower:* Pink to purplish.

Distribution.   Common on limestone; Pinyon-juniper Woodland to Alpine Zone, 7,000–12,500 ft (2,134–3,811 m).

Arabis lemmonii Watson var. *lemmonii*. **Lemmon Rock Cress.**   A perennial similar to *A. inyoensis* but a smaller plant. Stems are 2.5–8 in (6.4–20 cm) high, and siliques are usually spreading or ascending on one side of the stem. Pedicels are short, only 2/16–3/16 in (3–5 mm) long. *Flower:* Pink to purple.

Distribution. Open, rocky places; Pinyon-juniper Woodland to Alpine Zone, 8,500–13,800 ft (2,591–4,207 m).

Var. *depauperata* (A. Nels. & Kennedy) Rollins. Siliques ascending all around the stem. Its range is similar to that of var. *lemmonii,* but it is less common.

Arabis pulchra Jones. **Prince's Rock Cress.** (Plate 6.44) Perennial with green foliage but densely pubescent, with fairly showy flowers. Stems are 8–24 in (2–6 dm) high. Basal leaves are linear to obovate, 1–4 in (2.5–10 cm) long. Those on the stems are linear, are reduced in size, and lack ears or lobes at the base. Two varieties of this species occur in the range:

Var. *gracilis.* Flowers are $1/4–1/2$ in (6–13 mm) long. Pubescence is coarser than *A. pulchra* and less dense. Pedicels spread or arch downward, and the siliques, $1\,1/2–2$ in (3.8–5 cm) long, are pendulous. *Flower:* Red-purple.

Distribution. Relatively widespread but not abundant; Desert Scrub and Pinyon-juniper Woodland, 4,500–8,600 ft (1,372–2,622 m).

Var. *munciensis* Jones. The plant is densely pubescent and less robust than var. *gracilis,* and the flowers are less than $3/8$ in (10 mm) long. Pedicels curve gently downward. *Flower:* Pink-purple to purple.

Distribution. Uncommon; Desert Scrub to Pinyon-juniper Woodland, 4,500–7,000 ft (1,372–2,134 m).

Caulanthus crassicaulis Torr. Watson. **Woolly Caulanthus.** (Plate 6.45) A perennial with a stout, inflated stem $1–2\,1/2$ ft (3–7.5 dm) high. The leaves, tufted at the base, are oblanceolate, irregularly toothed, narrowing to stems longer than the blades, and 2–6 in (5–15 cm) long in all. Only a few leaves occur on the stem. The upper part of the stem bears single flowers. Each has a flask-shaped, white, densely hairy calyx about $1/2$ in (13 mm) long, with relatively inconspicuous petals protruding. Siliques are erect or ascending, 4–5 in (10–12 cm) long. This is a handsome and rather unusual plant. *Flower:* The purplish calyx, covered with white hairs, is more conspicuous than the white-margined purple petals.

Distribution. Mostly in Pinyon-juniper Woodland of the White Mountains and the northern part of the Inyo Mountains; Desert Scrub and Pinyon-juniper Woodland, 6,000–8,000 ft (1,829–2,439 m).

Caulanthus glaucus Watson. **Limestone Caulanthus, Cliff Cabbage.** (Plate 6.46) A perennial with several slender stems, 12–30 in (3–7.3 dm) tall. Leaves are light green, roundish to oblong, and some individuals lobed at the base; the blades are 2–7 in (5–17 cm) long, on stems about half their length. Leaves are mostly basal; those on the stems are usually narrower. The upper part of the main stem carries single flowers on slender pedicels. The calyx is about $3/8$ in (1 cm) long with petals protruding about $1/4$ in (6 mm). Siliques are slender, spreading, and 2–4 in (5–10 cm) long. *Flower:* Calyx is green, commonly purple tinged; petals are greenish yellow.

Distribution.   Limited, on limestone cliffs; Desert Scrub and Pinyon-juniper Woodland, 5,500–7,500 ft (1,677–2,287 m).

Caulostramina jaegeri (Rollins) Rollins. **Cliff dweller.** *(Thelypodium jaegeri)*   (Plate 6.47) Perennial from a tight mass of slender, woody stems packed in cliff crevices. The plant is green and leafy throughout, 4–12 in (1–3 dm) tall, with the inflorescence on the upper part of the stems. Leaves vary in shape but are mostly broadly ovate, 1–2 in (2.5–5 cm) long, on slender stems nearly as long. Flowers are ³⁄₈ in (1 cm) long, with the calyx half the length of the petals. Siliques are 1–2 in (2.5–5 cm) long, becoming spreading and contorted with age. This is a charming plant, one to enjoy in place but too rare to collect. *Flower:* Petals pale lavender or white with lavender veins.

Distribution.   Shaded crevices in limestone cliffs; Inyo Mountains; Pinyon-juniper Woodland, 6,000–9,200 ft (1,829–2,805 m).

Draba californica (Jepson) Rollins & Price. **White-flowered Draba.**   A small perennial with numerous stems 1¹⁄₂–5 in (4–12 cm) high from a tuft of basal leaves. Leaves are spatulate or obovate, coated with many-branched hairs. Flowers are minute but produce an abundance of elliptic silicles up to ³⁄₈ in (1 cm) long. *Flower:* White.

Distribution.   High meadows on dolomite in the White Mountains; Alpine Zone, 11,500–13,000 ft (3,506–3,963 m).

Draba oligosperma Hook. **White Mountain Draba.**   (Plate 6.48) A matted dwarf perennial with stems ¹⁄₂–4 in (1.3–10 cm) high. Leaves narrowly spatulate to linear, ¹⁄₈–¹⁄₂ in (6–13 mm) long, tufted on the branches of the spreading root crown. Flowers are minute, but the plump, ovate pods—hardly ¹⁄₄ in (6 mm) long—are impressively abundant. *Flower:* Yellow.

Distribution.   Common; open rocky places on limestone; White Mountains; Subalpine and Alpine zones, 8,900–14,250 ft (2,988–4,345 m).

Lepidium fremontii Watson. **Bush Peppergrass, Desert Alyssum.**   (Plate 6.49) A bushy perennial with a woody base and many branching stems, 8–20 in (2–5 dm) high. Leaves are linear, then divided, ³⁄₄–2 in (2–5 cm) long, well distributed. Flowers are very small but fragrant, and plentiful enough to make an attractive display. Silicles are flat, roundish to ovate, about ¹⁄₄ in (6 mm) long. *Flower:* White.

Distribution.   Rocky places, desert gullys and canyons; Desert Scrub, up to 6,000 ft (1,829 m).

Lesquerella kingii Watson ssp. *kingii.* **Beadpod.**   (Plate 6.50) A small, silvery-gray perennial with stems ¹⁄₂–6 in (1.3–15 cm) long. Blades of basal leaves are ovate to roundish, ¹⁄₈–1 in (6–25 mm) long, tapered to stems of about the same length. Those on the flowering stems are narrower. Flowers are about ¹⁄₄ in (6 mm) long, and silicles are beadlike, about ¹⁄₈ in (3 mm) in diameter. This plant is extremely variable in size, ranging from compact tufts only 1 in (2.5 cm) across at high elevations to well-developed stems spreading from a basal rosette of leaves, as found in the Pinyon-juniper Woodland. *Flower:* Bright yellow.

Distribution.   Limestone areas; Pinyon-juniper Woodland to Alpine Zone, 7,000–12,000 ft (2,134–3,658 m).

Stanleya elata Jones. **Prince's Plume.**   (Plate 6.51) A tall perennial, 2–6 ft (0.6–2 m) high. One or more erect stems rise from a clump of basal leaves. These are large, thick, oblong-ovate, and 4–8 in (1–2 dm) long. Flowering racemes are 6–18 in (15–45 cm) long on the upper portion of the tall stems, like tall yellow plumes. The sepals are petal-like, about ¼–⅜ in (7.5–10 mm) long. Those on the tall stems make a handsome sight when back-lit by an evening sun as one winds down the canyon roads toward Owens Valley. *Flower:* Sepals yellow, petals pale yellow.

Distribution.   Washes and canyon slopes; Desert Scrub and Pinyon-juniper Woodland, 4,200–8,000 ft (1,280–2,439 m).

Stanleya pinnata (Pursh) Britton var. *pinnata.* **Desert Plume.**   (Plate 6.52) A perennial 2–4 ft (0.6–1.3 m) high. Its stems are inclined to spread outward, and they are leafy on the lower portion. The leaves, 2–6 or 8 in (5–15 or 20 cm) long, are commonly divided into narrow segments, becoming simple and narrower above. The flowering racemes or "plumes" become 6–20 in (15–48 cm) long and are quite showy. Individual flowers are about ½ in (13 mm) long, both sepals and petals spreading, while the prominent stamens remain erect. *Flower:* Sepals pale yellow, petals bright yellow.

Distribution.   Reportedly indicates soil rich in selenium, slopes and washes; Desert Scrub, 4,000–6,000 ft (1,220–1,829 m).

Var. *inyoensis* (Munz & Ross) Reveal. **Inyo Desert Plume.**   A more robust plant than var. *pinnata,,* up to 5 ft (1.6 m) high and with a distinctly woody trunk 1½–3½ in (4–8 cm) thick. *Flower:* Same as var. *pinnata.*

Distribution.   Seepage areas or places of high groundwater, usually somewhat alkaline; Desert Scrub to Pinyon-juniper Woodland, up to nearly 7,500 ft (2,287 m).

Streptanthus cordatus Nutt. **Pinyon Streptanthus.**   (Plate 6.53) A short-lived perennial 8–30 in (2–7 dm) high. Basal leaves are spatulate-obovate, usually toothed, and 1–3 in (2.5–8 cm) high, and those on the stem are heart-shaped and clasping. Flowers are above the leaves. The plump sepals are about ¼ in (6 mm) long, with the less conspicuous petals protruding and curving outward. The entire plant is handsome. *Flower:* Calyx commonly purple or yellow, petals purple with white margins.

Distribution.   Common in Pinyon-juniper Woodland up to Subalpine Zone, 6,000–10,000 ft (1,829–3,049 m).

CACTACEAE (Cactus Family)

Succulent perennials, with fleshy stems that are columnar, globose, or flattened, commonly jointed. They are leafless except for small, narrow leaves on young *Opuntia* stems. Flowers have numerous petal-like segments, the outer sepals intergrading with the inner petals. The pistil is surrounded by many stamens. The ovary is inferior, that is, below the petals. The fruit is commonly dry, but in some species it is fleshy enough to be used as a food.

Echinocactus polycephalus **Engelm. & Bigelow. Cottontop Cactus.**   (Plate 6.54) Usually clumps of a few to many large cylindrical or spheroid stems, 6–20 in (1.5–5 dm) long, 8–12 in (2–3 dm) thick, gray-green in color. Spines are rigid and sturdy, the central ones $1^1/2$–$2^1/2$ in (3.8–6.4 cm) long. Flowers are at the apex of the stem, each bloom about 2 in (5 cm) across, surrounded with white, cottony growth. Few see them, however, because they appear in midsummer. Fruit is dry, partially buried in the "cotton." *Flower:* Yellow.

Distribution.   Dry, rocky slopes; Inyo Mountains; Desert Scrub, below 5,000 ft (1,524 m).

Echinocereus engelmannii **(Parry) Lemàine var.** *chrysocentrus* **(Engelm. & Bigelow) Engelm. Engelmann Cactus, Torch Cactus.**   (Plate 6.55) Usually 3 to 10 cylindrical stems, 5–12 in (12–30 cm) high, 2–$2^1/2$ in (5–6.4 cm) in diameter, ribbed. Spines vary in color, with the lower central one white, 1–3 in (2.5–8 cm) long. Flowers are borne laterally rather than terminally, each 2–3 in (5–8 cm) across. Fruit is green, turning red when mature, $3/4$–$1^1/4$ in (2–3 cm) long. It is edible and nutritious. *Flower:* Purple to magenta or lavender.

Distribution.   Rocky and gravelly places; Desert Scrub and Pinyon-juniper Woodland, below 7,000 ft (2,134 m).

Echinocereus triglochidiatus **Engelm. var.** *mojavensis* **(Engelm. & Bigelow) L. Benson. Mojave Mound Cactus.**   (Plate 6.56) Stems in dense mounds up to 1 ft (3 dm) high and 1–4 ft (3–12 dm) in diameter. They are ovoid to oblong, 2–6 in (5–15 cm) long, mostly 2–3 in (5–8 cm) in diameter, ribbed, and slightly nippled. Spines vary in color. Flowers are $1^1/2$–2 in (4–5 cm) across. Fruit is red, $1/2$–1 in (1.3–2.5 cm) long. *Flower:* Bright red.

Distribution.   Limestone outcrops; Desert Scrub to Subalpine Zone, 5,000–10,000 ft (1,524–3,049 m).

Opuntia basilaris **Engelm. & Bigelow. Beavertail.**   (Plate 6.57) Clumps 6–12 in (15–30 cm) high of flat, jointed stems. Joints are blue-green to purplish, mostly obovate or round, and 2–6 in (5–15 cm) long. There are no spines, but fine, barbed glochids are troublesome. Flowers are about 2–3 in (5–7.7 cm) across. Fruit is green, becoming tan or gray, dry, and 1–$1^1/4$ in (2.5–3 cm) long. *Flower:* Cerise or rose to orchid.

Distribution.   Widespread; dry gravelly and rocky places; Desert Scrub and Pinyon-juniper Woodland, up to 6,000 ft (1,829 m).

Opuntia erinacea Engelm. & Bigelow var. *erinacea*. **Mojave Prickly Pear.**   (Plate 6.58) Growth habit similar to Beavertail, but joints are more elongated and are spiny throughout, the spines somewhat flexuous. Flowers are 1 3/4–3 1/2 in (4.5–9 cm) across. Fruit is dry and densely spiny. *Flower:* Yellow.

Distribution.   Sandy or gravelly places; mostly in Joshua Tree and Pinyon-juniper Woodland, Desert Scrub and Pinyon-juniper Woodland, below 9,000 ft (2,743 m).

Var. *ursina* (A. Weber) Parish. Old Man Cactus, Grizzly Bear Cactus.   Growth habit similar to var. *erinacea*. Joints with long, flexuous, white or gray spines throughout. *Flower:* Yellow.
   Distribution.   Rocky places, such as Joshua Flats; Inyo Mountains; Desert Scrub and Pinyon-juniper Woodland, 5,500–7,500 ft (1,677–2,287 m).

Var. *utahensis* (Engelm.) L. Benson. Utah Prickly Pear.   Joints mostly 2–3 1/2 in (5–9 cm) long. Spines flexuous only on upper portion of stem. *Flower:* Yellow.
   Distribution.   Desert Scrub and Pinyon-juniper Woodland, much the same as Old Man Cactus, and they seem to intergrade.

Sclerocactus polyancistrus (Engelm. & Bigelow) Britton & Rose. **Mojave Fishhook Cactus, Pineapple Cactus.**   (Plate 6.59) A small barrel-like cactus with stems usually solitary, pineapple-shaped, 4–10 in (10–25 cm) long, ribbed, and with low nipples. The spines, which almost obscure the stem, include red hooked ones spreading outward and white radial ones close to the stem. Flowers, about 2 in (5 cm) across, are in a ring on the summit. Fruit is dry, about 1 in long. This is an endangered species because it appeals to collectors, but it does not survive when transplanted. *Flower:* Rose-purple to magenta.

Distribution.   Rocky places, mostly on limestone; Desert Scrub and Pinyon-juniper Woodland, 6,000–7,700 ft (1,829–2,348 m).

CAPRIFOLIACEAE (Honeysuckle Family)

Represented here by shrubs, most with opposite leaves and branches. Fruit is a berry.

Sambucus caerulea Raf. **Blue Elderberry.**   (Plate 6.60) A large shrub, 4–8 ft (1–2 dm) high, the branches brittle with a large core of pith. Leaves are large, with five to nine leaflets. These are finely toothed, mostly 2–4 in (5–10 cm) long, oblong, and with one side shorter than the other at the base. The inflorescence is a flat-topped cyme, usually about 6 in (15 cm) across. Flowers are small, 1/4 in (6 mm) or less wide, five-lobed. Fruit is a round berry, nearly black with a white bloom, appearing bluish. *Flower:* Creamy white.

Distribution.   Open, not too dry slopes and washes; mostly in the White Mountains, Pinyon-juniper Woodland and Subalpine Zone, 7,000–10,000 ft (2,134–3,049 m).

Symphoricarpos longiflorus Gray. **Desert Snowberry.**   (Plate 6.61) A spreading shrub with slender branches up to 4 ft (1.2 m) high. Leaves are simple and elliptical, mostly less than ½ in (13 mm) long. The dainty flowers are in the upper axils. The corolla is about ½ in (13 mm) long, slender and tubular, abruptly flaring to short lobes. Fruit is an elongated white berry, slightly shorter than the flower. *Flower:* Rose-pink or lavender to paler shades.

Distribution.   Rocky places, usually on limestone; Desert Scrub to Subalpine Zone, 5,000–9,700 ft (1,524–2,957 m).

CARYOPHYLLACEAE (Pink Family)

Annual or perennial herbs. Leaves mostly opposite, linear, often needle-like. Sepals separate or united in a tube. Petals small or lacking.

Arenaria aculeata Watson. **Prickly Sandwort.** (*Arenaria kingii* [Watson] Jones var. *glabrescens* [Watson] Maguire)   (Plate 6.62) Plants perennial with stems somewhat matted at the base, 4–8 in (1–2 dm) high. Leaves stiff and needle-like, up to ¾ in (2 cm) long, mostly basal, only two pairs on a stem. Flowers about ¼ in (16 mm) long with five petals, about the same length as the sepals, in loose terminal cymes. *Flower:* White.

Distribution.   Dry, rocky places; Desert Scrub to Alpine Zone, 6,000–12,600 ft (1,829–3,841 m).

Arenaria kingii (Watson) Jones ssp. *compacta* (Coville) Maguire. **Alpine Sandwort.**   (Plate 6.63) Similar to *A. aculeata* but more compact. Stems are less than 2½ in (6.4 cm) long, and leaves are only about ¼ in (6 mm) long. *Flower:* White.

Distribution.   Near or above timberline, mostly on limestone; Subalpine and Alpine zones; 10,000–12,500 ft (3,049–3,811 m).

Arenaria macradenia Watson ssp. *macradenia* var. *parishiorum* B.L. Robinson. **Lime Sandwort.**   (Plate 6.64) Perennial with stems 8–15 in (2–3.5 dm) tall. Basal leaves are like *A. kingii,* but most are about 1 in (2.5 cm) long, with the several pairs on the stem reduced. Petals are about ¼ in (6 mm) long, barely exceeding the sepals. *Flower:* Greenish yellow.

Distribution.   Rocky canyons, limestone areas; Desert Scrub, 4,000–6,500 ft (1,220–1,982 m).

Var. *macradenia* Watson. Mojave Sandwort. Similar to var. *parishiorum* but has larger flowers. Its petals are about 1 1/2 times as long as the sepals. *Flower:* White.

Distribution. Rare in southern part of the Inyo Mountains; Desert Scrub, 6,500 ft (1,982 m).

Scopulophila rixfordii (Bdg.) Munz & Johnston. Rixford Rockwort. (Plate 6.65) A rounded perennial, 4–8 in (1–2 dm) high, from a woody root crown. Tufts of pale beige wool at the base of the numerous stems are a distinguishing feature. The narrow leaves are in pairs on the stems. Although the flowers have no petals, they are so numerous that the tissuelike sepals give the plant a frosty appearance when in full bloom. *Flower:* Sepals translucent with a central green spot.

Distribution. Dry limestone cliffs; Inyo Mountains; Desert Scrub, 4,000–7,000 ft (1,463–2,134 m).

Silene bernardina Watson ssp. *maguirei.* Maguire Campion. Perennial with stems 6–18 in (15–45 cm) tall. Leaves in pairs on the stems, mostly linear-lanceolate, 1–2 in (2.5–5 cm) long. Flower calyx tubular, 1/2 in (13 mm) long, pale with vertical dark lines. Five 4-lobed petals protrude from the calyx. *Flower:* Whitish, commonly tinged with pink or purple.

Distribution. Rocky slopes; Pinyon-juniper Woodland and Subalpine Zone, 8,000–10,700 ft (2,439–3,262 m).

Note: Silene verecunda Watson ssp. *andersonii* (Clokey) Hitch & Maguire, Anderson Campion, is similar, but the petals are two-lobed and the flowers greenish white.

Stellaria longipes Goldie. Creek Stellaria. (Plate 6.66) Perennial from creeping rootstocks, 4–10 in (1–2.4 dm) high, somewhat tufted. Leaves lanceolate, 1/4–3/4 in (6–20 mm) long, in pairs on the slender stems. Flower petals deeply two-parted, about 3/16 in (5 mm) long. Although small, the dainty flowers with prominent dark stamens are most attractive. *Flower:* White.

Distribution. Streamlets and meadow borders; Desert Scrub and Subalpine Zone, 6,000–11,500 ft (1,829–3,506 m).

CHENOPODIACEAE (Goosefoot or Saltbush Family)

A family well represented throughout the range by herbs and shrubs, many of which tolerate alkaline conditions unfavorable to other species. Most of them are grayish and the leaf surfaces farinose (mealy) or scurfy. Many species, especially the shrubs, bear staminate (male) and pistillate (female) flowers on different plants, and some are polygamous, meaning that they bear unisexual and bisexual flowers on the same plant. Other species bear perfect flowers, having both staminate and pistillate parts. Flowers in this family lack corollas and are small and inconspicuous, so no flower colors are mentioned in this section. The fruits are more interesting, especially those with foliaceous bracts, which are distinctive for each species. Some species are difficult to determine, so only a few are listed.

Atriplex canescens (Pursh) Nutt. Fourwing Saltbush.   A much-branched, somewhat rounded shrub, 1 1/2–5 ft (0.5–1.6 m) high, grayish and scurfy. Leaves are narrowly linear, 1/2–1 1/2 in (13–38 mm) long. Staminate flower clusters are in terminal spikes. Pistillate flowers are also terminal, on different plants. They develop into four-winged fruit, mostly about 1/2 in (13 mm) broad. No other saltbush has such narrow leaves, and no other has fruit with wings on all four sides. The dry fruit, commonly persistent on the bush, is said to resemble popcorn.

Distribution.   Common along roadsides and wash borders, where there is a little extra moisture; Desert Scrub to Pinyon-juniper Woodland, below 7,000 ft (2,134 m).

Atriplex confertifolia (Torr. & Fremont) Watson. Shadscale.   (Plate 6.67) A rigidly branched, spiny shrub, 1–3 ft (3–9 dm) high. The branches are somewhat straw-colored and the foliage scurfy gray. Branchlets of the previous year become rigid spines. Leaf blades are mostly round-ovate, 1/4–3/4 in (6–20 mm) long. Staminate flowers are clustered on the short branchlets. Pistillate flowers, on different plants, develop into two-bracted fruit; that is, they have two oblong or roundish wings flaring above the seed cover, 1/4–3/8 in (6–10 mm) long.

Distribution.   A dominant shrub over vast areas of the dry lower slopes of the range; Desert Scrub, below 7,000 ft (2,134 m).

Atriplex polycarpa (Torr.) Watson. Allscale.   An intricately branched, pale scurfy-gray shrub, 2–6 ft (0.6–2 m) high. It has a rounded outline, and the upper twigs and branchlets are very fine. Leaves are small, 1/8–1/2 in (6–13 mm) long, with rosettes of tiny leaves bundled in their axils. Staminate and pistillate flowers are on separate plants. Bracts on the fruit are joined to well above the middle, the free upper edges shallowly toothed, and have various protrusions on the surface. They are somewhat triangular in outline, or rounded on the sides, and are about 1/8 in (6 mm) long. Everything about the shrub except its size is on a small scale. No other saltbush in the range has such small leaves.

Distribution.   Dry, moderately alkaline soils; Desert Scrub, below 6,000 ft (1,829 m).

Atriplex torreyi (Watson) Watson. Nevada Saltbush.   (Plate 6.68) A rather stiffly erect, scurfy, metallic-gray shrub, 2–5 ft (0.6–1.6 m) tall. The twigs are lined and angled longitudinally, and they become stiff and spiny as they lose their leaves. Leaf shape varies from ovate to bluntly arrow-shaped or triangular, 1/2–1 in long. Like the preceding saltbushes, the staminate and pistillate flowers are on separate plants. The fruiting bracts are roundish in outline but flattish at the base, with the upper margins free, finely scalloped, and about 1/8 in (3 mm) across.

Distribution.   Alkaline places with high roundwater or other reliable water source; Desert Scrub, below 6,000 ft (1,829 m).

Ceratoides lanata **Pursh. Winter Fat, Lamb's Tail.** *(Eurotia lanata)*   (Plate 6.69) An erect shrub 1–3 ft (0.3–1 m) high, the entire plant is whitish with a dense coat of silky hairs, commonly becoming rusty with age. The leaves are $1/2$–$1\,1/2$ in (13–38 mm) long and narrowly linear, with the margins strongly rolled under. Staminate and pistillate flowers are usually on separate plants, but not uncommonly they appear on the same one. They are on the upper part of the branches, the staminate flowers relatively inconspicuous. Pistillate bracts and the fruit are covered with long, white hairs and stand out well in a shrub community. It is the white-hairy fruiting stalks that give the plant its common name, *Lamb's Tail*. The name *Winter Fat* refers to its nutritional value for livestock.

Distribution.   It has a wide range and can tolerate some alkali; Desert Scrub and Pinyon-juniper Woodland, 3,500–9,400 ft (1,067–2,866 m).

Chenopodium atrovirens **Rydb. Pinyon Goosefoot.**   An erect annual usually 4–20 in (1–5 dm) high, although extremely dwarfed plants occur at high elevations. Foliage is green and the leaves ovate to triangular oblong, normally $1/2$–1 in long on somewhat shorter stems (petioles). Flower glomerules are farinose, in terminal spikes. The minute seeds are horizontal and enclosed by sharply ridged calyx lobes.

Distribution.   Relatively common in dry, open places; Desert Scrub to Subalpine Zone, 5,500–10,200 ft (1,677–3,110 m).

Chenopodium fremontii **Watson. Fremont Goosefoot.**   An erect annual, 6–36 in (1–9 dm) high, commonly branched. Leaves are bright green above and pale beneath, mostly $1/2$–1 in (13–25 mm) long, predominantly arrow-shaped, on slender stems shorter than the blades. Flowers are in small glomerules on terminal spikes. The minute seeds are horizontal and completely enclosed by the calyx lobes. Along with *C. atrovirens,* the most common of a number of *Chenopodium* species that occur in the range.

Distribution.   Common in the pinyon belt; Desert Scrub and Pinyon-juniper Woodland, 5,000–8,000 ft (1,524–2,439 m).

Grayia spinosa **(Hook.) Maguire. Hopsage.**   (Plate 6.70) A much-branched, evergreen shrub, 1–3 ft (3–9 dm) high. Branches are finely longitudinally lined, but this characteristic is lost in older wood. Its branchlets are commonly spinose-tipped. Leaves are small, $1/3$–1 in (8–25 mm) long, linear to obovate, and rather fleshy. They are most attractive in the spring, when they are gray-tipped as if dipped in powder. Staminate and pistillate flowers are inconspicuous and borne on the same plant or separate ones. It is the dense terminal clusters of fruiting bracts that attract attention. They are roundish and flattened, $1/4$–$1/2$ in (6–13 mm) across, and variously colored from flesh tones to deep rose red.

Distribution. Common and widespread on flats and slopes, commonly a dominant member of the scrub community; Desert Scrub to Pinyon-juniper Woodland, 3,500–8,000 ft (1,067–2,439 m). Stunted shrubs occur as high as 9,350 ft (2,851 m) in the Inyo Mountains.

Sarcobatus vermiculatus (Hook.) Torr. Greasewood. (Plate 6.71) A spiny, much-branched, deciduous shrub, 3–6 ft (1–2 m) high. Its leaves are linear, yellow-green, $1/2$–$1 1/2$ in (13–38 mm) long. Staminate and pistillate flowers are borne on the same or different plants. Staminate ones are in a terminal catkinlike spike $1/2$–1 in (13–25 mm) long. Pistillate flowers are in the upper leaf axils. In fruit the seed capsule is surrounded by a disklike wing about $1/2$ in (13 mm) across in all.

Distribution. Alkaline places where it is watered by groundwater, or around springs and seepage areas; Desert Scrub, below 7,000 ft (2,134 m).

CROSSOSOMATACEAE (Crossosoma Family)

Forsellesia nevadensis (Gray) Greene. Nevada Forsellesia. (Plate 6.72) Formerly placed in Celastraceae, the Staff-tree Family, a small, deciduous, intricately branched shrub, 8–36 in (2–9 dm) high. Branches are slender, ribbed, and yellowish green in color. Leaves are oblong to elliptic, usually less than $1/2$ in (13 mm) long. Although the leaves are closely set on young growth, the plant appears relatively leafless much of the time. The small flowers are in the leaf axils and have four or five slender, tongue-shaped petals about $1/4$ in (6 mm) long. The shrub might escape notice were it not one of the strong indicators of a certain type of limestone, usually with Littleleaf Mahogany (*Cercocarpus intricatus*). *Flower:* White.

Distribution. Limestone-, probably dolomite-rich soil; Desert Scrub, 4,500–7,000 ft (1,372–2,134 m).

CUSCUTACEAE (Dodder Family)

Also included in Convolvulaceae, the Morning Glory Family. Parasitic plants without chlorophyll. The twining yellow to orange stems resemble a tangle of coarse thread thrown over the host plant. The flowers are very small, waxy white, and usually clustered. A dodder germinates independently, then attaches itself by suckerlike parts to the first suitable plant it reaches. From then on, it lives on nourishment from the host plant.

Cuscuta salina Engelm. var. *apoda* (Yuncker) Yuncker. Nevada Dodder. *(Cuscuta nevadensis)* (Plate 6.73) The stems are very slender, orange-yellow. Flowers are about $1/8$ in (3 mm) long, with lanceolate calyx and corolla lobes. They are usually in dense clusters. Host plants are commonly shadscale or *Dalea* (*Psorothamnus*). *Flower:* White.

Distribution. Common; Desert Scrub and Pinyon-juniper Woodland, 4,500–8,000 ft (1,372–2,439 m).

Cuscuta suksdorfii Yuncker var. *subpedicellata* Yuncker. **Mountain Dodder.**
Stems are slender and pale yellowish. Flowers, which are in few-flowered clusters, are about ⅛ in (3 mm) long, with triangular calyx lobes and triangular-ovate corolla lobes. Host plants include aster, clover, and various shrubs. *Flower:* White.

Distribution. Common; Desert Scrub and Pinyon-juniper Woodland, 4,500–8,000 ft (1,372–2,439 m).

CYPERACEAE (Sedge Family)

A large family resembling grasses or rushes, usually spreading from rhizomes. Stems are solid (or rarely hollow) and mostly triangular, less commonly round. Leaves are parallel-veined, mostly three-ranked, with grass-like blades, or blades may be reduced or lacking. Inflorescence is in spikes or spikelets; flowers are very small and perfect, but some plants are dioecious. The perianth consists of one to six short or elongate bristles, or none; there are one to three stamens; the ovary is one-celled; the fruit is an achene. The species are numerous and difficult to identify, so they are not described individually; only the common genera are shown here.

Carex. **Sedge.** Common grasslike perennials with three-ranked leaves, closed sheaths, and solid stems. Floral spikes are in various forms and may be unisexual. Each is usually subtended by a bract, large and leafy, or much reduced and inconspicuous. There are three stamens, or less commonly two; pistillate flowers are enclosed by a saclike scale called a perigynium, as well as being subtended by an open scale; there are two or three stigmas with the achene accordingly lenticular or three-sided. This is the largest genus in the family by far and is represented in the range by about 30 species.

Eliocharis. **Spikebrush.** Stems round or flattened; leaves broad, reduced to mere sheaths or scales; spikelets solitary and terminal without subtending bracts; flowers perfect; perianth has zero to six (or nine) bristles; three stamens. The thickened base of the style persists as a tubercle at the apex of the achene. Members of this genus are relatively slender and dainty. Only four species are known in the range.

Scirpus. **Bulrush.** Stems mostly solid and triangular (except *S. acutus*); leaves long and grasslike or much reduced; inflorescence in various forms, subtended by one or more large and leafy or small bracts; flowers perfect, in the axils of the scales; perianth of one to six bristles; three stamens; style bifid or trifid; achene accordingly lenticular or three-sided, lacking a tubercle at the apex. Members of this genus are comparatively coarse. Only four species are known in the range.

EPHEDRACEAE (Ephedra Family)

Species in this family are gymnosperms as are pines. There is only one genus, which occurs in arid regions. The plants are broomlike shrubs and appear to be leafless.

They do have small, scalelike leaves, however, mostly in pairs in the species included here. The plants are dioecious. The miniature cones produce a pair of seeds.

Ephedra nevadensis Watson. Nevada Ephedra.   (Plate 6.74) An erect or sprawling dull-green shrub, 1–3 ft (3–9 dm) high, with rigid, somewhat spreading branches. The color is more bluish green than for other species, but there may be considerable variation. Male cones, about 1/4 in (6 mm) long, show an abundance of yellow stamens. Female plants bear small, stemmed cones about 3/8 in (1 cm) long containing a pair of smooth, dark brown seeds.

Distribution.   Common, dry places; from the valley floors to Desert Scrub to Pinyon-juniper Woodland, 7,000 ft (2,134 m).

Ephedra viridis Coville. Green Ephedra, Indian Tea.   (Plate 6.75) An erect yellowish green shrub, 1 1/2–4 ft (4.5–12 dm) high, with broomlike branches. Male cones are about 1/4 in (6 mm) long and yellow, with stamens. Female cones are 3/8 in (1 cm) long, have little or no stem, and contain two light brown to brown seeds. These are usually more slender than seeds of *E. nevadensis*. This shrub is a brighter green than Nevada Ephedra, and it usually occurs at higher elevations but there is some overlapping of their ranges and some hybridization between the two.

Distribution.   Common; dry, rocky places; Desert Scrub to Subalpine Zone, 4,500–10,300 ft (1,372–3,140 m).

EQUISETACEAE (Horsetail Family)

White-Inyo mountain species have annual stems, erect, jointed, hollow. Leaves are reduced to minute scales united to form a sheath at the nodes. Branches, if present, alternate with the scales at the base of the sheath. A conelike, spore-bearing body, 1/2–1 1/4 in long, tops each fertile stem. Stems are minutely ridged and somewhat rough to the touch.

Equisetum arvense L. Common Horsetail.   Stems are in two forms. Sterile stems are green with whorls of long branches; fertile ones are whitish or brown, unbranched, and soon wither. The sheath is greenish, 3/16–3/8 in (5–10 mm) long, with teeth 1–3 mm long; cone 3/16–1 3/8 in (0.5–3.5 cm) long, long-stemmed.

Distribution.   Wet places; Desert Scrub and Pinyon-juniper Woodland, 5,000–8,300 ft (1,524–2,530 m).

Equisetum laevigatum A. Bráun. Scouring Rush.   Stems all about alike, simple or some few-branched, 6–40 in (1.5–10 dm) tall and up to 5/16 in (8 mm) thick. Sheaths are generally 5/16–5/8 in (7–15 mm) long, mainly green, with a black band at apex only. Cone is 5/8–1 in (1–2.5 cm) long, short-stemmed.

Distribution.   Wet places; Desert Scrub and Pinyon-juniper Woodland, 4,000–9,200 ft (1,220–2,805 m).

EUPHORBIACEAE (Spurge Family)

Represented in the range by prostrate perennial plants with milky sap and glabrous foliage. Their slender, underground stems issue from heavy, deep-set roots. The tiny staminate flowers and the single pistillate flower are in a small, green, cuplike involucre. This is rimmed by dark glands bordered by petal-like appendages. The single pistillate flower bears a three-celled ovary that protrudes to one side.

Chamaesyce albomarginata (Torr. & Gray) Small. **Rattlesnake Weed.** *(Euphorbia albomarginata)* (Plate 6.76) Visible stems are 2–10 in (5–24 cm) long, closely hugging the ground. Leaves are rounded to oblong, 1/4 in (6 mm) long or less, and bluish green with a very thin white margin. Flowers are at the nodes throughout the plant. Glands are oblong and dark maroon, and the white appendages are conspicuously large, broader than the glands. The plant is small but is a most attractive groundcover. *Flower:* There are no true petals, but the white appendages are appealing.

Distribution.   Sandy slopes or flats; mostly in the Inyo Mountains; low elevations, Desert Scrub, up to nearly 6,000 ft (1,829 m).

Chamaesyce fendleri (Torr. & Gray) Small. **Fendler Spurge.** *(Euphorbia fendleri* Torr. & Gray) (Plate 6.77) Visible stems 2–6 in (5–15 cm) long, flat or slightly lifted. Leaves are triangular with rounded corners, minute to about 3/8 in (1 cm) long, and bright green. Like *C. albomarginata,* flowers are at the leaf nodes. Glands are oblong, reddish or paler, and the white appendages are only about the same width. *Flower:* The narrow appendages are white.

Distribution.   Common in limestone areas; Desert Scrub and Pinyon-juniper Woodland, 5,000–8,500 ft (1,524–2,591 m).

FABACEAE (LEGUMINOSAE) (Pea Family)

A large family represented in the range by herbs or shrubs with compound leaves composed of three to many leaflets. The common form is an odd-pinnate leaf with leaflets on either side of a rachis (leaf stem) plus a terminal leaflet. Lupines and clovers, however, have palmate leaves, in which the leaflets radiate from a central point, as fingers from the palm of a hand. Flowers are irregular and pealike with a tubular calyx. In lupines the calyces of some are enlarged or even shortly spurred at the upper side of the base. Two lower petals are united to form a keel. These are usually covered by two lateral petals known as the "wings," and a fifth petal, the "banner," is turned upward about midway. The fruit is a legume (pod) with few to many seeds.

Astragalus calycosus Torr. **Little Gray Milk-vetch.**   (Plate 6.78) A small, tufted, gray perennial, generally 2–4 in (5–10 cm) across. The leaves are 1–2 1/2 in (25–64 mm) long with obovate leaflets 1/4–1/2 in (6–13 mm) long. Flower racemes are slightly longer than the leaves, so they are inclined to form an outer ring around the foliage.

·Flowers are about 1/2 in (13 mm) long. Pods are papery, slender oblong, and up to 5/8 in (15 mm) long. Another common name for taxa of *Astragalus* is locoweed, or simply loco, which implies detrimental effects to livestock; however, few if any of the species here are guilty. *Flower:* Lavender or pinkish, fading bluish.

Distribution. Widespread on limestone flats or slopes, common in the Bristlecone Pine Forest; Pinyon-juniper Woodland and Subalpine Zone, 6,500–11,500 ft (1,982–3,506 m).

Astragalus cimae Jones var. *sufflatus* (Barneby). **Broad-shouldered Milk-vetch.** (Plate 6.79) A perennial with glabrous green foliage and stems up to 12 in (3 dm) long. Leaves are 2–4 in (5–10 cm) long with ovate to roundish leaflets, most about 1/2 in (13 mm) long. The flowers, 1/2 in (13 mm) or more long, are slender with the banner gently curved upward. The pods are thick-papery, inflated, 1 1/4–1 1/2 in (3–4 cm) long and 1/2–3/4 in (6–20 mm) wide, abruptly straight across the base and tapered toward a pointed tip. The distinguishing features are the pod's square end and its long stem (stipe), 1/4–1/2 in (6–13 mm) long, which protrudes from the calyx when mature. *Flower:* Petals purple with white wing tips.

Distribution. Endemic to the east side of the Inyo Mountains; Desert Scrub to Pinyon-juniper Woodland, 5,000–6,800 ft (1,524–2,073 m).

Astragalus coccineus Brandegee. **Scarlet Loco, Scarlet Milk-vetch.** (Plate 6.80) A tufted perennial with white-woolly foliage, only as tall as its 2–4 in (5–10 cm)–long leaves. Each leaf has seven to fifteen elliptic to broadly obovate leaflets, 1/4–1/2 in (6–12 mm) long. Flowering stems bear clusters of showy blooms just above the leaves. Although the flowers have the typical pea parts, they are long and slender. Their tubular appearance and bright color attract hummingbirds, which pollinate them. The calyx is 5/8 in (15 mm) long and the entire flower is at least twice that length. The pods are plump and white-furry, curving to a pointed tip, about 1 1/4 in (3 cm) long. *Flower:* Scarlet.

Distribution. Gravelly banks or pockets between rocks; infrequent, mostly on granitic or volcanic rocks; Desert Scrub, 3,500–6,500 ft (1,067–1,982 m).

Astragalus inyoensis Sheldon. **Inyo Milk-vetch.** (Plate 6.81) A spreading perennial with prostrate or ascending stems, 6–24 in (1.5–6 dm) long. Stems are slender and the foliage sparse. Leaves are only 1/2–1 1/2 in (13–38 mm) long, their crowded leaflets hardly 1/4 in (6 mm) long. The flowers, in terminal clusters, are about 3/8 in (1 cm) long. The distinctive, incurved little pods, about 1/2 in (13 mm) long, appear to have been mashed in the middle and are deeply grooved underneath. They are thinly leathery, commonly purplish, and are attached by a stipe about as long as the calyx. *Flower:* Dull pink-purple to yellowish.

Distribution. Gravelly flats, most common in Pinyon-juniper Woodland, 6,000–9,500 ft (1,829–2,896 m).

Astragalus kentrophyta Gray var. *elatus* (Watson) Barneby. Inyo Prickly Milk-vetch. (Plate 6.82) A grayish perennial with rigid, trailing stems, 4–16 in (1–4 dm) long, naked between the leaf nodes, which are an inch, more or less, apart. Leaves are stiff and prickly with linear, spine-tipped leaflets 1/4–1/2 in (6–13 mm) long. Flowers, too, are borne at the nodes and are relatively inconspicuous, only 1/4 in (6 mm) or less long. The teardrop-shaped pods are about the same length. This strange plant is much larger and coarser than other varieties of the genus. *Flower:* Off-white, commonly purplish-veined.

Distribution. Locally abundant; open places in the Bristlecone Pine Forest in the Inyo Mountains, scarce in the White Mountains; Subalpine Zone, 9,500–10,500 ft. This is a disjunct site. The nearest known population of this variety is in Lincoln County, Nevada, close to the Utah line, lower in elevation.

Var. *implexus* (Canby) Barneby. Dolomite Milk-vetch. A minute, compact variety growing in small tufts or mats. Leaves are 3/16 in (5 mm) long, closely set, and very fine in comparison to var. *elatus.* Flowers and pods are about the same size, however. *Flower:* Pink-purple with white wingtips.
    Distribution. Common on dolomite in the Bristlecone Pine Forest; White Mountains; Subalpine and Alpine zones, 9,000–12,000 ft (2,744–3,658 m).

Astragalus lentiginosus Douglas var. *fremontii* (Gray) Watson. Paper Loco, Freckled Milk-vetch. (Plate 6.83) A perennial or winter annual, bushy or sprawling, with stems 10–20 in (24–50 cm) long. Leaflets are mostly obovate and less than 1/2 in long, but they are extremely variable. Flower racemes rise well above the leaves. Flowers are 3/8–1/2 in (10–13 mm) long. Pods are papery and roundly inflated with an abruptly pointed beak, usually purplish or reddish mottled, and are about 3/4 in (2 cm) long. *Flower:* Purple.

Distribution. Widespread, commonly abundant on open slopes or flats; Desert Scrub to Subalpine Zone, 4,000–10,300 ft (1,220–3,140 m).

Var. *semotus* Jepson. Little Paper-pod. A perennial, much like var. *fremontii* but a smaller, more compact plant. Leaflets are smaller and more crowded, and flower racemes are short, not over 1 1/2 in (4 cm) long. The pods are usually highly colored, mottled in shades of rose red.
    Distribution. Open places, usually on flats; Pinyon-juniper Woodland and Subalpine Zone, 7,500–11,200 ft (2,287–3,415 m).

Astragalus minthorniae (Rydb.) Jepson var. *villosus.* Erect Milk-vetch. A sturdy perennial with rigidly erect stems, usually 12–18 in (3–4.5 dm) high. The plant is coated throughout with short, soft hairs. Leaflets are ovate, averaging 1/2 in (13 mm) long. Flowering spikes rise well above the leaves. Flowers are 1/2 in (13 mm) long, and the calyx, which has black hairs, is about half that length. Pods are slender but plumply cylindrical, 3/4 in (2 cm) long and about 1/8 in (3 mm) wide, nearly straight, and grooved underneath. They are angled upward or widely spreading. *Flower:* Rather dull pink-purple with white wing tips.

Distribution.   This is a disjunct population that appears to be narrowly restricted to the northern part of the Inyo Mountains; Desert Scrub and Pinyon-juniper Woodland, 4,500–7,600 ft (1,372–2,317 m).

Astragalus newberryi Gray. **Newberry Milk-vetch.**   (Plate 6.84) A small, tufted perennial, whitish with appressed silky hairs. The leaves are only a few inches high, the leaflets elliptic to obovate, 3/8–1/2 in (10–13 mm) long. The flower stalk, which does not exceed the leaves, carries three to eight showy blooms, each 1 in (2.5 cm) long. Pods are densely white-furry and plump, about 3/4 in (2 cm) long, abruptly curved to a short beak. *Flower:* Pink-lavender except for a white area in the banner, which is streaked with lavender.

Distribution.   Relatively common on rocky limestone slopes; Bristlecone Pine Forest; Desert Scrub and Pinyon-juniper Woodland, 5,000–9,500 ft (1,524–2,896 m).

Astragalus oophorus Watson. **Big-podded Milk-vetch, Spindle loco.**   (Plate 6.85) A perennial 4–10 in (1–2.4 dm) high, with green foliage and very large pods. Leaflets are broadly ovate, 1/8–3/4 in (3–20 mm) long. Flowers are 1/2 in (13 mm) long, with the banner abruptly turned upward. The hanging pods are bladdery and inflated, broadly spindle-shaped, papery, and strongly mottled, 1 1/4–1 1/3 in (3–4.5 cm) long. The entire plant is handsome. *Flower:* Purple with white wing tips.

Distribution.   Flats and loamy slopes; Pinyon-juniper Woodland to Subalpine Zone, 6,500–10,400 ft (1,982–3,170 m).

Astragalus purshii Douglas var. *tinctus* Jones. **Long-flowered Pursh Milk-vetch.** A tufted perennial, very similar to *A. newberryi*. The white hairs on the foliage and pods are dull with less sheen. Pods are not as abruptly curved. *Flower:* Lavender.

Distribution.   Relatively common on granitic and volcanic rocks; Desert Scrub to Subalpine Zone, 6,000–10,300 ft (1,829–3,140 m).

Dalea searlsiae (Gray) Barneby. **Prairie Clover.** *(Petalostemum searlsiae)*   (Plate 6.86) An erect perennial, 12–20 in (3–5 dm) high, from a branching root crown. The plant is dotted throughout with glands. The well-spaced leaves are 1–2 in (2.5–5 cm) long, with three to five narrowly oblong leaflets about 1/2 in (13 mm) long. The inflorescence is a very dense conical spike, 1/2–1 1/2 in (13–38 mm) long. The flowers are so small and densely packed that it takes a hand lens to study them, but they are richly colored and beautiful in detail. Pods are equally small, about 1/8 in (3 mm) long. *Flower:* Rose.

Distribution.   Unusual in California but reaches into the Inyo Mountains; Pinyon-juniper Woodland, 6,000–8,400 ft (1,829–2,561 m).

Lupinus argenteus Pursh var. *tenellus* (Douglas) D. Dunn. **Limestone Lupine.** (Plate 6.87) A bushy perennial, 15–25 in (36–63 cm) tall, with silvery foliage. Hairs on the stems and foliage are appressed, giving the plant a sleek, satiny appearance. All lupines have palmate leaves. They are well distributed throughout the bush, each with five to nine linear-oblanceolate leaflets up to 1 1/2 in (25–38 mm) long. The pealike flowers are 3/8 in (1 cm) long, and the calyx is enlarged at the base but not actually spurred. *Flower:* Blue or lilac, rarely white.

Distribution.   Common to abundant on limestone slopes in the White Mountains, making showy fields of color, but not common in the Inyo Mountains; Pinyon-juniper Woodland and Subalpine Zone, 6,400–11,000 ft (1,957–5,354 m).

Lupinus brevicaulis Watson. **Short-stemmed Blue Lupine.**   A small, densely hairy annual, 1–4 in (2.5–10 cm) high, the stem almost lacking. Leaf stems (petioles) are 1–3 in (2.5–8 cm) long, the leaflets spatulate and up to 1/2 in (13 mm) long. Flowers are 1/4 in (6 mm) long and the pods about 3/8 in (10 mm). *Flower:* Bright blue with some yellowish white.

Distribution.   Common on noncalcareous soils; Desert Scrub and Pinyon-juniper Woodland, 6,000–9,000 ft (1,829–2,744 m).

Lupinus flavoculatus Heller. **Yellow-eyes.**   (Plate 6.88) A tufted, softly hairy annual, 2–6 in (5–15 cm) high. Slender leaf stems (petioles) are 3/4–2 in (2–5 cm) long, and the green, broadly oblanceolate leaflets are 1/4–3/4 inch (6–20 mm) long. They are softly hairy below but glabrous above, and folded, boat-shaped. The spreading stems are slender, usually reddish purple, and up to 6 in (15 cm) long, with blooms in dense terminal clusters. Individual flowers are about 3/8 in (1 cm) long. Pods are short and broadly ovate, most less than 1/2 in (13 mm) long. This small annual makes colorful patches of groundcover in years of abundant precipitation. *Flower:* Rich deep violet with prominent yellow spot on the banner.

Distribution.   Open places; Desert Scrub to Pinyon-juniper Woodland, up to 7,500 ft (2,287 m).

Lupinus palmeri Watson. **Palmer Lupine.**   (Plate 6.89) A bushy perennial, 12–24 in (3–6 dm) tall, with grayish-green foliage. Hairs on the stems and foliage are looser than those on the bushy limestone lupine. The leaflets are inclined to be broader and longer, up to 2 in (5 cm) long. Flower racemes on this one are 4–8 in (1–2 dm) long and rather narrow. Flowers are roundish in outline, about 3/8 in (1 cm) long. The calyx on this one, too, is enlarged but not actually spurred at the base. These two bush lupines are very similar, but there are subtle differences in appearance. The foliage in *L. palmeri* lacks a sheen, the inflorescence is longer and narrower, and the flower color is duller. Also, the plant tolerates drier places, and it does not grow in dense colonies. *Flower:* Dull blue.

Distribution.   Dry flats and slopes; most common in Pinyon-juniper Woodland, 6,000–9,600 ft (1,829–2,927 m).

Lupinus tegeticulatus Eastwood var. *tegeticulatus.* (*Lupinus breweri* Gray var. *bryoides* C.P. Smith) **Silver Moss.**   (Plate 6.90) A matted perennial with silky, silvery foliage. The tiny leaves are crowded, the leaflets ¼ in (6 mm) long or less. The inflorescence is 1–2 in (2.5–5 cm) high, rising slightly above the leaves. Flowers are about ¼ in (6 mm) long. In the field the silvery foliage appears to be dotted with tiny flower clusters. Pods are oblong, up to ½ in (13 mm) long. *Flower:* Violet-blue with a prominent white area on the banner.

Distribution.   Mostly on the open sagebrush slopes high in the White Mountains; Subalpine Zone, 9,500–11,000 ft (2,896–3,354 m).

Oxytropis parryi Gray. **Parry Oxytropis.**   (Plate 6.91) A small but sturdy perennial with leaves tufted on branches of the root crown. The foliage is light gray with long, silky hairs. Leaflets are pinnate, as in *Astragalus.* They are commonly folded, boat-shaped, and usually less than ¼ in (6 mm) long. Naked flower stems rise above the leaves, 1 ½–4 in (4–10 cm) high. They usually carry two flowers, ¼ in (6 mm) long or slightly larger. Pods are erect, cylindric, and thinly leathery with a hairy surface, approximately ¾ in (2 cm) long. The keel petals of *Oxytropis* narrow to a point at the apex. *Flower:* Pink.

Distribution.   Open, rocky slopes and flats; White Mountains; Subalpine Zone, 10,400–11,000 ft (3,171–3,354 m).

Psorothamnus arborescens (Torr.) Barneby var. *minutifolius* (Parish) **Barneby.** **Indigo Bush, Blister Dalea.** *(Dalea sp.)*   (Plate 6.92) Rupert Barneby has placed the shrubby daleas in the genus *Psorothamnus.* According to him, however, this plant has been incorrectly called *Dalea fremontii,* a species that never occurred here. Therefore, we do not show that as a synonym. The considerable variation in leaf form, calyx color, number of glands on various parts, and other characteristics of plants observed in different locations, still leads to confusion. It is best to accept the fact that there are normal variations within this variety.

A rigid, spreading, white-barked shrub, 1–3 ft (3–9 dm) high. Leaves are pinnate, ¾–2 in (2–5 cm) long, the ovate leaflets up to ⅜ in (1 cm) long. Flowering spikes are mostly 1–2 in (2.5–5 cm) long and quite showy, elongating as they mature. The pealike flowers are ⅜ in (1 cm) long, the petals twice the length of the commonly reddish calyx. Pods are obliquely ovate, abruptly pointed, and about ⅜ in (1 cm) long. The distinguishing feature is the pods' blister-dotted surface, the blisters being amber glands containing an oil with a characteristic "dalea" odor. (On the true Fremont Dalea, the glands are confluent into ridges rather than being scattered dots.) *Flower:* Intense royal or deep purplish blue.

Distribution.   Common to nearly dominant in dry, gravelly places; Desert Scrub, low elevations to 6,000 ft (1,829 m).

Trifolium andersonii **Gray ssp.** *monoense* **(Greene) Gillett. Mono Clover.**   (Plate 6.93) A deep-rooted perennial, only 1 in (2.5 cm) or so high, with foliage tufted on the branches of a well developed root crown. Leaves are palmate, with four to six gray-hairy, spatulate leaflets, abruptly pointed at the apex, up to 3/4 in (2 cm) long. The naked flower stems are 1–3 in (2.5–7.5 cm) long, each bearing a single globose head 1/2–1 in (13–25 mm) broad. The calyx teeth are long and linear, feathery-hairy, exceeding the densely clustered flowers. The flowers are mostly hidden in the hairy heads, but it is an interesting plant—a most unusual clover. *Flower:* Pink to rose.

Distribution.   Common on high, open slopes, forming areas of groundcover; White Mountains; Subalpine and Alpine zones, 10,000–13,500 ft (3,049–4,116 m).

FERNS

Ferns are green vascular plants without seeds or flowers. They reproduce by microscopic spores contained in spore cases (sporangia). These are usually borne in clusters (sori) on the back of the leaf, sometimes near or on the margin. The leaves of ferns are known as fronds. Most of them begin as tightly coiled stalks emerging from the rootstocks, gradually uncoiling as they grow and expand. Each frond is divided one or more times, the divisions called segments. Ferns reach their best development in moist, tropical climates, but even the desert mountains support a number of species. These are relatively small, some of them able to survive lengthy dry periods.

Cheilanthes feei **T. Moore. Slender Lip Fern.**   Fronds densely tufted, 2–8 in (5–20 cm) long; blades narrowly ovate or oblong, thinly hairy above, somewhat woolly and pale brown beneath; the segments gray-green, oval to rounded, the margins narrowly rolled under.

Distribution.   Limestone crevices; Desert Scrub and Pinyon-juniper Woodland, 4,000–9,500 ft (1,220–2,896 m).

Cystopteris fragilis **L. Bernh. Brittle Fern.**   Fronds loosely tufted, 2–12 in (5–30 cm) long, lacking persistent stems from prior seasons; blades broadly lanceolate, bright green, thin and delicate, and the stem easily broken; segments variously lobed.

Distribution.   Moist, protected places; Pinyon-juniper Woodland to Alpine Zone, 8,000–13,700 ft (2,439–4,177 m).

Notholaena parryi **D.C. Eat. Parry Cloak Fern.**   Fronds clustered, 3–8 in (7.5–20 cm) long; blades narrowly ovate-oblong, densely woolly on both sides; segments round to oblong.

Distribution.   Dry places, usually under overhanging rocks or in crevices; Desert Scrub and Pinyon-juniper Woodland, 3,500–9,700 ft (1,062–2,957 m).

Pellaea breweri D.C. Eat. **Brewer Cliff Brake.**   Fronds 2–8 in (5–20 cm) long; blades with 6–12 pairs of leaflets that are essentially two-parted, with the upper part larger, firm; bases of old stems persistent.

Distribution.   Exposed, rocky places; Pinyon-juniper Woodland to Alpine Zone, 7,900–12,000 ft (2,408–3,658 m).

Woodsia scopulina D.C. Eat. **Rocky Mountain Woodsia.**   Similar to *Cystopteris fragilis,* but the leaves are not as thin and veiny, and they have gland-tipped hairs on the surface. Bases of old stems are conspicuously persistent.

Distribution.   Rocky places, commonly on moist talus slopes or high meadows; Pinyon-juniper Woodland and Subalpine Zone 8,000–11,000 ft (2,439–3,354 m).

GENTIANACEAE (Gentian Family)

Frasera puberulenta A. Davids. **Low Green Gentian, Inyo Gentian.**   (Plate 6.94) A gray-green perennial with sturdy stems 4–12 in (1–3 dm) high. Leaves are opposite, clasping the stem, narrowly white-margined, with those at the base obovate to spatulate, becoming smaller and more lanceolate upward. Flowers are on slender branches from the leaf nodes, making an open panicle of the upper half to two-thirds of the plant. Individual flowers are 1/4–1/2 in (6–13 mm) long, four-parted, the spreading, lanceolate sepals usually longer than the broader petals. Each petal has a circular or oblong fringed gland about midway. *Flower:* Sepals green, narrowly edged with white; petals pale green or cream, flecked with purple.

Distribution.   Dry places; Pinyon-juniper Woodland and Subalpine Zone, 8,000–10,500 ft (2,439–3,201 m).

Gentiana newberryi Gray. **Alpine Gentian.**   (Plate 6.95) A low perennial with one or more stems 1 1/2–3 in (4–7.5 cm) high from a tuft of spatulate basal leaves. Stem leaves are opposite and similar in shape but reduced in size. Each stem carries a single funnel-shaped flower, 1 in (2.5 cm) or more long. *Flower:* White with dark, vertical bands without.

Distribution.   Moist places, alpine meadows and streamlets; White Mountains; 11,000–12,000 ft (3,354–3,658 m).

Gentianella tenella Rottb. Boerner. **Lapland Gentian.** (*Gentiana tenella* Rottb.) (Plate 6.96) A biennial with slender stems 1 1/2–5 in (4–12 cm) long, curved ascending. Leaves are mostly basal, 1/2 in (13 mm) long, more or less oblanceolate. The stem has a few, reduced leaves. Calyx lobes are somewhat swollen at the base and unequal. The corolla is tubular, 1/4–5/8 in (6–15 mm) long with lobes about one-third the length of the flower. *Flower:* White or tinged blue.

Distribution.   Wet places throughout the White Mountains; Pinyon-juniper Woodland to Alpine Zone, 8,500–12,500 ft (2,591–3,801 m).

HYDROPHYLLACEAE (Waterleaf Family)

A large family that includes many desert annuals. These vary greatly in size, depending on the amount and the timing of precipitation. Flower parts here are mostly five-numerous, and the inflorescence is a scorpioid cyme (fiddleneck), but there is a wide variety of characteristics.

Phacelia crenulata Torr. **Purple Phacelia.** (Plate 6.97) A common robust annual, 4–24 in (1–6 dm) tall. The herbage is glandular-hairy and strongly scented. Leaves are mostly linear-oblong and coarsely notched, but there is considerable variation is size and form. Those at the base may be up to 4 in (10 cm) long, and the stem leaves are gradually reduced. The inflorescence is composed of branching, scorpioid cymes, large enough to be quite showy. The calyx has five spatulate, hairy parts, and the corolla is broadly bell-shaped, about 3/8 in (1 cm) long. Stamens are conspicuously exserted. *Flower:* Usually deep violet or blue-purple, uncommon occurrence in lighter shades.

Distribution. Common on dry canyon slopes and along gravelly washes; Desert Scrub and Pinyon-juniper Woodland, 3,500–9,000 ft (1,067–2,744 m).

Phacelia curvipes Torr. **Dwarf Phacelia.** (Plate 6.98) A small, tufted annual, 1–6 in (2.5–15 cm) high, usually branching from the base. Foliage is soft hairy. Leaf blades are elliptic to oblanceolate, up to 1 in long, on petioles of about the same length. The slender stems terminate in scorpioid cymes. Individual flowers have linear calyx lobes and a broadly bell-shaped corolla about 1/4 in (6 mm) long. *Flower:* Blue to violet, with a white throat.

Distribution. Dry, usually somewhat loamy places; Desert Scrub and Pinyon-juniper Woodland, 4,000–8,500 ft (1,220–2,591 m).

Phacelia fremontii Torr. **Yellow-throats.** (Plate 6.99) An annual with stems branching from the base, 2–12 in (5–30 cm) high. Leaves are mostly basal, or near the base, oblong or elliptic, divided into rounded lobes. The upper portions of the stems are leafless scorpioid cymes. Calyx lobes are spatulate and the corolla narrowly bell-shaped. *Flower:* Lavender to violet or blue, with a deep yellow throat.

Distribution. Common and widespread, making colorful displays on the lower deserts, but less abundant in the mountains; Desert Scrub and Pinyon-juniper Woodland, 3,500–9,500 ft (1,067–2,896 m).

Phacelia hastata Douglas. **Cordilleran Phacelia.** (Plate 6.100) A perennial with several stems from the branches of the root crown. Stems are 6–20 in (15–50 cm) long, prostrate or curving upward. Leaves are prominently veined, elliptic, largest at the base and reduced up the stems. The inflorescences are scorpioid but short and compact. The corolla is broadly bell-shaped, about ¹/₄ in (6 mm) long. Stamens are conspicuous. *Flower:* Dull white or pale lavender.

Distribution.   Dry, rocky places; Subalpine and Alpine zones, 9,500–13,000 ft (2,896–3,963 m).

Phacelia perityloides **Coville. Panamint Phacelia.**   (Plate 6.101) A perennial with slender stems spreading from a branched, woody root crown. Herbage is glandular-hairy throughout. Stems are leafy, 4–16 in (1–4 dm) long, forming dense mats, or sometimes pendulous. Leaf blades are nearly round, toothed, ¹/₄–³/₄ in (6–20 mm) long, on petioles longer than the blade. Flowers are in loose, few-flowered scorpioid cymes or scattered, with the corolla funnel-shaped with spreading lobes, about ³/₈ in (1 cm) long. The dense, green foliage dotted with flowers is most attractive, although this is a modest plant. *Flower:* White.

Distribution.   Crevices in limestone (dolomite) cliffs, mostly under overhangs or in shaded places on dry canyon walls; Desert Scrub and Pinyon-juniper Woodland, 4,000–7,000 ft (1,220–2,134 m).

Phacelia vallis-mortae **J. Voss. Death Valley Phacelia.**   (Plate 6.102) A tender annual, 2–24 in (5–60 cm) tall, from simple stems to openly branched plants. Its clear, spreading hairs make it attractive when back-lit. Hairs on the upper portion are tipped with black glands. Leaves are well distributed but somewhat sparse, the blades divided into narrow, toothed or lobed leaflets. Flowers are terminal on the branches in very short, scorpioid clusters, the calyces conspicuously bristly with fine, shining hairs. Corollas are broadly funnel-shaped, about ¹/₂ in (13 mm) long and some are wider, with spreading lobes. *Flower:* Lavender to violet.

Distribution.   Relatively common from desert canyons to flats in the Pinyon-juniper Woodland, commonly in colonies under pinyon trees; Desert Scrub and Pinyon-juniper Woodland, 3,500–8,500 ft (1,067–2,591 m).

Tricardia watsonii **Torr. Three Hearts.**   (Plate 6.103) A perennial with stems 5–16 in (12–40 cm) high from a stout root. Leaves are mostly basal, elliptic, up to 3 in (8 cm) long, the blade tapering to a petiole. The few leaves on the stem are ovate and reduced in size. The inflorescence is a terminal cluster of a few flowers. Three of the five calyx lobes are heart-shaped, about ¹/₄ in (6 mm) long; the two inner ones are narrow and inconspicuous. The corolla is cup-shaped with rounded lobes. It is inside of and about the same length as the calyx lobes, but upon maturity the heart-shaped lobes increase in length to ¹/₂–1 in (13–25 mm), enclosing the capsule—hence the common name, *three hearts. Flower:* White or yellowish with purple markings.

Distribution.   Limited, from Desert Scrub to Pinyon-juniper Woodland, especially abundant with Joshua Trees; Desert Scrub and Pinyon-juniper Woodland, 3,500–7,500 ft (1,067–2,134 m).

IRIDACEAE (Iris Family)

A family of perennial herbs, represented here by two genera. The leaves are equitant, parallel veined, and linear or sword-shaped. The inflorescence is subtended by two spathelike bracts. Flowers have six petal-like parts (tepals) in two series. The ovary is inferior, below the tepals, and the fruit is a capsule.

Iris missouriensis Nutt. **Wild Iris.** (Plate 6.104) Plants spreading by rhizomes; stems 8–20 in (20–50 cm) high. Leaves are narrow, up to $^1/4$ in (6 mm) wide and 18 in (4.5 dm) long, all basal. The showy flowers are terminal, one or two on a stem, the tissuelike spathe bracts 1 $^1/2$–2 $^1/2$ in (4–6 cm) long. The three spreading outer tepals are broadly oblanceolate, 2–2 $^1/2$ in (5–6 cm) long; the erect inner tepals are narrower. Mature seed capsules are ridged, up to 2 in (5 cm) long. *Flower:* Lavender or light blue to white, all with purplish veins.

Distribution. Common, moist meadows; Desert Scrub and Pinyon-juniper Woodland, 6,000–9,000 ft (1,829–2,744 m). An abundance of iris in a meadow indicates overgrazing.

Sisyrinchium idahoense Bickn. **Idaho Blue-eyed Grass.** (Plate 6.105) Stems 4–16 in tall, mostly leafless. Basal leaves are narrow, grasslike, and shorter than the stems. Flowers are terminal, several on a stem, their very slender, hairless pedicels issuing from unequal green spathe bracts. The six tepals are equal, about $^3/8$ in (1 cm) long, spreading. *Flower:* Blue-violet to deep violet-purple.

Distribution. Common, wet meadows and stream banks; Desert Scrub and Pinyon-juniper Woodland, 6,000–9,000 ft (1,829–2,744 m). Other species of *Sisyrinchium* can be expected at lower elevations. Their general appearance is much the same.

JUNCACEAE (Rush Family)

Resembling grasses or rushes, mostly perennial herbs; leaves with flat to channeled or round blades; inflorescence in different forms; flowers perfect, or rarely unisexual; perianth present but inconspicuous; six tepals in two sets of three; commonly greenish to brownish or blackish; usually six stamens; style three-branched; fruit a capsule. The genera follow.

Juncus. **Rush.** Glabrous perennials (except for the annual *J. bufonius*) with well-developed rhizomes; leaves divided into a sheath and blade; the inflorescence usually subtended by one or more leafy or tissuelike bracts, some of the lowest are elongate, appearing as a continuation of the stem; six tepals in two similar sets of three; three or six stamens; fruit a capsule with a short style at the apex. Represented by about 12 species, mostly in moist or wet places.

Luzula. **Woodrush.** Perennial, grasslike herbs, with spreading hairs on the leaf margins, at least when young; inflorescence in the species is in heads or short spikes;

flowers perfect; six tepals in two sets of three; six stamens; fruit a three-sectioned capsule. Represented by one relatively dainty plant at high elevations.

LAMIACEAE (LABIATAE) (Mint Family)

A family of aromatic herbs or shrubs. Leaves are opposite and the flowers commonly in whorls, the corollas tubular with irregular symmetry.

Monardella linoides Gray. **Flax-leaved Monardella.**   A strongly aromatic perennial with numerous stems, 8–20 in (2–5 dm) high, from a branching root crown. Leaves are lanceolate to elliptic, 1/2–3/4 in (13–20 mm) long, pale silvery green. Flowers are in terminal heads, about 3/4 in (2 cm) broad, subtended by rose-tinged, papery bracts 1/2 in (13 mm) long. Corollas are 1/2–1 in (13–25 mm) long, slender, tubular, with narrow lobes. *Flower:* Rose-lavender.

Distribution.   Dry places, mostly in granitic or volcanic rocks; Desert Scrub and Pinyon-juniper Woodland, 5,500–9,000 ft (1,677–2,744 m).

Monardella odoratissima Benth ssp. *parvifolia* (Greene) Epling. **Mountain Pennyroyal, Small-leaved Monardella.**   (Plate 6.106) Much like *M. linoides* Gray but not as robust. Stems are more slender, the leaves green and slightly smaller, and the heads mostly 1/2 in (13 mm) broad. Floral bracts are thicker and somewhat hairy, with lavender-tinged edges. *Flower:* Lavender to purple.

Distribution.   Dry places; Pinyon-juniper Woodland and Subalpine Zone, 8,500–10,500 ft (2,591–3,201 m).
   Note: A variation with finely puberulent leaves and reddish-purple flowers is called ssp. *glauca* (Greene) Epling.

Salvia columbariae Benth. **Chia.**   (Plate 6.107) An annual with square stems, 4–24 in (1–6 dm) tall. Leaves are essentially basal, 2–4 in (0.5–1 dm) long, divided one or more times into irregular lobes. The flowers are in one to three whorls, 1/2–1 in (13–25 mm) broad, subtended by spine-tipped, commonly purple bracts. The calyx has spine-tipped lobes also. The tubular corolla, 1/2 in (13 mm) long, has a short, notched upper lip and a much longer lower lip with an enlarged middle lobe. The seeds were valued by native peoples as a nutritious food, but the prickly flower heads must be handled gingerly. *Flower:* Blue.

Distribution.   Dry, gravelly places; Desert Scrub, below 6,500 ft (1,982 m).

Salvia dorrii (Kellogg) Abrams. var. *clokeyi* Strachan. **Clokey Blue Sage.**   (Plate 6.108) A low, silvery shrub, 4–12 in (1–3 dm) tall and commonly broader. Leaves are usually spatulate to ovate, broadly rounded at the apex and gradually narrowed to a short stem, 3/8–3/4 in (1–2 cm) long in all. The foliage is strongly aromatic. Flowering stems bear one to three whorls, about 1/2 in (13 mm) broad, subtended by purplish bracts. This *Salvia* has no prickles. The corolla, about 3/8 in (1 cm) long, resembles that of chia, but with more pronounced lobes. When in full bloom the plant is a colorful mass of flowers. *Flower:* Bright blue or blue-violet.

Distribution.   Dry, calcareous slopes and flats; Desert Scrub to Subalpine Zone, 6,000–10,000 ft (1,829–3,049 m).

> **Var. *dorrii* Abrams. Great Basin Blue Sage.**   Similar to var. *clokeyi* but usually larger, up to 20 in (5 dm) high, and leaves narrow abruptly at the base to the short stem. *Flower:* Pale to dark blue.
>
> **Distribution.**   Dry places, mostly on granitic or volcanic rocks; Desert Scrub to Subalpine Zone, 4,000–10,500 ft (1,220–3,201 m).

LILIACEAE (Lily Family)

Perennial herbs from bulbs, corms, or rhizomes. Leaves are mostly narrow, even grasslike, all parallel-veined. Flowers may be large and showy or very small in clusters. Their six parts are generally in two series. When these are not alike they are called sepals and petals, but when all are essentially the same they are referred to as tepals. The fruit is a capsule or a berry.

Allium atrorubens var. *inyonis.* **Inyo Onion.**   (Plate 6.109) An onion with stems 2–6 in high. Onions are readily recognized by the odor of their crushed foliage. Its single leaf, which may exceed the length of the flowering stems, is on some individuals coiled near the tip. The inflorescence is a many-flowered, rounded umbel with slender pedicels ¼–½ in (6–13 mm) long, the whole subtended by two or three ovate, pointed bracts about ½ in (13 mm) long. Each flower has six broadly lanceolate tepals ⅜ in (1 cm) long. The bracts are tissuelike and the tepals become so in maturity. *Flower:* Tepals pale pink or whitish with dark midveins.

Distribution.   Common, some in colonies, on dry slopes or flats; Desert Scrub and Pinyon-juniper Woodland, 5,000–9,500 ft (1,524–2,896 m).

Allium bisceptrum **Watson. Aspen Onion.**   An onion with stems 4–12 in (10–30 cm) high. It has three flat leaves. Two tissuelike bracts subtend the inflorescence. Flowers are in a rounded umbel on pedicels two to three times as long as the tepals. Tepals are lanceolate, tapered to a point, up to ⅜ in (1 cm) long, turning papery in age. This onion is taller and the flower parts daintier than the *A. atrorubens* variety. *Flower:* Bright rose-purple to pink.

Distribution.   Infrequent, shady moist places such as meadows and aspen groves; Pinyon-juniper Woodland and Subalpine Zone, 7,000–10,300 ft (2,134–3,140 m).

Calochortus bruneaunis **Nels. & Macbr. Sego Lily.** (*Calochortus nuttallii* Torr. var. *bruneaunis* [Nels. & Macbr.] Ownbey)   (Plate 6.110) A perennial with slender stems 6–16 in (15–40 cm) tall, bearing a few linear leaves that dry early. The flowers are bell-shaped but erect, each with three lanceolate sepals and three broad petals. The petals are obovate with a pointed apex, 1–1 1/2 in (2.5–4 cm) long. Each has a circular, depressed gland near the base, surrounded by a fringed membrane and with various hairs, deeply colored and showy. Anthers are oblong and relatively large. *Flower:* White, some individuals tinged lilac, each petal with a longitudinal greenish or silver stripe and a dark spot above the gland, yellowish in the gland area. Each sepal has some color and a dark spot also.

Distribution.   Limited, within sagebrush on dry slopes and flats or in open brushy places in wooded areas; Pinyon-juniper Woodland and Subalpine Zone, 6,000–10,000 ft (1,829–3,049 m).

Calochortus kennedyi Porter. Desert Mariposa.   (Plate 6.111) A perennial with stems 3–8 in (7.5–20 cm) high. Lower leaves are channeled, 4–8 in (1–2 dm) long, and commonly coiled on the ground; the few leaves on the stem are much reduced. The upper stem has short branches, each carrying a flower. This Mariposa Lily is sturdier and the flower parts broader than *C. bruneaunis,* but the general characteristics are much the same. Petals are wedge-shaped, 1–2 in (2.5–5 cm) long. Sepals are ovate. The gland area is colorful and hairy. *Flower:* Rich orange-red to orange, each petal and sepal with a dark brown-purple spot in the gland area.

Distribution.   Uncommon, desert slopes or flats; Desert Scrub; 5,000–6,500 ft (1,524–1,982 m).

Fritillaria atropurpurea Nutt. Wood Brownies, Chocolate Lily.   Erect perennial, 4–20 in (1–5 dm) high. Leaves are linear, 2–4 in (5–10 cm) long, on the upper half of the stem. Flowers have six spreading tepals, elliptic to rhombic, about 1/2 in (13 mm) long and half as wide, with an obscure gland at the base. Anthers are prominent. The flowers nod or face outward, one to four on a stem. *Flower:* Brown, streaked or mottled with white or yellow. Colors are rich but not bright and showy.

Distribution.   Uncommon, mostly in open forests or woodlands; Desert Scrub to Subalpine Zone, 6,000–11,000 ft (1,829–3,354 m).

Fritillaria pinetorum Davidson. Pine Fritillary.   (Plate 6.112) Erect perennial, 4–12 in high, the stems hollow. Leaves are linear, 2–6 in (5–15 cm) long, on the upper half of the hollow stem. Flowers are usually three to nine on a stem, erect or nearly so, broadly bell-shaped. Tepals are oblong, 1/4–3/4 in (6–20 mm) long and up to 1/4 in (6 mm) wide. *Flower:* Purplish, mottled with greenish yellow.

Distribution.   Uncommon, usually with pine trees; Pinyon-juniper Woodland and Subalpine Zone, 7,000–11,000 ft (2,134–3,354 m).

Smilacina stellata (L.) Desf. Starflower.   Leafy stems 12–24 in (3–6 dm) high, perennial from rhizomes. The largest leaves are up to 6 in (15 cm) long and 1 1/2 in (4 cm) wide, gradually reduced up the stem, broadly to narrowly lanceolate, somewhat clasping at the base. Flowers are small and relatively inconspicuous, in loose terminal racemes. Tepals are lanceolate to narrowly oblong, hardly 1/4 in (6 mm) long. The fruit is a berry up to 3/8 in (1 cm) broad, dark purple or black when mature. *Flower:* White.

Distribution.   Common throughout the range, riparian areas and other moist places; Desert Scrub to Subalpine Zone, 5,000–10,000 ft (1,524–3,049 m).

Zigadenus paniculatus **Nutt. Watson. Sand-corn.**   (Plate 6.113) Erect perennial 8–20 in (2–5 dm) tall, with a densely flowered terminal panicle 3–12 in (7.5–30 cm) long. Leaves are mostly basal, linear, 6–16 in (15–40 cm) long. Flowers are small and mostly perfect but may include some with only staminate parts. Tepals are in two series: the outer three are broadly ovate, about 1/4 in (6 mm) long, and the inner three are slightly longer and raised on a stemlike base. *Flower:* Yellowish white.

Distribution.   Uncommon, mostly in sagebrush or scattered pinyon; Desert Scrub and Pinyon-juniper Woodland, 5,500–7,500 ft (1,677–2,287 m).

Note: Although this species is not the one known as "Death Camas," it may be poisonous and should not be used as food.

LINACEAE (Flax Family)

Linum lewisii **Pursh. Blue Flax.**   (Plate 6.114) A slender perennial with leafy stems, 6–24 in (1.5–6 dm) high. Leaves are linear, most less than 1/2 in (13 mm) long. Flowers are loosely clustered on the branching upper part of the stem. There are five spreading petals, making the flower approximately 1 in (2.5 cm) across. *Flower:* Sky blue.

Distribution.   Common on dry slopes; Pinyon-juniper Woodland and Subalpine Zone, 7,200–11,500 ft (2,195–3,506 m).

LOASACEAE (Loasa or Stick-leaf Family)

Plants usually with harsh surfaces, sometimes with barbed or stinging hairs. Ovaries are inferior, meaning that they are situated below the petals. Most species are desert plants, but some occur in this range.

Eucnide urens **(Gray) Parry. Rock Nettle, Vegetable Velcro.**   (Plate 6.115) A rounded, bushy perennial, 8–30 in (2–7 dm) high, with a woody base. The stems are clothed with spreading hairs, along with shorter, hooked ones, which sting as well as cling to any soft surface. Leaves are ovate with toothed edges, mostly 1–2 in (2.5–5 cm) long. The hooked hairs on the undersurface will cling so tightly to a garment that the leaf will be torn apart in any effort to dislodge it. There are five broad petals up to 1 1/2 in (4 cm) long, making an open flower centered with a tuft of stamens. The plant's attractive foliage and large flowers are best admired without touching. *Flower:* Cream-colored.

Distribution.   Crevices in limestone cliffs or on rocky wash borders; Inyo Mountains; Desert Scrub, below 5,000 ft (1,524 m).

Mentzelia albicaulis (Douglas) Torr. & Gray. Little Blazing Star.   (Plate 6.116) An annual, 4–16 in (1–4 dm) high, with slender, somewhat brittle, shining white stems. Leaves are linear to lanceolate, mostly toothed or deeply lobed, 1–2 in (2.5–5 cm) long, the surfaces harsh. Flowers have five petals, $^1/_4$–$^3/_8$ in (6–10 mm) long. The inferior seed capsule, below the petals, is club-shaped, exceeding them in length. This species is extremely variable, so one should allow for minor differences. Similar species may occur also. *Flower:* Bright yellow.

Distribution.   Widespread and common, in dry places, such as Pinyon-juniper Woodland, up to 8,000 ft (2,439 m).

Mentzelia laevicaulis (Douglas) Torr. & Gray. Blazing Star.   (Plate 6.117) A coarse biennial that begins as an attractive rosette of wavy-lobed leaves, 8–20 in (2–5 dm) across. Then shining white stems grow to a height of 16–60 in (4–14.5 dm), often widely branching. Leaves on the stem are obovate, coarsely toothed, and harsh on the surface, about 2 in (5 cm) long. Flowers are very showy, with lanceolate or elliptic petals 2–3 in (5–6 cm) long. The conspicuous tuft of stamens is only a little shorter. The lanceolate sepals are reflexed. *Flower:* Bright yellow.

Distribution.   Widespread and locally relatively abundant in disturbed places; mostly in the White Mountains where it is not too dry; Desert Scrub and Pinyon-juniper Woodland, 5,000–9,000 ft (1,524–2,744 m).

Petalonyx nitidus Watson. Shiny-leaved Sandpaper Plant.   (Plate 6.118) An evergreen shrub, 6–26 in (15–65 cm) high. Stems are pale green to white with closely set, short-petioled leaves. These are obovate, shallowly toothed, about 1 in (2.5 cm) long, rigid, and shining but sandpapery to the touch. Flowers are in dense, terminal clusters about 2 in (5 cm) across. Individual flowers are small, each with five stamens that exceed the petals. *Flower:* White.

Distribution.   Locally on dry banks, wash borders, or talus slopes, especially in canyons cut through limestone; Desert Scrub and Pinyon-juniper Woodland, 4,000–7,000 ft (1,220–2,134 m).

MALVACEAE (Mallow Family)

A large family but with few species in the region. Only one has showy flowers, which resemble miniature hollyhocks.

Sphaeralcea ambigua Gray. Apricot Mallow.   (Plate 6.119) A hardy perennial, commonly bushy, with numerous stems, up to 30 in (7 dm) high. Stems are somewhat woody at the base and are coated with a feltlike surface of fine, star-shaped hairs. These may be irritating to the skin. Leaves are variable but are usually ovate with a heart-shaped base, somewhat three-lobed, and prominently wrinkle-veined. The inflorescence is a spike or narrow panicle. Flowers have petals ¹/₂–1 in long. They are showy and bloom over a long period. *Flower:* Deep apricot color, grenadine.

Distribution.   Common and widespread in canyons throughout the range; Desert Scrub and Pinyon-juniper Woodland, below 8,500 ft (2,591 m).

Ssp. *monticola* Kearney. Mountain Apricot Mallow.   Much like *S. ambigua*, but the stems are entirely herbaceous, the leaves thinner, and the inflorescence narrow and few-flowered. *Flower:* Same as *S. ambigua*.
   Distribution.   Pinyon-juniper Woodland, up to 9,000 ft (2,744 m).

Ssp. *rosacea* (Munz & Johnston) Kearney. Lavender Wand Mallow.   Stems slender and spreading but slightly woody at the base; leaves thinner and less prominently veined than *S. ambigua*. *Flower:* Lavender or paler.
   Distribution.   Locally in canyons cut through limestone in the Inyo Mountains; Desert Scrub, up to 6,000 ft (1,829 m).

NYCTAGINACEAE (Four O'Clock Family)

The family is represented here by perennial herbs. Flowers are subtended by bracts, some of which are united, making a cuplike container. The calyces are corollalike in form and color; petals are lacking.

Abronia nana **Watson ssp. *covillei* Heimerl. Munz. Limestone Sand-verbena.**
A tufted, somewhat glandular perennial from a branching root crown. Leaf blades are oblong to ovate, ¹/₄–³/₄ in (6–20 mm) long, on slender petioles several times longer than the blades. Flowers are in terminal heads on naked stems 1–4 in (2.5–10 cm) high. These are subtended by short, lanceolate bracts. Individual flowers are tubular, about ¹/₂ in (13 mm) long, flaring at the top. *Flower:* Pinkish to white.

Distribution.   Locally in open places in the Bristlecone Pine Forest and upper Pinyon-juniper Woodland and Subalpine Zone, 7,800–10,200 ft (2,378–3,110 m).

Mirabilis alipes **(Watson) Pilz. Hermidium, Rose Four O'clock.** (*Hermidium alipes* Watson)   (Plate 6.120) Stems are 8–16 in (2–4 dm) long from a perennial root, making a broad clump. Leaves are opposite, bluish green, glaucous and glabrous, broadly ovate, 1–2 in (2.5–5 cm) long. Flowers, subtended by green or purplish bracts, are clustered at the ends of the branches. They are funnel-shaped, up to 1 in (2.5 cm) long, abruptly flaring at the top. Like the other four o'clocks, they open in late afternoon. *Flower:* Rose to pink.

Distribution.   A Nevada species that has become established along routes from that state; dry canyons and roadsides; Desert Scrub, 4,000–6,500 ft (1,220–1,982 m).

Mirabilis bigelovii Gray var. *bigelovii*. **Wishbone Bush.**   (Plate 6.121) A much-branching, bushy perennial, 12–20 in (3–5 dm) high, with somewhat sticky foliage. Leaves are opposite, mostly ovate, 3/8–1 1/4 in (1–3 cm) long. Flowers are clustered at the ends of the branches. They are dainty, broadly bell-shaped, generally 3/8 in (1 cm) long, opening in late afternoon. Fruit is ovoid, commonly mottled. The common name comes from the wishbone shape of the branch forks. *Flower:* White to pale pink or lavender.

Distribution.   Common in canyons throughout the range; Desert Scrub and Pinyon-juniper Woodland, 4,500–7,200 ft (1,372–2,195 m).

> **Var. *aspera* (Greene) Munz. Wishbone Bush.**   Similar to var. *bigelovii* but stems more sticky-hairy. Fruit is roundish, with 10 pale vertical lines.
> **Distribution.**   Inyo Mountains and southern part of White Mountains; Desert Scrub, below 6,500 ft (1,982 m).

> **Var. *retrorsa* (Heller) Munz. Wishbone Bush.**   Similar to var. *aspera* but stems with hairs turned downward. Fruit is roundish, some striate.
> **Distribution.**   Same as for var. *aspera;* Desert Scrub, below 6,000 ft (1,829 m).

Mirabilis multiflora Torr. var. *pubescens* Watson. **Giant Four O'clock.** *(Mirabilis froebelii)*   (Plate 6.122) A much-branched perennial with ascending stems, 12–30 in (3–7 dm) long. The plant has a growth habit similar to *M. alipes,* but it usually forms broader clumps, up to 4 or 5 ft (1.3 or 1.6 m) across. Leaves are lightly to densely sticky-hairy, broadly ovate, rarely heart-shaped, 1–3 in (2.5–8 cm) long. Flowers, loosely clustered at the ends of the branches, are held in bell-shaped involucres about an inch deep, with toothlike lobes. The funnel-shaped flowers are about 1 1/2 in (4 cm) long, broadly flaring above. It is a showy plant when the flowers are open at the end of the day until morning, when the bright sunlight closes them. *Flower:* Rose-purple.

Distribution.   Locally on talus slopes and other rocky places; Desert Scrub and Pinyon-juniper Woodland, 4,000–8,000 ft (1,220–2,439 m).

Mirabilis pumila (Standl.) Standl. **Little Umbrella-wort.** *(Oxybaphus pumilus)* (Plate 6.123) An erectly branching perennial, 4–20 in (1–5 dm) tall. Leaves are triangular to ovate, mostly about 1 in (2.5 cm) long. The lower portion of the plant is leafy; the upper portion is in narrow, flowering spikes. The inflorescence is densely sticky-hairy. Flowers are about 3/8 in (1 cm) long and the calyx-like involucres enlarge to almost as long in fruit. *Flower:* Pale pink.

Distribution.   Uncommon, gravelly washes; Desert Scrub, 5,000–6,000 ft (1,524–1,829 m).

OLEACEAE (Olive or Ash Family)

A small family of trees and shrubs.

Forestiera neomexicana Gray. Desert Olive, Adelia.   (Plate 6.124) A stiffly erect, deciduous shrub, 4–12 ft (1.3–4 m) high. Leaves obovate to elliptic, narrowing at the base to a slender petiole, 1–2 in (2.5–5 cm) long in all. They are opposite, sometimes with additional ones on short spurs. Flowers are relatively inconspicuous and are clustered tightly against the branches. Pistillate and staminate parts are in separate flowers, commonly on different plants. The fruit is far more showy than the blooms. When mature, the clusters of 3/8 in (1 cm)–long blue-black "olives" are very attractive but unpalatable. *Flower:* White or yellowish.

Distribution.   Uncommon at springs; Inyo Mountains; Desert Scrub, below 6,500 ft (1,982 m).

Menodora spinescens Gray. Spiny Menodora.   (Plate 6.125) An extremely spiny shrub, 1–3 ft (0.3–1 m) high, with gray or yellowish green branches and commonly sparse foliage. Leaves are alternate, narrowly linear-oblong, up to 1/2 in (13 mm) long. Flowers are funnel-shaped, 1/8–1/4 in (3–6 cm) long, with five relatively long lobes. The fruit, shining and tinged with the same colors as the flowers, resembles twin berries but is actually a capsule parted almost to the base and covered with a thin membrane. The parts are roundish, about 1/4 in (6 mm) in diameter. *Flower:* White, tinged with purple or brown.

Distribution.   Common; Desert Scrub and Pinyon-juniper Woodland, 4,000–7,700 ft (1,220–2,348 m).

ONAGRACEAE (Evening Primrose Family)

A very large family represented here by annual or perennial herbs. Ovaries are inferior. The stigmas of *Camissonia* and *Gayophytum* are round, whereas those of *Epilobium* and *Oenothera* are four-parted, forming a cross. There are four petals and four sepals.

Camissonia boothii (Douglas) Raven ssp. *desertorum* (Munz) Raven.   (Plate 6.126) **Woody Bottle Washer.** *(Oenothera decorticans* var. *desertorum)* A white-stemmed, slender-branching annual, usually less than 14 in (3.5 dm) high. Leaves in a tuft at the base are broadly elliptic, up to 3 1/8 in (8 cm) long, on slender petioles about half the length of the blade. These lower leaves may dry before the blooms appear. Those above are smaller and gradually reduced upward. Flowers are in terminal clusters, nodding in bud but becoming erect in bloom. Petals are about 1/4 in (6 mm) long. The slender capsule, below the petals, twists as it matures, commonly until the tip is turned downward. After the seeds are shed, the persistent fibers of the capsule have the appearance of a bottle washer. *Flower:* White, aging pink.

Distribution.   Dry, open slopes and washes; Desert Scrub and Pinyon-juniper Woodland, 4,000–8,000 ft (1,220–2,439 m).

Note: The species *boothii* is so variable that some plants may be difficult to place
in a described subspecies.

Ssp. *intermedia* Munz. Hairy Primrose.   Similar to ssp. *desertorum,* but the
foliage is densely coated with soft, fine, white hairs. Stems vary from 2 to 12 in (5
to 30 cm) tall. Basal leaves are well developed, and all the others are very small.
Flower: White, aging pink.

Distribution.   Uncommon; Desert Scrub and Pinyon-juniper Woodland,
5,000–7,000 ft (1,524–2,134 m).

Ssp. *inyoensis* Munz. Inyo Primrose.   A dainty form of the species, 6–12 in
(15–30 cm) high. Basal leaves are elliptic, the blades mostly about 1 in (2.5
cm) long. Branches are very slender, and flowers are well spaced on the threadlike
stems. Petals are about 1/8 in (3 mm) long. *Flower:* Pinkish, aging deep pink.

Distribution.   Common in the Inyo Mountains; Desert Scrub and Pinyon-
juniper Woodland, up to 7,000 ft (2,134 m).

Camissonia chamaenerioides (Gray) Raven. Modest Primrose.   (*Oenothera
chamaenerioides* Gray)   A slender, erect annual, 4–20 in (1–5 dm) tall. A basal tuft of
small, ovate leaves may be present when the plant is young but usually withers before
maturity. Other leaves are elliptic, commonly sparse and much reduced. Flowers are
minute, the petals about 1/8 in (3 mm) long, but the very slender capsule is 1 1/2–2
in (4–5 cm) long. When mature the plant seems all capsules angling upward. *Flower:*
White, aging reddish.

Distribution.   Limited, on granitic or volcanic soils; Desert Scrub, below 6,500 ft
(1,982 m).

Camissonia claviformis (Torr. & Fremont) Raven ssp. *claviformis.* Brown-eyed
Primrose. (*Oenothera claviformis* Torr. & Fremont)   (Plate 6.127) An annual, 4–20 in
(1–5 dm) high, with leaves mostly in a basal rosette. These may have small, irregular
leaflets below a well-developed terminal leaflet that may be up to 2 1/2 in (6.5 cm)
long, narrowly ovate, and irregularly toothed. Some lesser leaves occur on the stems.
The foliage is highly variable. Tightly clustered buds nod until the flowers open.
Then the fruiting stems gradually become spikelike with ascending capsules. The
flowers, with petals about 1/4 in (6 mm) long, open in late afternoon. Capsules are
mostly about 3/4 in (2 cm) long and club-shaped on slender pedicels 1/2 in (13 mm)
long. *Flower:* White, aging purplish.

Distribution.   Locally in the Inyo Mountains and the southern part of the White
Mountains; Desert Scrub, from the valley floor up to 5,000 ft (1,524 m).

Ssp. *integrior* **(Raven) Raven. Northern Evening Primrose.** Similar to ssp. *claviformis,* but the leaves are nearly simple and slightly gray-hairy. *Flower:* White, aging purplish.

Distribution. North of the range of ssp. *claviformis;* especially on volcanic tuff and cinder slopes; Desert Scrub, up to 6,500 ft (1,982 m).

Camissonia pterosperma **(Watson) Raven. Pigmy Primrose.** (*Oenothera pterosperma* Watson) A small, hairy annual, 1–4 in (2.5–10 cm) high. Leaves are linear or narrowly obovate, seldom more than 1/2 in (13 mm) long. Flowers open in the morning. Petals are minute, hardly more than 1/16 in (2 mm) long, but the capsules are well developed, much like those of *C. claviformis,* 1/2–3/4 in (13–20 mm) long. *Flower:* Petals white with a yellow band near the base.

Distribution. Apparently not as rare as reported, but may appear only in climatically favorable years; dry places; Desert Scrub and Pinyon-juniper Woodland, 4,500–9,000 ft (1,372–2,744 m).

Camissonia refracta **(Watson) Raven. Narrow-leaved Primrose.** (*Oenothera refracta* Watson) A dainty-flowered annual with slender stems, usually branching from near the base. Stems have a reddish, shining coat that readily splits and peels. Leaves are linear or narrowly oblong, mostly shallowly toothed, 1–2 in (2.5–5 cm) long. They are well distributed, and the plant lacks a basal tuft. A characteristic of this species is its comparatively large, lanceolate sepals, turned downward, nearly as long as the 3/16 in (5 mm) petals. The ball-shaped stigma protrudes just beyond the petals. Flowers open in the evening. Capsules are very slender, 1 1/4–2 in (3–5 cm) long, spreading outward. *Flower:* White, aging pink.

Distribution. Common in canyons of the Inyo Mountains; below Desert Scrub, 5,500 ft (1,677 m).

Camissonia walkeri **(A. Nels.) Raven ssp.** *tortilis* **(Jepson) Raven. Rock or Limestone Primrose.** (*Oenothera multijuga* Watson var. *parviflora* [Watson] Munz) An erect annual or short-lived perennial, 4–30 in (1–7.5 dm) tall. The stems are nearly leafless, with a well-developed basal rosette. Leaves are divided, having a large terminal, ovate leaflet, 3/4–2 in (2–5 cm) long, and are dull green with purple dots. Flowers are very small, the petals about 1/4 in (6 mm) long. The linear capsules, 1–1 1/2 in (2.5–4 cm) long, are on slender pedicels about half their length, spreading at right angles from the stem. *Flower:* Yellow.

Distribution. Locally in rocky places, mostly near limestone cliffs; Desert Scrub, up to 6,000 ft (1,829 m).

Epilobium angustifolium **L. ssp.** *circumvagum* **Mosquin. Fireweed.** (Plate 6.128) An erect perennial with leafy stems, mostly 2–4 ft (6–12 dm) tall. Leaves are lanceolate, 3–6 in (8–15 cm) long and 3/4–1 in (2–2.5 cm) wide. Flowers are in showy racemes on the upper portion of the plant. Sepals are lanceolate, $3/8$ in (1 cm) long, and the spreading petals about $1/2$ in (13 mm) long, both four-parted and above the inferior ovary. Capsules are linear, $2-3\,1/2$ in (5–9 cm) long, and conspicuously spreading out from the stem. As they split open, they expose an abundance of silky hairs attached to the upper ends of the seeds. The comose seeds are a characteristic of the epilobiums and are carried by the slightest breeze. *Flower:* Lilac-purple, rarely pink or white. Sepals, too, are colored purple or red.

Distribution.   Cool, moist places; mostly in the White Mountains; Pinyon-juniper Woodland and Subalpine Zone, 7,000–11,500 ft (2,134–3,506 m).

Epilobium ciliatum Raf. ssp. *ciliatum*. **Slender Epilobium.** (*Epilobium adenocaulon Hausskn.* var. *parishii* [Trel.] Munz) (*Epilobium brevistylum* Barbey)   An erect perennial with slender, sometimes branching, leafy stems, 8–40 in (2–10 dm) tall. Leaves are willowlike, mostly opposite, 1–3 in (2.5–8 cm) long, reduced upward. The plant is also called "Willow Herb." The small flowers are terminal and at the upper leaf nodes. The petals, notched at the apex, are up to $1/4$ in (6 mm) long, situated over an inferior ovary that matures $1\,1/2-2\,1/2$ in (4–6.5 cm) long. Each seed carries a tuft of white, silky hairs. *Flower:* White, pink, or purplish.

Distribution.   Wet places, mostly streamside; Desert Scrub to Subalpine Zone, 3,500–10,000 ft (1,067–3,049 m). Other, similar species occur in the range.

Gayophytum diffusum Torr. & Gray ssp. *parviflorum* Lewis & Szweykowski. **Summer Snowflakes.**   A slender, upward-branching, sparsely leafy annual, 4–20 in (1–5 dm) tall. The stems may be tinged red or purplish throughout. Leaves are narrowly linear, $1/2-1\,1/4$ in (1.3–3 cm) long. Flowers are terminal on the delicate branchlets, well distributed on the plant. Petals are hardly $1/8$ in (6 mm) long, usually showing obviously staggered seeds. *Flower:* White, drying pink.

Distribution.   Common to abundant on dry slopes and flats; Pinyon-juniper Woodland and Subalpine Zone, 7,500–10,500 ft (2,287–3,201 m).

Gayophytum ramosissimum Torr. & Gray. **Pinyon Gayophytum.**   An annual, lower than *G. diffusum,* 3–8 in (8–20 cm) high, with very fine, spreading branches. Leaves are narrowly linear, less than 1 in (2.5 cm) long. Flowers are minute, about $1/16$ in (3 mm) long. The capsules are $1/4$ in (6 mm) long on very fine stems of equal length. *Flower:* White, drying pink.

Distribution.   Common on dry slopes and flats; Desert Scrub to Subalpine Zone, 4,500–10,500 ft (1,372–3,201 m).

Oenothera caespitosa Nutt. ssp. *crinita* (Rydb.) Munz. **Limestone Evening Primrose.**   (Plate 6.129) A densely hairy perennial with leaves tufted on branches of a thick root crown. Stems are lacking. Leaves are grayish with soft, long hairs, ovate with wavy, some with toothed edges. Blades are $1/2-1$ in (13–25 mm) long on petioles of about the same length. Stemlike flower tubes, up to 2 in (5 cm) long, rise above the leaves from the inferior ovaries below. Calyx lobes (sepals) are lanceolate, about 3/4 in (2 cm) long, turned downward. Petals are broad, 3/4–1 in (2–2.5 cm) long. The flowers, which open in the evening, are attractive and fragrant. *Flower:* White or faintly pink, aging pink.

Distribution.   Limited; limestone areas in the Inyo Mountains; Pinyon-juniper Woodland and Subalpine Zone, 8,000–10,200 ft (2,439–3,110 m).

Oenothera caespitosa Nutt. ssp. *marginata* (Nutt.) Munz. **Large White Evening Primrose.** (*Oenothera caespitosa Nutt.* var. *longiflora* [Heller] Munz)   (Plate 6.130) A robust form of *O. caespitosa.* Leaves are green, linear lanceolate, irregularly toothed, and 1 1/2–6 in (4–15 cm) long, including the petiole. Flower tubes from the ovary at the base are 3–7 in (8–18 cm) long. Flowers are fragrant and open in the evening. Sepals are 1–1 1/2 in (2.5–4 cm) long, and the broad petals 1–2 in (2.5–5 cm) long. *Flower:* White, aging pink.

Distribution.   Relatively common in open places of roadsides and wash borders; Desert Scrub to Subalpine Zone, 4,500–10,300 ft (1,372–3,140 m).

Oenothera hookeri Torr. & Gray ssp. *angustifolia* (Gates) Munz. **Tall Yellow Evening Primrose.**   A biennial with erect, leafy stems, 12–48 in (0.3–1.3 m) tall. Leaves are willowlike, the blades 1/2–6 in (1.3–15 cm) long. The inflorescence is on the upper portion of the plant, the inferior ovaries hugging the stem. From them issue the slender flower tubes, 1/2–2 in (13–50 mm) long. The reflexed, linear sepals are about 1 in (2.5 cm) long and the broad petals slightly longer. The tall stalks of flowers are in decided contrast to other oenotheras or Evening Primroses in the region. *Flower:* Yellow, aging orange-red or pinkish.

Distribution.   Moist or wet places; mostly in the White Mountains; Desert Scrub and Pinyon-juniper Woodland 4,000–8,500 ft (1,220–2,591 m).

ORCHIDACEAE (Orchid Family)

Represented here by two genera of perennial herbs. Flowers are irregular, in six segments. The outer series (sepals) may resemble petals, and the two lateral petals may be similar to the sepals. They may join with the upper sepal in forming a hood. The lower petal, known as the lip, is enlarged and leads to a basal nectary or into a spur. Stamens may be fused with the style and stigma to form a column. The ovary is inferior and the fruit a capsule.

Epipactis gigantea Douglas. **Desert Orchid, Stream Orchid.**   (Plate 6.131) A stout perennial with leafy stems 1–3 ft (0.3–1 m) high from creeping rhizomes. Lower leaves are ovate, up to 5 in (12 cm) long and 2 in (5 cm) wide, gradually reduced up the stem to shorter, narrower forms, all parallel-veined. Three to nine flowers are well spaced on the upper portion of the stem, usually on one side. The three sepals are triangular, spreading outward, about $^1/_2$ in (13 mm) long. Two petals resemble the sepals but are smaller and thinner. The long lower lip, unequally three-lobed, is the center of attraction. *Flower:* Sepals greenish with brownish veins, side petals more brownish purple, and the lip mostly yellowish with purple lines. Colors are rich but subdued.

Distribution.   Locally limited but widespread regionally, wet places; Desert Scrub, 4,000–6,000 ft (1,220–1,829 m).

Platanthera sparsiflora (Watson) Schlechter. **Green Canyon Orchid.** *(Habenaria sparsiflora)*   (Plate 6.132) Leafy stems 12–24 in (3–6 dm) tall. Leaves are lanceolate, the lower ones sheathing the stem, up to 4 in (10 cm) long and $^3/_4$ in (2 cm) broad, gradually reduced upward. The inflorescence is a narrow spike, each flower subtended by a narrow bract. The two lower sepals are spreading. The upper one curves forward together with the curving upper petals, forming a hood over the column. The lip is linear, about $^1/_4$ in (6 mm) long, extending downward. Its slightly curved spur is about the same length. The entire flower is about $^1/_2$ in (13 mm) long. *Flower:* Greenish.

Distribution.   Common, riparian areas; Desert Scrub to Subalpine Zone, 5,500–10,000 ft (1,677–3,049 m).

OROBANCHACEAE (Broomrape Family)

Fleshy root parasites lacking chlorophyll. The main stems are unusually thick, with scales in lieu of leaves. They are partially underground, attached at the base to the root of a host plant. Flowers are in spikes or clusters. The calyx is five-lobed and the corolla tubular with five irregular lobes.

Orobanche corymbosa (Rydb.) Ferris. **Flat-topped Broomrape, Sagebrush Strangler.**   Fleshy herbs 2–5 in (5–12 cm) tall, reddish purple to pale violet. The inflorescence is short and broadly corymbose, 1–2 in (2.5–5 cm) long, the flowers on slender individual stems about $^1/_2$ in (13 mm) long. Calyx lobes are long and slender. The corolla is up to 1 in (2.5 cm) long and slightly curved. Its two upper lobes are erect, and the lower ones curve outward. Anthers are hairy. *Flower:* Dull reddish with violet lines and yellow patches between the lobes of the lower lip.

Distribution.   Limited, parasitic mostly on sagebrush; Pinyon-juniper Woodland and Subalpine Zone, 7,000–10,400 ft (2,134–3,171 m).

Orobanche fasciculata Nutt. **Clustered Broomrape, Mountain Strangler.**   (Plate 6.133) Fleshy herbs 3–10 in (7.5–24 cm) tall, usually reddish purple. Inflorescence of 4 to 10 flowers, each on a long stem 1–4 in (2.5–10 cm) long. Calyx with short triangular lobes. The corolla is $^3/_4$–1 in (2–2.5 cm) long, strongly curved outward, all lobes about the same length. Anthers are not hairy but some are a bit woolly. *Flower:* Much the same as *O. corymbosa.*

Distribution.   Limited, parasitic on various species; Pinyon-juniper Woodland and Subalpine Zone, 7,000–10,600 ft (2,134–3,231 m).

PAPAVERACEAE (Poppy Family)

Plants with regular, broad-petaled flowers. Stamens may be numerous, tufted around a prominent pistil. The fruit is a capsule.

Argemone munita ssp. Dur. & Hilg. *rotundata* (Rydb.) Ownbey. **Prickly Poppy.** (Plate 6.134) A perennial with branching, leafy stems, 1–3 ft (0.3–1 m) tall, closely prickly throughout. Leaves, 1 1/2–6 in long, are lobed about halfway to the midribs, the lobes rounded and shallowly toothed. The flowers in terminal clusters are large and showy. The prickly sepals are ovate, each lobe tipped with a "tail." The six petals are thin, crepelike, and broadly wedge-shaped, 1 1/4–2 in (3–5 cm) long. Numerous yellow stamens surround the black-tipped ovary. The open flowers may be up to 4 in (10 cm) across. Local children call it the "fried egg flower." Mature seed capsules are elliptic-lanceolate, 1–2 1/4 in (2.5–5.6 cm) long, densely prickly, and tipped with the black pistil. The spreading prickles on this plant are up to 1/4 in (6 mm) long and very close. There is some variation, however, and this subspecies does gradually merge into ssp. *argentea*. The difference between them may not be well defined. *Flower:* Petals white.

Distribution.   Common, dryish canyons and slopes, especially along roadways; Desert Scrub and Pinyon-juniper Woodland, 5,000–9,500 ft (1,524–2,896 m).

Eschscholzia covillei Greene. **Coville Gold-poppy.** *(Eschscholzia minutiflora* var. *darwinensis)* (Plate 6.135) A small annual up to 12 in (30 cm) high, with a well-developed rosette of dissected basal leaves. The stems branch and carry some leaves also. It is much like a California Poppy in miniature form. It has the same conical cap, in lieu of sepals, which is pushed off by the expanding petals. Flowers are scattered among the upper branches. It has four petals, 1/4–1/2 in (6–13 mm) long, and 8 to 15 stamens tufted in the center. The seed capsule is linear, slightly curved, and about 1 1/2 in (3–8 mm) long. *Flower:* Yellow.

Distribution.   Common, dry gravelly places; Desert Scrub, 3,500–6,000 ft (1,067–1,829 m).

Note: The small annual poppies vary considerably in size and form, depending on the seasonal precipitation. In a dry year the plants may be no more than 1 in (2.5 cm) high. The flowers become smaller as the season progresses. A similar taxon, *E. minutiflora,* does occur in the Inyo Mountains. Its flowers are usually smaller, and the basal rosette may not be well developed.

POACEAE (GRAMINEAE) (Grass Family)

Although grasses are flowering plants, the flowers are minute, and it is commonly difficult to identify the species, even with a hand lens. They are interesting plants, however, and far too numerous and valuable to be ignored. Some are easy to recognize.

This is one of the largest plant families, and its usefulness surely exceeds all others. It supplies basic foods for the peoples of the world, as well as supporting their livestock. Both seeds and foliage are utilized by all levels of fauna. The value of native grasses cannot be overestimated. The White-Inyo Range has a generous share, but only a few of them are described here.

Stems of a grass plant are known as culms. The inflorescence is a spike or panicle, commonly called a head. The divisions are called spikelets, and they are composed of one or more florets. Leaves sheath the stems at the base, and the linear blades are parallel-veined. They may be tufted at the base or long enough to exceed the culms.

Festuca minutiflora **Rydb. Small-flowered Fescue.** *(Festuca brachyphylla schult)*   A densely tufted little alpine perennial, hardly more than $3/4$ in (2 cm) high on the slopes of White Mountain Peak. There the culms barely exceed the leaves, and the spikelike panicles may be no more than $5/8$ in (1.5 cm) long. The leaves are rolled round and so fine that they resemble stiff threads. The plant is taller in more favorable places, perhaps up to 4–5 in (10–12 cm), with the culms exceeding the leaves, and panicles close to 1 in (2.5 cm) long.

Distribution.   Open slopes of the high peaks; up to 14,100 ft (4,299 m).

Hilaria jamesii **(Torr.) Benth. James' Galleta.**   A common perennial in the desert ranges, widely spreading from rhizomatous roots. It forms a distinctive groundcover of rather rigid but curly leaves. Culms are 6–16 in (15–40 cm) tall with spikes up to 2 in (5 cm) long. The spikelets are attractive, long-haired at the base, and fringed at the apex.

Distribution.   Dryish flats and slopes; 5,000–7,500 ft (1,524–2,287 m). This hardy grass can take prolonged periods of drought. It is valued as a range species in desert mountains. Desert Bighorn may depend on it for 25% to 50% of their diet.

Koeleria macrantha **(Ledeb.) Sprengl. Junegrass.** *(Koeleria cristata* [L.] Pers., *Koeleria nitida)*   (Plate 6.136) A common tufted perennial with culms 10–26 in (2.5–6.5 dm) tall. Leaves are mostly basal, usually folded or rolled inward. It resembles a Poa but can be distinguished by the finely but densely hairy axis of the spike and the membranous shining surface of the florets.

Distribution.   Dryish slopes and flats; 7,000–13,000 ft (2,134–3,963 m). It is a good forage grass but too scattered to be of importance for grazing.

Leymus cinereus **(Scribn. & Merr.) A. Love. Ashy Wildrye, Great Basin Wildrye.** *(Elymus cinereus* Scribn. & Merr.)   A stout perennial bunchgrass, often forming large clumps, with culms 2–6 ft (0.6–2 m) tall. Leaves are firm, flat, and well developed, and the stiff spikes are mostly 4–8 in (1–2 dm) long. The plant's finely hairy surface gives it a gray or ashy cast.

Distribution.   Uncommon, usually an indication of a little extra moisture in depressions or gullies or on meadow borders; 4,000–10,000 ft (1,220–3,049 m).

Note: A similar species, *L. triticoides* (Buckl.), called Creeping Wildrye, is limited to riparian borders and sloughs where it is fairly wet. It is a brighter green and spreads by creeping rhizomes. Both of these coarse grasses are grazed to some extent when young. Their grains may be used as a food.

Melica stricta Boland. **Nodding Melic, Rock Melic.**   A tufted perennial with culms 8–20 in (2–5 dm) tall. Panicles are 2–6 in (5–15 cm) long. Its distinguishing feature is the well-spaced, nodding spikelets, $1/2$ in (1.5 cm) or more long, all on one side of the culm.

Distribution.   Relatively common but never abundant; rocky places; 5,000–11,000 ft (1,524–3,354 m).

Muhlenbergia richardsonis (Trin.) **Rydb. Mat Muhly.**   A mat-forming perennial from creeping rhizomes, its short culms mostly 4–10 in (10–25 cm) long, erect or sprawling. Leaf blades are very narrow, flat or rolled inward, $3/8$–2 in (1–5 cm) long. Panicles are $1/2$–$1 1/2$ in (1.5–4 cm) long, narrow and spikelike, green to blackish.

Distribution.   Common on moist slopes and about meadows; 7,000–11,300 ft (2,134–3,445 m). It is a good soil binder and an important forage where it occurs in abundance.

Oryzopsis hymenoides (Roemer & Schultes) **Ricker. Indian Ricegrass.**   (Plate 6.137) A densely tufted perennial with culms 8–24 in (2–6 dm) high. Leaf blades are very narrow and strongly rolled inward, nearly as long as the culms. The fine, threadlike branches of the panicle divide in pairs, delicately spreading. Spikelets are single-flowered, the florets with silky white hairs at the base.

Distribution.   Common to abundant in dry, usually sandy places; 4,000–10,400 ft (1,220–3,171 m). This is an adaptable grass, and a very nutritious one. Its seeds were a staple food for the native American people.

Poa secunda Presl. **Varied Bluegrass.** (*Poa ampla* Merr., *Poa gracillima* Vasey, *Poa incurva* Scribn. & Williams, *Poa nevadensis* Vasey, *Poa scabrella* [Thurb.] Benth., *Poa sandbergii* Vasey)   (Plate 6.138) A tufted perennial with culms 6–30 in (1.5–7.5 dm) tall. Leaves are mostly basal. The inflorescence is usually in spikelike panicles but some are more open with fine, spreading branches, some tinged purple. The poas or Varied Bluegrasses are common and are difficult to differentiate because morphologic differences are hard to define. A recent study has combined some of them, as evidenced by the list of synonyms, and placed them under a South American species. It allows for considerable variation within the species, many of which depend on elevation and local growing conditions. A distinctive characteristic of the genus is the way the tips of the leaves are shaped, like the prow of a boat. The spikelets of this species are not flattened or compressed.

Distribution.   Moist to dryish slopes; 3,500–12,600 ft (1,067–3,841 m). Its dense tufts make it a good soil stabilizer and turf builder. Some poas are used in lawn mixtures. All of them are valuable forage plants and tolerate heavy grazing.

Sitanion hystrix (Nutt.) S.G. Smith. Squirreltail.   (Plate 6.139) A tufted perennial with culms mostly 4–18 in (10–45 cm) high. Leaves are somewhat stiff and are well distributed on culms. Spikes are very broad with widely spreading, slender bristles—hence the common name. The stem of the spike (rachis) readily breaks apart when mature, allowing its segments to scatter and to penetrate anything within reach.

Distribution.   Common throughout the range; 6,500–14,000 ft (1,982–4,268 m). This grass is attractive when young but becomes a nuisance late in the season. The pointed stems and rough bristles injure the mouths, eyes, and ears of grazing animals. Tule Elk feed on it when green, however.

Note: S. jubatum, Big Squirreltail, is very similar but has a larger, bushier spike. It is usually at lower elevations, up to 10,000 ft.

Sporobolus airoides (Torr.) Torr. Alkali Sacaton.   (Plate 6.140) A stout perennial, an alkali-tolerant bunchgrass that may form broad, rounded clumps, densely clothed with the shining sheaths of old culms. Culms are slender, 16–40 in (4–10 dm) tall, with open pyramidal panicles 5–15 in (12–40 cm) long. The inflorescence is dainty. When observed in extensive populations, it appears as a beautiful purplish haze.

Distribution.   Seepage places and areas of high groundwater; 3,500–7,000 ft (1,067–2,134 m). Early desert travelers considered this grass a reliable indicator of water sufficiently fresh to drink within a few feet of the surface; however, with present-day water demands, the depth may be greater. It is an important forage grass in alkaline areas. When Desert Bighorn Sheep are present, it is heavily used by them. Native peoples used the fine seeds for food.

Stipa comata Trin. & Rupr. Needle and Thread.   A relatively stout, tufted perennial with culms 8–30 in (2–7.5 dm) tall. Leaves are mostly on the lower half of the plant. Panicles are 6–16 in (1.5–4 dm) long. The distinctive feature, unlike any other grass in the region, is the exceedingly long, flexuous bristles, 3–6 in (7–15 cm) long, of the inflorescence. When backlit by the sun, their shining forms are an impressive sight.

Distribution.   Common to abundant on dryish slopes; 6,000–9,500 ft. This grass provides good forage before maturity. When mature, the sharp base of the grain can damage the mouth parts of grazing animals.

Stipa speciosa Trin. & Rupr. Desert Needlegrass.   (Plate 6.141) A rather rigid, densely tufted perennial with culms 14–26 in (3.5–6.5 dm) high, scarcely exceeding the leaves. The spikelike panicles, 4–8 in (1–2 dm) long, are sometimes partially enclosed in the upper leaf sheath. The bristles of this species of *Stipa* are bent midway, and the lower portion is twisted and densely hairy. After maturity, the erect tufts of this grass become conspicuous straw-colored accents on rocky slopes.

Distribution.   Dry, rocky slopes; 3,500–8,000 ft (1,067–2,439 m). It is valuable as a forage, especially when young. It is relished by Bighorn Sheep and Tule Elk.

POLEMONIACEAE (Phlox Family)

A large family centered in California and well represented in the White-Inyo Range. The flowers are mostly five-parted. In most species the calyx is membranous between the lobes. Corollas are tubular, at least below, and may be campanulate (bell-shaped), funnelform, or salverform (a corolla with a slender tube abruptly expanding at right angles into petals or a rim). The narrow part at the base of the corolla is known as the tube and the flaring portion above as the throat, with the lobes above the throat. The leaves of many are prickle-tipped. *Gilia* leaves are usually toothed or lobed, some with a broad midrib (rachis). Most commonly they are in a basal rosette or tuft, with only a few reduced leaves above. One group, known as the cobwebby gilias, has cobwebby hairs about the base.

Collomia linearis Nutt. **Lesser Collomia.**   A slender annual, 4–12 in (1–3 dm) tall, with leafy stems. Leaves are thin, lanceolate to linear, mostly 1–2 in (2.5–5 cm) long, alternate on the stem. Flowers are in terminal clusters, mostly hidden by leaflike bracts. The dainty corolla is slender tubular with a slightly broader throat and flaring lobes, about ³⁄₈ in (1 cm) long in all. *Flower:* Pink or bluish to white.

Distribution.   Dry to moderately moist places; White Mountains; Desert Scrub to Subalpine Zone, up to 10,300 ft (3,140 m).

Eriastrum diffusum (Gray) Mason. **Spreading Eriastrum.**   A low annual with stems spreading from the base when well developed, up to 6 in (15 cm) long. Foliage is sparse on the reddish, wiry branches. Leaves are finely linear, ³⁄₈–1 in (1–2.5 cm) long, simple or with a pair of linear segments on the lower half. Flowers are in dense terminal clusters enclosed in prickle-tipped, woolly bracts, as is typical of the genus *Eriastrum*. The corolla is short tubular, about ¹⁄₄ in (6 mm) long, with slender lobes. *Flower:* Pale blue-lavender to white.

Distribution.   Dry, shady or gravelly places; Desert Scrub and Pinyon-juniper Woodland, 4,800–7,500 ft (1,463–2,287 m).

Eriastrum sparsiflorum (Eastwood) H. Mason var. *wilcoxii* (A. Nels.) Cronq. **Wilcox Woolly Star.**   (*Eriastrum wilcoxii* [A. Nels.] H. Mason)   An erect annual 4–12 in (1–3 dm) high, the stems freely branching in well-developed plants. The leaves are narrowly linear, mostly with one to three pairs of lateral segments. Heads are compact with woolly bracts, relatively few-flowered. The calyx lobes are woolly, lanceolate, and prickle-tipped, almost as long as the corolla tube. The corolla is short tubular, hardly ¹⁄₂ in (13 mm) long, with spreading lobes, all but the lobes fairly hidden. Stamens are on short filaments and barely protrude above the corolla throat. *Flower:* Pale blue-lavender to white.

Distribution.   Dryish slopes and washes; Desert Scrub and Pinyon-juniper Woodland, 4,200–8,000 ft (1,280–2,439 m).

Gilia aggregata (Pursh) Sprengel var. *arizonica* (Greene) Fosb. **Arizona Scarlet Gilia.** (*Ipomopsis aggregata* [Pursh] V. Grant ssp. *arizonica* [Greene] V. & A. Grant) (Plate 6.142) A perennial with several erect stems 4–10 in (1–2.4 dm) high. The plant is finely frosty-hairy above and has longer, curly hairs below. Leaves are tufted at the base and also on the stems. Basal blades are mostly ½–2 in (13–25 mm) long, divided into linear segments. Flowers are on the upper stems. The calyx is ¼ in (6 mm) long. The corolla has a gradually broadening tube, salverform, about ¾ in (2 cm) long. Its lobes are ⅜–½ in (10–13 mm) long. This variety has broader lobes and a shorter tube than others in the species. *Flower:* Bright red.

Distribution.   Uncommon; Inyo Mountains; Subalpine Zone, 10,000–10,500 ft (3,049–3,201 m).

Gilia brecciarum Jones ssp. *neglecta* A. & V. Grant. **Kern-Inyo Gilia.**   An erect annual 3–10 in (7.5–25 cm) high, commonly branching but with a rather rigid appearance. This is one of the cobwebby gilias with fine, web-like hairs about the base. Leaves are mostly in a semi-erect rosette. The blades are oblong or linear in outline, with a broad rachis and well-spaced toothlike lobes about as long as the rachis is wide. The inflorescence is stiffly branching. The corolla is ⅜–½ in (10–13 mm) long, the short, narrow tube expanding into a full, open throat, salverform, with lobes ¼ in (6 mm) long. This is a Showy Gilia with strong colors. Stamens are unequal and well exserted. *Flower:* The tube and lower throat are dark purple, the upper throat white with yellow spots, and the lobes light violet.

Distribution.   Open places; canyon mouths; Desert Scrub and Pinyon-juniper Woodland, to 9,000 ft (2,744 m).

Gilia campanulata Gray. **Bell Gilia.**   (Plate 6.143) A dainty annual, freely branching, making rounded plants 1–6 in (2.5–15 cm) high. They are leafy throughout, but the leaves are narrow and inconspicuous, up to ½ in (13 mm) long. Flowers are bell-shaped, ¼–⅜ in (6–10 mm) long, lobed. *Flower:* White with two yellow stripes below each lobe.

Distribution.   Uncommon; sandy places about the base of the range; Desert Scrub and Pinyon-juniper Woodland, up to 7,000 ft (2,134 m).

Gilia cana (Jones) Heller ssp. *triceps* (Brand) A. & V. Grant. **Showy Gilia.** (Plate 6.144) An erect annual with stems 4–12 in (1–3 dm) high. This is another of the cobwebby gilias. The leaves are in basal rosettes, the blades with a narrow rachis and prominent lobes. The inflorescence is loosely branched, the flowers on long, slender pedicels. The corolla is salverform; the tube is very slender, abruptly expanding to the throat; and the lobes are longer than broad, 1/2–1 in (13–25 mm) long in all. Stamens are slightly exserted. This is truly a showy species. Not only does it produce many flowers at once, but an entire slope may be colored with its blooms. *Flower:* The tube purple; the throat yellow below, commonly followed by a band of white, and violet above; and lobes pinkish violet.

Distribution.   Common, especially on limestone; dry, open places; Desert Scrub and Pinyon-juniper Woodland, 4,000–6,700 ft (1,220–2,043 m).

Gilia clokeyi **Mason. Clokey Gilia.**   A cobwebby gilia 2–12 in (5–30 cm) high with slender, branching stems. Leaves are in a dense or loose basal rosette. The rachis is narrow and the lobes short and blunt. A few small leaves appear at the branch forks. The corolla tube does not exceed the minute calyx, so only the narrow throat and corolla lobes are visible. The entire corolla length is about 3/16 in (5 mm). The capsules are globular. *Flower:* Throat pale yellow below, white above; the lobes pale or bluish.

Distribution.   Uncommon, apparently living in dolomitic soil; Desert Scrub, 4,000–5,500 ft (1,220–1,677 m).

Gilia congesta **Hook. var.** *montana* **(Nels. & Kennedy) Constance & Robbins. White Globe-gilia.**   (*Ipomopsis congesta* [Hook.] V. Grant ssp. *montana* [Nels. & Kennedy] V. Grant)   (Plate 6.145) A matted perennial that forms cushionlike rosettes with erect or spreading flowering stems 1 1/2–4 in (4–10 cm) long. The plants are grayish throughout with crinkly, white hairs. Leaves are narrowly divided, most with three to five lobes, forklike, 1/4–1 in (6–25 mm) long. Flowers are minute and in dense terminal heads or cymes. The calyx is about 1/8 in (3 mm) long, and the corolla is hardly twice that length, tubular, with out-turned lobes. Stamens are slightly exserted. The plant is appealing, but not at all showy. *Flower:* White with yellowish throat.

Distribution.   Common on high limestone or dolomite slopes; Pinyon-juniper Woodland to Alpine Zone, 7,200–12,000 ft (2,195–3,658 m).

Gilia filiformis **Parry. Yellow Gilia.**   A dainty annual, 1–6 in (2.5–15 cm) high, with very slender branches. Leaves are very narrow, mostly less than 1 in (2.5 cm) long, and well distributed but too fine to show up. Flowers, too, occur throughout the plant. The corolla is campanulate, fairly lacking a tube, but with lobes about 3/8 in (1 cm) long. *Flower:* Bright yellow.

Distribution.   Limited; dry sandy or gravelly places; Desert Scrub, 4,000–6,000 ft (1,120–1,829 m).

Gilia gilioides **(Benth.) Greene var.** *violacea* **(Heller) Cronq. Violet Gilia.** (*Allophyllum violaceum* [Heller] A. & V. Grant)   A slender annual, openly branched when well developed, 2–12 in (5–30 cm) high, leafy throughout. Leaves are narrowly linear or elliptic, some with a pair of teeth toward the base, and under 1 in (2.5 cm) long. The corolla is tubular or slender funnelform, 1/4 in (6 mm) long. *Flower:* Dark blue-violet.

Distribution. Uncommon; dry to moderately moist places; Pinyon-juniper Woodland, 7,000–9,000 ft (2,134–2,744 m).

Gilia hutchinsifolia Rydb. **Desert Pale Gilia.** A branching annual, 2–10 in (5–25 cm) high, with very fine tack-shaped glands throughout. The leaves, 1–2 in (2.5–5 cm) long, are in a well-developed basal rosette, along with some reduced forms on the branches. The rachis is narrow and the lobes prominent, commonly cut or toothed. The calyx is very short. The corolla is narrowly funnelform with a slender tube and flaring throat, topped by ascending lobes, 3/8–1/2 in (10–13 mm) long in all. Anthers are at the base of the lobes. *Flower:* Tube pale violet; lower throat yellow, upper white; lobes white with pale violet streaks.

Distribution. Uncommon; sandy slopes and washes; Desert Scrub, 4,200–5,000 ft (1,280–1,524 m).

Gilia latifolia Watson. **Holly Gilia.** (Plate 6.146) A finely glandular annual 4–12 in (1–3 dm) high. Leaves are broadly obovate and coarsely toothed, each tooth prickle-tipped. The blades, 1–3 in (2.5–8 cm) long, are on petioles equally long in basal leaves and much shorter above. The lower half of the plant is leafy, and the upper half is a branching inflorescence. The calyx is about 1/4 in (6 mm) long, its tapered and prickle-tipped lobes as long as its tube. The corolla is funnelform, 3/8 in (1 cm) long, five-lobed. *Flower:* Bright pink inside, pale or buff outside.

Distribution. Common; gravelly flats and in rocky gullies, especially in limestone areas; Desert Scrub, below 7,000 ft (2,134 m).

Gilia leptomeria Gray. **Sand Gilia.** A somewhat glandular annual, 3–8 in (8–20 cm) high, with leaves in a flat basal rosette. The shining leaves, 3/8–2 in (1–5 cm) long, are strap-shaped, shallowly lobed or bluntly toothed, usually bright green. The branching inflorescence has an abundance of small flowers. The corolla, about 3/16 in (5 mm) long, has a slender tube; a short, gently flaring throat; and pointed, commonly tridentate lobes. A hand lens will reveal their beautiful form. *Flower:* Tube pale pink or lavender, throat yellowish, and the lobes streaked with purple.

Distribution. Common; open, sandy places; Desert Scrub and Pinyon-juniper Woodland, 3,500–8,300 ft (1,067–2,530 m).

Gilia ochroleuca Jones. **Volcanic Pale Gilia.** A dainty annual, 2 1/2–6 in (6–15 cm) high, commonly with branches broadly spreading from the base. Leaves are at or near the base, but they are narrowly lobed and relatively inconspicuous. The flowers, on fine pedicels, are well distributed. The corolla is hardly 1/4 in (6 mm) long, twice the length of the calyx, which conceals the tube. The throat flares to a broad opening topped by spreading lobes. *Flower:* Lower throat yellow, the upper portion pale violet, and lobes violet or pink.

Distribution.   Limited; sandy or gravelly places on granitic or volcanic rocks; Desert Scrub, 4,000–6,500 ft (2,120–1,982 m).

Gilia ophthalmoides **Brand. Pinyon Gilia.**   (Plate 6.147) A cobwebby gilia 6–12 in high, glandular above. Plants are erect with a strict branching habit. Leaves have a narrow rachis, with lobes mostly longer than the width of the rachis, and are mostly in a basal tuft. The corolla is funnelform with an extremely slender tube expanding slightly to a narrow throat, topped by short lobes. *Flower:* Tube light violet, throat yellow except for pale blue-violet at the opening, and lobes violet to pink.

Distribution.   Most common in the Pinyon-juniper Woodland, Desert Scrub to Subalpine Zone, 4,500–10,000 ft (1,372–3,049 m).

Gilia polycladon **Torr. Spreading gilia.** (*Ipomopsis polycladon* [Torr.] V. Grant)   A low annual with branches 1–6 in (2.5–15 cm) long, spreading from the base. The branches are usually reddish and naked except for a single leaf at each node and terminal tufts of leaves and flowers. There are a few basal leaves also. The leaves are 3/8–1 in (1–2.5 cm) long, somewhat wedge-shaped, the upper half prominently toothed. Although they are green, they appear frosted with curly, white hairs. The flower clusters are almost hidden by the leaves. The corolla is tubular, 3/16 in (5 mm) long, hardly exceeding the calyx, with flaring lobes. *Flower:* White.

Distribution.   Limited; sandy or gravelly places; Desert Scrub to Pinyon-juniper Woodland, 4,000–7,600 ft (1,220–2,317 m).

Gilia scopulorum **Jones. Rock Gilia.**   A glandular-hairy annual, 4–16 in (1–4 dm) high, usually well branched. Leaves are 1/2–2 in (13–50 mm) long, deeply cut into teeth or toothed lobes, mostly in a basal tuft. Flowers have a relatively short calyx. The corolla is narrowly funnelform, about 1/2 in (13 mm) long, with rather short lobes. *Flower:* Tube purple-streaked; lower throat yellow, upper throat lavender; and lobes pink-lilac, usually pale pink or buff outside.

Distribution.   Uncommon; rocky places, commonly at the base of cliffs; usually on limestone; Desert Scrub, 3,500–6,000 ft (1,067–1,829 m).

Gilia sinuata **Douglas. Cinder Gilia.**   A stiffly erect branching annual, 3–12 in (8–30 cm) high, some individuals with multiple stems. The plant is moderately glandular-hairy on the upper portion, including the inflorescence, but the lower stems lack any hairs or glands. Leaves are strap-shaped and prominently lobed, grayish green above with a pale vein down the center, all in a basal rosette except for a few bractlike leaves on the stems. Flowers are small, only about 5/16 in (8 mm) long. The calyx is about one-third the length of the corolla. The latter is funnelform, with the narrow tube mostly enclosed in the calyx but some are well exserted. *Flower:* Tube purple with pale veins; throat yellowish, commonly with purple streaks coming up from the tube; and lobes violet to pinkish.

Distribution. Limited; dry, sandy places, especially on granitic and volcanic soils; Desert Scrub and Pinyon-juniper Woodland, 3,500–7,200 ft (1,067–2,195 m).

Gilia stellata Heller. **Dotted-throat Gilia.** An annual 4–20 in (1–5 dm) tall. The foliage at the base is not cobwebby but is gray with a dense coat of very fine, branched, white hairs. Leaves are usually 1–2 in (2.5–5 cm) long, divided to the middle into toothed lobes. Although they are mostly in a basal tuft, there are a few reduced leaves on the stems. The calyx is short, its green midribs tapering to slender lobes. The corolla is funnelform, about ³/₈ in (1 cm) long, with fairly long lobes. The stamens barely protrude at the mouth. A common characteristic is a row of purple dots around the throat, but these are absent on some individuals. *Flower:* Pale or off-white, some tinged lavender or pale blue.

Distribution. Limited, locally abundant; sandy and gravelly places; Desert Scrub, from low elevations up to 6,000 ft (1,829 m).

Gymnosteris parvula. **Gymnosteris.** (Plate 6.148) A diminutive annual, ¹/₂ in (13 mm) high, more or less. It has no foliage leaves, but a pair of tiny cotyledons persist at the base of the slender stems, and a whorl of bracts subtends the terminal flower cluster. The bracts are linear to ovate, ¹/₈–³/₈ in (3–10 mm) long. The corolla is tubular and lobed but only about ¹/₁₆ in (2 mm) long and hardly exceeding the calyx. This unusual little plant is worth examining under a lens. *Flower:* White or pinkish.

Distribution. Uncommon; moist slopes and meadow borders; Pinyon-juniper Woodland to Alpine Zone, 8,500–12,000 ft (2,591–3,658 m).

Langloisia setosissima (Torr. & Gray) ssp. *punctata* (Coville) Timbrook **Dotted Langloisia.** (*L. punctata* [Coville] Goodd.) (Plate 6.149) A prickly tuft of a plant or a much-branched, spreading annual, depending on the moisture available. It is ¹/₂–4 in (13–100 mm) high and is normally broader than tall. Leaves are triangular or wedge-shaped with three to five coarse, bristle-tipped teeth. Flowers are tubular, up to 1 in (2.5 cm) long, with flaring lobes. *Flower:* Lilac to whitish, purple-dotted.

Distribution. Dry, gravelly places on open slopes; Desert Scrub and Pinyon-juniper Woodland, 4,000–8,400 ft (1,222–2,561 m).

Leptodactylon pungens Torr. Rydb. var. *hallii* (Parish) Mason. **Prickly Phlox.** (Plate 6.150) A shrubby perennial with branches 4–24 in (1–6 dm) long and rigid but somewhat sprawling. Its branches are clothed with needle-like leaves up to ¹/₂ in (13 mm) long. Each has one or two pairs of lesser spine-tipped segments toward the base, so the middle segment is much the longest. It is commonly curved downward.

Flowers are nocturnal, opening in the evening, and commonly sweet-scented. The corolla is tubular with lobes about 3/8 in (1 cm) long, with lobes of some corolla equaling the length of tube. *Flower:* White, some tinged with lavender.

Distribution. Common on dryish flats and slopes; Desert Scrub to Alpine Zone, 6,000–12,000 ft (1,829–3,658 m).

> **Var. *pungens* (Torr.) Rydb. Granite Gilia.** (Ssp. *pulchriflorum* (Brand) Mason) Middle leaf segments are less than twice as long as the others, and there are more lateral segments. They are not as rigid as in var. *hallii.* The flowers are much the same.
>
> **Distribution.** Rocky places, mostly on granitic or volcanic rocks; Alpine Zone, 10,000–13,000 ft (3,049–3,963 m).

Linanthus nuttallii **(Gray) Greene ssp.** *pubescens* **Patterson. Bushy Linanthus.** *(Linanstrum nuttallii)* (Plate 6.151) A bushy perennial with a woody base and numerous slender stems 4–12 in (1–3 dm) high. The leaves are mostly 1/4–1/2 in (6–13 mm) long, divided to the base into five to nine linear segments. These, along with lesser leaves in the axils, make well-spaced whorls on the stems. Flowers are in terminal clusters subtended by leaflike bracts. The corolla is salverform, the tube 3/8 in (1 cm) long, with comparatively long lobes. The plant may vary from a fairly dense form to one with long internodes. These may be considered separate subspecies by some authors. *Flower:* White, commonly with a yellowish tube.

Distribution. Common on dryish slopes; Pinyon-juniper Woodland to Alpine Zone, 7,000–12,500 ft (2,134–3,811 m).

Linanthus parryae **(Gray) Greene. Sand Blossoms.** (Plate 6.152) A small annual, mostly only 3/4–2 in (2–5 cm) high, with a generous inflorescence hiding the rest of the plant. They appear to rest right on the ground. The inconspicuous leaves are divided into fine, linear segments. The 1/2 in (13 mm)–long corolla is showy, broadly funnelform, with the spreading lobes much longer than the very short tube. *Flower:* Usually blue-lavender, rarely paler to white, with a contrasting color in the throat.

Distribution. Limited populations; sandy or gravelly slopes; Desert Scrub, below 5,500 ft (1,677 m).

Navarretia breweri **(Gray) Greene. Yellow Navarretia.** A dainty annual 1/2–3 in (13–77 mm) high. Well-developed plants have wiry, branching stems, but more commonly they are no more than a short, single stem. Leaves are divided into very narrow, firm, prickly segments, up to 1 in (2.5 cm) long. Flowers are in dense terminal tufts subtended by leaflike bracts. The minute corollas are tubular, 1/4 (6 mm) long, and lobed. *Flower:* Yellow.

Distribution. Slightly moist places, such as flats or meadow borders; Pinyon-juniper Woodland and Subalpine Zone, 8,500–11,000 ft (2,591–3,354 m).

Phlox condensata (Gray) E. Nels. Cushion Phlox. (*Phlox covillei* E. Nels.)   (Plate 6.153) A perennial that forms dense, cushionlike mats composed of closely packed, erect stems, densely clothed with short, appressed leaves. The leaves are linear, two-grooved on the back, and sharply bristle-pointed. Each stem has a single flower, but the flowers are showy when covering the entire mound. The corolla is salverform, up to $1/2$ in (13 mm) long, with generous lobes. *Flower:* White to pink or blue-lavender.

Distribution.   Dense populations on dolomitic-soil flats; Pinyon-juniper Woodland to Alpine Zone, 8,400–13,500 ft (2,561–4,116 m).

Phlox hoodii Richards ssp. *canescens* (Torr. & Gray). Woolly Phlox.   A perennial, similar to *P. condensata,* but with a less dense growth habit, cushion-forming but not densely compact. The calyx and usually the leaf margins are cobwebby-woolly. The corolla, too, is similar to the cushion phlox but has longer lobes. *Flower:* Lavender or pink-purple to white.

Distribution.   Dry, rocky places; White Mountains; Pinyon-juniper Woodland and Subalpine Zone, 8,000–10,000 ft (2,439–3,049 m).

Phlox longifolia Nutt. var. *stansburyi* (Torr.) Gray. Stansbury Phlox. *(Phlox stansburyi {Torr.} Heller)*   (Plate 6.154) A perennial somewhat woody at the base. The leafy stems, 4–12 in high, usually come from horizontal underground stems. Leaves are firm, linear or narrowly lanceolate, in pairs, $1/2$–$1\,1/2$ in (13–38 mm) long. Corollas are salverform with straight tubes, 1 in (2.5 cm) long, and lobes $3/8$–$1/2$ in (10–13 mm) long. A short-flowered form, in which the corolla tube is only about twice the length of the calyx, also occurs in the range, but it is usually considered but a variation of the var. *stansburyi. Flower:* Deep pink to white.

Distribution.   Common; Desert Scrub to Subalpine Zone, 5,000–10,000 ft (1,524–3,049 m).

Polemonium chartaceum Mason. White Mountain Sky Pilot.   (Plate 6.155) A glandular perennial 2–6 in (5–15 cm) high. Stems and leaves are crowded on a short root crown, along with strawlike leaf bases persisting from prior years. Leaves are finely divided into minute leaflets, which are again divided almost to the base. Flowers are in dense, terminal heads. The corolla is funnelform, about $1/2$ in (13 mm) long, including its rounded lobes. Stamens are exserted. This species is like a smaller form of the Sierra Sky Pilot. *Flower:* Blue-violet.

Distribution.   Rocky places; White Mountains; Alpine Zone, above 13,000 ft (3,963 m).

POLYGONACEAE (Buckwheat Family)

A large family that is well represented in the range. It includes dainty annuals, perennials, and some shrubby forms. The flowers are minute but usually clustered, so the inflorescence may be fairly showy. There are no petals, but the two to six calyx segments are petal-like. The genus *Eriogonum* is by far the largest in number of species. Its determining characteristic is its involucres, like tiny containers that hold the flowers. These may be bell-shaped (campanulate), top-shaped (turbinate), or cylindric, and they may be on short stems (peduncles) or hugging the branchlets (sessile). The few to many flowers issuing from an involucre have six petal-like sepals, each with a darker midvein. They are in varying shades of white, pink, or yellow, usually changing color with age.

Many appealing forms show up in this family. Although the leaves of annuals commonly disappear by flowering time, the plants retain their shape when dry, turning to rich shades of reddish brown. The family is such an interesting one that it is worth the effort to become familiar with the botanical terms necessary to describe the species.

Chorizanthe brevicornu Torr. var. *spathulata* (Small) C.L. Hitchc. **Mountain Brittle Chorizanthe.** A yellowish-green annual, 1–12 in (2.5–30 cm) high. The plants may be grayish, however, with soft, white hairs, or they are rarely reddish throughout. Leaves are in a basal tuft, the blades spatulate to almost roundish, narrowed to a stem of nearly equal length, the whole 1–2 1/2 in (2.5–6.4 cm) long. Leaflike bracts occur at the nodes, becoming much reduced upward. Involucres are cylindric, ribbed, about 3/16 in (5 mm) long, and commonly curved outward with six curved teeth. Minute flowers are hidden in the involucres. *Flower:* White, rarely seen.

Distribution. Common; dry slopes and flats, from the valley elevations; Desert Scrub and Pinyon-juniper Woodland, to 9,000 ft (2,744 m), rarely higher.

Note: Var. *brevicornu,* with very narrow leaves, is common in Desert Scrub, below 5,000 ft (1,524 m), mostly in hotter, drier places.

Chorizanthe rigida (Torr.) Torr. & Gray. **Rosy-thorn.** (Plate 6.156) Short, stubby, extremely spiny annuals, 1–4 in (2.5–10 cm) high. Leaves are roundish to elliptic, 3/8–1 in (1–2.5 cm) long, on slender petioles 1–1 1/2 times as long. The plant is soft-hairy when young, but the leaves are soon shed, leaving only the spiny structure. The minute flowers are hidden in the spine-tipped involucres surrounded by other, longer spines. *Flower:* Yellowish.

Distribution. Very dry, open slopes; Desert Scrub, mostly below 4,500 ft (1,372 m).

Chorizanthe watsonii Torr. & Gray. **Watson Chorizanthe.** A small tufted annual, often reddish-tinged, 1–4 in (2.5–10 cm) high. Its foliage is grayish with soft, white hairs. Leaves are narrowly elliptic or oblanceolate, narrowing to a petiole. Involucral tubes are minute, slender, and five-lobed. Four of the lobes are outcurving or hooked teeth; the fifth is much larger and leaflike. The tip of the corolla protrudes from the involucre. *Flower:* Yellow.

Distribution.   Uncommon; dry slopes and flats; Desert Scrub and Pinyon-juniper Woodland, up to 7,500 ft (2,287 m).

Dedeckera eurekensis **Reveal & J.T. Howell. Dedeckera, July Gold, Eureka Gold.** (Plate 6.157) A rounded, deciduous shrub with a dense growth habit, generally 1–3 ft (0.3–1 m) high and 2–8 ft (0.6–2.6 m) broad. Branches are sturdy and woody at the base but increasingly slender upward. Leaves are elliptic, about 1/2 in (13 mm) long. Leaflike bracts occur at the nodes of the upper branches and are reduced upward. The inflorescence is corymbose, covering the entire bush. Involucres are lacking, but the flowers, like those of *Eriogonum,* have six petal-like sepals. *Flower:* Golden yellow.

Distribution.   Highly restricted to specific calcareous formations, probably dolomite rich; usually on north-facing slopes; Desert Scrub, 4,700–6,200 ft (1,433–1,890 m).

Eriogonum baileyi **Watson. Bailey Buckwheat.**   An annual, 4–6 in (1–4 dm) high, usually with branches spreading to make a rounded crown. Leaves are basal, roundish, 1/4–3/4 in (6–20 mm) broad, densely white-woolly on both surfaces. Involucres are elongated campanulate, close against the branches and at the nodes. The outer three calyx segments, about 1/16 in (2 mm) long, are oblong, somewhat constricted near the middle, and flaring above. The inner segments are narrower. *Flower:* White or pink.

Distribution.   Common in dry sandy or gravelly places; Desert Scrub to Pinyon-juniper Woodland, up to 7,500 ft (2,287 m).

Eriogonum brachyanthum **Torr. & Gray. Short-flowered Buckwheat.**   An annual much like *E. baileyi* in form and size. The leaves are similar also. Involucres are turbinate, hugging the branches. Calyx segments are very short, about half as long as those of *E. baileyi,* the inner ones slightly narrower than the outer. *Flower:* Yellow.

Distribution.   This species may not tolerate limestone; dry, sandy places; Desert Scrub to Pinyon-juniper Woodland, up to 7,500 ft (2,287 m).

Eriogonum brachypodum **Torr. & Gray. Glandular Buckwheat.**   A sturdy-stemmed annual, 3–10 in (8–24 cm) high. Leaves are basal, round to heart-shaped, 1/2–3 in (13–77 mm) broad, densely white-woolly below, less so above. The spreading branches are finely glandular throughout. Involucres are broadly turbinate on deflexed peduncles, so the flowers turn downward. Outer calyx segments are oblong and lobed or heart-shaped at the base; the inner three are smaller. *Flower:* White, aging pink or reddish.

Distribution.   Dry, gravelly places; Desert Scrub and Pinyon-juniper Woodland, 4,000–7,000 ft (1,220–2,134 m).

Eriogonum caespitosum **Nutt. Mat Buckwheat.**   A perennial that forms dense, pancake-size, whitish mats from much-branched, woody root crowns. Leaves are elliptic to spatulate, with the edges slightly rolled under, 1/4–1/2 in (6–13 mm) long, densely white-felted. Slender, leafless flowering stems rise 1–3 in (5–8 cm) from the mat. Each bears a single turbinate involucre with long, linear lobes turned downward. Under a hand lens the calyx shows a hairy base prolonged into a short stem. The inner and outer segments are similar. *Flower:* Yellow, aging reddish.

Distribution.   Common to abundant on dry limestone slopes; mostly in the Pinyon-juniper Woodland of the White Mountains; Pinyon-juniper Woodland and Subalpine Zone, 7,000–10,500 ft (2,134–3,201 m).

Eriogonum cernuum **Nutt. Nodding Buckwheat.**   A rather dainty annual, 2–12 in (5–30 cm) high, commonly branching at the base. Leaves are basal, round, 1/8–1/2 in (3–13 mm) broad, on petioles longer than the blade. Involucres are turbinate, five-lobed, on fine, deflexed peduncles 1/4–1 in (6–25 mm) long. Calyx segments are wavy-edged, somewhat narrowed toward the middle. *Flower:* White, aging rose-pink.

Distribution.   Uncommon but over a wide range; Pinyon-juniper Woodland and Subalpine Zone, 7,000–10,500 ft (2,134–3,201 m).

Eriogonum deflexum **var.** *deflexum.* **Skeleton Weed.**   See description of *E. brachypodum,* an annual that it closely resembles. This plant lacks glands, however, and the reflexed involucres have no peduncles or only very short ones. *Flower:* White, aging pink.

Distribution.   Sandy or gravelly places; Desert Scrub and Pinyon-juniper Woodland, 5,000–9,500 ft (1,524–2,896 m).

>   **Var.** *baratum* **(Elmer) Munz. Tall skeleton weed.**   A tall plant, up to 40 in (10 dm) high, the stems and some branches slightly inflated. The branching habit is strict, that is, sharply angling upward rather than spreading. Involucres are narrowly turbinate and the calyx segments relatively long. *Flower:* White, aging pink.
>
>   **Distribution.**   Common on gravelly surfaces, especially on volcanic cinders; Desert Scrub and Pinyon-juniper Woodland, 4,500–8,000 ft (1,372–2,439 m).

Eriogonum esmeraldense **Watson. Esmeralda Buckwheat.**   A dainty annual, 3–14 in (7.5–35 cm) high, the upper branches fine and threadlike. Leaves are basal, round-ovate, 1/4–1/2 in (6–13 mm) long, on petioles of equal length, and their surface is hairy rather than woolly. Involucres are turbinate, rather deeply five-lobed, on threadlike, reflexed peduncles about 1/4 in (6 mm) long. Calyx segments are oblong. *Flower:* White, tinged rose-red.

Distribution.   Uncommon; Pinyon-juniper Woodland and Bristlecone Pine Forest; Pinyon-juniper Woodland and Subalpine Zone, 7,000–10,400 ft (2,134–3,171 m).

Eriogonum fasciculatum Benth. var. *polifolium* (Benth.) Torr. & Gray. California Buckwheat. (Plate 6.158) A low, irregularly spreading shrub, 8–20 in (2–5 dm) high. It is leafy throughout except for the naked flowering stems. Leaves are narrowly linear or oblanceolate, with the edges slightly rolled under, 1/4–1/2 in (6–13 mm) long, and mostly in bundles along the branches. Their surfaces are densely white hoary or felted. Flowering stems rise 4–6 in (10–15 cm) above the leafy branches. The inflorescence is a head or short-branching cluster, the parts finely hairy throughout. Involucres are campanulate but angled. Outer calyx segments are broadly elliptic, the inner ones obovate. *Flower:* White or pinkish, but the general appearance is dirty white.

Distribution. Common; Desert Scrub and Pinyon-juniper Woodland, 4,500–7,500 ft (1,372–2,287 m).

Eriogonum gracilipes Watson. Raspberry Buckwheat. (Plate 6.159) A perennial with a turfy habit, the leaves densely clustered on a branching root crown. Leaves are elongated, mostly narrowly obovate, narrowing to a petiole, 1/4–1/2 in (6–13 mm) long in all, and covered with a loose, white-woolly coat. Flowers are in heads of five to seven crowded involucres on naked stems that rise 1–3 in (2.5–7.5 cm) above the leafy mat. Calyx segments are similar, tending to flare outward. *Flower:* White, turning deep pink to raspberry color.

Distribution. Mostly confined to dolomite areas in the White Mountains; Sub-alpine and Alpine zones, 10,000–13,000 ft (3,049–3,963 m).

Eriogonum heermannii Dur. & Hilg. ssp. *argense* (Jones) Munz. Rough Heermann Buckwheat. (Plate 6.160) A small, compact, rounded shrub, 4–8 in (1–2 dm) high, intricately branched, only 1/2 in (13 mm) or less between the nodes. Branchlets are very slender, with roughened surfaces. The small leaves are narrowly oblong and are located on the lower part of the plant. Involucres are sessile on the rigidly branched upper portion. Calyx segments are minute. *Flower:* Off-white.

Distribution. Dry, rocky places; most common in the Inyo Mountains; Desert Scrub and Pinyon-juniper Woodland, 4,500–9,000 ft (1,372–2,744 m).

Ssp. *humilius* Stokes. Common Heermann Buckwheat. A compact, rounded shrub, 12–28 in (3–7 dm) high, larger and coarser than the ssp. *argense*. Internodes are 1 in (2.5 cm) long, more or less. The intricate, rigidly geometric branching pattern is characteristic of Heermann Buckwheat, regardless of size. Leaves are obovate, most less than 1/2 in (13 mm) long, on the lower branches. Like ssp. *argense*, the turbinate involucres are sessile on the upper branches. Outer calyx segments are roundish and lobed at the base, and the inner three are oblong. They are large enough to show up well. *Flower:* White to yellowish white.

Distribution. Limestone slopes, especially on dolomite talus; Desert Scrub and Pinyon-juniper Woodland, 4,500–8,000 ft (1,372–2,439 m).

Eriogonum inflatum Torr. **Desert Trumpet.**   (Plate 6.161) A perennial, 8–40 in (2–10 dm) high, with bluish green stems openly branched above. The upper part of the main stem and the first branches are inflated, but the ultimate branchlets are extremely fine. Leaves are all basal, green, oblong to roundish, usually heart-shaped at the base, 1/2–1 1/4 in (13–30 mm) long, on slender petioles 1–2 1/4 in (2.5–5.6 cm) long. Involucres are turbinate, five-lobed, on threadlike stems. Calyx segments are hairy with pointed tips. *Flower:* Yellow.

Distribution.   Common in washes and along roadsides; below 6,500 ft (1,982 m).

Eriogonum kennedyi Porter var. *purpusii* (Brandeg.) **Reveal. Kennedy Buckwheat.**   A densely leafy mat on a woody root crown. Leaves are white-felted, oblong, the edges commonly curled under, 1/8–1/4 in (3–6 mm) long. Wiry, naked flowering stems rise 1 1/2–5 in (4–12 cm) above the leafy mat, each bearing a head about 3/8 in (1 cm) broad. Involucres are turbinate, tightly clustered. Calyx segments are short. *Flower:* White with greenish midribs.

Distribution.   On granitic flats and slopes; White Mountains; Pinyon-juniper Woodland, 6,000–8,000 ft (1,829–2,439 m).

Eriogonum maculatum Heller. **Spotted Buckwheat.**   An annual branching from the base, 2–8 in (5–20 cm) high, soft woolly almost throughout. Basal leaves are obovate, 1/2–1 in (13–25 mm) long, narrowing to a short petiole. Smaller leaves occur at the nodes and are reduced upward. The flowers, on threadlike peduncles, are well distributed over all but the basal part of the plant. Involucres are campanulate, finely glandular-hairy on the surface. Outer calyx segments are inflated in the lower portion, with the inner segments a little longer. This little buckwheat is easily identified by its leafy appearance and its spotted flowers. *Flower:* White to yellow, pink, or red, each outer segment with a conspicuous rose-purple spot.

Distribution.   Common on sandy and gravelly soils of dry places; Desert Scrub, 3,500–7,000 ft (1,067–2,134 m).

Eriogonum microthecum Nutt. var. *ambiguum* (Jones) **Reveal. Yellow Microthecum.**   A scraggly shrub, 1–2 ft high, with grayish, herbaceous stems issuing from slender, brown, woody branches. Leaves are on the lower portion of the herbaceous stems, the blades white woolly beneath and green above, elliptic in shape, 3/4 in (2 cm) long or less. The upper stem branches to form a relatively flat-topped cyme. Involucres, like the stems, are thinly white woolly. They are narrowly turbinate, and terminal on branches of the inflorescence. Outer calyx segments are broad, the inner ones narrower. *Flower:* Yellow with green midribs.

Distribution.   Dry, open places in forested areas; possibly restricted to granitic and volcanic soils or rocks; Pinyon-juniper Woodland and Subalpine Zone, 7,500–10,500 ft (2,287–3,201 m).

Var. *lapidicola* Reveal. Bristlecone Microthecum.   A small perennial with a branching root crown and slender stems ¹/₂–4 in (1.3–10 cm) high. Only the very bases of the stems are leafy. Leaves are white-woolly, especially underneath, elliptic with the edges turned under, ¹/₈–³/₈ in (6–10 mm) long. Stems are naked except for the leafy base, with a branching inflorescence at the top. Each of the fine branchlets carries a single, narrowly turbinate involucre. Outer calyx segments are broad, and the inner ones are narrower and elliptic. *Flower:* White or pink with rose midrib, maturing rose red.

Distribution.   Limestone areas; Inyo Mountains; open places in Pinyon-juniper Woodland and Subalpine Zone, 8,000–10,200 ft (2,439–3,110 m).

Var. *laxiflorum* Hook. Pinyon Microthecum.   A shrub similar to var. *ambiguum* but somewhat more compact and bushy, 4–16 in high. Leaves are obovate to elliptic, the edges turned under, whitish below, green above, ¹/₂–1 in (13–25 mm) long. The herbaceous part of the stem is green and leafy about half its length. The flat-topped inflorescence is similar in form to var. *ambiguum* but a little more compact. *Flower:* White or pink.

Distribution.   Dryish slopes and flats; Pinyon-juniper Woodland and Subalpine Zone, 7,500–10,000 ft (2,287–3,049 m).

***Eriogonum mummulare* Jones. Kearney Buckwheat.** (*Eriogonum kearneyi* Tides. var. *monoense* [Stokes] Reveal)   A scraggly perennial with dull-gray to brownish brittle stems, 12–40 in (3–10 cm) high. They may be somewhat woody at the base and are leafy above that area and below the branches. Leaves are elliptic, wavy-edged, whitish-coated, mostly ³/₄ in (2 cm) long. The branching inflorescence makes up more than half the plant. Involucres are tight on the branches, turbinate, and grayish. Calyx segments are joined at the base, hardly spreading above. The numerous flowers are not at all showy. In fact, the entire plant is drab. *Flower:* White with red midribs, maturing reddish.

Distribution.   Uncommon, but large populations occur on sandy soils, commonly on pumice; mostly Pinyon-juniper Woodland, 7,000–8,500 ft (2,134–2,591 m).

***Eriogonum nidularium* Coville. Bird's-nest Buckwheat.**   A small annual, 2–6 in high, repeatedly branched from the base upward, making a dense plant with a funnelform outline. The color is gray-green. Tips of the branches turn inward in age, creating a bird's-nest appearance. Leaves are basal, the blades roundish, ¹/₄–³/₄ in (6–20 mm) broad, on slender petioles up to 1 in (2.5 cm) long. Narrowly turbinate involucres hug the branches and their forks throughout the plant. Outer calyx segments are broadly fan-shaped, and the inner are narrower. The flowers of this little buckwheat are especially attractive. *Flower:* White or yellowish, aging rose-pink to red.

Distribution. Common along roadsides and other gravelly, open places; mostly between the valley elevations to Desert Scrub and Pinyon-juniper Woodland, 7,500 ft (2,287 m) rarely to 9,200 ft (2,805 m).

Eriogonum ovalifolium Nutt. var. *ovalifolium*. **Oval-leaved Buckwheat.** (Plate 6.162) A perennial that forms dense, leafy clumps on woody root crowns. Leaves are ovate rounded, 1/4–1/2 in (6–13 mm) long, densely white-felted. Lightly woolly flowering stems rise 2–6 in (5–15 cm) above the basal leaves, each carrying a dense head 1/2–1 1/4 in (13–30 mm) in diameter. These are quite showy. Outer calyx segments are lobed or heart-shaped at the base; the inner ones are spatulate. *Flower:* Whitish, pink, or soft yellow.

Distribution. Open slopes and flats; Pinyon-juniper Woodland to Alpine Zone, 6,000–13,000 ft (1,829–3,963 m).

Var. *nivale* (Canby) Jones. Fell-field Buckwheat. An extremely compact form of the species with leaves 1/4 in (6 mm) long or less, making dense mats. Stems may be less than 1/2 in (13 mm) high and the heads as small as 1/4 in (6 mm) in diameter. However, there are intermediates between the two varieties. *Flower:* White to rose red.

Distribution. Open places, commonly near or above timberline; Pinyon-juniper Woodland to Alpine Zone, 8,500–13,400 ft (2,591–4,085 m).

Eriogonum panamintense Morton var. *panamintense*. **Panamint Buckwheat.** A dull gray perennial with a spreading, somewhat woody root crown. Its stems begin branching fairly low and are commonly incurved above. They are 6–15 in (15–36 cm) high. Basal leaves are broadly elliptic or ovate, white-felted on both sides, 1/2–1 1/2 in (1.3–4 cm) long, on slender petioles about twice the length of the blade. Lesser leaves occur at the forks of the branches. Single involucres are scattered along the branches and in the forks. Calyx segments are broad above, tapering to a narrow base. *Flower:* White, shading to tan at the base, usually tinged pink.

Distribution. Rocky places; Pinyon-juniper Woodland, 6,500–9,500 ft (1,982–2,896).

Var. *mensicola* (Stokes) Reveal. Plain Panamint Buckwheat. This variety is less robust than var. *panamintense* and lacks leaves at the forks. Its basal leaves are round and usually smaller, and the flowers are smaller also. *Flower:* Whitish, tinged pink.

Distribution. Same as for var. *panamintense*. The two varieties commonly occur together.

Eriogonum pusillum Torr. & Gray. **Yellow Turbans.** An annual, 3–12 in (7.7–30 cm) high. The smaller plants are very dainty, with the first branches about midway and the ultimate branches fine and threadlike. With more moisture there may be several stems from the base, with the lower stems and branches sturdy and commonly somewhat inflated. Leaves are all basal, round, 1/4–3/4 in (6–20 mm) long, on petioles up to twice the length of the blade, densely white-felted beneath, less so above. Involucres are broadly turbinate, five-lobed, and finely glandular hairy, on fine peduncles 1/4–3/4 in (6–20 mm) long. Calyx segments differ, with the outer ones broadly obovate and the inner ones narrowly spatulate. They are lightly glandular on the central and lower portions. *Flower:* Yellow.

Distribution.   Sandy places on the lower slopes and flats; Desert Scrub, below 6,500 ft (1,982 m).

Eriogonum rosense A. Nels. & Kennedy. **Limestone Yellow-heads.**   (Plate 6.163) A perennial that forms loose, greenish gray mats, its leaves tufted on branches of the root crown. Leaves are obovate, 1/4–1/2 in (6–13 mm) long, densely white-felted below, less so above. Naked flowering stems rise 1/2–4 in (1.3–10 cm) high from the tufts of leaves. Involucres are crowded in terminal heads about 1/2 in (13 mm) across. Calyx segments are similar, all obovate. *Flower:* Bright yellow, aging reddish.

Distribution.   Open Alpine Fell-fields on limestone; White Mountains; Subalpine and Alpine zones, 10,000–12,500 ft (3,049–3,811 m).

Eriogonum rupinum Reveal. **Limber Pine Buckwheat.**   (Plate 6.164) A gray perennial, 6–20 in (1.5–5 dm) high, with stems rising from clumps of erect leaves. Leaf blades are oblong to obovate-elliptic, 3/4–1 1/2 in (2–3.8 cm) long, on petioles 1–2 1/2 in (2.5–6.1 cm) long. They are white-felted below, less so above, often rose-tinged. The inflorescence is showy throughout the upper part of the plant. Populations are somewhat variable. Those in the White Mountains seem to branch at narrower angles than those in the Inyo Mountains. Involucres are tubular campanulate, hug the stems, and are in the nodes. Calyx segments are broadly oblong. At its best this species is a beautiful study in rose and gray. *Flower:* Cream color or pink, aging rose-pink.

Distribution.   Uncommon; with sagebrush or scattered Limber Pine on noncalcareous soils; Pinyon-juniper Woodland and Subalpine Zone, 7,400–9,700 ft (2,256–2,957 m).

Eriogonum umbellatum Torr. var. *umbellatum.* **Sulphur Flower.**   (Plate 6.165) A shrubby perennial, commonly scraggly, 8–24 in (20–60 cm) high. Leaves are elliptic to ovate, 3/8–3/4 in (1–2 cm) long, greenish above, gray underneath. Flowering stems are usually 3–8 in (7.7–20 cm) long, topped by an umbel with rays mostly less than 1 in (2.5 cm) long, rarely up to 2 in (5 cm). Small, leaflike bracts are at the base of the umbel. Involucres have reflexed lobes as long as the tubular portion. Individual flowers are larger than in most buckwheats and far showier. They narrow below to a short, stemlike base. *Flower:* Yellow, becoming reddish tinged with age.

Distribution.   Common, usually on noncalcareous soils; Pinyon-juniper Woodland and Subalpine Zone, 7,000–10,200 ft (2,134–3,110 m).

Var. *chlorothamnus* Reveal. Narrow-leaved Sulphur Flower.   This plant is far more slender than var. *umbellatum* and has narrower leaves. Rays of the umbel are longer and more slender, commonly with small bracts midway. *Flower:* Yellow.

Distribution.   On granitic or volcanic rock or soil; Desert Scrub and Pinyon-juniper Woodland, 6,000–9,000 ft (1,829–2,744 m).

Var. *devestivum* Reveal. Pale Umbelled Buckwheat.   (Var. *dicrocephalum* Gand., var. *subaridum* Stokes)Leaves ovate, thinly woolly below. *Flower:* Whitish to cream color, tinged rose-pink.

Distribution.   Infrequent; Pinyon-juniper Woodland and Subalpine Zone, 9,000–10,000 ft (2,744–3,049 m).

Var. *versicolor* Stokes. Varicolored Buckwheat.   A low, matted perennial, less than 6 in (15 cm) high, with leaves broadly elliptic to round, less than 1/2 in (13 mm) long. Flowering stems are 1–6 in (2.5–15 cm) long. Umbels have short rays; some are compact and headlike. *Flower:* Whitish or cream color, becoming pink tinged, with prominent green midrib that quickly turns rose red.

Distribution.   Calcareous soils; common in the Bristlecone Pine Forests; Pinyon-juniper Woodland and Subalpine Zone, 7,500–11,000 ft (2,287–3,354 m).

Eriogonum wrightii Torr. var. *subscaposum* Watson. **Wright Buckwheat.**   (Plate 6.166) A woody, mat-forming perennial with narrowly branching flowering stems, 3–12 in (7.7–30 cm) high. Leaves are elliptic, 1/4–1/2 in (6–13 mm) long, densely white-felted. They are loosely to densely crowded, forming pale gray mats from which numerous stems rise. Involucres are angular-tubular, 1/8 in (3 mm) long, hugging the branches. Calyx segments are broadest in the upper portion. Flowers are numerous enough to make an attractive display. *Flower:* Pink or whitish.

Distribution.   Rocky slopes and flats, locally abundant; Pinyon-juniper Woodland and Subalpine Zone, 7,000–11,200 ft (2,134–3,415 m).

Oxyria digyna (L.) Hill. **Mountain Sorrel.**   (Plate 6.167) A tender perennial with acid juice. Leaves are tufted on the root crown. The blades are round kidney-shaped, mostly 1/2–1 in (13–25 mm) wide, on slender petioles up to several inches long. Naked flowering stems are 2–10 in (5–24 cm) tall, with the inflorescence crowded on the upper portion. There are no petals, and the minute flowers are relatively inconspicuous, but the broadly winged fruit becomes reddish tinged and attractive. *Flower:* Green or reddish.

Distribution.   Uncommon; sheltered places at the bases of boulders; White Mountains; Alpine Zone, 11,500–13,300 ft (3,506–4,055 m).

Oxytheca dendroidea Nutt. **Fine Oxytheca.** A very dainty annual, 4–16 in (1–4 dm) high, with branches spreading to make a rounded crown. Its leaves, tufted at the base, are narrowly elliptic or lanceolate, less than 1 in (2.5 cm) long, thinly hairy on the surface. Involucres are minute and four-lobed, each lobe spine-tipped. Calyx segments are finely hairy. The entire plant is so dainty that it cannot be appreciated without a hand lens. *Flower:* White or pink.

Distribution. Uncommon; sandy or gravelly places; Desert Scrub and Pinyon-juniper Woodland, 4,500–8,600 ft (1,372–2,622 m).

Oxytheca perfoliata Torr. & Gray. **Saucer Plant.** (Plate 6.168) An annual 2–10 in (5–25 cm) high. The main stem branches just above the base, and well-developed plants continue to branch repeatedly. The leaves, in a basal rosette, are broadest near the rounded apex, gradually tapering to short petioles, 1/2–1 1/2 in (13–38 mm) long in all. United bracts at each node form saucer-shaped disks about 3/4 in broad. This is the conspicuous feature of the plant. (It is unrelated to the tender Miner's Lettuce in the Purslane Family.) The seldom-noticed minute flowers are situated in the center of the "saucers." The entire plant may be reddish tinged and turns rosy brown when dry. *Flower:* White.

Distribution. Dry places; low elevations in Desert Scrub, to 6,500 ft (1,982 m).

Rumex crispus L. **Curly Dock.** A coarse perennial, 16–48 in (4–12 dm) high. Lower leaves are lanceolate to oblong-lanceolate, 4–12 in (1–3 dm) long, with wavy edges. Upper leaves are reduced. The inflorescence is a dense panicle, 4–20 in (1–50 dm) long. Flowers are inconspicuous but the fruit becomes showy. Seeds are enclosed by three "valves," which are enlarged sepals, each with a hardened callosity on the back. The plant is commonly tinged with red. *Flower:* Green.

Distribution. A common weed; Desert Scrub, usually below 6,000 ft (1,829 m).

Rumex paucifolius Nutt. ssp. *paucifolius*. **Mountain Dock.** (Plate 6.169) A perennial with few stems, 6–28 in (1.5–7 dm) high. Basal leaves are broadly lanceolate, 16–40 in (4–10 dm) long, narrowed to a petiole of equal length. The inflorescence is a dense panicle. The flowers, which may either be perfect or have the sexual parts in separate flowers on different plants, are minute. Valves of the fruit are heart-shaped, finely veined, and lacking callosities. *Flower:* Reddish.

Distribution. Moist meadows; Pinyon-juniper Woodland to Alpine Zone, 9,000–11,700 ft (2,744–3,567 m).

Ssp. *gracilescens* (Rech. f.) Rech. f. **Alpine Dock.** Stems numerous, less than 8 in (2 dm) high. Basal leaves are linear to linear lanceolate.
   Distribution. Very common in seasonally moist places; Subalpine and Alpine zones, 9,800–13,500 ft (2,988–4,116 m).

PORTULACACEAE (Purselane Family)

Represented here by small, relatively succulent herbs, from tender annuals to hardy perennials. All but one species have only two sepals and very small flowers; Bitterroot is the exception.

Calyptridium parryi Gray var. *nevadense* (J.T. Howell) Munz. Nevada Sandcress. (Plate 6.170) An annual with stems flat on the ground, radiating from the center, mostly 2–5 in (5–12 cm) long. The entire plant may be rose red. Leaves are teardrop-shaped, narrowing to a petiole longer than the blade, 3/8–1 1/4 in (1–3 cm) in all. They are mostly basal, but there are a few on the stems. Flowers are in short, scorpioid spikes, terminal and along the stems. The two sepals are tissue-margined and rose tinged, becoming quite enlarged, to about 1/8 in (3 mm) long. The outer one is broadly fan-shaped. There are four tissue-thin petals, shorter than the sepals. They unite to form a cap over the capsule as it matures. The seed capsules protrude above the sepals but are less than twice as long. Seeds are shining black. *Flower:* Petals white but inconspicuous. In general, the inflorescence is rose tinged.

Distribution. Limited, in dry places; Pinyon-juniper Woodland, 7,000–8,500 ft (2,134–2,591 m).

Calyptridium umbellatum Torr. Greene var. *caudiciferum* (Gray) Jepson. Pussy Paws. (Plate 6.171) A small perennial with slender stems, mostly 1–3 in (2.5–7.7 cm) long, but generally shorter at high elevations. As with *C. parryi,* stems radiate from the center and are flat on the ground, but this plant is far more compact. It has a branching, commonly woody root crown. The leaves, again much like *C. parryi,* are tufted at the ends of root branches. The inflorescence is a dense, terminal head, 1/2 in (13 mm), more or less, in diameter. Each flower has two broad, tissue-margined sepals up to 1/4 in (6 mm) long, and four shorter petals. The sepals are commonly tinged pink to rose or lavender, making the heads colorful and attractive. *Flower:* Petals white, inconspicuous.

Distribution. Common in open places; Subalpine and Alpine zones, up to 14,100 ft (4,299 m).

Claytonia parviflora (Douglas ex. Hook.) Torr. Miner's Lettuce. (*Montia perfoliata* [Donn] forma *parviflora* Douglas ex. Hook.) (Plate 6.172) A tender annual, mostly 2–6 in (5–15 cm) high, with leaves and stems rising from the base. Leaves are linear to oblanceolate, narrowing to a petiole longer than the blade. A characteristic of this plant is its fused leaves or bracts, which form a disk 1/2–1 in broad. These are high on the stems, just below the flower clusters. There are two sepals and several petals, which are less than 1/4 in (6 mm) long. The foliage attracts more attention than the flowers. *Flower:* White.

Distribution. Uncommon in shaded, somewhat moist places; Desert Scrub and Pinyon-juniper Woodland, below 7,000 ft (2,134 m).

Lewisia pygmaea (Gray) ssp. *pygmaea* B.L. Robins. Brooch Lewisia, Dwarf Lewisia.   A small perennial with stems partly underground, tufted on a thick root. Leaves are linear, 1–3 in (2.5–7.7 cm) long, spreading outward from the center. Each stem carries a pair of small bracts and one to three flowers. There are two rounded sepals, edged with pale glands, and about six petals ¼ in (6 mm) long. Well-developed plants are compact, with the flowers set in the rosette of leaves like jewels in a brooch. *Flower:* White or pinkish.

Distribution.   Moist, gravelly places; Alpine Fell-fields in the White Mountains; Alpine Zone, 11,900–14,100 ft (3,628–4,299 m).

Note: Ssp. *glandulosa* (Rydb.) Ferris is similar but has dark, stemmed glands on the edges of the sepals. Flowers and distribution are the same.

Lewisia rediviva Pursh var. *minor* (Rydb.) Munz. Bitterroot.   (Plate 6.173) No stems or leaves are evident on the little perennial when in bloom. Its tuft of linear leaves has dried and disappeared by the time flowers appear. The stems are only ½–1 in (13–25 mm) long and are jointed near the top. Thus, when the flower is mature, it drops intact, along with that part of the stem above the joint. Flowers are large, about 1 in (2.5 cm) across, with numerous petals slightly longer than the similar sepals. *Flower:* Waxy white or pinkish.

Distribution.   Limited, on open slopes; mostly in Pinyon-juniper Woodland, 7,000–9,400 ft (2,134–2,866 m).

Montia chamissoi (Ledeb.) Greene. Toad Lily.   (Plate 6.174) A tender perennial with long, slender runners, its leafy stems ½–6 in (1.3–15 cm) long. The leaves are opposite, oblong spatulate, and extremely variable in size. Flowers are mostly in loose, terminal clusters. Their petals are only about ¼ in (6 mm) long, but they show up well for such a small plant. *Flower:* White.

Distribution.   Wet meadows and streamlets; Pinyon-juniper Woodland to Alpine Zone, 7,000–11,600 ft (2,134–3,537 m).

PRIMULACEAE (Primrose Family)

A family with few representatives in desert country, but two species occur at high elevations in this range.

Androsace septentrionalis L. var. *subumbellata* A. Nels. Alpine Androsace. (Plate 6.175) It is worth a search to find this little miniature, which is far smaller than its name. Its numerous branched or simple, threadlike stems are mostly ¼–1 in (6–25 mm) long, rising from a dense tuft of minute leaves. The flowers are five-parted, the calyx lobes lanceolate, and the short-tubed corolla hardly showing above them. The stems and calyx are commonly reddish. *Flower:* White or pink.

Distribution.   Rocky places, Alpine Fell-fields; White Mountains; Alpine Zone, 11,000–14,100 ft (3,354–4,299 m).

Dodecatheon redolens (Hall) H.J. Thompson. Shooting Star.   (Plate 6.176) A lightly glandular perennial, 10–20 in (25–50 cm) tall. Leaves are erect, linear oblanceolate, tapering to their petioles, 6–14 in (15–35 cm) long in all. Flowers are in terminal clusters on naked stems. They are five-parted and about 1 1/4 in (3 cm) long. Petals are broadly elliptic, flaring back, and the five stamens protrude like a beak. *Flower:* Yellow at the base with petals lavender to magenta.

Distribution.   Damp meadows and streamsides; Subalpine and Alpine zones, 9,500–11,800 ft (2,896–3,598 m).

RANUNCULACEAE (Buttercup Family)

A large family that includes some unusual flower forms. Petals may be lacking or inconspicuous, and the sepals are commonly colored and showy. Stamens are usually numerous. In the genus *Ranunculus,* the sepals are commonly petal-like, in addition to the petals, and a prominent head of achenes occupies the center of the flower.

Aconitum columbianum Nutt. Monkshood.   (Plate 6.177) An erect, leafy perennial, 2–4 ft (6–12 dm) tall. Leaves are thin, deeply three-lobed and again divided and toothed, 2–5 in (5–12 cm) long and broad, somewhat reduced upward. Flowers are in terminal spikes, with some smaller ones at the nodes. The plant can be confused with the tall larkspur of similar habitats. Their leaves are similar, but their flowers are quite different in form. Monkshood has five showy, irregular flower parts known as sepals. The upper one forms a hood, the distinguishing feature of this species. A pair of broad sepals is directly under the hood, and a pair of lesser ones lies below. Two specialized petals under the hood go unnoticed. The entire flower is about 1 in (2.5 cm) long. *Flower:* Calyx parts deep blue-purple, petals whitish.

Distribution.   Cool, moist meadows and streamsides, commonly in willows; White Mountains; Pinyon-juniper Woodland and Subalpine Zone, 7,500–9,000 ft (2,287–2,744 m).

Aquilegia formosa Fisch. Red Columbine.   (Plate 6.178) An erect perennial, 18–36 in (0.5–1 m) tall. Leaves are twice divided, the leaflets broad or wedge-shaped at the base and with rounded teeth above. The flowers are on terminal branches, nodding when in bloom. They are unusual in form; the sepals flare out like petals, about 1/2 in (13 mm) long, and the petals are spurs topped by a short, erect, blunt lamina, about 1 in (2.5 cm) long in all. A cluster of yellow stamens protrudes conspicuously. This is considered one of the most beautiful of our mountain flowers. *Flower:* Calyces and petals red, except for yellow at the apex of the lamina.

Distribution.   Limited, along streams; White Mountains; Desert Scrub to Subalpine Zone, 5,000–10,000 ft (1,524–3,049 m).

Aquilegia shockleyi Eastwood. Mojave Columbine.   (Plate 6.179) A perennial so similar to *A. formosa* that it may be difficult to determine the difference. The sepals tend to be a little broader and the spurs slightly shorter. The leaves are three times divided, and the leaflets are smaller and slightly paler underneath. *Flower:* Same as *A. formosa.*

Distribution.   Moist or wet places, commonly at springs or seepage areas; can tolerate some alkali; Desert Scrub to Subalpine Zone, 4,900–9,800 ft (1,494–2,988 m).

Clematis ligusticifolia **Nutt. var.** *brevifolia* **Nutt. Virgin's Bower.**   (Plate 6.180) A perennial vine with branches 4–15 ft (1.3–5 m) long that climbs over bushes and up trees. Leaves have five to seven ovate leaflets, rounded or heart-shaped at the base and shallowly toothed above. Flowers are clustered toward the ends of the branches. There are four or five petal-like sepals, 1/4–1/2 in (6–13 mm) long, but no petals, and numerous stamens. When mature each seed has a feathery "tail" 1/2–1 in (13–25 mm) long. These are abundant enough to give an impressive mass effect, like silvery clouds over the riparian growth. *Flower:* Sepals creamy to greenish white.

Distribution.   Common at springs and along streams; Desert Scrub and Pinyon-juniper Woodland, 4,500–9,200 ft (1,372–2,805 m).

Delphinium parishii **Gray. Desert Larkspur.**   (Plate 6.181) A perennial with erect stems 6–24 in (1.5–6 dm) tall. Leaves are mostly basal but may dry and be gone by blooming time. They are triangular in outline, deeply cut into wedge-shaped to linear divisions, 1–3 in (2.5–7.7 cm) broad, on petioles 1 in (2.5 cm) to several inches long. Flowers are in a terminal spike on the upper part of the stem. They are about 3/4 in (2 cm) long, irregular in form, with the upper of the five sepals prolonged into a spur. The others are ovate and somewhat hairy. Two upper petals are whitish, and two lower ones are colored like the sepals and are also hairy. *Flower:* Sepals and lower petals sky blue.

Distribution.   Dry places, widespread; Desert Scrub and Pinyon-juniper Woodland, 3,500–7,800 ft (1,067–2,378 m).

Delphinium polycladon **Eastwood. Willow Larkspur.**   (Plate 6.182) A perennial with erect stems 6–30 in (1.5–7.3 dm) high. Leaves mostly basal, rounded in outline, and deeply divided, 1–3 in (2.5–7.7 cm) wide. The branching inflorescence is comparatively few-flowered. Flowers are much the same in form as those of the desert larkspur but not quite as open, about 1 in (2.5 cm) long. *Flower:* Dark blue or deep blue-purple.

Distribution.   Uncommon in wet meadows and along streams; White Mountains; Pinyon-juniper Woodland and Subalpine Zone, 8,500–11,500 ft (2,591–3,506 m).

Ranunculus andersonii **Gray. Pink Ranunculus.**   (Plate 6.183) A low perennial 4–8 in (1–2 dm) high. Leaves are in tufts, the blades about 1 in (2.5 cm) across, divided into narrow lobes, on petioles 1–3 in (2.5–7.7 cm) long that join the root below the ground surface. Naked stems carry one or two flowers 1 in (2.5 cm) broad.

The five broadly rounded petals exceed the ovate sepals. *Flower:* Petals rose-pink to pale pink, sepals reddish.

Distribution.   Uncommon, dry rocky places; mostly in Pinyon-juniper Woodland, 6,500–7,500 ft (1,982–2,287 m).

Ranunculus cymbalaria Pursh var. *saximontanus* Fernald. **Desert Buttercup.**   A perennial with running stems rooting at the nodes. Leaf blades are ovate with straight or heart-shaped bases, ¹/₂–1 in (13–25 mm) long, on petioles 1–4 in (2.5–10 cm) long. Flowers are on slender, often branching stems 2–10 in (5–25 cm) high. Sepals are quickly shed, leaving ³/₈ in (1 cm) petals at the base of an elongated head. *Flower:* Yellow.

Distribution.   Common and widespread in moist or wet places; can tolerate some alkali; Desert Scrub to Subalpine Zone, 4,000–10,500 ft (1,220–3,201 m).

Ranunculus eschscholtzii Schlecht. var. *oxynotus* (Gray) Jepson. **Snow Buttercup.** (Plate 6.184) A small perennial 2–6 in (5–15 cm) high from a branching rootstock clothed with persistent leaf stems. Leaves are roundish in outline, deeply lobed, ¹/₂–1 in (13–25 mm) broad, mostly basal with some linear-lobed leaves on stems. Flowers are ³/₄–1 in (2–2.5 cm) broad, with five sepals. This is a showy buttercup that appears near the borders of melting snowbanks. *Flower:* Bright yellow.

Distribution.   Gravelly places, moist from melting snow; Alpine Fell-fields in the White Mountains; Alpine Zone, 11,400–14,000 ft (3,475–4,258 m).

Ranunculus glaberrimus Hook. var. *ellipticus* (Greene) Greene. **Large-headed Buttercup.**   A perennial with prostrate or ascending stems 2–6 in (5–15 cm) long, not stoleniferous. Basal leaf blades are elliptic, narrowing to slender petioles 1–3 in (2.5–7.7 cm) long. Stems are leafy also, but these leaves lack petioles. The five petals are obovate and exceed the sepals. The akene head is globose and unusually large, ³/₈–³/₄ in (1–2 cm) in diameter, and is finely hairy. *Flower:* Yellow.

Distribution.   Uncommon, springs and moist meadows; White Mountains; Alpine Zone, 11,600 ft (3,537 m).

Thalictrum alpinum L. **Dwarf Meadow-rue.**   A perennial 2–10 in (0.5–2.4 dm) high with basal leaves and naked stems. The few leaves are divided into fan-shaped leaflets, thick and strongly veined, with margins turned under, dull green in color. The flowers are nodding, are minute, and lack petals, but have protruding stamens. This is an unusual, though not showy, species. *Flower:* Green.

Distribution.   Uncommon, moist meadows and springs fed by snowbanks; White Mountains; Alpine Zone, 10,500–12,000 ft (3,201–3,658 m).

Thalictrum sparsiflorum Turcz. **Few-flowered Meadow-rue.**   A perennial 1–4 ft (3–12 dm) high, leafy throughout. The green leaves are divided and strongly resemble those of columbine. The flowers of this species are nodding and similar to those of *T. alpinum*. The hanging stamens might be compared to tiny tassels. There is a difference between the leaves of the two species, and this one is much leafier. *Flower:* Green.

Distribution.   Cool, moist, or boggy places; White Mountains; Pinyon-juniper Woodland and Subalpine Zone, 8,000–10,000 ft (2,439–3,049 m).

ROSACEAE (Rose Family)

A large family including many shrubs. Flowers usually have five sepals and petals that are located at the edge of a short flower tube. Commonly there are bractlets somewhat smaller than the sepals and alternating between them. Flowers in many species have numerous stamens and pistils tufted in the center. The fruit may be a dry, podlike follicle, an achene that is hard and single-seeded, a dry or fleshy stone-fruit, or a small apple-like fruit.

Amelanchier pallida **Greene. Service Berry.**   A deciduous shrub, 3–8 ft (1–2.6 m) tall, with reddish to gray bark. The leaves, $1/2$–$1 1/2$ in (13–38 mm) long, are round-ovate, the upper half toothed, slightly paler on the underside. Flowers are in clusters, more or less throughout the shrub. Sepals are persistent, but the narrowly obovate petals, about $1/2$ in (13 mm) long, readily fall. The three or four styles are free almost to the base in this species. The fruit is round, reddish, fleshy, and edible, $1/4$ in (6 mm) in diameter. *Flower:* White.

Distribution.   Uncommon, Pinyon-juniper Woodland, 7,500–8,500 ft (2,287–2,591 m).

Cercocarpus intricatus **Watson. Little-leaf Mahogany.** (Plate 6.185)   An intricately branched evergreen shrub, 2–5 ft (0.6–1.6 m) high. The leaves are so tightly inrolled that they resemble grains of wheat, most $1/4$–$3/8$ in (6–10 mm) long. Flowers lack petals and are inconspicuous, but each has an achene with a feathery tail $1/2$ in (13 mm) or more long. The shrubs are dark green compared to other vegetation. *Flower:* Yellow-green.

Distribution.   Limited; restricted to specific calcareous geologic formations; Desert Scrub to Subalpine Zone, 5,000–10,000 ft (1,524–3,049 m).

Cercocarpus ledifolius **Nutt. Mountain Mahogany.** (Plate 6.186)   A sturdy, evergreen shrub or small tree, up to 20 ft (6.6 m) high. Leaves are about 1 in (2.5 cm) long, elliptic, and leathery with a hard surface. Flowers lack petals but are abundant enough to show up. Each flower produces a single achene (rarely two), which has a silvery tail 2–3 in (5–8 cm) long. These give the entire shrub a silvery appearance in late summer. *Flower:* Yellowish green from the stamens.

Distribution.   Locally common on dry slopes; Pinyon-juniper Woodland and Subalpine Zone, 7,000–10,500 ft (2,134–3,201 m).

Chamaebatiaria millefolium (Torr.) Maxim. **Fern Bush, Desert Sweet.** (Plate 6.187) An aromatic, evergreen shrub, 1½–5 ft (0.5–1.6 m) high. The leaves are finely divided, fernlike, 1–2 in (2.5–5 cm) long. The flowers, in heavily glandular, leafy panicles, are fairly large and attractive, up to ½ in (13 mm) across. The rounded petals exceed the sepals, and numerous stamens are clustered in the center. *Flower:* White.

Distribution.   Widespread on dry slopes; Pinyon-juniper Woodland and Subalpine Zone, 6,900–10,700 ft (2,104–3,262 m).

Coleogyne ramosissima Torr. **Blackbrush.**   (Plate 6.188) An intricately branched, deciduous shrub, 1–4 ft (0.3–1.3 m) high, with spinescent branches. Leaves are narrow, only about ¼ in (6 mm) long, in tiny bundles on the branchlets. The flowers, ¼ in (6 mm) long, are scattered along the branches. They lack petals, but the four sepals are yellowish inside. The shrub commonly occurs in pure stands, dark gray on the landscape. *Flower:* Sepals dull yellowish inside, gray-green outside.

Distribution.   Dry slopes and flats; Desert Scrub, below 6,000 ft (1,829 m).

Cowania mexicana D. Don var. *stansburiana* (Torr.) Jepson. **Cliff Rose.**   (Plate 6.189) An evergreen shrub, 2–8 ft (0.6–2.6 m) tall, the older branches with shreddy bark. Leaves are green, glandular, ovate in outline, ¼–½ in (6–13 mm) long, divided into five narrow segments that have the edges rolled under. Flowers are well distributed and showy, ½–1 in (13–25 mm) across. The broad petals much exceed the sepals. Each flower produces striate achenes, usually five, with feathery tails up to 1½ in (38 mm) long. *Flower:* Creamy white.

Distribution.   Dry canyons in limestone areas of the southern White Mountains and southward, especially on the east side of the White-Inyo Range; Desert Scrub and Pinyon-juniper Woodland, 4,700–8,200 ft (1,433–2,500 m).

Var. *dubia* **Bdg.**   A shrub with much smaller flowers. These usually produce only two achenes with short, hairy — not feathery — tails. This shrub is considered by some to be a hybrid between *Purshia tridentata* (Pursh) DC. and *C. mexicana.* *Flower:* Creamy white.

Distribution.   Rare in limestone areas; known on east side of Inyo Mountains; Desert Scrub, 4,600–4,800 ft (1,402–1,463 m).

Geum macrophyllum Willd. **Big-leaf Avens.**   An erect bristly-hairy perennial, 1–3 ft (0.3–1 m) high. The large basal leaves have a large, lobed terminal leaflet, along with pairs of lesser leaflets below it. The leaf, including the petiole, is 3–10 in (7.7–24 cm) long. There are also a few deeply divided leaves above the base. Flowers are in small, terminal cymes. They are about ⅜ in (1 cm) across. The fruit is a spherical head of achenes with elongated, hooked styles, the whole about ½ in (13 mm) in diameter. *Flower:* Petals yellow.

Distribution. Uncommon; cool, moist meadows and streamsides; White Mountains; Pinyon-juniper Woodland, 7,000–9,500 ft (2,134–2,896 m).

Holodiscus dumosus (Nutt.) Heller var. *glabrescens* (Greene) C.L. Hitchc. **Cream Bush.** *(Holodiscus microphyllus* Rydb.)   (Plate 6.190) A spreading or sprawling shrub, 1–4 ft (0.3–1.3 m) high. Leaves are less than $5/8$ in (1.6 cm) long, prominently veined, fanlike, the lower half wedge-shaped and the upper part rounded and toothed. They are green above and somewhat silvery below. Flowers are in numerous terminal spikes or simple panicles, 1–2 1/2 in (2.5–6.4 cm) long. Individual flowers are small, about 1/8 in (3 mm) broad, and showy only in their mass effect. Like most small flowers, they are beautiful in detail under a hand lens. *Flower:* White or pinkish.

Distribution. Cliffs and rocky places; Pinyon-juniper Woodland and Subalpine Zone, 6,900–10,500 ft (2,104–3,506 m).

Horkelia hispidula Rydb. **White Mountain Horkelia.**   An erect, hairy perennial herb, 4–10 in (10–24 cm) high. Leaves are finely divided with 6 to 12 pairs of leaflets, similar to those of the genus *Ivesia.* Those in a basal tuft are 2–6 in (5–15 cm) long; the few on the stem are reduced. Flowers are in a crowded terminal cluster. They are deeply cup-shaped, $3/16$ in (5 mm) broad, and the tiny, obovate petals relatively inconspicuous. There are 10 stamens with broadened filaments. *Flower:* Petals white.

Distribution. Uncommon; limestone slopes and outcrops; White Mountains; Subalpine Zone, 9,000–11,000 ft (2,744–3,354 m).

Ivesia lycopodioides Gray ssp. *scandularis* (Rydb.) Keck. **White Mountain Ivesia.** (Plate 6.191) A low perennial with a very thick, branching root. The leaves, 1/2–2 in (13–50 mm) long, have little or no petioles and are tufted on the root branches, so the plant forms a dense, green mound. Leaves are vermiform, wormlike, so small and dense are their parts, and somewhat hairy in this subspecies. The inflorescence is a dense cluster, about 1/2 in (13 mm) broad, terminal on a wiry stem, 1–3 in (2.5–8 cm) high. Flowers have minute bractlets, sepals, and petals, and eight or more pistils. *Flower:* Petals yellow.

Distribution. Moist, rocky or gravelly places; White Mountains; Subalpine and Alpine zones, 11,000–13,500 ft (3,354–4,116 m).

Ivesia shockleyi Watson. **Shockley Ivesia.**   A perennial with a thick, woody, branching root, similar to that of *I. lycopodioides* ssp. *scandularis.* Leaves are tufted but looser than in that subspecies, 1–2 in (2.5–5 cm) long, with only 7 to 10 divided leaflets, their surfaces densely glandular hairy. Petioles are equal to the blades. The inflorescence is a loose terminal cluster on slender stems, 1–4 in (2.5–10 cm) high. Flowers have minute bractlets and triangular sepals about 1/8 in (3 mm) long, exceeding the petals. *Flower:* Petals pale yellow.

Distribution.   Limestone talus or gravel; White Mountains; Subalpine and Alpine zones, 9,500–13,000 ft (2,896–2,963 m).

Peraphyllum ramosissimum **Nutt. Squaw Apple.**   A deciduous shrub, 3–6 ft (1–2 m) high, with leaves clustered at the ends of spurlike branchlets. Blades are oblanceolate to elliptic, $1/2$–$1\,1/2$ in (1.3–4 cm) long, and green. Flowers are along the branches, the petals roundish, $1/4$ in (6 mm) long. The fruit, like a tiny apple, $3/8$ in (1 cm) in diameter, is greenish yellow, bitter, and not edible. *Flower:* Pale pink.

Distribution.   Uncommon; mostly in water courses; Desert Scrub and Pinyon-juniper Woodland, 5,500–8,000 ft (1,677–2,439 m).

Petrophytum caespitosum **Nutt. Rydb. Rock Spiraea.**   (Plate 6.192) Woody plantꜱ that seem to be molded over rocks, forming dense mats. The spatulate, gray-green leaves, $1/8$–$1/2$ in (3–13 mm) long, are in small rosettes, making an attractive groundcover. The inflorescence is a dense terminal spike, usually less than 1 in (2.5 cm) long on slender, erect stems $1\,1/2$–4 in (4–10 cm) long, commonly arranged around the outer rim of the mat. Flowers are minute and crowded. *Flower:* Whitish.

Distribution.   Limestone ledges or outcrops; Desert Scrub to Subalpine Zone, 5,700–10,000 ft (1,738–3,049 m).

Physocarpus alterans **(Jones) J.T. Howell. Ninebark.**   (Plate 6.193) A deciduous shrub, 1–4 ft (0.3–1.3 m) high, densely branched and with shreddy bark. It resembles a currant bush, and the leaves are much the same. Leaves are roundish, mostly three-lobed, toothed, $3/8$–$3/4$ in (1–2 cm) long, finely stellate pubescent. Flowers are $3/8$ in (1 cm) broad, the roundish petals hardly exceeding the triangular sepals. Numerous stamens ring the floral tube. Although the flowers are small, they are numerous enough to be showy. The fruit is a densely hairy, small, dry pod. *Flower:* White.

Distribution.   Uncommon; along limestone cliffs; Desert Scrub to Subalpine Zone, 5,600–10,000 ft (1,707–3,049 m).

Potentilla biennis **Greene. Green Cinquefoil.**   Green, soft hairy and somewhat glandular, trifoliate, leaves well distributed throughout the plant. The three leaflets are roundish or obovate, coarsely toothed, mostly $3/8$–$3/4$ in (1–2 cm) long. Flowers are clustered in terminal cymes. The blooms are small, the petals shorter than the sepals. This is a weedy type and not particularly attractive. *Flower:* Petals yellow.

Distribution.   Moist or gravelly places; Pinyon-juniper Woodland and Subalpine Zone, 7,000–10,000 ft (2,134–3,049 m).

Potentilla breweri **Watson. Brewer Cinquefoil.**   A perennial with erect or ascending stems, 5–15 in (12–36 cm) long. There are few leaves, and they are mostly basal. They are pinnate, with four to six pairs of leaflets divided almost to the base, and pale gray with a felted coat of white hairs. Flowers are $1/2$ in (13 mm) across, the petals broad, exceeding the sepals. *Flower:* Yellow.

Distribution.   High, open places; White Mountains; Subalpine and Alpine zones, 11,000–13,000 ft (3,354–3,963 m).

Potentilla fruticosa L.. **Shrubby Cinquefoil.**   (Plate 6.194) A much-branched, leafy shrub, 8–40 in (2–10 dm) high. Leaves are pinnate, most with five leaflets, green, with soft, silky hairs. Each leaflet is $1/4-3/4$ in (6–20 mm) long, elliptic or narrowly oblong, with edges rolled under. Flowers are $1/2-1$ in (13–25 mm) across, the petals much exceeding the sepals and bractlets. *Flower:* Yellow.

Distribution.   Uncommon; high meadows and moist places; White Mountains; Pinyon-juniper Woodland to Alpine Zone, 8,500–12,000 ft (2,591–3,658 m).

Potentilla gracilis Douglas var. *flabelliformis* Lehm. Nutt. **Alkali Cinquefoil.** *(Potentilla flabelliformis* Lehm.)   A perennial with slender stems, 12–24 in (3–6 dm) high. Leaves are mostly basal, dark green above and silky gray beneath. They are palmate, with five to seven leaflets radiating from a central point. Leaflets are $3/4-2$ in (2–5 cm) long, divided nearly to the midrib into linear, spreading segments. Flowers are in branching clusters. Petals are somewhat heart-shaped, less than $3/8$ in (1 cm) long, exceeding the triangular sepals and narrow bracts. *Flower:* Yellow.

Distribution.   Limited, in moist meadows, where it may tolerate some alkali; Desert Scrub and Pinyon-juniper Woodland, 4,500–8,300 ft (1,372–2,530 m).

Var *glabrata* **(Lehm.) C.L. Hitchc.** (Ssp. *nutallii* [Lehm.] Keck)   A plant so similar to var. *flabelliformis* that there may be no clear dividing line. Leaflets are not divided so deeply in the typical form, and there is less contrast in color between the upper and lower surfaces. Flowers are slightly larger. *Flower:* Yellow.
   Distribution.   Moist meadows and streamsides; Pinyon-juniper Woodland and Subalpine Zone, 7,000–10,200 ft (2,134–3,110 m).

Potentilla pectinisecta **Rydb. Silky Potentilla.**   Much like *P. gracilis* but leaflets are white-silky on both sides and the linear segments are evenly and closely arranged like teeth in a comb. *Flower:* Yellow.

Distribution.   Moist places; Desert Scrub to Subalpine Zone, 6,000–11,500 ft (1,829–3,506 m).

Potentilla pennsylvanica **L. var.** *strigosa* **Pursh. Pennsylvania Potentilla.**   A fairly leafy perennial with a short-branching root and stems 3–12 in high. Leaves are pinnate, $2 1/2$ in (6.4 cm) long, including petioles. Leaflets are $3/8-1$ in (1–2.5 cm) long, deeply cut into linear segments. They are hairy on both surfaces but are greenish above and whitish beneath. Flowers are in dense terminal clusters. Petals are roundish but no longer than the sepals, about $^3/_{16}$ in (5 mm), so they hardly show. *Flower:* Petals yellow.

Distribution.   Moist slopes and meadows; Subalpine and Alpine zones, 9,500–14,050 ft (2,896–4,283 m).

Potentilla pseudosericea **Rydb. Small Silky Potentilla.**   A small perennial with erect or ascending stems, 2–6 in (5–15 cm) long. Leaves are pinnate, similar to those of *P. gracilis* Douglas & Hook. (Cinquefoil), but smaller and silky-gray on both sides. Flowers are in terminal clusters. Petals are no longer than the sepals, $^3/_{16}$ in (5 mm), and are more or less cupped within them. *Flower:* Pale yellow.

Distribution.   Moist places on dolomite slopes; White Mountains; Subalpine and Alpine zones, 9,800–13,500 ft (2,988–4,116 m).

Potentilla saxosa **Lemmon. Rock Potentilla.**   (Plate 6.195) A tufted perennial with slender, leafy stems, 1–10 in (2.5–25 cm) long. Basal leaves are pinnate with 5- to 15-toothed leaflets, round or fan-shaped, up to $^1/_2$ in (13 mm) long, green on both sides. Flowers are sparse and minute, the petals and sepals about $^1/_8$ in (3 mm) long. It is an interesting if not a showy plant. *Flower:* Petals pale yellow.

Distribution.   Uncommon; tufted in crevices of granite boulders or cliffs; Desert Scrub to Subalpine Zone, 5,800–10,800 ft (1,768–3,293 m).

Prunus andersonii **Gray. Desert Peach.**   (Plate 6.196) A spreading, deciduous shrub, 2–6 ft (0.6–2 m) high, with rigid, spinescent branches. Leaves are green, obovate, tapering at the base to a short petiole, $^1/_2$–1 in (13–25 mm) long in all. They are clustered in bundles along the branches, or are single on new growth. The flowers, about $^1/_2$ in (13 mm) broad, resemble peach blossoms. The fruit is like a dry, small peach, about $^1/_2$ in (13 mm) long. *Flower:* Rose-pink.

Distribution.   Uncommon; on granitic rocks in dry canyons; 5,700–8,500 ft (1,738–2,591 m).

Prunus fasciculata **Torr. Gray. Desert Almond.**   (Plate 6.197) A deciduous shrub, 2–6 ft (0.6–2 m) high, with stiff branches, more slender than *P. andersonii*. Leaves are narrowly spatulate, $^1/_4$–$^1/_2$ in (6–12 mm) long, clustered in bundles on short, budlike growths along the branches. Flowers are rarely more than $^1/_4$ in (6 mm) in diameter. Fruit is like a small almond, about $^1/_2$ in (13 mm) long. *Flower:* White.

Distribution.   Common in canyons cut through limestone, mostly in narrows or along cliffs; Desert Scrub; 4,200–6,000 ft (1,280–1,829 m).

Purshia glandulosa **Curran. Desert Bitterbrush.**   (Plate 6.198) An olive-green evergreen shrub, 2–8 ft (0.6–2.6 m) high. Leaves are thick, very glandular, $^1/_4$–$^3/_8$ in (6–10 mm) long, divided into three lobes with the edges rolled under. Flowers are up to $^1/_2$ in (13 mm) wide. The calyx lobes are turned downward and the petals are spreading, $^1/_4$ in (6 mm) long, spatulate, abruptly narrowing toward the base. The fruit is an achene that narrows to the style, about $^3/_4$ in (2 cm) long in all. *Flower:* Creamy white.

Distribution.   Common on dry slopes; Desert Scrub to Subalpine Zone, 5,000–10,000 ft (1,524–3,049 m).

Purshia tridentata (Pursh) DC. Bitterbrush.   A widely branched shrub, 1–6 ft (0.3–2 m) high. Leaves are evergreen, wedge-shaped, three-lobed, finely woolly and greenish above, gray underneath, $^1/_4$–$^3/_4$ in (6–20 mm) long. Flowers are similar to *P. glandulosa,* but the achenes are slightly shorter and broader. *Flower:* Creamy white.

Distribution.   Common where precipitation is greater than on the desert slopes; Pinyon-juniper Woodland, 7,000–9,500 ft (2,134–2,896 m).

Rosa woodsii Lindl. var. *ultramontana* (Watson) Jepson. Wild Rose.   (Plate 6.199) A prickly shrub, 2–6 ft (0.6–2 m) high. Leaves are pinnate with five to seven oval leaflets, $^1/_2$–1$^1/_2$ in (13–38 mm) long, and toothed. Flowers are loosely clustered, the roses 1–1$^1/_2$ in (2.5–3.8 cm) broad. The fruit, known as a rose hip, is roundish and becomes bright red, topped by the persistent sepals. The shrubs make dense thickets in favorable places. *Flower:* Pink.

Distribution.   Common to abundant; wet places such as springs, seeps, and stream-sides; Desert Scrub to Subalpine Zone, 4,500–10,000 ft (1,372–3,049 m).

RUBIACEAE (Madder Family)

Galium is the only genus described here. Leaves in the species listed are four in a whorl, well spaced on the stems. Some species have male (staminate) and female (pistillate) flowers on different plants; others have perfect flowers. The corollas are very small, with four petals spreading or bell-shaped. There are no sepals. The fruit is roundish and consists of two carpels that separate when ripe; these are covered with spreading hairs as long as or longer than the body.

Galium hypotrichium ssp. *hypotrichium.* Limestone Bedstraw.   A low perennial with many stems 1–5 in (2.5–12 cm) long. The plant is grayish and velvety with exceedingly fine hairs. Leaves are about $^1/_4$ in (6 mm) long, ovate to roundish, with a pointed apex. Flowers are perfect and minute, the corolla petals spreading or slightly cupped. The fruit is $^1/_8$ in (3 mm) broad, including the yellowish or brownish hairs. *Flower:* Pink.

Distribution.   Uncommon; rocky places, apparently restricted to limestone; Desert Scrub to Alpine Zone, 6,000–12,500 ft (1,829–3,811 m).

Galium hypotrichium Gray ssp. *inyoense* Demster & Ehrend. Inyo Bedstraw.   A perennial with stems 4–10 in (10–24 cm) high from a somewhat woody base. Leaves, about ¼ in (6 mm) long, are broadly ovate to roundish, pointed at the apex, the surfaces harsh with short, stiff hairs. Flowers are clustered on short, slender branches on the upper part of the stems. They are about ³⁄₁₆ in (5 mm) broad, with spreading or cupped petals. The fruit is ⁵⁄₁₆ in (8 mm) across, including its shining, white hairs. It is more conspicuous than the flowers. *Flower:* Yellowish.

Distribution.   Uncommon; on granitic or volcanic rocks; Pinyon-juniper Woodland and Subalpine Zone, 7,000–9,800 ft (2,134–2,988 m).

Galium matthewsii Gray. **Matthews Bedstraw.**   A glabrous perennial with numerous slender, some with tangled stems, 6–16 in (15–40 cm) long, from a woody base. The leaves are small and sparse, so the plant may appear relatively leafless. Leaves are firm, somewhat shiny, lanceolate to elliptic, ⅛–³⁄₈ in (3–10 mm) long, lacking a hairy surface. The inflorescence is more open than in the other species, the minute flowers in loose clusters on the fine, spreading branches. Male and female flowers are on separate plants. The corolla has rare to numerous long hairs on the outside. Fruit is ⅛ in (3 mm) broad, including its soft, pale hairs. *Flower:* Pale greenish yellow or pinkish.

Distribution.   Dry, rocky places, commonly in narrow canyons; Desert Scrub and Pinyon-juniper Woodland, 4,400–7,000 ft (1,341–2,134 m).

Galium multiflorum Kellogg forma *multiflorum*. **Shining Bedstraw.**   A glabrous perennial with numerous stems, 2–12 in (5–30 cm) high, from a woody base. Leaves are shining, varying from minute to ½ in (13 mm) long, ovate or broadly elliptic. Male and female flowers are on different plants, clustered on short branches. Corollas are somewhat bell-shaped. Fruit is up to ³⁄₈ in (1 cm) broad, including its long, tawny or off-white hairs. *Flower:* Greenish to cream color.

Distribution.   Uncommon; rocky north- or east-facing slopes; Desert Scrub and Pinyon-juniper Woodland, 5,000–8,000 ft (1,524–2,439 m).

forma *hirsutum* Gray. **Canyon Bedstraw.**   Differs from forma *multiflorum* in being stiff-hairy throughout. The fruit is about ³⁄₁₆ in (5 mm) across, including its shorter, somewhat sparse hairs.
    Distribution.   Rocky places; Desert Scrub and Pinyon-juniper Woodland, 5,900–7,500 ft (1,799–2,287 m).

Galium stellatum Kellogg. **Shrubby Bedstraw.**   A truly shrubby species, deciduous, 8–40 in (2–10 dm) high, harsh throughout, with short, stiff hairs. Leaves are very small, lanceolate, and relatively crowded. Some vigorous twigs, though, have larger, less crowded leaves. Corollas are minute, with the male and female flowers on different plants. The fruit, too, is minute, about ¹⁄₁₆ in (3 mm) broad, including its spreading whitish hairs. *Flower:* Pale greenish yellow.

Distribution.   Uncommon; hot, dry canyons; east side of Inyo Mountains; Desert Scrub, below 5,000 ft (1,524 m).

RUTACEAE (Rue Family)

Thamnosma montana Torr. & Fremont. **Turpentine Broom.**   (Plate 6.200) A strong-scented, yellowish green, broomlike shrub 1–2 ft (3–6 dm) high. Leaves are oblanceolate, 1/4–1/2 in (6–13 mm) long, soon deciduous, leaving naked stems. Flowers are erect, 1/4–1/2 in (6–13 mm) long, with four petals. The fruit is a leathery, two-lobed capsule. *Flower:* Dark purple.

Distribution.   Dry slopes; east side of Inyo Mountains; Desert Scrub, below 5,500 ft (1,677 m).

SAXIFRAGACEAE (Saxifrage Family)

A family represented here by only a few genera, including some well-known shrubs. The flowers have long or short tubes, commonly united to the ovary. In species of *Ribes* (currants and gooseberries), the sepals form a tube topped by generous lobes and inconspicuous petals. The sepals are colored and petal-like. Stamens usually number 5 to 10.

Heuchera duranni Bacig. **Duran Alum Root.**   A finely glandular-hairy perennial with slender, wiry stems, 5–14 in (12–35 cm) high, from a heavy root crown. Leaves are roundish or kidney-shaped, averaging 1/2 in (13 mm) wide, with five to nine blunt lobes, on petioles 3/4–2 in (2–5 cm) long. The inflorescence is 1 1/2 to 3 in (4–7.7 cm) long, the flowers close along the stem. Each tiny flower, 1/8 in (3 mm) wide, is composed of a top-shaped flower tube crowned by five triangular sepals, barely exceeded by the narrow petals. *Flower:* Petals yellowish, sepals tinged pink.

Distribution.   Uncommon; rocky limestone slopes or flats; White Mountains; Desert Scrub to Alpine Zone, 6,000–12,200 ft (1,829–3,720 m).

Heuchera rubescens Torr. var. *pachypoda* (Greene) Rosendahl. **Alum Root.**   (Plate 6.201) A perennial with the same growth habit as *H. duranni*. The plant is less glandular and the leaves slightly larger. Leaf lobes are more irregular and less blunt, and hairs on the edges are large and coarse. The inflorescence is a panicle with flowers loosely clustered on fine, threadlike branches. The flower tube is top-shaped, with five oblong lobes one-third as long as the tube, whitish or rose tinged and tipped with green. Narrow petals exceed the sepals, the entire flower hardly 1/4 in (6 mm) long. *Flower:* Petals white.

Distribution.   Widespread; crevices of cliffs and sheltered, rocky places, mostly where some moisture trickles down; Desert Scrub to Subalpine Zone, 5,800–10,000 ft (1,768–3,049 m).

Jamesia americana Torr. & Gray var. *californica* (Small) Jepson. **Cliffbush.** (Plate 6.202) A deciduous, sparsely leafy shrub, 1 1/2–4 ft (0.5–1.3 m) high, the branches usually supported by rocks or cliffs. Leaf blades are oblong to roundish, 1/2–1 1/2 in (13–38 mm) long, the upper portion coarsely toothed, green above and gray with dense hairs below. Petioles are short. Flowers are in small, dense clusters, terminal on the branchlets. They are five-parted. The calyx is hairy with triangular lobes, and the larger petals are 1/4–3/8 in (6–10 mm) long. The fruit is a many-seeded capsule almost 1/2 in (13 mm) long. *Flower:* Rose-pink.

Distribution.   Uncommon; about rocks or cliffs; Pinyon-juniper Woodland and Subalpine Zone, 7,200–10,000 ft (2,195–3,049 m).

Philadelphus stramineus Rydb. **Littleleaf Mock Orange.** (*Philadelphus microphyllus* Gray ssp. *stramineus* [Rydb.] C.L. Hitchc.)   (Plate 6.203) A deciduous shrub, 3–6 ft (1–2 m) high, with opposite branches and leaves. The leaves are narrowly ovate, 3/8–1/2 in (10–13 mm) long, and coated with appressed white hairs, which give them a gray-green color. Flowers are solitary, or a few may be grouped at the ends of short branchlets. The ovary is almost completely inferior, essentially below the four sepals and petals. The latter are 1/4–3/8 in (6–10 cm) long, broad and spreading above the base. The fruit is a dry capsule, hemispherical in shape, with the triangular sepals persistent at the top. *Flower:* White.

Distribution.   Uncommon; cliffs and rocky places; Desert Scrub and Pinyon-juniper Woodland, 5,700–9,000 ft (1,738–2,744 m).

Ribes aureum Pursh var. *aureum.* **Golden Currant.**   A relatively tall, deciduous shrub, 3–8 ft (1–2.6 m) high, without spines. Branches are smooth, erect or ascending, and the foliage green. Leaf blades are 1/2–1 1/2 in (13–64 mm) broad, most strongly three-lobed with shallow lobes or teeth between, on short petioles. Flowers are clustered on short stems from the leaf nodes along the branches. They are long-tubed with an interior ovary. The tube, nearly 1/2 in (13 mm) long, is topped with five broad sepal lobes 3/16 in (5 mm) long and five lesser petals. The fruit is a yellow to red or black berry, 1/4 in (6 mm) in diameter. This is a most attractive *Ribes* species, with showy flowers and wandlike branches. *Flower:* Tube, sepals, and petals yellow.

Distribution.   Uncommon; moist places; Pinyon-juniper Woodland, 7,000–8,500 ft (2,134–2,591 m).

Ribes cereum Douglas. **Wax Currant.**   (Plate 6.204) A rigid, intricately branched deciduous shrub, 2–6 ft (5–15 cm) high, lacking spines. The foliage is green, somewhat sticky glandular, and heavily fragrant. Leaves are 1/2–1 1/4 in (13–30 mm) broad, finely toothed, obscurely three-lobed, fan-shaped, and glossy. The flowers, which are in clusters on short stems from the leaf nodes along the branches, resemble those of *R. aureum,* but the entire ovary, tube, and sepals are hardly 1/2 in (13 mm) long. The fruit is a shining red berry up to $1/2$ in (13 mm) in diameter. *Flower:* Whitish to pink.

Distribution.   Common; rocky slopes; Pinyon-juniper Woodland to Alpine Zone, 7,000–12,500 ft (2,134–3,811 m).

Ribes inerme Rydb. **Straggly Gooseberry.** *(Ribes divaricatum* Douglas var. *inerme* (Rydb.) McMinn)   A deciduous shrub, 2–5 ft (0.6–1.6 m) high, with spreading, commonly simple stems, most with one to three short spines at the nodes. Leaves are 1–2 in (2.5–5 cm) broad and deeply divided into three to five main lobes, which are again toothed or lobed, on very slender petioles $1/2$–$3/4$ in (13–20 mm) long. They are thin and green. Flowers are similar to the other species of *Ribes* in form but shorter, only about $1/4$ in long. The clusters are few-flowered. Berries are smooth, $1/4$–$3/8$ in (6–10 mm) in diameter, dark purple. *Flower:* Greenish or purplish.

Distribution.   Uncommon; moist, shaded places; Pinyon-juniper Woodland, 7,000–8,500 ft (2,134–2,591 m).

Ribes velutinum var. *glanduliferum.* **Plateau Gooseberry.**   (Plate 6.205) A rigidly branched, leafy shrub, $1 1/2$–6 ft (0.5–2 m) high, with a single long, slender spine at each node. Leaf blades are deeply divided into three to five lobes, which are blunt-toothed. They are green, $3/8$–$3/4$ in (1–2 cm) broad, on petioles longer than the blades. Flowers are similar to the other taxa in this genus but have a short tube topped with five sepal lobes and minute petals, the whole only about $1/8$ in (3 mm) long. Berries are dark purple, $1/4$ in (6 mm) in diameter, and densely glandular hairy. *Flower:* Yellowish to white.

Distribution.   Common; dry slopes; Desert Scrub to Subalpine Zone, 5,500–10,000 ft (1,677–3,049 m).

SCROPHULARIACEAE (Figwort or Snapdragon Family)

A large family, widely distributed. Flowers are mostly tubular, four- or five-lobed and two-lipped, colorful and showy. When the two lips are well defined, the upper one usually has two lobes or teeth and the lower one has three. Some have a palate on the lower lip, mostly hairy and ridged or raised to some degree, fairly closing the throat, as in a snapdragon. The fruit is a two-celled capsule.

Antirrhinum kingii Watson. **Least Snapdragon.**   (Plate 6.206) A dainty, erect annual, 4–24 in (1–6 dm) high. Leaves are usually narrowly linear, $1/4$–$1 1/4$ in (6–30 mm) long. The small flowers are at the leaf axils, all along the stems and branches, one at a node on short, threadlike pedicels. The short calyx is irregular, with one lobe larger than the other four, increasing in size to $1/4$ in (6 mm) when mature. The flowers, like miniature snapdragons, are $1/4$ in (6 mm) long. *Flower:* White with purple veins.

Distribution. Gravelly places or talus slopes; Creosote Bush Scrub to Pinyon-juniper Woodland, Desert Scrub, 4,200–6,000 ft (1,280–1,829 m).

Castilleja chromosa A. **Nels. Desert Paintbrush.** (Plate 6.207) A perennial with leafy stems, 6–14 in (15–35 cm) high. The plants are somewhat grayish with white hairs. The leaves, 1–2 in (2.5–5 cm) long, are narrow with one or two pairs of lateral segments. The inflorescence is a dense terminal cluster of brightly colored bracts and calyx lobes, fairly hiding the obscure corollas. The bracts have one to three rounded lateral segments, making a rather full "paintbrush." The tubular calyx is deeply cleft on either side, and each part has two rounded lobes, colored like the bracts. The corolla is also tubular, 3/4–1 1/4 in (2–3 cm) long, with a narrow upper lip (galea) about half its length. The lower lip is only a row of short, incurved, green teeth. *Flower:* Galea margins, calyx lobes, and bracts bright red.

Distribution. Common on dry slopes or canyon bottoms, with sagebrush or other shrubs; Desert Scrub and Pinyon-juniper Woodland, below 7,000 ft (2,134 m).

Castilleja linarieafolia **Benth. Long-leaved Paintbrush.** (Plate 6.208) A perennial from a somewhat woody root crown, the stems 12–40 in (3–10 dm) tall, often branched above. Leaves are narrowly linear, most 1–2 in long, the upper ones of some with narrow segments. The inflorescence is more elongated than in most *Castilleja* species, the flowers rarely well spaced. The tubular calyx is 3/4–1 in (2–2.5 cm) long and deeply cleft in front, allowing the corolla to curve outward. The corolla is up to 1 1/2 in (3.8 mm) long, with the galea half that length, and the lower lip consists of the typical incurved teeth. Bracts are sparse and very narrow. This is one of the taller paintbrushes. It is known by its very narrow leaves and well-exposed corolla. *Flower:* The galea is greenish to yellowish with thin, red margins, and the calyx and bracts are red.

Distribution. Limited populations in moist places; Desert Scrub and Pinyon-juniper Woodland, 4,000–9,500 ft (1,220–2,896 m).

Castilleja martinii **Abrams** var. *clokeyi* **(Penn.) N. Holmgren. Clokey Paintbrush.** (Plate 6.209) A perennial 6–20 in (15–50 cm) high. The plants are soft-hairy and glandular throughout. Leaves are 1/2–1 1/2 in (13–38 mm) long, somewhat wavy, with one or two pairs of linear, lateral segments. The usual appearance is of short, deeply divided leaves. Those on the lower stem are longer, sometimes simply linear and undivided. The inflorescence is dense, but the bracts are not as full and broad as those of species *chromosa;* some are quite narrow and hardly divided. The corolla is 1–1 1/2 in (2.5–3.8 cm) long, the galea about half its length. *Flower:* Galea margins and lobes of calyx and bracts red.

Distribution. Common on dry slopes; Pinyon-juniper Woodland and Subalpine Zone, 7,000–10,500 ft (2,134–3,201 m).

Castilleja miniata Douglas. Streamside Paintbrush.   (Plate 6.210) A perennial 10–30 in (24–73 cm) tall. Leaves are simple, lanceolate, 1–3 in (2.5–7.7 cm) long. Bracts are lanceolate, with one or two pairs of pointed segments. Calyx segments, too, are narrow and sharply tapered. The corolla is 1–1³/₄ in (2.5–4.5 cm) long, the galea less than half its length. *Flower:* Galea margins and lobes of calyx and bracts red or orange-red.

Distribution.   Wet meadows and streamsides; Pinyon-juniper Woodland and Subalpine Zone, 7,500–10,500 ft (2,287–3,201 m).

Castilleja minor (Gray). Alkali Paintbrush. *(Castilleja exilis)*   An annual 1–3 ft (0.3–1 m) tall. Leaves are 1–3 in (2.5–7.7 cm) long, lanceolate. The inflorescence is elongated, with flowers well separated along the stem. Bracts are leaflike, lanceolate, and colored above. The corolla is about ³/₄ in (2 cm) long, with the galea only ¹/₃ its length. *Flower:* Colored parts red or pink.

Distribution.   Uncommon; wet, common in alkaline places; Desert Scrub and Pinyon-juniper Woodland, 4,000–8,000 ft (1,220–2,439 m).

Castilleja nana Eastwood. Dwarf Paintbrush.   (Plate 6.211) A low perennial, 1¹/₂–10 in (13–24 cm) high, commonly branching at the base. The plants are soft-hairy throughout. Leaves are mostly less than 1 in (2.5 cm) long and narrow, those above with very narrow lateral segments. The foliage varies in color from pale gray to purplish. Bracts are three-lobed. The corolla is about ¹/₂ in (13 mm) long, including its very short galea. The lower lip is fairly large, about two-thirds the length of the galea. *Flower:* Colored parts mostly off-white to yellowish, or shades of dull pink to lavender.

Distribution.   Common and widespread; rocky places; Subalpine and Alpine zones, 9,500–14,250 ft (2,896–4,345 m).

Collinsia parviflora Douglas. Meadow Collinsia.   An annual with slender stems, 2–8 in (5–20 cm) high, with opposite leaves and branches. Leaves are remotely spaced, more or less oblong, ¹/₂–1 in (13–25 mm) long, except for the lowest pair, which are very small, round ones. Flowers issue from the leaf nodes on slender pedicels about ¹/₄ in (6 mm) long. The calyx, ¹/₈ in (3 mm) long, has five teeth about half its length, the whole enlarging in fruit. The irregular corolla, ³/₈ in (1 cm) long, is pouched at the base and two-lipped. The upper lip is broadly two-lobed and erect, and the lower lip, with three smaller lobes, projects horizontally. The lower branches of this plant are broadly spreading, the lowest commonly as long as the main stem. *Flower:* Blue with a white upper lip.

Distribution.   Uncommon; moist places bordering streams and meadows; Pinyon-juniper Woodland and Subalpine Zone, 7,000–10,500 ft (2,134–3,201 m).

Cordylanthus kingii Watson ssp. *helleri* (Ferris) Chuang & Heckard. **Heller Bird's-beak.** (*Cordylanthus helleri* [Ferris] Macbride)   A branching annual 2–12 in (5–30 cm) tall, glandular hairy throughout. The stems and foliage are usually purplish, but the soft hairs are white, giving the plant a frosty appearance. Leaves are mostly ½–1 in (13–25 mm) long, with very narrow, linear lobes. Flowers are in terminal clusters, resembling a paintbrush. The corolla is fairly hidden by bracts, which resemble the leaves, and the calyx is approximately the same length. It is ½–1¼ in (13–30 mm) long and the lips are about equal in length, but the lower lip is broader than the upper and pouched. *Flower:* Upper lip violet with a greenish yellow tip, lower lip purple.

Distribution.   Common and widespread; mostly in Pinyon-juniper Woodland but also in the Subalpine Zone, 6,500–10,400 ft (1,982–3,171 m).

Keckiella rothrockii (Gray) Straw. **Buckskin Keckiella.** (*Penstemon rothrockii* Gray) A low shrub, 1–2 ft (3–6 dm) high, with slender stems, sometimes broomlike, from a woody base. Leaves are opposite, ¼–¾ in (6–20 mm) long, ovate, with wavy edges. Flowers are at the upper nodes. The corolla is ½ in (13 mm) long, tubular, and conspicuously two-lipped. The upper lip is erect, and the lower has three reflexed lobes. Because of their small size and dull color, the flowers may go unnoticed. *Flower:* Dull brownish yellow, some tinged with pink or purple.

Distribution.   Limited; dry, rocky places; Pinyon-juniper Woodland, 6,500–9,500 ft (1,982–2,896 m).

Mimulus bigelovii (Gray) Gray var. *bigelovii.* **Bigelow Mimulus.**   (Plate 6.212) A small annual, 1–6 in (2.5–15 cm) high, with simple or broadly branching stems. Leaves are elliptic or obovate, ½–1¼ in (13–30 mm) long. Flowers are on very short pedicels clustered at the ends of branches and at the nodes. The calyx is ¼–⅜ in (6–10 mm) long, irregular with one longer side, with reddish ribs. The corolla is up to 1 in (2.5 cm) long, funnel-shaped, and two-lipped but with its rounded lobes nearly equal. It persists after withering. Anthers are included in the tube, so the corolla throat appears empty. *Flower:* Magenta, with two yellow patches on the palate.

Distribution.   Dry sandy or gravelly places; Desert Scrub, up to 6,000 ft (1,824 m).

Var. *cuspidatus* A. & V. Grant. Desert Mimulus. *(Mimulus spissus* A.L. Grant) Differs from var. *bigelovii* in having broadly obovate leaves that abruptly narrow to a pointed apex.
Distribution.   Common; gravelly places, especially on volcanic cinders; Desert Scrub and Pinyon-juniper Woodland, 4,500–7,500 ft (1,372–2,287 m).

Mimulus cardinalis Douglas. **Scarlet Mimulus.**   (Plate 6.213) A rhizomatous perennial, 10–30 in (24–73 cm) high. Leaves are opposite, broadly elliptic or ovate,

1–3 $1/2$ in (2.5–8 cm) long, clasping at the base, irregularly toothed. Flower pedicels are 1–4 in (2.5–10 cm) long. The tubular calyx is about half the length of the corolla, which is 1 $1/2$–2 in (4–5 cm) long. The upper lip is erect and arched, its lobes broad, and the lower lip spreads outward or downward. The corolla readily drops after blooming, leaving the long style protruding from the calyx. The flowers are large and handsome. *Flower:* Red.

Distribution.   Limited; wet places such as streambanks and springs; Desert Scrub and Pinyon-juniper Woodland, 5,000–7,000 ft (1,524–2,134 m).

Mimulus densus. **Elfin Mimulus.**   A small annual, 1–4 in (2.5–10 cm) high, with simple or branching stems, the smaller plants appearing tufted. The leaves, $3/8$–$3/4$ in (1–2 cm) long, are elliptic to oblanceolate and relatively inconspicuous. Flowers are in terminal clusters and at the nodes on very short pedicels. The corolla is funnelform, about $3/4$ in (2 cm) long, the flaring lips forming five nearly equal lobes. It persists after withering. The anthers show at the opening of the corolla throat. This feature helps distinguish it from *M. bigelovii,* which also has larger flowers and leaves. *Flower:* Yellow or magenta, each with contrasting dots and streaks. Both colors may appear in the same population.

Distribution.   Limited; dry slopes and flats; open places in the Pinyon-juniper Woodland and Subalpine Zone, 6,400–10,000 ft (1,951–3,049 m).

Mimulus guttatus Fisch. **Common Monkey-flower.**   (Plate 6.214) Annual or perennial rooting at the lower nodes, 2–24 in (0.5–6 dm) high. On larger plants the stems are stout and hollow, although tender; smaller forms have slender stems. The species is extremely variable, especially in leaf form and size. Leaves are opposite and commonly clasp the stem, but more commonly they are on petioles of various lengths. Leaf blades, $1/4$–3 in (0.6–7.7 cm) long, are usually ovate and commonly toothed. Flowers are on slender pedicels, $1/2$–1 $1/2$ in (13–38 mm) long. The calyx is bell-shaped, $1/4$–$1/2$ in (6–12 mm) long, enlarging in fruit, and the shorter, lower lobes curve around the seed capsule. Ribs are prominent, ending in five triangular teeth. The corolla is $3/8$–1 $3/8$ in (1–3.5 cm) long, distinctly two-lipped. Margins of the upper lip are reflexed, and lobes of the lower lip are longer and spreading. The hairy palate is raised, closing the throat. The corolla readily drops off after blooming. Regardless of variations in this species, the flowers are bright and showy. *Flower:* Yellow, the palate red-dotted.

Distribution.   Common and widespread; wet places, springs, seeps, and stream-sides; Desert Scrub and Pinyon-juniper Woodland, 4,000–9,500 ft (1,220–2,896 m).

Mimulus primuloides Benth. var. *primuloides.* **Meadow Mimulus.** (*Mimulus primuloides* Benth. var. *pilosellus* [Greene] Smiley) (Plate 6.215) A very small perennial, stonoliferous and rhizomatous, with naked, flowering stems $3/4$–3 in (2–7.7

cm) high. Leaves are obovate, mostly 1/4– 1/2 in (6–12 mm) long, all basal, commonly in rosettes. They are sparsely to densely hairy on the upper surface, usually sparklings with drops of moisture. The plants are mat forming. Each slender stem bears a single flower. The calyx is tubular, 1/4 in (6 mm) long, with reddish ribs. The corolla, 1/2–3/4 in (13–20 mm) long, is funnelform, obscurely two-lipped, with five spreading lobes. These small plants make cheery splashes of color in wet places. *Flower:* Yellow with reddish dots on the palate.

Distribution.   Wet meadows, springs, and streamlets; Desert Scrub to Alpine Zone, 6,000–12,500 ft (1,829–3,811 m).

Mimulus suksdorfii Gray. **Suksdorf Miniature Mimulus.**   (Plate 6.216) A tiny, usually tufted annual, 1/2–3 in (1.3–8 cm) high, with simple or much-branched stems. The narrow leaves rarely reach 1/2 in (13 mm) in length. There are blooms throughout, as if this tiny mimulus were determined to see how many flowers it could crowd onto one plant. Pedicels are 1/8– 1/4 in (3–6 mm) long. The corolla is narrowly funnelform, about 1/2 in (13 mm) long, the lips barely apparent, with five nearly equal lobes. The corolla readily drops after blooming. *Flower:* Yellow with red lines or dots on the palate.

Distribution.   Relatively common; moist sandy or gravelly places; Pinyon-juniper Woodland to Alpine Zone, 8,000–12,300 ft (2,439–3,750 m).

Mohavea breviflora Coville. **Small Mohavea, Desert Snapdragon.**   (Plate 6.217) A small annual, 1–6 in (2.5–15 cm) high, broadly branching when moisture lasts. The herbage is yellowish green, glandular-puberulent. Leaves are 1/2–1 1/2 in (13– 38 mm) long, ovate, the upper leaves narrowing to a slender tip. Flowers are on short pedicels at the axils. The calyx of five distinct segments is about 3/8 in (1 cm) long. The snapdragon-like corolla is 1/2–3/4 in (13–20 mm) long, the upper lip turned upward and the lower lip reflexed, the palate closing the throat. *Flower:* Lemon yellow with some red streaks and dots.

Distribution.   Uncommon; dry sandy or gravelly places; southern Inyo Mountains; Desert Scrub, up to 4,100 ft (1,250 m).

Pedicularis attollens Gray. **Little Elephant Heads.**   (Plate 6.218) A perennial with simple stems 4–14 in (10–35 cm) high. The leaves are divided, fernlike, 2 1/2–4 in (6.4–10 cm) long. They are mostly basal. The inflorescence is a rather dense spike, 1–2 1/2 in (2.5–6.4 cm) long. The corolla is about 1/4 in (6 mm) long; the upper lip is curved, hoodlike, with an upturned "trunk," and the lower lip, three-lobed, projects outward. The common name comes from its resemblance to an elephant's head. *Flower:* White or pink with violet lines.

Distribution.   Uncommon; wet meadows and streamsides; White Mountains; Alpine Zone, 11,000–12,500 ft (3,354–3,811 m).

Penstemon floridus Brandegee var. *floridus*. Rose Penstemon.   (Plate 6.219) A sturdy perennial with wandlike stems 18–40 in (4.5–10 dm) tall and blue-green, glaucous foliage. Leaves are large, thickish, and toothed, with those on the stem opposite, 2–4 in (5–10 cm) long. The inflorescence, on the upper part of the stem, is up to 20 in (5 dm) long. Flowers are as much as 1 1/4 in (3 cm) long, the calyx only about 1/8 in (3 mm), and the corolla large and plump. The short corolla tube abruptly expands underneath to a full throat about 1/2 in (13 mm) broad, constricting again toward the mouth. The upper lip has two short lobes and is usually exceeded by the three-lobed lower lip so that the opening angles upward. The entire plant is handsome with attractive leaves and tall stems of showy flowers. *Flower:* Rose-pink.

Distribution.   Dry slopes and washes; Desert Scrub and Pinyon-juniper Woodland, 5,500–8,500 ft (1,677–2,591 m).

Var. *austinii* (Eastwood) Keck. Austin Penstemon.   Differs from var. *floridus* in having a narrower corolla, gradually expanding to about half as wide as in the former variety, and a perpendicular opening at the mouth. *Flower:* Rose red to magenta.

Distribution.   Slightly drier places than for var. *floridus*; mostly in the Inyo Mountains; Desert Scrub and Pinyon-juniper Woodland, 6,000–8,500 ft (1,829–2,591 m).

Penstemon fruticiformis Coville. Desert Mountain Penstemon.   (Plate 6.220) A shrubby perennial, 12–24 in (3–6 dm) high, with pale green, glaucous foliage. Leaves are narrowly linear lanceolate, 3/4–2 1/2 in (2–6 cm) long. Flowering stems spread from the upper nodes. The calyx is 1/4 in (6 mm) long and the corolla 1–1 1/4 in (2.5–3 cm) long, broadly expanding to a throat nearly 1/2 in (13 mm) wide. The wide mouth shows a hairy palate and curved stamens in the throat. This plant forms a rounded bush, fairly covered with flowers in season. *Flower:* White or flesh-colored with pale lavender lobes and lavender lines.

Distribution.   Dry, rocky canyons or slopes; Inyo Mountains; Desert Scrub and Pinyon-juniper Woodland, 4,000–7,000 ft (1,220–2,134 m).

Penstemon heterodoxus Gray. Whorlflower Penstemon.   (Plate 6.221) A perennial with stems rising 2–8 in (5–20 cm) long from a spreading rootstock. Basal leaves are well developed, forming mats, and there are several pairs of leaves on each stem. They are narrowly spatulate to obovate, narrowing to a petiole, 1/2–2 in (13–50 mm) long in all. Flowers are in one to four dense whorls on the stem. The corolla is tubular, 3/8–5/8 in (1–1.6 cm) long, the two lips small-lobed. *Flower:* Deep blue-purple.

Distribution.   Common; moist slopes and meadow borders; Subalpine and Alpine zones, 9,500–12,800 ft. (2,896–3,902 m).

Penstemon monoensis Heller. Mono Penstemon.   (Plate 6.222) A sturdy perennial, 4–14 in (1–3.5 dm) high, with leafy stems and a thick inflorescence. Leaves are oblong-ovate to lanceolate, 1 1/2–4 1/2 in (3.8–11 cm) long. Flowers are in four to six dense whorls, rather closely spaced. The corolla is tubular funnelform, about 3/4 in (2 cm) long, two-lipped with spreading lobes. The inflorescence is finely glandular hairy, giving it a somewhat frosty appearance. *Flower:* Wine red to reddish pink with a pale palate.

Distribution.   Uncommon; dry places on limestone; Desert Scrub, 4,000–6,500 ft (1,220–1,982 m).

Penstemon patens (Jones) N. Holmgren. Owens Valley Penstemon.   *(Penstemon confusus patens* [Jones] Keck)   (Plate 6.223) A perennial, 2 1/2–12 in (6–30 cm) high, with leaves mostly basal. Blades are thickish, 1–2 in (2.5–5 cm) long, oblanceolate, the basal ones tapering to a petiole. Flowers are in loose whorls, spreading on pedicels of varying lengths. The corolla is about 5/8 in (1.6 cm) long, tubular funnelform, two-lipped, with lobes spreading outward, the lower ones reflexed. *Flower:* Violet to magenta lobes with paler throat.

Distribution.   Rocky slopes; Pinyon-juniper Woodland, 6,500–9,500 ft (1,982–2,896 m).

Penstemon rostiflorus Kellogg. Scarlet Penstemon.   *(Penstemon bridgesii* Gray)   (Plate 6.224) A perennial with many stems, 4–24 in (1–6 dm) tall, from a somewhat shrubby base, forming large clumps. Leaves are 3/4–2 1/2 in (2–6.4 cm) long, those below oblanceolate, becoming lanceolate to linear above. The inflorescence is long and showy, the flowers in loose whorls, most turning to one side of the stem. The corolla is about 1 in (2.5 cm) long, tubular, and gradually expanding. The upper lip protrudes beaklike, and the three-lobed lower lip is reflexed. *Flower:* Scarlet to orange-red.

Distribution.   Common and widespread; dry slopes and roadsides; Pinyon-juniper Woodland and Subalpine Zone, 6,500–10,000 ft (1,982–3,049 m).

Penstemon scapoides Keck. Westgard Penstemon.   (Plate 6.225) A perennial with slender stems, 6–18 in (15–45 cm) high, from a dense basal mat. Leaves, mostly on the mat, are velvety-hairy, often folded. The blades are ovate to nearly round, 1/4–3/4 in (6–20 mm) long, on longer petioles. The inflorescence is sparse, the flowers few on elongated pedicels. The corolla is tubular, gradually widening, its two lips gently flaring, and with two ridges in the throat. This is the daintiest of the penstemons and is easily recognized here by its leafy mat. *Flower:* Pale lavender to deeper shades.

Distribution.   Common in the Pinyon-juniper Woodland, less common above; Pinyon-juniper Woodland and Subalpine Zone, 6,500–10,300 ft (1,982–3,140 m).

Penstemon speciosus Douglass. Showy Penstemon.   (Plate 6.226) A short-lived perennial, 2–18 in (5–45 cm) high. Leaves are basal and on the stems. Those below are obovate, narrowing to a petiole, and the stem leaves gradually become narrower and clasping. The inflorescence is relatively dense and the flowers large and showy. The corolla is 1–1 1/2 in (2.5–3.8 cm) long, with the short tube expanding to a gradually broadening throat up to 3/8 in (1 cm) wide. The lips spread, exposing the open throat. The height is variable, but even when the stems are very short the flowers are showy. *Flower:* Blue-violet throat with blue lobes.

Distribution.   Common and widespread; Pinyon-juniper Woodland and Subalpine Zone, 6,400–10,500 ft (1,951–3,201 m).

Scrophularia desertorum (Munz) R.J. Shaw. Desert Figwort. *(Scrophularia californica* Cham. & Schlecht. var. *desertorum* Munz)   (Plate 6.227) A leafy, branching perennial with robust stems 2–5 ft (0.6–1.6 m) tall. Leaf blades are 1–4 in (2.5–10 cm) long, ovate to triangular, irregularly toothed, on petioles 1/2–1 1/2 in (13–38 mm) long. Flowers are numerous but small, in terminal panicles up to 18 in (45 cm) long. The corolla is barely 1/4 in (6 mm) long, bicolored, with a globular tube constricted at the throat. The two-lobed upper lip is erect, as are the short side lobes of the lower lip; the middle lobe of the lower lip is reflexed. *Flower:* Brownish red or maroon above, and cream with a pinkish tinge below.

Distribution.   Somewhat moist places in dry areas, usually in canyons; Desert Scrub and Pinyon-juniper Woodland, 4,800–9,500 ft (1,463–2,896 m).

Verbascum thapsus L. Wooly Mullein.   (Plate 6.228) A stout biennial with stems 1–5 ft (0.3–1.6 m) tall. A rosette of woolly leaves appears the first year and the robust, flowering stem the next. The basal leaves are 3–20 in (7.7–48 cm) long, obovate to oblanceolate, thick, and densely woolly. Those on the stem are progressively smaller, their bases attached to the stem, winglike, below the nodes. Flowers are in a dense terminal spike. Calyx lobes are lanceolate, about 3/8 in (1 cm) long, densely woolly also. The corolla is about 1 in (2.5 cm) broad, with five spreading lobes. This species was introduced from Eurasia and has rapidly become a weedy invader. *Flower:* Yellow.

Distribution.   Roadsides and waste places; Desert Scrub, 4,000–6,000 ft (1,219–1,829 m).

Veronica americana (Raf.) Schw. American Brooklime.   A rhizomatous perennial, 2–14 in (5–35 cm) tall, rooting at the lower nodes. The opposite leaves are 1/2–1 1/4 in (13–30 mm) long, ovate to lanceolate, with short petioles. Racemes issue from the upper nodes. The corolla is up to 3/8 in (1 cm) across, irregularly four-lobed. The seed capsule is broader than long, scarcely notched. *Flower:* Bright blue with white center.

Distribution.   In streamlets and wet stream borders; Pinyon-juniper Woodland and Subalpine Zone, 6,000–10,200 ft (1,829–3,110 m).

Veronica peregrina L. ssp. *xalapensis* (HBK.) Penn. Purslane Speedwell.   An annual 2–8 in (5–20 cm) high, the leafy stems simple or branched at the base. Leaves are 3/16–3/4 in (5–20 mm) long, linear or narrowly oblong. Flowers are so small that they are inconspicuous. Seed capsules are heart-shaped. *Flower:* White.

Distribution.   Damp meadows or other wet places; Pinyon-juniper Woodland, 7,000–9,000 ft (2,134–2,744 m).

SOLANACEAE (Nightshade Family)

This is a large family but one not well represented in this range. Flowers listed here are tubular, flaring at right angles at the mouth. Other species with open, bell-shaped flowers occur in the range, but only rarely.

Lycium andersonii Gray. Desert Tomato.   (Plate 6.229) A spiny shrub, 1–4 ft (0.3–1.3 m) high. Leaves are plump and fleshy but narrow, linear or oblanceolate, tapering toward the base, 1/4–3/4 in (6–20 mm) long. The flowers are numerous but somewhat drab and obscure. The short calyx has five triangular lobes. The corolla is a slender tube about 3/8 in (1 cm) long, gently broadening, with five short, flaring lobes. More showy are the fleshy red fruits, which resemble miniature tomatoes, about 1/4 in (6 mm) in diameter. *Flower:* Whitish to dull yellowish tube with bluish lavender lobes.

Distribution.   Common on dry, rocky slopes; Desert Scrub, below 6,000 ft (1,829 m).

Lycium cooperi Gray. Peach-thorn.   (Plate 6.230) A sturdy, very leafy, somewhat spiny shrub, 3–6 ft (1–2 m) high. Its leaves are 1/2–1 1/4 in (13–30 mm) long, obovate, tapered to a short petiole. They are clustered on knobby growths along the branches. The calyx has a broad tube 1/4 in (6 mm) long, topped by five lanceolate lobes about half as long. The corolla tube is about 1/2 in (13 mm) long and has five triangular lobes. The distinctive fruit is dry, greenish, constricted above the middle, and somewhat notched at the sides. *Flower:* Greenish white, some with lavender veins.

Distribution.   Mostly along cliffs at its lower elevations, but on open flats in its upper range; Desert Scrub to Pinyon-juniper Woodland, 4,000–7,000 ft (1,220–7,000 m).

Nicotiana attenuata Torr. Coyote Tobacco.   A somewhat glandular-hairy annual, 12–20 in (3–5 dm) tall. The leaf blades are ovate-lanceolate, 1 1/2–3 in (4–8 cm) long, on petioles up to 1 in long. They are mostly basal, but there are some narrower leaves on the stems. Flowers are in loose racemes. The calyx is 1/4 in (6 mm) long, enlarging in fruit. The corolla is narrowly tubular, 1–1⅜ in (2.5–3.5 cm) long, with a narrow limb. *Flower:* White to greenish white.

Distribution.   Limited, along roadways and disturbed places; Desert Scrub and Pinyon-juniper Woodland, 5,000–9,000 ft (1,524–2,744 m).

Nicotiana trigonophylla **Dunal. Desert Tobacco.**   (Plate 6.231) An ill-smelling glandular-hairy perennial, 1–2 ft (3–6 dm) high, leafy throughout. Leaves on the stem are ovate to obovate, sometimes narrowing and then flaring just above the base, usually clasping. The lower ones are about 3 in (1 dm) long, gradually reduced upward. The calyx, including its five lanceolate teeth, is ⅜ in (1 cm) long. The comparatively broad corolla tube is ¾ in (2 cm) long, with a broad limb. *Flower:* Creamy white to greenish.

Distribution.   Common in lower canyons, usually on or about cliffs; Inyo Mountains; Desert Scrub, up to 4,600 ft (1,402 m).

TAMARICACEAE (Tamarisk Family)

Introduced shrubs or trees with scale-like leaves. Minute flowers in plumelike inflorescence. A shrubby species is the common one in the region.

Tamarix ramosissima **L. Salt Cedar.**   (Plate 6.232) A deciduous shrub, usually with many stems up to 10 ft (2.6 m) high. The bark is dull reddish brown. Twigs and branchlets are covered with fine, scale-like leaves. Flowers are in numerous, slender racemes, mostly ⅜–3 in (1.5–7 cm) long, ⅛ in (3–4 mm) wide, spreading on terminal branchlets. The minute individual flowers are five-petaled. Seeds have terminal tufts of fine hairs. This very aggressive, weedy shrub is extremely water-greedy. It has become a serious threat to springs and seeps, especially those low in the White-Inyo Range facing Owens Valley, where there is a widespread infestation. The windblown seeds readily become established in any moist spot. *Flower:* Pale to deep pink.

Distribution.   Springs and seeps or other moist places; Desert Scrub, up to 6,000 ft (1,829 m).

URTICACEAE (Nettle Family)

Urtica dioica **L. ssp. *gracilis* (Ait.) Seland var. *holosericea* (Nutt.) C.L. Hitchcock. Stinging Nettle.** *(Urtica holosericea* Nutt.)   A perennial from spreading rootstocks, the stout stems 3–6 ft (1–2 m) tall. Leaves are opposite, lanceolate to ovate, coarsely toothed, 2–5 in (5–12 cm) long. The herbage has scattered bristles as well as fine hairs. Any contact with the skin causes painful stinging, which may persist for some time. The plants are monoecious. Flower clusters are located at the nodes on the upper part of the stems. The male clusters are almost as long as the leaves, the female clusters short and dense. *Flower:* Inconspicuous.

Distribution.   Common to abundant in riparian areas; Desert Scrub and Pinyon-juniper Woodland, up to 9,000 ft (2,744 m).

VIOLACEAE (Violet Family)

Viola nephrophylla **Greene. Northern Bog Violet.**   A stemless perennial with leaves rising 2–6 in (5–15 cm) high. The blades are mostly heart-shaped, shallowly scalloped, 3/4–2 1/2 in (2–6.4 cm) wide. Naked peduncles, 2 1/2 to 6 in (6.4–15 cm) long, bear single flowers. Petals are 1/2–3/4 in (13–20 mm) long. The flower is a typical violet in form with a short, blunt spur. *Flower:* Deep blue-violet with white bearding and dark veins.

Distribution.   Uncommon; cool, wet places; Desert Scrub and Pinyon-juniper Woodland, 5,500–9,100 ft (1,677–2,774 m).

VISCACEAE (Mistletoe Family)

Small shrubby plants parasitic on trees, obtaining nourishment from a single attachment to the tree. Leaves are opposite, some in the form of scales. Flowers are minute, the staminate (male) and pistillate (female) parts on different plants. The fruit is a fleshy berry.

Arceuthobium divaricatum **Engelm. Pinyon Dwarf Mistletoe.**   Very small, olive-green to brownish plants with fragile stems several inches long. Leaves are reduced to scales. The greenish berries are compressed, spindle-shaped, about 1/8 in (3 mm) long. *Host:* Pinyon Pine (*Pinus monophylla*). *Flower:* Inconspicuous.

Distribution.   Locally common in certain areas in the Inyo Mountains, rarely in the White Mountains; Pinyon-juniper Woodland, 6,500–7,800 ft (1,982–2,378 m).

Phoradendron bolleanum **Seem. Eichler ssp.** *densum* **Torr. Wiens. Leafy Juniper Mistletoe.**   (Plate 6.233) Woody plants with branching, brittle stems up to 10 in (24 cm) long. They form dense, rounded growths up to the size of a basketball. Leaves are thick, oblanceolate, 3/8–3/4 in (1–2 cm) long. The straw-colored berries are roundish, 3/8 in (1 cm) in diameter. *Host:* Utah Juniper (*Juniperus osteosperma* [Torr.] Little). *Flower:* Inconspicuous.

Distribution.   Limited; mostly in the Inyo Mountains; Pinyon-juniper Woodland, 5,700–7,500 ft (1,738–2,287 m).

Phoradendron juniperinum **Engelm. ssp.** *juniperinum.* **Juniper Mistletoe.**   Woody plants with branching stems up to about 6 in (15 cm) long. Although the growth may be dense, it is not as large and bulky as *P. bolleanum* ssp. *densum.* Leaves are reduced to minute, united scales. The fruit, straw- or wine-colored, is roundish and slightly smaller than the preceding variety. *Host:* Utah Juniper (*Juniperus osteosperma*). *Flower:* Inconspicuous.

Distribution.   Limited; mostly in the Inyo Mountains; Pinyon-juniper Woodland, 6,500 ft (1,982–2,470 m).

Note: Rare hybridization occurs between these two species of *Phoradendron* where they occur together in the Inyo Mountains. The hybrid more resembles the species *juniperinum* but has linear to oblanceolate leaves ³/₁₆–³/₈ in (0.5–1 cm) long. No blooms or fruit have been found on them.

ZYGOPHYLLACEAE (Caltrop Family)

Larrea tridentata L. Creosote Bush.   (Plate 6.234) An evergreen shrub with an open growth form, 3–12 ft (1–4 m) high. Leaves are opposite with two olive-green, obliquely ovate leaflets ¼–³/₈ in (6–10 mm) long, attached at the base. Flowers are five-parted with round-ovate, hairy sepals ¼ in (6 mm) long. The petals, ³/₈ in (1 cm) long, are twisted sideways like the vanes of a windmill. The fruit is covered with white hairs like a furry ball, about ³/₁₆ in (5 mm) long. This shrub, with green leaves and wandlike branches, is an attractive contrast to the predominantly gray, intricately branched desert shrubs. It is the dominant shrub in the Mohave Desert. *Flower:* Yellow.

Distribution.   Dominant on the lower slopes of the southern Inyo Mountains; Desert Scrub, below 5,400 ft.

WILDFLOWER KEY BY COLOR AND FORM

White, Cream, or Green	Yellow, Orange, or Brown	Red, Pink, or Rose	Blue to Purple
A. Leaves Parallel-veined, Flower Parts in Threes or Sixes (Except for Some Grasses)			
AGAVACEAE	LILIACEAE	LILIACEAE	IRIDACEAE
Yucca brevifolia	*Calochortus kennedyi*	*Allium atrorubens* var. *inyonis*	*Iris missouriensis*
Joshua Tree	Desert Mariposa	Inyo Onion	Wild Iris
LILICEAE	*Fritillaria atropurpurea*	*Allium bisceptrum*	*Sisyrinchium idahoense*
Allium atrorubens var. *inyonis*	Wood Brownies,	Aspen Onion	Idaho Blue-eyed Grass,
Inyo Onion	Chocolate Lily		Blue-eyed Grass
Calochortus bruneaunis	ORCHIDACEAE		
Sego Lily	*Epipactis gigantea*		
Smilacina stellata	Desert Orchid,		
Starflower	Stream Orchid		
Zigadenus paniculatus			
Sand-corn			
ORCHIDACEAE			
Plantanthera sparsiflora			
Green Canyon Orchid			
POACEAE			
Festuca minutiflora			
Small-flowered fescue			
Hilaria jamesii			
James Galleta			
Koeleria macrantha			
Junegrass			

WILDFLOWER KEY BY COLOR AND FORM

White, Cream, or Green	Yellow, Orange, or Brown	Red, Pink, or Rose	Blue to Purple
Leymus cinereus Ashy Wildrye, Great Basin Wildrye			
Leymus tritocoides Creeping Wildrye			
Melica stricta Nodding Melic, Rock Melic			
Muhlenbergia richardsonis Mat Muhly			
Oryzopsis hymenoides Indian Ricegrass			
Poa secunda Varied Bluegrass			
Sitanion hystrix Squirreltail			
Sitanion jubatum Big Squirreltail			
Sporobolus airoides Alkali Sacaton			
Stipa comata Needle and Thread			
Stipa speciosa Desert Needlegrass			
See also Cyperaceae and Junaceae			

WILDFLOWER KEY BY COLOR AND FORM

White, Cream, or Green	Yellow, Orange, or Brown	Red, Pink, or Rose	Blue to Purple
		All Following Species Have Leaves Net-veined	
		B. Four Petals or Petal-like Sepals, Separate to Base	
BRASSICACEAE	**BRASSICACEAE**	**BRASSICACEAE**	**BRASSICACEAE**
Arabis holboelli	*Draba oligosperma*	*Arabis holboelli*	*Arabis inyoensis*
Holboell Rock Cress	White Mountain Draba	Holboell Rock Cress	Inyo Rock Cress
Caulanthus glaucus	*Lesquerella kingii* ssp. *kingii*	*Arabis inyoensis*	*Arabis lemmonii* var. *lemmonii*
Limestone Caulanthus,	Beadpod	Inyo Rock Cress	Lemmon Rock Cress
Cliff cabbage	*Stanleya elata*	*Arabis lemmonii* var. *lemmonii*	*Caulanthus crassicaulis*
	Princeś Plume	Lemmon Rock Cress	Woolly Caulanthus
Caulostramina jaegeri			
Cliff Dweller	*Stanleya pinnata* var. *pinnata*	**ONAGRACEAE**	*Streptanthus cordatus*
	Desert Plume	*Camissonia boothii* ssp.	Pinyon Streptanthus
Draba californica		*inyoensis*	
White-flowered Draba	*Stanleya pinnata* var. *inyoensis*	Inyo Primrose	**ONAGRACEAE**
	Inyo Desert Plume		*Epilobium angustifolium*
Lepidium fremontii		*Epilobium ciliatum* ssp. *ciliatum*	ssp. *circumvagum*
Bush Peppergrass,	*Streptanthus cordatus*	Slender Epilobium	Fireweed
Desert Alyssum	Pinyon Streptanthus (calyx)		
		POLYGONACEAE	*Epilobium ciliatum* ssp. *ciliatum*
CROSSOSOMATACEAE	**ONAGRACEAE**	*Oxyria digyna*	Slender Epilobium
Forsellesia nevadensis	*Camissonia walkeri* ssp. *tortilis*	Mountain Sorrel (sepals)	
Nevada Forsellesia	Rock Primrose,		**PORTULACACEAE**
		PORTULACACEAE	*Calyptridium umbellatum* var.
CUSCUTACEAE	Limestone Primrose	*Calyptridium parryi* var. *nevadense*	*caudiciferum*
Cuscuta salina var. *apoda*	*Oenothera hookeri* ssp.	Nevada Sand-cress (sepals)	Pussy Paws (sepals)
Nevada Dodder	*angustifolia*		
(parasitic, threadlike)	Tall Yellow Evening Primrose	*Calyptridium umbellatum* var.	**RUTACEAE**
		caudiciferum	*Thamnosma montana*
		Pussy Paws (sepals)	Turpentine Broom

WILDFLOWER KEY BY COLOR AND FORM

White, Cream, or Green	Yellow, Orange, or Brown	Red, Pink, or Rose	Blue to Purple
Cuscuta suksdorfii var. *subpedicellata*	**PAPAVERACEAE**	**RUBIACEAE**	
Mountain Dodder (parasitic, threadlike)	*Eschscholzia covillei* Coville Gold-poppy	*Galium hypotrichium* ssp. *hypotrichium* Limestone Bedstraw	
GENTIANACEAE	**ROSACEAE**	*Galium mathewsii* Mathews Bedstraw	
Frasera puberulenta Inyo Gentian, Low Green Gentian	*Coleogyne ramosissima* Blackbrush (sepals)		
ONAGRACEAE	**RUBICACEAE**		
Camissonia boothii ssp. *desertorum* Woody Bottlewasher	*Galium hypotrichium* ssp. *inyoense* Inyo Bedstraw		
Camissonia boothii ssp. *intermedia* Hairy Primrose	*Galium mathewsii* Mathews Bedstraw		
Camissonia boothii ssp. *inyoensis* Inyo Primrose	*Galium stellatum* Shrubby Bedstraw		
Camissonia chamaenerioides Modest Primrose			
Camissonia claviformis ssp. *claviformis* Brown-eyed Primrose			
Camissonia claviformis ssp. *integrior* Northern Evening Primrose			

WILDFLOWER KEY BY COLOR AND FORM

White, Cream, or Green	Yellow, Orange, or Brown	Red, Pink, or Rose	Blue to Purple
Camissonia pterosperma Pigmy Primrose			
Camissonia refracta Narrow-leaved Primrose			
Epilobium ciliatum ssp. *ciliatum* Slender Epilobium			
Gayophytum diffusum ssp. *parvilorum* Summer Snowflakes			
Gayophytum ramosissimum Pinyon Gayophytum			
Oenothera caespitosa ssp. *crinita* Limestone Evening Primrose			
Oenothera caespitosa ssp. *marginata* Large White Evening Primrose			
POLYGONACEAE			
Oxyria digyna Mountain Sorrel (sepals)			
PORTULACACEAE			
Calyptridium parryi var. *nevadense* Nevada Sand-cress (sepals)			
Calyptridium umbellatum var. *caudiciferum* Pussy Paws (petals inconspicuous)			

WILDFLOWER KEY BY COLOR AND FORM

White, Cream, or Green	Yellow, Orange, or Brown	Red, Pink, or Rose	Blue to Purple
RANUNCULACEAE			
Clematis ligusticifolia var. *brevifolia*			
Virgin's Bower (sepals)			
Thalictrum alpinum			
Dwarf Meadow-rue (sepals)			
Thalictrum sparsiflorum			
Few-flowered Meadow-rue (sepals)			
RUBIACEAE			
Galium multiflorum forma *multiflorum*			
Shining Bedstraw			
Galium multiflorum forma *hirsutum*			
Canyon Bedstraw			
Galium stellatum			
Shrubby Bedstraw			
SAXIFRAGACEAE			
Philadelphus stramineous			
Littleleaf Mock-orange			

White, Cream, or Green	Yellow, Orange, or Brown	Red, Pink, or Rose	Blue to Purple
	C. Four Petals, More or Less United, Including Tubular Corollas with Four Lobes		
GENTIANACEAE	SCROPHULARIACEAE	SCROPHULARIACEAE	SCROPHULARIACEAE
Gentiana newberryi	*Castilleja miniata*	*Castilleja chromosa*	*Castilleja nana*
Alpine Gentian	Streamside Paintbrush (calyx)	Desert Paintbrush (calyx)	Dwarf Paintbrush
Gentianella tenella		*Castilleja linariaefolia*	*Pedicularis attollens*
Lapland Gentian		Long-leaved Paintbrush (calyx)	Little Elephant's Heads
SCROPHULARIACEAE		*Castilleja martinii* var. *clokeyi*	*Veronica americana*
Castilleja nana		Clokey Paintbrush (calyx)	American Brooklime
Dwarf Paintbrush (calyx)		*Castilleja miniata*	
Pedicularis attollens		Streamside Paintbrush (calyx)	
Little Elephant's Heads		*Castilleja minor*	
Veronica peregrina ssp. *xalapensis*		Alkali Paintbrush (calyx)	
Purslane Speedwell			
	D. Five Petals, Separate to Base; Flowers Regular		
APIACEAE	APIACEAE	RANUNCULACEAE	APIACEAE
Angelica lineariloba	*Lomatium mohavense*	*Aquilegia formosa*	*Lomatium mohavense*
Tall Angelica,	Mojave Parsley	Red Columbine	Mojave Parsley
Sierra Soda-straw	*Pteryxia petraea*	(sepals spurred)	LINACEAE
Cymopterus aboriginum	Rock Pteryxia	*Aquilegia shockleyi*	*Linum lewisii*
White Cymopterus,		Mojave Columbine	Blue Flax
Indian Parsley		(sepals spurred)	
LOASACEAE			
Mentzelia albicaulis			
Little Blazing Star			

WILDFLOWER KEY BY COLOR AND FORM

White, Cream, or Green	Yellow, Orange, or Brown	Red, Pink, or Rose	Blue to Purple
Lomatium foeniculaceum ssp. *inyoense* Inyo Mountain Parsley	*Mentzelia laevicaulis* Blazing Star	*Ranunculus andersonii* Pink Ranunculus	MALVACEAE
Lomatium foeniculaceum ssp. *fimbriatum* White Mountain Parsley	MALVACEAE	ROSACEAE	*Sphaeralcea ambigua* ssp. *rosacea* Lavendar Wand Mallow
CARYOPHYLLACEAE	*Sphaeralcea ambigua* Apricot Mallow	*Petaphyllum ramosissimum* Squaw Apple	SAXIFRAGACEAE
Arenaria aculeata Prickly Sandwort	*Sphaeralcea ambigua* ssp. *monticola* Mountain Apricot Mallow	*Prunus andersonii* Desert Peach	*Ribes inerme* Straggly Gooseberry
Arenaria kingii ssp. *compacta* Alpine Sandwort	RANUNCULACEAE	*Rosa woodsii* var. *ultramontana* Wild Rose	
Arenaria macradenia ssp. *macradenia* var. *parishiorum* Lime Sandwort	*Ranunculus cymbalaria* var. *saximontanus* Desert Buttercup	SAXIFRAGACEAE	
Arenaria macradenia ssp. *macradenia* var. *macradenia* Mojave Sandwort	*Ranunculus eschscholtzii* var. *oxynotus* Snow Buttercup	*Jamesia americana* var. *californica* Cliffbrush	
Scopulophila rixfordii Rixford Rockwort	*Ranunculus glaberrimus* var. *ellipticus* Large-headed Buttercup	*Ribes cereum* Wax Currant	
Silene bernardina ssp. *maguirei* Maguire Campion	ROSACEAE	TAMARICACEAE	
Stellaria longhipes Creek Stellaria	*Geum macrophyllum* Big-leaf Avens	*Tamarix ramosissima* Salt Cedar	
	Ivesia lycopodioides ssp. *scandularis* White Mountain Ivesia		
	Ivesia shockleyi Schockley Ivesia		

White, Cream, or Green	Yellow, Orange, or Brown	Red, Pink, or Rose	Blue to Purple
CROSSOMATACEAE	*Potentilla biennis*		
Forsellesia nevadensis	Green Cinquefoil		
Nevada Forsellesia	*Potentilla breweri*		
	Brewer Cinquefoil		
CUSCUTACEAE	*Potentilla fruticosa*		
Cuscuta salina var. *apoda*	Shrubby Cinquefoil		
Nevada Dodder	*Potentilla gracilis* var.		
(parisitic, threadlike)	*flabelliformis*		
Cuscuta suksdorfii var.	Alkali Cinquefoil		
subpedicellata	*Potentilla pectinisecta*		
Mountain Dodder	Silky Potentilla		
(parasitic, threadlike)			
	Potentilla pennsylvania var.		
LOASACEAE	*strigosa*		
Eucnida urens	Pennsylvania Potentilla		
Rock Nettle,	*Potentilla pseudosericea*		
Vegetable Velcro	Small Silky Potentilla		
Petalonyx nitidus			
Shiny-leaved Sandpaper	*Potentilla saxosa*		
Plant	Rock Potentilla		
PORTULACACEAE	**SAXIFRAGACEAE**		
Claytonia parviflora	*Heuchera duranii*		
Miner's Lettuce	Duran Alum Root		
Montia chamissoi	*Ribes aureum* var. *aureum*		
Toad Lily	Golden Currant		

WILDFLOWER KEY BY COLOR AND FORM

White, Cream, or Green	Yellow, Orange, or Brown	Red, Pink, or Rose	Blue to Purple
RANUNCULACEAE	*Ribes velutinum* var.		
Clematis ligusticifolia var.	*glanduliferum*		
brevifolia	Plateau Gooseberry		
Virgin's Bower	ZYGOPHYLLACEAE		
ROSACEAE	*Larrea tridentata*		
Cowania mexicana var.	Creosote bush		
stansburiana			
Cliff Rose			
Holodiscus dumosus var.			
glabrescens			
Cream Bush			
Horkelia hispidula			
White Mountain Horkelia			
Petrophytum caespitosum			
Rock Spiraea			
Physocarpus alternans			
Ninebark			
Prunus fasciculata			
Desert Almond			
Purshia glandulosa			
Desert Bitterbrush			
Purshai tridentata			
Bitterbrush			

WILDFLOWER KEY BY COLOR AND FORM

White, Cream, or Green	Yellow, Orange, or Brown	Red, Pink, or Rose	Blue to Purple
SAXIFRAGACEAE			
Heuchera rubescens var. *pachypoda* — Alum Root			
Ribes cereum — Wax Currant			
Ribes inerme — Straggly Gooseberry			
Ribes velutinum var. *glanduliferum* — Plateau Gooseberry			

E. Five Petals, Separate to Base; Flowers Irregular

White, Cream, or Green	Yellow, Orange, or Brown	Red, Pink, or Rose	Blue to Purple
FABACEAE	FABACEAE	FABACEAE	FABACEAE
Astragalus kentrophyta var. *elata* — Inyo Prickly Milk-vetch	*Astragalus inyoensis* — Inyo Milk-vetch	*Astragalus coccineus* — Scarlet Loco, Scarlet Milk-vetch	*Astragalus calycosus* — Little Gray Milk-vetch
Astragalus lentiginosus var. *semotus* — Little Paper-pod		*Dalea searlsiae* — Prairie Clover	*Astragalus cimae* var. *sufflatus* — Broad-shouldered Milk-vetch
		Oxytropis parryi — Parry Oxytropis	*Astragalus inyoensis* — Inyo Milk-vetch
		Trifolium andersonii ssp. *monoense* — Morio Clover	*Astragalus kentrophyta* var. *elata* — Inyo Prickly Milk-vetch

WILDFLOWER KEY BY COLOR AND FORM

White, Cream, or Green	Yellow, Orange, or Brown	Red, Pink, or Rose	Blue to Purple
			Astragalus kentrophyta var. *implexas* Dolomite Milk-vetch
			Astragalus lentiginosus var. *fremontii* Paper Loco, Freckled Milk-vetch
			Astragalus lentiginosus var. *semotus* Little Paper-pod
			Astragalus mintborniae var. *villosus* Erect Milk-vetch
			Astragalus newberryi Newberry Milk-vetch
			Astragalus oophorus Big-podded Milk-vetch, Spindle Loco
			Astragalus purshii var. *tinctus* Long-flowered Pursh Milk-vetch
			Dalea searlsiae Prarie Clover

WILDFLOWER KEY BY COLOR AND FORM

White, Cream, or Green	Yellow, Orange, or Brown	Red, Pink, or Rose	Blue to Purple
			Lupinus argenteus var. *tenellus* Limestone Lupine
			Lupinus brevicaulis Short-stemmed Blue Lupine
			Lupinus flavoculatus Yellow-eyes
			Lupinus palmeri Palmer Lupine
			Lupinus tegeticulatus var. *tegeticulatus* Silver Moss
			Psorothamnus arborescens var. *minutifolius* Indigo Bush, Blister Dalea
			RANUNCULACEAE *Aconitum columbianum* Monkshood
			Delphinium parishii Desert Larkspur
			Delphinium polycladon Willow Larkspur
			VIOLACEAE *Viola nephrophylla* Northern Bog Violet

WILDFLOWER KEY BY COLOR AND FORM

F. Five Petals, More or Less United, Including Tubular Corollas with Five Lobes; Flowers Regular

White, Cream, or Green	Yellow, Orange, or Brown	Red, Pink, or Rose	Blue to Purple
BORAGINACEAE	**BORAGINACEAE**	**CAPRIFOLIACEAE**	**BORAGINACEAE**
Cryptantha flavoculata Sulphur-throated Forget-me-not	*Amsinckia tessellata* Fiddleneck	*Symphoricarpos longiflorus* Desert Snowberry	*Hackelia brevicula* White Mountain Forget-me-not
Cryptantha cinerea var. *abortiva* Bow-nut Forget-me-not	*Cryptantha confertifolia* Golden Forget-me-not	**NYCTAGINACEAE**	*Hackelia floribunda* Tall Hackelia
Cryptantha pterocarya Wing-nut Forget-me-not	*Gilia filiformis* Yellow Gilia	*Abronia nana* ssp. *covillei* Limestone Sand-verbena	**CAPRIFOLIACEAE**
Cryptantha rostorum Roos Forget-me-not	*Navarretia breweri* Yellow Navarretia	*Mirabilis alipes* Hermidium, Rose Four O'clock	*Symphoricarpos longiflorus* Desert Snowberry
Cryptantha utahensis Fragrant Forget-me-not, Nievitas		*Mirabilis bigelovii* Wishbone Bush	**HYDROPHYLLACEAE**
Cryptantha virginensis Virgin Valley Forget-me-not		*Mirabilis pumila* Little Umbrella-wort	*Phacelia crenulata* Purple Phacelia
Sambucus caerulea Blue Elderberry		**POLEMONIACEAE**	*Phacelia curvipes* Dwarf Phacelia
GENTIANACEAE		*Collomia linearis* Lesser Collomia	*Phacelia fremontii* Yellow-throats
Gentiana newberryi Alpine Gentian		*Gilia aggregata* var. *arizonica* Arizona Scarlet Gilia	*Phacelia hastata* Cordilleran Phacelia
Gentianella tenella Lapland Gentian		*Gilia latifolia* Holly Gilia	*Phacelia vallis-mortae* Death Valley Phacelia
		Phlox condensata Cushion Phlox	**NYCTAGINACEAE**
			Mirabilis bigelovii Wishbone Bush

WILDFLOWER KEY BY COLOR AND FORM

White, Cream, or Green	Yellow, Orange, or Brown	Red, Pink, or Rose	Blue to Purple
HYDROPHYLLACEAE		*Phlox longifolia*	*Mirabilis multiflora*
Phacelia hastata		var. *stansburyi*	var. *pubescens*
Cordilleran Phacelia		Stansbury Phlox	Giant Four O'clock
Phacelia perityloides		**PRIMULACEAE**	**POLEMONIACEAE**
Panamint Phacelia		*Androsace septentrionalis*	*Collomia linearis*
Tricardia watsonii		var. *subumbellata*	Lesser Collomia
Three Hearts		Alpine Androsace	*Eriastrum diffusum*
			Spreading Eriastrum
NYCTAGINACEA		**SAXIFRAGACEAE**	*Eriastrum sparsiflorum*
Abronia nana ssp. *covellei*		*Heuchera rubescens*	var. *wilcoxii*
Limestone Sand-verbena		var. *pachypoda*	Wilcox Woolly Star
Mirabilis bigelovii var. *bigelovii*		Alum Root	*Gilia breacciarum*
Wishbone Bush			ssp. *neglecta*
			Kern-Inyo Gilia
OLEACEAE			*Gilia cana* ssp. *triceps*
Menodora spinescens			Showy Gilia
Spiny Menodora			*Gilia clokeyi*
			Clokey Gilia
POLEMONIACEAE			*Gilia gilioides* var. *violacea*
Collomia linearis			Violet Gilia
Lesser Collomia			*Gilia leptomeria*
Eriastrum diffusum			Sand Gilia
Spreading Eriastrum			*Gilia ochroleuca*
Eriastrum sparsiflorum			Volcanic Pale Gilia
var. *wilcoxii*			
Wilcox Woolly Star			
Gilia campanulata			
Bell Gilia			

WILDFLOWER KEY BY COLOR AND FORM

White, Cream, or Green	Yellow, Orange, or Brown	Red, Pink, or Rose	Blue to Purple
Gilia clokey Clokey Gilia			*Gilia opthalmoides* Pinyon Gilia
Gilia congesta var. *montana* White Globe-gilia			*Gilia scropulorum* Rock Gilia
Gilia hutchinsifolia Desert Pale Gilia			*Gilia sinuata* Cinder Gilia
Gilia leptomeria Sand Gilia			*Langlosia punctata* Dotted Langlosia
Gilia polycladon Spreading Gilia			*Linanthus parryae* Sand Blossoms
Gilia stellata Dotted-throat Gilia			*Phlox condensata* Cushion Phlox
Gymnosteris parvula Gymnosteris			*Phlox boodii* ssp. *canescens* Woolly Phlox
Langloisia punctata Dotted Langlosia			*Polemonium chartaceam* White Mountain Sky Pilot
Leptodactylon pungens var. *hallii* Prickly Phlox			PRIMULACEAE *Dodecatheon redolens* Shooting Star
Leptodactylon pungens var. *pungens* Granite Gilia			SOLANACEAE *Lycium andersonii* Desert Tomato
Linanthus nuttallii ssp. *pubescens* Bushy Linanthus			

WILDFLOWER KEY BY COLOR AND FORM

White, Cream, or Green	Yellow, Orange, or Brown	Red, Pink, or Rose	Blue to Purple
Linanthus parryae Sand Blossoms			
Phlox condensata Cushion Phlox			
Phlox boodii ssp. canescens Woolly Phlox			
Phlox longifolia var. *stansburyi* Stansbury Phlox			
PRIMULACEAE *Androsace septentrionalis* var. *subumbellata* Alpine Androsace			
ROSACEAE *Amelanchier pallida* Service Berry			
Chamaebatiaria millefolium Fern Bush, Desert Sweet			
SAXIFRAGACEAE *Heuchera rubescens* var. *pachypoda* Alum Root			
SOLANACEAE *Lycium andersonii* Desert Tomato			

WILDFLOWER KEY BY COLOR AND FORM

White, Cream, or Green	Yellow, Orange, or Brown	Red, Pink, or Rose	Blue to Purple
Lycium cooperi			
Peach-thorn			
Nicotiana attenuata			
Coyote Tobacco			
Nicotiana trigonophylla			
Desert Tobacco			

G. Five Petals, More or Less United, Commonly Tubular; Flowers Irregular

White, Cream, or Green	Yellow, Orange, or Brown	Red, Pink, or Rose	Blue to Purple
SCROPHULARIACEAE	OROBANCHACEAE	SCROPHULARIACEAE	LAMIACEAE
Antirrhinum kingii	*Orobanche corymbosa*	*Mimulus cardinalis*	*Monardella linoides*
Least Snapdragon	Flat-topped Broomrape,	Scarlet Mimulus	Flax-leaved Monardella
Collinsia parviflora	Sagebrush Strangler	*Penstemon floridus*	*Monardella odoratissima*
Meadow Collinsia	*Orobanche fasciculata*	var. *floridus*	ssp. *parviflora*
Penstemon fructiformis	Clustered Bloomrape,	Rose Penstemon	Mountain Pennyroyal
Desert Mountain Penstemon	Mountain Strangler	*Penstemon floridus*	*Salvia columbariae*
	SCROPHULARIACEAE	var. *austinii*	Chia
	Keckiella rothrockii	Austin Penstemon	*Salvia dorrii* var. *clokeyi*
	Buckskin Keckiella	*Penstemon monoensis*	Clokey Blue Sage
	Mimulus densus	Mono Penstemon	*Salvia dorrii* var. *dorrii*
	Elfin Mimulus	*Penstemon rostiflorus*	Great Basin Blue Sage
	Mimulus guttatus	Scarlet Penstemon	SCROPHULARIACEAE
	Common Monkey-flower	*Scrophularia desertorum*	*Collinsia parviflora*
	Mimulus primuloides	Desert Figwort	Meadow Collinsia
	var. *primuloides*		
	Meadow Mimulus		

WILDFLOWER KEY BY COLOR AND FORM

White, Cream, or Green	Yellow, Orange, or Brown	Red, Pink, or Rose	Blue to Purple
	Mimulus suksdorfii		*Cordylanthus kingii*
	Suksdorf Miniature Mimulus		ssp. *belleri*
			Heller Bird's-beak
	Mohavea breviflora		*Mimulus bigelovii*
	Small Mohavea,		var. *bigelovii*
	Desert Snapdragon		Bigelow Mimulus
	Verbascum thapsus		*Mimulus bigelovii*
	Wooly Mullein		var. *cuspidatus*
			Desert Mimulus
			Mimulus densus
			Elfin Mimulus
			Penstemon heterodoxus
			Whorlflower Penstemon
			Penstemon patens
			Owens Valley Penstemon
			Penstemon scapoides
			Westgard Penstemon
			Penstemon speciosus
			Showy Penstemon

WILDFLOWER KEY BY COLOR AND FORM

White, Cream, or Green	Yellow, Orange, or Brown	Red, Pink, or Rose	Blue to Purple
	H. Six Petals or Petal-like Sepals (Tepals)		
PAPAVERACEAE	POLYGONACEAE	POLYGONACEAE	
Argemone minuta	*Chorizanthe rigida*	*Eriogonum baileyi*	
ssp. *rotundata*	Rosy-thorn	Bailey Buckwheat	
Prickly Poppy	*Chorizanthe watsonii*	*Eriogonum gracilipes*	
POLYGONACEAE	Watson Chorizanthe	Raspberry Buckwheat	
Chorizanthe brevicornu	*Dedeckera eurekensis*	*Eriogonum kearneyi*	
var. *spathulata*	Dedeckera, July Gold	var. *monoense*	
Mountain Brittle Chorizanthe	*Eriogonum brachyantham*	Kearney Buckwheat	
Eriogonum baileyi	Short-flowered Buckwheat	*Eriogonum maculatum*	
Bailey Buckwheat	*Eriogonum caespitosum*	Spotted Buckwheat	
Eriogonum brachypodum	Mat Buckwheat	*Eriogonum microthecum*	
Glandular Buckwheat	*Eriogonum inflatum*	var. *lapidicola*	
Eriogonum cernuum	Desert Trumpet	Bristlecone Microthecum	
Nodding Buckwheat	*Eriogonum microthecum*	*Eriogonum microthecum*	
Eriogonum deflexum	var. *ambiguum*	var. *laxiflorum*	
var. *deflexum*	Yellow Microthecum	Pinyon Microthecum	
Skeleton Weed	*Eriogonum nidularium*	*Eriogonum ovalifolium*	
Eriogonum deflexum	Bird's-nest Buckwheat	var. *ovalifolium*	
var. *baratum*	*Eriogonum ovalifolium*	Oval-leaved Buckwheat	
Tall Skeleton Weed	var. *ovalifolium*	*Eriogonum ovalifolium*	
Eriogonum esmeraldense	Oval-leaved Buckwheat	var. *nivale*	
Esmeralda Buckwheat	*Eriogonum pusillum*	Fell-field Buckwheat	
	Yellow Turbans	*Eriogonum rufinum*	
		Limber pine Buckwheat	

WILDFLOWER KEY BY COLOR AND FORM

White, Cream, or Green	Yellow, Orange, or Brown	Red, Pink, or Rose	Blue to Purple
Eriogonum fasciculatum var. *polifolium* California Buckwheat	*Eriogonum roseum* Limestone Yellow-heads	*Eriogonum umbellatum* var. *versicolor* Varicolored Buckwheat	
Eriogonum gracilipes Raspberry Buckwheat	*Eriogonum umbellatum* var. *umbellatum* Sulphur-flower	*Eriogonum wrightii* var. *subscaposum* Wright Buckwheat	
Eriogonum heermannii ssp. *argense* Rough Heermann Buckwheat	*Eriogonum umbellatum* var. *chlorothamnus* Narrow-leaved Sulphur-flower	*Oxytheca dendroidea* Fine Oxytheca	
Eriogonum heermannii ssp. *humulus* Common Heermann Buckwheat		*Rumex paucifolius* ssp. *paucifolius* Mountain Dock (three sepals enlarged)	
Eriogonum kearneyi var. *monoense* Kearney Buckwheat		*Rumex paucifolius* ssp. *gracilescens* Alpine Dock	
Eriogonum kennedyi var. *purpusii* Kennedy Buckwheat			
Eriogonum maculatum Spotted Buckwheat			
Eriogonum microthecum var. *lapidicola* Bristlecone Microthecum			

WILDFLOWER KEY BY COLOR AND FORM

White, Cream, or Green	Yellow, Orange, or Brown	Red, Pink, or Rose	Blue to Purple
Eriogonum microthecum			
var. *laxiflorum*			
Pinyon Microthecum			
Eriogonum nidularium			
Bird's-nest Buckwheat			
Eriogonum ovalifolium			
var. *ovalifolium*			
Oval-leaved Buckwheat			
Eriogonum ovalifolium			
var. *nivale*			
Fell-field Buckwheat			
Eriogonum panamintense			
var. *panamintense*			
Panamint Buckwheat			
Eriogonum panamintense			
var. *mensicola*			
Plain Panamint Buckwheat			
Eriogonum rupinum			
Limber Pine Buckwheat			
Eriogonum umbellatum			
var. *devestivum*			
Pale Umbelled Buckwheat			
Eriogonum umbellatum			
var. *versicolor*			
Varicolored Buckwheat			

WILDFLOWER KEY BY COLOR AND FORM

White, Cream, or Green	Yellow, Orange, or Brown	Red, Pink, or Rose	Blue to Purple
Eriogonum wrightii var. *subscaposum* Wright Buckwheat			
Oxytheca dendroidea Fine Oxytheca			
Oxytheca perfoliata Saucer Plant			
Rumex crispus Curly Dock (three sepals enlarged)			
PORTULACACEAE			
Lewisia pygmaea ssp. *pygmaea* Brooch Lewisia Dwarf Lewisia			

I. More Than Six Petals or Petal-like Sepals

White, Cream, or Green	Yellow, Orange, or Brown	Red, Pink, or Rose	Blue to Purple
PORTALACACEAE *Lewisia rediviva* var. *minor* Bitterroot	CACTACEAE *Echinocactus polycephalus* Cottontop Cactus	CACTACEAE *Echinocereus triglochidiatus* var. *mojavensis* Mojave Mound Cactus	CACTACEAE *Echinocereus engelmannii* var. *chrysocentrus* Engelmann Cactus, Torch Cactus
	Opuntia erinacea var. *erinacea* Mojave Prickly Pear	*Opuntia basilaris* Beavertail	*Opuntia basilaris* Beavertail

WILDFLOWER KEY BY COLOR AND FORM

White, Cream, or Green	Yellow, Orange, or Brown	Red, Pink, or Rose	Blue to Purple
	Opuntia erinacea var. *ursina* Old Man Cactus, Grizzly Bear Cactus		*Sclerocactus polyancistrus* Mojave Fishhook Cactus, Pineapple Cactus
	Opuntia erinacea var. *utahensis* Utah Prickly Pear		
	RANUNCULACEAE *Ranunculus cymbalaria* var. *saximontanus* Desert Buttercup		

J. Flowering Heads Composite, or Few to Many Individual Flowers;
Marginal (Ray) Flowers Petal-like; Central (Disk) Flowers, Small, Tubular, If Present

White, Cream, or Green	Yellow, Orange, or Brown	Red, Pink, or Rose	Blue to Purple
ASTERACEAE *Antennaria microphylla* Rosy Everlasting Flowers, Pussytoes	ASTERACEAE *Acamptopappus shockleyi* Shockley goldenhead	ASTERACEAE *Antennaria microphylla* Rosy Everlasting Flowers, Pussytoes	ASTERACEAE *Cirsium nidulum* Red Thistle
Artemisia tridentata Big Sagebrush, Great Basin Sagebrush	*Ambrosia dumosa* Burro-bush, Bur Sage	*Erigeron compositus* var. *glabratus* Cut-leaf Daisy	*Machaeranthera canescens* Sticky Aster
			Machaeranthera shastensis var. *montana* Shasta Aster

WILDFLOWER KEY BY COLOR AND FORM

White, Cream, or Green	Yellow, Orange, or Brown	Red, Pink, or Rose	Blue to Purple
Artemisia arbuscula Dwarf Sagebrush	*Anisocoma acaulis* Scale Bud	*Stephanomeria pauciflora* Desert Milk-aster	*Townsendia scapigera* Ground Daisy
Artemisia nova Broom Sagebrush	*Calycoseris parryi* Yellow Tack-stem	*Stephanomeria spinosa* Wool Cache Plant, Thorny Skeleton Plant	*Xylorhiza tortifolia* Mojave Aster
Brickellia oblongifolia var. *linifolia* Pinyon Brickellia	*Chrysothamnus viscidiflorus* ssp. *viscidiflorus* Curly Rabbitbrush	*Townsendia scapigera* Ground Daisy	
Calycoseris wrightii White Tack-stem	*Chrysothamnus viscidiflorus* ssp. *axillaris* Fine-leaved Rabbit brush		
Chaenactis carphoclinia Pebble Pincushion	*Chrysothamnus viscidiflorus* ssp. *puberulus* Pinyon Rabbitbrush		
Chaenactis douglasii Douglas Pincushion	*Crepis intermedia* Hawksbeard		
Erigeron compositus var. *glabratus* Cut-leaf Daisy	*Encelia virginensis* ssp. *actoni* Bush Sunflower, Brittlebush		
Layia glandulosa White Tidy-tips	*Ericameria cooperi* Cooper Goldenbush		
Leucelene ericoides Heath Daisy	*Ericameria cuneata* Cliff Goldenbrush		
Stephanomeria pauciflora Desert Milk-aster	*Erigeron aphanactis* Gold Buttons (no rays)		

WILDFLOWER KEY BY COLOR AND FORM

White, Cream, or Green	Yellow, Orange, or Brown	Red, Pink, or Rose	Blue to Purple
	Gutierrezia microcephala		
	Threadleaf, Yellow-green		
	Matchweed		
	Hulsea algida		
	Alpine Gold		
	Hulsea vestita		
	ssp. *inyoensis*		
	Inyo Gold,		
	Inyo Hulsea		
	Hymenopappus filifolium		
	var. *nanus*		
	Inyo Cutleaf (no rays)		
	Hymenooxys cooperi		
	var. *canescens*		
	Gray Goldenflower		
	Perityle inyoensis		
	Inyo Perityle (no rays)		
	Perityle megalocephala		
	Tall Perityle (no rays)		
	Petradoria discoidea		
	Rock Goldenrod (no rays)		
	Senecio canus		
	Rock Senecio		
	Senecio douglasii		
	var. *monoensis*		
	Mono Senecio		

WILDFLOWER KEY BY COLOR AND FORM

White, Cream, or Green	Yellow, Orange, or Brown	Red, Pink, or Rose	Blue to Purple
	Senecio multilobatus Basin Senecio		
	Solidago multiradiata Alpine Goldenrod		
	Tetradymia canescens Gray Horsebrush (no rays)		
	Viguiera multiflora var. *nevadensis* Nevada Viguiera		

Annuals   Perennial Herbs   Shrubs

K. Petals Lacking, Inconspicuous, or Difficult to Classify;
Staminate (Male) and Pistillate (Female) Reproductive Parts May Be on Separate Plants

White, Cream, or Green	Yellow, Orange, or Brown	Red, Pink, or Rose	Blue to Purple
CHENOPODIACEAE	EUPHORBIACEAE	ASTERACEAE	
Chenopodium atrovirens Pinyon Goosefoot	*Chamaesyce albomarginata* Rattlesnake Weed	*Ambrosia dumosa* Burro-bush Bur Sage	
Chenopodium fremontii Fremont Goosefoot	*Chamaesyce fendleri* Fendler Spurge	*Artemisia tridentata* Big Sagebrush, Great Basin Sagebrush	
		Artemisia arbuscula Dwarf Sagebrush	
		Artemisia nova Broom Sagebrush	

REFERENCES

DeDecker, Mary. 1984. *Flora of the Mojave Desert, California.* Special Publication no. 7, California Native Plant Society, Sacramento.

Kartesz, J. T., and Rosemarie Kartesz. 1980. *A synonymized checklist of the vascular flora of the United States, Canada, and Greenland. Vol. II: The biota of North America.* University of North Carolina Press, Chapel Hill.

Lloyd, R. M., and R. S. Mitchell. 1973. *A flora of the White Mountains, California and Nevada.* University of California Press, Berkeley.

Munz, P. A., and D. D. Keck. 1970. *A California flora.* University of California Press, Berkeley and Los Angeles.

Munz, P. A., and D. D. Keck. 1973. *Supplement to a California flora.* University of California Press, Berkeley and Los Angeles.

Raven, P. H. 1977. The California flora. In Michael G. Barbour and Jack Major (eds.). *Terrestrial vegetation of California,* pp. 109–137. John Wiley & Sons, New York.

PART III

ANIMALS

7

Common Insects
and Other Arthropods

John Smiley and Derham Giuliani

Insects, members of the Phylum Arthropoda (arthropods, or "jointed-legged" creatures), are small animals that usually have six legs and whose adult forms usually bear wings. They are the most varied group of organisms on Earth; nearly a million species have been described. Insects are primarily terrestrial, although many inhabit freshwater streams, ponds, and lakes. In the oceans, insects are replaced by their relatives, the crustaceans. Other arthropods common in terrestrial habitats are the spiders, mites, ticks, and scorpions (collectively known as arachnids); a few species of terrestrial crustaceans, such as pillbugs and sowbugs; and the centipedes and millipedes. This chapter emphasizes species of insects but also lists and illustrates other types of arthropods commonly encountered in the vicinity of the White Mountains.

The small size and great diversity of arthropods make determination of species difficult; therefore, it is usually a job for experts. However, recognition of major groups is not difficult, and one can obtain as much satisfaction from recognizing a particular family or order as from identifying an interesting bird species. For example, identifying an insect family provides information about the intricate (and commonly fascinating) life cycle of the insect in question, its relations with its environment, and its interactions with other species of plants and animals. In our discussions of major groups, we encapsulate some of the more interesting facets of arthropod life history along with species distributions and aids to identification. Names are given for some of the more common, large species, most of which are illustrated as well. Our selection is necessarily somewhat arbitrary, because we have neither the space nor the collected material to systematically list species or even genera. Useful books to aid in insect identification are *California Insects* by J. A. Powell and C. H. Hogue, the *Peterson Field Guide to the Study of Insects* by D. J. Borror and C. L. White, and *Introduction to the Study of Insects* by D. J. Borror, D. M. Delong, and C. A. Triplehorn.

Most terrestrial arthropods are small, but adult individuals range considerably in size, depending on the amount of food available during the juvenile stages. For this reason, and because we wish to emphasize major groups rather than species, we do not report sizes for most species. Instead, we indicate size in general terms. "Large" generally refers to insects over 0.4 in (10 mm) in length, and "small" refers to insects under 0.2 in (4 mm) long.

Most of the species discussed in this chapter occur along the road from Big Pine to Westgard Pass, or from there up the road to the Bristlecone Pine forest and the Barcroft facilities of the White Mountain Research Station (WMRS). Many of the species occur in the vicinity of the Crooked Creek facilities (WMRS), at 10,150 ft (3,094 m), Barcroft Laboratory, at 12,470 ft (3,801 m), and White Mountain Peak, at 14,250 ft (4,343 m). Most species listed as occurring at low elevations are present in the vicinity of the Owens Valley facilities (WMRS), 3 mi (5 km) east of Bishop, California.

SPIDERS, MITES, TICKS, SCORPIONS, AND OTHERS
(Class Arachnida)

Arthropods of the Class Arachnida generally bear eight legs, and the head and thorax are usually fused into a single body section, the cephalothorax. The arachnids generally prey on other arthropods (e.g., spiders), but some are herbivorous (e.g., Spider Mites) and others are parasitic (e.g., ticks). Still other types feed on decaying matter.

Scorpion (Order Scorpiones)

Scorpions (Fig. 7.1) are common at lower elevations and are generally nocturnal. These predaceous arthropods have a stinger at the tip of the tail-like abdomen and should be handled with care. Smaller forms are common around houses and woodpiles.

Spiders (Order Araneae)

The spiders are a diverse group of predatory arthropods. In many habitats they are extremely abundant and consume vast numbers of tiny insects and other small prey. They are also a favorite food of many birds and other insectivorous vertebrates.

Tarantulas (Family Theraphosidae). (Fig. 7.1) Large spiders with very hairy bodies. Although the Tarantula can bite, North American species are relatively harmless. Tarantulas are nocturnal and serve as prey for several large spider-killing wasps, including those of the genus *Pepsis*. During the day they hide in silk-lined burrows in the ground.

Black Widow Spider, *Latrodectus hesperus* (Family Theridiidae). (Fig. 7.1) Produces tangled webs made of exceptionally strong, thick silk, commonly occur in buildings and sheds. The female is black with an hourglass-shaped red patch on the underside. The venom is very toxic, and bites should be treated medically. Black Widows are known to catch their prey by "spitting" strands of silk, entangling it.

Orb-weaving Spiders (Family Araneidae). (Fig. 7.1) A large family of spiders that weave the familiar circular "orb" web, which is used to catch flying insect prey.

Wolf Spiders, *Lycosa* spp. (Family Lycosidae). (Fig 7.1) Terrestrial hunters, often abroad by day. The females of these hairy brown spiders are commonly seen carrying a large, spherical egg case or newly hatched young on their back. Small Wolf Spiders

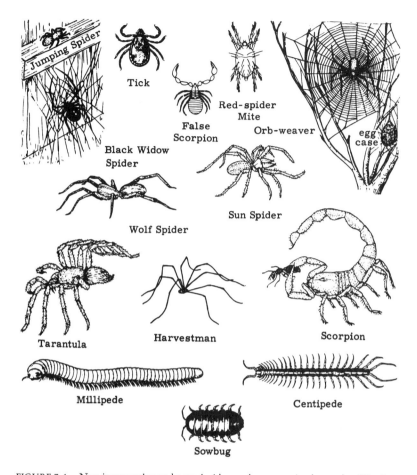

FIGURE 7.1 Non-insect arthropods: arachnids, sowbugs, centipedes, and millipedes.

may be extremely abundant in grasslands and meadows up to 14,000 ft (4,300 m) elevation.

Jumping Spiders (Family Salticidae). (Fig. 7.1) An easily recognized family of spiders with very short legs, which they use to rapidly run and jump in search of their prey. Diurnal, they have large eyes and hunt their prey visually, jumping on it and delivering a paralyzing bite. Some species are brightly colored with red, metallic green, or blue.

Harvestmen (Order Opiliones)

Harvestmen have the entire body fused into a circular or oval shape and commonly have very long legs. Most species are predaceous.

Daddy Longlegs (Suborder Palpatores).   (Fig. 7.1) Some Daddy Longlegs huddle together in masses of hundreds in cool, damp spots, their legs resembling masses of brown hair.

Mites and Ticks (Order Acarina)

Mites and ticks are usually small, with very short legs as compared with spiders. They have sucking mouthparts.

Ticks (Families Ixodidae and Argasidae).   (Fig. 7.1) Ticks are blood-sucking parasites of vertebrates, to which they attach themselves and feed until they are engorged. In large numbers they may cause temporary paralysis until removed. Tick bites can become infected, particularly when a feeding tick is removed carelessly, its head broken off and left in the wound. Ticks also serve as vectors for disease.

Red-spider Mites (Family Tetranychidae).   (Fig. 7.1) An important group of extremely tiny arthropods (less than 0.04 in or 1.0 mm) that are herbivorous, causing severe economic damage to certain crops and cultivated plants, particularly indoors. They are slow-moving and sedentary. Other mites, larger and more active, are predaceous and commonly seen at all elevations on the ground and in foliage. They are usually red or orange.

False Scorpions, or Pseudoscorpions (Order Pseudoscorpiones)

False Scorpions (Fig. 7.1) are small arthropods that lack the tail-like stinger of true scorpions but possess a pair of pincers and otherwise look very much like true scorpions. These animals overwinter under stones and logs, in a silken case.

Wind Scorpions (Order Solifugidae)

Wind Scorpions are a group of large, conspicuous athropods. They are fast-running predators chiefly active at night.

Sun Spiders.   (Fig. 7.1) Yellow-brown arachnids that look like large spiders except that the abdomen is segmented, like that of a scorpion, and the head bears large, foreward-facing jaws. They do not produce venom.

ISOPODS
(Class Crustacea)

The Class Crustacea is an extremely diverse group of arthropods found primarily in aquatic or marine habitats, including such forms as shrimp, crabs, lobsters, and barnacles. Only one group, the isopods, have invaded terrestrial habitats.

Sowbugs (Order Isopoda).   (Fig. 7.1) The Sowbug is a widespread, extremely successful crustacean. Sowbugs have a gray-black segmented carapace, have seven pairs of legs, and are commonly seen around habitations or where the ground is watered. Some are capable of rolling up into a ball and are known as pillbugs.

MILLIPEDES
(Class Diplopoda)

Millipedes are long, wormlike arthropods with two pairs of legs on each body segment and commonly 60–100 legs overall. Usually occurring in damp places, millipedes are generally scavengers and do not bite.

Cylindrical Millipedes (Order Opisthospermophora). Cylindrical millipedes (Fig. 7.1) are relatively large and have a hard shell. They occur in leaf litter and on the ground.

CENTIPEDES
(Class Chilopoda)

Like millipedes, centipedes are long and slender and composed of many segments. Unlike millipedes, centipedes bear only one pair of legs per segment and are predaceous, actively running and seeking out prey. Larger individuals are capable of delivering a painful bite.

Centipedes (Several orders). Centipedes (Fig. 7.1) range from small to very large (up to 6 in long) and are capable of biting or pinching with both their mandibles and their tail appendage. The venom is generally not toxic in North American species.

INSECTS
(Class Insecta)

Insects have an inelastic, external skeleton that must be shed as the animal grows. After hatching from the egg, a typical insect undergoes a fixed number of moults until it reaches adulthood; the stages between moults are called instars. When the insect reaches the adult stage, it may develop wings; this change is called metamorphosis. Juvenile insects never have wings. Adult insects are capable of reproduction but not of growth since no further moults are possible. Thus, a small insect with wings is a fully formed adult and will grow no further, whereas a large insect without wings may be a juvenile or, in some cases, a wingless adult. In insects with incomplete metamorphosis, the juveniles resemble the adults and are usually called nymphs. In species with complete metamorphosis, the juveniles differ greatly from the adult and are usually called larvae (singular: larva). Figure 7.2 illustrates these differences.

Because they are small, insects cannot store large amounts of water, food, or heat in their bodies. Under ideal growth conditions insects grow and multiply rapidly, but they must pass seasons of cold or drought by hiding in a state of dormancy, or

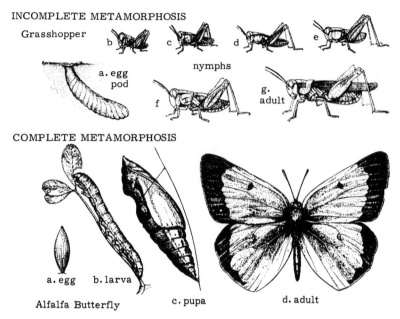

FIGURE 7.2   Complete and incomplete metamorphosis.

diapause. In the White Mountains region, most insects are active in the springtime and dormant during the dry summers and the cold winters. Other insects are active in the summer and fall, and a few species are adapted to cold conditions, active on melting snow or under the snow during the winter months. Owing to differences in the regimes of temperature and moisture at different elevations, the period of spring activity begins in March or April in the Owens Valley, but this period does not begin at Barcroft or White Mountain Peak until July or August. There "spring" commonly lasts until the first snows in September or October.

Figure 7.3 illustrates the external anatomy of a typical insect, a grasshopper. An insect has a head, thorax, and abdomen. The head contains the eyes, which may be simple or compound (i.e., composed of hundreds of simple eyes). Also on the head is a single pair of segmented antennae. They are primarily used for detecting odors, although some species with long antennae may use them as "feelers" for detecting objects or vibrations. The head also bears the mouthparts, including mandibles (jaws), maxillae, and various jointed palps for manipulating food. During the course of evolution, insect mouthparts have taken many different forms, including piercing "syringes," beaks, and coiled tubes. Each group of insects has characteristic mouthparts that are very useful in identification.

The thorax consists of three segments: the prothorax, mesothorax, and metathorax from front to back, each of which bears a pair of legs. The top of each segment is protected by a hardened plate. In addition to legs, the meso- and metathorax each bear a pair of wings in most adult insects. The anterior wing is called the

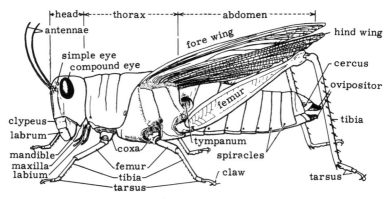

FIGURE 7.3   External anatomy of a grasshopper.

forewing, and the posterior the hindwing. The wings of insects are membranous, with a framework of rigid veins. The arrangement of these veins is very important in insect identification.

A typical insect leg has four visible jointed segments: the coxa, femur, tibia, and tarsus. The coxa is usually rounded and attached to the body. The femur usually extends out from the body and is the first long segment. The tibia usually extends downward from the femur, nearly touching the substrate. The tarsus functions like a foot, with claws, hairs, and pads for clinging to surfaces. The tarsus is itself composed of several segments, the number of which is useful in identification.

The abdomen of insects usually has 6 to 10 visible segments. The upper (dorsal) and lower (ventral) surfaces of each segment may bear hardened plates, but in some species the abdomen is soft. The posterior end of the abdomen bears the anal opening, appendages for copulation, and, in female insects, the ovipositor for laying eggs. In a few insects, such as grasshoppers, roaches, and related groups, a pair of sense organs are borne on the upper surface of the posterior end of the abdomen. These are called cerci (singular: cercus).

The Class Insecta is divided into approximately 20 orders and 750 families, 500 of which occur in North America. In this natural history guide we introduce most of these orders and a few of the most easily distinguished families occurring in the White Mountains. Because there may be as many as 5,000 to 10,000 insect species present in the region, we can only present a sampling of the most common and interesting species. The only large group that is nearly completely represented here is that of the butterflies, for which identification may be accomplished by reference to the color plates.

Dragonflies and Damselflies (Order Odonata)

Members of the Order Odonata are easily recognized in the adult form. Species that hold their wings extended laterally when resting are known as Dragonflies (Suborder Anisoptera), and species that hold their wings pressed together dorsally at rest are

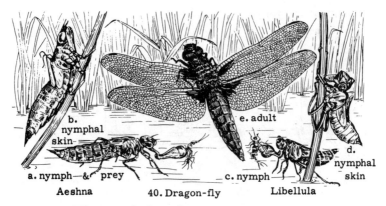

FIGURE 7.4   Life stages of a dragonfly.

known as Damselflies (Suborder Zygoptera). These insects are predators, capturing other insects in flight with their basketlike legs. Individuals copulate in flight and frequently are seen flying in tandem, with the male clasping the female behind the head using appendages at the tip of his abdomen. The female may also lay eggs in the water while in tandem with the male. The nymphs live in fresh water, where they are predators of small animals. Adults are common on the floor of the Owens Valley and have been recorded as high as White Mountain Peak, at over 14,000 ft (4,300 m). Figure 7.4 illustrates the life stages of dragonflies.

Green Jacket Dragonfly, *Erythemis simplicicollis* **(Family Libellulidae).**   Occurs from the Owens Valley floor to Crooked Creek (10,000 ft, or 3,100 m). The large, green adults fly in July and August, commonly at some distance from water.

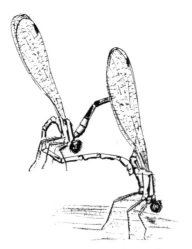

FIGURE 7.5   Dancer Damselfly
(*Argia* sp.).

Dancers, *Argia* spp. (Family Coenagrionidae).   (Fig. 7.5) Damselfly genus occurs from the Owens Valley Floor to Crooked Creek (10,000 ft, or 3,100 m), usually near water.

Termites (Order Isoptera)

Termites are highly social insects. Some species can be very destructive due to their feeding activities on wooden structures. They are soft-bodied, are whitish in color, and live in large colonies with a well-defined caste system. Their gut contains diverse symbiotic microorganisms that aid in the digestion of wood.

Dampwood Termites, *Zootermopsis* spp. (Family Hodotermitidae).   (Fig. 7.6) Occupy dead logs and stumps, especially places where wood is damp. Another termite, the Subterranean Termite (*Reticulotermes* spp.), does not occur at relatively high elevations in the White Mountains but is present in the Owens Valley, where it can damage structural wood in contact with the soil.

Grasshoppers, Roaches, Mantids, and Related Groups (Order Orthoptera)

The Order Orthoptera is a highly diverse group, including many large, common species. The crickets, katydids (Family Tettigoniidae), and grasshoppers (Family Acrididae) are primarily herbivorous and have enlarged, powerful hind legs that enable them to jump (see Fig. 7.3). Many grasshoppers take flight during their jump and display brightly colored wings, which carry them up to 100 ft (30 m). The roaches, which have long antennae and long abdominal cerci, are primarily nocturnal scavengers. The phasmids, or walking sticks, are herbivorous. The mantids are highly

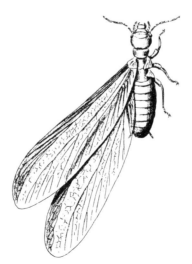

FIGURE 7.6 Dampwood Termite (*Zootermopsis* sp.).

predaceous, with forelegs modified into striking claws that can grab prey with lightning speed.

Most adult orthopterans are winged, including roaches, but some species of montane grasshoppers and crickets are flightless. Crickets, katydids, and grasshoppers commonly possess sound-producing organs on their legs and wings; in most species the males produce trilling, buzzing, or clicking sounds that attract females for mating. Grasshoppers are common in open, dry habitats and are well-represented in the White Mountain region. Here is also present a flightless species (*Agnostokasia sublima*) that occurs nowhere else.

American Cockroach, *Periplaneta americana* (Family Blattidae). (Fig. 7.7) A house and yard pest species that occurs at lower elevations in the Owens Valley. They apparently do not reach Crooked Creek, at 10,000 ft (3,100 m).

Short-horned Grasshoppers (Family Acrididae). Short-horned Grasshoppers may be recognized by their antennae, which are much shorter than the body. Many species have brightly colored wings, visible in flight.

Migratory Grasshopper, *Melanoplus sanguinipes.* (Plate 7.1) Commonly present in swarms between 11,000 and 13,000 ft (3,300 and 4,000 m). At lower elevations it rarely occurs in large numbers but can be a devastating crop pest when it does.

Pallid-winged Grasshopper, *Trimerotropis pallidipennis.*(Plate 7.1) Occurs in the Owens Valley at elevations as high as 5,000 ft (1,500 m).

Sierran Blue-winged Grasshopper, *Circotettix thalassinus.* Common at middle elevations (6,000–9,000 ft, 1,800–2,700 m), where males display by flying up and making loud popping or crackling noises.

Agnostokasia sublima. (Plate 7.1) Known only from 12,000 to 13,000 ft (3,600 to 4,000 m) in the White Mountains, including Barcroft area. A flightless species.

Mormon Cricket, *Anabrus simplex* (Family Tettigoniidae). (Plate 7.1) Occurring near Crooked Creek and near Barcroft, 10,000–12,000 ft (3,000–3,600 m), always associated with sagebrush (*Artemisia*). Flightless, the males call in late morning with a loud stridulation. This species is a member of a subfamily of crickets (the Decticinae)

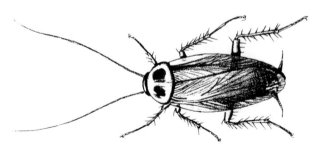

FIGURE 7.7   American Cockroach (*Periplaneta americana*).

that is very diverse in the Owens Valley region. Known as the Shield-backed Katydids, Decticinae are commonly flightless, especially the females.

Camel Cricket, *Ceuthophilus lamellipes* (Family Gryllacrididae). (Fig. 7.8) Occurs from the Owens Valley to elevations of 11,000 ft (3,400 m), usually present under stones and logs.

California Mantid, *Stagmomantis californica* (Family Mantidae). (Fig. 7.9) Occurs in Owens Valley up to higher elevations. Mantids have been collected at Crooked Creek, at 10,150 ft (3,100 m), but not at higher sites.

True Bugs (Order Hemiptera)

Members of the Order Hemiptera, or true bugs, possess a slender, segmented beak, arising from the anterior tip ("forehead") of the insect, and front wings divided into two parts, with the basal portion thick and leathery and the rest transparent. The antennae are fairly long and consist of four or five segments. Many hemipterans have scent glands, which give off an acrid scent when the insect is disturbed. Juvenile hemipterans look like the adults, except they lack wings. Juveniles eat the same food as the adults and occur in the same habitats. Most species feed on plant juices, and some are considered serious pests. Other hemipterans are considered beneficial to man because they attack harmful insects. Still other hemipterans suck blood, and a few of these insects act as vectors for disease. Some hemipterans resemble ants in appearance and mode of walking, presumably to deceive their predators.

Say's Stink Bug, *Chlorochroa sayi* (Family Pentatomidae). (Fig. 7.10) Green bugs widespread and common in the White Mountains from 4,000–14,000 ft (1,200 to 4,300 m). They can be found feeding on a variety of plants from spring to fall.

FIGURE 7.8   Camel Cricket
(*Ceuthophilus lamellipes*).

FIGURE 7.9   California Mantid
(*Stagmomantis californica*).

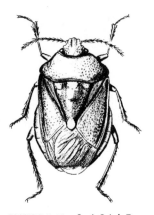

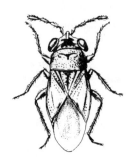

FIGURE 7.10　Say's Stink Bug
(*Chlorochroa sayi*).

FIGURE 7.11　Big-eyed Bug
(*Geocoris bullatus*).

Big-eyed Bug, *Geocoris bullatus* **(Family Lygaeidae).**　(Fig. 7.11) Abundant, very small insect occurring in the Mount Barcroft area under low vegetation, where it probably eats seeds and soft-bodied insects.

Alydus pluto **(Family Alydidae).**　(Plate 7.1) The bright red-orange abdomen shows in flight but is covered by dark wings when the insect is at rest. Common at middle elevations (6,000–10,000 ft; 1,800–3,100 m). Nymphs resemble ants and feed on plants.

Common Milkweed Bug, *Lygaeus kalmii* **(Family Lygaeidae).**　(Plate 7.1) A common member of the Seed Bug Family that occurs at elevations as high as 11,000 ft (3,400 m) in the White Mountains. Red with black markings, this bug prefers milkweed seeds for its food but will also feed on a wide range of other plants.

Cicadas, Leafhoppers, Aphids, Scale Insects, and Others (Order Homoptera)

The large and diverse Order Homoptera is related to the Order Hemiptera. Homopterans exhibit a large variation in body structure, but the most distinguishing characteristic is the beak, which is located near the insect's neck (on the "chin"). The antennae are very short and bristlelike, and the compound eyes are usually large. Winged homopterans usually have four membranous wings, which at rest are usually held rooflike over the body.

All homopterans feed on plant sap, and many species are serious pests of cultivated plants. A few homopteran species are beneficial, used to make shellac, dyes, and other materials.

Giant Willow Aphid, *Tuberolachnus salignus* **(Family Aphididae).**　(Fig. 7.12) An aphid common on willows (*Salix* spp.) in the region, feeding in large colonies on the trunks and branches. Also known as Plant Lice, members of the Aphid Family

FIGURE 7.12   Giant Willow Aphid
(*Tuberolachnus salignus*).

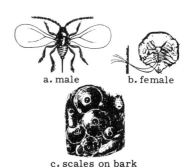

a. male   b. female

c. scales on bark
FIGURE 7.13   Scale insect.

are sedentary insects that feed on plant sap. Many aphids are "tended" by ants, which obtain sugary "honeydew" excretion in return for protection from enemies such as Ladybird Beetles and maggots (larvae) of Syrphid Flies. Adult aphids may be winged sexual reproductives or wingless females that reproduce parthenogenically (i.e., without mating). Aphids may occur at all elevations in the White Mountains.

Scale insects (Family Coccidae).   (Fig. 7.13) The body of a scale insect is hidden under a waxy shell that resembles fish scales attached to the bark of trees and shrubs. Some species secrete honeydew and are tended by ants. They occur in the Owens Valley, and probably on trees and shrubs at elevations below 12,000 ft (3,700 m).

Leafhoppers (Family Cicadellidae).   (Fig. 7.14) Occurring at all elevations in the White Mountains, Leafhoppers are highly active homopterans that live on twigs of trees, shrubs, and herbs. Usually cylindrical and bullet-shaped, many Leafhoppers have the habit of quickly moving to the opposite side of the twig when approached so as to be shielded from view.

Cicadas (Family Cicadidae).   (Fig. 7.15) Occur at elevations below 12,000 ft (3,700 m). Usually heard but not seen, most male cicadas produce a loud, musical buzz or whine that is easily distinguished from the trills and intermittent buzzes/clicks of most orthopterans. Cicadas are large-bodied, and the juveniles feed underground on

FIGURE 7.14   Leafhopper.

FIGURE 7.15   Cicada.

plant roots for two to five years. One species, *Okanagana cruentifera*, is locally very abundant in sagebrush (*Artemisia*).

Beetles (Order Coleoptera)

The Order Coleoptera contains about 40% of all known insect species. Beetles occur in virtually every habitat except the ocean. The wings are the most distinguishing characteristic of Coleoptera. The hard, shell-like front pair, called elytra, are used mainly for protection. The second pair of wings, membranous and longer than the elytra, are used for flying and are folded under the elytra when not in use. Beetles have chewing mouthparts and undergo complete metamorphosis. Overwintering can occur at any stage of development, depending on the species. The larvae vary considerably in form among different families. Beetles and beetle larvae are known to feed on all types of plant and animal materials. Many beetles are considered valuable because they destroy injurious insects or act as scavengers.

Tiger Beetles, *Cicindela* spp. (Family Cicindelidae). (Fig. 7.16) Very active, predaceous beetles commonly seen at elevations up to 12,000 ft (3,700 m). They may be metallic green, blue, or plain brown, but their colors are difficult to see because they move so rapidly. Two species, *C. plutonica* and *C. montana,* are common at high elevations (11,000–12,000 ft, 3,300–3,700 m).

Ground Beetles, *Pterostichus* spp. (Family Carabidae). (Fig. 7.17) Occurs near 9,000 ft (2,700 m) in July. Ground Beetles are common insects that forage for prey mainly on the ground. Species are often similar in shape but may differ greatly in size. They are usually black or brown and have fine "lines" on the wing covers parallel to the margins. There are very many species. Another genus that occurs in the White Mountains is *Callisthenes,* near 10,000 ft (3,100 m) in July and August.

River Beetle, *Agabus lutosus* (Family Dytiscidae). (Fig. 7.18) A water beetle that commonly occurs in small ponds at elevations up to 12,500 ft (3,800 m). Both the larvae and the adults are predaceous.

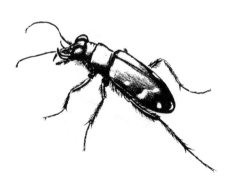

FIGURE 7.16   Tiger Beetle (*Cicindela* sp.).

FIGURE 7.17   Ground Beetle (*Pterostichus* sp.).

FIGURE 7.18 River Beetle
(*Agabus lutosus*).

FIGURE 7.19 *Serica* sp.

Burying Beetle, *Nicrophorus hecate* (Family Silphidae). (Plate 7.1) Two varieties—one black, the other red and black—are found on carrion from 4,000 to 10,000 ft (1,200 to 3,100 m), from spring to fall. These beetles bury small carrion, remove the hair, and feed and lay eggs in an underground chamber.

***Serica* spp. (Family Scarabidae).** (Fig. 7.19) Occurs near 8,000 ft (2,400 m) elevation in summer, commonly on trees and shrubs.

Twig Girdler, *Agrilus walshinghami* (Family Buprestidae). (Fig. 7.20) Occurs from 4,000 to 6,000 ft (1,200–1,800 m) in August and September on flowers of Rabbit Brush *Chrysothamnus nauseosus*.

Cactus Flower Beetles, *Carpophilus* spp. (Family Nitulidae). (Fig. 7.21) Occur in cactus flowers at lower elevations (4,000–9,000 ft, 1,200–2,700 m) in spring.

Common Checkered Beetle, *Trichodes ornatus* (Family Cleridae). (Fig. 7.22) Commonly occurs on flowers, including cactus flowers, and probably occurs up to 10,000 ft (3,100 m).

Blister Beetles (Family Meloidae). A family of beetles common and diverse in the low-elevation areas of the Owens Valley. Many are brightly colored. Eggs are laid on

FIGURE 7.20
Twig Girdler
(*Agrilus walshinghami*).

FIGURE 7.21
Cactus Flower Beetle
(*Carpophilus* sp.).

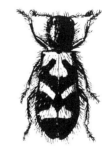

FIGURE 7.22
Common Checkered Beetle
(*Trichodes ornatus*).

the ground or on flowers, and the first instar larvae actively seek out host insects such as bees or grasshopper eggs, feeding on the host eggs and larvae.

Meloe spp. May occur up to 12,000 ft (3,700 m). The larvae are parasites of bees.

Epicauta oregona. A small and grey species with black spots that occurs in the Owens Valley. Its larvae probably feed on grasshopper eggs.

Soldier Blister Beetle, *Tegrodera latecincta.* (Plate 7.1) A large meloid occurring in the Owens Valley and up into the foothills to 4,500 ft (1,400 m). This and the following two species may be seen feeding on flowers in summer.

Pleurospasta mirabilis. (Plate 7.1) Occurs below 5,000 ft (1,500 m) in the Owens Valley.

Phodaga alticeps. (Plate 7.1) Occurs below 5,000 ft (1,500 m) in the Owens Valley.

Armored Stink Beetle, *Eleodes armatus* (Family Tenebrionidae). (Plate 7.1) A large, black beetle that occurs commonly during all seasons from 4,000 to 7,000 ft (1,200 to 2,100 m), where it is usually found walking on open ground. When disturbed, it raises the tip of its abdomen into the air, sometimes emitting a foul-smelling vapor. These beetles superficially resemble Ground Beetles (Family Carabidae), but their behavior and the lack of prominent jaws are usually sufficient to distinguish the two families. Other common species include *Eleodes obscura,* which occurs from 5,000 to 8,000 ft (1,500 to 2,400 m), spring to fall; *Eleodes pilosa,* at 10,000 ft (3,100 m) in July; and *Eleodes (Blapylus)* species, which occur from 10,000 to 13,000 ft (3,100 to 4,000 m) in summer and fall.

Convergent Ladybird Beetle, *Hippodamia convergens* (Family Coccinellidae). (Plate 7.1) A familiar beetle occurring at all elevations. Thousands of "ladybugs" may locally occur clustered in watered canyons or on mountain peaks, especially in fall and winter. This and the following species are important predators of other insects, especially homopterans.

Neomysia spp. (Family Coccinellidae). Occurring from 6,000 to 9,000 ft (1,800 to 2,700 m), pale, faintly striped species montane in distribution and common on Pinyon Pine.

Leaf Beetles, *Altica* spp. (Family Chrysomelidae). Small (0.1 in, 3mm) metallic blue or purple beetles common at higher elevations (10,000–12,000 ft, 3,100–3,700 m). Members of this abundant, diverse family are commonly green, blue, or black and resemble the ladybird beetles in shape. They are commonly very small and feed primarily on the leaves of plants. Also common are the *Trirhabda* species, whose irridescent green larvae feed on sagebrush.

Long-horn Beetles (Family Cerambycidae). Adult beetles of the Family Cerambycidae have thick, long antennae and so are collectively known as "long-horn beetles." Larvae of most species bore into wood.

FIGURE 7.23
Banded Alder Borer
(*Rosalia funebris*).

Banded Alder Borer, *Rosalia funebris*. (Fig. 7.23) A large, conspicuous beetle that occurs along Owens River, where its larvae bore into alder, willow, and other hardwood trees.

Crossidius hertipes nubilis. (Plate 7.1) Occurs from 7,000 to 8,000 ft (2,100 to 2,400 m), where it is commonly seen feeding on flowers of Rabbit Brush *Chrysothamnus viscidiflorus*.

Arhopalus asperatus. A large, black cerambycid whose larvae bore into pine and other conifers.

Judolia instabilis. (Plate 7.1) Commonly occur on flowers, especially lupine. Larvae bore into pine species. Adults of this species may be yellow and black, or all black. Occurs from 7,000 to 13,000 ft (2,100 to 4,000 m).

Butterflies and Moths (Order Lepidoptera)

Lepidoptera is a familiar group of insects commonly known as butterflies and moths. The adults possess minute scales on their wings that, in many species, produce brilliant color patterns. The mouthparts are modified into a thin, coiled tube through which they drink fluids. Most butterflies have six functional legs, but adults of one family, the Nymphalidae, possess only four.

Lepidoptera are almost entirely herbivorous: only in the larvae stage, when they are known as caterpillars, do they eat solid food. They are voracious eaters and can quickly defoliate a plant, particularly when feeding in groups. Lepidopteran caterpillars can be recognized by the gap (of at least two segments) between their thoracic " true" legs and their abdominal "prolegs," which are not jointed legs but simply extensions of the abdominal body wall. Other insect larvae that might be mistaken for Lepidoptera caterpillars either: (1) have prolegs on every abdominal segment (Sawflies, of the Order Hymenoptera), (2) lack prolegs except for an anal "clasper" (Ladybird and Leaf Beetles, of the families Coccinellidae and Chrysomelidae, respectively), or (3) lack thoracic legs entirely (Hover flies, of the Family Syrphidae).

Most adult moths are gray or brown and are easily distinguished from butterflies, which are usually brightly colored. However, there are some exceptions. In such cases, butterflies may usually be distinguished by the presence of clubbed antennae, unlike the usual hairlike or plumose antennae of moths.

Lepidoptera, particularly the butterflies, are a favorite of collectors. Consequently, their habits and distributions are relatively well known. Most species of butterfly are brightly colored and may be recognized by comparison with drawings or photographs; we have included most of the species known from the White Mountain area in Plates 7.1–7.5. Good specimens of most butterflies may be obtained by locating the caterpillars and raising them to adults in a jar or plastic bag, feeding them leaves of the host plant they were found upon.

Tent Caterpillar, *Malacosoma americana* (Family Lasiocampidae). Commonly weaves large, conspicuous "tents" of silk in shrubs belonging to the Rose Family (locally plants in other families are used). Each tent contains 50 or more caterpillars. The adults, plain brown moths, occur in desert scrub up to 9,000 ft (2,700 m).

White-lined Sphinx Moth, *Hyles lineata* (Family Sphingidae). (Plate 7.2) Occurs up to 13,000 ft (4,000 m) in spring, summer, and fall. These moths are commonly attracted to lights at night, sometimes in large numbers, and may be seen visiting flowers at dusk or on overcast days.

Skippers (Family Hesperiidae). Skippers derive their common name from their rapid, "skipping" flight, usually seen when they visit flowers. At rest, many male skippers do not fold their wings together over their back but hold them at an angle, with the fore- and hindwings separated. Many skipper caterpillars feed on monocot plants, such as grasses, and are green or brown with very large heads.

Common Sootywing, *Pholisora catullus*. (Plate 7.2) Found at 6,000 ft (1,800 m) in May. Larvae feed on pigweeds such as *Chenopodium* and *Amaranthus*.

Great Basin Sootywing, *Pholisora libya lena*. (Plate 7.2) Adults occur at 6,000 ft (1,800 m) in June.

Sandhill Skipper, *Polites sabuleti tecumseh*. (Plate 7.2) Adults occur from 10,000 to 13,000 ft (3,100 to 4,000 m) in the summer. Larvae feed on grasses such as *Distichlis* and lawn grass.

Sierra Skipper, *Hesperia miriamae*. (Plate 7.2) Adults occur from 13,000 to 14,000 ft (4,000 to 4,300 m) during the summer. Larvae of this high-altitude species probably feed on grasses.

Uncas Skipper, *Hesperia uncas macswaini*. Looks like *H. miriamae* but with a dusky border on the upper surface of the hindwing. It flies at very high elevations in the

White Mountains, in grassy areas in June and July. Larvae feed on Needlegrass *Stipa nevadensis*.

Common Banded Skipper, *Hesperia comma harpalus*. (Plate 7.2) Occurs from 4,000 to 14,000 ft (1,200 to 4,300 m) from spring to fall. Larvae feed on grasses and sedges.

Juba Skipper, *Hesperia juba*. (Plate 7.2) May occur from 6,000 to 10,000 ft (1,800 to 3,100 m) in summer. Larvae feed on grasses.

Mexican Cloudy-wing, *Thorybes mexicana blanca*. A skipper medium brown in color, with black-bordered white spots on the forewing. It occurs above 7,000 ft (2,100 m) in June–August. Larval food plants are unknown.

Whites and Sulfurs (Family Pieridae). As their names suggest, Whites and Sulfurs are butterflies that are usually white or yellow in coloration. They are typically fragile animals, losing their legs and scales easily. They have six functional legs. The caterpillars are mostly green or yellow-green, lack long spines or hairs, and feed on plants in the Mustard and Caper families (White Butterflies) or in the Legume Family (Sulfur Butterflies).

Cabbage White, *Pieris rapae*. A species common around gardens and fields on the Owens Valley floor and occasionally at higher elevations. It has whitish or yellowish underwings, in contrast to the other whites of the region, which have dark markings below.

Checkered White Butterfly, *Pontia protodice*. (Plate 7.2) The underside has relatively few brownish markings. Occurs from 4,000 to 14,000 ft (1,200 to 4,300 m) from spring to fall. Larvae feed on plants in the Mustard Family (Brassicaceae).

Becker's White Butterfly, *Pontia beckerii*. (Plate 7.2) A white with black spotting on the tips and margins of the forewings; the undersides of the wings have greenish brown markings. Adults occur from 4,000 to 8,000 ft (1,200 to 2,400 m) in June and July. Larvae feed on mustard plants such as the Black Mustard (*Brassica nigra*).

Hyantis Marble Butterfly, *Euchloe hyantis lotta*.(Plate 7.2) A small white with green markings on the underside of the wings. The adults occur from 4,000 to 8,000 ft (1,200 to 2,400 m) in May. Larvae feed on several species of mustard.

Orange Sulfur, *Colias eurytheme*. (Plate 7.2) Occurs from 4,000 to 14,000 ft (1,200 to 4,300 m) from spring to fall. Larvae feed on several species of plants in the Legume Family, including alfalfa (*Medicago* spp.), clover (*Trifolium* spp.), vetches and locoweeds (*Astragalus* spp.), and lupines (*Lupinus* spp.).

Swallowtails (Family Papilionidae). Members of the Family Papilionidae derive their common name from the "tails" attached to the hindwing. Swallowtails are large, sturdy butterflies, usually black and yellow. They are commonly seen gliding

FIGURE 7.24   Western Tiger Swallowtail
(*Papilio rutulus*).

effortlessly across open ground, visiting flowers and searching for host plants. Adults
have six legs.

Western Tiger Swallowtail, *Papilio rutulus*. (Fig. 7.24) Commonly occur in watered
canyons and around towns. Larvae feed on willow, poplar, and sycamore trees.

Short-tailed Black Swallowtail, *Papilio indra nevadensis*. (Plate 7.3) Adults occur
from 6,000 to 9,000 ft (1,800 to 2,700 m) in June. Larvae usually feed on plants
in the Carrot Family (Apiaceae), but they are also known to feed on sagebrush
(e.g., *Artemisia tridentata*).

Blues and Coppers (Family Lycaenidae).   Lycaenidae is a family of butterflies diverse in the White Mountains region, and many of its members are associated with
ants in various ways. The caterpillars are sluglike, with a thick skin that is resistant to ant attack. Some species have glands and pores that secrete nectar and
amino acids. This functions to attract a protective "guard" of ants, much in the
way that many homopterans attract ants. For unknown reasons, male lycaenids have
somewhat reduced forelegs compared with the females, which have six functional
legs.

Mormon Metalmark Butterfly, *Apodemia mormo*. (Plate 7.3) Occurs from 4,000 to
7,000 ft (1,200 to 2,100 m) in the fall. Larvae feed on buckwheat (*Eriogonum*
spp.).

Edward's Blue, *Plebejus (Lycaeides) melissa paradoxa*. (Plate 7.3) Occurs from 4,000
to 11,000 ft (1,200 to 3,400 m) in the summer. The larvae feed on species in the
Legume Family, including lupines, vetches, and locoweed (*Oxytropis* spp.).

Greenish Blue, *Plebejus saepiolus*. (Plate 7.3) Occurs at 12,000 ft (3,700 m)
throughout the summer. Larvae feed on clover (*Trifolium* spp.).

Boisduval's Blue, *Plebejus (Icaricia) icarioides*. (Plate 7.3) Occurs from 9,000 to
12,000 ft (2,700 to 3,700 m) during the summer. Larvae feed on lupine (*Lupinus*
spp.).

Alpine Blue, *Plebejus shasta*. (Plate 7.3) Occurs from 10,000 to 13,000 ft (3,100 to 4,000 m) during the summer. Larvae feed on lupines, clover, and locoweed (e.g., *Astragalus*).

Lupine Blue, *Plebejus lupini*. (Plate 7.3) Occurs from 10,000 to 13,000 ft (3,100 to 4,000 m) during the summer.

Acmon Blue, *Plebejus acmon*. (Plate 7.3) Adults occur from 4,000 to 11,000 ft (1,200 to 3,400 m) in July. Larvae feed on buckwheat (*Eriogonum* spp.).

Arrowhead Blue, *Glaucopsyche piasus*. (Plate 7.4) The underside of the wing bears white "arrowhead" markings. The adults occur in June at 9,000–11,000 ft (2,700–3,400 m). Larvae feed on lupine (*Lupinus* spp.).

Silvery Blue, *Glaucopsyche lygdamus*. (Plate 7.4) The underside of the wing bears a single jagged row of small black dots ringed with white. The adults occur in May between 6,000 and 10,000 ft (1,800 and 3,000 m). Larvae feed on lupine (*Lupinus*), and locoweed (e.g., *Oxytropis* and *Astragalus*).

Spring Azure, *Celastrina ladon*. (Plate 7.4) Occurs from 5,000 to 10,000 ft (1,500 to 3,100 m) during the spring and summer.

Pygmy Blue, *Brephidium exilis*. (Plate 7.4) Small, with a wingspread less than 3/4 in (1.9 cm). Occurs between 4,000 and 11,000 ft (1,200 and 3,400 m) from spring to fall. Larvae feed on pigweed (*Chenopodium* spp. and *Amaranthus* spp.) and saltbush (*Atriplex* spp.).

Blue Copper, *Lycaena (Chalceria) heteronea*. (Plate 7.4) Occurs from 10,000 to 12,000 ft (3,100 to 3,700 m) during the summer. Larvae feed on buckwheat (*Eriogonum* spp.).

Edith's Copper, *Lycaena (Gaeides) editha*. (Plate 7.4) Occurs from 10,000 to 13,000 ft (3,100 to 4,000 m) during the summer. Larval food plants are unknown.

Cupreus Copper, *Lycaena cuprea*. (Plate 7.4) Occurs from 10,000 to 13,000 ft (3,100 to 4,000 m) during the summer and fall. Larvae feed on Mountain Sorrel (*Oxyria*).

Thicket Hairstreak, *Mitoura spinetorum*. (Plate 7.4) A species with short "tails" on the hindwings. Wings have dull blue upper surfaces and brown lower surfaces. It occurs from 6,000 to 9,000 ft (1,800 to 2,700 m) during the summer. Larvae are known to feed on mistletoe (*Arceuthobium*) species that parasitize conifers.

Siva Hairstreak, *Mitoura siva*. (Plate 7.4) Has "tails" like *M. spinetorum*, but wings have brown upper surfaces and greenish lower surfaces. It occurs from 6,000 to 8,000 ft (1,800 to 2,400 m) during the spring. Larvae resemble the twigs of their host plant, juniper (*Juniperus* spp.).

Comstock's Green Hairstreak, *Callophrys comstocki*. A tailless hairstreak light grey above with a broken white band on the underside of the hindwing, edged inwardly with black. The undersurface of the wing is greenish. It occurs from 5,000 to 7,000 ft (1,500 to 2,100 m) in the spring. Larvae feed on buckwheat (*Eriogonum*).

Brush-footed Butterflies (Family Nymphalidae). Nymphalids are commonly large and showy, and may be easily recognized by the presence of only four functional legs, the forelegs being modified into "drumming" organs used by the females to "taste" the host plants. Nymphalid caterpillars are commonly spiny or brightly colored, although the grass feeders tend to be green and difficult to see.

Monarch Butterfly, *Danaus plexippus.* (Plate 7.5) Occurs from 4,000 to 14,000 ft (1,200 to 4,300 m) from spring to fall. Larvae feed on milkweed (*Asclepias* spp.).

Dark Wood Nymph, *Cercyonis oetus.* (Plate 7.5) Occurs from 10,000 to 12,000 ft (3,100 to 3,700 m) in the summer. Larvae feed on grass.

Riding's Satyr, *Neominois ridingsii.* (Plate 7.1) Occurs from 9,000 to 11,000 ft (2,700 to 3,100 m). It "flushes" when disturbed, flies a short distance, and quickly alights, camouflaging itself on rocks or lichens. Its larvae probably feed on grass.

Neumoegen's Checkerspot, *Chlosyne (Charidryas) neumoegeni.* (Plate 7.5) Occurs from 4,000 to 6,000 ft (1,200 to 1,800 m) in the spring. Larvae feed on plants in the Sunflower Family (Asteraceae).

Leanira Checkerspot, *Chlosyne (Thessalia) leanira alma.* (Plate 7.5) Occurs from 5,000 to 8,000 ft (1,500 to 2,400 m) in the spring. Larvae feed on Indian Paintbrush (*Castelleja* spp.).

Anicia Checkerspot, *Euphydryas (Occidryas) anicia wheeleri.* (Plate 7.5) Occurs from 9,000 to 11,000 ft (2,700 to 3,400 m) in summer. Larvae feed on plants in the Scrophulariaceae, including species of *Penstemon* and *Castelleja.*

Milbert's Tortoiseshell, *Nymphalis (Aglais) milberti.* (Plate 7.5) Occurs from 10,000 to 13,000 ft (3,100 to 4,000 m) in the summer and fall. Larvae usually feed on nettles (*Urtica* spp.) but have been reported on species of willow (*Salix* spp.) and sunflower (*Helianthus* spp.).

Mourning Cloak, *Nymphalis antiopa.* (Plate 7.1) A large, easily recognized species that occurs along streams and in the Owens Valley. The larvae feed on willow (*Salix* spp.) and other trees.

Painted Lady, *Vanessa cardui.* (Plate 7.5) Occurs from 4,000 to 14,000 ft (1,200 to 4,300 m), spring to fall. Larvae feed on plants in the Sunflower Family (Asteraceae).

West Coast Lady, *Vanessa annabella.* (Plate 7.5) Adults occur in June near 7,000 ft (2,100 m). Larvae feed on plants in the Mallow Family (Malvaceae).

Red Admiral, *Vanessa atalanta.* (Plate 7.1) Occurs from 4,000 to 11,000 ft (1,200 to 3,400 m), spring to fall. This large species feeds on nettle (*Urtica* spp.).

Lorquin's Admiral, *Limenitis lorquini.* (Plate 7.1) Larvae feed on willow, poplar, and other trees along streams and in the Owens Valley. The adults fly with quick wingbeats interspersed with gliding and are large and striking.

Flies, Gnats, and Mosquitoes (Order Diptera)

Dipterans, also known as the "true flies," may be recognized by the possession of only two wings instead of the four that other adult insects have. In Diptera, the hindwings have been modified into tiny, clublike halteres, which are used as organs of balance. Most dipterans lack mandibles, and adults are common visitors to flowers, where they drink nectar with their spongelike or sucking mouthparts. Adult female dipterans of many species are blood suckers and require one or more blood meals for egg production. The larvae of many dipterans are aquatic or feed in anaerobic decaying matter; others feed on plant material or are predaceous on other insects. One family (Tachinidae) is particularly important as parasites of caterpillars; the larvae feed internally until the entire host is consumed. Dipteran larvae are legless and maggotlike except for specialized aquatic forms, such as mosquito larvae.

Crane flies, *Tipula* spp. (Family Tipulidae).   (Fig. 7.25) Crane flies have the appearance of very large mosquitoes but are completely harmless. They occur at elevations up to 13,000 ft (4,000 m).

Mosquitoes, *Anopheles* spp. (Family Culicidae).   (Fig. 7.26) Mosquitoes are common in wet areas, such as along the Owens River or boggy areas at higher elevations. Members of this genus are the principal vectors of malaria in California.

Robber Flies, (Family Asilidae).   (Fig. 7.27) Robber Flies are common and easily recognized by their stout thorax, wings, and legs, and by their behavior of perching in exposed positions and sallying forth after flying prey. They are very diverse in the White Mountains at all elevations.

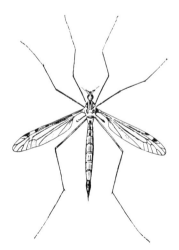

FIGURE 7.25   Crane Fly (*Tipula* sp.).

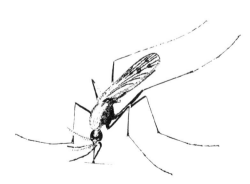

FIGURE 7.26   Mosquito (*Anopheles* sp.).

FIGURE 7.27   Robber Fly.

Hover Flies (Family Syrphidae).   Hover Flies are commonly seen visiting flowers. Many species look very much like bees or wasps. They also commonly hover in midair, holding a fixed position relative to the surrounding vegetation, and abruptly changing position when approached. Larvae of some species are caterpillarlike and feed on aphids and small herbivorous insects. Some species occur at elevations as high as the top of White Mountain Peak.

Common Hover Fly, *Metasyrphus aberrantis*. (Plate 7.1) Occurs on flowers from 6,000 to 10,000 ft (1,800 to 3,100 m). The larvae crawl on plants and eat aphids and other small insects. They are legless, yet manage to cling to vegetation very efficiently.

Sawflies, Wasps, Bees, and Ants (Order Hymenoptera)

Adult hymenopterans possess four wings, with the hindwings smaller than the forewings. Except for the Sawflies, hymenopterans also have a constricted "waist" between the first and second abdominal segments and, in females, an ovipositor modified into a stinger. The larvae of Sawflies are mainly herbivorous and greatly resemble lepidopteran caterpillars. The wasps are mainly predaceous or parasitic on other insects and are very important in controlling their numbers. Some wasps and Sawflies parasitize plants by laying their eggs in plant tissues. The egg or resulting larvae then induces the plant to form a gall, which surrounds the insect. These galls are particularly common on oaks and willows. The bees feed primarily on pollen and nectar and are probably the most important agents of flower pollination.

Many hymenopterans live in tightly coordinated social groups usually dominated by one or more reproductive "queens." The queen's efforts at reproduction are aided by numerous "workers," which may be temporarily or permanently sterile. Ants represent the extreme of this type of social evolution, and the sterile, wingless workers are among the most common, visible insects in many habitats. They feed on small insects and obtain sugary "honeydew" secretions from Homoptera. They are very important in controlling the numbers of other insects in many habitats.

Sawflies, *Tenthredo* spp. (Family Tenthredinidae).   (Fig. 7.28) Adult Sawflies resemble wasps, except that they have a stout "waist" instead of the threadlike waist of the true wasps and bees. Sawflies are commonly encountered as larvae feeding on the leaves of plants. Many Sawfly larvae look very much like caterpillars of Lepidoptera,

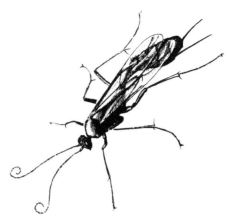

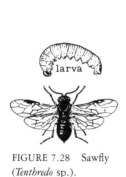

FIGURE 7.28   Sawfly
(*Tenthredo* sp.).

FIGURE 7.29   Ichneumon (*Ophion* sp.).

except that they possess prolegs on every abdominal segment rather than on five or fewer segments (as seen in Lepidoptera). Many Sawflies lay their eggs internally in the host plant leaves rather than externally, as in most Lepidoptera. Some Sawflies make galls in their host plants. Sawflies occur as high as Crooked Creek in the White Mountains (10,150 ft, 3,100 m).

Ichneumons, *Ophion* spp. (Family Ichneumonidae).   (Fig. 7.29) Ichneumons are elongated wasps, the larvae of which are parasitic on other insects. They are frequently seen searching vegetation for their hosts by quivering their long, curled antennae and making short flights between branches or plants. They occur at all elevations below 13,000 ft (4,000 m).

Cuckoo Wasps, *Chrysis* spp. (Family Chrysididae).   Cuckoo Wasps are brillant green and reproduce by parasitizing larvae of other wasps in their burrows. They occur at all elevations below 13,000 ft (4,000 m), where they may be seen drinking from flowers.

Tarantula Hawks, *Pepsis* spp. (Family Pompilidae).   (Plate 7.1) Easily recognized wasps because of their very large size and black and orange wings, they occur from 4,000 to 8,000 ft (1,200 to 2,400 m) in summer and fall. These and other spider wasps actively hunt spiders, which they paralyze by stinging and drag to a burrow. Then they deposit an egg and seal up the burrow. Eventually the egg hatches, and the wasp larva consumes the spider. Smaller spider wasps in the same family occur at elevations up to 13,000 ft (4,000 m).

Resin Bees, *Dianthidium* spp. (Family Megachilidae).   (Fig. 7.30) Occur at elevations below 8,000 ft (2,400 m), and possibly higher. Commonly found in deserts and foothills in California, they nest alone rather than in colonies. Resin Bees are common pollinators of *Phacelia* and other desert flowers.

FIGURE 7.30   Resin Bee
(*Anthidium* sp.).

FIGURE 7.31   Honey Bee
(*Apis mellifera*).

Bumble Bees, *Bombus centralis* and *B. morrisoni* (Family Apidae). (Plate 7.1) Bumble bees occur at elevations up to 11,000 ft (3,400 m). Commonly seen visiting flowers, these bees live in nests underground.

Honey Bee, *Apis mellifera* (Family Apidae). (Fig. 7.31) Abundant at lower elevations, an introduced bee that has established itself in the wild, nesting in hollows in trees, caves, and underground.

Carpenter Bee, *Xylocopa californica arizonensis* (Family Anthophoridae). (Fig. 7.32) Adults are large, black bees that bore into dead wood to make nest chambers. They occur between 6,000 and 8,000 ft (1,800 and 2,400 m).

Ants (Family Formicidae). Ants are familiar organisms at all elevations in the White Mountains. Protected underground and by numerous worker individuals willing to sacrifice their lives in defense of the colony, ants are among the most successful creatures on earth. Perhaps because of the ants' abundance, many insects have evolved specific adaptations to survive with them. For example, aphids and many butterflies of the Family Lycaenidae secrete sugary honeydew, which attracts ants, which in return protect the insects from enemies such as parasitic wasps and Ladybird Beetles.

FIGURE 7.32   Carpenter Bee
(*Xylocopa* sp.).

FIGURE 7.34 Carpenter Ant
(*Camponotus* sp.).

FIGURE 7.33 Mound Ant (*Formica* sp.).

Mound Ants, *Formica* spp. (Fig. 7.33) Occur from the Owens Valley to 12,500 ft (3,800 m) in large, mound-shaped nests on bare ground. These ants may be very aggressive. The species *F. subpolita* occurs at Barcroft Laboratory at 12,500 ft (3,800 m).

Carpenter ants, *Camponotus* spp. (Fig. 7.34) Large, black ants that usually nest in or near dead wood, which they hollow out. In spite of their large size, these ants are commonly timid and nonaggressive. They occur in dead wood to 11,000 ft (3,400 m). *C. sansabeanus* and *C. ochreatus* nest in dry wood near Westgard Pass.

REFERENCES

Borror, D. J., D. Delong, and C. A. Triplehorn. 1976. *Introduction to the Study of Insects.* Holt, Rinehart, and Winston, New York.

Borror, D. J., and R. E. White. 1970. *A Field Guide to the Insects of America North of Mexico.* Peterson Field Guide Series, Houghton Mifflin, Boston.

Emmel, T. C., and J. F. Emmel. 1973. *The Butterflies of Southern California.* Natural History Museum, Los Angeles.

Garth, J. S., and J. W. Tilden. 1986. *California Butterflies.* University of California Press, Berkeley.

Powell, J. A., and C. L. Hogue. 1979. *California Insects.* University of California Press, Berkeley.

8

Fishes

Edwin P. Pister

INTRODUCTION

For all practical purposes, the fishes of the White Mountains are introduced species. It is unlikely that native species ever existed in these mountains except in the very lowest reaches of either easterly or westerly drainages.

Perhaps the terms *introduced species* and *native species* should be clarified. When Europeans first arrived in the Owens Valley, only four fishes were found there, all of them considered nongame species: the Owens Pupfish (*Cyprinodon radiosus* Miller), Owens Chub (*Gila bicolor snyderi* Miller), Owens Dace (*Rhinichthys osculus* sp.), and Owens Sucker (*Catostomus fumeiventris* Miller). On the east side of the range, in Fish Lake Valley, only a chub (*Gila* sp.) was found. These constitute the native fish fauna of the White Mountains area, and through many years of neglect only one of them, the Owens Sucker, now occurs in abundance. The others are endangered, threatened, or of undetermined status. Recovery programs are in progress for the endangered and threatened fauna, under the provisions of the federal and state endangered species acts.

The streams flowing from the White Mountains are spring-fed. Being a desert range, the White Mountains seldom hold the summer snowbanks that typify the Sierra Nevada, just a few miles to the west. Once the winter snows have melted, the stream flows quickly stabilize except during occasional summer thundershowers.

A glance at a map of the Inyo National Forest reveals a large number of streams flowing from the crest of the White Mountains. However, only a few of them contain significant fish populations, and these generally only in the upper reaches. The vast majority of these streams, whether they flow east or west, have for many years been diverted for irrigation.

EARLY TROUT PLANTING

The exact history of fish introductions into the White Mountains is unknown. Accurate records of early fish planting, unfortunately, were not kept. It is safe to assume, however, that most introductions occurred in this century prior to World War II. Some introductions were made by the California Division (now Department) of Fish and Game, and others were made by the Rainbow Club, an early sportsmen's club headquartered in Bishop. The club has planted no fish since before World War II.

Most White Mountain streams have been planted with trout, and one may expect to find Eastern Brook Trout, *Salvelinus fontinalis* (Mitchill), and Rainbow Trout, *Oncorhynchus mykiss gairdnerii* (Richardson), in the higher elevations and Brown Trout,

Salmo trutta Linnaeus, in the lower elevations. However, the California streams are no longer being stocked with trout; all populations are self-sustaining. The Nevada Department of Wildlife, however, occasionally stocks Rainbow Trout in streams flowing into northern Fish Lake Valley.

Paiute Trout

An exception to the general rule concerning trout species composition and distribution is found in Cottonwood Creek, which flows easterly into Fish Lake Valley from near White Mountain Peak. In 1946, when Department of Fish and Game and U.S. Forest Service biologists noted that the Paiute Cutthroat Trout, *Oncorhynchus clarki seleniris* (Snyder), populations of the upper East Fork Carson River (Alpine County, California) were seriously threatened, a limited number were planted in the previously fishless upper North Fork Cottonwood Creek. This stream has been generally closed to angling since that time. The subspecies is currently listed as threatened under the federal Endangered Species Act.

The North Fork Cottonwood Creek Paiute Cutthroat population is perhaps the only genetically pure population left in the world, and it is being protected as part of the recovery plan for the subspecies. Should the subspecies recover sufficiently, management plans may allow a very limited harvest. Until that time, however, the North Fork Cottonwood Creek will remain closed to angling. To accelerate the recovery of the Paiute Cutthroat Trout, it may be spread to other suitable streams as part of a plan under consideration by the Department of Fish and Game and the U.S. Forest Service. At present, however, the only stream area in the White Mountains with a special restriction is the North Fork Cottonwood Creek. Anglers planning to fish anywhere in California should check current fishing regulations, which are available at most sporting goods stores.

SPECIES DESCRIPTIONS

Rainbow Trout, *Oncorhynchus mykiss gairdneri* (Richardson).   (Fig. 8.1) Other than the Paiute Trout, the Rainbow Trout is the only trout species in the White Mountains that is native to California. It may be distinguished from the other species by its generally silvery appearance and profusion of spots, including a spotted tail. It also commonly has a reddish lateral band extending from head to tail. However, look for the spotted tail as the definitive characteristic. None of the other trout species in the White Mountains has a heavily spotted tail.

Eastern Brook Trout, *Salvelinus fontinalis* (Mitchill).   (Fig. 8.2) Although called a trout, the Eastern Brook Trout is actually a char. It is native to the eastern United States and was brought to California many years ago. It has been introduced widely throughout the Sierra Nevada and occurs in several streams in the White Mountains.

Eastern Brook Trout are generally olive green with light spots on the sides. They may be distinguished from the trout species by vermiculations, or wavy lines, along

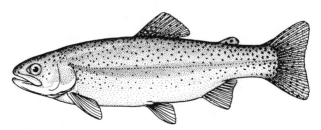

FIGURE 8.1 Rainbow Trout, *Oncorhynchus mykiss gairdnerii* (Richardson).

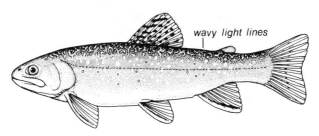

FIGURE 8.2 Eastern Brook Trout, *Salvelinus fontinalis* (Mitchill).

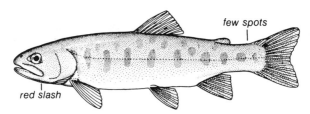

FIGURE 8.3 Paiute Cutthroat Trout, *Oncorhynchus clarki seleniris* (Snyder).

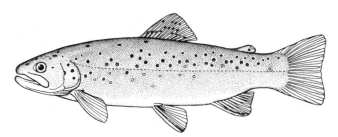

FIGURE 8.4 Brown Trout, *Salmo trutta* Linnaeus.

the back from head to tail. They also have distinct white borders along the anterior margins of the ventral and anal fins.

Paiute Cutthroat Trout, *Oncorhynchus clarki seleniris* **(Snyder).** (Fig. 8.3) The Paiute Cutthroat Trout, which is native to the Great Basin, was introduced into the North Fork Cottonwood Creek in 1946 in one of the first recorded efforts toward species preservation in California. It has survived in Cottonwood Creek in limited numbers, but the North Fork is closed to angling to ensure its protection. The Paiute Cutthroat Trout evolved through geographic isolation from the Lahontan Cutthroat Trout, *Oncorhynchus clarki henshawi* (Gill and Jordan), in upper Silver King Creek, Alpine County.

This trout normally has an overall purplish hue, which distinguishes it from the other trout species in the White Mountains. It also has very few (if any) spots and possesses the distinctive reddish cutthroat marks under the jaw.

Brown Trout, *Salmo trutta* **Linnaeus.** (Fig. 8.4) The Brown Trout, a native of Europe, was brought into California many years ago and eventually found its way into the White Mountains. It is common there, especially in the lower stream areas. It is an excellent game fish and is sought after by anglers, especially fly fishermen.

The Brown Trout is usually dark or olive brown on the back and golden brown on the sides. It generally has red spots surrounded by a halo on its sides. It may have spots on the tail, but they are sparse in contrast to the profusion of tail spotting present in Rainbow Trout.

CONCLUSION

Some researchers are now questioning the general advisability of introducing nonnative species into a naturally balanced ecosystem. The trout stocking that occurred in the early 1900s was a result of resource management procedures in practice at that time, but current research is beginning to recognize the long-term implications of stocking to the ecosystem. Such introduction invariably harms native organisms and is now considered unacceptable ecological practice.

REFERENCES

California Department of Fish and Game. 1969. *Trout of California*. Calif. Dept. of Fish and Game, Sacramento.

Hubbs, C. L., and R. R. Miller. 1948. Correlation between fish distribution and hydrographic history in the desert basins of western United States. In *The Great Basin, with emphasis on glacial and postglacial times*. Bulletin of the University of Utah, no. 38, pp. 17–166.

Miller, R. R. 1948. *The cyprinodont fishes of the Death Valley system of eastern California and southwestern Nevada*. Miscellaneous Publications of the Museum of Zoology, University of Michigan, no. 68.

Miller, R. R. 1973. *Two new fishes*, Gila bicolor snyderi *and* Catostomus fumeiventris, *from the Owens River basin, California*. Occasional Papers, Museum of Zoology, University of Michigan, no. 667.

Miller, R. R., and E. P. Pister. 1971. Management of the Owens pupfish, *Cyprinodon radiosus*, in Mono County, California. *Transactions of the American Fisheries Society* 100:502–509.

Pister, E. P. 1974. Desert fishes and their habitats. *Transactions of the American Fisheries Society* 103:531–540.

Pister, E. P. 1976. A rationale for the management of nongame fish and wildlife. *Fisheries* 1:11–14.

Pister, E. P. 1979. Endangered species: Costs and benefits. *Environmental Ethics* 1:341–352.

Pister, E. P. 1981. The conservation of desert fishes. In R. J. Naiman and D. L. Soltz (eds.).*Fishes in North American deserts*, pp. 411-455. John Wiley & Sons, New York.

Schumacher, Genny (ed.). 1969. *Deepest valley: Guide to Owens Valley and its mountain lakes, roadsides, and trails.* Wilderness Press, Berkeley, Calif.

Soltz, D. L., and R. J. Naiman. 1978. *The natural history of native fishes in the Death Valley system.* Natural History Museum of Los Angeles County, Science Series, no. 30.

Vestal, E. H. 1947. A new transplant of the Paiute trout (*Salmo clarkii seleuiris*) from Silver King Creek, Alpine County, California. *California Fish and Game* 33(2):89–95.

9

Amphibians

J. Robert Macey and Theodore J. Papenfuss

INTRODUCTION

Amphibians are cold-blooded vertebrates with moist, scaleless skin. These animals either occur in close association with permanent water or are active only during wet times of the year. There are approximately 3,200 species in the world, and amphibians are present on all continents except Antarctica.

Amphibians are divided into three groups: caecilians, salamanders, and frogs and toads. Caecilians are elongate, "wormlike," burrowing or aquatic forms that lack limbs and functional eyes. The approximately 165 species are restricted to the tropical regions of the world; no species occur in the United States. Most caecilians are less than 2 ft (0.6m) long; however, one species in South America reaches a length of 5 ft (1.5m).

Most salamanders have a lizardlike shape with four legs and a tail. They have smooth, moist skin that lacks scales. In the New World there are three areas with high species diversity. One is the mountainous region of southern Mexico and northern Central America, with some 50 species. Another is the Appalachian Mountains of the eastern United States, with about 45 species. The third region comprises the Pacific states of California, Oregon, and Washington, with about 35 species.

The species that are present in California have two very different developmental patterns. Some breed in water, and the adults return to streams and ponds during the rainy season to lay eggs. Gilled larvae develop in the water and later transform into terrestrial adult salamanders. Other salamanders are completely terrestrial. The eggs are laid on land in moist places. The larval stage takes place in the egg, and small, fully transformed salamanders emerge. All western fully terrestrial salamanders lack lungs, and respiration takes place through the skin.

Three species of salamanders are known to occur in the California portion of the White-Inyo mountains region. The only state with no native salamanders is Nevada. There have been several reports of salamanders in Nevada, but none have been confirmed. Although the species accounts included here for salamanders have been brought up to date, they are probably incomplete and may even be lacking a species. We would appreciate receiving any additional information, such as a new distribution or a salamander that does not fit the descriptions.

The frogs and toads are the largest group of amphibians. Approximately 2,600 species of frogs and toads are known, and they occur on every continent except Antarctica. The greatest species diversity is in the tropics, but frogs and toads are

THE VALLEYS OF THE INYO AND WHITE MOUNTAINS REGION

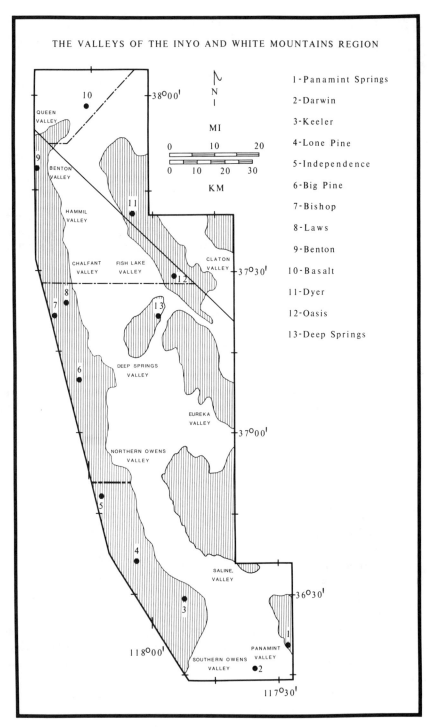

1-Panamint Springs
2-Darwin
3-Keeler
4-Lone Pine
5-Independence
6-Big Pine
7-Bishop
8-Laws
9-Benton
10-Basalt
11-Dyer
12-Oasis
13-Deep Springs

MAP 9.1

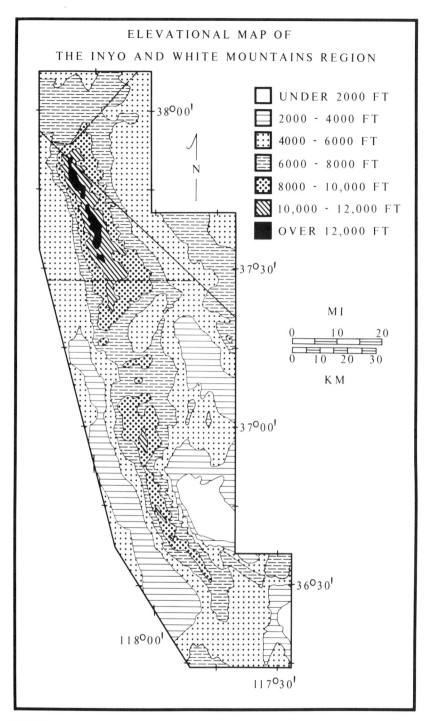

ELEVATIONAL MAP OF
THE INYO AND WHITE MOUNTAINS REGION

UNDER 2000 FT
2000 - 4000 FT
4000 - 6000 FT
6000 - 8000 FT
8000 - 10,000 FT
10,000 - 12,000 FT
OVER 12,000 FT

38°00'

N

37°30'

MI

0   10   20

0   10   20   30

KM

37°00'

36°30'

118°00'

117°30'

MAP 9.2

well represented in temperate regions. These amphibians occur in a great variety of habitats. Some species occur in arid regions, where they spend most of their lives underground, coming to the surface only during occasional rains. Others are fully aquatic and never leave the water. A few species in tropical regions spend their entire lives in the tree canopy. There are 23 families of frogs and toads worldwide, of which 5 occur in California and Nevada. The families that occur in the area under study are the True Toads (Family Bufonidae), Treefrogs (Hylidae), Spadefoot Toads (Pelobatidae), and True Frogs (Ranidae).

SPECIES ACCOUNTS

The following species accounts cover the three salamanders and seven frogs and toads that occur in the White-Inyo mountains region. Accounts are ordered by main group, then alphabetically by family name, and finally alphabetically by species name. Each account consists of a brief identification, information on habitat, and a remarks section, which treats natural history. A brief summary of the range and a list of the exact localities corresponding to the dots on the range maps are also included. When the locality is vague, it is not plotted on a map. In these lists the first reference to a place name is listed in its entirety, and all other references to that place name follow it as separate localities. These localities are based on museum specimens. The majority of specimens from this region are deposited in the Museum of Vertebrate Zoology, University of California at Berkeley (MVZ). Other museums represented in the localities sections are: American Museum of Natural History, New York (AMNH); California Academy of Sciences, San Francisco (CAS); Carnegie Museum of Natural History, Pittsburgh (CMNH); Field Museum of Natural History, Chicago (FMNH); University of Kansas (KU); Natural History Museum of Los Angeles County (LACM); Museum of Comparative Zoology, Harvard University (MCZ); San Diego Natural History Museum (SDSNH); University of Michigan Museum of Zoology (UMMZ); University of Nevada, Reno (UN); and United States National Museum, Washington, D.C. (USNM). The acronym of the museum follows each locality. Absence of an acronym indicates that the locality is based on a specimen from the Museum of Vertebrate Zoology. For accuracy, elevations and distances of localities are cited as recorded by the collector and have not been converted to or from the English or metric system.

The color plates of species will aid in identification. All amphibians in the color plates are from the White-Inyo mountains region except the Northern Leopard Frog (*Rana pipiens*), which is from Churchill County, Nevada. For each species, pertinent literature references are listed; the complete citations are at the end of the chapter. General references to the amphibians of the region are: Macey (1986), Papenfuss (1986), Stebbins (1951), and Stebbins (1985). All scientific names are after Collins (1990). In addition, the following chapter of this book, on reptiles, has two sections that contain general information on amphibians of the White-Inyo mountains region.

Lungless Salamanders (Family Plethodontidae)

Kern Plateau Slender Salamander, *Batrachoseps* sp. (no author, not yet described). (Plate 9.1) 3–4 in (7.5–10 cm); dorsal pattern variable; black with a brown middorsal stripe or black with an overlay of silver specks; only four toes on each foot. *Habitat:* This species occurs around permanent springs and creeks with riparian vegetation. The salamanders live in the daytime under cover objects such as rocks and logs. *Remarks:* This salamander is related to the Inyo Mountains Slender Salamander (*B. campi*) and was the second salamander to be discovered in the White-Inyo mountains region. The Kern Plateau Slender Salamander has a narrower head and shorter legs than the Inyo Mountains Slender Salamander. The ranges of the two species do not overlap. Species of the genus *Batrachoseps* are the only salamanders in California that have just four toes on each hind foot. Other species of *Batrachoseps*, known as Slender Salamanders, are widely distributed throughout California. They commonly occur in urban areas under rocks and boards. This species is currently known from the Kern Plateau and the southeastern slopes of the Sierra Nevada, but it may have a more extensive range. *Range:* Kern Plateau and the eastern slopes of the Sierra Nevada south and west of Owens Lake. *Reference:* Stebbins (1985).

Inyo Mountains Slender Salamander, *Batrachoseps campi* (Marlow, Brode & Wake, 1979). (Plates 9.2 [from Hunter Canyon] and 9.3 [from French Spring], Map 9.3) 2–3 in (5–7.5 cm); dorsal pattern variable; background color dark brown to black; in some populations scattered green, lichenlike spots on body; in others the background color is completely overlain with silver flecks; only four toes on each foot. *Habitat:* Occurs only around permanent springs and seeps that provide a riparian habitat. Inyo Mountains Slender Salamanders are active at night. During the day they take shelter under moist rocks or in damp crevices. They have been found at springs as low as 1,800 ft (550 m) and as high as 8,600 ft (2,600 m). *Remarks:* The discovery in 1973 of these salamanders in the arid Inyo Mountains was unexpected. In the past, numerous biologists had visited many of the springs where these salamanders live without detecting them, because salamanders are not considered desert animals. Doubtless, additional populations will be found. These salamanders are relicts that entered the Inyo Mountains prior to the rise of the Sierra Nevada and the formation of the Mojave and Great Basin deserts. In some instances these isolated populations may consist of only a few hundred individuals. They are protected by state law and should not be collected. At the present time, capping of springs is the major threat to these populations. *Range:* Both east and west slopes of the Inyo Mountains. *References:* Marlow, Brode, and Wake (1979); Yanev and Wake (1981).

Localities: California, Inyo Co.: 6,800–7,000, 8,000–8,300 ft, Addie Canyon; 6,400 ft, Barrel Springs; 6,400 ft, Cove Springs; 3,500 ft, Craig Canyon; 6,000 ft, French Spring (LACM, MVZ); 1,800 ft, 2,200 ft, Hunter Canyon; 4,000 ft, Keynot Canyon; 6,500 ft, Lead Canyon (LACM, MVZ); 5,600 ft, Long John Canyon (LACM, MVZ); 3,500 ft, McElvey Canyon; 7,500 ft, top of ridge between Lead and Addie canyons; 7,200 ft, Waucoba Canyon; 4,700 ft, Willow Creek Canyon.

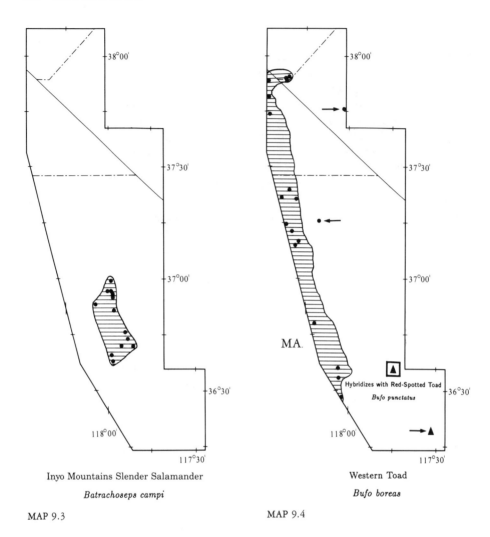

Inyo Mountains Slender Salamander

Batrachoseps campi

MAP 9.3

Western Toad

Bufo boreas

MAP 9.4

Owens Valley Web-toed Salamander, *Hydromantes* **sp. (no author, not yet described).** (Plate 9.4) $3^1/_2$–$4^1/_2$ in (9–11.5 cm); body and head very flattened; dorsal pattern variable; greenish brown to silver with scattered black spots; scattered lichenlike silver spots on ventral surface; feet with extensive webbing; four toes on front feet and five toes on hind feet. *Habitat:* The Owens Valley Web-toed Salamander occurs in the vicinity of permanent springs and mountain streams with riparian vegetation. Although this salamander is nocturnal, it can be encountered under wood and rocks in areas with moist soil. *Remarks:* The Genus *Hydromantes* is distributed in California, Italy, and Sardinia. The species in Europe are the only members of the lungless salamander family, Plethodontidae, in the Old World. The Owens Valley Web-toed Salamander was discovered in 1985 during field work in preparation for this chapter.

Range: Eastern slopes of the Sierra Nevada, at least from the area around Owens Lake to Big Pine. *Reference:* Wake, Maxson, and Wurst (1978).

True Toads (Family Bufonidae)

Western Toad, *Bufo boreas* (Baird & Girard, 1852).   (Plate 9.5, Map 9.4) 3–5 ½ in (7.5–13.75 cm); marbled dorsal pattern of brown, gray, and green in equal proportions; distinct white or light yellow line down middle of back; ventral background color cream with black spots; small warts scattered over back; oblong gland (parotoid gland) behind eye is longer than upper eyelid. *Habitat:* In White-Inyo Range, occurs around permanent ponds and slow-moving streams. Western Toads are generally nocturnal; however, recently discovered populations in the northern White Mountains (see Map 9.4) are also active during the day, at least in spring and summer. *Remarks:* Western Toads are a common, wide-ranging species in much of the western United States, occurring from sea level to above 9,000 ft (2,740 m). They are often seen at night on roads and in yards in rural areas. In the White-Inyo mountains region, this species is generally restricted to valleys, but it has been found above 7,000 ft (2,130 m) in the Pinyon-juniper Woodland of the northern White Mountains. A Creosote Bush Scrub outpost for this species is Darwin Falls Canyon in the northern Argus Mountains. Here the Western Toad and the Red-spotted Toad (*B. punctatus*) coexist and occasionally hybridize (see Red-spotted Toad account). At a second isolated locality, Fish Lake in Fish Lake Valley, Western Toads may be extinct due to the introduction of Bullfrogs (*Rana catesbeiana*) (see Bullfrog account). *Range:* Darwin Falls Canyon, northern Argus Mountains; Owens Valley; vicinity of Fish Lake, Fish Lake Valley; extreme northern White Mountains. *Reference:* Karlstrom (1962).

    Localities: California, Inyo Co.: Alvord (USNM); 3.0 mi S Bartlet; Batchelder Spring, Westgard Pass; Big Pine; 1.5 mi SW; 4 mi NW (LACM); Bishop; 0.5 mi NW (UMMZ); 5 mi E (LACM); 4000 ft, Bishop Creek (USNM); Darwin Falls, Argus Mtns.; Diaz Lake, Owens Valley (CAS); Fish Lake Spring (CAS); Independence; Laws (CAS, MVZ); near (UMNZ); Lone Pine (MCZ, MVZ, USNM); 2.9 mi S (CAS). Mono Co.: Benton; 5 mi N (SDSNH); 3 mi from Nevada State line, spring, Taylor Ranch, 5 mi N Benton (UMMZ). Nevada, Esmeralda Co.: Fish Lake (MVZ, UMMZ); 7,820 ft, Buffalo Canyon. Mineral Co.: Orchard Spring, Buffalo Canyon; Queen Canyon.

Black Toad, *Bufo exsul* (Myers, 1942).   (Plate 9.6, Map 9.5) 1 ½–2 ½ in (3.75– 6.25 cm); dorsal color predominantly black; faint white line down middle of back; ventral color black, with white mottling becoming more extensive on chin; small warts scattered over back; oblong gland (parotoid gland) behind eye is longer than upper eyelid. *Habitat:* This species is the most aquatic toad in the region. It never occurs far from permanent water. Black Toads prefer marshy areas around pools or slow-moving streams. They are generally diurnal but may be active at night during the summer. *Remarks:* The Black Toad along with the three salamanders are the only amphibians endemic to the White-Inyo mountains region. It is native only to the Deep Springs Valley but has been introduced to Batchelder Spring on the west side of

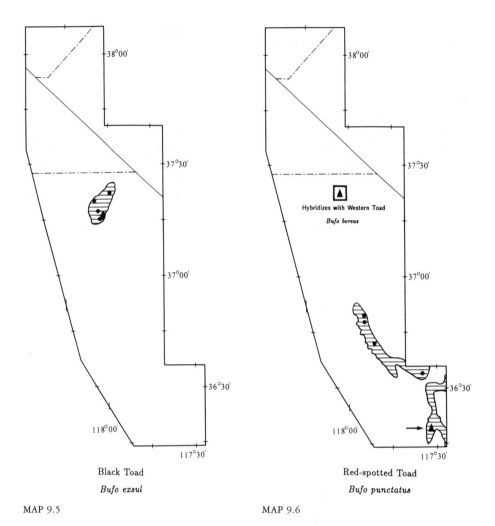

Black Toad

Bufo exsul

MAP 9.5

Red-spotted Toad

Bufo punctatus

MAP 9.6

Westgard Pass. However, no toads have been seen at Batchelder Spring in recent years, and that population may be extinct. The Black Toad is closely related to the Western Toad (*B. boreas*). It has been isolated from the Western Toad for at least 12,000 years, since the last Pleistocene moist period. The Black Toad, and the Amargosa Toad (*B. nelsoni*) in Nye County, Nevada, have commonly been regarded as subspecies of the Western Toad. However, a recent genetic study suggests that these two forms be recognized as full species. The only other amphibian in Deep Springs Valley is the Great Basin Spadefoot (*Spea intermontana*). Spadefoots have light-colored, smooth skin and spades on the hind feet (see Great Basin Spadefoot Toad account). Black Toads are protected by California law and should not be collected. *Range:* Areas of permanent water in the Deep Springs Valley; introduced to Batchelder Spring, Westgard Pass, but may be extinct. *References:* Myers (1942), Schuierer (1962).

Localities: California, Inyo Co.: Antelope Spring; Deep Springs Valley (CAS, LACM); Batchelder Spring, Westgard Pass; Bog Mounds Spring, Deep Springs Valley; Buckhorn Spring, Deep Springs Valley (CAS, MVZ); Deep Springs (CAS, CMNH, FMNH, SDSNH, USNM, KU, MCZ); 6 mi S (LACM, MVZ); 7 mi S; 7.5 mi S (AMNH, UMMZ); 8 mi S (LACM); Deep Springs Lake (CAS, MCZ, USNM); 0.5 mi E; Warm Spring at Deep Springs Lake.

Red-spotted Toad, *Bufo punctatus* (Baird & Girard, 1852).   (Plate 9.7, Map 9.6)
2–3 in (5–7.5 cm); greenish gray background color; small warts scattered over back, arms, and legs; each wart is reddish brown and surrounded by a black circle; round gland (parotoid gland) slightly smaller than upper eyelid, located behind each eye. *Habitat:* This toad occurs near springs and semipermanent streams in and around Creosote Bush Scrub. Red-spotted Toads are nocturnal but may be found during the day under rocks adjacent to streams. *Remarks:* This species can be distinguished from other toads in the area by the small red spots and the round parotoid gland that is smaller than the eyelid. It is a wide-ranging, predominantly Creosote Bush Scrub species that reaches the northern limits of its distribution in our area. At Darwin Falls in the northern Argus Mountains (see Map 9.6), Red-spotted Toads and Western Toads (*B. boreas*) occur together. Locally, hybrids between the two species have been found; this is the only reported case in California of hybridization between Red-spotted Toads and other toads. *Range:* East side of the Argus and Inyo mountains in canyons draining into the Panamint and Saline valleys. *Reference:* Feder (1979).

Localities: California, Inyo Co.: Darwin Falls, Argus Mtns. (CAS, MVZ); Grapevine Canyon, Nelson Mtns.; Hunter Creek, Saline Valley (CAS, MVZ); below Jackass Spring, Panamint Mtns. (E of study area) (USNM); Pat Keyes Canyon, Saline Valley; Willow Creek, Saline Valley.

Treefrogs (Family Hylidae)

Pacific Treefrog, *Pseudacris regilla* (Baird & Girard, 1852).   (Plate 9.8, Map 9.7) 1–2 in (2.5–5 cm); dorsal pattern variable, gray with brown blotches or uniform green; individual frogs can change color; dark stripe extends from nose through eye and beyond jaw; smooth skin; toe tips enlarged to form small adhesive pads. *Habitat:* In the White-Inyo Range this species is restricted to permanent streams and marshy areas. Treefrogs are mainly nocturnal and form breeding choruses during the spring and early summer. Some live during the day next to streams and on vegetation in marshes. The adhesive pads on their toes allow them to climb. *Remarks:* The Pacific Treefrog is a widespread and common frog in California. However, in the White-Inyo mountains region its distribution is limited. It appears to be restricted to the southern Owens Valley from Owens Lake to Independence, and it is present in the Queen Valley. It seems to be absent not only from the rest of the Owens Valley, but also from the White-Inyo Range. Suitable habitat is present in both areas, but

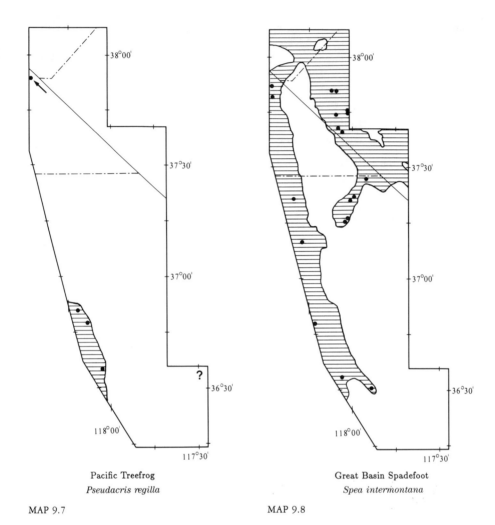

Pacific Treefrog
Pseudacris regilla

Great Basin Spadefoot
Spea intermontana

MAP 9.7   MAP 9.8

no specimens have been reported. It is common, however, in several canyons in the Panamint Mountains. The 1891 U.S. Department of Agriculture Death Valley expedition collected two specimens in Cottonwood Canyon, in the northern Panamint Mountains. This locality is just east of the area covered in this chapter, and it is possible that Pacific Treefrogs may occur in the Panamint Mountain portion (see ? on Map 9.7). *Range:* Owens Lake to Independence in the southern Owens Valley; Queen Valley. Expected in the northwestern Panamint Mountains. *References:* Hedges (1986); Jameson, Mackey, and Richmond (1966).

Localities: California, Inyo Co.: 3,800 ft, Cottonwood Canyon, below Jackass Spring, Panamint Mtns. (E of study area) (USNM); 3 mi E Independence; 3 mi N; 0.8 mi S Lone Pine. Mono Co.: 40 N Bishop [= Bramlett-Taylor Ranch Springs, 8 mi N Benton] (UMMZ).

Spadefoot Toads (Family Pelobatidae)

Great Basin Spadefoot Toad, *Spea intermontana* (Cope, 1883).   (Plate 9.9, Map 9.8) 1–2 ½ in (2.5–6.25 cm); dorsal background light gray with dark gray spots; skin smooth; a jet black oval protrudes from the bottom of each hind foot; eyes relatively large; fleshy bump; known as a boss, between eyes. *Habitat:* This species is the only amphibian in the area that is not restricted to the vicinity of permanent water. Typical habitat in our area is Great Basin Scrub below 6,500 ft (1,980 m). However, on the east side of Owens Lake they have been found in Creosote Bush Scrub (see Map 9.8). Spadefoots are strictly nocturnal. They are most active in the fall, in the spring, and during summer rains. *Remarks:* The smooth skin, black spades, and boss between the eyes distinguish this toad from all others in the region. Spadefoots may be observed on roads at night, most commonly during or after rains. In the day and during dry times of the year, they use their spades to dig backward into the soil. These toads are very resistant to water loss and may remain underground for long periods of time. A related species in southeastern California, the Couch's Spadefoot Toad (*S. couchii*), has been known to remain underground for two years waiting for rains. The Great Basin Spadefoot Toad usually breeds during the spring in temporary ponds. The hatching of eggs into tadpoles and the transformation of tadpoles into toads may take place in a few weeks. Although Great Basin Spadefoots have not been observed in the White-Inyo mountains region above 6,500 ft (1,980 m), they have been found at an elevation of 9,200 ft (2,800 m) in the Bodie Hills north of Mono Lake. *Range:* West side of the White-Inyo Range in the entire Owens Valley, Chalfant Valley, Hammil Valley, Benton Valley, and Queen Valley; south and east side of the White Mountains in the Deep Springs and Fish Lake valleys. *Reference:* Mayhew (1962).

Localities: California, Inyo Co.: Big Pine; 0.5 mi NE; 5.6 mi NE; 27.8 mi NE; 0.3 mi E; Bishop; 3.0 mi N; Deep Springs (CAS); 7 mi S; Deep Springs Lake; NE end (LACM); Diaz Lake (CAS); 0.5 mi SE of Hwy. 168 on Eureka Valley Rd.; 1.4 mi W Independence; 2.0 mi SE; Lone Pine; 8.1 mi SE; 10.0 mi SE; 1.0 mi S Mono County line on Hwy. 168. Mono Co.: Benton; 3.2 mi N (LACM); 1.6 mi W (LACM). Nevada, Esmeralda Co.: 1 mi W Hwy. 264 along Chiatovich Creek, Fish Lake Valley; 5,000 ft, Chiatovich Ranch, Fish Lake Valley; Dyer; 1.8 mi S; 4.0 mi N; Fish Lake (MVZ, UMMZ); 1 mi S.

True Frogs (Family Ranidae)

Bullfrog, *Rana catesbeiana* (Shaw, 1802).   (Plate 9.10, Map 9.9) 4–8 in (10–20 cm); background color light to dark green, uniform on back with crossbars on legs; conspicuous large eardrum behind eye. *Habitat:* This frog prefers slow-moving streams and rivers. It is also common in marshes associated with permanent ponds and lakes. Bullfrogs are active both during the day and at night. They are very wary, and when approached they commonly escape by jumping from the bank into the water. *Remarks:* Bullfrogs are not native to the area. They were originally introduced from the eastern United States to parts of western North America to provide a fresh source of meat. Natural expansion of this frog's range and further introductions have greatly

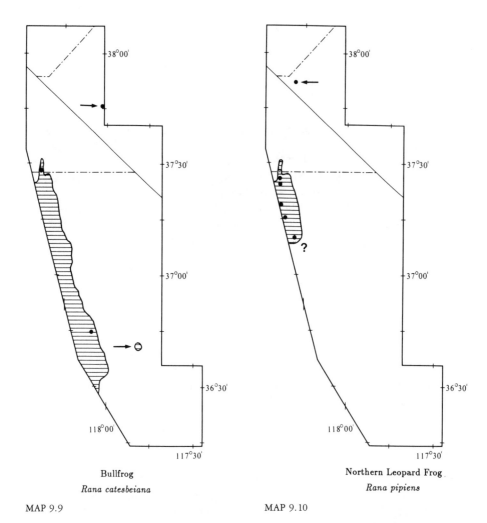

Bullfrog

Rana catesbeiana

MAP 9.9

Northern Leopard Frog

Rana pipiens

MAP 9.10

increased the area in which Bullfrogs live. Unfortunately, they have had a disastrous effect on native amphibians because they prey on them. A large Bullfrog is capable of eating the young and even adults of the native frogs and toads. Red-legged Frogs (*R. aurora*) and Foothill Yellow-legged Frogs (*R. boylei*) are now extinct in many areas of central California due to the presence of Bullfrogs. In our area, they were recently introduced into the Fish Lake Valley, where Western Toads (*Bufo boreas*) were formerly common. During the preparation of this chapter, extensive field work was conducted in the Fish Lake Valley, but no Western Toads were seen. *Range:* Introduced into the Owens Valley; Fish Lake, Fish Lake Valley; marshes around Salt Works, Saline Valley. *References:* Moyle (1973).

Localities: California, Inyo Co.: Owens River, 2 mi S Independence. Mono Co.: Fish Slough, 0.4 mi N Inyo County line. Nevada, Esmeralda Co.: Fish Lake.

Northern Leopard Frog, *Rana pipiens* (Schreber, 1782). (Plate 9.11, Map 9.10)
2 ½–4 in (6.25–11.25 cm); background color gray or tan; distinct dark-brown or black spots over back and sides; spots on legs forming bars; pale-colored ridge runs down each side of the back from top of eyelid to hind leg; ventral surface uniformly pale. *Habitat:* Northern Leopard Frogs occur around permanent ponds and streams. They are active both during the day and at night. This is a wary species that usually jumps into the water when approached. *Remarks:* Leopard Frogs, which range from Panama to the Northwest Territories, Canada, are the most widely distributed group of frogs in North America. Until recently they were all considered one species. The Northern Leopard Frog is the widest-ranging species currently recognized in this group; it occurs from New Foundland to the western Great Basin. This species' wide range is presumed to be due to major expansions since the recession of the last glacial period, which started 18,000 years ago. Leopard Frogs are commonly used in biology class dissections and laboratories around the country. This practice has led to many introductions of this species where they did not formerly occur. *Range:* Northern Owens Valley from Big Pine to north of Bishop; may occur further south in the Owens Valley (see ? on Map 9.10); reported from the east side of the White Mountains below Boundary Peak. *References:* Hillis, Frost, and Wright (1983); Sage and Selander (1979).

    Localities: California, Inyo Co.: 1 mi W Big Pine; 4 mi W Bishop (W of study area); 3.2 mi N (UMMZ); 5 mi N (LACM, MVZ); 8 mi S. Nevada, Esmeralda Co.: 7,100 ft, east side of White Mountains below Boundary Peak (UN).

REFERENCES

Collins, J. T. 1990. *Standard common and current scientific names for North American amphibians and reptiles,* 3d ed. Society for the Study of Amphibians and Reptiles, Herpetological Circular no. 19.

Feder, J. H. 1979. Natural hybridization and genetic divergence between the toads *Bufo boreas* and *Bufo punctatus. Evolution* 33:1089–1097.

Hedges, B. S. 1986. An electrophoretic analysis of Holarctic hylid frog evolution. *Systematic Zoology* 35:1–21.

Hillis, D. M., J. S. Frost, and D. A. Wright. 1983. Phylogeny and biogeography of the *Rana pipiens* complex: A biochemical evaluation. *Systematic Zoology* 32:132–143.

Jameson, D. L., J. P. Mackey, and R. C. Richmond. 1966. The systematics of the pacific tree frog, *Hyla regilla. Proceedings of the California Academy of Sciences* 19:551–620.

Karlstrom, E. L. 1962. The toad genus *Bufo* in the Sierra Nevada of California. *University of California Publications in Zoology* 62:1–104.

Macey, J. R. 1986. The biogeography of a herpetofaunal transition between the Great Basin and Mojave deserts. In C. A. Hall, Jr. and D. J. Young (eds.), *Natural history of the White-Inyo Range, eastern California and western Nevada, and high altitude physiology,* pp. 119–128. University of California White Mountain Research Station Symposium, August 23–25, 1985, Bishop, Calif. vol. 1.

Marlow, R. W., J. M. Brode, and D. B. Wake. 1979. A new salamander, genus *Batrachoseps,* from the Inyo Mountains of California with a discussion of relationships in the genus. Natural History Museum of Los Angeles County, Contributions in Science, no 308.

Mayhew, W. W. 1962. *Scaphiopus couchi* in California's Colorado Desert. *Herpetologica* 18:153–161.

Moyle, D. B. 1973. Effects of introduced Bullfrogs, *Rana catesbeiana*, on the native frogs of the San Joaquin Valley, California. *Copeia* 1973:18–22.

Myers, G. S. 1942. The Black Toad of Deep Springs Valley, Inyo County, California. Occasional Papers, Museum of Zoology, University of Michigan, no. 469.

Papenfuss, T. J. 1986. Amphibian and reptile diversity along elevational transects in the White-Inyo Range. In C. A. Hall, Jr. and D. J. Young (eds.), *Natural history of the White-Inyo Range, eastern California and western Nevada and high altitude physiology*, pp. 129–136. University of California White Mountain Research Station Symposium, August 23–25, 1985, Bishop, Calif. vol. 1.

Sage, R. D., and R. K. Selander. 1979. Hybridization between species of the *Rana pipiens* complex in central Texas. *Evolution* 33:1069–1088.

Schuierer, F. W. 1962. Remarks upon the natural history of *Bufo exsul* Myers, the endemic toad of Deep Springs Valley, Inyo County, California. *Herpetologica* 17:260–266.

Stebbins, R. C. 1951. *Amphibians of western North America*. University of California Press, Berkeley and Los Angeles.

Stebbins, R. C. 1985. *A field guide to western amphibians and reptiles*. Houghton Mifflin, Boston.

Wake, D. B., L. R. Maxson, and G. Z. Wurst. 1978. Genetic differentiation, albumin evolution, and their biogeographic implications in Plethodontid salamanders of California and southern Europe. *Evolution* 32:529–539.

Yanev, K. P., and D. B. Wake. 1981. Genic differentiation in a relic desert salamander, *Batrachoseps campi*. *Herpetologica* 37:16–28.

10

Reptiles

J. Robert Macey and Theodore J. Papenfuss

INTRODUCTION

The great majority of living reptiles are in the Order Squamata, which includes three major groups. The smallest is the Suborder Amphisbaenia. These are elongate, blind, burrowing reptiles. Most of the 200 or so species live in South America and Africa. All are limbless except for three species of the Genus *Bipes* in Mexico that have front legs. Only one amphisbaenian, the Florida Worm Lizard (*Rhineura floridana*), occurs in the United States. The largest groups of squamate (scaly) reptiles are the snakes and lizards, with about 2,500 and 3,000 species, respectively. Snakes and lizards are the only reptiles present in the White-Inyo mountains region. By western North American standards, the White-Inyo mountains region, accommodating 37 known species, is relatively rich in reptiles.

Using the Chapter

Each species in the region is discussed in a species account, listed alphabetically by species name within each family, and illustrated with a color plate. All reptiles in the color plates are from the White-Inyo mountains region except the juvenile Southern Alligator Lizard (*Elgaria multicarinata*), which is from Kern County, California; the juvenile Western Whiptail (*Cnemidophorus tigris*), which is from Nye County, Nevada; and the Mojave Shovel-nosed Snake (*Chionactis occipitalis occipitalis*), Striped Whipsnake (*Masticophis taeniatus*), Spotted Leaf-nosed Snake (*Phyllorhynchus decurtatus*), and Lyre Snake (*Trimorphodon biscutatus*), which are from San Bernardino County, California. A range map shows the distribution of each species in the area. The species account gives a brief description that should be used in conjunction with the color plate for positive identification. Sizes are given for adult specimens; naturally, juveniles and hatchlings will be much smaller. The size stated is total length, from head to tip of tail. In most lizards the actual body length is only one-third to one-half the total length. The remarks section provides information of general biological interest for each species. The range of the species is summarized for the region, and this summary should be used in conjunction with the range map for the species. One or more literature references are listed for each species; the complete citations are at the end of the chapter. Two references, Stebbins (1954) and Stebbins (1985), provide general information on western reptiles. All scientific names are after Collins (1990). Five references that discuss detailed studies on the reptiles of this region or nearby desert areas are: Banta (1962) (Saline Valley), Macey (1986) (White-Inyo region), Miller and Stebbins (1964) (Joshua Tree National Monument), Papenfuss

(1986) (White-Inyo region), and Tanner and Jorgensen (1963) (Nevada Test Site, Nye County).

Finally, a list of exact localities based on museum specimens is provided. These localities correspond to dots on each range map. When the locality is vague, it is not plotted on a map. In these lists the first reference to a place name is listed in whole, and other references to that place name follow it as separate localities. Refer to maps 9.1 and 9.2 for a guide to place names, valleys, and elevation. The majority of the specimens are housed at the Museum of Vertebrate Zoology, University of California at Berkeley. The acronym for this institution (MVZ) does not follow the locality unless one or more other institutions have specimens from the same locality. In order to assist biologists who may wish to examine specimens from the region, the localities for specimens in other institutions are followed by the museum acronyms. The institutions with specimens from the area include: American Museum of Natural History, New York (AMNH); Brigham Young University (BYU); California Academy of Sciences, San Francisco (CAS); Carnegie Museum of Natural History, Pittsburgh (CMNH); Field Museum of Natural History, Chicago (MNH); University of Kansas (KU); Natural History Museum of Los Angeles County (LACM); Museum of Comparative Zoology, Harvard University (MCZ); Nevada State Museum (NSM); San Diego Natural History Museum (SDSNH); University of California at Santa Barbara (UCSB); University of Colorado Museum (UCM); University of Michigan Museum of Zoology (UMMZ); University of New Mexico (UNM); and the National Museum of Natural History (USNM). For accuracy, elevations and distances of localities from reference points are cited as recorded by the collector and have not been converted to or from the English or metric system.

Two additional sections are included. "Amphibian and Reptile Diversity in Selected Habitats" provides outlined information on how to find the species that occur in selected areas. This will aid in finding and observing amphibians and reptiles in the region. "Amphibian and Reptile Biogeography," which follows this introduction, presents a synthesis of the distributional data in this chapter and in Chapter 9, on amphibians. This section will help the observer understand why a particular species occurs in an area.

Observing Reptiles

Exact localities and habitats are listed in each account. Using this information along with the section "Amphibian and Reptile Diversity in Selected Habitats," at the end of the chapter, will facilitate the observation of reptiles.

Most of the lizard species are easy to observe. Except for the Western Banded Gecko (*Coleonyx variegatus*), all are diurnal, and many are common in preferred habitats. Lizards are most easily seen when they are basking in the morning during the spring and early summer. In low-elevation desert areas, they are not active during the hot, dry midsummer. There is a second period of activity during September and October, followed by hibernation from November through March. At intermediate and high elevations, lizards come out of hibernation in May or June and are active throughout the summer. Lizards tend to be wary, but by walking slowly and quietly, the observer can approach most species within a few feet.

Snakes are more difficult to find than lizards. Ten of the 19 species in the area are always active at night, and 5 more are nocturnal during hot weather. These species are best found by "night driving," a technique used by herpetologists that involves driving slowly at night along deserted paved roads and watching for snakes either lying on or crossing the road. This method works best on warm nights when the moon is not full. Snakes tend to be much less active during the full moon, perhaps because they are more easily seen by predators then. When snakes are on the road, they can be approached and even picked up with ease. Rattlesnakes, of course, should be avoided. Several of the little-traveled roads in the region are good for night driving. These include the Lone Pine–Death Valley road (Hwy. 136), the Big Pine–Eureka Valley road (Eureka Valley Road), the Big Pine–Westgard Pass road (Hwy. 168) below 6,000 ft (1,830 m), the road across Deep Springs Valley (Hwy. 168), the Fish Lake Valley roads (east–west Hwy. 168 and Hwy. 266, north–south Hwy. 266 and Hwy. 264), and the Benton-Lee Vining road (Hwy. 120). Highway 395 through the Owens Valley and Hwy. 6 through the Chalfant, Hammil, Benton, and Queen valleys have too much traffic, but short side roads in these valleys are alternatives.

Diurnal snakes are occasionally seen by hikers, but they are more commonly seen on the road in the morning and late afternoon. During the daytime snakes tend to be more alert and wary. Species such as the Coachwhip (*Masticophis flagellum*), the Striped Whipsnake (*M. taeniatus*), and the Western Patch-nosed Snake (*Salvadora hexalepis*) are surprisingly quick and will flee when approached. Aquatic species such as the Sierra Garter Snake (*Thamnophis couchii*) and the Western Terrestrial Garter Snake (*T. elegans*) are slow on land, but once in the water they can escape with ease.

AMPHIBIAN AND REPTILE BIOGEOGRAPHY

The amphibians and reptiles that occur in the White-Inyo mountains region show several different distributional patterns. This is due in part to changes in desert vegetation in the area. The southern valleys, which are relatively low in elevation, have Creosote Bush (*Larrea tridentata*) as the dominant plant. This is typical of the Mojave Desert as well as other southern deserts in North America. Panamint Valley, Saline Valley, Eureka Valley, and the western slopes of the Inyo Mountains in southern Owens Valley all have Creosote Bush Scrub. The higher, northern valleys, where Creosote Bush is absent, have other dominant plants, such as Shadscale (*Atriplex confertifolia*). Fish Lake Valley, Deep Springs Valley, Owens Valley (except the southwestern part), Chalfant Valley, Hammil Valley, Benton Valley, and Queen Valley all feature this Great Basin Scrub desert. The change in desert foliation causes a south-to-north transition in species of amphibians and reptiles.

The amphibians and reptiles can be grouped into five distributional patterns (see Table 10.1). The southern group consists of species whose ranges are primarily south of the area in Creosote Bush Scrub; these species typically occur in the Mojave Desert. In the White-Inyo mountains region, two species appear to follow the distribution

					SOUTHERN					
	GR	PA	SA	EU	SO	NO	CH	DS	FL	PL
Red-spotted Toad *Bufo punctatus*	X	X	X	—	—	—	—	—	—	—
Desert Tortoise *Gopherus agassizii*	X	—	—	—	—	X	—	—	—	—
Western Banded Gecko *Coleonyx variegatus*	X	X	X	X	X	—	—	—	—	—
Desert Iguana *Dipsosaurus dorsalis*	X	X	X	X	X	—	—	—	—	—
Common Chuckwalla *Sauromalus obesus*	X	X	X	X	X	X	—	—	—	—
Mojave Fringe-toed Lizard *Uma scoparia*	X	—	—	—	—	—	—	—	—	—
Long-tailed Lizard *Urosaurus graciosus*	X	—	—	—	—	—	—	—	—	—
Desert Night Lizard *Xantusia vigilis*	X	X	X	X	X	X	X*	—	—	—
Rosy Boa *Lichanura trivirgata*	X	X	—	—	X	—	—	—	—	—
Glossy Snake *Arizona elegans*	X	X	X	—	X	—	—	—	—	—
Western Shovel-nosed Snake *Chionactis occipitalis*	X	X	X	—	X	—	—	—	—	—
Spotted Leaf-nosed Snake *Phyllorhynchus decurtatus*	X	X	—	—	—	—	—	—	—	—
Southwestern Black-headed Snake *Tantilla hobartsmithi*	X	X	X	—	X	X	—	—	—	—
Lyre Snake *Trimorphodon biscutatus*	X	X	—	X	—	—	—	—	—	—
Western Blind Snake *Leptotyphlops humilis*	X	X	X	X	X	—	—	—	—	—
Sidewinder *Crotalus cerastes*	X	X	—	—	X	X	X	—	—	—
Speckled Rattlesnake *Crotalus mitchelli*	X	X	X	X	X	X	X*	X	X	—
Mojave Rattlesnake *Crotalus scutulatus*	X	—	—	—	—	—	—	—	—	—

		GR	PA	SA	EU	SO	NO	CH	DS	FL	PL
		WIDE-RANGING									
Zebra-tailed Lizard	Callisaurus draconoides	X	X	X	X	X	X	X	—	X	X
Great Basin Collard Lizard	Crotaphytus bicinctores	X	X	X	X	X	X	X*	X	X	X
Long-nosed Leopard Lizard	Gambelia wislizenii	X	X	X	X	X	X	X	X	X	X
Desert Horned Lizard	Phrynosoma platyrhinos	X	X	X	X	X	X	X	X	X	X
Desert Spiny Lizard	Sceloporus magister	X	X	X	X	X	X	X	X	X	X
Side-blotched Lizard	Uta stansburiana	X	X	X	X	X	X	X	X	X	X
Western Whiptail	Cnemidophorus tigris	X	X	X	X	X	X	X	X	X	X
Night Snake	Hypsiglena torquata	X	X	X	X	X	X	X*	X	X	X
Common Kingsnake	Lampropeltis getula	X	X	X	X	X	X	X*	X	X	X
Coachwhip	Masticophis flagellum	X	X	X	X	X	X	X*	X	X	X
Gopher Snake	Pituophis catenifer	X	X	X	X	X	X	X	X	X	X
Long-nosed Snake	Rhinocheilus lecontei	X	X	X	X	X	X	X*	X	X	X
Western Patch-nosed Snake	Salvadora hexalepis	X	X	X*	X*	X	X	X	X	X	X*
Ground Snake	Sonora semiannulata	X	X	X*	X	X*	X	X*	X	X*	X
		NORTHERN									
Western Toad	Bufo boreas	—	X	—	—	X	X	X	—	X	X
Pacific Treefrog	Pseudacris regilla	—	X	—	—	X	—	X	—	—	X
Great Basin Spadefoot	Spea intermontana	—	—	—	—	X	X	X	X	X	X
Northern Leopard Frog	Rana pipiens	—	—	—	—	—	X	X*	—	X	X
Sagebrush Lizard	Sceloporus graciosus	—	—	—	—	X	X	X	—	X	X
Western Fence Lizard	Sceloporus occidentalis	X	—	X	X	X	X	X	X	X	X
Western Skink	Eumeces skiltonianus	—	—	—	—	X	X	—	—	X	X
Racer	Coluber constrictor	—	—	—	—	—	—	—	—	—	X
Striped Whipsnake	Masticophis taeniatus	—	—	—	—	—	X	X	X*	X	X
Western Terrestrial Garter Snake	Thamnophis elegans	—	—	—	—	X	X	X	X	X	X
Western Rattlesnake	Crotalus viridis	—	—	—	—	—	—	X	—	—	X

TABLE 10.1 *(Concluded)*

		GR	PA	SA	EU	SO	NO	CH	DS	FL	PL
ENDEMIC											
Kern Plateau Slender Salamander	*Batrachoseps sp.*	—	—	—	—	X	—	—	—	—	—
Inyo Mountains Salamander	*Batrachoseps campi*	—	—	X	—	X	X	—	—	—	—
Owens Valley Web-toed Salamander	*Hydromantes sp.*	—	—	—	—	X	X	—	X	—	—
Black Toad	*Bufo exsul*	—	—	—	—	—	—	—	X	—	—
Panamint Alligator Lizard	*Elgaria panamintina*	—	X	X	—	X	X	X*	—	—	—
WESTERN											
Southern Alligator Lizard	*Elgaria multicarinata*	—	—	—	—	X	X	—	—	—	—
Gilbert Skink	*Eumeces gilberti*	X	X	X	X	—	X	—	X	X	—
Sierra Garter Snake	*Thamnophis couchii*	X	X	—	—	X	X	X	—	—	X
INTRODUCED											
Bullfrog	*Rana catesbeiana*	—	—	X*	—	X	X*	X	—	X	X

Notes: GR = Granite Mountains
        PA = Panamint Valley
        SA = Saline Valley
        EU = Eureka Valley
        SO = Southern Owens Valley
        NO = Northern Owens Valley
        CH = Chalfont Valley (included together with Hammil, Benton, and Queen valleys)
        DS = Deep Springs Valley
        FL = Fish Lake Valley
        PL = Pyramid Lake

Lists for valleys include species that occur up to 1,500 ft (460 m) above the valley floor.

Asterisks indicate sites for which no museum records exist, but where species are certain to occur.

of Creosote Bush closely: the Desert Iguana (*Dipsosaurus dorsalis*) and the Western Blind Snake (*Leptotyphlops humilis*). However, the Western Banded Gecko (*Coleonyx variegatus*), Common Chuckwalla (*Sauromalus obesus*), Desert Night Lizard (*Xantusia vigilis*), Southwestern Black-headed Snake (*Tantilla hobartsmithi*), Sidewinder (*Crotalus cerastes*), and Speckled Rattlesnake (*Crotalus mitchellii*), extend north of the Creosote Bush Scrub into Great Basin Scrub. The Red-spotted Toad (*Bufo punctatus*), the only southern amphibian in the area, requires a moist habitat with permanent water. It is absent from the Eureka and southern Owens valleys. The Glossy Snake (*Arizona elegans*) and Sidewinder (*Crotalus cerastes*) seem to be absent from the Saline and Eureka valleys. The Western Shovel-nosed Snake (*Chionactis occipitalis*) has not been found in the Eureka Valley. The Rosy Boa (*Lichanura trivirgata*), Spotted Leaf-nosed Snake (*Phyllorhynchus decurtatus*), and Lyre Snake (*Trimorphodon biscutatus*) have yet to be recorded from any valley except the Panamint.

The wide-ranging species have distributions in both the Mojave Desert and the Great Basin Desert. These species occur in every valley, with the exception of the Zebra-tailed Lizard (*Callisaurus draconoides*), which appears to be absent from Deep Springs Valley.

Species in the northern group generally avoid Creosote Bush Scrub. They have distributions to the north in the Great Basin Desert. Many of these species also occur to the west of the Sierra Nevada, and some are found isolated on high mountains in the Mojave Desert. The Northern Leopard Frog (*Rana pipiens*) is restricted to the Owens River and its tributaries in the northern Owens Valley, and apparently along creeks draining the eastern White Mountains, since there is one record from 7,100 ft (2,160 m). The Western Toad (*Bufo boreas*), Pacific Treefrog (*Pseudacris regilla*), and Great Basin Spadefoot Toad (*Spea intermontana*), which tend to be near water, each have one record in the range of Creosote Bush. The Western Skink (*Eumeces skiltonianus*) is mainly distributed in mountain areas in the vicinity of water and avoids Creosote Bush Scrub in this area. The Sagebrush Lizard (*Sceloporus graciosus*) mainly occurs in high mountain areas but it also occurs on the valley floors of the southern Owens, northern Owens, Chalfant, Hammil, Benton, Queen, and Fish Lake valleys. The Western Fence Lizard (*Sceloporus occidentalis*) occurs in or around all valleys, but at higher elevations around the Panamint Valley. The Western Rattlesnake (*Crotalus viridis*) is present only in the Queen and Fish Lake valleys, where it may be hybridizing with the Speckled Rattlesnake (*Crotalus mitchellii*). The Striped Whipsnake (*Masticophis taeniatus*) is present in all northern valleys, as is the Western Terrestrial Garter Snake (*Thamnophis elegans*). The latter is also in the southern Owens Valley.

The five endemic species occur only in the White-Inyo mountains region and directly adjacent areas. The Inyo Mountains Salamander (*Batrachoseps campi*) occurs at 13 springs in the Inyo Mountains, and is in the Saline Valley and southern and northern portions of the Owens Valley. The Kern Plateau Salamander (*Batrachoseps* sp.) occurs along creeks draining the Sierra Nevada in the southern Owens Valley. The Owens Valley Web-toed Salamander (*Hydromantes* sp.) is present along creeks draining the Sierra Nevada in the southern and northern portions of the Owens Valley. The Black Toad (*Bufo exsul*), a close relative of the Western Toad (*Bufo boreas*), occurs only in the Deep Springs Valley, where the Western Toad (*Bufo boreas*) is absent. The Panamint Alligator Lizard (*Elgaria panamintina*) is recorded from the Panamint and Saline valleys and throughout the eastern portion of the Owens valley. A site record for the west side of the White Mountains in the Hammil Valley also exists.

Species in the western group have distributions mainly to the west of the Sierra Nevada. The Southern Alligator Lizard (*Elgaria multicarinata*) is distributed along the east side of the Sierra Nevada at least from Olancha to Grant Lake, Mono County. The Gilbert Skink (*Eumeces gilberti*) is present in springs at low elevations and in a variety of habitats at higher elevations. It occurs in many mountain ranges throughout the Mojave Desert and in all Creosote Bush Scrub valleys, but it appears to be absent from the western slopes of the Inyo Mountains in the southern Owens Valley. It also occurs on the western slopes of the White Mountains in the northern Owens Valley and in the southeastern slopes of the White Mountains in the Deep Springs and Fish Lake valleys. The Sierra Garter Snake (*Thamnophis couchii*) is present in the southern Owens, northern Owens, and Chalfant valleys.

Figures 10.1 and 10.2 show the percentages of southern, wide-ranging, northern, endemic, and western species in each of the valleys. In general, as southern species decline in number, northern species increase. The valleys to the east of the White-Inyo Range show an abrupt transition between the northern fauna of the Great Basin Desert and the southern fauna of the Mojave Desert. In the Panamint, Saline, and Eureka valleys, which contain Creosote Bush, a few northern species occur. In contrast, the Fish Lake Valley to the north, in which no Creosote Bush is present, has 8 northern species. Additionally, the only southern species in the Fish Lake Valley is the Speckled Rattlesnake (*Crotalus mitchellii*). To the south in the Eureka Valley there are 6 southern species, in the Saline Valley 9, and in the Panamint Valley 14.

On the west side of the White-Inyo Range a more gradual transition between the two desert fauna exists. The southern Owens Valley has 7 northern species, although it contains Creosote Bush desert. The northern Owens Valley contains 8, and the Chalfant, Hammil, Benton and Queen valleys together have 9 northern species. In the latter grouping of valleys only 3 southern species—the Desert Night Lizard (*Xantusia vigilis*), Sidewinder (*Crotalus cerastes*), and Speckled Rattlesnake (*Crotalus mitchellii*)—occur, yet the northern Owens Valley, which lacks Creosote Bush, has 6 species. In the southern Owens Valley there are 10 southern species.

The Deep Springs Valley between the Inyo and White mountains contains Great Basin Scrub desert. The Speckled Rattlesnake (*Crotalus mitchellii*) is the only southern species present in the valley. The wide ranging Zebra-tailed Lizard (*Callisaurus draconoides*) appears to be absent from this valley. In addition, only four northern species occur here, along with one western species and one endemic.

To illustrate the relationships among valleys, two trees are included. These trees were derived from two formulas, called faunal resemblance factors. The Braun-Blanquet faunal resemblance factor (BFRF) emphasizes the differences between the species compositions of different geographic regions (Braun-Blanquet, 1932). It is calculated by taking the number of species in common (C) to two sites and dividing it by the total number present at the site with the larger number of species (N_L).

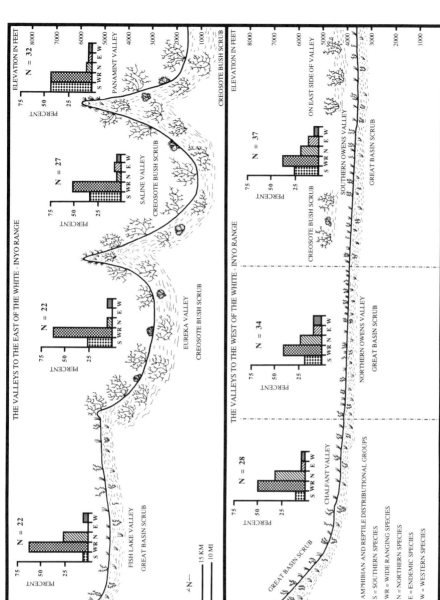

FIGURE 10.1   Amphibian and reptile distributional patterns on the two sides of the White-Inyo Range. Above are the valleys to the east of the White-Inyo Range. Below are the valleys to the west of the White-Inyo Range. Note that the Chalfant Valley is included with Hammil, Benton, and Queen valleys.

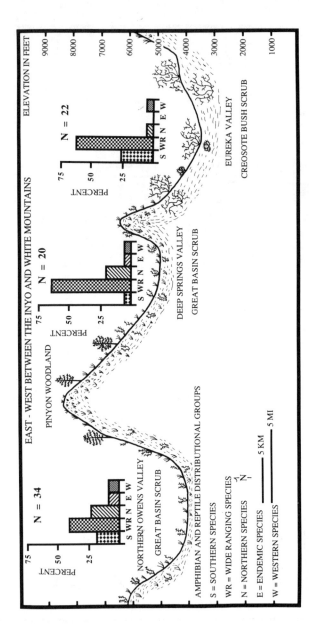

FIGURE 10.2 Amphibian and reptile distributional patterns across the White-Inyo Range.

The resulting value is multiplied by 100 to take the form of a percentage.

$$BFRF = (C/N_L)100$$

Alternatively, the Simpson faunal resemblance factor (SFRF) emphasizes the similarities between the species compositions of different geographic regions (Simpson, 1960). It is calculated by taking the number of species in common (C) to two sites and dividing it by the total number present at the site with the smaller number of species (N_S).

$$SFRF = (C/N_S)100$$

The numbers that were derived are presented in Table 10.2. To show the relation between the valleys in the White-Inyo mountains region, two sites outside the area were included. In the Mojave Desert, the Granite Mountains south of Kelso, San

TABLE 10.2   Comparison of species compositions between regions

	GR	PA	SA	EU	SO	NO	CH	DS	FL	PL
GR	34	29	25	22	25	22	18	16	17	15
PA	—	32	25	21	27	23	20	15	17	16
SA	—	—	27	22	25	23	18	16	17	15
EU	—	—	—	22	21	20	17	16	17	15
SO	—	—	—	—	37	31	25	17	21	22
NO	—	—	—	—	—	34	26	19	24	23
CH	—	—	—	—	—	—	28	18	22	24
DS	—	—	—	—	—	—	—	20	19	17
FL	—	—	—	—	—	—	—	—	24	22
PL	—	—	—	—	—	—	—	—	—	26
	GR	PA	SA	EU	SO	NO	CH	DS	FL	PL
GR	34	85	74	65	68	65	53	47	50	44
PA	91	32	78	66	73	68	63	47	53	50
SA	93	93	27	81	68	68	64	59	63	56
EU	100	95	100	22	57	59	61	73	71	58
SO	74	84	93	95	37	84	68	46	57	59
NO	65	72	85	91	91	34	76	56	71	68
CH	64	71	67	77	89	93	28	64	79	86
DS	80	75	80	80	85	95	90	20	79	65
FL	71	71	71	77	88	100	92	95	24	85
PL	58	62	58	68	85	88	92	85	92	26

Note: The number of species in a particular region appears on the diagonals. The number of species common to two regions appears above the upper diagonal. The BFRF percent similarity between two regions is found above the lower diagonal. The SFRF percent similarity is found below the lower diagonal.

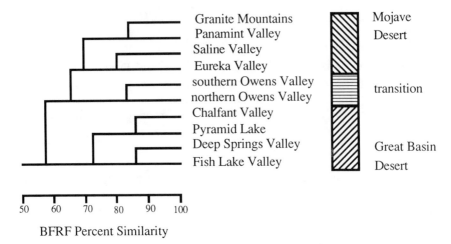

FIGURE 10.3   The Baun-Blanquet faunal resemblance factor (BFRF) percent similarity tree, which emphasizes differences.

Bernardino County, California, was used. In the Great Basin Desert, Pyramid Lake, Washoe County, Nevada, was used.

The trees are presented in Figs. 10.3 and 10.4. They illustrate the abrupt transition between the two desert fauna present on the east side of the White-Inyo Range. Both trees cluster the Panamint, Saline, and Eureka valleys with the Granite Mountains in the Mojave Desert. Both trees also cluster the Chalfant (including the Hammil, Benton, and Queen valleys), Deep Springs, and Fish Lake valleys with Pyramid Lake

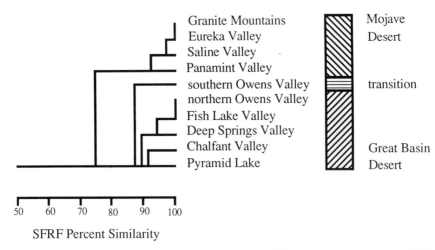

FIGURE 10.4   The Simpson faunal resemblance factor (SFRF) percent similarity tree, which emphasizes similarities.

in the Great Basin Desert. The two trees differ on the positioning of the southern Owens and northern Owens valleys. The BFRF, emphasizing differences, places the southern and northern portions of the Owens Valley together in a subcluster of the Mojave desert cluster. The SFRF, emphasizing similarities, places the southern Owens Valley furthest out from the Great Basin Desert cluster and puts the northern Owens Valley with the Fish Lake Valley. This illustrates a more gradual and broad transition between the two fauna in the Owens Valley to the west of the White-Inyo Range. This is due to a wider range of habitats present in the Owens Valley. The Owens River and the creeks that drain the eastern Sierra Nevada provide riparian habitat and cooler conditions for northern species. The Creosote Bush Scrub in the southern Owens Valley and the gradual elevational increase from Owens Lake to the Queen Valley provide a corridor for southern species to range further north (Macey, 1986; Murphy, 1983).

SPECIES ACCOUNTS

Alligator Lizards (Family Anguidae)

Southern Alligator Lizard, *Elgaria multicarinata* (Blainville, 1835). (Plates 10.1 and 10.2, Map 10.1) 8–16 in (20–40 cm); brown to gray dorsal background color; narrow light brown bands, about one scale wide, across top of back, turning darker on sides; white fleck at end of each scale in dark brown bands on side; distinct fold with granular scales between side and belly; up to two-thirds of total length may be tail. *Habitat:* In the White-Inyo mountains region this species seems to be restricted to the vicinity of permanent water. Southern Alligator Lizards are active during the day and early evening, but they are seldom seen because they are secretive and spend much of their time in leaf litter. *Remarks:* The subspecies of Southern Alligator Lizard occurring in this area is the San Diego Alligator Lizard (*E. m. webbii*), which is known from a single locality in the Alabama Hills near Lone Pine (see Map 10.1). It is a wide-ranging species in California west of the Sierra Nevada that enters the area from the south and extends north along the east side of the Sierra Nevada. The five localities (four outside of our area) in Inyo County are all west of the Owens River. The only species that could be confused with this lizard is the Panamint Alligator Lizard (*E. panamintina*), which has body bands three to four scales wide rather than one scale wide. Although the two species have not yet been found together, it is possible that they coexist in the Owens Valley. *Range:* Owens Valley west of the Owens River and canyons draining the east slope of the Sierra Nevada at least between Olancha, Inyo County, and Grant Lake, Mono County. *References:* Fitch (1935), Fitch (1938), Good (1988a), Good (1988b), Stebbins (1985).

   Localities: California, Inyo Co.: 1,730 m, Division Creek, 13 mi NNW Independence (W of area); 6,000 ft, 5 mi W and 1.25 mi S Independence (W of area); 4,400 ft, 2.75 mi NW Lone Pine, Alabama Hills; 5,700 ft, south fork of Oak Creek, 5.0 mi W Independence (W of area); 5,200 ft, Walker Creek, 4 mi SW Olancha (S of area).

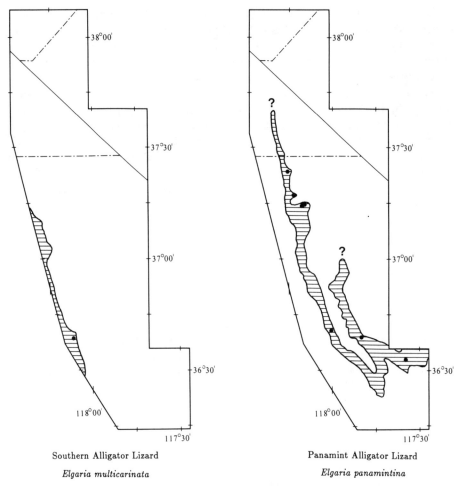

Southern Alligator Lizard

Elgaria multicarinata

MAP 10.1

Panamint Alligator Lizard

Elgaria panamintina

MAP 10.2

Panamint Alligator Lizard, *Elgaria panamintina* **(Stebbins, 1958).** (Plates 10.3 and 10.4, Map 10.2) 7–14 in (17.5–35 cm); gray dorsal background with light to dark-brown bands three to four scales wide, circling the top and sides; white flecks on sides behind each band; ventral coloration cream with gray flecks; banded tail longer than body. *Habitat:* This lizard is most common in rocky canyons in the vicinity of springs and streams. Panamint Alligator Lizards are not commonly encountered because they spend much of their time in rock piles or brush. They can sometimes be seen during the late afternoon and early evening basking in the open. *Remarks:* This species was first discovered in 1954 in Surprise Canyon, Panamint Mountains. It has since been found in the Argus, Nelson, Inyo, and southern White mountains. Panamint Alligator Lizards at French Spring in the Inyo Mountains occur less than

10 mi (16 km) east of the Alabama Hills, where Southern Alligator Lizards (*E. multicarinata*) live (see Maps 10.1 and 10.2). Although it is geographically close to the Southern Alligator Lizard, its nearest relative is the Madrean Alligator Lizard (*E. kingii*), which occurs 300 mi (480 km) to the southeast, in Arizona. At one time a single species of alligator lizard ranged from Arizona to the White-Inyo mountains region. The formation of the Great Basin Desert and the drying of the Mojave Desert separated this population, leaving the Panamint Alligator Lizard isolated. Since its discovery, fewer than 30 specimens have been deposited in the collections of major museums. This species is now protected by state law and should not be collected. *Range:* Panamint, eastern Argus, Nelson, Inyo, and western White mountains below 7,500 ft (2,290 m); site record for the western slopes of the White Mountains above Hammil Valley; may occur more widely (see ? on Map 10.2). *References:* Banta (1962), Good (1988a), Good (1988b), Stebbins (1958).

   Localities: California, Inyo Co.: 1 mi E Batchelder Spring, Westgard Pass (LACM); 1.5 mi NE; 9.8 mi NE Big Pine; 6,650 ft, 10.1 mi NE; Daisy Canyon, Saline Valley (CAS); 6,000 ft, French Spring, Inyo Mtns.; 4,850 ft (CAS, LACM), 5,000 ft (CAS), 5,030 ft (CAS), 5,100 ft (CAS), Grapevine Canyon, Nelson Mtns.; 6,800 ft, Marble Canyon, White Mtns.; Silver Creek Canyon, White Mtns.

Geckos (Family Gekkonidae)

Western Banded Gecko, *Coleonyx variegatus* (Baird, 1858). (Plate 10.5, Map 10.3) 3–6 in (7.5–15 cm); pale yellow or cream background with brown bands on body and tail; in large individuals body bands may separate into blotches; regenerated tails short, fat, and unbanded; eyes large and catlike with vertical pupils. *Habitat:* This species is most abundant in rocky areas where Creosote Bush is present, but it has also been found in Great Basin Desert Scrub below 6,000 ft (1,830 m). These geckos are active only at night. During the day they take shelter under rocks, in cracks, or in rodent burrows. *Remarks:* The subspecies of the Western Banded Gecko in this area is the Desert Banded Gecko (*C. v. variegatus*). Geckos from the Owens Valley have a more distinct banded pattern than those found in the other valleys, which tend to have more broken bands and speckling. This is the only member of the gecko family in our area. Geckos are primarily a tropical group. Over 800 species are known worldwide, only 5 of which are native to the southwestern United States. The northernmost known locality for this species is in the Eureka Valley. They can commonly be seen at night on roads that go through rocky areas. They are especially abundant during the late spring and early summer on the Eureka Valley Road. Banded Geckos readily lose their tails as a defense mechanism against predators, and many adults have regenerated tails. *Range:* Throughout the Panamint, Saline, and Eureka valleys and extending into the mountains surrounding those valleys; Owens Valley to at least Big Pine and Westgard Pass; a site record for east of Bishop (see ? on Map 10.3). *References:* Congdon, Vitt, and King (1974); Klauber (1945).

   Localities: California, Inyo Co.: Big Pine; 4,500 ft, 4.7 mi NE; 4,850 ft, 5.5 mi NE; 6.0 mi NE; 7.0 mi NE; Darwin Falls; 0.4 mi SE of Hwy. 168 on Eureka Valley

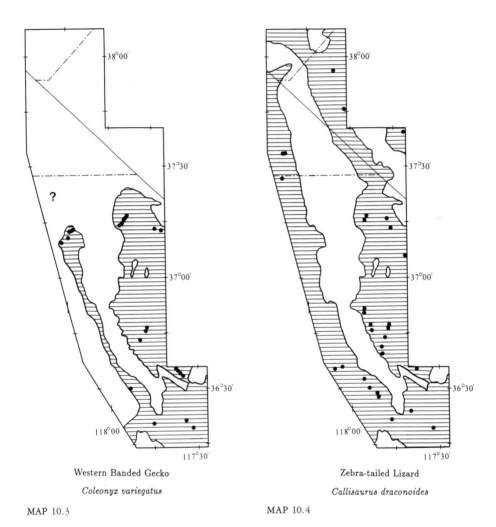

Western Banded Gecko

Coleonyx variegatus

MAP 10.3

Zebra-tailed Lizard

Callisaurus draconoides

MAP 10.4

Rd.; 5,750 ft, 22.3 mi SE; 5,600 ft, 22.6 mi SE; 24.0 mi SE; 24.4 mi SE; 24.5 mi SE; 24.6 mi SE; 24.8 mi SE; 24.9 mi SE; 25.2 mi SE; 25.5 mi SE; 25.9 mi SE; 26.0 mi SE; 26.3 mi SE; 26.7 mi SE; 27.5 mi SE; 27.7 mi SE; 27.8 mi SE; 28.2 mi SE; 37.3 mi SE; 40.3 mi SE; 2,300–4,030 ft, Grapevine Canyon, Nelson Range (CAS); 8.9 mi SE of Hwy. 136 on Hwy. 190; 7.5 mi W Panamint Valley Rd. on Hwy. 190 (CAS); 37.2 mi W; 1,060–1,200 ft along Warm Springs Rd., Saline Valley (CAS).

Iguanids (Family Iguanidae)

Zebra-tailed Lizard, *Callisaurus draconoides* (Blainville, 1835).   (Plates 10.6 and 10.7, Map 10.4) 5–9 in (12.5–22.5 cm); dorsal pattern gray, mottled with white flecks; faint black blotches down middle of back, forming bands on tail; ventral surface white with paired black bars on each side; in males the bars are surrounded by blue; underside of tail black- and white-banded. *Habitat:* Zebra-tailed Lizards are most common in valley floors and along sandy washes below 5,000 ft (1,520 m). This diurnal lizard has a high tolerance to heat and may be active in the middle of the day, even during the hot summer. *Remarks:* The subspecies of Zebra-tailed Lizard in the area is the Common Zebra-tailed Lizard (*C. d. draconoides*). This species, which ranges to the tip of Baja California and Sinoloa, Mexico, is common throughout much of the western deserts. The dorsal pattern provides good camouflage for these animals. They commonly are not seen until they run. This is an extremely fast and wary lizard that has been clocked at nearly 20 miles (30 km) per hour for short distances. Just before they run, they usually curl and wag their banded tail over their back. *Range:* On the west side of the White-Inyo Range, in the entire length of the Owens Valley, and the Chalfant, Hammil, Benton, and Queen valleys; on the east side of the White-Inyo Range, in the Panamint, Saline, Eureka, and Fish Lake valleys below 6,000 ft (1,830 m). Appears to be absent from the Deep Springs Valley. *References:* Kay, Miller, and Miller (1970); Pianka and Parker (1972).

Localities: California, Inyo Co.: Aeolian Sand Dunes, Saline Valley (CAS); 5.5 mi N Bishop (UCSB); 4,600 ft, 12.5 mi N, 0.5 mi W (LACM); Darwin Falls (CAS, LACM, SDSNH); Darwin Wash; 1,900 ft, Daisy Canyon, Saline Valley (CAS); 27.7 mi SE of Hwy. 168 on Eureka Valley Rd.; 29.1 mi SE; jct. Eureka Valley Rd. and North Eureka Valley Rd.; 3.9 mi N of Eureka Valley Rd. on North Eureka Valley Rd.; E side of Eureka Valley sand dunes; 2,280–3,225 ft, Grapevine Canyon, Nelson Range (CAS); Grapevine Canyon, Nelson Range (SDSNH); Keeler; 1 mi S (LACM); between Lone Pine and Independence (CAS); Lone Pine (MVZ, USNM); 2.3 mi W (LACM); 2.9 mi W (LACM); 1.5 mi S, 7 mi E (UCM); 10.0 mi SE; 23 mi E; 5.6 mi N of Hwy. 190 on Saline Valley Rd.; 1,100 ft, center along dirt rd., Saline Valley (CAS); 1,175–2,350 ft, N end along dirt rd. (CAS); Seven Springs, Saline Valley (CAS); 1,090 ft, Tramway, Saline Valley (CAS); 890–1,200 ft, Warm Springs Rd., Saline Valley (CAS); Willow Creek, Saline Valley (MVZ, SDSNH). Mono Co.: Chalfant (SDSNH). Nevada, Esmeralda Co.: Fish Lake; Jct. Hwy. 264 and Hwy. 774; 7.9 mi SSW Silver Peak.

Great Basin Collard Lizard, *Crotaphytus bicinctores* (Smith & Tanner, 1972). (Plate 10.8, Map 10.5) 8–14 in (20–35 cm); tan background color with narrow, broken yellow bands and small gray spots on back; a distinct black collar around neck, which is split in the middle with a white and gray band; head appears very large in proportion to body; tail long, about twice body length. *Habitat:* Collard Lizards occur in rocky areas throughout the study area up to an elevation of at least 6,500 ft (1,980 m) at the lower extent of the Pinyon-juniper Woodland. They are commonly observed basking on boulders. *Remarks:* The diet of this species consists mainly of insects and other lizards. The collared lizards (Genus *Crotaphytus*) and the leopard lizards (Genus *Gambelia*) are closely related and have considerable dietary overlap. They avoid competing by living in different habitats (see Long-nosed Leopard Lizard,

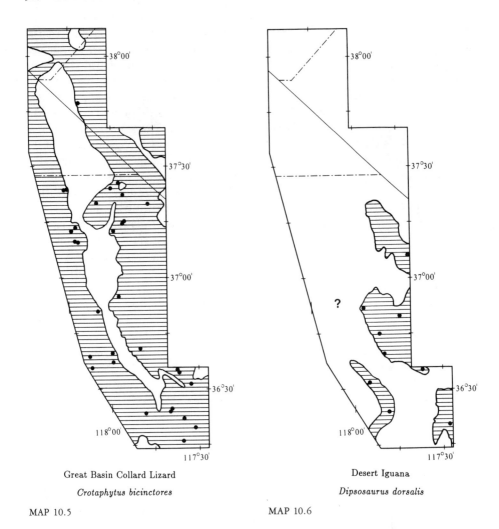

Great Basin Collard Lizard

Crotaphytus bicinctores

MAP 10.5

Desert Iguana

Dipsosaurus dorsalis

MAP 10.6

G. wislizenii). Until recently, only two species of collard lizards were recognized: the Reticulate Collard Lizard (*C. reticulatus*), occurring in a limited area of southern Texas and northern Mexico, and a wide-ranging species occurring from Idaho to southern Baja California and from California to eastern Missouri. Recent studies suggest that the latter species be partitioned into three species: the Common Collard Lizard (*C. collaris*), ranging from western Arizona to eastern Missouri; the Baja California Collard Lizard (*C. insularis*), occurring from southern California to southern Baja California; and the Great Basin Collard Lizard, which lives from southern California and western Arizona to Idaho. Some workers consider *C. bicinctores* a subspecies of *C. insularis*. *Range:* Throughout the White-Inyo mountains region below about 6,500 ft (1,980 m). *References:* Axtell (1972); Montanucci (1983); Montanucci, Axtell, and Dessauer (1975); Sanborn and Loomis (1979); Smith and Tanner (1974).

Localities: California, Inyo Co.: Antelope Spring, Deep Springs Valley (LACM); 5 mi E Big Pine; 6,000 ft, 9 mi NE (AMNH); Darwin (CAS); Darwin Falls (CAS, LACM, MVZ); 6,200 ft, 4.0 mi NE Deep Springs (LACM); NW end Deep Springs Valley (LACM); 3 mi SE Hwy. 168 on Eureka Valley Rd., (BYU); 4.5 mi SE; 19.8 mi SE; 24.1 mi SE; 25.2 mi SE; 9.1 mi N Eureka Valley Rd. on North Eureka Valley Rd.; French Spring, Inyo Mtns.; 2,300–4,480 ft, Grapevine Canyon, Nelson Range (CAS); 0.5 mi W Inyo National Forest on Hwy. 168; 8 mi SE Keeler (CAS, SDSNH); 4.0 mi E Laws; 4,200 ft, Long John Canyon, Inyo Mtns.; 4.5 mi NE Lone Pine; Lone Pine Creek, ridge S of Wilson Ranch; Mazourka Canyon, Inyo Mtns. (SDSNH); 7.5 mi W Panamint Springs (CAS); Pearly Gates, 7 mi S Saline Valley; S end Saline Valley (CAS, BYU); W end Saline Valley (CAS); 5.6 mi N of Hwy. 190 on Saline Valley Rd.; 7 mi N; 1 mi W Salt Lake, Saline Valley (LACM); 4,600 ft, 7,000 ft, Silver Creek Canyon, White Mtns.; Waucoba Wash area, 33.3 mi from Big Pine, W end Saline Valley (CAS). Nevada, Esmeralda Co.: Indian Canyon, White Mtns.

Desert Iguana, *Dipsosaurus dorsalis* **(Baird & Girard, 1852).**   (Plate 10.9, Map 10.6) 12–16 in (30–40 cm); dorsal coloration light brown to gray with darker reddish brown mottling; mottling forms bands on tail; sides and belly cream with some reddish flecks on sides; dorsal pattern fades during heat of day, giving this species a bleached appearance; row of enlarged scales runs down middle of back. *Habitat:* Desert Iguanas almost always occur near Creosote Bush. Although this species is a habitat generalist, it prefers flat, sandy washes below 5,000 ft (1,520 m). These lizards are active on warm days and can be seen basking when it is too hot for other lizards. *Remarks:* The diet of Desert Iguanas consists mainly of plants. The flowers and leaves of the Creosote Bush provide a major source of food. These lizards are active at very high temperatures and have been recorded with body temperatures as great as 115°F (64°C), which is higher than for any other species of lizard in the area. Desert Iguanas are widely distributed in the southwestern United States and northwestern Mexico. This species, along with the Chuckwalla (*Sauromalus*), is related to the giant iguanas of Mexico and Central and South America, including the well-known Galapagos Marine Iguana. Desert Iguanas are very common in the Panamint and Saline valleys, where they may be observed basking on small rocks or under Creosote Bush along roads. They are not very wary and can be approached closely. *Range:* On the east side of the Inyo Mountains in the Panamint, Saline, and Eureka valleys; on the west side of the Inyo Mountains in the southern Owens Valley, north to at least the vicinity of Lone Pine (see ? on Map 10.6). *References:* Norris (1953), Pianka (1971).

Localities: California, Inyo Co.: Near Big Horn Mine, Hunter Canyon, Saline Valley (USNM); Darwin Falls; sand dunes, S end Eureka Valley; 8 mi SE Keeler (SDSNH); 2,280 ft, 3,150 ft, Grapevine Canyon, Nelson Range (CAS); 10.0 mi SE Lone Pine; 4,100 ft, 3 mi E Owens Lake (USNM); Panamint Springs; N Saline Valley (CAS); 5 mi N Salt Works, Saline Valley; upper Warm Springs Valley, Saline Valley (LACM); Willow Creek, Saline Valley.

Long-nosed Leopard Lizard, *Gambelia wislizenii* (Baird & Girard, 1852). (Plate 10.10, Map 10.7) 10–16 in (25–40 cm); narrow cream-colored bands across back, extending to the tail; areas between bands are brown with cream rings, making back appear spotted; tail very long, about twice body length; brown stripes on chin fading toward throat; belly uniform cream or with small gray spots. *Habitat:* In our area, leopard lizards occur in all habitats up to at least 7,500 ft (2,290 m) in the White Mountains. They are most common in flat, sandy Great Basin Scrub and Creosote Bush Scrub areas but also occur in rocky areas and well into the Pinyon-juniper zone. They are very numerous in the Eureka Valley, where they can be seen in the early morning basking on rocks along the side of the road. *Remarks:* The subspecies of Long-nosed Leopard Lizard occurring in the White-Inyo mountains region is the Large-spotted Leopard Lizard (*G. w. wislizenii*). In addition to feeding on insects, this large, aggressive lizard feeds on other lizards, occasionally even members of its own species. They are sit-and-wait predators that perch on rocks or lie under bushes until a prey item wanders by. This is a species with a wide range that occurs from Idaho to southern Baja California and from California to Texas. The only other member of the genus is the Blunt-nosed Leopard Lizard (*G. sila*), which occurs in the San Joaquin Valley of California. It is on the Federal Endangered Species List due to extensive habitat loss from agricultural development. *Range:* Throughout the White-Inyo mountains region below 7,500 ft (2,290 m). *References:* Parker and Pianka (1976), Tollestrup (1982).

Localities: California, Inyo Co.: Aberdeen (LACM); 5.6 mi N Bishop (UCSB); Darwin (USNM); 15 mi N; Darwin Falls, Argus Mtns. (CAS, MVZ); Deep Springs; 4 mi SW; NW end Deep Springs Valley (LACM); 6.3 mi SE of Hwy. 168 on Eureka Valley Rd.; within 1.0 mi W of North Eureka Valley Rd. on Eureka Valley Rd.; 1.6 mi E; 10.4 mi N Eureka Valley Rd. on North Eureka Valley Rd.; Fish Lake Valley; French Spring, Inyo Mtns.; 2,300–5,570 ft, Grapevine Canyon, Nelson Range (CAS); Independence (MVZ, USNM); 0.5 mi W (AMNH); Keeler; 1 mi S (LACM); Lone Pine (LACM, MCZ, USNM); Lone Pine Creek; between Lone Pine and Independence (CAS); Mazourka Canyon, Inyo Mtns.; 14.6 mi NE Olancha (LACM); N Saline Valley (CAS); 1 mi W Salt Lake, Saline Valley (LACM); 1,190–1,300 ft, Warm Springs Rd., Saline Valley (CAS). Mono Co.: Benton; 4,840 ft, Cinnamon Ranch, 10 mi SSE; 6.0 mi S Nevada state line on Hwy. 266. Nevada. Esmeralda Co.: 8 mi S Hwy. 6 on Hwy. 264; 7,000 ft, Chiatovich Creek, White Mtns.; 4,900 ft, Chiatovich Ranch, Fish Lake Valley; 4,800 ft, 7 mi E (E of area); Fish Lake; 7,400 ft, Indian Canyon, White Mtns.; 3.7 mi S of Leidy Creek Rd. on Hwy. 264, Fish Lake Valley (BYU); 6,000 ft, 9 mi W Lida Summit; jct. of rd. to Middle Creek and Hwy. 264, Fish Lake Valley; 8.4 mi SSW Silver Peak. Mineral Co.: 1.6 mi NE of California state line on Hwy. 6.

Desert Horned Lizard, *Phrynosoma platyrhinos* (Girard, 1852).   (Plate 10.11, Map 10.8) 4–6 in (10–15 cm); dorsal background gray to light brown with broken black stripe running down back; ventral color white; flattened oval body; horns at back of head; tail short. *Habitat:* In this area Desert Horned Lizards are present in

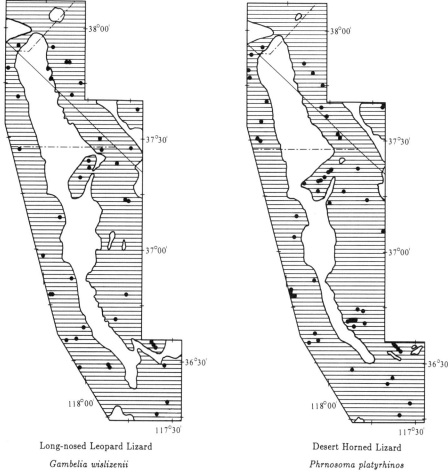

Long-nosed Leopard Lizard

Gambelia wislizenii

MAP 10.7

Desert Horned Lizard

Phrnosoma platyrhinos

MAP 10.8

all habitats up to about 7,000 ft (2,130 m) in the Pinyon-juniper Woodland. They are most common in valley floors and sandy washes. These lizards are often seen in the early morning and late afternoon basking on small rocks at the edge of roads. They are especially abundant in low-elevation Creosote Bush Scrub valleys. *Remarks:* The White-Inyo mountains region is an area of intergradation between the Southern Desert Horned Lizard (*P. p. calidiarum*) and the Northern Desert Horned Lizard (*P. p. platyrhinos*). The northern form has shorter horns than the southern form. Horned lizards, commonly called "horned toads," are one of the most specialized groups of lizards in North America. There are 14 species in the genus *Phrynosoma*, which occurs from southern Canada to northern Guatemala. They are all similar in body shape and feed in large part on ants. Horned lizards are easily approached and can be picked up by hand because they rely on camouflage and their horns for protection. *Range:* Throughout the White-Inyo mountains region below 7,000 ft (2,130 m). *References:* Pianka and Parker (1975), Tanner and Krogh (1973).

Localities: California, Inyo Co.: 2,200 ft, 3,800 ft, 6,200–6,400 ft, near Big Horn Mine, Hunter Canyon, Saline Valley (USNM); 20.8 mi NE Big Pine; 23.3 mi NE; 26.3 mi NE; Bog Mound Spring, Deep Springs Valley; 4,500 ft, Daisy Canyon, Inyo Mtns. (CAS); Darwin; Darwin Falls; Deep Springs (BYU, LACM); 5.0 mi W (UNM); 5.2 mi W (UNM); 7.5 mi S (UMMZ); 12 mi W (UNM); Deep Springs Lake (LACM); 2,800 ft, 2,930 ft S end Eureka Valley (LACM); 3.3 mi SE Hwy. 168 on Eureka Valley Rd.; 27.7 mi SE; Jct. of North Eureka Valley Rd. and Eureka Valley Rd.; 1.3 mi S of Canyon Rd. on North Eureka Valley Rd.; Fish Lake Valley; 2,950–5,570 ft, Grapevine Canyon, Nelson Range (CAS); Independence (MVZ, USNM); 4,000 ft, 0.5 mi W (AMNH); 2 mi NE; Joshua Flats, 21.2 mi SE of Hwy. 168 on Eureka Valley Rd., Inyo Mtns.; Keeler; Lone Pine (USNM); 2.0 mi ENE; 3 mi W; 6,000 ft, Mazourka Canyon, Inyo Mtns.; 1,200 ft, Mesquite Sand Dunes, Saline Valley (CAS); Oak Creek, Owens Valley (UMMZ); 5.6 mi N Hwy. 190 on Saline Valley Rd.; Saline Valley 1 mi W Salt Lake (LACM); Santa Rosa Hills, 25 mi NE Olancha (LACM); E side Tinemaha Reservoir, Owens Valley; 1,090 ft, 2 mi ESE Tramway, Saline Valley (CAS); 860 ft, 990 ft, 1,000 ft, Warm Springs Rd., Saline Valley (CAS), Mono Co.: Benton; 2 mi S; 5 mi N (SDSNH); 5,100 ft, Cinnamon Ranch, 10 mi SSE; 10 mi N Bishop (USNM); 10.5 mi N, 1 mi W (SDSNH); Arrowhead Knoll, 15 mi N (UCSB); 3.2 mi S Nevada state line on Hwy. 266; 4.6 mi S. Nevada, Esmeralda Co.: 1.5 mi N California state line on Hwy. 264, Fish Lake Valley (NSM); 2 mi W of Hwy. 264 along Chiatovich Creek; 5,500 ft, 7 mi W Chiatovich (E of area); 2.5 mi SE Dyer; 8.6 mi N; Fish Lake; 6.3 mi SSW Silver Peak; 6.5 mi SSW; 6.7 mi SSW; 6.8 mi SSW; 6.9 mi SSW; 7.2 mi SSW; 7.5 mi SSW; 7.7 mi SSW. Mineral Co.: 1.4 mi E Janes Ranch at Hwy. 6, Queen Valley.

Common Chuckwalla, *Sauromalus obesus* **(Baird, 1858).** (Plate 10.12, Map 10.9) 12–18 in (30–45 cm); heavy-bodied; dorsal coloration generally brown or black; small granular scales; tail uniform tan or banded with black; juvenile body coloration brown to green. *Habitat:* This lizard is restricted to rock outcrops, where it is commonly seen basking on large boulders during the day. It is most common in Creosote Bush Scrub below 5,000 ft (1,520 m). *Remarks:* The subspecies of Common Chuckwalla present in the area is the Western Chuckwalla (*S. o. obesus*). This is the largest species of lizard in the region and, next to the Gila Monster (*Heloderma suspectum*), the largest in the United States. The leaves and flowers of Creosote Bush are one of the primary foods of this mainly plant-eating lizard. Most of the range of this species overlaps with Creosote Bush. An exception is in the foothills of the Inyo Mountains between Independence and Big Pine, where Creosote Bush is absent. Chuckwallas live in cracks in boulders, where they readily take shelter when approached. Once in a crack, they inflate their lungs and tightly wedge themselves in, making it virtually impossible for a predator to extract them. This is a highly social species; a large, dominant male controls a harem of several females. It has been estimated that it takes

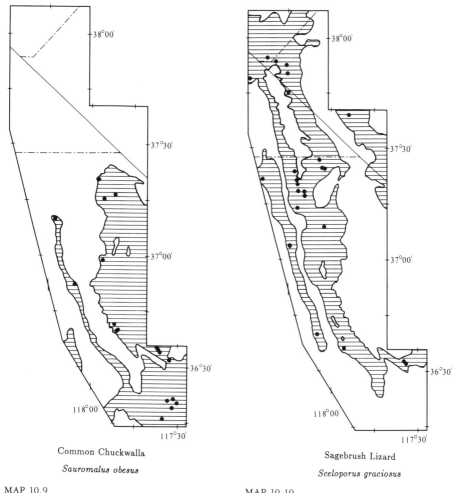

Common Chuckwalla
Sauromalus obesus

MAP 10.9

Sagebrush Lizard
Sceloporus graciosus

MAP 10.10

a male 10 or more years to reach this status. *Range:* In the Owens Valley, restricted to the Alabama Hills and the lower slopes of the Inyo Mountains from Big Pine south; rocky areas in the Panamint, Saline, and Eureka valleys. *Reference:* Berry (1974).

Localities: California, Inyo Co.: 3,800 ft, near Big Horn Mine, Hunter Canyon, Saline Valley (USNM); 3,500–4,300 ft, Daisy Canyon, Inyo Mtns. (CAS); Darwin; Darwin Falls (CAS, LACM, MVZ); 25.2 mi SE of Hwy. 168 on Eureka Valley Rd.; 29.2 mi SE; 2,250–4,630 ft, Grapevine Canyon, Nelson Range (CAS); Mazourka Canyon, Inyo Mtns.; 2.5 mi SE of Hwy. 168 on Eureka Valley Rd., Owens Valley; 1.8 mi NW Panamint Springs, 4 mi NW (CAS); 6 mi NW (CAS); Pearly Gates, 7 mi S, Saline Valley; 4,500 ft, Soldier Pass Canyon, Eureka Valley; Waucoba Wash area, 37 mi from Big Pine, N Saline Valley (CAS).

Sagebrush Lizard, *Sceloporus graciosus* (Baird & Girard, 1852). (Plate 10.13, Map 10.10) 4–6 in (10–15 cm); dorsal coloration brown with turquois-blue stripe from top of head to base of tail; two white stripes on each side; throat and belly dark blue in males, pale blue in females; midventral region black, commonly divided by white in males, lacking black in females. *Habitat:* Sagebrush Lizards occur in a variety of habitats mostly below about 9,000 ft (2,740 m). They are most common in the Pinyon-juniper Woodland. This species is absent from desert areas and is usually not present below 5,000 ft (1,520 m), except in the Owens Valley. These lizards are commonly seen basking on small rocks or on the ground at the edges of bushes. *Remarks:* The subspecies of Sagebrush Lizard present in the area is the Northern Sagebrush Lizard (*S. g. graciosus*). The Sagebrush Lizard is one of three species of the genus *Sceloporus* that occur in the White-Inyo mountains region. It can be distinguished from the Desert Spiny Lizard (*S. magister*) by its striped dorsal pattern and small size, and from the Western Fence Lizard (*S. occidentalis*) by the striped dorsal pattern rather than irregular black bands. All three species occur together in the Owens Valley and at the lower edge of the Pinyon-juniper zone. Sagebrush Lizards reach higher elevations than any other species of reptile in the region. *Range:* Owens Valley, White-Inyo Range, Nelson Range, Last Chance Range, Silver Peak Range. *References:* Stebbins (1944), Stebbins and Robinson (1946), Tinkle (1973).

Localities: California, Inyo Co.: 6,000 ft, 6 mi E [NE] Big Pine; 7.5 mi S (LACM); 13 mi NE; Bishop (LACM); Dead Horse Meadow, White Mtns. (LACM); Pass over Inyo Mtns. on Eureka Valley Rd.; 8,200 ft, Grandview Campground, White Mtns. (LACM); 5,480–5,977 ft, Grapevine Canyon, Nelson Range (CAS); 4 mi N Lone Pine (LACM); 7.0 mi E; Sierra View Point, White Mtns. (LACM); between old and new Silver Creek Canyon (LACM); 7,500 ft, Waucoba Pass, Inyo Mtns.; Westgard Pass (LACM, MVZ); 6,500 ft, White Mtn. Rd. (AMNH); 8,000 ft sign, White Mtn. Rd. (LACM); 9,100 ft, White Mtn. Rd. (AMNH); Wyman Canyon, White Mtns. (LACM); 7,500 ft; Roberts Ranch, Wyman Canyon, White Mtns.; 1 mi E. Mono Co.: Benton (LACM, MVZ); 8,400 ft, Indian Creek, White Mtns. Nevada, Esmeralda Co.: Chiatovich Creek, White Mtns.; 7,700 ft, 2 mi S Piper Peak, Silver Peak Range; Alberta Mine, Queen Canyon, White Mtns.; 2,430 m, Trail Canyon, White Mtns. Mineral Co.: Orchard Spring, Buffalo Canyon, White Mtns.

Desert Spiny Lizard, *Sceloporus magister* (Hallowell, 1854). (Plates 10.14 and 10.15, Map 10.11) 8–12 in (20–30 cm); body covered with large spiny scales; dorsal background gray to pale yellow with six or seven transverse crossbars, which are more pronounced in females; black neck collar; females with uniform cream ventral coloration; males have extensive blue and black ventral coloration with green and yellow flecks. *Habitat:* This species occurs in a variety of vegetation types, from low-elevation Creosote Bush Scrub up to the lower edge of the Pinyon-juniper Woodland. It is most common in wooded or rocky areas below 7,000 ft (2,130 m). This wary lizard can be observed basking on rocks and tree trunks. *Remarks:* The subspecies of Desert Spiny Lizard present in this area is the Barred Spiny Lizard (*S. m. transversus*). Other subspecies range from northern Nevada to the tip of Baja California, Sinoloa,

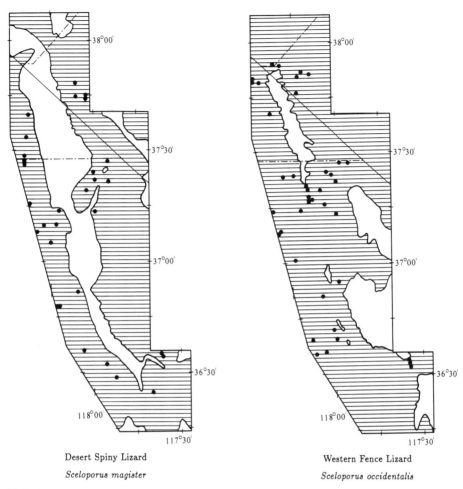

Desert Spiny Lizard

Sceloporus magister

MAP 10.11

Western Fence Lizard

Sceloporus occidentalis

MAP 10.12

and northeastern Mexico, and from the Coast Range of central California to western Texas. In our area Desert Spiny Lizards are very common at Joshua Flats in the Inyo Mountains on the road from Big Pine to Eureka Valley. The spiny leaves of the Joshua Tree provide protection from predators. This large, heavy-bodied lizard feeds mainly on insects but will also eat small lizards. *Range:* Entire White-Inyo mountains region below 7,000 ft (2,150 m). *References:* Parker and Pianka (1973), Phelan and Brattstrom (1955).

Localities: California, Inyo Co.: Batchelder Spring, 9.8 mi E Big Pine (CMNH, UNM); Big Pine (CAS, MVZ); 4 mi W (SDSNH); 6 mi E; 1,620 m, 21.3 mi NE; Deep Springs (CAS); NW end Deep Springs Valley (LACM); 4,400 ft, NW end Eureka Valley; 2.0 mi SE of Hwy. 168 on Eureka Valley Rd.; Fish Slough, 5 mi N Bishop

(UCSB); 3,430–4,850 ft, Grapevine Canyon, Nelson Range (CAS); Independence; 0.5 mi W (UMMZ); 1.4 mi W; 21.5 mi N (LACM); Joshua Flats, 21.2 mi SE of Hwy. 168 on Eureka Valley Rd.; Keeler (SDSNH); Keough's Hot Springs, 7 mi S Bishop (CAS, LACM); Lone Pine (CAS, USNM); 8.1 mi SE; Mazourka Canyon, 7.0 mi ENE Independence; 1.0 mi S Mono County line on Hwy. 168; 5.6 mi N of Hwy. 190 on Saline Valley Rd.; 1,380 m, Silver Canyon, 2.0 mi E Laws; 4,500 ft, Soldier Pass Canyon, Eureka Valley. Mono Co.: 5,040 ft, Cinnamon Ranch, 10 mi SSE Benton; Fish Slough, 8 mi N Bishop (UMMZ). Nevada, Esmeralda Co.: 1,570 m, along Chiatovich Creek, 1.5 mi W of Hwy. 264; 4.6 mi N Dyer; 8.2 mi N; Fish Lake (MVZ, UMMZ): 0.5 mi S; 1 mi S.

Western Fence Lizard, *Sceloporus occidentalis* **(Baird & Girard, 1852).** (Plate 10.16, Map 10.12) 5–9 in (12.5–22.5 cm); dorsal coloration gray to brown with irregular black bands across top of back; blue patch on each side of belly, outlined with black; throat blue, some are outlined with black. *Habitat:* This lizard occurs in a variety of habitats from below 4,000 ft (1,220 m) to 9,000 ft (2,740 m) but is absent from Creosote Bush Scrub areas. It is the most abundant lizard in the pinyon-juniper belt, where it is commonly seen basking on rocks or logs. *Remarks:* The subspecies of Western Fence Lizard present in the area is the Great Basin Fence Lizard (*S. o. biseriatus*). The Western Fence Lizard, commonly called the "blue-belly lizard," is the most wide-ranging species of lizard in California, occurring in all habitats except alpine regions and Creosote Bush Scrub. There are two similar species in the area. The Desert Spiny Lizard (*S. magister*) is larger and has distinct black patches on each side of the neck. The Sagebrush Lizard (*S. graciosus*) has stripes running down the back. Over 60 species of *Sceloporus*, ranging from the United States to Panama, are known. It is the largest genus of lizards present exclusively in North America. Most of the species occur in Mexico, where as many as six are known to live together at a single place. *Range:* On the west side of the White-Inyo Range in the entire Owens, Chalfant, Hammil, Benton, and Queen valleys; White-Inyo Range, Nelson Range, Panamint Mountains (at higher elevations), Last Chance Range, Silver Peak Range, and Deep Springs and Fish Lake valleys. *References:* Fitch (1940a), Tanner and Hopkin (1972).

Localities: California, Inyo Co.: 2.6 mi W of Hwy. 395 on Hogback Rd., Alabama Hills (SBMNH); Antelope Spring, Deep Springs Valley (LACM); Batchelder Spring, 9.8 mi E Big Pine (CMNH, MVZ); 3 mi W Big Pine (LACM); 4 mi W (SDSNH); 6,000 ft, 9 mi NE (AMNH); 4 mi NW Black Rock Springs; Cedar Flat, White Mtns.; Cottonwood Creek, Mono County line, Fish Lake Valley (UMMZ); Deep Springs (CAS, MVZ, UMMZ); Deep Springs Lake (LACM); French Spring, Inyo Mtns.; 4,000–5,977 ft, Grapevine Canyon, Nelson Range (CAS); Joshua Flats, 21.2 mi SE of Hwy. 168 on Eureka Valley Rd.; Keough Hot Springs, 7.0 mi S Bishop (SDSNH); Lone Pine (MCZ); 2.9 mi W (LACM); 3 mi W (LACM); 7.5 mi NE; 1.0 mi S Mono County line on Hwy. 168; Payson Canyon, 2 mi W Deep Springs Valley; Pinyon Picnic Area, White Mtns.; Roberts Ranch, Wyman Canyon; 1 mi E; Sierra View Point, White Mtn. Rd. (LACM); 4,600 ft, Silver Creek Canyon; 2,060 m,

Silver Creek Canyon, 7.2 mi E Laws; 7,300 ft, E base Waucoba Mtn., Inyo Mtns.; 8,000 ft, White Mtn. Rd. (LACM, MVZ); Willow Springs Canyon, 8.0 mi ENE Independence; Wyman Canyon (LACM); 6,400 ft; 6,750 ft. Mono Co.: Benton; 1.25 mi N, 2.5 mi E; 5,400 ft, Cinnamon Ranch, 10 mi SSE Benton. Nevada, Esmeralda Co.: Albert Mine, Queen Canyon; 1,680 m, Chiatovich Creek, Fish Lake Valley; 7,000 ft; 2,080 m, Dry Creek, White Mtns.; 7,400 ft, south fork Indian Creek, White Mtns. Mineral Co.: Orchard Spring, Buffalo Canyon, White Mtns.

Side-blotched Lizard, *Uta stansburiana* (Baird & Girard, 1852). (Plate 10.17, Map 10.13) 4–6 in (10–15 cm); variable dorsal pattern of spots, speckles, or bands; ventral color pale, distinct small dark blue to black patch on side behind each arm. *Habitat:* In this area, Side-blotched Lizards occur in all habitats up to at least 7,000 ft (2,130 m). This is the most common species of lizard in the region, but because of its small size, it is easily overlooked. *Remarks:* This wide-ranging species occurs in arid and semi-arid regions of the western United States and Mexico. Side-blotched Lizards occur over a broader geographic range than any other species of desert lizard in western North America. They occur from Washington to the tip of Baja California and northern Mexico, and from the coast of central California to Oklahoma. The number of individuals may exceed 20 per acre in some areas, and females may lay two to four clutches of eggs in a single season. Studies have shown that this species has a short life span and that there may be an almost complete turnover in the adult population from one year to the next. Side-blotched Lizards are a major source of food for lizard-eating predators because of their abundance. *Range:* Throughout the White-Inyo mountains region below 8,000 ft (2,440 m). *References:* Parker and Pianka (1975), Tinkle (1967).

Localities: California, Inyo Co.: Antelope Spring, Deep Springs Valley (LACM); Batchelder Spring, 9.8 mi NE Big Pine (CMNH, MVZ); near Bighorn Mine, Hunter Canyon, Inyo Mtns. (USNM); 4 mi W Big Pine (SDSNH); 9.7 mi N (LACM); 16.6 mi S (UMMZ); 1,620 m, 21.3 mi NE; 5.4 mi S Bishop (UMMZ); 6 mi S (SDSNH); Cedar Flat, 11 mi NE Big Pine; 2,250–4,800 ft, Daisy Canyon, Inyo Mtns. (CAS); Darwin (CAS); 8 mi N (SDSNH); 15 mi N; Darwin Falls (LACM); Deep Springs (CAS, UMMZ); 7.5 mi S (UMMZ); 8.2 mi W (UMMZ); Deep Springs Lake (LACM); W end Deep Springs Valley (LACM); 3.4 mi SE of Hwy. 168 on Eureka Valley Rd.; Eureka Valley sand dunes; 2,800 ft, near (LACM); Fish Slough pond, 5.4 mi N Bishop (UMMZ); Fish Slough, 6.25 mi N Bishop (UCSB); 2,250–5,977 ft, Grapevine Canyon, Nelson Range (CAS); 3,800 ft (LACM); Independence; 4,000 ft, 0.5 mi W (AMNH); 1.4 mi W; Joshua Flats, 21.2 mi SE of Hwy. 168 on Eureka Valley Rd.; Keeler (MVZ, USNM); Keough's Hot Springs, 7 mi S Bishop (LACM); Laws; Lee Flat, 15 mi E Keeler; Lone Pine; 2.3 mi W (LACM); 4,000 ft, 3.0 mi W (LACM); 8.1 mi SE; 10.0 mi SE (MVZ, UMMZ); 4,200 ft, Long John Canyon, Inyo Mtns.; Mesquite Sand Dunes, Saline Valley (CAS); 1.0 mi S Mono County line on Hwy. 168; 7.5 mi W Panamint Springs (CAS); 11.7 mi W (UMMZ); Payson Canyon, 2 mi W Deep Springs Valley; N end Saline Valley (CAS); 4,450 ft, Silver Creek Canyon, White Mtns.; 1,380 m, Silver Creek Canyon, 7.2 mi E.

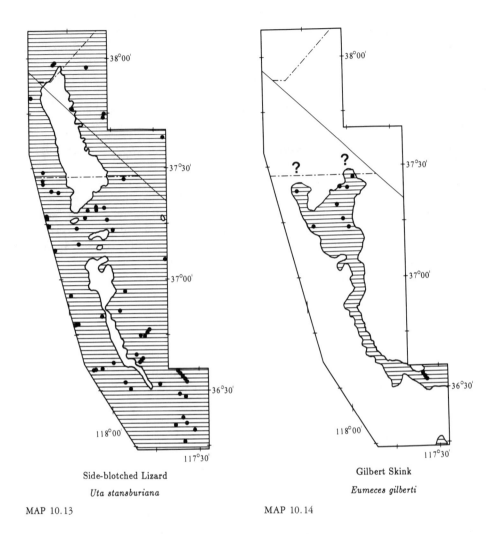

Side-blotched Lizard

Uta stansburiana

MAP 10.13

Gilbert Skink

Eumeces gilberti

MAP 10.14

Laws; 1,080–1,350 ft, Warm Springs Rd., Saline Valley (CAS); Willow Creek, Saline Valley; Willow Springs Canyon, 8.0 mi ENE Independence; mouth, Wyman Canyon, White Mtns.; 6,750 ft. Mono Co.: Benton; Fish Slough, 8 mi N Bishop (UMMZ). Nevada, Esmeralda Co.: Fish Lake (MVZ, UMMZ); 0.75 mi SSW; 7,400 ft, Indian Creek, White Mtns.; 9.1 mi SSW Silver Peak. Mineral Co.: 7,000 ft, 0.7 mi W Montgomery Pass (CAS).

Skinks (Family Scincidae)

Gilbert Skink, *Eumeces gilberti* **(Van Denburgh, 1896).** (Plates 10.18 and 10.19, Map 10.14) 6–10 in (15–25 cm); dorsal coloration uniform brown in adults; juveniles with two white lateral stripes running from top of head to base of tail, dividing brown dorsal coloration into three stripes; a middorsal brown stripe extending onto tail, and a brown stripe on each side stopping at hind legs, not extending onto base of tail; adults with brown tails; juveniles with pink tails. *Habitat:* In this area Gilbert Skinks are most common around springs and streams between 4,000 and 8,000 ft (1,220 and 2,440 m). They also occur in habitats away from water between 6,000 and 8,000 ft (1,830 and 2,440 m). This secretive lizard is rarely observed but can sometimes be seen in leaf litter or at the base of bushes during the midmorning or late afternoon. It is most easily found by turning rocks near springs or streams. *Remarks:* The subspecies of Gilbert Skink present in the area is the Western Red-tailed Skink (*E. g. rubricaudatus*). A juvenile Gilbert Skink can be distinguished from the Western Skink (*E. skiltonianus*) by differences in tail coloration. In the former, the tail color is predominantly pink, and in the latter, it is blue. One exception is that juvenile Gilbert Skinks in the Panamint Mountains have blue tails. In both subadult Gilbert Skinks and adult Western Skinks the tail coloration fades. They can still be distinguished by the length of the brown stripes on the sides, which extend onto the base of the tail in the Western Skink and stop at the hind legs in the Gilbert Skink (Fig. 10.5). (See Western Skink, *E. skiltonianus*, account for a discussion on distributional interactions between the two species.) *Range:* Mid-elevations of Argus Mountains, Nelson Range, Panamint Mountains, Inyo Mountains, and White Mountains

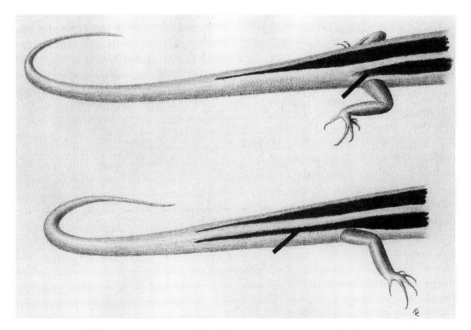

FIGURE 10.5   Gilbert Skink (*Eumeces gilberti*): Brown stripes on the sides of the body stop at hind legs (above). Western Skink (*Eumeces skiltonianus*): Brown stripes on the sides of the body extend onto the base of the tail (below).

at least as far north as the Mono County line (see ? on Map 10.14). *Reference:* Rodgers and Fitch (1947).

Localities: California, Inyo Co.: Batchelder Spring, 9.8 mi NE Big Pine; 1,840 m, Cottonwood Canyon, 3.7 mi W of Hwy. 168 on rd., White Mtns.; Deep Springs Lake (LACM); NW end, Deep Springs Valley (LACM); 4,000–5,977 ft, Grapevine Canyon, Nelson Range (CAS); 4,850 ft (BYU); Joshua Flats, 21.2 mi SE of Hwy. 168 on Eureka Valley Rd.; 2,060 m, Silver Creek Canyon, 7.2 mi E Laws; sec. 18, T. 6 S., R. 36 E., Wyman Canyon, White Mtns. (CMNH).

Western Skink, *Eumeces skiltonianus* (Baird & Girard, 1852). (Plate 10.20, Map 10.15) 5–8 in (12.5–20 cm); dorsal coloration brown with two white lateral stripes running from top of head onto tail; two lateral brown stripes below white stripes extend beyond hind legs onto base of tail; tail blue, sometimes fading in adults, especially in individuals with regenerated tails. *Habitat:* In this area, the Western Skink is a high-elevation species that has not been found below 7,000 ft (2,130 m) and may occur as high as 10,000 ft (3,050 m). An exception to this are populations on the eastern slope of the Sierra Nevada that occur a little lower. It appears to inhabit only Pinyon-juniper Woodland. These lizards are rarely seen because they spend most of their time under rocks and logs and in leaf litter. *Remarks:* The subspecies of Western Skink that occurs in the area is the Great Basin Skink (*E. s. utahensis*). See Gilbert Skink (*E. gilberti*) account for distinguishing characteristics between these two species. The Western Skink and the Gilbert Skink are very closely related species. It is possible that they interbreed where their ranges contact in the White-Inyo mountains region, but not enough specimens have been obtained to come to any definitive conclusions. Only a single Western Skink is recorded from the White Mountains. A skink with a blue tail was seen at 6,300 ft (1,920 m) in Beveridge Canyon, Inyo Mountains (see small ? on Map 10.15). A young specimen from 6,100 ft (1,860 m) in Cottonwood Canyon on the east side of the White Mountains has a pink tail with a blue tip. An adult from the same area has typical Gilbert Skink coloration. *Range:* Sight record from Inyo Mountains (see small ? on Map 10.15); White Mountains above 7,000 ft (2,130 m); Silver Peak Range above 7,000 ft (2,130 m); expected in the mountains north of Queen Valley (see large ? on Map 10.15); eastern slope of the Sierra Nevada. *References:* Rodgers and Fitch (1947), Tanner (1957).

Localities: California, Inyo Co.: 8,000–8,200 ft, corner Secs. 17, 18, 19, 20, R. 35 E, T. 7 S, N of Westgard Pass, White Mtns. Nevada, Esmeralda Co.: 7,120 ft, Birch Creek, Spring, Palmetto Mtns. (E of area); 7,300 ft, Valcalda Spring, Silver Peak Range (NE of area).

Whiptails (Family Teiidae)

Western Whiptail, *Cnemidophorus tigris* (Baird & Girard, 1852). (Plates 10.21 and 10.22, Map 10.16) 8–14 in (20–35 cm); four middorsal pale yellow stripes, distinct on front part of body, less distinct on back part; reticulate pattern of black and gray between stripes, on sides of body, and on limbs; reticulate pattern on underside of body, with neck and chest nearly completely black in some individuals; tail very

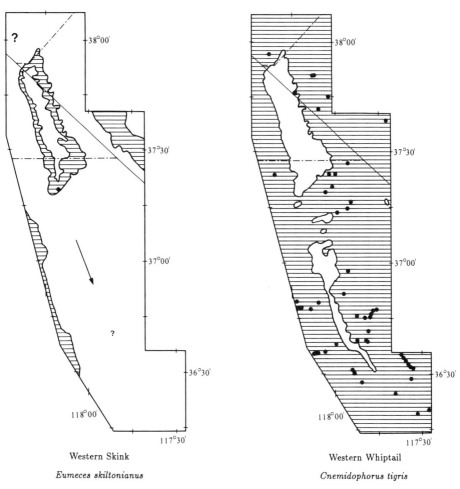

Western Skink

Eumeces skiltonianus

MAP 10.15

Western Whiptail

Cnemidophorus tigris

MAP 10.16

long, usually more than twice body length; in juveniles pale yellow stripes continuous and tail blue (see Plate 10.22). *Habitat:* In this area, Western Whiptails occur in all terrestrial habitats up to about 7,500 ft (2,290 m) in the Pinyon-juniper Woodland. This species is most common in washes and sandy areas. They are active lizards and are commonly seen moving from bush to bush in search of food. These lizards feed on invertebrates, which are captured on the surface or dug out of the ground. *Remarks:* The subspecies of Western Whiptail present in the area is the Great Basin Whiptail (*C. t. tigris*). Members of the genus *Cnemidophorus* range from Minnesota to Argentina and from California to Maryland. There are about 45 species, of which 15 are all-female. These species reproduce asexually, from eggs laid by the female and each offspring is a clone of the mother. These all female species have a larger-than-normal chromosome number (polyploidy) because of the original hybridization of two different species and the incorporation of chromosomes from both parent species into the new asexual species. The Western Whiptail is not an all-female species, but it is an ancestral parent for some of the all-female species that occur in Arizona, New Mexico, Texas, and northern Mexico. *Range:* Throughout the White-Inyo mountains region below 7,500 ft (2,290 m). *References:* Bezy and Sites (1987), Cole (1984), Parker (1972), Wright and Low (1968).

Localities: California, Inyo Co.: 3,800 ft, 6,600–6,800 ft, Near Big Horn Mine, Hunter Canyon, Inyo Mtns. (CAS); 1,620 m, 21.3 mi NE Big Pine; 5,000 ft, 24 mi NE; 2,400–4,850 ft, Daisy Canyon, Inyo Mtns. (CAS); 5,200 ft, 15 mi N Darwin; Darwin Falls (CAS, MVZ); NW end Deep Springs Valley (LACM); 23.6 mi SE of Hwy. 168 on Eureka Valley Rd.; 27.7 mi SE; 2,250–5,977 ft, Grapevine Canyon, Nelson Range (CAS); Independence; 4,000 ft, 0.5 mi W (AMNH); 1.4 mi W; 2 mi N; 3,800 ft, 2.5 mi E; 6,000–6,100 ft, 2 mi W Jackass Spring, Nelson Range; Joshua Flats, 21.2 mi SE of Hwy. 168 on Eureka Valley Rd.; 1 mi S Keeler (LACM); Laws; 4,200 ft, Long John Canyon, Inyo Mtns.; Lone Pine (FMNH, USNM); 4,300 ft, 2.3 mi W (LACM); 2.9 mi W (LACM); 4,700 ft, 3 mi W, 0.5 mi S; 4 mi W; 10.0 mi SE; 4,000 ft, Mazourka Canyon, Inyo Mtns.; 1 mi S Mono County line on Hwy. 168; 1,200 ft, Mesquite Sand Dunes, Saline Valley (CAS); Panamint Springs (CAS, MVZ); 5.6 mi N of Hwy. 190 on Saline Valley Rd.; near Freshwater Pond, W side, Saline Valley (CAS); NW end, Saline Valley (CAS); 5 mi N Salt Works; near Seven Springs, S of Lower Warm Spring, Saline Valley (CAS); 850–1,400 ft, Warm Springs Rd., Saline Valley (CAS); Willow Creek, Saline Valley; 6,750 ft, Wyman Creek, White Mtns. Mono Co.: Benton. Nevada, Esmeralda Co.: 0.25 mi W of Hwy. 264 along Chiatovich Creek, Fish Lake Valley; 5,000 ft, 0.75 mi W; 4,800 ft, 1.5 mi N Dyer; Fish Lake; 7,400 ft, Indian Creek, White Mtns.; 9.1 mi SSW Silver Peak; Mineral Co.: 3.9 mi NE California state line on Hwy. 6.

Night Lizards (Family Xantusiidae)

Desert Night Lizard, *Xantusia vigilis* (Baird, 1858). (Plate 10.23, Map 10.17) 2–4 in (5–10 cm); background coloration gray or brown with tiny black flecks that form indistinct stripes; belly uniform cream with scales arranged in transverse rows; eyelids absent. *Habitat:* This secretive, rarely seen lizard occurs in a variety of habitats up to at least 6,800 ft (2,070 m) in the White-Inyo mountains region. However, it has been found above 9,000 ft (2,750 m) in the Panamint Mountains of Death Valley National Monument. Specimens are most commonly found under the rubble of fallen Joshua Trees but have also been taken from under rocks, logs, and piles of brush. At Joshua Flats and Lee Flat in the Inyo Mountains, where no specimens have been seen, they appear not to live in Joshua Trees. *Remarks:* The subspecies of Desert Night Lizard present in the area is the Common Night Lizard (*X. v. vigilis*). Although the common name implies that this species is nocturnal, they are in fact active during the day under cover objects. This is the smallest species of lizard in the area and is easily overlooked. There are very few records of Desert Night Lizards from north of the Panamint Valley, and the range of this species is certainly more extensive than is

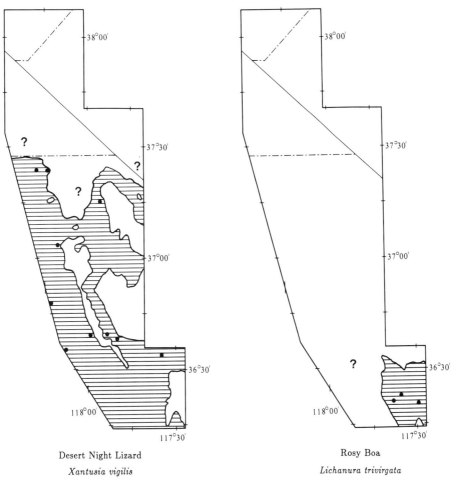

Desert Night Lizard
Xantusia vigilis

MAP 10.17

Rosy Boa
Lichanura trivirgata

MAP 10.18

presently known. The farthest north that Desert Night Lizards are known to occur in the west is the vicinity of Bishop. In the east, they are known from southeastern Utah. One record, for 6,800 ft (2,070 m) in Silver Creek Canyon, east of Laws in the White Mountains, is at the northern edge of the known range of this species. This high-elevation locality indicates that this species should be expected further north (see ? on Map 10.17). The Night Lizard family (Xantusiidae) consists of about 12 species, most of which are present in Mexico. A single species occurs in Cuba, and one species is present on three of the Channel Islands of California. *Range:* Valleys and mountains of the southern White-Inyo mountains region up to at least 6,800 ft (2,070 m). Presently known from the Panamint Valley, Argus Mountains, Saline Valley, Last Chance Range, Eureka Valley, Owens Valley north to the Mono County line, and the west side of the White Mountains. *Reference:* Bezy and Sites (1987), Zweifel and Lowe (1966).

Localities: California, Inyo Co.: Near Big Horn Mine, Hunter Canyon, Inyo Mtns. (USNM); 4,500 ft, 5 mi N, 2 mi W Bishop (W of area); BLM Ecology Center, 9 mi NW Bishop on Hwy. 395 (NW of area) (UNM); 4,500 ft, Daisy Canyon, Inyo Mtns. (CAS); 25.1 mi SW Hwy. 168 on Eureka Valley Rd.; French Spring, Inyo Mtns.; 4,200–4,400 ft, Grapevine Canyon, Nelson Range (CAS); 1.4 mi W Independence; 5,800 ft, Last Chance Spring, Last Chance Range; 5 mi W Lone Pine (LACM); Montezuma Mine, 1 mi NE Tinemaha Reservoir; 1,380 m, Silver Creek Canyon, 2.0 mi E Laws; 2,060 m, Silver Creek Canyon, 7.2 mi E Laws.

Boas (Family Boidae)

Rosy Boa, *Lichanura trivirgata* **(Cope, 1861).**   (Plate 10.24, Map 10.18) 24–36 in (60–90 cm); heavy-bodied with head small in proportion to body; background color gray with three broad, distinct reddish stripes running the length of the body; tail short and blunt. *Habitat:* In our area, Rosy Boas are restricted to Creosote Bush Scrub below about 5,000 ft (1,500 m). They occur in rocky hills and canyons and are very rare or absent on valley floors. This species is mainly nocturnal but is occasionally active in the early morning and late afternoon during the spring. *Remarks:* The subspecies of Rosy Boa present in the area is the Desert Rosy Boa (*L. t. gracia*). Two other subspecies occur in coastal southern California and in Baja California and Sonora, Mexico. The Rosy Boa and the Rubber Boa (*Charina bottae*) are the only members of the Boa Family in the United States. These two species are tiny in comparison with the giant pythons of Africa and Asia, the Anaconda of the Amazon Basin, and the Boa Constrictor, which occurs from Mexico into South America. The Rosy Boa, like other boas and pythons, kills its prey by constriction. This species feeds on rodents, birds, and occasionally lizards. Rosy Boas are gentle, slow-moving snakes. They usually remain motionless when approached and never attempt to bite when picked up. *Range:* Known only from the foothills of the Panamint Mountains and Argus Range surrounding the Panamint Valley. Suitable habitat exists in the Owens Valley in the foothills of the Inyo Mountains east of Owens Lake, and in the hills surrounding the Saline and Eureka valleys, but no specimens have been recorded (see ? on Map 10.18). *References:* Gorman (1965), Klauber (1931).

Localities: California, Inyo Co.: 0.2 mi E Darwin Wash Rd. on Hwy. 190; 10 mi W; 8.9 mi W Panamint Valley Rd. on Hwy. 190.

Colubrids (Family Colubridae)

Glossy Snake, *Arizona elegans* **(Kennicott, 1859).**   (Plate 10.25, Map 10.19) 24–28 in (60–95 cm); cream to light gray background with narrow light brown blotches running down back; black flecks around edges of blotches; ventral surface uniform white; scales smooth. *Habitat:* This nocturnal snake usually occurs in valley floors and sandy washes. In the area, Glossy Snakes have been found only in

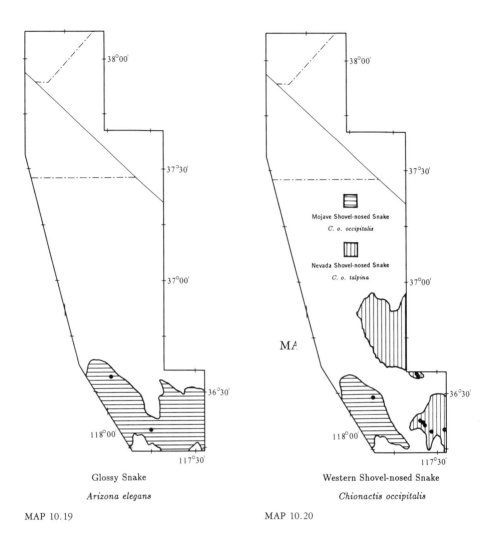

Mojave Shovel-nosed Snake
C. o. occipitalis

Nevada Shovel-nosed Snake
C. o. talpina

Glossy Snake

Arizona elegans

MAP 10.19

Western Shovel-nosed Snake

Chionactis occipitalis

MAP 10.20

and around Creosote Bush Scrub. These active snakes are rarely seen because they do not lie on roads at night, like many other species, but move rapidly across them. *Remarks:* The subspecies of Glossy Snake present in the area is the Mojave Glossy Snake (*A. e. candida*). Other subspecies occur throughout much of the southwestern United States and northern Mexico. Glossy Snakes resemble juvenile Gopher Snakes (*Pituophis catenifer*) but are readily distinguished by their smooth scales and lighter background color and blotches. This species has a flattened head, enabling it to bury in sand or loose soil. Food consists of small rodents, lizards, and reptile eggs. *Range:* Panamint Valley; foothills of northern Argus and southern Inyo Mountains; southern Owens Valley in the vicinity of Owens Lake; expected in the Saline and Eureka valleys. *Reference:* Klauber (1946).

Localities: California, Inyo Co.: 8.1 mi SE of Hwy. 136 on Hwy. 190; 4 mi SE Lone Pine.

Western Shovel-nosed Snake, *Chionactis occipitalis* (Hallowell, 1854). (Plates 10.26 and 10.27, Map 10.20) 10–16 in (25–40 cm); a small, banded snake; background yellow with brown bands; faint reddish-brown band in middle of each yellow band (absent in snakes from southern Owens Valley); pale ventral color, with brown bands crossing belly in some individuals; snout flattened. *Habitat:* This species occurs in Creosote Bush Scrub below about 5,000 ft (1,500 m). These generally nocturnal snakes are most common in sandy areas. *Remarks:* There are two subspecies of Western Shovel-nosed Snake in our area. The Mojave Shovel-nosed Snake (*C. o. occipitalis*) is present in the extreme southern Owens Valley around Owens Lake. This subspecies lacks the faint reddish-brown band in the middle of each yellow band. The Nevada Shovel-nosed Snake (*C. o. talpina*), which occurs in the Panamint and Saline valleys, has the faint reddish-brown band (see Map 10.20). This snake uses its flattened snout to aid in burying itself in the ground. In areas of loose sand they can crawl beneath the surface of the sand for great distances. In Arizona, where Western Shovel-nosed Snakes occur together with venomous Arizona Coral Snakes (*Micruroides euryxanthus*), the Shovel-nosed Snakes have a similar color pattern with red bands. The two species resemble each other, with the harmless Western Shovel-nosed Snake mimicking the venomous Arizona Coral Snake. *Range:* Vicinity of Owens Lake in the southern Owens Valley (*C. o. occipitalis*); Panamint and Saline valleys (*C. o. talpina*). *References:* Elvin (1963), Klauber (1951), Norris and Kavanau (1966).

Localities: California, Inyo Co.: Darwin Falls; 6.8 mi W of Darwin Rd. on Hwy. 190; 9.2 mi W; 2,340–3,750 ft, Grapevine Canyon, Nelson Range (CAS); Owens Lake (dot on Map 10.20 is the position of an additional site record) (FMNH); 2.1 mi E Panamint Springs; 9.5 mi E of Saline Valley Rd. on Hwy. 190.

Night Snake, *Hypsiglena torquata* (Günther, 1860). (Plate 10.28, Map 10.21) 12–24 in (30–60 cm); a slender snake with a wide, flattened head; gray background coloration with numerous brown spots running the length of body; a series of paired dorsal spots may be fused or slightly offset, giving a checkered appearance; belly uniform cream; distinct dark brown neck band which extends along side of head to eye, commonly with a projection extending to middle of top of head. *Habitat:* Night Snakes occur in all habitats below about 7,000 ft (2,130 m). They are most common in rocky places in low- to moderate-elevation desert areas. This is a strictly nocturnal species that is sometimes seen crossing roads at night. They are fairly common on the Westgard Pass road (Hwy. 168) west of Tollhouse Spring and on the Eureka Valley Road between Joshua Flats and the Eureka Valley floor. *Remarks:* The subspecies of Night Snake present in the region is the Desert Night Snake (*H. t. deserticola*). This wide-ranging species occurs from extreme southern British Columbia to southern Mexico and from coastal central California to Texas. These small snakes have enlarged, grooved teeth in the back of the upper jaw. These teeth are used in channeling venom into prey, which usually consists of small lizards. It is unlikely that this small species could envenomate a human, but care should be taken if these snakes

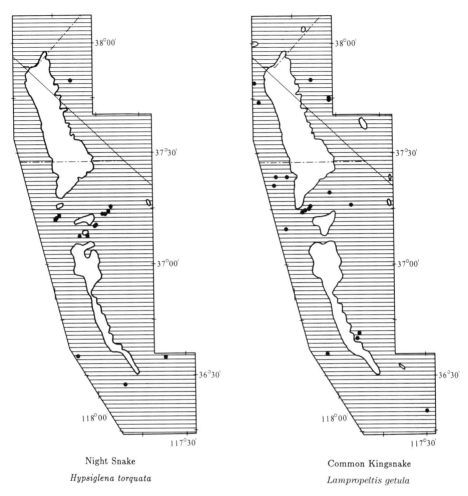

Night Snake

Hypsiglena torquata

MAP 10.21

Common Kingsnake

Lampropeltis getula

MAP 10.22

are handled. *Range:* Throughout the White-Inyo mountains region below 7,000 ft (2,130 m). *Reference:* Tanner (1944).

Localities: California, Inyo Co.: 4.7 mi NE Big Pine; 5 mi NE; 6.4 mi NE; pass over Inyo Mtns. on Eureka Valley Rd.; 11.3 mi SE of Hwy. 168 on Eureka Valley Rd.; 1,920 m, 19.5 mi SE; 1,840 m, 19.9 mi SE; 24.1 mi SE; 24.9 mi SE; 26.3 mi SE; 27.4 mi SE; 3,630 ft, Grapevine Canyon, Nelson Range (CAS); 3 mi W Lone Pine; 15.3 mi SE. Nevada, Esmeralda Co.: 5,200 ft, 2 mi W of Hwy. 264 along Chiatovich Creek, Fish Lake Valley.

Common Kingsnake, *Lampropeltis getula* **(Linnaeus, 1766).** (Plate 10.29, Map 10.22) 30–48 in (75–120 cm); black- and white-banded; black bands cross belly; black bands wider on top than on sides and belly. *Habitat:* Kingsnakes occur in all habitats below about 7,500 ft (2,290 m). They are active both during the day and on warm nights. *Remarks:* The subspecies of Common Kingsnake present in the area is the California Kingsnake (*L. g. californiae*). Common Kingsnakes are one of the widest-ranging snakes in the United States. They occur across North America from the Pacific coast to the Atlantic coast. There are a number of subspecies with varying color patterns. Kingsnakes eat a variety of vertebrate animals, including mammals, small birds, and reptiles. They are well known for eating other snakes, even rattlesnakes. They are generally not affected by the venom and will continue eating a rattlesnake even if bitten. It has been shown that rattlesnakes sense the odor of kingsnakes and attempt to avoid them. The only similar-looking species in the area is the Western Long-nosed Snake (*Rhinocheilus lecontei lecontei*). In the black- and white-banded color phase of this species, the black bands do not encircle the belly. In this region, Common Kingsnakes are relatively rare in Creosote Bush Scrub areas. They appear to be more common in Great Basin Scrub areas, especially in the vicinity of springs and streams. *Range:* Throughout the White-Inyo mountains region below 7,500 ft (2,290 m). *Reference:* Carpenter and Gillingham (1975).

Localities: California, Inyo Co.: Beveridge Canyon, Saline Valley (FMNH); Big Pine; 6,300 ft, 7 mi NE; 7.8 mi NE; 1,800 m, 8.2 mi NE; 9.0 mi NE; 22.0 mi NE; 2 mi E Bishop; 6,600–6,800 ft, Big Horn Mine, Hunter Canyon, Saline Valley (USNM); 0.3 mi E Darwin Wash Rd. on Hwy. 190; 27.7 mi SE of Hwy. 168 on Eureka Valley Rd.; Laws; Lone Pine; 5.9 mi S of Mono County line on Hwy. 6; 4.6 mi E Hwy. 6 on Silver Creek Canyon Rd.; White Mtns. Mono Co.: 1.0 mi W Benton; 18.9 mi N of Inyo County line on Hwy. 6. Nevada, Esmeralda Co.: 1,640 m, Chiatovich Creek, Fish Lake Valley; Fish Lake (LACM); 0.5 mi S.

Coachwhip, *Masticophis flagellum* (Shaw, 1802).   (Plate 10.30, Map 10.23) 36–84 in (90–210 cm); a long, slender snake with large eyes; dorsal background red or reddish brown; indistinct narrow tan or cream crossbands on front half of body; between two and six distinct dark brown or black crossbands on neck; ventral surface pale with small black spots on chin and throat; juveniles are banded or blotched, usually less red than adults, with dark neck bands less distinct. *Habitat:* Coachwhips are diurnal snakes that occur in all habitats up to about 6,500 ft (1,980 m) in the lower Pinyon-juniper Woodland. They are relatively common in desert canyons where riparian vegetation is present. *Remarks:* The subspecies of Coachwhip present in the area is the Red Coachwhip (*M. f. piceus*). The seven subspecies of this wide-ranging snake occur from coastal southern California across the southern half of the country to the Carolinas and Florida, and south in Mexico to the states of Veracruz, Sinoloa, and the tip of Baja California. Other subspecies are variable in color pattern and may not look like individuals from the White-Inyo mountains region. Coachwhips eat a variety of food, including lizards, snakes, birds, mammals, and even insects. This is the fastest-moving snake in the region. In the open, it will flee if approached and usually disappear into a clump of vegetation or down a rodent burrow. This evil-tempered species always tries to bite when picked up. Although it is not poisonous, the tiny,

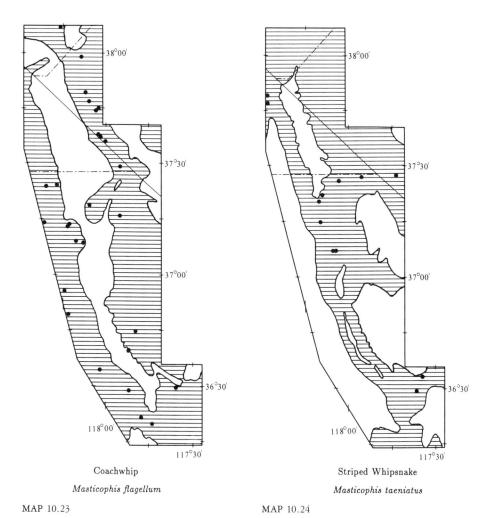

Coachwhip

Masticophis flagellum

MAP 10.23

Striped Whipsnake

Masticophis taeniatus

MAP 10.24

razor-sharp teeth will draw blood. *Range:* Entire White-Inyo mountains region below about 6,500 ft (1,980 m). *References:* Ortenburger (1928), Wilson (1970).

Localities: California, Inyo Co.: 1.5 mi SW Batchelder Spring, Westgard Pass; near Big Horn Mine, Hunter Canyon, Inyo Mtns. (USNM); 5,500 ft, 6 mi E Big Pine; 19.9 mi NE; 31 mi S Bishop; Charcoal Kilns off Hwy. 395, N Independence (LACM); W end Deep Springs Valley (LACM); 5,000 ft, 4.9 mi SE of Hwy. 168 on Eureka Valley Rd.; 7.3 mi SE; 26.9 mi SE; 9.8 mi E of Hwy. 136 on Hwy. 190; 2 mi N Independence; 4 mi N (SDSNH); Keeler (USNM); 9 mi SE (SDSNH); Keough Hot Springs, 7 mi S Bishop (SDSNH); Laws; Lee Flat, 3.3 mi S of summit on Saline Valley Rd. (CAS); 2 mi SE Lone Pine; 1,200 ft, Mesquite Sand Dunes, Saline Valley (CAS); 6,000 ft, Silver Creek Canyon, White Mtns. Mono Co.: Oasis (BYU, MVZ).

Nevada, Esmeralda Co.: 1.7 mi E California state line on Hwy. 264 (LACM); 4.9 mi E; 1 mi W of Hwy. 264 on Chiatovich Creek, Fish Lake Valley; 2 mi S Chiatovich Creek on Hwy. 264, Fish Lake Valley; 4.8 mi S Dyer (LACM); Fish Lake; 1 mi SW. Mineral Co.: 8.1 mi N of Hwy. 6 on Hwy. 360.

Striped Whipsnake, *Masticophis taeniatus* (Hallowell, 1852). (Plate 10.31, Map 10.24) 30–60 in (75–150 cm); a slender snake with a narrow neck, wide head, and large eyes; dorsal background coloration brown, commonly with a bluish cast; white lateral stripe on each side divided in half by a narrow black line; two additional narrow black stripes on lower part of each side; midventral coloration yellow, becoming pale toward neck and pink toward tail; small black spots on chin and throat; black spot on the side of each ventral scale. *Habitat:* In this area, Striped Whipsnakes occur from mid-elevation Great Basin Scrub, above 5,000 ft (1,520 m), to at least 8,400 ft (2,560 m) in the Pinyon-juniper Woodland of the White Mountains. The species has been recorded at 9,400 ft (2,870 m) in the Panamint Mountains. This active, diurnal form is very alert and will flee when approached. *Remarks:* The subspecies of Striped Whipsnake present in the region is the Desert Striped Whipsnake (*M. t. taeniatus*). The species ranges from eastern Washington south throughout the Great Basin and east into central Texas. It occurs in Mexico at least as far south as the state of Michoacán. A detailed study of Striped Whipsnakes was conducted between 1969 and 1973 in northern Utah, at a site where the snakes hibernate in communal dens. A total of 242 whipsnakes were marked and studied. It was found that young snakes ate only lizards, but adult snakes ate both lizards and small mammals. During the summer, individual snakes commonly moved 400–500 ft (122–152 m) in a day, and one snake traveled more than a mile (1.6 km) from the den. *Range:* Entire White-Inyo mountains region, between about 5,000 ft (1,520 m) and 9,000 ft (2,740 m) elevation. *References:* Bennion and Parker (1976), Ortenburger (1928), Parker and Brown (1980).

Localities: California, Inyo Co.: 6,620 ft, 9.8 mi NE Big Pine; Dead Horse Meadow, Crooked Creek, White Mtns. (LACM); 6,600 ft, 10 mi SE of Hwy. 168 on Eureka Valley Rd. (LACM); 6,750 ft, 10.7 mi SE (LACM); 5,400 ft, Grapevine Canyon, Nelson Range [Willow Creek] (USNM); Inyo Lodge Camp, Inyo Mtns. (LACM); 1.2 mi S Mono County line on Hwy. 168, White Mtns.; 15.5 mi NE of Hwy. 190 on Saline Valley Rd., Nelson Range (LACM); 3.1 mi N of Hwy. 168 on White Mtn. Rd. (LACM); 8,400 ft, 6.0 mi N. Mono Co.: Benton; 5,200 ft, 2 mi S. Nevada, Esmeralda Co.: 12 mi E Oasis, Silver Peak Range (KU).

Spotted Leaf-nosed Snake, *Phyllorhynchus decurtatus* (Cope, 1868). (Plate 10.32, Map 10.25) 12–20 in (30–50 cm); light reddish brown to gray dorsal background coloration with brown blotches running down back; uniform white ventral coloration; black stripe through each eye; enlarged, leaf-shaped rostral scale at tip of nose. *Habitat:* In the White-Inyo mountains region Spotted Leaf-nosed Snakes occur in Creosote Bush Scrub below about 3,000 ft (910 m). They are most common in sandy or gravelly areas. This strictly nocturnal species is commonly seen crossing roads on warm nights in the late spring and early summer. *Remarks:* The subspecies

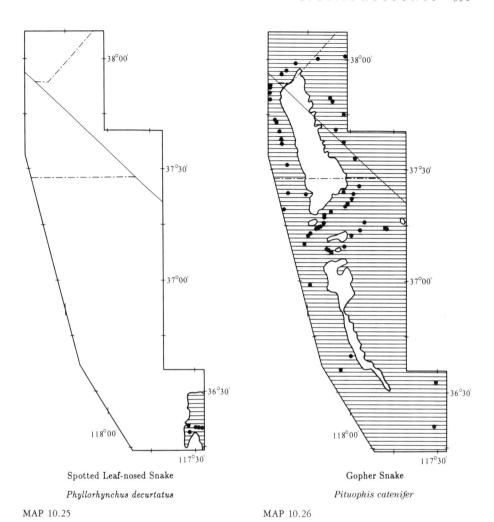

Spotted Leaf-nosed Snake

Phyllorhynchus decurtatus

MAP 10.25

Gopher Snake

Pituophis catenifer

MAP 10.26

of Spotted Leaf-nosed Snake present in the region is the Western Leaf-nosed Snake (*P. d. perkinsi*). Until 1922, only six specimens were known to science, and it was considered one of the rarest North American snakes. At about this time, biologists discovered that nocturnal snakes could easily be collected by driving on paved roads at night. It was soon learned that Spotted Leaf-nosed Snakes were one of the most abundant snakes in the southern California deserts. The diet of this species is very specialized. Occasionally small lizards are eaten, but the majority of food taken consists of the eggs of other reptiles. The enlarged scale on the snout of this snake aids in digging in the sand in search of eggs. *Range:* Recorded only from the Panamint Valley. Suitable habitat is present in the extreme southern Owens Valley, Saline Valley, and Eureka Valley, but no specimens are recorded. *References:* Brattstrom (1953), Klauber (1935).

Localities: California, Inyo Co.: Darwin Falls; 3.9 mi W of Darwin Rd. on Hwy. 190; 0.5 mi E Panamint Springs; 1 mi NW; 1.3 mi E; 1.5 mi E; 1.7 mi E; 4.7 mi E; 5.7 mi E; 2.6 mi W of Panamint Valley Rd. on Hwy. 190; 4.3 mi W.

Gopher Snake, *Pituophis catenifer* (Blainville, 1835). (Plate 10.33, Map 10.26) 30–60 in (75–150 cm); large, blotched snake with distinctly keeled scales; dorsal coloration gray to tan; large black to brown blotches running down back; blotches often fused in neck region. *Habitat:* Gopher Snakes occur in all habitats below about 8,000 ft (2,440 m). They are active during the day and on warm nights, and they are commonly seen resting on paved roads during the late afternoon and at night. *Remarks:* The subspecies of Gopher Snake present in the area is the Great Basin Gopher Snake (*P. c. deserticola*). Other subspecies of this wide-ranging snake occur from the Pacific coast to the Great Plains and from Canada to Mexico. In the past, many of these subspecies were recognized as distinct species. Some of the forms in the United States look very different from each other, and future studies may determine that they are, in fact, distinct species. This large, heavy-bodied snake feeds primarily on rodents, which are first killed by constriction. The Gopher Snake is occasionally mistaken for a rattlesnake because it sometimes coils its body and vibrates its tail, making a rattling sound in dry leaves. Young Gopher Snakes are similar in color pattern to Glossy Snakes (*Arizona elegans*). The former has keeled scales, and the latter has smooth scales. *Range:* Throughout the White-Inyo mountains region below 8,000 ft (2,440 m). *References:* Klauber (1947), Parker and Brown (1980).

Localities: California, Inyo Co.: 4,000 ft, 1 mi E Big Pine; 5.1 mi NE; 6.0 mi NE; 8.2 mi NE; 8.6 mi NE; 10.3 mi NE; 11.9 mi NE; 15.4 mi NE; 21.9 mi NE; 22.8 mi NE; 24.5 mi NE; 27.2 mi NE; 3.5 mi ESE Bishop; Hwy. 190 between Darwin Wash Rd. and 4,000 ft Vista Lookout; 6.9 mi SE of Hwy. 168 on Eureka Valley Rd.; 5,750 ft, 7.4 mi SE; 8.4 mi SE; 7,150 ft, 16.1 mi SE; 20.3 mi SE; 22.7 mi SE; 35.1 mi SE; 35.4 mi SE; French Spring, Inyo Mtns.; 5,750 ft, Grapevine Canyon, Nelson Range (CAS); 13 mi N Independence (LACM); Jackass Spring, 20 mi N Darwin, Panamint Mtns. (USNM); Lone Pine (CAS, USNM); 4.6 mi N; 3.1 mi S Mono County line on Hwy. 168; 6.8 mi S Mono County line on Hwy. 6; Westgard Pass (BYU); 6,000 ft; Wyman Canyon, 2 mi W Deep Springs Valley, White Mtns. Mono Co.: Benton; 5 mi N (SDSNH, UMMZ); 6 mi S (SDSNH); N end Fish Slough, 19 mi N Bishop (UCSB); 4.4 mi N Inyo County line on Hwy. 6; 10.9 mi N; 11.9 mi N; Silver Canyon, 4.5 mi E Laws; 18.6 mi N; 3.2 mi SW Nevada state line on Hwy. 6; 4.8 mi SW; Nevada state line on Hwy. 266, N Oasis. Nevada, Esmeralda Co.: 1 mi W of Hwy. 264 along Chiatovich Creek, Fish Lake Valley; 1 mi S Chiatovich Creek on Hwy. 264, Fish Lake Valley; 0.3 mi N Dyer; Fish Lake; jct. Hwy. 6 and Hwy. 264; 11.3 mi E Mineral County line on Hwy. 6; 5.1 mi N California state line on Hwy. 264. Mineral Co.: 1.6 mi E Montgomery Pass on Hwy 6; 2.4 mi NE California state line on Hwy. 6; 4.6 mi NE.

Long-nosed Snake, *Rhinocheilus lecontei* (Baird & Girard, 1853). (Plate 10.34, Map 10.27) 20–40 in (50–100 cm); a speckled snake with distinct black saddles across back and sides; white flecks on the sides of each saddle; in most individuals the area

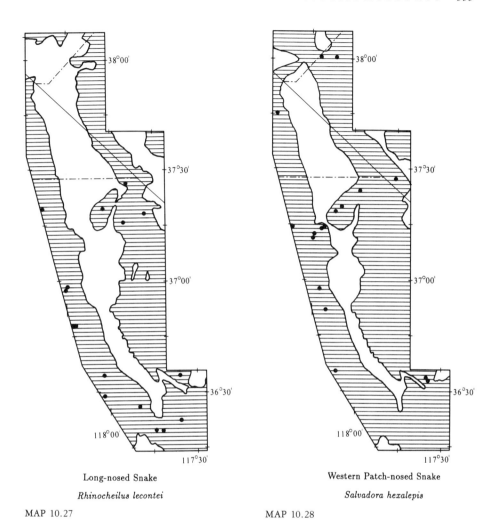

Long-nosed Snake

Rhinocheilus lecontei

MAP 10.27

Western Patch-nosed Snake

Salvadora hexalepis

MAP 10.28

between the saddles is white with red and black speckles; in some specimens the area between the saddles is uniform white; belly pale, some with black blotches; snout pointed. *Habitat:* Long-nosed Snakes occur throughout the White-Inyo mountains region below about 6,000 ft (1,830 m). They are most common in sandy Creosote Bush Scrub and Great Basin Scrub areas. This species is almost exclusively nocturnal and is usually seen crossing roads at night during the spring and summer. It is a fast-moving snake that rarely rests on the pavement as Gopher Snakes (*Pituophis catenifer*) and rattlesnakes (*Crotalus*) do. *Remarks:* The subspecies of Long-nosed Snake in the area is the Western Long-nosed Snake (*R. l. lecontei*). At one time the black and white color phase was recognized as a distinct subspecies (*R. l. clarus*). Owing, in part, to reports of both color phases being hatched from a single clutch of eggs, this taxonomic distinction has been dropped for the present. However, more research is needed on the *clarus* phase. In some areas, such as parts of the Coachella Valley in Riverside County, California, all Long-nosed Snakes lack red speckles. The *clarus* phase may be distinguished from the similarly colored Common Kingsnake (*Lampropeltis getula*) by the pointed snout and the absence of black bands connecting across the belly. Long-nosed Snakes feed on lizards and lizard eggs, small snakes, small mammals, and occasionally birds. *Range:* Throughout the White-Inyo mountains region below 6,000 ft (1,830 m). *References:* Klauber (1941), Shannon and Humphrey (1963).

Localities: California, Inyo Co.: 0.6 mi E Aberdeen; 1.3 mi S; Bartlett (SDSNH); 12 mi N Big Pine (LACM); 20.1 mi NE on Hwy. 168; 30.7 mi NE; 10 mi S Bishop; 5.7 mi N of Eureka Valley Rd. on North Eureka Valley Rd.; 26.9 mi SE of Hwy. 168 on Eureka Valley Rd.; 3,850 ft, Grapevine Canyon, Nelson Range (CAS); Independence; 1.4 mi W; 2 mi SE Lone Pine (SDSNH); 16.6 mi SE; 38 mi E; 1.3 mi W of Saline Valley Rd. on Hwy. 190; 0.8 mi E.

Western Patch-nosed Snake, *Salvadora hexalepis* (Cope, 1866). (Plate 10.35, Map 10.28) 24–36 in (60–90 cm); gray to light brown dorsal coloration with two narrow, broken stripes running down back; ventral coloration uniform cream; enlarged scale on tip of snout (rostral scale). *Habitat:* This snake occurs throughout the entire White-Inyo mountains region up to about 6,500 ft (1,980 m). It is most common in sandy valley floors. This is a fast-moving diurnal species. Patch-nosed snakes are sometimes seen in the late afternoon basking on roads. *Remarks:* The subspecies of Western Patch-nosed Snake in the area is the Mojave Patch-nosed Snake (*S. h. mojavensis*). This genus contains eight species that range from northern Nevada to Guatemala. They occur in arid and semi-arid regions. The Western Patch-nosed Snake ranges the farthest north of any species, occurring from northern Nevada into central western Mexico, and from coastal southern California to western Texas. This wary, alert snake will attempt to escape when approached. In this area, it is more common in Great Basin Scrub habitats than in Creosote Bush Scrub habitats. Patch-nosed Snakes feed mainly on lizards and reptile eggs. *Range:* Throughout the White-Inyo mountains region below 6,500 ft (1,980 m). *Reference:* Bogert (1939).

Localities: California, Inyo Co.: Antelope Spring, Deep Springs Valley (LACM); 5,000 ft, 5 mi E Big Pine; 6,000 ft, 6 mi NE; 6,400 ft, 7 mi NE; 20.4 mi NE; 2 mi NE Deep Springs (LACM); 8.1 mi SW (LACM); 1 mi NE of Eureka Valley Rd. on Hwy. 168 (CMNH); 4,480 ft, 5,100 ft, Grapevine Canyon, Nelson Range (CAS); 5.0 mi NE Independence; 11.0 mi N; Keough Hot Springs, 7 mi S Bishop (LACM); 2.8 mi W Lone Pine (LACM); 9 mi W Panamint Springs on Hwy. 190; 6,000 ft, 3.1 mi S of summit on Saline Valley Rd. (CAS). Mono Co.: 4.4 mi S of Hwy. 120 at Benton on Hwy. 6. Nevada, Esmeralda Co.: 10 mi E Basalt (UMMZ); 4.0 mi E California state line on Hwy. 266; 0.5 mi E Mineral County line on Hwy. 6.

Ground Snake, *Sonora semiannulata* (Baird & Girard, 1853). (Plate 10.36, Map 10.29) 10–16 in (25–40 cm); black- and orange-banded; width of bands about equal; bands not sharply defined and not continuous ventrally except on tail. *Habitat:* The few specimens recorded from the region have been found in mountainous areas in

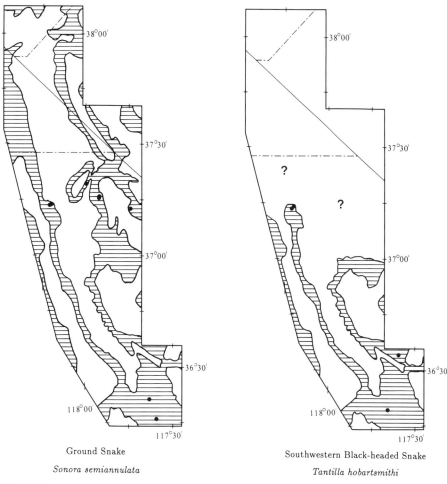

Ground Snake

Sonora semiannulata

MAP 10.29

Southwestern Black-headed Snake

Tantilla hobartsmithi

MAP 10.30

both Creosote Bush Scrub and Great Basin Desert Scrub below 6,000 ft (1,830 m). Ground Snakes may occasionally be found under rocks near streams but are most commonly encountered on roads at dusk. *Remarks:* Ground Snakes range from Texas to California and from Idaho to the tip of Baja California and northeastern Mexico. They may be locally abundant but are seldom seen throughout most of their range. In some places striped or uniformly colored populations exist. In the past, some of these populations were regarded as separate species, but currently only a single species is recognized. Ground Snakes prey on spiders and other invertebrates. The only other snake in the region likely to be confused with this species is the Western Shovel-nosed Snake (*Chionactis occipitalis*), which has a flattened snout and yellow rather than orange bands. There is also usually a faint brown saddle in each yellow band, in the latter species. *Range:* Presumed to occur throughout the White-Inyo mountains region below 6,500 ft (1,980 m). May be absent from valley floors. *Reference:* Frost (1983).

Localities: California, Inyo Co.: 7 mi NE Big Pine; 7.7 mi NE; 4,000–5,000 ft, Darwin Vicinity on Hwy. 190; E end Deep Springs Valley (SDSNH); 27.3 mi SE of Hwy. 168 on Eureka Valley Rd.; 27.7 mi SE; 38.7 mi SE; 4,500 ft, Grapevine Canyon, Nelson Range (CAS); 6.8 mi E of Saline Valley Rd. on Hwy. 190.

Southwestern Black-headed Snake, *Tantilla hobartsmithi* (Taylor, 1936). (Plate 10.37, Map 10.30) 8–14 in (20–35 cm); small, thin brown snake with a black head; ventral color red. *Habitat:* In the White-Inyo mountains region, Black-headed Snakes have been found in rocky, mountainous places below 6,500 ft (1,980 m). These snakes occur both in Creosote Bush Scrub and Great Basin Scrub and into the Pinyon-juniper Woodland. They are most common around springs and streams. This is a nocturnal species that can occasionally be found by turning rocks. *Remarks:* This secretive, small snake is seldom observed. There are only four museum specimens from the White-Inyo mountains region. The northernmost known record for the species is on the Westgard Pass road (see Map 10.30), but it is probable that they occur farther north in suitable habitat. Black-headed Snakes have a very specialized diet, feeding almost exclusively on centipedes. Although they are not considered dangerous to humans, this species has enlarged rear fangs and venom to aid in killing prey. Outside of our area, the range of the Southwestern Black-headed Snake extends southeast into Nevada, Utah, Colorado, Arizona, New Mexico, Texas, and northern Mexico. *Range:* Northern Argus Mountains, Nelson Range above the Saline Valley, western slopes of the Inyo Mountains; may occur further north (see ? on Map 10.30). *Reference:* Cole and Hardy (1981).

Localities: California, Inyo Co.: 5,550 ft, 7.2 mi NE Big Pine; 8.5 mi NE; 4,020–4,030 ft, Grapevine Canyon, Nelson Range (CAS); Hogback Creek, 6 mi S Olancha (S of area); 3.4 mi E of Saline Valley Rd. on Hwy. 190.

Sierra Garter Snake, *Thamnophis couchii* (Kennicott, 1859). (Plate 10.38, Map 10.31) 24–42 in (60–105 cm); dorsal background color olive-brown with black spots arranged in four rows running down the body; pale chin; ventral surface light to dark brown, commonly with black line at posterior margin of each ventral scale; long, narrow, triangular head with black neck collar. *Habitat:* This highly aquatic snake is restricted to the vicinity of marshes, streams, and rivers. It is a wary diurnal species that readily enters the water if disturbed while basking. Once in the water, these snakes usually hide under rocks at the bottoms of pools. *Remarks:* This was formerly regarded as one wide-ranging species with six subspecies in California and western Nevada. It has now been split up into four species. In the western Sierra Nevada this snake has a typical striped garter snake pattern, but in our area it is spotted with no stripes. The snakes from the Owens Valley have not been studied yet and may actually represent a fifth species in this group. A second species of garter snake, the Western Terrestrial Garter Snake (*T. elegans*) is also found here. Where the two species coexist

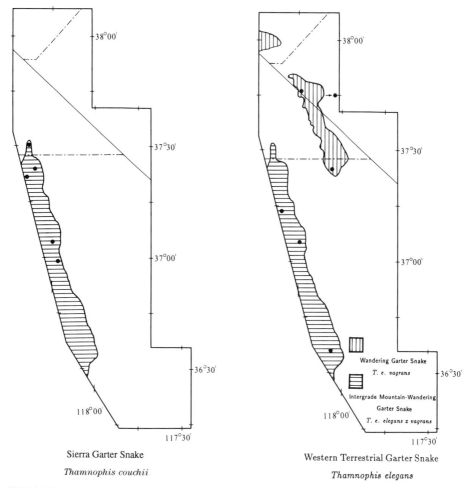

Sierra Garter Snake

Thamnophis couchii

MAP 10.31

Western Terrestrial Garter Snake

Thamnophis elegans

MAP 10.32

in the Owens Valley, the Western Terrestrial Garter Snake has a middorsal stripe (see following account). Sierra Garter Snakes feed primarily on fish and frogs. Like other garter snakes, this species is live-bearing, and the young are born at a size of about 6 in (10 cm) in the late summer. *Range:* Owens Valley from Bishop to Lone Pine and streams draining the eastern slopes of the Sierra Nevada. *References:* Fitch (1940b), Fitch (1941), Rossman and Stewart (1987).

Localities: California, Inyo Co.: Owens River just above Aberdeen (UMMZ); 4,000 ft, Alvord, Owens Valley (USNM); Bishop; 4,200 ft, 2 mi W; 4,100 ft, Laws; Lone Pine (USNM); Tinemaha Creek, 0.5 mi NW of Hwy. 395, 7 mi S Big Pine (LACM). Mono Co.: Fish Slough, 10 mi N Bishop (USNM).

Western Terrestrial Garter Snake, *Thamnophis elegans* **(Baird & Girard, 1853).**
(Plate 10.39, Map 10.32) 18–36 in (45–90 cm); dorsal background light to dark
brown with black spots forming irregular bands; in Owens Valley individuals, a
middorsal yellow stripe is present; ventral surface light brown with irregular black
patches, which sometimes completely cover the belly; black neck band may extend
to top of head. *Habitat:* This species usually occurs in the vicinity of permanent
water but may wander some distance. It frequents mountain streams, rivers, ponds,
marshes, and lakes. These snakes are mainly diurnal but are occasionally active at
night during the summer. *Remarks:* This variable species occurs throughout much
of the western United States. In the northern portion of the White-Inyo mountains
region, the Wandering Garter Snake (*T. e. vagrans*) is present; this subspecies has no
middorsal stripe. In the Owens Valley, intergrades between this subspecies and the
Mountain Garter Snake (*T. e. elegans*) occur (see Map 10.32); these intergrades have
a middorsal stripe. The stripe will distinguish this species from the Sierra Garter
Snake (*T. couchii*), which also occurs in the Owens Valley. In addition to fish and
frogs, Terrestrial Garter Snakes feed on lizards, mice, and even nestling birds. Young
are born in the late summer. *Range:* Entire length of Owens Valley (*T. e. elegans* ×
vagrans);[1] Fish Lake Valley, streams on the eastern and southern slopes of the White
Mountains to at least 8,200 ft (2,500 m), (*T. elegans vagrans*). *References:* Fitch (1941),
Fox (1951), White and Kolb (1974).

Localities: California, Inyo Co.: 4,000 ft, 5 mi NW Big Pine; 5.4 mi S (UMMZ);
4,200 ft, 2 mi W Bishop; Lone Pine (USNM); Roberts Ranch, Wyman Canyon,
White Mtns. Nevada, Esmeralda Co.: 8,200 ft, Chiatovich Creek, White Mtns; Fish
Lake.

Lyre Snake, *Trimorphodon biscutatus* **(Duméril, Bibron & Duméril, 1854).**
(Plate 10.40, Map 10.33) 24–36 in (60–90 cm); gray dorsal coloration with brown
blotches running down back; gray saddle within each brown blotch; white ventral
coloration with small brown blotches fringing belly; head wide and flattened with
blunt nose; brown V-shaped stripe behind eyes. *Habitat:* This nocturnal species occurs in rocky Creosote Bush Scrub areas below 5,000 ft (1,520 m). Lyre Snakes are
uncommon but can occasionally be observed crossing roads at night. *Remarks:* The
subspecies of Lyre Snake in this area is the California Lyre Snake (*T. b. vandenburghi*).
The Lyre Snake is a wide-ranging desert and tropical species occurring from Inyo
County, California, southern Nevada, and southern Utah to Costa Rica, and from
coastal southern California to western Texas. In the past, Lyre Snakes were classified
as six distinct species, but recent work suggests that they represent a single, geographically variable species. In tropical Mexico, Lyre Snakes may reach a length of
over 5 ft (1.5 m). This is a mildly venomous snake that has enlarged rear fangs.
The venom is used to kill small lizards and perhaps small rodents. Lyre Snakes
are not considered dangerous to humans but should be handled with caution. *Range:*
In our area, known only from the Panamint Valley below 5,000 ft (1,520 m). Suitable

---

[1] × refers to intergrades between the subspecies *T. e. elegans* and *T. e. vagrans*

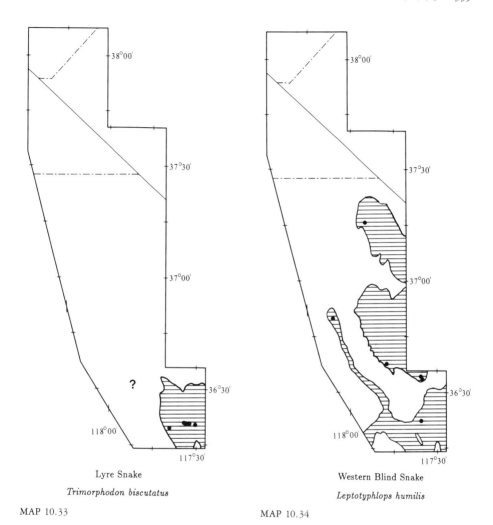

Lyre Snake

Trimorphodon biscutatus

MAP 10.33

Western Blind Snake

Leptotyphlops humilis

MAP 10.34

habitat is present in the Saline, Eureka, and southern Owens valleys, but no specimens have been recorded (see ? on Map 10.33). *References:* Cowles and Bogert (1953), Gehlbach (1971), Klauber (1940a).

Localities: California, Inyo Co.: 1 mi W of Darwin Falls Rd. on Hwy. 190; 3 mi W; 3.2 mi W; 4.6 mi W; Hwy. 190, between Darwin Wash Rd. and 4,000 ft Vista Point; 4.7 mi W Panamint Springs (CAS); 3.5 mi E of Saline Valley Rd. on Hwy. 190 (LACM).

Slender Blind Snakes (Family Leptotyphlopidae)

Western Blind Snake, *Leptotyphlops humilis* (Baird & Girard, 1853). (Plate 10.41, Map 10.34) 6–12 in (15–30 cm); shiny in appearance; dorsal color silver or light brown with a silver cast; eyes reduced to black spots covered by scales; head, body, and tail of uniform diameter. *Habitat:* In our area this species appears to be restricted to Creosote Bush Scrub below 5,000 ft (1,520 m). Most specimens have been found in rocky canyons where streams or springs are present. Worm Snakes, as they are commonly called, spend most of the time underground but occasionally are active on the surface at night. *Remarks:* Blind Snakes of the genus *Leptotyphlops* occur in Africa, Southwest Asia, South America, Central America, and North America. Most species occur in the tropics, and only two are present in the United States. Western Blind Snakes do not look like typical snakes and could be mistaken for worms because of their small size, uniform diameter, and lack of an obvious head. The greatly reduced eyes are covered by scales and function only to distinguish light intensity. They live underground, commonly in association with termite colonies. Termites, ants, and ant eggs are a major part of their diet. Blind snakes are rarely encountered in the White-Inyo mountains region but are commonly found in the Colorado River region of the Arizona-California border. *Range:* Canyons draining into the Panamint, Saline, Eureka, and Southern Owens valleys. *References:* Klauber (1940b), Brattstrom and Schwenkmeyer (1951).

Localities: California, Inyo Co.: 3,900 ft, Daisy Canyon, Saline Valley (CAS); 27.7 mi SE of Hwy. 168 on Eureka Valley Rd.; 4,000 ft, 4,480 ft, 4,500 ft, 4,630 ft, Grapevine Canyon, Nelson Range (CAS); 5 mi ENE Independence; 9.5 mi W Panamint Valley Rd. on Hwy. 190.

Vipers (Family Viperidae)

Sidewinder, *Crotalus cerastes* (Hallowell, 1854). (Plate 10.42, Map 10.35) 14–24 in (35–60 cm); light-gray background color with a single row of dark gray to brown oval blotches running down the center of the back; black speckling, occasionally forming indistinct blotches, along sides of body; no distinct black bands at base of rattle; enlarged scale forms a hornlike process above each eye; white stripe across top of each brown eye horn. *Habitat:* Sidewinders are most commonly encountered in sandy areas below 5,000 ft (1,520 m); however, individuals are occasionally found in rocky areas. They are primarily nocturnal but may be active in the late afternoon. *Remarks:* The subspecies of Sidewinder in the White-Inyo mountains region is the Mojave Desert Sidewinder (*C. c. cerastes*). The Sidewinder reaches its northern distributional limits in the Hammil Valley. It probably ranges as far north as the Queen Valley in Mineral County, Nevada (see ? on Map 10.35). This species is unique among all New World snakes in that it moves sideways. This adaptation allows Sidewinders to move easily over sand dunes. Sidewinding has evolved independently in a few species of sand dune–dwelling vipers that occur in the deserts of northern and southern Africa. Sidewinders are the only rattlesnakes that bury themselves in the sand. It is possible to follow the distinctive S-shaped tracks of this snake and locate the site where the animal has buried itself for the day. Look for a circular depression in the sand, usually at the base of a bush, and watch for the top of the head protruding from the sand. Do not get too close because this is a venomous species. *Range:* On the west side

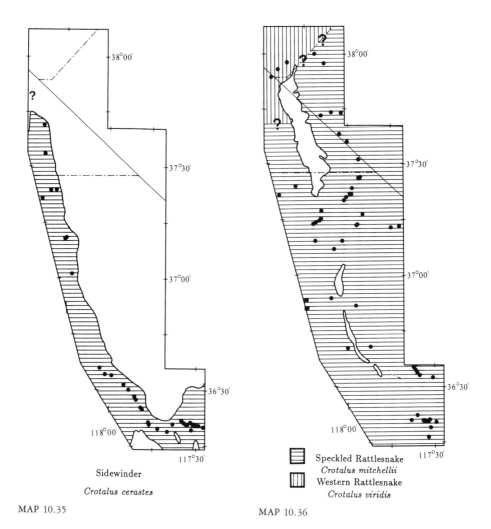

Sidewinder
Crotalus cerastes

MAP 10.35

Speckled Rattlesnake
Crotalus mitchellii
Western Rattlesnake
Crotalus viridis

MAP 10.36

of the Panamint Mountains in the Panamint Valley; on the west side of the White-Inyo Range in the Owens Valley, Chalfant Valley, and Hammil Valley; absent from the Deep Springs Valley and the eastern side of the White-Inyo Range. *References:* Klauber (1944), Klauber (1972).

Localities: California, Inyo Co.: 1.9 mi NE Big Pine; 2.4 mi NE; Bishop (SDSNH); Darwin Falls, Argus Mtns.; jct. of Darwin Falls Rd. and Hwy. 190; 0.5 mi W; 3.3 mi E; jct. Hwy. 136 and Hwy. 190; 5.5 mi SE of Hwy. 136 on Hwy. 190; 10.0 mi SE; Keeler; 1 mi S (CMNH); 4 mi SE (SDSNH); 8 mi SE; Laws; Lone Pine; 1.5 mi SE; 3.5 mi SE; 8.6 mi E; 10.0 mi SE; 3.4 mi NW Panamint Springs; 1.6 mi W; 4.1 mi W; 5.2 mi W; 6.1 mi W; 6.3 mi W; 6.5 mi W; 7 mi W; 8.0 mi W; 11.5 mi W; 2.6 mi E Saline Valley Rd. on Hwy. 190; 4,450 ft, Silver Creek Canyon, 5 mi ENE Bishop; E side Tinemaha Reservoir. Mono Co.: 4,840 ft, Cinnamon Ranch, 10 mi SSE Benton; 6.9 mi N Inyo County line on Hwy. 6.

Speckled Rattlesnake, *Crotalus mitchellii* (Cope, 1861). (Plate 10.43, Map 10.36) 24–36 in (60–100 cm); background color light gray to light brown with narrow gray to dark brown bands running from neck to rattle; bands wider on middle of back than on sides; commonly scattered black and white flecks at margin of bands; ventral coloration cream with scattered black flecks; end of tail and base of rattle black; top of head with two internasal scales in contact with the rostral scale, and supraocular scales pitted or with outer edges broken. *Habitat:* This snake prefers rocky canyons and rocky slopes surrounding valleys but is occasionally found on valley floors. Speckled Rattlesnakes occur as high as 9,000 ft (2,740 m) in the White Mountains. This species is active during the day in the spring and fall and at high elevations. At lower elevations, it is nocturnal during the summer. *Remarks:* The subspecies of Speckled Rattlesnake present in this area is the Panamint Rattlesnake (*C. m. stephensi*). This snake may be confused with the Western Rattlesnake (*C. viridis*) because the two species are similar in size and color pattern. They can be distinguished by careful examination of the scales on the top of the head. The Panamint Rattlesnake has two internasal scales in contact with the rostral scale and has supraocular scales that are pitted or with broken outer edges. The Western Rattlesnake has three or four internasal scales touching the rostral scale, and the supraocular scales are smooth and regular in shape. Speckled Rattlesnakes occur from the tip of Baja California through southern California, western Arizona, and southern Nevada. The northern known limit of its distribution is the Fish Lake Valley. A detailed discussion of the distributional interactions between this species and the Western Rattlesnake is found in the following account. Owing to their size and tendency to rattle when approached, Speckled Rattlesnakes are easily observed. These snakes feed primarily on rodents but will also eat birds and lizards. *Range:* On the west side of the White-Inyo Range north to at least the Mono County line (see ? on Map 10.36); on the east, in the Panamint, Saline, Eureka, Deep Springs, and Fish Lake valleys; surrounding mountains to around 9,000 ft (2,740 m). *References:* Klauber (1936), Klauber (1972).

Localities: California, Inyo Co.: 2 mi S Aberdeen [old Aberdeen at railroad] (SD-SNH); Barrel Springs, 9 mi NE Independence; Batchelder Spring, 8 mi NE Big Pine; Beveridge Canyon, Saline Valley (FMNH); 6 mi NE Big Pine; 6.3 mi NE; 6.6 mi NE; 7.2 mi NE: 8.2 mi NE; 10.7 mi NE; 23.3 mi NE; 25.6 NE; 27.1 mi NE; 29.4 mi NE; 31.9 mi NE; near Bishop (SDSNH); Darwin Falls; 5.2 mi W of Darwin Falls Rd. on Hwy. 190; 7 mi S of Hwy. 190 on Darwin Rd.; Deep Springs (CMNH); near; E end Deep Springs Valley (SDSNH); 3.7 mi SE of Hwy. 168 on Eureka Valley Rd.; 2,070 m, 10.6 mi SE; 2,150 m, 14.5 mi SE; 1,790 m, 21.8 mi SE; 24.1 mi SE; 24.3 mi SE; 28.1 mi SE; 37.4 mi SE; 40.1 mi SE; 3,300–5,320 ft, Grapevine Canyon, Nelson Range (CAS); 5,500 ft, Grapevine Canyon, Nelson Range [Willow Creek] (USNM); 5–8 mi N Independence (SDSNH); Jackass Spring, 20 mi N Darwin, Panamint Mtns. (SDSNH); 39 mi E Lone Pine; 8.7 mi SE; 1.9 mi S Mono County line on Hwy. 168; 5 mi NW Panamint Springs; 6.5 mi W; 4.1

mi W of Panamint Valley Rd. on Hwy. 190; 10.1 mi W; 5.7 mi E of Saline Valley Rd. on Hwy. 190; Silver Creek Canyon, White Mtns.; 3.4 mi S Nevada state line on Hwy. 266; summit of Westgard Pass (CAS); Mt. Whitney Fish Hatchery, 5 mi N Independence (LACM); Willow Springs, Saline Valley (AMNH). Nevada, Esmeralda Co.: 3 mi S Dyer (LACM); 3.4 mi N; 7.2 mi S; 1 mi S Fish Lake; 4.0 mi S of Hwy. 6 on Hwy. 264; 2,150 m, Indian Creek, White Mtns.; 7,150 ft, Trail Canyon, White Mtns.

Western Rattlesnake, *Crotalus viridis* (Rafinesque, 1818). (Plate 10.44, Map 10.36) 28–50 in (70–125 cm); background color light gray to light brown, with narrow gray to dark brown bands running from neck to rattle; bands wider on middle of back than on sides; commonly scattered black and white flecks at margin of bands; ventral coloration cream with scattered black flecks; end of tail and base of rattle black; top of head with three or four prenasal scales in contact with rostral; supraocular scales smooth and regular in shape. *Habitat:* This snake occurs in valley floors, rocky canyons, and well into the mountains. Western Rattlesnakes are active during the day and are also nocturnal on warm nights. *Remarks:* The subspecies of Western Rattlesnake that occurs in the area is the Great Basin Rattlesnake (*C. v. lutosus*). (See preceding account for characteristics that distinguish this species from the similar Speckled Rattlesnake, *C. mitchellii.*) There are eight subspecies of the Western Rattlesnake, ranging from Canada to Mexico. In most places where Western Rattlesnakes occur together with or near other species of rattlesnakes, there are differences in size and color pattern that make it easy to tell the species apart. This is not the case in the White-Inyo mountains region. The Speckled Rattlesnake has been found as far north as Silver Creek Canyon, just south of the Mono County line in the Owens Valley, and at the northern edge of the Fish Lake Valley. The only three specimens of Western Rattlesnake known from the area were collected in the vicinity of the California-Nevada state line in the Queen Valley. These three specimens are similar in color pattern to specimens of Speckled Rattlesnakes taken in the region to the south. These two species may hybridize in the northern White Mountains and adjacent valleys. Unfortunately, no specimens have been obtained from these areas. *Range:* Northwestern slopes of White Mountains, Queen Valley, and areas north to edge of study area (see ? on Map 10.36). *References:* Fitch and Glading (1947), Klauber (1972).

Localities: California, Mono Co.: 0.5 mi SW Nevada state line on Hwy. 6. Nevada, Mineral Co.: 6,400 ft, 3.2 mi W Montgomery Pass; 2.3 mi NE California state line on Hwy. 6.

AMPHIBIAN AND REPTILE DIVERSITY IN SELECTED HABITATS

A variety of amphibian and reptile habitats are present in the White-Inyo mountains region. In this section, eight sites that are representative of particular habitats have been selected. Each site is on or near a main road and is easily accessible to people who may wish to observe a particular species or the species assemblage at a specific habitat.

Southern Owens Valley

The rocky slopes at the base of the Inyo Mountains are drained by canyons. At the mouth of each canyon a rocky, boulder-strewn alluvial fan gradually merges into the sand dunes around Owens Lake (Fig. 10.6). Scattered Creosote Bushes are present at the base of the mountains.

Amphibians

Great Basin Spadefoot (*Spea intermontana*). Nocturnal; breeds in temporary pools in sand dunes.

Lizards

Western Banded Gecko (*Coleonyx variegatus*). Nocturnal; most common in rocky areas.

Zebra-tailed Lizard (*Callisaurus draconoides*). Diurnal; very common on gravel flats and at bases of sand dunes.

Great Basin Collard Lizard (*Crotaphytus bicinctores*). Diurnal; basks on boulders.

Desert Iguana (*Dipsosaurus dorsalis*). Diurnal; uncommon on alluvial fans and around bushes in sand dunes.

Long-nosed Leopard Lizard (*Gambelia wislizenii*). Diurnal; basks on small rocks and under bushes; rare on rocky slopes.

Desert Horned Lizard (*Phrynosoma platyrhinos*). Diurnal; most common in sandy areas; well camouflaged except when basking on small rocks.

Chuckwalla (*Sauromalus obesus*). Diurnal; basks on boulders on slopes and in canyons.

Desert Spiny Lizard (*Sceloporus magister*). Diurnal; occurs in rocky areas and around large bushes in sand dunes.

Side-blotched Lizard (*Uta stansburiana*). Diurnal; occurs in all habitats; most common lizard in the area.

Western Whiptail (*Cnemidophorus tigris*). Diurnal; present in all habitats; less common in rocky areas.

Desert Night Lizard (*Xantusia vigilis*). Diurnal; secretive; active under cover objects such as logs and brush piles.

Snakes

Glossy Snake (*Arizona elegans*). Nocturnal; usually occurs in sandy areas.

Western Shovel-nosed Snake (*Chionactis occipitalis*). Nocturnal; most common among sand dunes.

Night Snake (*Hypsiglena torquata*). Nocturnal; usually occurs on rocky slopes and in canyons.

FIGURE 10.6   East side of Owens Lake, southern Owens Valley.

Common Kingsnake (*Lampropeltis getula*). Nocturnal during summer, diurnal during spring and fall; occurs in all habitats but rare in sand dunes.

Coachwhip (*Masticophis flagellum*). Diurnal; lives in all habitats but less common in rocky areas.

Gopher Snake (*Pituophis catenifer*). Both nocturnal and diurnal; occurs in all habitats.

Long-nosed Snake (*Rhinocheilus lecontei*). Nocturnal; most common in sandy areas.

Western Patch-nosed Snake (*Salvadora hexalepis*). Diurnal; most common in sandy areas.

Ground Snake (*Sonora semiannulata*). Nocturnal; active in the early evening; prefers rocky areas.

Southwestern Black-headed Snake (*Tantilla hobartsmithi*). Nocturnal; occurs in rocky areas.

Western Blind Snake (*Leptotyphlops humilis*). Nocturnal; occurs in washes of rocky areas; can be common in areas with permanent surface water.

Sidewinder (*Crotalus cerastes*). Usually nocturnal; occurs in all habitats but most common in sandy areas.

Speckled Rattlesnake (*Crotalus mitchellii*). Both nocturnal and diurnal; most common in rocky areas.

Southern White Mountains

Tollhouse Spring (Fig. 10.7) is the only source of permanent surface water along the Westgard Pass road (Hwy. 168). There is a fairly extensive area of riparian vegetation around the spring. The Pinyon-juniper Woodland starts just above the spring. A wide, gravelly, boulder-strewn wash below the spring separates the rocky lower slopes of the Inyo Mountains to the south from the White Mountains to the north.

Amphibians

Western Toad (*Bufo boreas*). Both nocturnal and diurnal; breeds in stream below Tollhouse Spring; may be extinct.

Black Toad (*Bufo exsul*). Diurnal except during heat of midsummer; introduced to Tollhouse Spring; may be extinct.

Great Basin Spadefoot (*Spea intermontana*). Nocturnal; expected but not confirmed from Tollhouse Spring; known to occur nearby.

Lizards

Panamint Alligator Lizard (*Elgaria panamintina*). Usually diurnal but sometimes active after dusk; may climb in vegetation in search of food; sometimes on road at dusk.

Western Banded Gecko (*Coleonyx variegatus*). Nocturnal; commonly observed at night on road below spring at around 5,000 ft (1,520 m) elevation.

Zebra-tailed Lizard (*Callisaurus draconoides*). Diurnal; occurs in sandy or gravelly washes.

Great Basin Collard Lizard (*Crotaphytus bicinctores*). Diurnal; basks on boulders.

Long-nosed Leopard Lizard (*Gambelia wislizenii*). Diurnal; basks on small rocks and under bushes in wash.

Desert Horned Lizard (*Phrynosoma platyrhinos*). Diurnal; occurs in wash; may bask on small rocks.

Sagebrush Lizard (*Sceloporus graciosus*). Diurnal; occurs from Tollhouse Spring up into Pinyon-juniper Woodland.

Desert Spiny Lizard (*Sceloporus magister*). Diurnal; basks on rocks and tree trunks.

Western Fence Lizard (*Sceloporus occidentalis*). Diurnal; basks on rocks, logs, and tree trunks; most common lizard from Tollhouse Spring up into Pinyon-juniper Woodland.

Side-blotched Lizard (*Uta stansburiana*). Diurnal; most common in wash below spring.

FIGURE 10.7   Vicinity of Tollhouse Spring, Westgard Pass, southern White Mountains.

Gilbert Skink (*Eumeces gilberti*). Diurnal but secretive; occurs in riparian vegetation around Tollhouse Spring.

Western Whiptail (*Cnemidophorus tigris*). Diurnal; most common around bushes in wash below spring.

Desert Night Lizard (*Xantusis vigilis*). Diurnal but secretive; active under cover objects such as logs and rocks.

Snakes

Night Snake (*Hypsiglena torquata*). Nocturnal; relatively common on road at night below Tollhouse Spring.

Common Kingsnake (*Lampropeltis getula*). Diurnal during spring and fall, nocturnal in heat of midsummer; very common around Tollhouse Spring.

Coachwhip (*Masticophis flagellum*). Diurnal; present in all habitats but most common in wash.

Striped Whipsnake (*Masticophis taeniatus*). Diurnal; occurs in all habitats.

Gopher Snake (*Pituophis catenifer*). Diurnal during spring and fall, nocturnal during heat of summer; commonly seen on road around Tollhouse Spring.

Long-nosed Snake (*Rhinocheilus lecontei*). Nocturnal; occasionally seen crossing road below Tollhouse Spring.

Western Patch-nosed Snake (*Salvadora hexalepis*). Diurnal; most common in sandy or gravelly washes.

Ground Snake (*Sonora semiannulata*). Nocturnal; active in early evening; during the day, expected under rocks around spring.

Southern Black-headed Snake (*Tantilla hobartsmithi*). Nocturnal; two records from about 5,500 ft (1,680 m) elevation on road below spring and 6,500 ft (1.980 m) on road above spring.

Sidewinder (*Crotalus cerastes*). Usually nocturnal; occurs in all habitats at lower elevations below spring but most common in sandy areas.

Speckled Rattlesnake (*Crotalus mitchellii*). Both nocturnal and diurnal; occurs in all habitats around Tollhouse Spring.

Central Owens Valley

Along the Owens River are extensive, large tree stands with other riparian vegetation. Such growth is also present around creeks draining the Sierra Nevada (Fig. 10.8). Along the Owens River many side pools provide breeding habitat for amphibians.

In this list only riparian-associated species are discussed. For other species in the area, refer to the southern White Mountains list (except for the Panamint Alligator Lizard, *Elgaria panamintina*, and the Gilbert Skink, *Eumeces gilberti*).

Amphibians

Owens Valley Web-toed Salamander (*Hydromantes* sp.). Nocturnal; active in spring; occurs under wood and rocks along streams draining the Sierra Nevada.

Western Toad (*Bufo boreas*). Both nocturnal and diurnal; breeds in side pools.

Pacific Treefrog (*Pseudacris regilla*). Both nocturnal and diurnal; breeds in side pools; occurs along streams and in marsh areas.

Great Basin Spadefoot (*Spea intermontana*). Nocturnal; breeds in temporary pools.

Lizards

Southern Alligator Lizard (*Elgaria multicarinata*). Diurnal but secretive; active in the late afternoon; occurs under wood and rocks along streams draining the Sierra Nevada.

Western Skink (*Eumeces skiltonianus*). Diurnal but secretive; occurs under wood and rocks along streams draining the Sierra Nevada.

Snakes

Sierra Garter Snake (*Thamnophis couchii*). Diurnal and wary; highly aquatic; occurs along the Owens River and large streams draining the Sierra Nevada.

FIGURE 10.8   East side of the Sierra Nevada in the central Owens Valley.

Western Terrestrial Garter Snake (*Thamnophis elegans*). Mainly diurnal but also nocturnal during warm weather; occurs along the Owens River and streams draining the Sierra Nevada; may wander from permanent water.

Queen Valley and Northern White Mountains

The floor of Queen Valley, at an elevation of about 6,000 ft (1,830 m), is covered with typical Great Basin Scrub vegetation (Fig. 10.9). On the southeast side of the valley, Pinyon-juniper Woodland starts on the slopes of the White Mountains at an elevation of 6,800 ft (2,070 m). Springs with dense riparian vegetation are present in Queen and Buffalo canyons.

Amphibians

Western Toad (*Bufo boreas*). Both nocturnal and diurnal; occurs in riparian areas in Queen and Buffalo canyons.

Great Basin Spadefoot (*Spea intermontana*). Nocturnal; breeds in temporary pools; occasionally seen on roads at night during and after rains.

FIGURE 10.9   Queen Valley and northern White Mountains.

Lizards

Zebra-tailed Lizard (*Callisaurus draconoides*). Diurnal; expected in sandy and gravelly areas below Pinyon-juniper Woodland.

Great Basin Collard Lizard (*Crotaphytus bicinctores*). Diurnal; occurs in rocky areas below about 6,500 ft (1,980 m).

Long-nosed Leopard Lizard (*Gambelia wislizenii*). Diurnal; basks on small rocks and under bushes; rare on rocky slopes.

Desert Horned Lizard (*Phrynosoma platyrhinos*). Diurnal; most common in sandy areas; not present above 7,000 ft (2,130 m).

Sagebrush Lizard (*Sceloporus graciosus*). Diurnal; common in Pinyon-juniper Woodland.

Desert Spiny Lizard (*Sceloporus magister*). Diurnal; occurs in rocky slopes and around large bushes below 7,000 ft (2,130 m).

Western Fence Lizard (*Sceloporus occidentalis*). Diurnal; commonly seen basking on rocks and logs in Pinyon-juniper Woodland; may climb trees to escape when approached.

Side-blotched Lizard (*Uta stansburiana*). Diurnal; most common in sandy areas on valley floor; absent above 7,000 ft (2,130 m).

Western Skink (*Eumeces skiltonianus*). Diurnal but secretive; not confirmed but expected in canyons draining the White Mountains.

Western Whiptail (*Cnemidophorus tigris*). Diurnal; occurs up to about 7,500 ft (2,290 m); most common in Great Basin Scrub areas.

Snakes

Night Snake (*Hypsiglena torquata*). Nocturnal; expected in rocky foothills below 6,500 ft (1,980 m).

Common Kingsnake (*Lampropeltis getula*). Nocturnal during summer, diurnal during spring and fall; occurs in all habitats below about 7,500 ft (2,290 m).

Coachwhip (*Masticophis flagellum*). Diurnal; expected on valley floor; usually absent above 6,000 ft (1,830 m).

Striped Whipsnake (*Masticophis taeniatus*). Diurnal; occurs from valley floor well into Pinyon-juniper Woodland in the foothills.

Gopher Snake (*Pituophis catenifer*). Both nocturnal and diurnal; occurs in all habitats below about 8,000 ft (2,440 m).

Long-nosed Snake (*Rhinocheilus lecontei*). Nocturnal; expected in sandy areas on valley floor up to about 6,000 ft (1,830 m).

Western Patch-nosed Snake (*Salvadora hexalepis*). Diurnal; most common in sandy areas on valley floor; not expected above 6,500 ft (1,980 m).

Ground Snake (*Sonora semiannulata*). Nocturnal; active in the early evening; expected in rocky areas up to about 6,000 ft (1,830 m).

Western Rattlesnake (*Crotalus viridis*). Both nocturnal and diurnal; present on valley floor; expected in foothills.

Northeastern Argus Mountains

The Panamint Valley has the most Creosote Bush Scrub species. The slopes of the Argus Mountains provide a good habitat for species restricted to rocky Creosote Bush Scrub. Darwin Falls (Fig. 10.10) has an extensive riparian-vegetated area.

All species covered in the southern Owens Valley account occur here (except the Great Basin Spadefoot, *Spea intermontana*) and are found in a similar manner. Additional species are discussed in the following list.

Amphibians

Western Toad (*Bufo boreas*). Mostly nocturnal but also diurnal; occurs in riparian areas at Darwin Falls; hybridizes with the Red-spotted Toad (*Bufo punctatus*).

Red-spotted Toad (*Bufo punctatus*). Nocturnal; breeds in pools in Darwin Canyon; hides during the day in rodent burrows or under rocks; hybridizes with the Western Toad (*Bufo boreas*).

FIGURE 10.10   Darwin Falls, northeastern Argus Mountains.

Snakes

Rosy Boa (*Lichanura trivirgata*). Nocturnal; diurnal in late evening and morning during spring; during midsummer nocturnal only; in rocky areas to 5,000 ft (1,520 m).

Spotted Leaf-nosed Snake (*Phyllorhynchus decurtatus*). Nocturnal; usually present in sandy or gravelly places.

Lyre Snake (*Trimorphodon biscutatus*). Nocturnal; in rocky areas to 5,000 ft (1,520 m).

Base of East Side of Inyo Mountains

Hunter Canyon (Fig. 10.11) is one of several canyons draining the east side of the Inyo Mountains that contains extensive riparian vegetation and surface water all year. The rocky canyon mouth is located at an elevation of about 1,600 ft (490 m) in rocky Creosote Bush Scrub. Only riparian-restricted amphibians and reptiles are discussed here. General lowland Creosote Bush Scrub species that occur here (except for the Great Basin Spadefoot, *Spea intermontana*, the Glossy Snake, *Arizona elegans*, and the Sidewinder, *Crotalus cerastes*) are covered in the Southern Owens Valley account.

FIGURE 10.11   Hunter Canyon, east side of the Inyo Mountains.

Amphibians

Inyo Mountains Slender Salamander (*Batrachoseps campi*). Nocturnal; restricted to vicinity of water; lives in mossy, damp crevices and under rocks where ground is wet.

Red-spotted Toad (*Bufo punctatus*). Nocturnal; breeds in pools in canyon; hides during the day in rodent burrows or under rocks.

Lizards

Panamint Alligator Lizard (*Elgaria panamintina*). Usually diurnal but sometimes active after dusk; may climb in vegetation in search of food.

Gilbert Skink (*Eumeces gilberti*). Diurnal but secretive; commonly forages in leaf litter.

Northeast Slopes of Inyo Mountains

Joshua Flats (Fig. 10.12), at an elevation of about 6,200 ft (1,890 m) on the Eureka Valley Road, is covered with an extensive stand of Joshua Trees. Pinyon-juniper Woodland is present on the surrounding hills. Several narrow, rocky canyons drain into the flats.

FIGURE 10.12   Joshua Flats, northeastern Inyo Mountains.

Lizards

Zebra-tailed Lizard (*Callisaurus draconoides*). Diurnal; occurs in sandy or gravelly washes.

Great Basin Collard Lizard (*Crotaphytus bicinctores*). Diurnal; basks on boulders.

Long-nosed Leopard Lizard (*Gambelia wislizenii*). Diurnal; basks on small rocks and under bushes.

Desert Horned Lizard (*Phrynosoma platyrhinos*). Diurnal; most common in sandy parts of Joshua Flats.

Sagebrush Lizard (*Sceloporus graciosus*). Diurnal; active on ground around bushes; basks on small rocks and logs; occurs in Pinyon-juniper Woodland above flats.

Desert Spiny Lizard (*Sceloporus magister*). Diurnal; very common at Joshua Flats; climbs high in Joshua Trees.

Western Fence Lizard (*Sceloporus occidentalis*). Diurnal; basks on rocks and fallen Joshua Trees.

Side-blotched Lizard (*Uta stansburiana*). Diurnal; most common in sandy part of flats.

Gilbert Skink (*Eumeces gilberti*). Diurnal but secretive; occurs under large rocks and in piles of Joshua Tree rubble.

Western Whiptail (*Cnemidophorus tigris*). Diurnal; most common around bushes in sandy areas.

Desert Night Lizard (*Xantusia vigilis*). Diurnal but secretive; should live in piles of Joshua Tree rubble but has not been found at this site.

Snakes

Night Snake (*Hypsiglena torquata*). Nocturnal; can be found during the day under fallen Joshua Tree logs; common along road at night.

Common Kingsnake (*Lampropeltis getula*). Diurnal during spring and fall, nocturnal during midsummer; occurs in all habitats.

Coachwhip (*Masticophis flagellum*). Diurnal; occurs in all habitats but most common in sandy flats.

Striped Whipsnake (*Masticophis taeniatus*). Diurnal; occurs in all habitats.

Gopher Snake (*Pituophis catenifer*). Nocturnal during midsummer, diurnal during spring and fall; occurs in all habitats.

Long-nosed Snake (*Rhinocheilus lecontei*). Nocturnal; expected in sandy areas of Joshua Flats.

Patched-nosed Snake (*Salvadora hexalepis*). Diurnal; most common in sandy areas but present in all habitats.

Ground Snake (*Sonora semiannulata*). Nocturnal; occasionally found by turning rocks and fallen logs.

Speckled Rattlesnake (*Crotalus mitchellii*). Both nocturnal and diurnal but not active in heat of day during midsummer.

Deep Springs Valley

Most of the sandy floor of Deep Springs Valley is covered with Great Basin desert vegetation. The lowest point is about 5,000 ft (1,520 m) at Deep Springs Lake. At the southeastern edge of the valley, the flow from Deep Springs forms a marsh of a few acres around Deep Springs Valley (Fig. 10.13). The rocky foothills of the White-Inyo Range, which surround the valley, support stands of pinyon and juniper.

Amphibians

Black Toad (*Bufo exsul*). Diurnal, becoming nocturnal during heat of summer; restricted to pools and marshes around springs.

Great Basin Spadefoot (*Spea intermontana*). Nocturnal; breeds in pools; occasionally seen on road at night.

FIGURE 10.13   Deep Springs Valley.

Lizards

Great Basin Collard Lizard (*Crotaphytus bicinctores*). Diurnal; basks on boulders in foothills surrounding valley.

Long-nosed Leopard Lizard (*Gambelia wislizenii*). Diurnal; basks on small rocks and under bushes; most common in sandy areas.

Desert Horned Lizard (*Phrynosoma platyrhinos*). Diurnal; common throughout the valley; commonly seen along the highway.

Sagebrush Lizard (*Sceloporus graciosus*). Diurnal; absent from valley floor; occurs in Pinyon-juniper Woodland of foothills.

Desert Spiny Lizard (*Sceloporus magister*). Diurnal; occurs in rocky hills and around large bushes on valley floor.

Western Fence Lizard (*Sceloporus occidentalis*). Diurnal; lives in rocky foothills; commonly seen basking on rocks along lower Wyman Canyon Road and along highway east of Deep Springs College.

Side-blotched Lizard (*Uta stansburiana*). Diurnal; most common in sandy areas on valley floor.

Gilbert Skink (*Eumeces gilberti*). Diurnal but secretive; rarely seen; appears to be restricted to the vicinity of springs.

Western Whiptail (*Cnemidophorus tigris*). Diurnal; occurs throughout valley and surrounding foothills; very common around bushes on valley floor.

Snakes

Night Snake (*Hypsiglena torquata*). Nocturnal; occurs in rocky foothills surrounding valley.

Common Kingsnake (*Lampropeltis getula*). Nocturnal during summer, diurnal during spring and fall; occurs in all habitats.

Coachwhip (*Masticophis flagellum*). Diurnal; most common on valley floor.

Striped Whipsnake (*Masticophis taeniatus*). Diurnal; occurs from valley floor well into Pinyon-juniper Woodland.

Gopher Snake (*Pituophis catenifer*). Both nocturnal and diurnal; occurs in all habitats.

Long-nosed Snake (*Rhinocheilus lecontei*). Nocturnal; occurs on valley floor.

Western Patch-nosed Snake (*Salvadora hexalepis*). Diurnal; most common in sandy areas on valley floor.

Ground Snake (*Sonora semiannulata*). Nocturnal; active in the early evening; prefers rocky areas.

Speckled Rattlesnake (*Crotalus mitchellii*). Both nocturnal and diurnal; most common in rocky areas but present on valley floor.

REFERENCES

Axtell, R. W. 1972. Hybridization between western collard lizards with a proposed taxonomic rearrangement. *Copeia* 1972:707–727.

Banta, B. H. 1962. A preliminary account of the herpetofauna of the Saline Valley hydrographic basin, Inyo County, California. *Wasmann Journal of Biology* 20:161–251.

Bennion, R. S., and W. S. Parker. 1976. Field observations of courtship and aggressive behavior in desert striped whipsnakes, *Masticophis t. taeniatus*. *Herpetologica* 32:30–35.

Berry, K. 1974. The ecology and social behavior on the chuckwalla, *Sauromalus obesus obesus* Baird. *University of California Publications in Zoology* 101:1–60.

Bezy, R. L., and J. W. Sites, Jr. 1987. A preliminary study of allozyme evolution in the lizard family Xantusiidae. *Herpetologica* 43:280–292.

Bogert, C. M. 1939. A study of the genus *Salvadora*, the patch-nosed snakes. *Publications of the University of California at Los Angeles in Biological Sciences* 1:177–236.

Brattstrom, B. H. 1953. Notes on a population of leaf-nosed snakes *Phyllorhynchus decurtatus perkinsi*. *Herpetologica* 9:57–64.

Brattstrom, B. H., and R. C. Schwenkmeyer. 1951. Notes on the natural history of the worm snake, *Leptotyphlops humilis*. *Herpetologica* 7:193–196.

Braun-Blanquet, J. (translated by G. D. Fuller and H. S. Conrad). 1932. *Plant sociology: The study of plant communities.* McGraw-Hill, New York.

Carpenter, C. C., and J. C. Gillingham. 1975. Postural responses to kingsnakes by crotaline snakes. *Herpetologica* 31:293–302.

Cole, C. J. 1984. Unisexual lizards. *Scientific American* 250(1):94–100.

Cole, C. J., and L. M. Hardy. 1981. Systematics of North American colubrid snakes related to *Tantilla planiceps* (Blainville). *Bulletin of the American Museum of Natural History* 171:199–284.

Collins, J. T. 1990. *Standard common and current scientific names for North American amphibians and reptiles,* 3d ed. Society for the Study of Amphibians and Reptiles, Herpetological Circular no. 190.

Congdon, J. D., L. J. Vitt, and W. W. King. 1974. Geckos: Adaptive significance and energetics of tail autotomy. *Science* 184:1379–1380.

Cowles, R. B., and C. M. Bogert. 1935. Observations on the California lyre snake, *Trimorphodon vandenburghi* Klauber, with notes on the effectiveness of its venom. *Copeia* 1935:80–85.

Elvin, D. W. 1963. Variation and distribution of the shovel-nosed snakes (*Chionactis occipitalis*) in the northern Mojave Desert, California and Nevada. *Herpetologica* 19:73–76.

Fitch, H. S. 1935. Natural history of the alligator lizards. *Transactions of the Academy of Science at Saint Louis* 29:1–38.

Fitch, H. S. 1938. A systematic account of the alligator lizards (*Gerrhonotus*) in the western United States and lower California. *American Midland Naturalist* 20:381–424.

Fitch, H. S. 1940a. A field study of the growth and behavior of the fence lizard. *University of California Publications in Zoology* 44:151–172.

Fitch, H. S. 1940b. A biogeographical study of the *ordinoides* artenkreis of garter snakes (genus *Thamnophis*). *University of California Publications in Zoology* 44:1–150.

Fitch, H. S. 1941. The feeding habits of California garter snakes. *California Fish and Game* 27(2):2–32.

Fitch, H. S., and B. Glading. 1947. A field study of a rattlesnake population. *California Fish and Game* 33(2):103–123.

Fox, W. 1951. Relationships among the garter snakes of the *Thamnophis elegans* rassenkreis. *University of California Publications in Zoology* 50:485–530.

Frost, D. 1983. Relationships of the Baja California ground snakes, genus *Sonora*. *Transactions of the Kansas Academy of Science* 86:31–37.

Gehlbach, F. R. 1971. Lyre snakes of the *Trimorphodon biscutatus* complex: A taxonomic resume. *Herpetologica* 27:200–211.

Good, D. A. 1988a. Allozyme variation and phylogenetic relationships among the species of *Elgaria* (Squamata; Anguidae). *Herpetologica* 44:154–162.

Good, D. A. 1988b. Phylogenetic relationships among Gerrhonotine lizards: An analysis of external morphology. *University of California Publications in Zoology.* 121:1–139.

Gorman, G. C. 1965. The distribution of *Lichanura trivirgata* and the status of the species. *Herpetologica* 21(4): 283–287.

Kay, F. R., B. W. Miller, and C. L. Miller. 1970. Food habits and reproduction and *Callisaurus draconoides* in Death Valley, California. *Herpetologica* 26:431–436.

Klauber, L. M. 1931. A new subspecies of the California boa, with notes on the genus *Lichanura. Transactions of the San Diego Society of Natural History* 6:305–318.

Klauber, L. M. 1935. Phyllorhynchus, *the leaf-nosed snake.* Bulletins of the Zoological Society of San Diego, no. 12.

Klauber, L. M. 1936. *Crotalus mitchellii,* the speckled rattlesnake. *Transactions of the San Diego Society of Natural History* 8:149–184.

Klauber, L. M. 1940a. The lyre snakes (genus *Trimorphodon*) of the United States. *Transactions of the San Diego Society of Natural History* 9:163–194.

Klauber, L. M. 1940b. The worm snakes of the genus *Leptotyphlops* in the United States and northern Mexico. *Transactions of the San Diego Society of Natural History* 9:87–162.

Klauber, L. M. 1941. The long-nosed snakes of the genus *Rhinocheilus. Transactions of the San Diego Society of Natural History* 9:289–332.

Klauber, L. M. 1944. The sidewinder, *Crotalus cerastes,* with description of a new subspecies. *Transactions of the San Diego Society of Natural History* 10:91–126.

Klauber, L. M. 1945. The geckos of the genus *Coleonyx* with descriptions of new subspecies. *Transactions of the San Diego Society of Natural History* 10:133–216.

Klauber, L. M. 1946. The glossy snake, *Arizona,* with descriptions of new subspecies. *Transactions of the San Diego Society of Natural History* 10:311–398.

Klauber, L. M. 1947. *Classification and ranges of the gopher snakes of the genus* Pituophis *in the western United States.* Bulletins of the Zoological Society of San Diego, no. 22.

Klauber, L. M. 1951. The shovel-nosed snake, *Chionactis,* with descriptions of two new subspecies. *Transactions of the San Diego Society of Natural History* 11:141–204.

Klauber, L. M. 1972. *Rattlesnakes: Their habits, life histories, and influence on mankind,* 2d ed. 2 vols. University of California Press, Berkeley.

Macey, J. R. 1986. The biogeography of a herpetofaunal transition between the Great Basin and Mojave deserts. In C. A. Hall, Jr. and D. J. Young (eds.). *Natural history of the White-Inyo Range, eastern California and western Nevada, and high altitude physiology,* pp. 119–128. University of California White Mountain Research Station Symposium, August 23–25, 1985, Bishop, Calif., vol. 1.

Miller, A. H., and R. C. Stebbins. 1964. *The lives of desert animals in Joshua Tree National Monument.* University of California Press, Berkeley.

Montanucci, R. R. 1983. Natural hybridization between two species of collard lizards (*Crotaphytus*). *Copeia* 1983:1–11.

Montanucci, R. R., R. W. Axtell, and H. C. Dessauer. 1975. Evolutionary divergence among collard lizards (*Crotaphytus*), with comments on the status of *Gambelia. Herpetologica* 31:336–347.

Murphy, R. W. 1983. *Paleobiogeography and genetic differentiation of the Baja California herpetofauna.* Occasional Papers of the California Academy of Sciences, no. 137.

Norris, K. S. 1953. The ecology of the desert iguana *Dipsosaurus dorsalis. Ecology* 34:265–287.

Norris, K. S., and S. L. Kavanau. 1966. The burrowing of the western shovel-nosed snake, *Chionactis occipitalis* Hallowell, and the undersand environment. *Copeia* 1966:650–664.

Ortenburger, A. I. 1928. *The whip snakes and racers: Genera* Masticophis *and* Coluber. Memoirs of the University of Michigan Museums, no. 1.

Papenfuss, T. J. 1986. Amphibian and reptile diversity along elevational transects in the White-Inyo Range. In C. A. Hall, Jr. and D. J. Young (eds.). *Natural history of the White-Inyo Range, eastern California and western Nevada, and high altitude physiology,* pp. 129–136. University of California White Mountain Research Station Symposium, August 23–25, 1985, Bishop, Calif., vol. 1.

Parker, W. S. 1972. Ecological study of the western whiptail lizard, *Cnemidophorus tigris gracilis,* in Arizona. *Herpetologica* 28:360–369.

Parker, W. S., and W. S. Brown. 1980. *Comparative ecology of two colubrid snakes,* Masticophis t. taeniatus *and* Pituophis deserticola, *in northern Utah.* Milwaukee Public Museum Publications in Biology and Geology, no. 7.

Parker, W. S., and E. R. Pianka. 1973. Notes on the ecology of the iguanid lizard, *Sceloporus magister. Herpetologica* 29:143–152.

Parker, W. S., and E. R. Pianka. 1975. Comparative ecology of populations of the lizard *Uta stansburiana. Copeia* 1975:615–632.

Parker, W. S., and E. R. Pianka. 1976. Ecological observations on the leopard lizard (*Crotaphytus wislizeni*) in different parts of its range. *Herpetologica* 32:95–114.

Phelan, R. L., and B. H. Brattstrom. 1955. Geographic variation in *Sceloporus magister. Herpetologica* 11:1–14.

Pianka, E. R. 1971. Comparative ecology of two lizards. *Copeia* 1971:129–138.

Pianka, E. R., and W. S. Parker. 1972. Ecology of the iguanid lizard *Callisaurus draconoides. Copeia* 1972:493–508.

Pianka, E. R., and W. S. Parker. 1975. Ecology of horned lizards: A review with special reference to *Phrynosoma platyrhinos*. *Copeia* 1975:141–162.

Rodgers, T. L., and H. S. Fitch. 1947. Variation in the skinks (Reptilia: Lacertilia) of the *skiltonianus* group. *University of California Publications in Zoology* 48:169–220.

Rossman, D. A., and G. R. Stewart. 1987. *Taxonomic reevaluation of* Thamnophis couchii *(Serpentes: Colubridae)*. Occasional Papers of the Museum of Zoology, Louisiana State University, no. 63.

Sanborn, S. R., and R. B. Loomis. 1979. Systematics and behavior of collard lizards (*Crotaphytus*, Iguanidae) in southern California. *Herpetologica* 35:101–106.

Shannon, F. A., and F. L. Humphrey. 1963. Analysis of color pattern polymorphism in the snake, *Rhinocheilus lecontei*. *Herpetologica* 19:153–160.

Simpson, G. G. 1960. Notes on the measurement of faunal resemblance. *American Journal of Science* 258:300–311.

Smith, N. M., and W. W. Tanner. 1974. *A taxonomic study of the western collard lizards*, Crotaphytus collaris *and* Crotaphytus insularis. Brigham Young University Science Bulletin, Biological Series, vol. 19, no. 4.

Stebbins, R. C. 1944. Field notes on a lizard, the mountain swift, with special reference to territorial behavior. *Ecology* 25:233–245.

Stebbins, R. C. 1954. *Amphibians and reptiles of western North America*. McGraw-Hill, New York.

Stebbins, R. C. 1958. *A new alligator lizard from the Panamint Mountains, Inyo County California*. American Museum Novitates, no. 1883.

Stebbins, R. C. 1985. *A field guide to western amphibians and reptiles*. Houghton Mifflin, Boston.

Stebbins, R. C., and H. B. Robinson. 1946. Further analysis of a population of the lizard *Sceloporus graciosus gracilis*. *University of California Publications in Zoology* 48:149–168.

Tanner, W. W. 1944. A taxonomic study of the genus *Hypsiglena*. *Great Basin Naturalist* 5:25–92.

Tanner, W. W. 1957. A taxonomic and ecological study of the western skink (*Eumeces skiltonianus*). *Great Basin Naturalist* 17:59–94.

Tanner, W. W., and J. M. Hopkin. 1972. *Ecology of* Sceloporus occidentalis longipes Baird *on Rainier Mesa, Nevada Test Site, Nye County, Nevada*. Brigham Young University Science Bulletin, Biological Series, vol. 15, no. 4.

Tanner, W. W., and C. D. Jorgensen. 1963. *Reptiles of the Nevada Test Site*. Brigham Young University Science Bulletin, Biological Series, vol. 3, no. 31.

Tanner, W. W., and J. E. Krogh. 1973. Ecology of *Phrynosoma platyrhinos* at the Nevada Test Site, Nye County, Nevada. *Herpetologica* 29:327–342.

Tinkle, D. W. 1967. *The life and demography of the side-blotched lizard*, Uta Stansburiana. Miscellaneous Publications, Museum of Zoology, University of Michigan, no. 132.

Tinkle, D. W. 1973. A population analysis of the sagebrush lizard, *Sceloporus graciosus*, in southern Utah. *Copeia* 1973:284–296.

Tollestrup. K. 1982. Growth and reproduction in two closely related species of leopard lizards, *Gambelia silus* and *Gambelia wislizenii*. *American Midland Naturalist* 108:1–20.

White, M., and J. A. Kolb. 1974. A preliminary study of *Thamnophis* near Sagehen Creek, California. *Copeia* 1974:126–136.

Wilson, L. D. 1970. The coachwhip snake, *Masticophis flagellum* (Shaw): Taxonomy and distribution. *Tulane Studies in Zoology and Botany* 16:31–99.

Wright, J. W., and C. H. Lowe. 1968. Weeds, polyploids, parthenogenesis, and the geographical and ecological distribution of all-female species of *Cnemidophorus*. *Copeia* 1968:128–138.

Zweifel, R. G., and C. H. Lowe. 1966. *The ecology of a population of* Xantusia vigilis, the desert night lizard. American Museum Novitates, no. 2247.

11

Breeding Birds

Ned K. Johnson and Carla Cicero
Illustrated by N. John Schmitt and Gene M. Christman

A rich variety of birds nest in the White-Inyo Range, including a number of species not widely distributed elsewhere in California. In this chapter, our chief objective is to introduce the reader to the most frequently seen nesting species and to supplement this list with comments on life history, habitats, and distribution. For reasons of space, we emphasize the montane species and exclude from treatment a host of other, equally interesting kinds of birds that breed in the lowland habitats of the region, for example, Owens Valley, Deep Springs Valley, and Fish Lake Valley. Furthermore, we pass over species known solely in the region as transients, winter visitants, or vagrants. The list of such species is long; both Oasis and Deep Springs Ranch, on the east side of the mountains, are popular birding localities where many unusual distributional records have been gathered in recent years. For an up-to-date summary of the status in the region of all excluded species, we refer the reader to Garrett and Dunn (1981). Johnson and Cicero (1986) have recently summarized records of all species of birds thought to breed in the White-Inyo mountains. Their analysis provided the basis for a quantitative comparison of the boreal avifaunas of the two ranges with those of several nearby mountain systems. Common names, scientific names, and the sequence of species follow the style of the American Ornithologists' Union (1983).

In each of the following species accounts, our goal is to provide an accurate statement on the relative abundance, seasonal status, local distribution, and known elevational range of each form. Descriptions of relative abundance (e.g., "common," "fairly common," "uncommon") are based on the definitions and philosophy offered by Grinnell and Miller (1944). Names of ecologic formations (capitalized) follow Miller (1951). Elevations were determined from specimen labels and field notes, and through direct measurement with an altimeter. Accurate determination of elevational range in this region is especially important because some of the highest known records for certain species are from the White Mountains. The data on lengths and weights are offered to allow gross estimates of body size. These estimates assist in field identification and enable rough comparisons of species. We hasten to note that the information on length is too imprecise to serve any other useful purpose. Figures on lengths and weights are averages of at least five individuals of each sex from study specimens in the Museum of Vertebrate Zoology, University of California, Berkeley (MVZ). Where possible, specimens from Mono County or Inyo County were used for these size data. Measurements in the metric system have been converted to English units; the former were taken directly from specimens and therefore are more accurate.

Each species account contains information on habitat occurrence, foraging and nesting habits, voice and other useful identifying features of behavior, and, occasionally, unusual characteristics of life history or ecology. Much of this information is derived from our own annual field experience in the Great Basin and eastern Sierra Nevada, which for the first author dates more than 30 years and includes many visits to the White-Inyo mountain region. For some species, however, we have drawn details from the literature cited at the end of each account. These citations also serve to introduce the serious student of birds to other sources of information for each species.

For general information on distribution, the notes and collections in MVZ were particularly useful. These were obtained by field parties that visited the White Mountains in 1917 and 1955. The notes of Joseph G. Hall, Ward C. Russell, and Francis S. L. Williamson were especially helpful. In addition, Ward C. Russell (*pers. comm.*) provided information on the habitat of Blue Grouse in the White Mountains. We sincerely thank these individuals for the detailed permanent record they left on the status of the avifauna 30 years ago.

We do not emphasize field identification in the accounts because such information is now readily available in several excellent, new pocket guides. Thus, the beginner will want to carry a guide to the identification of North American birds, along with this book, when exploring these fascinating mountains.

CATHARTIDAE (New World Vultures)

Turkey Vulture, *Cathartes aura*. (Fig. 11.1) Male length 25 1/2 in (65 cm), female length 27 in (68 cm); male weight 3 1/2 lb (1,559 g), female weight 3 2/3 lb (1,660 g). Uncommon summer resident in the White-Inyo Range; occurs at all elevations.

Turkey Vultures scavenge over open woods, brush, and grassland in varied terrain. Ranches and farming country are also visited. Although most common over valleys and foothills, they occasionally appear at higher elevations. The species is easily recognized by its very small head and broad wings held in a dihedral while soaring. Turkey Vultures forage singly, in pairs, or in loose groups. Odors wafting from carrion are picked up by their keen sense of smell, a rare trait in birds. Because vultures depend largely on thermals for uplift, they are less active on windless days or during stormy weather. This species generally roosts in two separate sites; the main one is used during the night. The second roost, used at dawn and dusk, serves mainly for sunning and preening. These bulky birds prefer to perch in open-branching live or dead trees, on poles, or even on the ground. Such perches enable easy takeoffs and landings. Nest sites are sheltered pockets in cliff faces or among large rocks on steep, brushy slopes. *References:* D. Davis (1979), Rea (1983).

ACCIPITRIDAE (Hawks and Eagles)

Cooper's Hawk, *Accipiter cooperi*. (Fig. 11.2) Male length 15 1/2 in (39 cm), female length 17 1/2 in (45 cm); male weight 10 1/3 oz (291 g), female weight 16 1/2 oz (466

FIGURE 11.1   Turkey Vulture.

FIGURE 11.2   Cooper's Hawk.

g). Scarce permanent resident in the White Mountains from the valleys to 9,500 ft (2,896 m).

This hawk prefers to nest in aspens, willows, and cottonwoods in canyon bottoms. Foraging takes them over adjacent slopes grown to pines, broken woodland, and brush. A skilled hunter, the Cooper's Hawk maneuvers through openings in foliage, around trees, and over clearings in search of small birds and mammals. Reptiles, amphibians, and large insects are taken infrequently. Like other accipiters, it actively pursues its prey while using vegetation to screen its approach. It may also dash toward prey from a concealed perch in dense foliage. Prey are commonly seized near the ground, in shrubs, or in the canopy of low cover. The hawk usually returns with its kill to feed within 100 ft (30 m) of the nest tree. *References:* Snyder and Wiley (1976), Reynolds and Meslow (1984).

Red-tailed Hawk, *Buteo jamaicensis.* (Fig. 11.3) Male length 20½ in (52 cm), female length 23 in (58 cm); male weight 2 lb (910 g), female weight 2⅔ lb (1,223 g). Common permanent resident in the White-Inyo Range, at all elevations up to 10,500 ft (3,200 m).

FIGURE 11.3   Red-tailed Hawk.

Red-tailed Hawks are one of the most widespread species in the region, occurring throughout a variety of habitats. They hunt for small and medium-sized mammals over broken woodland, brushy slopes, and grassland. Invertebrates, birds, reptiles, and amphibians are taken less commonly. Red-tailed Hawks search for terrestrial prey while soaring high above the ground or while perching quietly in a tree or on a pole. They attack with long dives or sudden plunges. The bulky stick nest is built on a cliff shelf or in a tree and, once abandoned, may serve importantly as a nesting site for large owls. During the breeding season, male Red-tailed Hawks swoop and ascend in exaggerated flight while carrying a snake or other conspicuous prey item in their talons. This courtship display may signify to the female that he is a competent hunter. *References:* Fitch, Swenson, and Tillotson (1946); Weathers (1983).

Golden Eagle, *Aquila chrysaetos.* (Fig. 11.4) Male length 32 in (81 cm), female length 34 in (87 cm); male weight 7 1/4 lb (3,293 g), female weight 8 7/8 lb (4,030 g). Uncommon resident in the White-Inyo Range, from the valley floors to the summits of the highest peaks.

Golden Eagles soar throughout these mountains over all available habitats, including brushland, Pinyon-juniper Woodland, Subalpine Forest, riparian cover in canyon bottoms, and alpine steppes. Open country is preferred for foraging. Mammals are taken primarily, but birds and some snakes may also be eaten. The composition

FIGURE 11.4   Golden Eagle.

of the diet depends on prey availability, but all animals ranging in size from mice to fawns and songbirds to grouse are fair game. This species is notorious for killing domestic livestock, especially lambs, but such events occur uncommonly. Golden Eagles hunt either from a perch or from the air while near the ground or soaring at great heights. The large stick nest is built on an inaccessible cliff ledge or in tall trees. Early in the breeding season, pairs of eagles conduct elaborate aerial courtship displays that involve mutual dives and other acrobatics. *References:* Brown and Amadon (1968), Olendorff (1975).

FALCONIDAE (Falcons)

American Kestrel, *Falco sparverius.* (Fig. 11.5) Male length 10 in (26 cm), female length 10 1/2 in (27 cm); male weight 3 3/8 oz (97 g), female weight 4 1/8 oz (116 g). Uncommon permanent resident in the White-Inyo Range at all elevations.

This species forages in open terrain where vegetation is sparse and low-growing, and where suitable perch sites are available; meadows, unforested slopes, sagebrush flats, and rocky outcrops are frequented. The American Kestrel is a generalized

FIGURE 11.5   American Kestrel.

predator of invertebrates and small vertebrates. Grasshoppers, crickets, and other insects make up the bulk of their diet, but reptiles, mammals, and birds may also be taken. This small falcon typically searches for and attacks its prey from an exposed perch at a moderate height, striking on or near the ground surface. On windy days, however, the birds may hunt by hovering over the ground, especially where perches are sparse or lacking. American Kestrels also "hawk" insects on the wing or, uncommonly, forage directly on the ground for nonflying invertebrates. This species nests commonly in tree cavities, especially in old Northern Flicker holes, and rarely in earth banks or cliff crevices. Being highly maneuverable, American Kestrels harass larger birds of prey and Common Ravens by long stoops and swift ascents. *Reference:* Balgooyen (1976).

Prairie Falcon, *Falco mexicanus*.   (Fig. 11.6) Male length 15 1/2 in (39 cm), female length 18 in (46 cm); male weight 1 1/8 lb (519 g), female weight 1 7/8 lb (849 g). Scarce resident in the White-Inyo Range at all elevations.

An arid-adapted species, the Prairie Falcon avoids heavily wooded areas. Open rocky canyons and ridgetops grown to Singleleaf Pinyon, sagebrush flats and slopes, alpine scrub, and grassland are preferred. There it searches for small mammals, birds, and invertebrates such as grasshoppers and crickets. Horned Larks are a common food item in open terrain. Prairie Falcons are swift and highly maneuverable in flight, and they deftly take prey from either the air or the ground. They also hunt while perched on a post or pole. Nests are built on rocky ledges or in cliff cavities, commonly far from water but near suitable foraging habitat. The Prairie Falcon can travel long distances daily away from the nest site in search of food. *Reference:* Cade (1982).

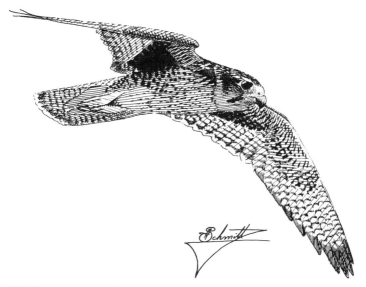

FIGURE 11.6   Prairie Falcon.

PHASIANIDAE (Partridge, Grouse, and Quail)

Chukar, *Alectoris chukar*. (Fig. 11.7) Male length 13 in (33 cm), female length 13 in (33 cm); male weight 21⅔ oz (614 g), female weight 17⅔ oz (500 g). Introduced. Common resident from the foothills to at least 10,000 ft (3,050 m) in the Inyo Mountains and 13,400 ft (4,090 m) in the White Mountains. Most numerous between 4,000 and 8,000 ft (1,220 and 2,440 m). Scarce in the northern portion of the region and at very high elevations.

Initially released into California in 1932, this partridge is now widely established in many arid portions of the state. It favors rough and inhospitable canyonsides where scattered clumps of brush and cheatgrass are interspersed with rock outcrops and steep talus slopes. Water from tiny seeps, steadily flowing streams, or tanks must be accessible daily during warm periods and may dictate the local occurrence of birds. Chukars feed primarily on the blades, seeds, and buds of cheatgrass and annuals, although grasshoppers and caterpillars are taken in the spring. Seeds are most important in the summer diet. The birds move continually while feeding, walking up steep boulder faces with agility and skulking across openings. When flushed, the covey explodes into the air and typically heads downhill, alternating rapid wing beats with short glides. Shrill alarm notes accompany the departure of disturbed adults. Foraging adults utter a throaty, resonant chuckling call, which carries for great distances in mountain canyons. *Reference:* Christensen (1954).

FIGURE 11.7 Chukar.

Blue Grouse, *Dendragapus obscurus.* (Fig. 11.8) Male length 19 in (49 cm), female length 16 in (41 cm); male weight 2⅝ lb (1,213 g), female weight 1¾ lb (803 g). Rare to fairly common, but local, permanent resident in the northern and central White Mountains; recorded between 8,000 and 10,200 ft (2,440 and 3,110 m) elevation. Numbers fluctuate annually. No known records from the Inyo Mountains.

Blue Grouse occur primarily on the east side of the White Mountains, inhabiting upper stream canyons lined with willow and aspen, as well as open Limber Pine forest on adjacent north- and northeast-facing slopes. The diet is well known for populations in the Sierra Nevada and other regions but has been poorly documented in the White Mountains. Spring and summer food in the Sierra Nevada reportedly consists of buds, twigs, catkins, and conifer needles, with fir needles becoming predominant during fall and winter. Because no native firs occur in the White Mountains, it is uncertain what the local grouse eat during those months. However, Limber Pine needles could be an important food. The species supplements its diet with willow leaves in the summer. Blue Grouse leave piles of characteristic droppings on the ground. Each dropping, approximately

FIGURE 11.8   Blue Grouse.

1 in (2.5 cm) long and ¼ in (0.6 cm) in diameter, is slightly curved and composed of tightly stacked, coarse plant material that shears neatly into individual cylinders. Males "boom" from trees during the breeding season, amplifying these hoots by expelling air held in vivid orange neck sacs. *Reference:* Johnsgard (1973).

Sage Grouse, *Centrocercus urophasianus.* (Fig. 11.9) Male length 25 in (63 cm), female length 19 in (48 cm); male weight 4¼ lb (1,954 g), female weight 2⅜ lb (1,085 g). Scarce summer resident in the White Mountains between 8,500 and 12,000 ft (2,590 and 3,660 m) elevation, especially in alpine sagebrush north of White Mountain Peak.

Sage Grouse are strictly tied to the sagebrush association, especially on flat or gently rolling terrain. Sage leaves constitute the main diet of adult birds, although herbaceous legumes and grasses are also eaten; chicks feed primarily on insects. The nest is usually well hidden underneath a sage bush. Prior to breeding, males congregate in large arenas or "leks" subdivided into individual territories. Here they conduct elaborate courtship displays for a group of females. The more dominant males typically occupy central territories in the lek and perform most of the matings. After courtship, the two sexes separate until the fall, when flocks are formed. The range and abundance of the Sage Grouse in California have declined dramatically during this century as a result of the devastation of sagebrush habitat by livestock and agriculture. *Reference:* Wiley (1973).

California Quail, *Callipepla californica.* (Fig. 11.10) Male length 8½ in (22 cm), female length 9 in (23 cm); male weight 5⅝ oz (159 g), female weight 5½ oz (155 g). Relatively common resident in the White-Inyo Range; occurs between 3,300 and 8,400 ft (1,010 and 2,560 m), although scarce at higher elevations.

This species occurs in localized areas of favorable habitat near streams and springs. Willows and other riparian vegetation, as well as sagebrush and Pinyon-juniper Woodland on adjacent slopes, are frequented. The quail forage mainly in the drier habitats but prefer to nest and roost under the concealing thicket cover. Seeds of Rabbitbrush and sagebrush make up the bulk of their diet in the Great Basin, although in other regions legumes and annuals are a more important seed source. Grass or legume leaves and the fruits, buds, and catkins of brush and juniper are also eaten. In addition, adults take small quantities of animal food, especially during the spring and summer; chicks subsist mainly on such food for the first month. Nests are typically placed on the ground in tall, dense cover of herbaceous vegetation. The California Quail is highly gregarious except during the breeding season. In the fall and winter, coveys forage together in alleyways through brush or alongside roads and other corridors. The social structure of coveys is strictly organized. *Reference:* Leopold (1977).

Mountain Quail, *Oreortyx pictus.* (Fig. 11.11) Male length 10 in (25.5 cm), female length 9½ in (24 cm); male weight 8½ oz (242 g), female weight 7⅝ oz (218 g). Scarce permanent resident in the White-Inyo Range; current status unclear.

FIGURE 11.9   Sage Grouse.

FIGURE 11.10   California Quail.

FIGURE 11.11   Mountain Quail.

Mountain Quail occur locally in the region on slopes and in canyon bottoms where dense brush is interspersed with open woodland. Sagebrush, Rabbitbrush, and currant within either broken Pinyon-juniper Woodland or Mountain Mahogany are favored. Water is required on a daily basis. Seeds of various perennial plants are taken year-round, with leaves and some fruits, flowers, and insects supplementing the diet. Young chicks subsist primarily on insects. Nests are well concealed under fallen branches, in tall weeds and dense shrubs, or near large, shaded rocks surrounded by thick vegetation. Like other species of quail, Mountain Quail spend the year in coveys except when breeding. Pairs form within coveys while these social groups are intact. In spring, males give a far-reaching, single inflected whistle that resembles the call of the Northern Pygmy-Owl. Males call frequently in the morning during the early breeding season. This species is highly secretive and prefers to remain hidden in dense brushy cover. In other regions, especially where the birds summer at high elevations, postbreeding coveys are thought to migrate downslope on foot into snow-free, warmer environments. *References:* Gutiérrez (1980), Miller and Stebbins (1964).

COLUMBIDAE (Pigeons and Doves)

Mourning Dove, *Zenaida macroura*.   (Plate 11.1) Male length 11 in (28 cm), female length 10 1/2 in (26.5 cm); male weight 4 1/4 oz (122 g), female weight 4 oz

(113 g). Fairly common summer (permanent?) resident in the White-Inyo Range; occurs up to approximately 10,000 ft (3,050 m).

This species inhabits a variety of habitats, including pinyon woodland, sagebrush, riparian thickets, and meadows. The birds travel long distances daily in search of both food and water. Mourning Doves feed primarily in open areas such as meadows and grassland, where they can find an ample supply of seeds from herbaceous plants. Grain can also constitute an important part of the diet; this is taken mainly in cultivated fields at lower elevations. Tiny pebbles and gravel are also consumed to help grind seeds in the muscular stomach. Nesting habitat requirements are flexible. The preferred nesting substrate consists of a horizontal branch in a tree or shrub, but the flimsy nest may also be built on the ground if woody vegetation is lacking. In addition, Mourning Doves commonly use abandoned nests, either of their own species or of others. Strongly monogamous, Mourning Doves are commonly seen in pairs. This species is easily detected by its characteristic call, a mournful *awoo-coo-coo-coo*. *Reference:* Johnsgard (1975).

STRIGIDAE (Typical Owls)

Western Screech-Owl, *Otus kennicottii*.   (Fig. 11.12) Male length 8 1/2 in (22 cm), female length 9 in (22.5 cm); male weight 4 3/4 oz (133 g), female weight 5 1/2 oz (155 g). Uncommon permanent resident in the White-Inyo Range; recorded from 7,200 to 8,200 ft (2,200 to 2,500 m) elevation.

Although this species is locally common in old-growth cottonwoods and tree willows in Owens Valley, only small numbers occur in the White-Inyo mountains. There they prefer the warmer portions of the Singleleaf Pinyon belt. Western Screech-Owls dwell in the lower stretches of canyons in mature trees on gently sloping ground. Natural or woodpecker-excavated cavities in large pinyon trunks are used for roosting and nesting. Foraging takes these owls into more open habitats, but at least some scattered pinyons or junipers seem essential for the presence of this species. Western Screech-Owls feed on a variety of insects, including grasshoppers, crickets, beetles, moths, caterpillars, and spiders. Vertebrates are occasionally eaten, especially during the winter months. The bouncing-ball song of the local subspecies (*O. k. inyoensis*) is shorter and composed of fewer notes than the vocalizations of related forms. Like all small owls, the Western Screech-Owl has suffered from fuel-wood cutting in the Singleleaf Pinyon Woodland and from the removal of riparian trees generally. Numbers nearly everywhere have been declining over the past several decades. *Reference:* Miller and Stebbins (1964).

Great Horned Owl, *Bubo virginianus*.   (Fig. 11.13) Male length 18 in (45.75 cm), female length 19 1/2 in (49.75 cm); male weight 2 lb (914 g), female weight 2 1/2 lb (1,142 g). Fairly common permanent resident in the White-Inyo Range; occurs at all elevations up to approximately 9,500 ft (2,896 m).

The Great Horned Owl is widespread through the region in a variety of habitats. Mammals of small to medium size predominate in their diet, but birds such as quail,

FIGURE 11.12   Western Screech-Owl.

woodpeckers, and passerines are also taken. To a lesser extent, the species may eat reptiles or amphibians, large insects (e.g., crickets, beetles), and carrion found along highways. Great Horned Owls are most active at night, but they can be seen abroad during the day under overcast conditions. However, most days are spent roosting in large pinyons, in other conifers or aspens, or in cavities in canyon walls. Stick nests abandoned by other raptors, either on cliff shelves or in trees, serve as the primary nesting sites. This species breeds in late winter or early spring. Toward the onset of the nesting season and during the breeding period, both sexes emit deep, resonant hoots. These hoots are deeper pitched in males despite their smaller size relative to females. Great Horned Owls are generally shy and difficult to approach, even at night. *References:* Burton (1973), Fitch (1947).

Long-eared Owl, *Asio otus*.   (Plate 11.2) Male length 13 in (33.25 cm), female length 13 in (33.5 cm); male weight 8⅝ oz (245 g), female weight 9⅞ oz (279 g). Uncommon permanent resident throughout the White-Inyo region, occurring up to 9,500 ft (2,900 m).

Although in this region the Long-eared Owl favors dense pinyon forest, it also frequents stands of cottonwoods, tree willows, aspens, and Mountain Mahogany. At night, the owls hunt through woodland and along the edges of clearings in search of prey, which consists primarily of small mammals. These owls also feed occasionally on

FIGURE 11.13   Great Horned Owl.

small birds and, more rarely, on reptiles or amphibians. During the day, the species roosts in dense clumps of Singleleaf Pinyon, Mountain Mahogany, cottonwoods, or aspens. Long-eared Owls are generally solitary except during the winter, when they form loose roosting aggregations in riparian thickets in the foothills and lowlands. Breeding takes place in abandoned nests of other large birds, particularly Red-tailed Hawks, Common Ravens, and, in the lower valleys, Black-billed Magpies. The Long-eared Owl is shy and difficult to attract by means of imitated calls. *References:* Grinnell and Storer (1924), Marti (1976).

Northern Saw-whet Owl, *Aegolius acadicus.* (Fig. 11.14) Male length 7 in (17.75 cm), female length 7 1/2 in (18.75 cm); male weight 2 5/8 oz (75 g), female weight 3 1/4 oz (91 g). Uncommon resident in the White Mountains. Winter status is uncertain; at that time, individuals from other regions may augment the local population. Recorded up to approximately 9,000 ft (2,740 m).

This owl occurs in dense riparian thickets and on remote canyon slopes far from water. They forage at the edges of meadows or clearings, particularly among open

FIGURE 11.14   Northern Saw-whet Owl.

stands of small to medium-sized conifers. There, mice and an occasional bird are taken. Nest sites consist of abandoned woodpecker holes or natural cavities at medium heights in trees. During the day, individuals roost in the dense foliage of small trees, commonly within 10 ft (3.0 m) of the ground. Mated males call infrequently. In contrast, unmated Northern Saw-whet Owls call steadily in the late winter and spring. These calls carry up to 0.5 mi (0.8 km), and thus the owls can easily be detected. They are difficult to locate, however, because the steady whistles quaver in pitch and fade in and out in intensity. Once a Northern Saw-whet Owl is found, either during the day or at night, commonly it can be closely approached. *Reference:* Earhart and Johnson (1970).

CAPRIMULGIDAE (Nightjars)

Common Nighthawk, *Chordeiles minor*.   (Fig. 11.15) Male length 9 in (22.75 cm), female length 9 in (22.75 cm); male weight 2 1/4 oz (63 g), female weight 2 1/2 oz (72 g). Scarce summer resident in the White Mountains; more common in the northern part of Owens Valley to the west. Recorded from 4,000 to 6,750 ft (1,220 to 2,060 m) elevation.

FIGURE 11.15   Common Nighthawk.

Common Nighthawks breed in the sagebrush-pinyon–covered alluvial fans on both sides of the White Mountains, and in adjacent ranch country with riparian growth in the valleys. Each evening in June and early July, they perform spectacular courtship dives in which the male plunges toward the ground and recovers suddenly with a loud, muffled *vvrrrr* sound. The call commonly delivered during high aerial foraging flights is a nasal *peent*. Females lay their eggs directly on the ground among gravel, sticks, and other plant debris, either in brushland or in large openings in forest. If disturbed while incubating, she flops awkwardly across the ground with fanned wings and tail, luring the intruder away from the nest site. This species feeds exclusively on insects caught on the wing, commonly over water surfaces. *References:* Armstrong (1965), Caccamise (1974).

Common Poorwill, *Phalaenoptilus nuttalli*. (Fig. 11.16) Male length 7 1/2 in (18.75 cm), female length 7 in (18 cm); male weight 1 3/4 oz (48 g), female weight 1 3/4 oz (48 g). Fairly common summer resident in the White-Inyo Range; winter status uncertain. Recorded up to 9,500 ft (2,900 m).

Poorwills prefer warm, open terrain with scattered trees or brush where there is an abundance of exposed sand, gravel, and rocks. This habitat is common in both the sagebrush and Pinyon-juniper zones of the region. Mountain Mahogany is also

FIGURE 11.16   Common Poorwill.

visited, especially when mixed with pinyon. Poorwills commonly rest on gravel road beds, where in the evening their reflected eye shine can be seen in car headlights or with a flashlight. They feed at dusk and dawn, when they take short flights from the ground in search of flying insects such as moths. The whistled *poor-will* call is followed by a brief *dup* note, delivered at a somewhat lower pitch and audible only at very close range. This species can become torpid during cold weather; such dormant individuals hide in protected crannies in rocks. *References:* Jaeger (1948), Marshall (1957).

APODIDAE (Swifts)

White-throated Swift, *Aeronautes saxatalis*.   (Plate 11.3) Male length 5 3/4 in (14.5 cm), female length 5 1/2 in (14 cm); male weight 1 1/10 oz (31 g), female weight 1 oz (29 g). Locally common summer resident in the White-Inyo Range, between 6,000 and 10,300 ft (1,830 and 3,140 m).

White-throated Swifts inhabit deep, rocky canyons that offer steep cliff faces for nesting and roosting. Foraging birds fly over a wide variety of habitats where insects are taken on the wing. The daily cruising range of the White-throated Swift exceeds that of most other species of birds in the region. Nests of twigs are cemented together and attached to cliff crevices by means of saliva. Granitic rock is apparently preferred as a nest substrate because it provides for easier nest attachment. White-throated Swifts commonly nest and roost colonially. They forage singly or in groups, darting swiftly at heights from near the treetops to high overhead. A series of excited shrill notes is commonly uttered in flight. During cold snaps, this species becomes dormant and individuals remain together in rocky crevices until warmer temperatures resume. *Reference:* Weathers (1983).

TROCHILIDAE (Hummingbirds)

Broad-tailed Hummingbird, *Selasphorus platycercus.* (Fig. 11.17) Male length 3 1/2 in (9 cm), female length 3 3/4 in (9.5 cm); male weight 1/10 oz (3.8 g), female weight 1/8 oz (4.5 g). Relatively common summer resident locally in the White-Inyo Range; occurs between approximately 6,000 and 9,000 ft (1,829 and 2,743 m) elevation.

This hummingbird inhabits the pinyon–juniper–Mountain Mahogany belt, where it prefers riparian thickets along wet or dry watercourses or near springs. There it feeds primarily on nectar from a variety of plants. Insects and spiders on flowers, near sapsucker borings, or in the air are also taken. The small, cup-shaped nests are typically placed on low horizontal branches of streamside trees. Like most hummingbirds, the Broad-tailed Hummingbird constructs its nest with spider webs, fine leaves, shreds of bark, and cottony material. Prior to breeding, one or several males display with U-shaped dives to a perched female from 20 ft (6 m) or more above the ground. During this display, sharp clicking notes are commonly uttered. In ordinary flight, males produce with specialized wing feathers a characteristic cricketlike trill. *Reference:* Johnsgard (1983).

PICIDAE (Woodpeckers)

Red-naped Sapsucker, *Sphyrapicus nuchalis.* (Plate 11.4) Male length 7 in (18 cm), female length 7 1/2 in (19 cm); male weight 1 1/2 oz (44 g), female weight 1 1/2 oz (43 g). Locally fairly common summer resident in the White Mountains, between approximately 9,000 and 9,600 ft (2,740 and 2,930 m).

FIGURE 11.17   Broad-tailed Hummingbird.

This woodpecker lives in canyons on the east side of the range, in streamside growth of aspens and willows. Mountain Mahogany and Bristlecone Pine are visited to a lesser extent. The adults drill linear rows of rectangular holes in the trunks and limbs of these trees and dip up the exuding sap with their brushy-tipped tongues. Such borings commonly lure insects, which, in turn, attract other species of birds. The Red-naped Sapsucker usually excavates its nest cavity in a large dying aspen, where decaying wood provides for easy digging. As the nestlings mature, their loud begging cries can be heard up to 100 yd (91 m) from the nest. In response to these cries, the parents arrive independently every few minutes carrying billsfull of large Timber Ants and other insects. Other cavity-nesting species of birds commonly use abandoned sapsucker nests for raising their own young. Consequently, sapsuckers and other woodpeckers play an important role as primary cavity excavators for a significant group of secondary hole-nesting species. For decades this form was combined with the Yellow-bellied Sapsucker (*S. varius*) and the Red-breasted Sapsucker (*S. ruber*) as a single species. *References:* Johnson and Johnson (1985), Short (1982).

Hairy Woodpecker, *Picoides villosus.* (Fig. 11.18) Male length 8 in (20.25 cm), female length 8 1/4 in (21 cm); male weight 2 1/8 oz (60 g), female weight 2 1/5 oz (62 g). Fairly common permanent resident in the White-Inyo Range, between 6,750 and 9,600 ft (2,060 and 2,930 m).

This species is perhaps the most generalized of all North American woodpeckers. In the White-Inyo mountain region, it is at home in such diverse habitats as Pinyon-juniper Woodland, aspen-willow associations, and coniferous forest of Limber and Bristlecone pines. Pinyon is used less commonly toward the south; there the trees must be large and in relatively thick groves on cool slopes or in canyons. Nest cavities are excavated in dead trees of any kind. The species forages mostly in dead or dying trees, where adult and larval insects are obtained by digging into decaying wood. In these vast mountains, Hairy Woodpeckers are sparsely distributed, and usually only one or two pairs may be encountered in a single day. *Reference:* Short (1971).

Northern Flicker, *Colaptes auratus.* (Plate 11.1) Male length 11 1/4 in (28.5 cm), female length 11 in (28.25 cm); male weight 5 3/8 oz (151 g), female weight 5 oz (141 g). Relatively common permanent resident in the White-Inyo Range, up to 10,350 ft (3,155 m).

Northern Flickers breed throughout the region in all types of woodland habitats, preferably where there are extensive tracts of good-sized trees near openings. Large, dying pinyons, aspens, or pines are all used for excavating nest cavities. Similar flexibility is shown in foraging behavior. Flickers search for ants, caterpillars, grubs, termites, beetles, and other terrestrial or foliage insects in live and dead tree trunks, leaf litter, bare soil, and ant hills. Because of its unusual terrestrial habits, this woodpecker is likely to be flushed from the ground in meadows, sagebrush flats, or other openings in wooded country. The attractive salmon-red color underneath the wings and tail, clearly seen in flight, is based on red pigments obtained through the diet. Occasional individuals that exhibit yellowish wing or tail feathers have not

FIGURE 11.18   Hairy Woodpecker.

eaten sufficient pigment-containing food prior to and during feather growth. *Reference:* Short (1965).

TYRANNIDAE (Tyrant Flycatchers)

Olive-sided Flycatcher, *Contopus borealis.*   (Fig. 11.19) Male length $6\frac{1}{2}$ in (16.5 cm), female length $6\frac{1}{2}$ in (16.5 cm); male weight $1\frac{1}{8}$ oz (32.6 g), female weight $1\frac{1}{8}$ oz (32.6 g). Fairly common summer resident locally in the White Mountains. Recorded from 8,200 to 10,500 ft (2,500 to 3,200 m).

This large flycatcher breeds only in the higher coniferous forests of Limber Pine, Bristlecone Pine, and Lodgepole Pine. It prefers open stands of mature timber, particularly where high perches and prominent song posts are available. Such perches are in the tops of tall dead and dying conifers. Olive-sided Flycatchers have the highest foraging beat of all North American members of their family, the Tyrannidae.

FIGURE 11.19   Olive-sided Flycatcher.

They feed mainly on large, flying insects. In contrast, nests are typically built at lower heights, on the outer live branches of Limber or Bristlecone pines. Males may sing continuously, but pairs are usually widely spaced on extensive territories. The easily recognizable song, *quick-three-beers*, accented on the second note, can be heard from up to 0.5 mi (0.8 km) away. Late migrants passing through the valleys and foothill canyons during late May and early June may also sing occasionally. *Reference:* Grinnell and Storer (1924).

Western Wood-Pewee, *Contopus sordidulus*.   (Fig. 11.20) Male length 5 3/4 in (14.5 cm), female length 5 1/2 in (14 cm); male weight 1/2 oz (13 g), female weight 1/2 oz (13 g). Common summer resident in the White Mountains, between 7,400 and 9,000 ft (2,260 and 2,740 m) elevation.

This flycatcher is most common in woodland and coniferous forest along streams. Because it prefers to forage from tall trees of open branchwork, dense pinyon and Mountain Mahogany are shunned. Large Quaking Aspen, Bristlecone Pine, and Limber Pine are frequented most commonly. Western Wood-Pewees seek flying insects from moderate heights above the ground; their foraging beat is therefore between that of the Dusky Flycatcher and that of the Olive-sided Flycatcher, with overlap at both

FIGURE 11.20   Western Wood-Pewee.

the upper and lower levels. Wood-Pewees migrate well into June. Then they may occur in Pinyon-juniper Woodland, willow thickets, and other nonbreeding habitats. The nasal buzz of the Western Wood-Pewee is commonly given throughout the day, even on sunny summer afternoons when few other species of birds are calling. *Reference:* Marshall (1957).

Dusky Flycatcher, *Empidonax oberholseri.*   (Fig. 11.21) Male length 5 1/4 in (13.5 cm), female length 5 in (13 cm); male weight 2/5 oz (11.6 g), female weight 2/5 oz (11.6 g). Common summer resident in the White-Inyo Range, between 8,200 and 10,500 ft (2,500 and 3,200 m).

Although this species avoids Singleleaf Pinyon except occasionally during migration, most other trees as well as willow thickets are used for breeding. In particular, it frequents Mountain Mahogany groves, streamside aspen woodland, and open forests of Bristlecone and Limber pines. Nests are usually built within 5 ft (1.5 m) of the ground in upright twigs of tall, dense shrubs (such as Wild Rose), aspen saplings, and willows. The adults feed near the nest and higher up in the openings between tall trees. The singing and sentry posts are often well above the ground. Dusky Flycatchers feed on miscellaneous flying insects such as small beetles, wasps, flies, and bugs, all of which are snapped from the air. *Reference:* Johnson (1963).

Gray Flycatcher, *Empidonax wrightii.*   (Fig. 11.22) Male length 5 1/4 in (13.25 cm), female length 5 in (13 cm); male weight 2/5 oz (11.6 g), female weight 2/5 oz

FIGURE 11.21   Dusky Flycatcher.

(11.6 g). Common summer resident in the White-Inyo Range from 7,200 to 10,500 ft (2,200 to 3,200 m).

Gray Flycatchers are most numerous in the vast tracts of Singleleaf Pinyon growing on either flat or sloping terrain. They also breed sparingly in sunny stands of Limber and Bristlecone pines up to 10,500 ft (3,200 m) elevation in the Inyo Mountains. This is the highest known nesting station for the species. In other regions, such as near the south end of Mono Lake, they breed in stands of tall sagebrush and Bitterbrush. Such growth does not seem to be used extensively in the White-Inyo mountain area. Nesting pairs prefer medium to large Singleleaf Pinyons near openings with relatively sparse brush. The nest straddles a horizontal branch and is commonly placed right near the trunk. Males commonly perch on a bare twig near the nest tree, where they are conspicuous by virtue of their silvery white underparts and tail-dipping mannerism. Typical perch sites for singing or foraging are within 12 ft (3.7 m) of the ground. Insects are caught from bare or nearly bare patches of ground between sagebrush, Bitterbrush, lupine, and small Beavertail Cactus. Like its relative, the Dusky Flycatcher, the Gray Flycatcher catches small insects while in flight. Although they maintain separate territories, the two species commonly occur side by side where their preferred habitats meet in these mountains. *Reference:* Johnson (1966).

FIGURE 11.22   Gray Flycatcher.

Say's Phoebe, *Sayornis saya*.   (Plate 11.1) Male length 6¾ in (17 cm), female length 6¾ in (17 cm); male weight ¾ oz (21.6 g), female weight ⁷/₁₀ oz (20.4 g). Sparse summer resident in the White-Inyo region, between 5,900 and 9,500 ft (1,800 and 2,900 m).

Say's Phoebes inhabit the pinyon-juniper-sagebrush zone in the region. Although the species is not numerous, nesting pairs can usually be seen in arid canyon mouths where sunny gravel banks and/or human constructs are present. Nests are placed on protected shelves in cliffs or buildings, and the adults forage nearby. Insect food is snapped from the air or the ground as the birds momentarily leave their low perches on bushtops or rocks, or as they hover. Postbreeding adults and independent young are widespread in shrubland or ranch country, where they perch singly on fenceposts, wires, or bushtops. *Reference:* Weathers (1983).

Ash-throated Flycatcher, *Myiarchus cinerascens*.   (Fig. 11.23) Male length 7 ½ in (18.75 cm), female length 7 in (18 cm); male weight 1 oz (28.6 g), female weight ⁹/₁₀ oz (26.4 g). Uncommon summer resident in the White-Inyo Range, from the valley floors to approximately 7,500 ft (2,290 m).

This flycatcher inhabits Pinyon-juniper Woodland and brush on warm, dry slopes, and open riparian growth with at least scattered trees. Because much of the foraging

FIGURE 11.23   Ash-throated Flycatcher.

activity occurs within 20 ft (6 m) of the ground, low perching sites are essential. Bushtops or exposed dead twigs in a dead or dying tree are used most typically. The Ash-throated Flycatcher captures large wasps, flies, beetles, and bugs by means of aerial sorties. Nests are built of twigs and lined with grass in a natural or woodpecker-excavated cavity in an old Singleleaf Pinyon or juniper. Both parents are usually conspicuous near the nest site. Pairs are widely spaced through the habitat on large territories and announce their presence with a loud, rolling *ka-brick* or *prit-wherr* call (accented on the second syllable). *Reference:* Miller and Stebbins (1964).

ALAUDIDAE (Larks)

Horned Lark, *Eremophila alpestris.* (Fig. 11.24) Male length 6 1/4 in (16 cm), female length 6 in (15 cm); male weight 1 oz (29.2 g), female weight 9/10 oz (26.5 g). Locally common summer resident in the White-Inyo Range. Occurs in two separate elevational belts: from the valley floors to 8,000 ft (2,440 m), and from 10,000 ft (3,050 m) to the summit of the White Mountains (14,246 ft or 4,340 m).

The Horned Lark nests over the widest elevational span of any bird species in the region. Because it prefers open and flat or gently sloping terrain, its local distribution is sharply divided into two main parts: lower valleys and flats covered with brush, up to 8,000 ft (2,440 m); and rolling upper sagebrush steppes and alpine fell-fields above timberline, from approximately 10,000 ft (3,050 m) to the highest peaks. This species is most at home in the skimpy grass, herbs, and rocks of windswept wastes,

FIGURE 11.24   Horned Lark.

where all nesting and foraging activities take place. Grass seeds and insects compose the diet. Breeding males announce their territories by spectacular song flights above their nesting areas. Early in the breeding period, two or more males swiftly chase over bushtops and high overhead. After being aloft for several minutes, they plunge from the sky and perch on the ground, on the tops of rocks, or on prominent shrubs. Postbreeding flocks of coalesced family groups or scattered singles wheel over open country and then land in the rocks and grass, each individual vanishing by virtue of its remarkable concealing coloration. *References:* Behle (1942), Verbeek (1967).

HIRUNDINIDAE (Swallows)

Violet-green Swallow, *Tachycineta thalassina.* (Plate 11.3) Male length $4^{3}/4$ in (12 cm), female length $4^{1}/2$ in (11.5 cm); male weight $^{1}/2$ oz (15.6 g), female weight $^{1}/2$ oz (15.5 g). Common summer resident in the White-Inyo mountain region, between 6,750 and 10,300 ft (2,060 and 3,140 m).

The Violet-green Swallow, one of the most conspicuous birds in the mountains, can be seen overhead on virtually any day. It is most common near cliffs or rocky outcrops above 7,500 ft (2,290 m), with numbers declining in the warmer areas below. Several pairs may form loose colonies in the vicinity of such cliff sites. Unlike most other swallows, this species build nests in two distinct kinds of places: either in rock crevices or in abandoned woodpecker cavities in aspens and conifers. The adults commonly perch on dead limbs of pines or aspens near the nest. This species feeds entirely on small insects caught on the wing. *Reference:* Grinnell and Storer (1924).

CORVIDAE (Crows and Jays)

Steller's Jay, *Cyanocitta stelleri.* (Fig. 11.25) Male length 10³/₄ in (27.5 cm), female length 10¹/₂ in (26.5 cm); male weight 3⁷/₁₀ oz (105 g), female weight 3¹/₂ oz (98 g). Fairly common permanent resident locally in the White-Inyo Range. Recorded between 6,200 and 9,500 ft (1,890 and 2,900 m).

Most records of this jay are from streamside willows and aspens, especially where the latter are mixed in canyon bottoms with large Singleleaf Pinyons or, at higher elevations, with Bristlecone and Limber pines. Diet is exceptionally varied; conifer seeds, fruits, large adult insects, caterpillars, and eggs and young of small birds are all devoured. Steller's Jays are also known to pilfer the seed stores of the Clark's Nutcracker. Nests in the White Mountains have been found in dense willow thickets. The breeding cycle starts in early spring so that stubby-tailed young, attended by

FIGURE 11.25   Steller's Jay.

parents, can be seen in late May. In other regions, Steller's Jays have been shown to defend group territories, where each pair is dominant to other members of the group on a portion of the total territory. These jays are therefore gregarious year-round. The handsome crest reveals the relative degree of aggressiveness (crest erect) or submissiveness (crest flattened) displayed during interactions with other members of their own species or with potential enemies. *Reference:* Brown (1964).

Scrub Jay, *Aphelocoma coerulescens.*   (Fig. 11.26) Male length 11 1/2 in (29.3 cm), female length 10 3/4 in (27.3 cm); male weight 2 4/5 oz (79 g), female weight 2 3/4 oz (77 g). Fairly common permanent resident in the White-Inyo Range, from 6,000 to 9,500 ft (1,830 to 2,900 m).

This species occurs in Pinyon-juniper Woodland on the slopes of the White-Inyo Range. Willows in canyon bottoms and groves of Mountain Mahogany are also visited if the preferred Singleleaf Pinyon is nearby. Brush near pinyon is used sparingly. The Scrub Jay is omnivorous wherever it occurs: seeds, nuts, fruits, large insects, and eggs and nestlings of small birds are all taken when available. Pinyon nuts are a particularly important food in these mountains. Scrub Jays living in pinyon

FIGURE 11.26   Scrub Jay.

woodlands of southeastern California are grayer and have longer, thinner bills than the oak-chaparral birds west of the Sierra Nevada. Presumably, the drabber coloration in the arid pinyon environment aids in concealment, and the bill shape is adapted for extracting pinyon seeds from cones. *Reference:* Ritter (1983).

Pinyon Jay, *Gymnorhinus cyanocephalus.* (Fig. 11.27) Male length 10 1/2 in (26.5 cm), female length 10 in (25 cm); male weight 4 oz (112 g), female weight 3 1/2 oz (97 g). Common permanent resident in the White-Inyo Range; recorded between 7,200 and 10,500 ft (2,195 and 3,200 m) elevation. Annual numbers fluctuate dramatically in any one place in concert with the availability of pinyon seeds.

Pinyon Jays are one of the most characteristic species of the interior Pinyon-juniper Woodland. The loud *kraw* call, given in chorus from the tops of trees or in flight, usually announces the presence of these conspicuous birds. When foraging, garrulous flocks, commonly numbering into the hundreds, sift through arid woodlands and over adjacent sagebrush country. Pinyon seeds are the major component of their diet and are also important in feeding displays and other courtship rituals. During the fall and early winter, large quantities of the seeds are harvested, transported in the throat, and stored on traditional nesting grounds. Because pinyon seed production is highly sporadic, the foraging range as well as the size of the flock depend on local seed availability. Pinyon Jays also eat some insects, which are taken from open ground by probing or from bark crevices. Pairs nest in loose colonies in large pinyons or junipers in fairly open woodland. Like other jays, the Pinyon Jay is very aggressive and will commonly harass hawks and other threatening birds of prey, especially when the latter are near the nesting area. *Reference:* Balda and Bateman (1973).

Clark's Nutcracker, *Nucifraga columbiana.* (Plate 11.2) Male length 11 1/2 in (29.5 cm), female length 11 1/4 in (28.7 cm); male weight 5 oz (139 g), female weight 4 5/8 oz (131 g). Common permanent resident in the White-Inyo Range; recorded from 6,800 to approximately 11,000 ft (2,073 to 3,353 m).

The Clark's Nutcracker is one of the more conspicuous species in the region and is commonly seen or heard overhead in a variety of habitats. The loud, grating *kraaa* call reveals its presence 0.5 mi (0.8 km) away. According to other studies, this species conducts seasonal altitudinal migrations in the Sierra Nevada, and it may show similar behavior in the White Mountains. Summers are commonly spent in the timber at higher elevations, and the onset of winter initiates a downslope movement into Pinyon-juniper Woodland. Although Clark's Nutcrackers are opportunistic feeders, they subsist mainly on the seeds of various conifers. Whitebark Pine and Jeffrey Pine are the primary trees utilized in the Sierra Nevada, but in the virtual absence of these conifers in the White Mountains, the local populations must eat the seeds of Limber pine and possibly Bristlecone Pine; little work has been done to document this, however. Nutcrackers also commonly visit pinyon in the summer, and when pinyon nuts are plentiful, they may be an important food source. This species is known to store vast seed reserves throughout the year in the Sierra Nevada. A small sac behind the tongue, unique to nutcrackers in the crow family, enables individuals

FIGURE 11.27   Pinyon Jay.

to carry seeds long distances between sources and storage sites. In addition to conifer seeds, Clark's Nutcrackers also eat insects and spiders, especially during the warmer months. Uncommonly, berries, freshly killed vertebrates (small mammals, nestling birds), and carrion are eaten. Nests are preferably built in fairly small conifers such as junipers. Typically, the birds begin nesting in late winter or early spring, so that by early summer the fully grown young are able to accompany their parents on long feeding flights. *References:* Tomback (1978a, 1978b).

Common Raven, *Corvus corax.*   (Fig. 11.28) Male length 21³/₄ in (55.25 cm), female length 21¹/₄ in (54 cm); male weight 2 lb (891 g), female weight 1⁷/₁₀ lb (767 g). Relatively common permanent resident at all elevations in the White-Inyo Range.

Although the species is conspicuous, total numbers in the region are probably small. Typically a bird of open country, the species is attracted to carrion of livestock and rabbits, large insects such as grasshoppers, and small mammals. Ravens move long distances daily in search of food. Postbreeding movements bring groups of ravens

FIGURE 11.28   Common Raven.

to largely barren alpine wastes. Nests are bulky piles of sticks placed on shelves in cliffs; buildings may also be used. The Common Raven is commonly harassed in the air by smaller birds such as American Kestrels and Violet-green Swallows. Our largest perching bird, the Common Raven soars like a hawk near windswept crags and over ridges. *Reference:* Goodwin (1976).

PARIDAE (Titmice)

Mountain Chickadee, *Parus gambeli*.   (Plate 11.4) Male length 5 in (12.5 cm), female length 5 in (12.5 cm); male weight $2/5$ oz (11.4 g), female weight $3/8$ oz (10.7 g). Very common resident in the White-Inyo Range, from 6,750 to 10,500 ft (2,057 to 3,200 m).

This species is most at home in the coniferous forests of Limber Pine, Bristlecone Pine, and Lodgepole Pine occurring above 8,900 ft (2,710 m). However, it also uses lower-elevation habitats of pinyon woodland and streamside thickets of willow-rose-birch, particularly during the nonbreeding season. Nesting activities are concentrated in small cavities in dead conifers or aspen snags. The species forages in the lower foliage layers, where it takes caterpillars and various insects from needle clusters, twigs, and small branches. When the birds are not breeding, they are gregarious and forage in flocks, either with other chickadees or in mixed groups with nuthatches, creepers, and other small insect-eating species. Mountain Chickadees utter a plaintive series of whistles, *teeee-tee-tee*, with the first note on a higher pitch and all three or four notes given in a minor key. This vocalization is a common sound in the White Mountains, especially early in the nesting period, and functions in territorial defense. The species also has a variety of buzzy and sputtering calls. *References:* Dixon (1965), Grinnell and Storer (1924).

Plain Titmouse, *Parus inornatus.* (Fig. 11.29) Male length 5 in (13 cm), female length 5 1/4 in (13.25 cm); male weight 5/8 oz (16.3 g), female weight 1/2 oz (15.4 g). Uncommon permanent resident in the White-Inyo Range; occurs from 7,200 to 7,900 ft (2,200 to 2,410 m).

This species is distributed sparsely through the warm, arid portion of mixed Pinyon-juniper Woodland; cool tracts of pure pinyon on northeast slopes are usually avoided. Plain Titmice favor open groves with at least some large, old trees that offer substantial limbs and trunks containing rotted cavities for nest placement. They hop

FIGURE 11.29 Plain Titmouse.

leisurely on large branches and twigs while searching the foliage for adult insects and caterpillars. Pinyon seeds are pounded open with the stout bill. The species commonly delivers a clear, ringing *pee-two, pee-two, pee-two* song while foraging. *References:* Dixon (1949); Johnson, Bryant, and Miller (1948).

AEGITHALIDAE (Long-tailed Tits and Bushtits)

Bushtit, *Psaltriparus minimus.* (Fig. 11.30) Male length 4 1/3 in (11 cm), female length 4 1/4 in (10.75 cm); male weight 1/5 oz (5.5 g), female weight 1/5 oz (6.1 g). Fairly common resident in the White-Inyo Range, from 6,750 to 8,200 ft (2,060 to 2,500 m).

Despite their small size, Bushtits are conspicuous in the summer as they forage in areas of pinyon-juniper intermixed with sagebrush and Mountain Mahogany. Streamside willow thickets are also inhabited. During the breeding season, in early spring, pairs are generally quiet and fairly shy. By June, however, they join other Bushtits to form tight flocks commonly comprising 20 or more individuals. Such flocks move widely through tree canopies and tracts of tall brush, following lead birds from one foraging site to another while constantly conversing in soft, twittery notes. Small insects and some vegetable matter are eaten as the birds forage among outer leaves and twigs in an acrobatic manner, moving with agility in the fine foliage. The Bushtit nest is an elongated pouch woven from fine plant materials and usually suspended from the end of a pinyon bough. *References:* Ervin (1977), Marshall (1957).

FIGURE 11.30   Bushtit.

SITTIDAE (Nuthatches)

Red-breasted Nuthatch, *Sitta canadensis.*   (Fig. 11.31) Male length 4 1/4 in (10.75 cm), female length 4 in (10.25 cm); male weight 2/5 oz (10.9 g), female weight 3/8 oz (10.3 g). Uncommon summer (permanent?) resident of the White Mountains; recorded from 8,900 to 9,500 ft (2,710 to 2,900 m).

This nuthatch occurs very sparingly and only in Subalpine Forest of Limber and Bristlecone pines. It is the least numerous of the three species of nuthatch that breed in the mountains. Red-breasted Nuthatches feed in the thickly foliaged tops of pines, where they can be extremely difficult to watch. They decoy readily, however, to imitated calls of small owls and will approach to within a few feet if one sits motionless next to a tree trunk. Like other nuthatches, this species excavates its own nest cavity in dead trunks or large limbs by digging vigorously with the bill. *References:* Anderson (1976), Kilham (1973).

White-breasted Nuthatch, *Sitta carolinensis.*   (Plate 11.2) Male length 5 1/3 in (13.5 in), female length 5 1/4 in (13.25 cm); male weight 5/8 oz (16.6 g), female

FIGURE 11.31   Red-breasted Nuthatch.

weight ³/₅ oz (16.3 g). Relatively common permanent resident in the White-Inyo Range, from 7,200 to 10,500 ft (2,200 to 3,200 m).

This species prefers relatively large Singleleaf Pinyon and Limber pines for foraging but will also use Bristlecone and Lodgepole pines to a lesser extent. An agile climber, the White-breasted Nuthatch ascends, descends, and circles large limbs and trunks in search of insects. Most prey is taken from the bark and from bark fissures. However, they also retrieve insects from deeper inside the wood by woodpeckerlike pounding and digging with their bills. Occasionally, this species drops to the ground to secure fallen items. During the breeding season, pairs of White-breasted nuthatches are widely spaced through the coniferous forest. At other times, they may join other nuthatches and insect-eating species in loose foraging groups. Like the Red-breasted and Pygmy nuthatches, the White-breasted Nuthatch nests in cavities in dead pine or aspen trees. *References:* Kilham (1972), McEllin (1979).

Pygmy Nuthatch, *Sitta pygmaea.* (Plate 11.4) Male length 4 in (10.25 cm), female length 4 in (10.25 cm); male weight ⁴/₁₀ oz (10.1 g), female weight ³/₈ oz (10.8 g). Relatively common resident in the White and northern Inyo mountains, between 9,500 and 10,500 ft (2,900 and 3,200 m).

The Pygmy Nuthatch typically inhabits Ponderosa Pines and other Yellow Pine associations throughout most of its range. In the White Mountains, in contrast, where Yellow Pines are virtually absent, it occurs almost exclusively in Bristlecone Pines. Aspen stands may be surveyed infrequently for possible nest sites, but the Bristlecone Pines largely fulfill requirements for food, nesting, and roosting. Pygmy Nuthatches feed on both plant and animal matter. Through the year, the bulk of their diet is composed of pine seeds, but insects predominate during the warmer months. Unlike the Red-breasted and White-breasted nuthatches, these small birds prefer to forage at upper levels in the pines, on the smallest, outermost twigs and needle clusters; trunks and large limbs are usually avoided. This species commonly forages in groups. Occasional individuals dart out after flying insects. The Pygmy Nuthatch uses its bill to dislodge insects from crevices in bark and also to wedge pine seeds into fissures before cracking them open. Some seeds are also stored in such crevices. Nest and roost sites are in tree cavities that they or other species excavate. Occasionally, several birds in addition to the nesting pair may assist in the digging. Some nests may also be shared by three nuthatches instead of two, the third individual typically being an unmated male helper. This species is gregarious when roosting in cavities. This occurs year-round, from before sunset to well after sunrise. *Reference:* Norris (1958).

CERTHIIDAE (Creepers)

Brown Creeper, *Certhia americana.* (Fig. 11.32) Male length 4 ¹/₂ in (11.75 cm), female length 4 ³/₄ in (12 cm); male weight ³/₁₀ oz (8 g), female weight ³/₁₀ oz (7.9 g). Uncommon permanent resident in the White-Inyo Range; recorded from 7,700 to 10,000 ft (2,350 to 3,200 m).

FIGURE 11.32   Brown Creeper.

Brown Creepers inhabit Subalpine Forest of Limber Pine, Bristlecone Pine, and Lodgepole Pine and woodlands of large Singleleaf Pinyon. They prefer mature timber in fairly dense stands for both foraging and nesting. These birds are excellent climbers, spiraling up tree trunks while probing into bark fissures for insects with their long, decurved bills. Their pale white throats may aid in reflecting light into these dark cracks. After attaining a certain height in the tree, creepers drop to the base of the same or another tree and continue their foraging. Brown Creepers nest in crevices or spaces underneath slabs of loosened tree bark. Although the back is camouflaged and resembles bark, the species can be detected by its constant movement. *Reference:* C. Davis (1979).

TROGLODYTIDAE (Wrens)

Rock Wren, *Salpinctus obsoletus.*   (Plate 11.3) Male length 5 in (13 cm), female length 5 in (12.75 cm); male weight $1/2$ oz (15.1 g), female weight $3/5$ oz (16 g). Common resident in the White-Inyo Range, from the base of the ranges to the summit of White Mountain Peak, at 14,246 ft (4,342 m).

Rock Wrens occur through an exceptionally wide elevational range in the region, on generally arid canyon slopes or flats wherever rocky outcrops or surfaces occur. They even persist in areas inhabited by few other species, such as the high-elevation, windswept wastes covered sparsely by low scrub, grass, and rocks. Insects are removed from rock crevices and exposed rock surfaces. This species also uses such crevices for nesting, although it may nest in tunnels in earth banks. Rock Wrens sing from prominent rocks, their buzzes and trills ringing and echoing across canyon walls. *References:* Kroodsma (1975), Weathers (1983).

Canyon Wren, *Catherpes mexicanus.* (Plate 11.3) Male length 5 in (12.5 cm), female length 4 3/4 in (12.25 cm); male weight 2/5 oz (10.8 g), female weight 3/8 oz (9.7 g). Rare to locally relatively common resident in the White-Inyo Range, with records between 5,100 and 7,400 ft (1,555 and 2,256 m).

Canyon Wrens occur as very widely scattered pairs in the region, their local presence dictated by the availability of either steep, rocky canyon walls, with shady overhangs near pools, or boulder piles with deep, shady crevices. The surrounding vegetation can be varied, ranging from brush or woods to open forest. Males announce their presence by a cascading series of clear, mournful whistles that reverberate through the habitat during the nesting period. The adults sneak through shady cracks among the boulders, apparently using their stark white throats to reflect light into the dark recesses, revealing prey of insects and spiders. Nests are also hidden in such crannies. *Reference:* Grinnell and Storer (1924).

Bewick's Wren, *Thryomanes bewickii.* (Fig. 11.33) Male length 4 3/4 in (12 cm), female length 4 3/4 in (12 cm); male weight 3/8 oz (9.3 g), female weight 3/8 oz (9.7 g). Common permanent resident in the White-Inyo Range; recorded from 6,750 to 9,500 ft (2,060 to 2,900 m).

This species frequents mountain slopes and canyons grown to Pinyon-juniper Woodland and mixed brush, especially sagebrush. Nearby Mountain Mahogany will occasionally be entered, but it is not preferred. There is some evidence for a partial winter exodus of the population into riparian willows at lower elevations in canyons and valleys. Bewick's Wrens are active near the ground, where they are commonly out of sight, but foraging birds visit the upper and outer foliage of pinyons and junipers. A variety of insects are gleaned from needle surfaces, twigs, and cracks in bark or trunks. The male sings from exposed perches 5 to 15 ft (1.5 to 4.6 m) above the ground. Members of a pair typically forage within several yards of each other. Nests are hidden in or near the ground in natural hollows or crannies in pinyons and junipers as well as in cavities or protected nooks in human-made structures such as cabins and woodpiles. *References:* Miller and Stebbins (1964), E. Miller (1941).

House Wren, *Troglodytes aedon.* (Fig. 11.34) Male length 4 1/2 in (11.5 cm), female length 4 2/5 in (11.25 cm); male weight 3/8 oz (9.8 g), female weight 2/5 oz (10.4 g). Common resident in the White Mountains; recorded from 6,750 to 9,950 ft (2,060 to 3,030 m).

FIGURE 11.33   Bewick's Wren.

FIGURE 11.34   House Wren.

House Wrens live in riparian settings, where they nest in natural cavities or in abandoned woodpecker holes in aspens. Preferred nest sites are commonly within 5 ft (1.5 m) of the ground. However, in areas of human settlement, they may also nest under the eaves or in cracks in walls of cabins. Foraging similarly takes place at low levels, in brush, willows, or other such growth around fallen trees and rocks. A diversity of insects, especially those of small size, make up their diet. The bubbling song of male House Wrens is a characteristic summer sound of the aspen zone in the range. *References:* Kendeigh (1941), Marshall (1957).

CINCLIDAE (Dippers)

American Dipper, *Cinclus mexicanus.* (Fig. 11.35) Male length 7 in (17.5 cm), female length 6 3/4 in (17 cm); male weight 2 1/8 oz (60 g), female weight 1 3/4 oz (49 g). Small numbers of this species occur year-round in the deep, wet canyons of the White Mountains, up to elevations of approximately 10,000 ft (3,050 m).

The American Dipper occurs only along permanently flowing streams characterized by cool, swift, clear water. Aquatic insect larvae compose the bulk of their diet, but small fish and other invertebrates are occasionally eaten. Dippers get most of their prey directly from the fast-moving waters. They also flycatch and pick insect larvae from streamside rocks. The ability of dippers to forage in mountain streams is truly remarkable. With their strong feet they grasp the rubble on the bottom and wade

FIGURE 11.35 American Dipper.

underwater in search of food; in deeper, faster water, they typically use their wings while diving and swimming. The American Dipper usually stands on emerged rocks at the water's edge while foraging. Flight between such perches is rapid and low over the water. This species also breeds in the dampness of the stream environment. Preferred nest substrates are overhanging cliff ledges in areas protected from predators and inclement weather but exposed to water spray. Large rocks, tree roots, and undercut banks are commonly used. The mossy covering of the nest is moist and springy. Birds tend to breed in early spring, an adaptation that allows them to take advantage of an ample insect supply before late spring runoff decreases the availability of food. *References:* Morse (1979), Price and Bock (1983).

MUSCICAPIDAE (Muscicapids). SYLVIINAE (Kinglets and Gnatcatchers)

Ruby-crowned Kinglet, *Regula calendula.* (Fig. 11.36) Male length 4 in (10.25 cm), female length 4 in (10 cm); male weight $1/5$ oz (6.2 g), female weight $1/5$ oz (6 g). Relatively common summer resident locally in the White-Inyo Range; occurs between approximately 9,500 and 10,600 ft (2,900 and 3,230 m) elevation.

This species is most common in coniferous forest of Bristlecone, Limber, and Lodgepole pines. Aspen groves are visited occasionally. Foraging is concentrated on the terminal needle clusters at low to middle heights in the canopy. Here, this kinglet picks small insects from the foliage while nervously flicking its wings. Perches

FIGURE 11.36   Ruby-crowned Kinglet.

are changed frequently. Occasional sorties after flying insects and hovering flights near foliage are additional common foraging maneuvers. *References:* Franzreb (1984), Grinnell and Storer (1924).

Blue-gray Gnatcatcher, *Polioptila caerulea.* (Fig. 11.37) Male length 4 1/4 in (10.75 cm), female length 4 in (10.5 cm); male weight 1/5 oz (5.4 g), female weight 1/5 oz (5.7 g). Common summer resident in the White-Inyo Range, from 5,100 to 9,400 ft (1,555 to 2,870 m).

Blue-gray Gnatcatchers frequent arid Oak Woodland and Chaparral throughout most of their breeding range west of the White-Inyo mountain region. However, in these desert mountains, the species switches to a more xeric habitat of Pinyon-juniper Woodland interspersed with sagebrush and, in some areas, Mountain Mahogany. Nearby streamside thickets of willows and tall sagebrush are used less commonly. Gnatcatchers are conspicuous where they occur, uttering a series of high, thin, wheezy notes while actively foraging among the dense foliage of trees and shrubs. Alighting momentarily on a branch, the bird quickly scans the area for food before flying to the next perch. Large insects are usually picked from leaves and twigs, but some may also be taken on the wing. Nests are small, compact cups attached to upright branch

FIGURE 11.37   Blue-gray Gnatcatcher.

forks in a tree or bush. Although sometimes placed in the open, they are nonetheless well hidden by virtue of their camouflaging outer material. Blue-gray Gnatcatchers respond readily to human squeaks and imitated owl calls. *References:* Root (1967), Root (1969).

TURDINAE (Thrushes)

Mountain Bluebird, *Sialia currucoides.*   (Plate 11.2) Male length 6 3/5 in (16.75 cm), female length 6 1/2 in (16.5 cm); male weight 1 oz (28.7 g), female weight 1 oz (28.8 g). Common summer resident in the White-Inyo Range, from 7,200 to 10,500 ft (2,200 to 3,200 m).

This species lives in exposed places: meadows, sagebrush flats, sparsely vegetated slopes, and open coniferous forest. There they perch on bush tops, prominent rocks, fences, or dead treetops. Insects are taken from either the air, the ground, or the foliage and woody parts of trees and shrubs. The Mountain Bluebird commonly hovers buoyantly before securing its prey. Nests are mostly placed in cavities in dead conifers or aspens. In late summer, postbreeding family groups forage widely over open country. The Mountain Bluebird winters in flocks at lower elevations, either in agricultural regions in valleys, in the desert, or on mountain slopes grown to juniper, the berries of which are often a staple food during that season. *References:* Power (1966), Power (1980).

Townsend's Solitaire, *Myadestes townsendi.*   (Fig. 11.38) Male length 7 9/10 in (20 cm), female length 8 1/10 in (20.5 cm); male weight 1 1/8 oz (31.9 g), female weight 1 1/4 oz (35.6 g). Rare summer resident in the White-Inyo Range, between 9,300 and 10,500 ft (2,840 and 3,200 m) elevation. The solitaire also occurs in winter on the lower slopes of these ranges, although these birds are not necessarily from the local summering population.

As a nesting species, solitaires occur only in the best stands of subalpine Limber and Bristlecone Pine forest. Males sing a far-reaching, jumbled series of warbles from spires in the treetops. A more commonly heard vocalization, however, is the brief, haunting whistle that simulates a creaky hinge. Townsend's Solitaires commonly take shady perches near the trunk, below the main foliage canopy of pines. They obtain insects in summer, occasionally by flycatching; winter birds commonly feed on juniper berries. Nests are built in protected crevices in banks, stumps, and exposed tree roots. *Reference:* Salomonson and Balda (1977).

Hermit Thrush, *Catharus guttatus.*   (Plate 11.4) Male length 6 3/4 in (17.25 cm), female length 6 1/4 in (16 cm); male weight 1 oz (28.5 g), female weight 1 oz (28.8 g). Common summer resident in the White-Inyo Range; recorded from 7,700 to 10,500 ft (2,350 to 3,200 m).

This species lives in the shadiest habitats of the White-Inyo Range: aspen woodland, willow thickets, and coniferous forest of Limber, Bristlecone and Lodgepole pines. Dense groves of Mountain Mahogany, especially on northeast slopes or in

FIGURE 11.38   Townsend's Solitaire.

ravines, are also suitable; these provide good shade and a ground layer of plant debris in which the thrushes forage. In the morning and again at dusk, males deliver their enchanting, fluty song from prominent perches. The environment occupied by the Hermit Thrush in these mountains seems more open and arid than places where the species occurs in the Sierra Nevada. *References:* Dilger (1956), Morse (1971).

American Robin, *Turdus migratorius.*   (Fig. 11.39) Male length 9 1/8 in (23.25 cm), female length 9 1/4 in (23.5 cm); male weight 2 5/8 oz (74 g), female weight 2 3/4 oz (78 g). Common summer resident in the White Mountains, from 6,750 to 10,500 ft (2,060 to 3,200 m). Scarce in the Inyo Mountains; there is one June record from Waucoba Canyon, at 7,200 ft (2,200 m).

In the White Mountains region, this familiar species breeds in moist canyon bottoms where meadows and dense thickets of willow, rose, and birch prevail. Such habitats provide soft, open ground for foraging, where worms and other ground invertebrates may be taken. Mud for nest construction is also available in these places. The American Robin builds its nest in many kinds of trees situated near wet areas. Typically, the cup-shaped nest is placed on a branch or in a fork at moderate heights. Males begin to sing on their breeding territories in early spring. They sing most vigorously at dawn and during the early morning hours, and their caroling

FIGURE 11.39   American Robin.

song can often be heard continuously along streamcourses throughout the summer. *References:* Howell (1942), James and Shugart (1974), Shedd (1982).

MIMIDAE (Mockingbirds and Thrashers)

Sage Thrasher, *Oreoscoptes montanus.*   (Fig. 11.40) Male length 7 7/8 in (20 cm), female length 7 7/10 in (19.5 cm); male weight 1 2/5 oz (40 g), female weight 1 1/2 oz (44 g). Present in both ranges during the spring and summer months, from approximately 6,000 to 11,000 ft (1,830 to 3,350 m) elevation in the White Mountains.

Although never numerous, Sage Thrashers are most common in the tall, dense sagebrush present on the alluvial fans in the northern White Mountains. Populations at high elevations, where the brush is of short stature, are sparse. In those areas, however, the birds typically seek out the scattered, thicker patches of brush and use the tallest available sages for both song posts and nest sites. This species inhabits no other plant assemblage in the region. Foraging concentrates on the ground between and below the shrubs, but insects in the foliage are also taken; preferred prey items include grasshoppers, cicadas, beetles, and other large species. The Sage Thrasher builds its bulky nest in a well-concealed position in the top of a sage bush. Four or five spotted blue eggs are laid. Males also sing their rich, warbled song from bush

FIGURE 11.40   Sage Thrasher.

tops and may commonly be heard across the open terrain for at least 0.5 mi (0.8 km). These birds can also be detected by their strong and direct flight just above the sagebrush tops. *Reference:* Reynolds and Rich (1978).

VIREONIDAE (Vireos)

Solitary Vireo, *Vireo solitarius*.   (Fig. 11.41) Male length 5 4/5 in (14.3 cm), female length 5 2/5 in (13.8 cm); male weight 3/5 oz (16.2 g), female weight 3/5 oz (16.8 g). Relatively common summer resident in the White-Inyo Range, between 6,200 and 8,200 ft (1,890 and 2,500 m).

In these mountains, Solitary Vireos inhabit wooded canyon slopes, draws, and flats dominated by large pinyons, junipers, and, to a lesser extent, Mountain Mahogany. Foraging activity ranges from the tree crowns to near the ground. There birds forage for adult and larval insects by moving deliberately through clumps of foliage. The nest is a cup constructed of fine plant fibers, delicate inner bark strips, and grass tops. It is camouflaged externally with grayish or greenish lichens or dried leaves, and it is suspended by its rim from the horizontal fork of a pinyon or juniper branch. Solitary Vireos can be detected from a distance of over 0.25

FIGURE 11.41   Solitary Vireo.

mi (0.4 km) by their song of rich, inflected slurs or burred phrases, often uttered in a question-and-answer pattern. Occasionally, the male may sing from the nest while covering the eggs in the absence of the female. Pairs of these vireos are generally widely spaced, so that four or five territories at most are encountered in a hike of several miles through favorable habitat. The form *V. solitarius plumbeus*, which inhabits the White-Inyo Range, is a clean, grayish white bird, in contrast to the yellowish green form, *V. solitarius cassinii*, that breeds on the west side of the Sierra Nevada. *V. s. plumbeus* is a relative newcomer to the region, unrecorded there prior to the 1960s. *Reference:* James (1981).

Warbling Vireo, *Vireo gilvus*.   (Fig. 11.42) Male length 4 3/4 in (12 cm), female length 4 3/4 in (12 cm); male weight 3/8 oz (10.8 g), female weight 2/5 oz (11.8 g). Common summer resident in the White-Inyo Range, between 6,200 and 10,500 ft (1,890 and 3,200 m).

Warbling Vireos dwell in the canopy foliage of riparian aspen, willows, and Water Birch. They take insects from their leafy surroundings by deliberate foraging motions. This species can be difficult to find in the treetops, but its presence is revealed by incessant singing, which commonly continues to midday or even into the afternoon, when other birds are silent. In the early morning, especially in spring soon after their arrival, chases of male vireos in territorial encounters, and males and females in pairing flights, are announced by silvery white flashes through the foliage. The nest is a neatly woven cup suspended from a horizontal fork and placed 8–25 ft (2.4–7.6 m) above the ground in deciduous foliage. Brown-headed Cowbirds commonly

FIGURE 11.42   Warbling Vireo.

parasitize Warbling Vireo nests in the Sierra Nevada, and possibly also do so in the White Mountains. In favorable habitat, the linear territories of the species occur in uninterrupted succession along mountain streams. *References:* Grinnell and Storer (1924), Walsberg (1981).

EMBERIZIDAE (Emberizids). PARULINAE (Wood Warblers)

Orange-crowned Warbler, *Vermivora celata.*   (Fig. 11.43) Male length 4 2/5 in (11.25 cm), female length 4 5/8 in (11.75 cm); male weight 2/5 oz (9.2 g), female weight 2/5 oz (9.1 g). Relatively common summer resident in the White Mountains and locally in the Inyo Mountains, between 6,650 and 9,500 ft (2,030 and 2,900 m).

The interior form of this species lives only in moist canyon bottoms, in the cool riparian strip of aspen, Water Birch, and associated thickets of willow and Wild Rose. Such habitat contrasts greatly with the warm Oak-Chaparral growth at low elevations occupied by the form on the west side of the Sierra Nevada. Like most other species in the genus *Vermivora*, the Orange-crowned Warbler builds its nest in a concealed place on the ground. The adults are well hidden as they search for insects and spiders in the foliage of willow, rose, and aspen saplings. Most challenging of all is to pinpoint the male as he sings from the crowns of aspen, birch, or willow along the stream. His song—a continuous, insectlike trill of two or three parts, each on a slightly different pitch—is usually delivered in long series from a concealed perch. Although exposed briefly while flying between song perches, he quickly vanishes again in the leafy treetops. *References:* Mengel (1964), Morrison (1981).

Virginia's Warbler, *Vermivora virginiae.*   (Fig. 11.44) Male length 4 1/4 in (11 cm), female length 4 1/4 in (11 cm); male weight 2/5 oz (8.4 g), female weight 1/4 oz (7.5

FIGURE 11.43   Orange-crowned Warbler.

FIGURE 11.44   Virginia's Warbler.

g). Relatively common summer resident locally in the White Mountains, between 6,750 and 9,500 ft (2,060 and 2,900 m).

This warbler is most abundant on upper slopes in groves of Mountain Mahogany, but it also occurs sparingly in riparian willows and around clumps of seviceberry in the pinyon zone. The plant growth these birds occupy is often clumped among boulder piles or near rock slides. A secretive species, it perches in the leaves just below the foliage top and can be difficult to find even when it is singing. Nonetheless, a squeak or hissing note will usually bring the bird into view. Then it characteristically flicks its tail while uttering *chip* notes in alarm. Virginia's Warblers take insect food from twigs and leaves of deciduous brush; thus, their sphere of activity is focused within several feet of the ground. *Reference:* Johnson (1976).

Yellow Warbler, *Dendroica petechia.*   (Fig. 11.45) Male length 4 1/2 in (11.25 cm), female length 4 1/4 in (10.5 cm); male weight 3/10 oz (9.3 g), female weight 3/10 oz (8.5 g). Uncommon local summer resident in the White Mountains, between 6,750 and 8,200 ft (2,060 and 2,500 m).

This species dwells in the canopy of riparian vegetation, mainly in canyons on the east side of the range. It also breeds at scattered oases in the valleys on each side of the mountains. Yellow Warblers prefer tree willows and cottonwoods but will venture sparingly into aspen at higher elevations. Low willow and alder growth along streams is used for foraging, although much insect food is also taken well up in the foliage of large trees. Nests too are placed in these trees from near the ground to middle heights. Elsewhere this species is heavily parasitized by Brown-headed Cowbirds, and

FIGURE 11.45   Yellow Warbler.

this activity is suspected to contribute to the uncommonness of the Yellow Warbler in the White Mountains. *References:* Biermann and Sealy (1982), Griscom and Sprunt (1957).

Yellow-rumped Warbler, *Dendroica coronata.* (Plate 11.4) Male length 5 in (13 cm), female length 5 in (13 cm); male weight $^2/_5$ oz (12.3 g), female weight $^2/_5$ oz (12.5 g). Common summer resident in the White-Inyo Range, occurring from 8,200 to 10,500 ft (2,499 to 3,200 m).

This species summers in Subalpine Forest of Bristlecone Pine, Limber Pine, or Lodgepole Pine, and in associated riparian trees such as aspen. One of the most generalized foragers of all warblers, it takes insects from the foliage by gleaning and hovering and from the air by flycatching. All levels of the habitat are visited, from the ground to the tops of tall conifers. During the nonbreeding season, berries are often eaten. The Yellow-rumped Warbler also varies its nest sites from near the ground to high in the conifers. *Reference:* Hubbard (1969).

Black-throated Gray Warbler, *Dendroica nigrescens.* (Plate 11.2) Male length $4^5/_8$ in (11.8 cm), female length $4^1/_2$ in (11.5 cm); male weight $^1/_4$ oz (8.1 g), female weight $^3/_{10}$ oz (8.9 g). Very common summer resident in the White-Inyo Range, from 6,750 to 9,500 ft (2,060 to 2,900 m).

This warbler's preference for sunny and warm environments is reflected in its increasing abundance from north to south in the woodlands of the White-Inyo mountains. Arid portions of Pinyon-juniper Woodland are favored, with occasional use of Mountain Mahogany. The Black-throated Gray Warbler must occur in huge numbers, as it is one of the most commonly encountered species in the region. Its "see-saw," buzzy song, rising in pitch near the end, is a characteristic sound of the pinyon zone through the spring and summer. Adult Black-throated Grays hunt for insects and spiders in dense terminal needle clusters of pinyon. Nests are built in pinyons or in nearby brush. *References:* Marshall (1957), Morrison (1982).

MacGillivray's Warbler, *Oporornis tolmiei.* (Fig. 11.46) Male length $4^4/_5$ in (12.25 cm), female length $4^3/_4$ in (12 cm); male weight $^3/_8$ oz (10.8 g), female weight $^3/_8$ oz (10.7 g). Common summer resident in the White Mountains, between 6,750 and 9,500 ft (2,060 and 2,900 m).

This warbler inhabits thick undergrowth along streams, attaining its greatest numbers between 8,200 and 9,000 ft (2,500 and 2,740 m) in willows, alder, Water Birch, nettles, and aspen saplings. Shade and dampness are prominent features of the species' habitat. MacGillivray's Warblers forage for insects and nest near the ground in dense foliage and branchwork; thus, they can be very difficult to observe. When singing, however, males are commonly exposed in bush tops from 5 to 15 ft (1.5 to 4.6 m) above the ground. During migration, this species occurs much more widely and can be found even in very open country near damp spots, as long as there is relatively thick brush nearby with shady hiding places. *References:* Grinnell and Storer (1924), Hutto (1981).

FIGURE 11.46   MacGillivray's Warbler.

FIGURE 11.47   Yellow-breasted Chat.

Yellow-breasted Chat, *Icteria virens.* (Fig. 11.47) Male length 6 7/8 in (17.5 cm), female length 7 in (17.75 cm); male weight 7/8 oz (24.9 g), female weight 1 oz (27.8 g). Local and rare summer resident in the White Mountains, with records at 6,750 ft (2,060 m), an unusually high elevation for the species.

The Yellow-breasted Chat nests only in the densest riparian thickets in foothill canyons on the east side of the range. Total numbers in the region are probably very small. Lush growth of willows, Wild Rose, nettles, and cottonwood saplings are used for all activities. Because of these habitat preferences, chats are usually very difficult to see in their impenetrable haunts. Their presence is typically revealed by an unusual song, a mixture of harsh and varied rattles interspersed with clear whistles. The singing male is commonly obscured by foliage, but patience will be rewarded by a spectacular song flight occurring between thickets, in which the legs are dangled and wings slowly fluttered. Food consists of insects, spiders, and small fruits. *References:* Petrides (1938), Thompson (1977).

THRAUPINAE (Tanagers)

Western Tanager, *Piranga ludoviciana.* (Plate 11.4) Male length 6 1/4 in (16 cm), female length 6 1/4 in (16 cm); male weight 1 oz (27.5 g), female weight 1 oz (27.8 g). Relatively common summer resident in the White-Inyo Range, from 6,750 to 9,800 ft (2,060 to 2,990 m).

This species shuns open Singleleaf Pinyon as breeding habitat in favor of the larger conifers occurring at higher elevations. Occasionally, however, tall pinyon trees intermixed with Mountain Mahogany, as well as aspen, may be used for nesting. Pinyon Woodland is visited much more extensively when the birds are migrating, which may occur well into June. Western Tanagers forage for wasps, ants, beetles, and other insects in the pine canopies, either by picking the insects from the branches and foliage or by snapping them from the air during short jaunts from their perches. Other foods, particularly fruits, are eaten by postbreeding or migrating individuals. Nests of twigs and fine roots are placed on the outer ends of large limbs, from middle heights to the top of the canopy. Although this species prefers the security afforded by dense conifer foliage, dead limbs or trees are known to be used. Brightly colored males are easily spotted by flashes of yellow as they traverse openings in the forest. The short, melodious, languid warble given by the male, or the short *pit-er-ic* call uttered by both sexes, also announces the presence of the species. *Reference:* Grinnell and Storer (1924).

CARDINALINAE (Cardinals, Grosbeaks, and Allies)

Black-headed Grosbeak, *Pheucticus melanocephalus.* (Fig. 11.48) Male length 7 in (18 cm), female length 7 1/4 in (18.25 cm); male weight 1 1/2 oz (41 g), female weight 1 1/2 oz (44 g). Very common summer resident in the White-Inyo Range, between 6,750 and 8,900 ft (2,060 and 2,710 m).

FIGURE 11.48   Black-headed Grosbeak.

This species is a characteristic mid-elevation bird of the region in diverse woodlands such as pinyon, aspen-willow, and Mountain Mahogany. Between approximately 7,000 and 8,000 ft (2,130 and 2,440 m) elevation, it is very prominent and is almost constantly within sight or sound. The male's rich, warbled song is so loud that it virtually drowns out the voices of most other singing birds in its neighborhood. Male Black-headed Grosbeaks even sing loudly from the nest as they cover the eggs during the absence of the female. Extensive edges and diverse plant mixtures are preferred, these providing the species with foliage insects, buds, and fruits for consumption. *References:* Weston (1947), Bent (1968).

Lazuli Bunting, *Passerina amoena.*   (Fig. 11.49) Male length 5 in (12.75 cm), female length 4⁹/₁₀ in (12.5 cm); male weight ½ oz (14.7 g), female weight ½ oz (13.6 g). Fairly common summer resident in the White Mountains, recorded between 6,750 and 9,000 ft (2,060 and 2,740 m), but rare above 8,200 ft (2,500 m) except as a postbreeding vagrant.

Lazuli Buntings are restricted in the White Mountains to streamside thickets and are most common in the middle and lower reaches of canyons. Dense tangles of willows, Wild Rose, and Water Birch are chosen for both foraging and nesting, especially where the plant growth is mixed in terms of species composition and stature. The colorful male commonly sings from the tops of tall bushes or small

FIGURE 11.49   Lazuli Bunting.

trees. Occasionally, however, he ascends to the top of an aspen, pinyon, or other conifer and sings from 30 to 40 ft (9 to 12 m) above the ground. The song is characteristically variable, with phrases and short trills at different pitches and often in couplets. The closely related Indigo Bunting (*P. cyanea*), with which the Lazuli Bunting is known to hybridize, has been expanding its range southwestward in recent years, and males have been recorded in the White-Inyo mountains. *References:* Emlen, Rising, and Thompson (1975); Thompson (1976).

EMBERIZINAE (Towhees, Sparrows, and Allies)

Green-tailed Towhee, *Pipilo chlorurus*.   (Fig. 11.50) Male length 6 3/4 in (17 cm), female length 6 1/2 in (16.75 cm); male weight 1 oz (28.9 g), female weight 7/8 oz (24.9 g). Locally common summer resident in the White-Inyo Range, from 6,200 to 10,000 ft (1,890 to 3,050 m).

Green-tailed Towhees breed in brushland in this region, occurring in greatest numbers in open pinyon with mixed brushland. High-elevation habitats of sagebrush mixed with willows and birch are visited sparingly. A particularly favorable site is sagebrush interspersed with serviceberry, currant, and scattered pinyons in a canyon bottom. Arid flats of pure sagebrush are avoided. The adults are skilled runners, moving while crouched in alleyways between the shrubs. They forage on the ground

FIGURE 11.50   Green-tailed Towhee.

for insects and fruit in leaf litter. Nests are placed near the ground in bushes. Adult Green-tailed Towhees decoy readily to a squeak and commonly respond with a catlike *mew*. Males sing from open perches in pinyon tops at approximately 20 ft (6 m) above the ground. *Reference:* Grinnell and Storer (1924).

Rufous-sided Towhee, *Pipilo erythrophthalmus.*   (Fig. 11.51) Male length 7 3/4 in (20 cm), female length 7 1/2 in (19.5 cm); male weight 1 3/10 oz (37.4 g), female weight 1 3/10 oz (37.6 g). Common resident in the White-Inyo Range, recorded from 6,000 to 9,000 ft (1,830 to 2,740 m).

This species frequents dense brushy habitats along slopes and canyon bottoms in the pinyon-juniper-mahogany belt. Sagebrush and streamside growth of willow-rose-birch are particularly favored. A ground cover of litter is essential to the presence of Rufous-sided Towhees; there the species rakes up seed of herbaceous vegetation and insects by simultaneously scratching with both feet. While foraging, it stays well hidden in the dense cover of brush or riparian thickets. Nests are usually placed on or near the ground at the base of a shrub or in an otherwise concealed place. During the breeding season, males commonly sing from more exposed areas, such as branches of small pinyons, junipers, or Mountain Mahogany. Although this species is difficult to see except when singing, it will readily announce its presence by a buzzy trill, which is subordinated in this region by one or more harsh introductory notes. *References:* Kroodsma (1971), Davis (1960).

Chipping Sparrow, *Spizella passerina.*   (Fig. 11.52) Male length 5 1/4 in (13 cm), female length 5 in (12.5 cm); male weight 1/2 oz (12.6 g), female weight 2/5 oz (12.1

FIGURE 11.51   Rufous-sided Towhee.

FIGURE 11.52   Chipping Sparrow.

g). Very common summer resident in the White-Inyo Range, from 7,200 to 10,400 ft (2,200 to 3,170 m).

This sparrow is very numerous in open woods of pinyon, juniper, and Mountain Mahogany. Territories are defended in areas of scattered trees, open brush, rocks and grass; heavy brush is avoided. Chipping Sparrows search the ground for small seeds and insects but will also take buds in bushes and trees, especially during the spring. The dry, harsh trill of the male is a common summertime song in this area. *References:* Grinnell and Storer (1924), Reynolds and Knapton (1984).

Brewer's Sparrow, *Spizella breweri.* (Fig. 11.53) Male length 5 1/4 in (13 cm), female length 5 in (12.5 cm); male weight 3/8 oz (11 g), female weight 3/8 oz (10.4 g). Very common summer resident in the White-Inyo region, from 6,750 to 10,300 ft (2,060 to 3,140 m).

Although the Brewer's Sparrow nests over an impressively wide elevational range in these mountains, only sagebrush is occupied. Extensive stands, such as those on the alluvial fans below the pinyon zone or those on benches and flats at high elevations, are used most commonly. Small numbers also nest in sagebrush growth in local openings of otherwise narrow canyons. This sparrow compensates for its plain plumage by emitting an elaborate song—a series of buzzes and trills given at different pitches, one of the longest vocalizations of any species in the region. Brewer's Sparrows forage

FIGURE 11.53   Brewer's Sparrow.

on the ground or in bushes for insects and seeds. Nests are well hidden in sagebrush tops. *References:* Reynolds (1981), Weathers (1983).

Black-chinned Sparrow, *Spizella atrogularis.*   (Fig. 11.54) Male length 5 1/4 in (13 cm), female length 5 1/4 in (13 cm); male weight 3/8 oz (10.6 g), female weight 3/8 oz (10.9 g). Rare and local summer resident in the White Mountains; recorded between 6,750 and 7,000 ft (2,060 and 2,130 m).

The Black-chinned Sparrow occurs sparingly in the White Mountains, at the northern edge of the species' distribution, where it lives in a rather distinctive and characteristic habitat. Although sagebrush is usually prevalent where this sparrow breeds in eastern California, it typically requires a diverse mixture of shrubs in addition to the sage, including Rabbitbrush, Bitterbrush, and Mormon Tea. Furthermore, most records of the species are from brushland sites in varied, sloping terrain, often with jumbled rock outcrops and a scattering of pinyon and/or juniper. Males sing from either the tops of these small trees or from the tops of prominent shrubs and usually fly substantial distances between song perches. Thus, territories

FIGURE 11.54   Black-chinned Sparrow.

are large, and pairs are widely spaced. The easiest way to detect this trim, handsome sparrow is through its distinctive song—a rapid trill introduced by three clear, sweet notes and increasing in cadence toward the end. *Reference:* Johnson, Bryant, and Miller (1948).

Vesper Sparrow, *Poocetes gramineus.*   (Fig. 11.55) Male length 6 in (15 cm); female length 5 3/4 in (14.75 cm); male weight 7/8 oz (24.9 g), female weight 4/5 oz (22.7 g). Uncommon summer resident in the White-Inyo Range, from approximately 7,800 to 10,500 ft (2,380 to 3,200 m).

This species occurs in the sagebrush-grassland habitat both below and above the pinyon belt. There only small numbers can be found. Vesper Sparrows are shy birds and commonly remain undetected even when present because of their inconspicuous habits. They forage mostly on the ground, but males usually perch on prominent sage tops when delivering their advertising song. *References:* Kroodsma (1972), Grinnell and Storer (1924).

Black-throated Sparrow, *Amphispiza bilineata.*   (Fig. 11.56) Male length 5 1/4 in (13 cm), female length 5 in (12.5 cm); male weight 1/2 oz (13.5 g), female weight 1/2 oz (13.2 g). Fairly common summer resident in the White-Inyo Range, occurring from the valley bottoms up to approximately 6,800 ft (2,070 m) elevation.

Black-throated Sparrows occur only in brushland on the alluvial fans on both slopes of the mountains. They generally prefer the warmer, drier areas to the south. Consequently, greatest densities are attained in the southern Shadscale zone, with the species becoming relatively scarce on the cooler sagebrush slopes to the north. The sparrows favor areas that are sparingly vegetated and where an exposed hard rock or gravel surface is evident. Seeds taken from the ground between shrubs constitute the primary food. Nests are placed on the ground in a thick cover of brush. During

FIGURE 11.55   Vesper Sparrow.

FIGURE 11.56   Black-throated Sparrow.

the breeding season, these birds can be seen or heard singing from bush tops, and after June, postbreeding family groups filter through the brushland. This strikingly patterned species is often easy to watch and seems tamer than its somewhat plainer relative, the Sage Sparrow. *References:* Heckenlively (1970), Weathers (1983).

Sage Sparrow, *Amphispiza belli.* (Fig. 11.57) Male length 5 3/4 in (14.5 cm), female length 5 1/2 in (14 cm); male weight 3/5 oz (16.5 g), female weight 1/2 oz (14.7 g). Very common summer resident in the White-Inyo Range; occurs from the valley floors to approximately 7,500 ft (2,290 m) elevation. Postbreeding birds occur higher, to 8,500 ft (2,590 m), even in early June.

This species occurs continuously along the west-facing slope from the north end of the White Mountains to the southern portion of the Inyos. Curiously, it is rare or lacking on the east side of the mountains south of Trail Canyon. Flats and alluvial fans between 3,500 and 6,500 ft (1,067 and 1,981 m) support the greatest numbers; very high altitudes are avoided. Like its close relative the Black-throated Sparrow, the Sage Sparrow lives only in brushland, and both species commonly occur side by side in the White-Inyo Range. In the north the Sage Sparrow occupies essentially pure sagebrush, while in the south Shadscale (saltbush) is the predominant habitat. Seeds of annual plants provide the primary food source. This sparrow also uses the tops of

FIGURE 11.57   Sage Sparrow.

bushes for song posts as well as for concealed nest sites. Occasionally, several males can be heard singing from very close range. The tinkling song carries for several hundred yards unless the bird is downwind. Nesting begins in April in the south, so that fully grown juveniles abound in the saltbush scrub by June, when family groups are commonly encountered. Northern populations breed several weeks later. These birds are typically shy and difficult to approach in the open brushland; when pressed, they will fly long distances and may drop to the ground and run among the shadows below well-spaced shrubs. *References:* Moldenhauer and Wiens (1970), Wiens (1982).

Fox Sparrow, *Passerella iliaca.*   (Fig. 11.58) Male length 6 ½ in (16.75 cm), female length 6 ½ in (16.75 cm); male weight 1 oz (29.7 g), female weight 1 oz (28.1 g). Locally common summer resident in the White Mountains, between 6,750 and 9,600 ft (2,060 and 2,930 m) elevation. Known to occur locally in the Inyo Range (Lead Canyon, 9,600 ft [2,930 m]).

Fox Sparrows breed in dense riparian thickets of willows, Water Birch, aspen saplings, and Wild Rose, especially in the deep canyons on the east side of the mountains. This habitat, shared by all Great Basin and Rocky Mountain subspecies, contrasts strikingly with the chaparral used primarily by all forms in the Sierra Nevada. In favorable streamside growth, Fox Sparrow territories are placed in a

FIGURE 11.58   Fox Sparrow.

continuous linear sequence, and two or more males are commonly heard at once. Song perches, from 5 to 15 ft (1.5 to 4.6 m) high, are typically in bush tops, which offer partial concealment by sprays of foliage. This species forages principally on the ground in leaf litter, which is kicked away by vigorous backward strokes of the legs. Insects exposed in this way are fed to the nestlings. *References:* Martin (1977), Martin (1979).

Song Sparrow, *Melospiza melodia.*   (Fig. 11.59). Male length 5 3/4 oz (14.75 cm), female length 5 1/2 in (14.25 cm); male weight 3/4 oz (21.7 g), female weight 3/4 oz (20.4 g). Locally common summer resident in the White Mountains with records up to 9,600 ft (2,930 m); more numerous in Owens Valley to the west of the White-Inyo Range.

The highest elevational record for the form *M. m. fisherella* occurs in Cottonwood Basin in the White Mountains. There, and throughout this generally arid region, the species is restricted to canyon bottoms with thick, low cover near water. Willow and Wild Rose thickets along streams are commonly occupied. Song Sparrows forage near the water's edge or on damp ground below the willows. Males sing from exposed bush tops, usually no more than several feet above the ground. Food consists of insects and seeds taken from the ground. *References:* Nice (1937); Smith, Yom-Tov, and Moses (1982).

FIGURE 11.59   Song Sparrow.

FIGURE 11.60   White-crowned Sparrow.

White-crowned Sparrow, *Zonotrichia leucophrys*.   (Fig. 11.60) Male length 6 1/2 in (16.5 cm), female length 6 in. (15.5 cm); male weight 1 oz (30 g), female weight 9/10 oz (26.1 g). Common summer resident in the White Mountains, between 8,200 and 10,500 ft (2,500 and 3,200 m).

White-crowned Sparrows frequent high-altitude meadows where willow thickets, young or stunted pines, scattered aspen saplings, and wildflowers are clumped on the boggy ground. Because they favor places with running water, the headwaters of mountain streams are a good place to find the species. The adults are sleek and appear clean-cut. During the summer, they forage for insects on the damp ground, never far from cover. Nests are placed either on the ground under willows or other bushes, or a few feet above the ground in willows or small conifers. In the Subalpine Zone of the high Sierra Nevada, the volume of winter and spring snowfall drastically influences both the timing of summer breeding and the amount of space available for nesting. When the snowpack is heavy, fewer birds breed, and these individuals nest two weeks later than during normal years. Populations in the White Mountains presumably respond in a similar fashion. *References:* Morton (1978); Morton, Horstman, and Osborn (1972).

Dark-eyed (Oregon) Junco, *Junco hyemalis*.   (Fig. 11.61) Male length 5 1/2 in (14.25 cm), female length 5 1/2 in (14 cm); male weight 3/5 oz (17 g), female weight 5/8 oz (18.3 g). Common summer resident in the White-Inyo Range, between 7,400 and 10,500 ft (2,260 and 3,200 m).

Gray-headed Junco, *Junco caniceps*.   (Fig. 11.62) Male length 6 in (15.25 cm), female length 6 in (15 cm); male weight 5/8 oz (18.4 g), female weight 5/8 oz (18.8 g). Rare to relatively common summer resident in the White-Inyo Range, between 7,400 and 10,500 ft (2,260 and 3,200 m).

Because these two forms hybridize in the region, some authorities combine them into one species (Dark-eyed Junco, *Junco hyemalis*). However, most individuals encountered in this area appear to be either pure parental types or very close to one species or the other; thus, we prefer to consider them as two full species. Furthermore, studies from several areas where both forms coexist have shown that each kind prefers to pair with a mate of similar appearance, further evidence that two distinct species are involved.

Juncos prefer cool and shady places where grass or forb cover provides a substrate for foraging and nesting. Thus, woodland of large pinyons on north- or east-facing slopes, riparian growth of willows and aspen, shady groves of large Mountain Mahogany, and Subalpine Forest of Bristlecone, Limber, and Lodgepole pines are all used. Openings in these habitats are favored. Most activities are concentrated on or near the ground. There juncos take insects and seeds and commonly conceal their nests under overhanging plants or turf. However, exposed twigs or tree tops at heights ranging from 10 to 50 ft (3 to 15 m) are chosen by males for song posts. The song is a ringing, musical trill. Juncos give their distinctive popping note when an intruder is

FIGURE 11.61 Dark-eyed (Oregon) Junco.

FIGURE 11.62 Gray-headed Junco.

near the nest, especially after the eggs have hatched. *References:* Balph (1977), Hadley (1969), A. Miller (1941).

ICTERINAE (Blackbirds, Orioles, and Allies)

Brewer's Blackbird, *Euphagus cyanocephalus*.   (Plate 11.1) Male length 9 1/4 in (23.5 cm), female length 8 1/4 in (21 cm); male weight 2 5/8 oz (76 g), female weight 2 1/10 oz (59 g). Common summer visitant and local summer resident in the White-Inyo mountain region; recorded up to 9,500 ft (2,900 m) elevation.

This blackbird is a common resident in the vicinity of towns, ranches, and other centers of human activity. It nests in parks, hedgerows, windbreaks of ornamental trees, and riparian growth. In the White Mountains, the Brewer's Blackbird is most likely to be seen as a visitant near meadows and along streams. Wandering individuals may turn up in any kind of habitat and terrain, even at high elevations. *References:* La Rivers (1944), Williams (1952).

Brown-headed Cowbird, *Molothrus ater*.   (Plate 11.1) Male length 6 3/4 in (17 cm), female length 6 1/4 in (15.75 cm); male weight 1 1/2 oz (41 g), female weight 1 3/10 oz (37 g). Fairly common summer resident in the White-Inyo Range; recorded from the lowland valleys up to 11,600 ft (3,540 m) elevation.

Being nest parasites with no fixed breeding territory, Brown-headed Cowbirds are most commonly seen on the move. The males wander widely when advertising for mates, stopping for several minutes in a treetop or on a power pole to display before departing. This display consists of a gurgling call uttered while the chest is expanded and the tail is spread. A similar liquid note given in flight usually announces the presence of this species. The Brown-headed Cowbird is typically recorded overhead in areas of Pinyon-juniper Woodland, riparian willows, and tall sagebrush. Streamside habitats are especially frequented; thus, the small birds of these environments suffer most from cowbird parasitism. Wandering birds commonly mingle with blackbirds around agricultural areas and pack stations, where they forage on the ground for insects, seeds, grass leaves, and gravel. They feed near piles of manure, prying it forward with their bills to uncover food items. Cowbirds drink water daily in arid regions. *References:* Scott and Ankney (1983), Verner and Ritter (1983).

Scott's Oriole, *Icterus parisorum*.   (Fig. 11.63) Male length 7 1/2 in (19 cm), female length 7 1/4 in (18.5 cm); male weight 1 3/8 oz (38 g), female weight 1 1/2 oz (41 g). Summer resident in the White-Inyo Range; rare in the north, uncommon in the south.

This species occupies arid woodlands of pinyon, juniper, and, in the northern Mojave Desert, Joshua Tree. Because of their huge territories, the population densities of Scott's Orioles in the region are low. Males announce their positions with a far-reaching song of great beauty—rich, clear whistles reminiscent of the Western Meadowlark. Insect food is taken from the foliage of pinyon or yucca. Nests of these

FIGURE 11.63   Scott's Oriole.

northern populations are commonly built in pinyons; more southerly populations nest in Joshua trees. *References:* Marshall (1957), Weathers (1983).

FRINGILLIDAE (Finches and Allies)

Rosy Finch, *Leucosticte arctoa.* (Fig. 11.64) Male length 6 in (15.5 cm), female length 6 in (15 cm); male weight $9/10$ oz (26 g), female weight $7/8$ oz (25 g). Fairly common summer resident in the White Mountains, from above timberline to the summit, at 14,246 ft (4,340 m) elevation. The species does not nest in the Inyo Mountains, where breeding habitat is lacking.

The Rosy Finch is the only species of bird strictly confined to the Alpine Zone in these mountains during the summer. These birds prefer to feed at the edges of snowfields and cirques, and in alpine rocklands or other areas with much exposed bare ground. Seeds and insects, even those frozen in snow, are taken. Strong fliers, Rosy Finches are highly mobile and forage over wide reaches of the Alpine Zone. Nests are placed in damp cracks below cliffs or in rock piles. In winter, flocks have been encountered in the pinyon-sagebrush zone near old mines. There they roost for the

FIGURE 11.64   Gray-crowned Rosy Finch.

night in protected niches in the walls of abandoned vertical shafts. *References:* Grinnell and Storer (1924), Johnson (1965).

Cassin's Finch, *Carpodacus cassinii*.   (Fig. 11.65) Male length 5 3/4 in (14.75 cm), female length 5 3/4 in (14.5 cm); male weight 1 oz (27.3 g), female weight 1 oz (26.6 g). Common summer resident in the White-Inyo Range, between 6,750 and 10,500 ft (2,060 and 3,200 m).

In the White and Inyo mountains, Cassin's Finches have been recorded most commonly in the aspen-willow association and in both Bristlecone and Lodgepole pines. They prefer open forest growth in cool, dry places. Locally, they may nest in cool portions of the pinyon zone, particularly where trees are large and mixed with Mountain Mahogany. This finch takes seeds from the ground and nips buds of aspen and conifers. Females of all ages and males up to approximately 14 months old are similar in appearance, with a streaked gray and brown plumage. Older males contrast strikingly, with their vivid hues of pinkish and rose-red. Studies in other areas have shown that the population size of Cassin's Finches fluctuates annually, presumably in response to the abundance of tree buds. Furthermore, males usually outnumber females. Like most true finches, this species demonstrates no real territorial system. Instead, the male defends the space around his mate wherever she goes rather than the area of the nest site. *References:* Mewaldt and King (1985), Samson (1976).

House Finch, *Carpodacus mexicanus*.   (Fig. 11.66) Male length 5 1/4 in (13.25 cm), female length 5 in (13 cm); male weight 5/8 oz (18.4 g), female weight 5/8 oz

FIGURE 11.65   Cassin's Finch.

FIGURE 11.66   House Finch.

(19 g). Uncommon and local summer resident in the White-Inyo Range; occurs from the lowlands to 9,000 ft (2,740 m) elevation.

Although this species is common around lowland ranches and urban plantings, it is sparse in the mountains proper. Most records are from the pinyon-juniper belt. Springs are especially favored because they can fulfill the species' daily water requirements. Desert cactus fruits, when available, also provide some moisture. House Finches feed on a variety of seeds and small fruits. Nests are commonly placed in steep canyon walls or bluffs. Because they prefer warm and sunny environments, there is minimal overlap in the region between this species and its congener, the Cassin's Finch. *References:* Thompson (1960), Weathers (1983).

Red Crossbill, *Loxia curvirostra.*   (Fig. 11.67) Male length 5 3/4 in (14.75 cm), female length 5 3/4 in (14.5 cm); male weight 1 1/8 oz (33 g), female weight 1 1/5 oz (34 g). Irregular permanent resident in the White-Inyo Range; recorded from 6,750 to 10,500 ft (2,060 to 3,200 m). Numbers fluctuate annually; usually the species is either uncommon or relatively common.

This erratic species has been recorded uncommonly from the ranges, where its presence and numbers depend on conifer seed production, which also varies annually.

FIGURE 11.67   Red Crossbill.

Trees producing requisite seeds include Singleleaf Pinyon, Limber Pine, Bristlecone Pine, and Lodgepole Pine. Lodgepole Pine, an important food source for crossbills in the Sierra Nevada and the Cascade Mountains, is presumably of slight importance in the White-Inyo Range because of its very local occurrence there. This finch is usually first detected overhead by its *kip-kip* or *jip-jip* call notes. With good fortune, one may encounter a feeding group in a conifer top. The birds quietly work over terminal cones but then burst away without notice in a flurry of call notes. Breeding may occur in any season if seeds are abundant. In the White Mountains, family groups were recorded in the pinyon zone in early June. By the third week of June, these groups had coalesced into larger flocks. *References:* Beedy and Granholm (1985), Grinnell and Storer (1924).

REFERENCES

American Ornithologists' Union. 1983. *Check-list of North American birds*, 6th ed. Allen Press, Lawrence, Kansas.

Anderson, Stanley H. 1976. Comparative food habits of Oregon Nuthatches. *Northwest Science* 50:213–221.

Armstrong, Joseph T. 1965. Breeding home range in the nighthawk and other birds; its evolutionary and ecological significance. *Ecology* 46:619–629.

Balda, Russell P., and Gary C. Bateman. 1973. The breeding biology of the Pinyon Jay. *Living Bird* 11:5–42.

Balgooyen, Thomas G. 1976. Behavior and ecology of the American Kestrel (*Falco sparverius* L.) in the Sierra Nevada of California. *University of California Publications in Zoology* 103:1–83.

Balph, Martha H. 1977. Winter social behavior of Dark-eyed Juncos: Communication, social organization, and ecological implications. *Animal Behaviour* 25:859–884.

Beedy, Edward C., and Stephen L. Granholm. 1985. *Discovering Sierra birds*. Yosemite Natural History Association and Sequoia Natural History Association.

Behle, William H. 1942. Distribution and variation of the Horned Larks (*Otocoris alpestris*) of western North America. *University of California Publications in Zoology* 46:205–316.

Bent, Arthur C. 1968. *Life histories of North American cardinals, grosbeaks, buntings, towhees, finches, sparrows, and allies*. U.S. National Museum Bulletin 237, Smithsonian Institution, Washington, D.C.

Biermann, Gloria C., and Spencer G. Sealy. 1982. Parental feeding of nestling Yellow Warblers in relation to brood size and prey availability. *Auk* 99:332–341.

Brown, Jerram L. 1964. The integration of agonistic behavior in the Steller's Jay, *Cyanocitta stelleri* (Gmelin). *University of California Publications in Zoology* 60:223–328.

Brown, Leslie, and Dean Amadon. 1968. *Eagles, hawks, and falcons of the world*. 2 vols. McGraw-Hill, New York.

Burton, John A. (ed.). 1973. *Owls of the world*. E. P. Dutton Inc., New York.

Caccamise, Donald. 1974. Competitive relationships of the Common and Lesser Nighthawks. *Condor* 76:1–20.

Cade, Thomas J. 1982. *Falcons of the world*. Cornell University Press, Ithaca, N.Y.

Christensen, Glen C. 1954. *The Chukar Partridge in Nevada*. Nevada Fish and Game Commission Biological Bulletin no. 1, State Printing Office, Carson City, Nevada.

Davis, Cheyleen M. 1979. A nesting study of the Brown Creeper. *Living Bird* 17:237–263.

Davis, Deborah. 1979. Morning and evening roosts of Turkey Vultures at Malheur Refuge, Oregon. *Western Birds* 10:125–130.

Davis, John. 1960. Nesting behavior of the Rufous-sided Towhee in coastal California. *Condor* 62:434–456.

Dilger, William C. 1956. Hostile behavior and reproductive isolating mechanisms in the avian genera *Catharus* and *Hylccichla*. *Auk* 73:313–353.

Dixon, Keith L. 1949. Behavior of the Plain Titmouse. *Condor* 51:110–136.

Dixon, Keith L. 1965. Dominance-subordination relationships in Mountain Chickadees. *Condor* 67:291–299.

Earhart, Caroline M., and Ned K. Johnson. 1970. Size dimorphism and food habits of North American owls. *Condor* 72:251–264.

Emlen, Stephen T., James D. Rising, and William L. Thompson. 1975. A behavioral and morphological study of sympatry in the Indigo and Lazuli Buntings of the Great Plains. *Wilson Bulletin* 87:145–179.

Ervin, Stephen. 1977. Flock size, composition, and behavior in a population of Bushtits. *Bird-Banding* 48:97–109.

Fitch, Henry S. 1947. Predation by owls in the Sierran foothills of California. *Condor* 49:137–151.

Fitch, Henry S., Freeman Swenson, and Daniel F. Tillotson. 1946. Behavior and food habits of the Red-tailed Hawk. *Condor* 48:205–237.

Franzreb, Kathleen E. 1984. Foraging habits of Ruby-crowned and Golden-crowned Kinglets in an Arizona montane forest. *Condor* 86:139–145.

Garrett, Kimball, and Jon Dunn. 1981. *The birds of southern California*. Los Angeles Audubon Society, Los Angeles.

Goodwin, Derek. 1976. *Crows of the world*. Cornell University Press, Ithaca, N.Y.

Grinnell, Joseph, and Alden H. Miller. 1944. *The distribution of the birds of California*. Pacific Coast Avifauna no. 27, Cooper Ornithological Club, Berkeley, California.

Grinnell, Joseph, and Tracy I. Storer. 1924. *Animal life in the Yosemite*. University of California Press, Berkeley.

Griscom, Ludlow, and Alexander Sprunt, Jr. 1957. *The warblers of America*. Devin-Adair, New York.

Gutiérrez, Ralph J. 1980. Comparative ecology of the Mountain and California Quail in the Carmel Valley, California. *Living Bird* 18:71–93.

Hadley, N. F. 1969. Breeding biology of the Gray-headed Junco, *Junco caniceps* (Woodhouse) in the Colorado Front Range. *Colorado Field Ornithologist* 5:15–21.

Heckenlively, Donald B. 1970. Song in a population of Black-throated Sparrows. *Condor* 72:24–36.

Howell, J. C. 1942. Notes on the nesting habits of the American Robin. *American Midland Naturalist* 28:529–603.

Hubbard, John P. 1969. The relationships and evolution of the *Dendroica coronata* complex. *Auk* 86:393–432.

Hutto, Richard L. 1981. Seasonal variation in the foraging behavior of some migratory western wood warblers. *Auk* 93:765–777.

Jaeger, Edmund C. 1948. Does the Poor-will "hibernate"? *Condor* 50:45–46.

James, Frances C., and Hank H. Shugart, Jr. 1974. The phenology of the nesting season of the American Robin (*Turdus migratorius*) in the United States. *Condor* 76:159–168.

James, Ross D. 1981. Factors affecting variation in the primary song of North American Solitary Vireos (Aves: Vireonidae). *Canadian Journal of Zoology* 59:2001–2009.

Johnsgard, Paul A. 1973. *Grouse and quails of North America*. University of Nebraska Press, Lincoln.

Johnsgard, Paul A. 1975. *North American game birds of upland and shoreline.* University of Nebraska Press, Lincoln.

Johnsgard, Paul A. 1983. *The hummingbirds of North America.* Smithsonian Institution Press, Washington, D.C.

Johnson, David H., Monroe D. Bryant, and Alden H. Miller. 1948. Vertebrate animals of the Providence Mountains area of California. *University of California Publications in Zoology* 48:221–376.

Johnson, Ned K. 1963. Biosystematics of sibling species of flycatchers in the *Empidonax hammondii-oberholseri-wrightii* complex. *University of California Publications in Zoology* 66:79–238.

Johnson, Ned K. 1966. Bill size and the question of competition in allopatric and sympatric populations of Dusky and Gray Flycatchers. *Systematic Zoology* 15:70–87.

Johnson, Ned K. 1976. Breeding distribution of Nashville and Virginia's Warblers. *Auk* 93:219–230.

Johnson, Ned K., and Carla Cicero. 1986. Richness and distribution of montane avifaunas in the White-Inyo region, California. *In* C. A. Hall, Jr. and D. J. Young (eds.). *Natural history of the White-Inyo Range, eastern California and western Nevada, and high altitude physiology,* pp. 137–159. University of California White Mountain Research Station Symposium, August 23–25, 1985, Bishop, Calif., vol. 1.

Johnson, Ned K., and Carla B. Johnson. 1985. Speciation in sapsuckers (*Sphyrapicus*): II. Sympatry, hybridization, and mate preference in *S. ruber daggetti* and *S. nuchalis. Auk* 102:1–15.

Johnson, Richard E. 1965. Reproductive activities of Rosy Finches, with special reference to Montana. *Auk* 82:190–205.

Kendeigh, S. Charles. 1941. *Territorial and mating behavior of the House Wren.* Illinois Biological Monograph no. 18, University of Illinois Press, Urbana.

Kilham, Lawrence. 1972. Reproductive behavior of White-breasted Nuthatches. II. Courtship. *Auk* 89:115–129.

Kilham, Lawrence. 1973. Reproductive behavior of the Red-breasted Nuthatch. I. Courtship. *Auk* 90:597–609.

Kroodsma, Donald E. 1971. Song variations and singing behavior in the Rufous-sided Towhee, *Pipilo erythrophthalmus oregonus. Condor* 73:303–308.

Kroodsma, Donald E. 1972. Variations in songs of Vesper Sparrows in Oregon. *Wilson Bulletin* 84:173–178.

Kroodsma, Donald E. 1975. Song patterning in the Rock Wren. *Condor* 77:294–303.

La Rivers, Ira. 1944. Observations on the nesting mortality of the Brewer Blackbird, *Euphagus cyanocephalus. American Midland Naturalist* 32:417–437.

Leopold, A. Starker. 1977. *The California Quail.* University of California Press, Berkeley.

Marshall, Joe T., Jr. 1957. *Birds of Pine-oak Woodland in southern Arizona and adjacent Mexico.* Pacific Coast Avifauna no. 32, Cooper Ornithological Society, Berkeley, California.

Marti, Carl D. 1976. A review of prey selection by the Long-eared Owl. *Condor* 78:331–336.

Martin, Dennis J. 1977. Songs of the Fox Sparrow. I. Structure of song and its comparison with song in other Emberizidae. *Condor* 79:209–221.

Martin, Dennis J. 1979. Songs of the Fox Sparrow. II. Intra- and interpopulation variation. *Condor* 81:173–184.

McEllin, Shaun M. 1979. Nest sites and population demographics of White-breasted and Pygmy Nuthatches in Colorado. *Condor* 81:348–352.

Mengel, Robert M. 1964. The probable history of species formation in some northern wood warblers (Parulidae). *Living Bird* 3:9–43.

Mewaldt, L. Richard, and James R. King. 1985. Breeding site faithfulness, reproductive biology, and adult survivorship in an isolated population of Cassin's Finches. *Condor* 87:494–510.

Miller, Alden H. in 1941. Speciation in the avian genus *Junco*. *University of California Publications in Zoology* 44:173–434.

Miller, Alden H. 1951. An analysis of the distribution of the birds of California. *University of California Publications in Zoology* 50:531–644.

Miller, Alden H., and Robert C. Stebbins. 1964. *The lives of desert animals in Joshua Tree National Monument*. University of California Press, Berkeley.

Miller, Edwin V. 1941. Behavior of the Bewick Wren. *Condor* 43:81–99.

Moldenhauer, Ralph R., and John A. Wiens. 1970. The water economy of the Sage Sparrow, *Amphispiza belli nevadensis. Condor* 72:265–275.

Morrison, Michael L. 1981. The structure of western warbler assemblages: Analysis of foraging behavior and habitat selection in Oregon. *Auk* 98:578–588.

Morrison, Michael L. 1982. The structure of western warbler assemblages: Ecomorphological analysis of the Black-throated Gray and Hermit Warblers. *Auk* 99:503–513.

Morse, Douglass H. 1971. Effects of the arrival of a new species upon habitat utilization by two forest thrushes in Maine. *Wilson Bulletin* 83:57–65.

Morse, Pamela J. 1979. Pairing and courtship in the North American dipper. *Bird-Banding* 50:62–65.

Morton, Martin L. 1978. Snow conditions and the onset of breeding in the Mountain White-crowned Sparrow. *Condor* 80:285–289.

Morton, Martin L., Judith L. Horstman, and Janet M. Osborn. 1972. Reproductive cycle and nesting success of the Mountain White-crowned Sparrow (*Zonotrichia leucophrys oriantha*) in the central Sierra Nevada. *Condor* 74:152–163.

Nice, Margaret M. 1937 (reprinted 1964). *Studies in the life history of the Song Sparrow*. 2 vols. Dover, New York.

Norris, Robert A. 1958. Comparative biosystematics and life history of the nuthatches *Sitta pygmaea* and *Sitta pusilla. University of California Publications in Zoology* 56:119–300.

Olendorff, Richard R. 1975. *Golden Eagle Country*. Knopf, New York.

Petrides, George A. 1938. A life history of the Yellow-breasted Chat. *Wilson Bulletin* 50:184–189.

Power, Harry W. 1966. Biology of the Mountain Bluebird in Montana. *Condor* 68:351–371.

Power, Harry W. 1980. *The foraging behavior of Mountain Bluebirds with emphasis on sexual foraging differences*. Ornithological Monographs no. 28, American Ornithologists' Union, Washington, D.C.

Price, Frank E., and Carl E. Bock. 1983. *Population ecology of the Dipper* (Cinclus mexicanus) *in the Front Range of Colorado*. Studies in Avian Biology no. 7, Allen Press, Lawrence, Kansas.

Rea, Amadeo M. 1983. *Once a river*. University of Arizona Press, Tucson.

Reynolds, John D., and Richard W. Knapton. 1984. Nest site selection and breeding biology of the Chipping Sparrow. *Wilson Bulletin* 96:488–493.

Reynolds, Richard T., and E. Charles Meslow. 1984. Partitioning of food and niche characteristics of coexisting *Accipiter* during breeding. *Auk* 101:761–779.

Reynolds, Timothy D. 1981. Nesting of the Sage Thrasher, Sage Sparrow, and Brewer's Sparrow in southeastern Idaho. *Condor* 83:61–64.

Reynolds, Timothy D., and Terrell D. Rich. 1978. Reproductive ecology of the Sage Thrasher (*Oreoscoptes montanus*) on the Snake River Plain in south-central Idaho. *Auk* 95:580–582.

Ritter, Lyman V. 1983. Nesting ecology of Scrub Jays in Chico, California. *Western Birds* 14:147–158.

Root, Richard B. 1967. The niche exploitation pattern of the Blue-gray Gnatcatcher. *Ecological Monographs* 37:317–350.

Root, Richard B. 1969. The behavior and reproductive success of the Blue-gray Gnatcatcher. *Condor* 71:16–31.

Salomonson, Michael G., and Russell P. Balda. 1977. Winter territoriality of Townsend's Solitaires (*Myadestes townsendi*) in a Pinyon-Juniper-Ponderosa Pine ecotone. *Condor* 79:148–161.

Samson, Fred B. 1976. Territory, breeding density, and fall departure in Cassin's Finch. *Auk* 93:477–497.

Scott, David M., and C. Davison Ankney. 1983. The laying cycle of Brown-headed Cowbirds: Passerine chickens? *Auk* 100:583–592.

Shedd, Douglas H. 1982. Seasonal variation and function of mobbing and related antipredator behaviors of the American Robin (*Turdus migratorius*). *Auk* 99:342–346.

Short, Lester L. 1965. Hybridization in the flickers (*Colaptes*) of North America. *Bulletin of the American Museum of Natural History* 129:307–428.

Short, Lester L. 1971. Systematics and behavior of some North American woodpeckers, genus *Picoides* (Aves). *Bulletin of the American Museum of Natural History* 145:1–118.

Short, Lester L. 1982. *Woodpeckers of the world*. Monographs, Delaware Museum of Natural History, Greenville.

Smith, James N. M., Yoram Yom-Tov, and Richard Moses. 1982. Polygyny, male parental care, and sex ratio in Song Sparrows: An experimental study. *Auk* 99:555–564.

Snyder, Noel F. R., and James W. Wiley. 1976. *Sexual size dimorphism in hawks and owls of North America*. Ornithological Monographs no. 20, American Ornithologists' Union, Washington, D.C.

Thompson, Charles F. 1977. Experimental removal and replacement of territorial male Yellow-breasted Chats. *Auk* 94:107–113.

Thompson, William L. 1960. Agonistic behavior in the House Finch. Part II: Factors in aggressiveness and sociality. *Condor* 62:378–402.

Thompson, William L. 1976. Vocalizations of the Lazuli Bunting. *Condor* 78:195–207.

Tomback, Diana F. 1978a. Foraging strategies of Clark's Nutcracker. *Living Bird* 16:123–161.

Tomback, Diana F. 1978b. Pre-roosting flight of the Clark's Nutcracker. *Auk* 95:554–562.

Verbeek, Nicolaas A. M. 1967. Breeding biology and ecology of the Horned Lark in alpine tundra. *Wilson Bulletin* 79:208–218.

Verner, Jared, and Lyman V. Ritter. 1983. Current status of the Brown-headed Cowbird in the Sierra National Forest. *Auk* 100:355–368.

Walsberg, Glenn E. 1981. Nest-site selection and the radiative environment of the Warbling Vireo. *Condor* 83:86–88.

Weathers, Wesley W. 1983. *Birds of Southern California's Deep Canyon*. University of California Press, Berkeley.

Weston, Henry G., Jr. 1947. Breeding behavior of the Black-headed Grosbeak. *Condor* 49:54–73.

Wiens, John A. 1982. Song pattern variation in the Sage Sparrow (*Amphispiza belli*): Dialects or epiphenomena? *Auk* 99:208–229.

Wiley, R. Haven. 1973. Territoriality and non-random mating in Sage Grouse, *Centrocercus urophasianus*. *Animal Behaviour Monographs* 6:87–169.

Williams, Laidlaw. 1952. Breeding behavior of the Brewer Blackbird. *Condor* 54:3–47.

12

Mammals

Hannah V. Carey and John D. Wehausen

Approximately 60 species of mammals occur in the White Mountains. The diversity of mammalian species in this mountain range is low compared with lower-elevation areas in the temperate zone. This paucity of species reflects the island-like conditions characteristic of montane regions. The dry valleys on either side of the range present major barriers to colonization for many species, particularly those adapted to high-elevation habitats.

The distinguishing feature of this group of vertebrates is the presence of mammary tissue in females, which provides milk to help the young grow quickly. High metabolic rates enable mammals to maintain high and relatively invariant body temperatures. This allows them to inhabit a wide range of environmental conditions but is costly in terms of energy requirements. Such energy requirements are difficult or impossible to meet at higher elevations during the cold season. Mammals inhabiting these elevations in the White Mountains have evolved a variety of solutions to this problem. Some abandon their high body temperatures by hibernating (e.g., marmots and ground squirrels), thus regulating body temperature at a lower setpoint. Some subsist entirely on stored food through the winter, such as the Pika, or use it as a supplement to what they obtain through foraging in winter, as is the case with some mice. Some, such as deer and Mountain Sheep, migrate to lower elevations. Others simply endure the harsh conditions by subsisting on the limited available food. Such species include the White-tailed Hare, which feeds mostly where wind or sun has cleared snow, and shrews and mice, which can forage beneath the snow.

INSECTIVORES (Order Insectivora)

Shrews, *Sorex*.   Although shrews are active both day and night and are relatively abundant in some areas, they are rarely seen. Their high metabolic rate and small size require continual foraging, especially in cold weather, when body temperature is more difficult to maintain. Their diet includes insects, snails, earthworms, and spiders. Owls and Stellar Jays are known to feed on shrews, but many predators appear to avoid them. The White Mountains are home to three species of shrews.

Water Shrew, *S. palustris*.   (Fig. 12.1) Head and body about 3.3 in (8.4 cm), tail 2.5–3 in (6.3–7.6 cm); black, frosted with gray-tipped hairs dorsally, underparts whitish and tinged with brown; tail bicolored, 70–105% of total body length; hind feet with a conspicuous fringe of hairs along the sides and toes. Water Shrews live near edges of clear, cold streams up to 11,600 ft (3,540 m). The stiff, thick hairs

FIGURE 12.1   Water Shrew.

on the hind feet are effectively used as paddles to propel this relatively large shrew through rushing streams. Thick body fur helps protect this shrew from icy waters as it swims below the surface in search of tadpoles, minnows, and aquatic insects.

Merriam Shrew, S. merriami.   Head and body 2.2–2.5 in (5.7–6.3 cm); tail 1.5 in (3.8cm); upper parts light brownish grey, underparts white. The Merriam Shrew has been reported up to 9,500 ft (2,896 m) in the Pinyon-juniper Woodland and in Cottonwood Creek basin. This is the only species of *Sorex* to occur regularly in arid habitats, far from streams or meadows.

Inyo Shrew, S. tennellus.   Body length 2.4 in (6.1 cm), tail about 1.6 in (4 cm); upper surface dark gray, underparts pale, smoky gray. This shrew occurs along streams up to 9,500 ft (2,896 m).

BATS (Order Chiroptera)

Bats are the only mammals capable of true flight. This is accomplished by modification of the long bones of the arm and hand into a wing. Also, the hind limbs are rotated such that the knee joint bends backward instead of forward. The small eyes of the bat contribute little to visual orientation; rather, bats have well-developed ears that allow them to use echolocation for orientation as well as for hunting insects in flight. All species of bats that occur in the White Mountains are insectivorous. Two survival mechanisms are exhibited by bats during the winter, when insects are absent. Some species migrate to more favorable regions, returning months later to their summer ranges. Other species hibernate during the winter to minimize energy expenditure when food is scarce. The following bat species are known from records to occur in the White Mountains: Long-eared Myotis *(Myotis evotis)*, Hairy-winged Myotis *(Myotis volans)*, Small-footed Myotis *(Myotis subulatus)*, Western Pipistrelle *(Pipistrellus hesperus)*, and Big Brown Bat *(Eptesicus fuscus)*. Species that are likely to occur at least seasonally in the White Mountains include: Little Brown Myotis *(Myotis lucifugus)* (Fig. 12.2), Yuma Myotis *(Myotis yumanensis)*, Fringed Myotis *(Myotis thysanoides)*, California Myotis *(Myotis californicus)*, Leib's Myotis *(Myotis Leibii)*, Hoary

FIGURE 12.2   Bat: Little Brown Myotis.

Bat *(Lasiurus cinereus)*, Silvery-haired Bat *(Lasionycteris noctivagans)*, Pallid Bat *(Antrozous pallidus)*, Brazilian Free-tailed Bat *(Tadarida brasiliensis)*, and Western Big-eared Bat *(Plecotus townsendii)*.

PIKAS, RABBITS, AND HARES (Order Lagomorpha)

Pika, *Ochotona princeps.*   (Fig. 12.3) Body length 6.2–8.5 in (15.8–21.6 cm); no visible tail; ears round, much shorter than head, with white edges; fur grayish buff to dark brown. Pikas range from about 8,200 ft (2,500 m) to White Mountain Peak summit, at 14,246 ft (4,340 m), but are most common in the upper elevations above timberline. Like the Yellow-bellied Marmot, they prefer to live on talus slopes bordering alpine meadows, where they forage on grasses and forbs. Pikas may be seen carrying food in their mouths from feeding areas to their burrows among the talus; there they stack the food into "haypiles" for subsistence during the winter. Pikas and their relatives, rabbits and hares, are active year-round. Pikas can be located by listening for their distinctive *eenk-eenk* call. Pika calls may signal approaching predators or represent territorial and mating displays. An annual molt produces a mottled coloration of the fur. Pikas are eaten by weasels, hawks, falcons, Coyotes,

FIGURE 12.3   Pika carrying vegetation for haypiles.

and other predators. Litter size ranges from one to five, and young are born naked with eyes closed in May or June.

Black-tailed Hare, *Lepus californicus.*   (Fig. 12.4) Head and body 18–25 in (46–63 cm), tail 2–4.4 in (5.0–11.2 cm); ears 3.9–5.7 in (10–14.5 cm); weight 3–7 lb (1.4–3.2 kg); upper surface gray, nearly white beneath; ears with blackish tips; upper side of tail black, running up onto rump, buff gray below. The Black-tailed Hare, also known as the Black-tailed Jackrabbit, ranges from the floor of Owens Valley to about 12,500 ft (3,811 m) but is most common in open, brushy vegetation below

FIGURE 12.4   Black-tailed Hare.

the Pinyon-juniper Woodland. Black-tailed Hares eat a variety of herbs and shrubs and have wide habitat preferences. Predators include Coyotes, eagles, hawks, owls, and snakes. An annual molt takes place in late summer or early fall. The new coat is dark grayish brown and thick; with time the fur lightens and becomes thinner, which aids in heat dissipation in hot weather. Black-tailed Hares can be distinguished from White-tailed Hares in areas where they co-occur by their smaller size and the brownish underside of the tail (the tail of the White-tailed Hare is white). As many as seven young can be born to a litter.

White-tailed Hare, *Lepus townsendii*. (Fig. 12.5) Head and body 22–26 in (56–65 cm), tail 2.6–4.3 in (6.6–10.9 cm); ears 3.7–4.8 in (9.5–12.2 cm); weight 5–10 lb (2.3–4.5 kg); grayish brown in summer, white in winter; tail white. White-tailed Hares (or Jackrabbits) range from about 10,000 ft (3,050 m) up to the summit of White Mountain Peak (14,246 ft, 4,340 m). They are common among sagebrush in open areas and feed on grasses and shrubs. This hare undergoes two annual molts, turning white in winter. This most likely aids in making it less conspicuous to its predators, which include Coyotes, Bobcats, owls, and eagles. One may approach a White-tailed Hare quite easily during the summer months without being aware of it, for its gray-brown coat blends in well with the surrounding rocks and shrubs of the Alpine Zone. As with all hares, the young are born fully furred with the eyes open. Litters can contain eight young and are produced once per year.

Nuttall Cottontail, *Sylvilagus nuttalli*. (Fig. 12.6) Head and body 13.8–15.4 in (35–39 cm), tail 1.6–2 in (4–5 cm); ears 2.1–2.5 in (5.4–6.4 cm); weight 1.2–1.8 lb (0.5–0.8 kg); grayish brown above, white below; tail hairs white to roots; feet densely covered with long hairs. Also known as the Mountain Cottontail, this rabbit frequents the dense cover of brush in the Pinyon-juniper Woodland and in Sagebrush Scrub. It occurs up to 11,000 ft (3,354 m) and feeds on currants, willows, junipers, sagebrush, and grasses. Predators include Bobcats, hawks, owls, and Coyotes. In

FIGURE 12.5 White-tailed Hare.

FIGURE 12.6 Nuttall Cottontail.

contrast to the hares, the young of rabbits are born naked with the eyes closed. Litter size is about eight.

RODENTS (Order Rodentia)

Marmots, Ground Squirrels, and Chipmunks (Family Sciuridae)

Yellow-bellied Marmot, *Marmota flaviventris.*   (Fig. 12.7) Head and body 14–19 in (36–48 cm); tail 4.5–9 in (11–23 cm); weight 5–10 lb (2.3–4.6 kg); upper surface yellowish brown with white-tipped hairs, underside yellow; white band below eyes. Marmots occur from 9,000 ft (2,744 m) to 13,500 ft (4,115 m) elevation. They inhabit rocky terrain near vegetated areas, preferably alpine meadows bordering talus slopes. White Mountain marmots hibernate from September to late April. During the active season they forage on grasses, sedges, and forbs, storing body fat for overwinter sustenance. When not feeding, marmots usually bask in the sun on rocks, which also serve as refuges from predators. Sharp alarm whistles are given when a predator, such as a Coyote or Golden Eagle, is suspected to be nearby. Yellow-bellied Marmots live in colonies of related adult females and their young. Juveniles are born in early June and first emerge aboveground in early July. Litter size averages five to six.

Golden-mantled Ground Squirrel, *Spermophilus lateralis.*   (Fig. 12.8) Head and body 6–8 in (15–20 cm), tail 2.5–4.8 in (6–12 cm); head and shoulders golden; one white stripe bordered by two long black stripes on each side of back. Golden-

FIGURE 12.7   Yellow-bellied Marmot.

FIGURE 12.8   Golden-mantled Ground
Squirrel.

mantled Ground Squirrels occur from about 7,000 ft (2,130 m) to 14,000 ft (4,270 m) in most habitats within this range. Their diet consists primarily of seeds, nuts, and fruits. In winter these hibernators subsist on body fat stored during the summer months, and may also eat food cached in their burrows during periodic arousals. Hawks, eagles, Coyotes, and weasels are their main predators. Young appear above-ground in July; litter size is two to six.

Antelope Ground Squirrel, *Ammospermophilus leucurus*.   (Fig. 12.9) Head and body 5.5–6.5 in (14–16.5 cm), tail 2–3 in (5–7.6 cm); grayish brown with one stripe on each side and no dark stripes; tail usually held closely over the back while running, exposing white underside. This fast-moving desert ground squirrel occurs from the floor of Owens Valley to 8,300 ft (2,530 m) in the White Mountains. Whereas most other rodents that live in such hot and arid environments are nocturnal, the Antelope Ground Squirrel is day-active and avoids overheating by allowing its body temperature to rise up to 109°F (43°C)—higher than that of any other nonsweating mammal. Once it reaches this high body temperature, the Antelope Ground Squirrel cools itself by going into an underground burrow, where it dissipates the excess body heat. Highly efficient kidneys and evaporative cooling by fur licking also help this rodent maintain body temperature and water balance in a hot environment. Its diet consists mainly of seeds and fruits, but some animal matter is also eaten. Litter size is six to eight.

FIGURE 12.9   Antelope Ground Squirrel.

Chipmunks, *Eutamias*.   The chipmunk has alternate dark and light stripes on the body that extend to the head, in contrast to ground squirrels, which lack head stripes. Sides are yellowish to reddish brown, with the undersurface whitish. There are three species of chipmunks in the White Mountains. Identification of individual species requires careful observation of physical characteristics as well as locality and habitat type.

Sagebrush Chipmunk, *E. minimus*. Head and body 3.7–4.5 in (9.3–11.4 cm), tail 3–4.5 in (7.6–11.4 cm); short, grayish fur with contrasting stripes—dorsal stripe black, outer light stripe white, all stripes extending to base of tail; tail held vertically when moving, yellowish underneath. Occurs from 7,000 ft (2,134 m) to at least 11,800 ft (3,598 m) in sagebrush, mixed Pinyon-juniper Woodland, and Alpine Fell-field habitats.

Panamint Chipmunk, *E. panamintinus*. Head and body 4.5–4.7 in (11.4–11.9 cm), tail 3.5–4 in (8.9–10.2 cm); crown of head noticeably gray; shoulders and back reddish; outer dark stripes, below the outer white stripes, are inconspicuous; other dorsal dark stripes are reddish or grayish. Occurs above 5,900 ft (1,800 m) to 9,500 ft (2,900 m) in Pinyon-juniper Woodland.

Uinta Chipmunk, *E. umbrinus*. (Fig. 12.10) Head and body 4.5–5 in (11.4–12.7 cm), tail 3.5–4.6 in (8.9–11.7 cm); back of neck and crown grayish; outer light stripes pure white, dorsal stripes well demarcated, outer dark stripes indistinct. Distribution restricted in the White Mountains to the Bristlecone Pine Forest, 9,500–11,500 ft (2,900–3,510 m).

Chipmunks store large caches of seeds and fruits in their burrows for sustenance during the winter. They may hibernate in some years, but their periods of torpor are not as predictable as those of ground squirrels and marmots. Chipmunks also eat insects and fungi and are themselves eaten by hawks, weasels, Coyotes, snakes, and other carnivores. Litter size is three to six, and young are generally active aboveground by June or July.

FIGURE 12.10   Uinta Chipmunk.

Pocket Gophers (Family Geomyidae)

Pocket Gophers, *Thomomys*.   Head and body 4.8–7 in (12–18 cm), tail 2–3.8 in (5–9.5 cm); yellowish brown-gray fur; head small and flattened; neck short; shoulders and forearms broad and muscular; eyes small; fur-lined internal cheek pouches on either side of mouth. Two species of pocket gophers inhabit the White Mountains: the Northern Pocket Gopher (*T. talpoides*), which ranges from the floor of Owens Valley to 8,200 ft (2,500 m); and the Valley Pocket Gopher (*T. bottae*) (Fig. 12.11), occurring from the valley floor to about 10,500 ft (3,200 m). Preferred habitat for both is around meadows in soft soil, rarely in densely wooded or rocky areas. Pocket Gophers are strictly herbivorous, feeding on a wide range of foods including roots and succulent vegetation. The long, curved claws and chisel-like incisors are used to excavate tunnels below the ground surface. Gopher activity is apparent from the characteristic fan-shaped pile of soil marked by concentric rings where soil has been pushed up from below. Predators include owls, hawks, Badgers, Coyotes, and weasels. Young are born in the spring, and number three to six to a litter.

Pocket Mice, and Kangaroo Rats and Mice (Family Heteromyidae)

Pocket Mice, *Perognathus*.   Head and body 2.5–4.8 in (6.4–12.2 cm), tail 3.2–4.8 in (8.1–12.2 cm); upper surface yellowish brown, white below; ears small; an external fur-lined pouch at each side of mouth; forelegs and feet small, hind feet and tail long; hind feet without hair. Two species of these nocturnal rodents are present in the White Mountains. The Long-tailed Pocket Mouse (*P. formosus*) (Fig. 12.12) ranges up to 7,100 ft (2,165 m) and is common in rocky areas. It is distinguished by its bicolored tail that is heavily crested with a tuft at its end and darker than the rest of the body. The Great Basin Pocket Mouse (*P. parvus*) occurs in sagebrush and Pinyon-juniper Woodland up to about 8,300 ft (2,530 m). Pocket Mice are quadrupedal except for isolated bipedal leaps away from danger. Their cheek pouches serve to transport seeds to underground food caches. During times of extreme weather conditions or food scarcity, Pocket Mice go into torpor, (i.e., lower their body temperature, heart

FIGURE 12.11   Valley Pocket Gopher.

FIGURE 12.12   Long-tailed Pocket Mouse.

rate, and metabolic rate to conserve energy). Their main predators include owls and Coyotes. Litter size is two to six, and young are born in June or July.

Kangaroo Rats, *Dipodomys*.   Head and body 4–5 in (10.2–12.7 cm), tail 5–7.3 in (12.7–18.5 cm); body yellowish brown above, whitish below; ears small; external cheek pouches; hind legs large; tail always longer than head and body, has dark dorsal and ventral longitudinal bands with lateral longitudinal stripes and is tufted with long hairs. The White Mountains contain three species of kangaroo rats: Ord's Kangaroo Rat (*D. ordii*) (Fig. 12.13) ranges up to 6,500 ft (1,982 m); Merriam's Kangaroo Rat (*D. merriami*) occurs up to 7,200 ft (2,195 m); and the largest of the three species, the Great Basin Kangaroo Rat *(D. microps)*, has been reported up to 7,100 ft (2,165 m). Kangroo Rats are bipedal, foraging at night mostly on seeds. The Great Basin Kangroo Rat is also known as Chisel-tooth, because it uses its flattened incisors to shave off the salty outer layers of saltbush (*Atriplex*) leaves before consumption. Kangaroo Rats are noted for their highly developed water conservation ability. Water is derived solely from oxidation of carbohydrates, fats, and protein and is conserved by kidneys that are able to dispose of wastes with an extremely small output of water. Their large auditory chambers help to alert them to attack by owls and Coyotes, their main predators.

FIGURE 12.13   Ord's Kangaroo Rat.

Mice, Rats, Lemmings, and Voles (Family Cricetidae)

Western Harvest Mouse, *Reithrodontomys megalotis*.   Head and body 2.8–3 in (7.1–7.6 cm), tail 2.3–3.2 in (5.8–8.1 cm); upper parts and sides buffy, underparts grayish brown; tail indistinctly bicolored; no external cheek pouches. Western Harvest Mice have been reported up to 6,700 ft (2,040 m) in the White Mountains, inhabiting damp grassy meadows and marshy areas, but they may occur in other habitats during population peaks. They eat mainly seeds and fruits, with some insects, and they are preyed upon by owls, snakes, and a number of mammalian predators. They commonly use the runways of meadow mice (*Microtus* spp.) during their nightly foraging periods. Litters are produced several times per year and average four to six young.

Deer Mice, *Peromyscus*.   There are three species of Deer Mice present in the White Mountains. They can be distinguished from other mice by several characteristics, including their large, membranous ears, lack of external cheek pouches, and a tail exceeding 70% of the head and body length. Their diets consist of seeds, fruits, and insects, particularly butterfly and moth larvae. They are active year-round and store caches of food for winter consumption. Deer Mice are preyed upon by many avian and mammalian predators.

Pinyon Mouse, *P. truei*. Head and body 3.6–4 in (9.1–10.2 cm), tail 3.4–4.8 in (8.6–12.2 cm); brown to dark brown above, creamy white underneath; feet whitish; tail bicolored, whitish below, length exceeds 90% of head and body length; ears very large. Pinyon Mice have been documented up to 9,500 ft (2,896 m) and are common in the Pinyon-juniper Woodland, where they feed on juniper berries and Pinyon Pine nuts. Much of their time is spent in trees.

Deer Mouse, *P. maniculatis*. (Fig. 12.14) Head and body 2.8–4 in (7.1–10.2 cm), tail 2–5 in (5–12.7 cm); yellowish brown to grayish above, pure white below; feet white; bicolored tail usually less than 90% of head and body length. The Deer Mouse, probably the most common mammal in North America, has the greatest elevational range of any mammal in California. The same subspecies of Deer Mouse that lives on the floor of Death Valley also occurs on White Mountain Peak (14,246 ft, 4,340 m). Deer Mice live in nearly all habitat types.

FIGURE 12.14   Deer Mouse.

Canyon Mouse, *P. crinitus.* Head and body 3–3.4 in (7.6–8.6 cm), tail 3.5–4.3 in (8.9–10.9 cm). Fur long and soft, pale yellowish buff above and creamy white below; long hairs on tip of tail; feet white; tail usually longer than the head and body, with a broad, light brown dorsal stripe, creamy white below. Canyon Mice frequent rocky areas up to 8,250 ft (2,515 m) in the White Mountains.

Southern Grasshopper Mouse, *Onychomys torridus.* Head and body 3.5–4 in (8.9–10.2 cm), tail 1.6–2 in (4–5 cm); light cinnamon above, white below. The Grasshopper Mouse has been found up to 5,000 ft (1,524 m), most commonly in canyons. The diet is 90% animal matter, most of which is arthropods. These nocturnal rodents emit high-pitched calls and usually nest in burrows dug by other mammals. Predators include snakes, weasels, owls, Bobcats, and other carnivores.

Wood Rats, *Neotoma.* The scaly tail of the largely nocturnal Wood Rat is covered by overlying hairs. Wood Rats eat mostly vegetation and are preyed upon by Coyotes, foxes, owls and large snakes. Litter size is three to four, and young are born in the spring. There are two species of wood rats present in the White Mountains.

Desert Wood Rat, *N. lepida.* Head and body 5.8–7 in (14.7–17.8 cm), tail 4.3–6.4 in (10.9–16.3 cm); fur grayish, mixed with black hairs above, underparts white or buffy; tail hairs short. Also known as the Pack Rat, this species occurs up to 8,000 ft (2,440 m) in Sagebrush Scrub and Pinyon-juniper Woodland and frequents rocky areas in these regions. It uses cactus for water and nesting material.

Bushy-tailed Wood Rat, *N. cinerea.* (Fig. 12.15) Head and body 7–9.4 in (17.8–23.9 cm), tail 5.2–7.4 in (13.2–18.8 cm); fur cinnamon brown to buffy, some tipped with black above; white or grayish below; tail with hairs over 2 cm long. Bushy-tailed Wood Rats have been recorded up to 10,300 ft (3,140 m) in the White Mountains; however, a single individual was collected from the summit hut on White Mountain Peak (14,246 ft, 4,340 m) during the summer of 1983. Whether this is an accurate representation of their usual range in these mountains is uncertain.

FIGURE 12.15   Bushy-tailed Wood Rat.

Sagebrush Vole, *Lagurus curtatus*.   Head and body 3.8–4.5 in (9.6–11.4 cm), tail 0.6–1.1 in (1.5–2.8 cm); fur long and fine, light grayish above and almost white below. Sagebrush Voles occur up to 12,500 ft (3,810 m) in Sagebrush Scrub and Pinyon-juniper Woodland. Similar to meadow voles, they are active both day and night. They feed on nearly anything green and do not require additional drinking water. This species is endemic to the Great Basin. Litters average five young.

Meadow voles, *Microtus*.   There are three species of meadow mice or voles in the White Mountains. All are active both day and night and are preyed upon by hawks, owls, falcons, Coyotes, weasels, and snakes. They feed on stems and leaves of forbs and grasses. The litter size usually ranges from five to eight young.

Montane Vole, *M. montanus*. Head and body 4–5.5 in. (10.2–14 cm), tail 1.2–2.6 in (3–6.6 cm); fur dark brown, some reddish tinged; undersurface dark gray; tail usually less than one-third of total body length, nearly unicolored. The Montane Vole occurs up to at least 12,500 ft (3,810 m), commonly in alpine meadows or other high-elevation grassy areas. It builds conspicuous runways through grasses and sedges, and it tunnels beneath the snow during the winter. It feeds chiefly on succulent stems and leaves of forbs, rarely grasses.

Long-tailed Meadow Vole, *M. longicaudus*. (Fig. 12.16) Head and body 4.5–5.3 in (11.4–13.5 cm), tail 2–3.5 in (5–8.9 cm); dorsal band of reddish brown fur with grayish sides and bluish gray underparts; tail usually more than one-third of total body length and more or less bicolored. The Long-tailed Meadow Vole is common along streams and in wet meadows in higher elevations up to 11,500 ft (3,510 m). Unlike the Montane Vole, it does not construct extensive runways.

California Meadow Vole, *M. californicus*. Head and body 4.6–5.7 in (11.7–14.5 cm), tail 1.6–2.8 in (4–7.1 cm); buffy or dark brown above, commonly with a reddish tinge on the middle of the back; undersurface blue-gray to white; ears project well above fur. This species has been recorded up to 4,500 ft (1,370 m) in Silver Canyon, but occurs mostly along the Owens River.

FIGURE 12.16   Long-tailed Meadow Vole.

Beavers (Family Castoridae)

Beaver, *Castor canadensis*. Beavers were introduced to the east side of the White Mountains in the Cottonwood Creek area about 1950. Environmental damage caused by beavers led to an apparently successful program to remove them in the mid-1970s. Remnants of their dams may still be visible on some creeks.

Porcupines (Family Erethizontidae)

Porcupine, *Erethizon dorsatum*. (Fig. 12.17) Head and body 18–22 in (46–56 cm), tail 7–9 in (18–23 cm); weight usually 9–15 lb (4–7 kg); yellowish to blackish above; stiff quills and spines, especially on rump and tail. Porcupines exhibit a distinct habitat and diet shift with season. In winter they inhabit wooded areas, where they consume tree bark; a variety of habitats and foods are used in summer. During the summer they may range up to 13,500 ft (4,115 m), where they forage on flowers and leaves of alpine forbs. The spines of these slow-moving rodents are actually modified hairs that are loosely attached to the body. When under attack by a Mountain Lion, Bobcat, or Coyote, a slap of the tail is enough to drive the quills into the predator.

CARNIVORES (Order Carnivora)

Coyote, *Canis latrans*. (Fig. 12.18) As large as a medium-sized dog, with long, bushy tail; 3–5 ft (1–1.5 m) long, including tail; adults 20–30 lb (9–14 kg); pelage nonuniform in color due to color banding of the hairs, usually appearing grayish with reddish tint, the red commonly more noticeable around the erect ears and neck. Coyotes are distributed throughout the White Mountains at all seasons. Although they are primarily predators of rodents, hares, and rabbits, their diet may include berries, grasshoppers, and carrion. Coyotes generally pose little threat to adult Mule Deer, Mountain Sheep, Pronghorn Antelope, and Tule Elk, but they can prey on the young of these species. Most Coyotes in the White Mountains occur singly or in family groups of a mother with young pups. Most hunting occurs at dawn and dusk,

FIGURE 12.17 Porcupine.

FIGURE 12.18   Coyote.

but it is nevertheless common to observe Coyotes during the day. Young are born in the spring.

Gray Fox, *Urocyon cinereoargenteus.*   (Fig. 12.19) As large as a small dog, head and body about 2 ft (60 cm), tail about 1 ft (30 cm) long; weight 9–11 lb (4–5 kg); pelage pepper and salt gray with black on tip of long, bushy tail and tips of prominent, erect, pointed ears. The Gray Fox is uncommon in the White Mountains, probably distributed mostly at middle to low elevations on both sides of the range. Its diet

FIGURE 12.19   Gray Fox.

includes rodents, hares, rabbits, birds, insects, and fruit, depending on availability. Young are born in spring, usually three to five in a litter.

Ringtail, *Bassariscus astutus*.   (Fig. 12.20) Head and body length 14–16 in (36–41 cm), tail 15 in (38 cm); weight 2–2.5 lb (0.9–1.1 kg); body pelage tan, somewhat lighter beneath, with black-tipped hairs on back; dark eyes conspicuously ringed with white; light spot in front of each ear. A small, very agile relative of the raccoon, with a long, bushy, banded tail, pointed face, and prominent, erect ears, Ringtails commonly have been called the Miner's Cat (although not a cat at all) due to their propensity to take up residence in and around cabins. Ringtails occur in canyons of the White Mountains, living mostly near water. They are very nocturnal, and thus rarely seen by people. Their diet is highly varied, including small mammals, birds, reptiles, carrion, insects, spiders, and fruit. Litters are usually born in late spring.

Marten, *Martes americana*.   About the size of a house cat, but longer and narrower, with bushy tail and sharply pointed face; head and body 14–17 in (36–43 cm), tail 7–9 in (18–23 cm); weight 1–2.5 lb (0.4–1.1 kg); pelage golden brown with yellowish patch on throat and chest. The Marten is apparently a rare inhabitant of timberline coniferous forests, probably occcuring mostly in Limber Pine on the east side of the White Mountains. An opportunistic predator that can climb trees, it preys on birds and small mammals as large as hares but also eats berries and carrion when available. The Marten commonly hunts beneath the snow in winter and is largely solitary. Young are born in spring and litter size is generally two to four.

Wolverine, *Gulo luscus*.   A large, stocky member of the weasel family; head and body 29–32 in (74–81 cm), tail 7–9 in (18–23 cm); weight 35–60 lb (16–27 kg); shaggy, blackish brown pelage, with pale stripe from shoulder to rump on each side, joining at the base of bushy tail; pale patch from eye to ear on either side of head. The Wolverine is a rare inhabitant of the White Mountains, reported on only three

FIGURE 12.20   Ringtail.

FIGURE 12.21   Badger.

occasions in over 30 years. Its range is probably the crest and east side of the range. Wolverines are known to eat virtually any animal matter, including carrion, and will eat berries in summer. Young are born in late winter or spring, usually numbering two to four.

Badger, *Taxidea taxus*.   (Fig. 12.21) Head and body 18–22 in (46–56 cm), tail 4–6 in (10–15 cm); weight 13–25 lb (6–11 kg); stature broad and low such that the body fur appears to drag on the ground; pelage yellowish brown to silver gray, with white stripe down middle beginning at nose and sometimes extending to base of the tail; face with upturned snout and black and white patterning. Badgers are distributed throughout the White Mountains, up to at least 12,000 ft (3,660 m). Their feet and legs are adapted for digging out burrowing animals, which is its main food (especially ground squirrels). Insects and other terrestrial animals are eaten opportunistically, but vegetative matter is virtually absent from the diet. Litters of one to five are born in spring.

Long-tailed Weasel, *Mustela frenata*.   (Fig. 12.22) Head and body 8–10.5 in (20–27 cm), tail 4–6 in (10–15 cm); weight less than 0.75 lb (0.34 kg); pelage whitish underneath and brown above, with black on tip of tail; upper pelage usually changes to white in winter in snowy environments. A small, voracious carnivore, whose long and slender body is adapted for hunting small animals in burrows and rocks, this weasel is distributed throughout the White Mountains. Long-tailed Weasels have been recorded as high as 12,500 ft (3,810 m) but probably occur higher. Their diet

FIGURE 12.22   Long-tailed Weasel.

consists mostly of small mammals but may include insects, reptiles, birds, and eggs. Litters of six to nine are born in spring.

Skunks. Two skunk species inhabit the White Mountains. The Striped Skunk (*Mephitis mephitis*) (Fig. 12.23) is about the size of a house cat, with a conspicuous bushy tail, weighing 6–14 lb (2.7–6.4 kg). It is glossy black with two conspicuous white stripes on either side of its back that meet at the neck. The Spotted Skunk (*Spilogale putorius*) (Fig. 12.24) is considerably smaller, weighing 0.8–2.5 lb (0.4–1.1 kg). Its black pelage is broken by numerous white stripes and spots, including a white tip on the tail. Striped Skunks occur up to about 7,000 ft (2,130 m) and Spotted Skunks to 10,500 ft (3,200 m) in the White Mountains. Both species consume a highly varied diet consisting of invertebrates, small vertebrates, bird eggs, and some fruit, nuts, grains, and roots. Young are generally born during May for both species, with litters of three to six for Spotted Skunks and four to eight for Striped Skunks.

Mountain Lion, *Felis concolor.* (Fig. 12.25) A large cat with a long tail; head and body 42–54 in (107–137 cm), tail 30–36 in (76–91 cm); adults 80–150 lb (36–68 kg); pelage tawny with white underside, black on back of ears and on tip of long, prominent (but not bushy) tail; kittens spotted with banded tail. The primary food of Mountain Lions is deer, which they hunt by stalking and ambushing. Hares

FIGURE 12.23 Striped Skunk.

FIGURE 12.24   Spotted Skunk.

may be eaten if locally abundant, and other ungulates, such as Mountain Sheep and Tule Elk, are generally hunted only where their ranges overlap the deer range. Mountain Lions occur throughout the White Mountains where Mule Deer are present. Their dependence on concealment for hunting keeps them mostly in canyons, where vegetation and rocks meet this need. They are extremely shy of humans and hence rarely seen. They usually occur singly or as a mother with young. Young can be born any month of the year, and litter size is generally two to four.

FIGURE 12.25   Mountain Lion.

FIGURE 12.26   Bobcat.

Bobcat, *Lynx rufus*. (Fig. 12.26) About twice the size of a house cat with proportionately longer legs, especially rear legs, and a short tail; head and body 25–30 in (63–76 cm), tail 5 in (13 cm); weight 15–35 lb (7–16 kg); pelage yellowish to reddish brown and variously streaked and spotted; tail with dark bands toward the tip; prominent ears pointed with tufts of black hair at the tips. Like Coyotes, Bobcats feed mostly on rodents, hares, and rabbits, occasionally catching larger prey. They differ from Coyotes in their method of hunting, using only stealth to stalk and ambush, never running down prey. Consequently, like their relatives the Mountain Lions, Bobcats mostly inhabit areas where they can hide. They occur throughout the White Mountains but rarely use the high, open slopes where the visitor might hope to see one. Bobcats are generally solitary, except when a female is accompanied by kittens. Litter size is usually three to five. Young are generally born in spring and summer.

EVEN-TOED UNGULATES (Order Artiodactyla)

Tule Elk, *Cervus elaphus*. (Fig. 12.27) Large, standing well over 3 ft (1 m) at the shoulders; adult males up to about 700 lb (320 kg), females about three-quarters the weight of males; pelage light reddish brown with dark brown neck and large, cream-colored rump patch; males carry antlers that are cast and regrown each year and may become very massive with numerous branches in prime adults. Tule Elk are native only west of the crest of the Sierra Nevada in the foothills, Great Valley, and Coast Ranges. They were introduced to Owens Valley in 1933 and 1934 in an attempt to establish a large, free-roaming population. At the time, this subspecies (*nannodes*) numbered fewer than 300, and most were in enclosures. The Owens Valley population now extends from Owens Lake to Laws and numbers about 500. The west slope of the White Mountains is used by Tule Elk up to about 8,000 ft (2,440 m) in the region from the Westgard Pass Road to just south of Silver Canyon. This area is used largely in winter and spring and includes calving grounds.

FIGURE 12.27   Tule Elk.

Mule Deer, *Odocoileus hemionus*.   (Fig. 12.28) Shoulder height about 3 ft (91 cm); weight about 100 lb (45 kg) for females and 130 lb (59 kg) for males; gray-brown pelage with small white rump patch covered by tail; conspicuous, large ears; males carry antlers that increase in length and degree of branching with body size and are cast and regrown each year. Mule deer are widely distributed in the White Mountains. Similar to Mountain Sheep, they migrate seasonally up and down the mountain to obtain the best yearly diet, occurring as high as 14,000 ft. (4,270 m) in summer. They are long-legged and fleet and escape predators by outrunning them. Habitats used by Mule Deer include the open Desert Scrub and alpine communities, as well as the more closed Pinyon Pine, Limber Pine, Bristlecone Pine, and Mountain Mohogany belts in the middle elevations. Common to all habitats is topography that allows fleetness in escaping predators. Consequently, Mule Deer rarely are present on the steep, rocky slopes preferred by Mountain Sheep.

Pronghorn Antelope, *Antilocapra americana*.   (Fig. 12.29) Shoulder height about 33 in (85 cm); weight about 75 lb (34 kg) for females and 110 lb (50 kg) for males; pelage rusty brown on back, with conspicuous white belly, rump patch, and neck stripes; females with very short, inconspicuous (some lacking) horns; males with black horns rarely exceeding 16 in (40 cm) with a short, forward-protruding branch in the middle and hooked tips; horn sheaths are cast and regrown each year in males, unlike

FIGURE 12.28 Mule Deer.

FIGURE 12.29 Pronghorn Antelope.

any other horned mammal in the world. Pronghorn Antelopes were once common residents of valleys surrounding the White Mountains. They probably used the lower slopes of the range in spring and migrated to high sagebrush flats in summer. An attempt beginning in 1982 to reintroduce these antelopes to Adobe Valley northwest of Benton has resulted in populations that winter at the base of the White Mountains from Hammil Valley to Queen Valley; occasionally they have been observed high in the range in summer.

Mountain Sheep, *Ovis canadensis.* (Fig. 12.30) Shoulder height about 36 in. (91 cm); maximum weight about 140 lb (64 kg) for females and 200 lb (91 kg) for males; gray pelage with large, conspicuous white rump patch; females with short, narrow horns that curve back and outward toward tips; adult males with massive horns that grow back and then curve forward to form an arc. Mountain (Bighorn) Sheep are usually found in rugged topography due to their need for steep rocks to escape predators. They also use less rocky terrain if visibility is good and safe rocks are within running distance. Consequently, Mountain Sheep range is usually discontinuous. Where possible, Mountain Sheep exhibit seasonal altitudinal migration in order to

FIGURE 12.30   Mountain Sheep.

feed on the greenest, most nutritious forage. In the White Mountains they range in elevation from 5,700 ft (1,740 m) to 14,000 ft (4,270 m). Their main predator in the White Mountains is the Mountain Lion, with Coyotes and Bobcats possible predators on lambs. Historically, Mountain Sheep occurred in scattered localities in the southern White Mountains, including Wyman Canyon and the Cottonwood Creek basin, and all west-side canyons from White Mountain Peak to Montgomery Peak in the northern half of the range. Loss of part of this range was probably due to diseases introduced from domestic livestock. Today, Mountain Sheep remain only in the most rugged and inaccessible portion of their original range, from White Mountain Peak to Montgomery Peak. These canyons become less steep and rocky as they approach the crest of the range. Consequently, Mountain Sheep are uneasy and very flighty when feeding high in the mountains in summer. They usually flee into the canyons at such great distances from people that few untrained observers ever see them. There is concern that increased human use north of White Mountain Peak in summer might cause serious displacement of this species from its nutritious summer range.

ODD-TOED UNGULATES (Order Perissodactyla)

Wild Horses, *Equus caballus*.   Like Tule Elk, Wild Horses are a nonnative species. Their origin, however, is unintentional, stemming from escaped domestic horses. Their range encompasses the canyons on the east side of the White Mountains from around Cottonwood Creek to the northern end of the range. They range in elevation from the alluvial fans of Fish Lake Valley to high alpine flats, such as Pellisier Flats. A U.S. Forest Service policy to regulate their numbers has been only partially implemented. There is concern over the potentially detrimental impact these large animals may have on fragile alpine ecosystems. Wild Horses live in year-round harems, with bachelor males living in separate groups until dominant enough to obtain a harem.

PART IV

ARCHAEOLOGY AND ANTHROPOLOGY

PLATE 1.1   Cirrus and cumulus clouds,
White Mountain Rd., and Bristlecone Pines.

PLATE 1.2   Altocumulus clouds over
White Mountains at sunrise.

PLATE 1.3   Boundary and Montgomery
peaks, Pellisier Flats, and cumulus clouds.

PLATE 1.4   Approaching snowstorm viewed
from summit of White Mountain Peak.

PLATE 1.5   Cirrostratus and altostratus
clouds over the crest of the Sierra Nevada.

PLATE 1.6   Thunderstorm approaching
Chiatovich Flats from Fish Lake Valley.

PLATE 1.7   Lee wave cloud, altocumulus
lenticularis, over Westgard Pass.

PLATE 1.8   Developing thunderstorm over
Silver Canyon area of the White Mountains.

PLATE 6.1
Yucca brevifolia (p. 109).

PLATE 6.2
Angelica lineariloba
(p. 109).

PLATE 6.3
Cymopterus aboriginum
(p. 112).

PLATE 6.4
Lomatium foeniculaceum ssp.
inyoense (p. 112).

PLATE 6.5
Lomatium mohavense
(p. 112).

PLATE 6.6
Acamptopappus shockleyi
(p. 113).

PLATE 6.7
Ambrosia dumosa (p. 113).

PLATE 6.8
Anisocoma acaulis (p. 113).

PLATE 6.9
Antennaria microphylla
(p. 114).

PLATE 6.10   *Brickellia oblongifolia* var. *linifolia* (p. 115).

PLATE 6.11   *Calycoseris parryi* (p. 115).

PLATE 6.12   *Chaenactis carphoclinia* (p. 116).

PLATE 6.13   *Chrysothamnus viscidiflorus* ssp. *viscidiflorus* (p. 116).

PLATE 6.15   *Crepis intermedia* (p. 117).

PLATE 6.14   *Cirsium nidulum* (p. 116).

PLATE 6.16
Encelia virginensis ssp.
actonii (p. 117).

PLATE 6.17
Erigeron aphanactis
(p. 118).

PLATE 6.18
Erigeron argentatus
(p. 118).

PLATE 6.19
Erigeron clokeyi (p. 118).

PLATE 6.20
Erigeron compositus var.
glabratus (p. 118).

PLATE 6.21
Hulsea algida (p. 119).

PLATE 6.22
Hulsea vestita ssp. *inyoensis*
(p. 119).

PLATE 6.23
Hymenoxys cooperi var.
canescens (p. 119).

PLATE 6.24
Layia glandulosa (p. 120).

PLATE 6.25
Leucelene ericoides (p. 120).

PLATE 6.26
Senecio canus (p. 121).

PLATE 6.27
Senecio douglasii var.
monoensis (p. 121).

PLATE 6.28
Senecio multilobatus
(p. 122).

PLATE 6.29
Solidago multiradiata
(p. 122).

PLATE 6.30
Stephanomeria pauciflora
(p. 122).

PLATE 6.31
Stephanomeria spinosa
(p. 122).

PLATE 6.32
Tetradymia canescens
(p. 122).

PLATE 6.33
Townsendia scapigera
(p. 123).

PLATE 6.34
Viguiera multiflora var.
nevadensis (p. 123).

PLATE 6.35
Xylorhiza tortifolia
(p. 123).

PLATE 6.36
Amsinkia tessellata
(p. 124).

PLATE 6.37   *Cryptantha confertiflora* (p. 124).   PLATE 6.38   *Cryptantha flavoculata* (p. 124).

PLATE 6.39   *Cryptantha pterocarya* (p. 125).

PLATE 6.40
Cryptantha roosiorum
(p. 125).

PLATE 6.41
Cryptantha utahensis
(p. 125).

PLATE 6.42
Cryptantha virginensis
(p. 125).

PLATE 6.43   *Arabis holboellii* (p. 127).

PLATE 6.44   *Arabis pulchra* (p. 128).

PLATE 6.45
Caulanthus crassicaulis
(p. 128).

PLATE 6.46   *Caulanthus glaucus* (p. 128).

PLATE 6.48   *Draba oligosperma* (p. 129).

PLATE 6.47   *Caulostramina jaegeri* (p. 129).

PLATE 6.49
Lepidium fremontii (p. 129).

PLATE 6.50
Lesquerella kingii ssp. *kingii*
(p. 129).

PLATE 6.51
Stanleya elata (p. 130).

PLATE 6.52
Stanleya pinnata var.
pinnata (p. 130).

PLATE 6.53
Streptanthus cordatus
(p. 130).

PLATE 6.54
Echinocactus polycephalus
(p. 131).

PLATE 6.55
Echinocereus engelmannii var.
chrysocentrus (p. 131).

PLATE 6.56
Echinocereus triglochidiatus
var. *mojavensis* (p. 131).

PLATE 6.57
Opuntia basilaris (p. 131).

PLATE 6.58
Opuntia erinacea var.
erinacea (p. 132).

PLATE 6.59
Sclerocactus polyancistrus
(p. 132).

PLATE 6.60
Sambucus caerulea (p. 132).

PLATE 6.61
Symphoricarpos longiflorus
(p. 133).

PLATE 6.62
Arenaria aculeata (p. 133).

PLATE 6.63
Arenaria kingii ssp.
compacta (p. 133).

PLATE 6.64   *Arenaria macradenia* ssp. *macradenia* var. *parishiorum* (p. 133).

PLATE 6.65   *Scopulophila rixfordii* (p. 134).

PLATE 6.66   *Stellaria longipes* (p. 134).

PLATE 6.67   *Atriplex confertifolia* (p. 135).   PLATE 6.68   *Atriplex torreyi* (p. 135).

PLATE 6.69   *Ceratoides lanata* (p. 136).

PLATE 6.70
Grayia spinosa (p. 136).

PLATE 6.71
Sarcobatus vermiculatus
(p. 137).

PLATE 6.72
Forsellesia nevadensis
(p. 137).

PLATE 6.73
Cuscuta salina var. *apoda*
(p. 137).

PLATE 6.74
Ephedra nevadensis (p. 139).

PLATE 6.75
Ephedra viridis (p. 139).

PLATE 6.76
Chamaesyce albomarginata
(p. 140).

PLATE 6.77
Chamaesyce fendleri
(p. 140).

PLATE 6.78
Astragalus calycosus
(p. 140).

PLATE 6.79
Astragalus cimae var.
sufflatus (p. 141).

PLATE 6.80
Astragalus coccineus
(p. 141).

PLATE 6.81
Astragalus inyoensis
(p. 141).

PLATE 6.82
Astragalus kentrophyta var.
elatus (p. 142).

PLATE 6.83
Astragalus lentiginosus var.
fremontii (p. 142).

PLATE 6.84
Astragalus newberryi
(p. 143).

PLATE 6.85
Astragalus oophorus
(p. 143).

PLATE 6.86
Dalea searlsiae (p. 143).

PLATE 6.87
Lupinus argenteus var.
tenellus (p. 144).

PLATE 6.88
Lupinus flavoculatus
(p. 144).

PLATE 6.89
Lupinus palmeri (p. 144).

PLATE 6.90
Lupinus tegeticulatus var.
tegeticulatus (p. 145).

PLATE 6.91
Oxytropis parryi (p. 145).

PLATE 6.92
Psorothamnus arborescens var.
minutifolius (p. 145).

PLATE 6.93
Trifolium andersonii ssp.
monoense (p. 146).

PLATE 6.94
Frasera puberulenta (p. 147).

PLATE 6.95
Gentiana newberryi
(p. 147).

PLATE 6.96
Gentianella tenella (p. 147).

PLATE 6.97
Phacelia crenulata (p. 148).

PLATE 6.98
Phacelia curvipes (p. 148).

PLATE 6.99
Phacelia fremontii (p. 148).

PLATE 6.100
Phacelia hastata (p. 148).

PLATE 6.101
Phacelia perityloides
(p. 149).

PLATE 6.102
Phacelia vallis-mortae
(p. 149).

PLATE 6.103
Tricardia watsonii (p. 149).

PLATE 6.104
Iris missouriensis (p. 150).

PLATE 6.105
Sisyrinchium idahoense
(p. 150).

PLATE 6.106 *Monardella odoratissima* ssp. *parvifolia* (p. 151).

PLATE 6.107 *Salvia columbariae* (p. 151).

PLATE 6.108 *Salvia dorrii* var. *clokeyi* (p. 151).

PLATE 6.109
Allium atrorubens var.
inyonis (p. 152).

PLATE 6.110
Calochortus bruneaunis
(p. 152).

PLATE 6.111
Calochortus kennedyi
(p. 153).

PLATE 6.112   *Fritillaria pinetorum* (p. 153).

PLATE 6.113   *Zigadenus paniculatus* (p. 154).

PLATE 6.114   *Linum lewisii* (p. 154).

PLATE 6.115
Eucnide urens (p. 154).

PLATE 6.116
Mentzelia albicaulis
(p. 155).

PLATE 6.117
Mentzelia laevicaulis
(p. 155).

PLATE 6.118   *Petalonyx nitidus* (p. 155).   PLATE 6.119   *Sphaeralcea ambigua* (p. 155).

PLATE 6.120   *Mirabilis alipes* (p. 156).

PLATE 6.121
Mirabilis bigelovii var.
bigelovii (p. 157).

PLATE 6.122
Mirabilis multiflora var.
pubescens (p. 157).

PLATE 6.123
Mirabilis pumila (p. 157).

PLATE 6.124   *Forestiera neomexicana* (p. 158).

PLATE 6.125   *Menodora spinescens* (p. 158).

PLATE 6.126   *Camissonia boothii* ssp. *desertorum* (p. 158).

PLATE 6.127
Camissonia claviformis ssp.
claviformis (p. 159).

PLATE 6.128
Epilobium angustifolium ssp.
circumvagum (p. 160).

PLATE 6.129
Oenothera caespitosa ssp.
crinita (p. 161).

PLATE 6.130
Oenothera caespitosa ssp.
marginata (p. 162).

PLATE 6.131
Epipactis gigantea (p. 162).

PLATE 6.132
Platanthera sparsiflora
(p. 163).

PLATE 6.133
Orobanche fasciculata
(p. 163).

PLATE 6.134
Argemone munita ssp.
rotundata (p. 164).

PLATE 6.135
Eschscholzia covillei
(p. 164).

PLATE 6.136
Koeleria macrantha (p. 165).

PLATE 6.137
Oryzopsis hymenoides
(p. 166).

PLATE 6.138
Poa secunda (p. 166).

PLATE 6.139
Sitanion hystrix (p. 167).

PLATE 6.140
Sporobolus airoides (p. 167).

PLATE 6.141
Stipa speciosa (p. 167).

PLATE 6.142
Gilia aggregata var.
arizonica (p. 169).

PLATE 6.143
Gilia campanulata
(p. 169).

PLATE 6.144
Gilia cana ssp. *triceps*
(p. 169).

PLATE 6.145
Gilia congesta var. *montana*
(p. 170).

PLATE 6.146
Gilia latifolia (p. 171).

PLATE 6.147
Gilia ophthalmoides
(p. 172).

PLATE 6.148
Gymnosteris parvula
(p. 173).

PLATE 6.149
Langloisia setosissima ssp.
punctata (p. 173).

PLATE 6.150
Leptodactylon pungens var.
hallii (p. 173).

PLATE 6.151
Linanthus nuttallii ssp.
pubescens (p. 174).

PLATE 6.152
Linanthus parryae (p. 174).

PLATE 6.153
Phlox condensata (p. 175).

PLATE 6.154
Phlox longifolia var.
stansburyi (p. 175).

PLATE 6.155
Polemonium chartaceum
(p. 175).

PLATE 6.156
Chorizanthe rigida (p. 176).

PLATE 6.157
Dedeckera eurekensis
(p. 177).

PLATE 6.158
Eriogonum fasciculatum var.
polifolium (p. 179).

PLATE 6.159
Eriogonum gracilipes
(p. 179).

PLATE 6.160
Eriogonum heermannii ssp.
argense (p. 179).

PLATE 6.161
Eriogonum inflatum
(p. 180).

PLATE 6.162
Eriogonum ovalifolium var.
ovalifolium (p. 182).

PLATE 6.163
Eriogonum rosense (p. 183).

PLATE 6.164
Eriogonum rupinum
(p. 183).

PLATE 6.165
Eriogonum umbellatum var.
umbellatum (p. 183).

PLATE 6.166
Eriogonum wrightii var.
subscaposum (p. 184).

PLATE 6.167
Oxyria digyna (p. 184).

PLATE 6.168
Oxytheca perfoliata (p. 185).

PLATE 6.169
Rumex paucifolius ssp.
paucifolius (p. 185).

PLATE 6.170
Calyptridium parryi var.
nevadense (p. 186).

PLATE 6.171
Calyptridium umbellatum
var. *caudiciferum* (p. 186).

PLATE 6.172
Claytonia parviflora
(p. 186).

PLATE 6.173
Lewisia rediviva var. *minor*
(p. 187).

PLATE 6.174
Montia chamissoi (p. 187).

PLATE 6.175
Androsace septentrionalis var.
subumbellata (p. 187).

PLATE 6.176
Dodecatheon redolens
(p. 188).

PLATE 6.177
Aconitum columbianum
(p. 188).

PLATE 6.178 *Aquilegia formosa* (p. 188).

PLATE 6.179 *Aquilegia shockleyi* (p. 188).

PLATE 6.180 *Clematis ligusticifolia* var. *brevifolia* (p. 189).

PLATE 6.181 *Delphinium parishii* (p. 189).   PLATE 6.182 *Delphinium polycladon* (p. 189).

PLATE 6.183 *Ranunculus andersonii* (p. 189).

PLATE 6.184   *Ranunculus eschscholtzii* var. *oxynotus* (p. 190).

PLATE 6.185   *Cercocarpus intricatus* (p. 191).

PLATE 6.186   *Cercocarpus ledifolius* (p. 191).

PLATE 6.187 *Chamaebatiaria millefolium* (p. 192).

PLATE 6.188 *Coleogyne ramosissima* (p. 192).

PLATE 6.189 *Cowania mexicana* var. *stansburiana* (p. 192).

PLATE 6.190
Holodiscus dumosus var.
glabrescens (p. 193).

PLATE 6.191
Ivesia lycopodioides ssp.
scandularis (p. 193).

PLATE 6.192
Petrophytum caespitosum
(p. 194).

PLATE 6.193
Physocarpus alternans
(p. 194).

PLATE 6.194
Potentilla fruticosa (p. 195).

PLATE 6.195
Potentilla saxosa (p. 196).

PLATE 6.196
Prunus andersonii (p. 196).

PLATE 6.197
Prunus fasciculata (p. 196).

PLATE 6.198
Purshia glandulosa (p. 196).

PLATE 6.199
Rosa woodsii var.
ultramontana (p. 197).

PLATE 6.200
Thamnosma montana
(p. 199).

PLATE 6.201
Heuchera rubescens var.
pachypoda (p. 199).

PLATE 6.202
Jamesia americana var.
californica (p. 200).

PLATE 6.203
Philadelphus stramineus
(p. 200).

PLATE 6.204
Ribes cereum (p. 200).

PLATE 6.205
Ribes velutinum var.
glanduliferum (p. 201).

PLATE 6.206
Antirrhinum kingii
(p. 201).

PLATE 6.207
Castilleja chromosa (p. 202).

PLATE 6.208   *Castilleja linarieafolia* (p. 202).

PLATE 6.209   *Castilleja martinii* var. *clokeyi* (p. 202).

PLATE 6.210   *Castilleja miniata* (p. 203).

PLATE 6.211
Castilleja nana (p. 203).

PLATE 6.212
Mimulus bigelovii var.
bigelovii (p. 204).

PLATE 6.213
Mimulus cardinalis
(p. 204).

PLATE 6.214
Mimulus guttatus (p. 205).

PLATE 6.215
Mimulus primuloides var.
primuloides (p. 205).

PLATE 6.216
Mimulus suksdorfii (p. 206).

PLATE 6.217
Mohavea breviflora (p. 206).

PLATE 6.218
Pedicularis attollens
(p. 206).

PLATE 6.219
Penstemon floridus var.
floridus (p. 207).

PLATE 6.220
Penstemon fruticiformis
(p. 207).

PLATE 6.221
Penstemon heterodoxus
(p. 207).

PLATE 6.222
Penstemon monoensis
(p. 208).

PLATE 6.223 *Penstemon patens* (p. 208).

PLATE 6.224 *Penstemon rostiflorus* (p. 208).

PLATE 6.225 *Penstemon scapoides* (p. 208).

PLATE 6.226
Penstemon speciosus (p. 209).

PLATE 6.227
Scrophularia desertorum
(p. 209).

PLATE 6.228
Verbascum thapsus (p. 209).

PLATE 6.229
Lycium andersonii (p. 210).

PLATE 6.230
Lycium cooperi (p. 210).

PLATE 6.231
Nicotiana trigonophylla
(p. 211).

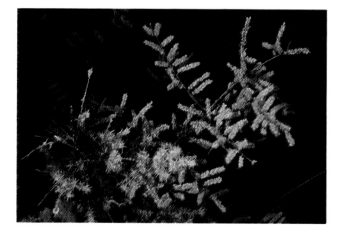

PLATE 6.232
Tamarix ramosissima
(p. 211).

PLATE 6.233
Phoradendron bolleanum ssp.
densum (p. 212).

PLATE 6.234
Larrea tridentata (p. 213).

70 mm

Trimerotropis pallidipennis
(p. 254)

Nymphalis antiopa (p. 266)

Melanoplus sanguinipes
(p. 254)

Agnostokasia sublima
(p. 254)

Limenitis lorquini (p. 266)

Anabrus simplex
(p. 254)

Eleodes armatus
(p. 260)

Phodaga alticeps
(p. 260)

*Tegrodera
latecincta*
(p. 260)

*Pleurospasta
mirabilis*
(p. 260)

Pepsis sp.
(p. 269)

Vanessa atalanta
(p. 266)

Judolia instabilis
(p. 261)

*Crossidius
hertipes nubilis*
(p. 261)

Nicrophorus hecate
(p. 259)

Neominois ridingsii
(p. 266)

*Metasyrphus
aberrantis*
(p. 268)

*Lygaeus
kalmii*
(p. 256)

*Alydus
pluto*
(p. 256)

*Hippodamia
convergens*
(p. 260)

*Bombus
centralis*
(p. 270)

PLATE 7.1   Nymphalid butterflies and miscellaneous insects. (*Arranged and photographed by J. Smiley.*)

—81 mm—

Hyles lineata
(p. 262)

Pholisora catullus
(p. 262)

Pholisora libya lena
(p. 262)

Polites sabuleti tecumseh (p. 262)

Hesperia miriamae
(p. 262)

Hesperia comma harpalus
(p. 263)

♂

♀

Hesperia juba
(p. 263)

♂

♀

Pontia protodice (p. 263)

♂

♀

Pontia beckerii (p. 263)

♂

Pontia beckerii
(p. 263)

♀

Euchloe hyantis lotta
(p. 263)

Colias eurytheme
(p. 263)

♀

Colias eurytheme (p. 263)

♂

PLATE 7.2 Sphinx moth, skippers, and pierid butterflies. (*Butterfly specimens courtesy of County Museum of Los Angeles and Museum of Systematic Biology, University of California, Irvine. Arranged and photographed by N. Rank.*)

Papilio indra
nevadensis (p. 264)

Plebejus melissa paradoxa (p. 264)   underside

Plebejus saepiolus (p. 264)

Plebejus icarioides
(p. 264)

Plebejus shasta   Plebejus lupini   Plebejus acmon
(p. 265)   (p. 265)   (p. 265)

underside   Apodemia mormo
Plebejus acmon (p. 265)   (p. 264)

PLATE 7.3   Swallowtail and lycaenid butterflies. (*Butterfly specimens courtesy of County Museum of Los Angeles and Museum of Systematic Biology, University of California, Irvine. Arranged and photographed by N. Rank.*)

|←— 29 mm —→|

Glaucopsyche piasus
(p. 265)

Glaucopsyche lygdamus (p. 265)

underside

♂

Celastrina ladon (p. 265)

♂

♀

underside

Brephidium exilis
underside (p. 265)

Lycaena heteronea (p. 265)

♂

♀

Lycaena editha (p. 265)

♀

♂

Lycaena cuprea (p. 265)

♂

Mitoura siva
(p. 265)

♂

♀

Mitoura spinetorum
(p. 265)

PLATE 7.4   Lycaenid butterflies. (*Butterfly specimens courtesy of County Museum of Los Angeles and Museum of Systematic Biology, University of California, Irvine. Arranged and photographed by N. Rank.*)

|←——— 90 mm ———→|

Danaus plexippus (p. 266)

Cercyonis oetus (p. 266)

Chlosyne neumoegeni (p. 266)

Chlosyne leanira alma (p. 266)

Euphydryas anicia wheeleri (p. 266)

Nymphalis milberti (p. 266)

Vanessa cardui (p. 266)

Vanessa annabella (p. 266)

PLATE 7.5 Nymphalid butterflies.(*Butterfly specimens courtesy of County Museum of Los Angeles and Museum of Systematic Biology, University of California, Irvine. Arranged and photographed by N. Rank.*)

PLATE 9.1   Kern Plateau Slender Salamander, *Batrachoseps* sp. (p. 281).

PLATE 9.2   Inyo Mountains Slender Salamander, *Batrachoseps campi* (p. 281).

PLATE 9.3   Inyo Mountains Slender Salamander, *Batrachoseps campi* (p. 281).

PLATE 9.4   Owens Valley Web-toed Salamander, *Hydromantes* sp. (p. 282).

PLATE 9.5   Western Toad, *Bufo boreas* (p. 283).

PLATE 9.6   Black Toad, *Bufo exsul* (p. 283).

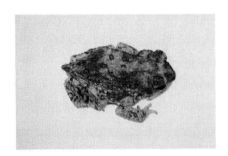

PLATE 9.7   Red-spotted Toad, *Bufo punctatus* (p. 285).

PLATE 9.8   Pacific Treefrog, *Pseudacris regilla* (p. 285).

PLATE 9.9 Great Basin Spadefoot Toad, *Spea intermontana* (p. 287).

PLATE 9.10 Bullfrog, *Rana catesbeiana* (p. 287).

PLATE 9.11 Northern Leopard Frog, *Rana pipiens* (p. 289).

PLATE 10.1 Southern Alligator Lizard, *Elgaria multicarinata*, adult (p. 303).

PLATE 10.2 Southern Alligator Lizard, *Elgaria multicarinata*, juvenile (p. 303).

PLATE 10.3 Panamint Alligator Lizard, *Elgaria panamintina*, adult (p. 304).

PLATE 10.4 Panamint Alligator Lizard, *Elgaria panamintina*, juvenile (p. 304).

PLATE 10.5 Western Banded Gecko, *Coleonyx variegatus* (p. 305).

PLATE 10.6 Zebra-tailed Lizard, *Callisaurus draconoides*, male dorsal (p. 306).

PLATE 10.7 Zebra-tailed Lizard, *Callisaurus draconoides*, male ventral (p. 306).

PLATE 10.8 Great Basin Collard Lizard, *Crotaphytus bicinctores*, male (p. 307).

PLATE 10.9 Desert Iguana, *Dipsosaurus dorsalis* (p. 309).

PLATE 10.10 Long-nosed Leopard Lizard, *Gambelia wislizenii* (p. 310).

PLATE 10.11 Desert Horned Lizard, *Phrynosoma platyrhinos* (p. 310).

PLATE 10.12 Common Chuckwalla, *Sauromalus obesus* (p. 312).

PLATE 10.13 Sagebrush Lizard, *Sceloporus graciosus* (p. 314).

PLATE 10.14   Desert Spiny Lizard,
Sceloporus magister, male (p. 314).

PLATE 10.15   Desert Spiny Lizard,
Sceloporus magister, female (p. 314).

PLATE 10.16   Western Fence Lizard,
Sceloporus occidentalis, male (p. 316).

PLATE 10.17   Side-blotched Lizard,
Uta stansburiana, male (p. 317).

PLATE 10.18   Gilbert Skink,
Eumeces gilberti, adult (p. 318).

PLATE 10.19   Gilbert Skink,
Eumeces gilberti, juvenile (p. 318).

PLATE 10.20   Western Skink,
Eumeces skiltonianus, adult (p. 320).

PLATE 10.21   Western Whiptail,
Cnemidophorus tigris, adult (p. 320).

PLATE 10.22 Western Whiptail, *Cnemidophorus tigris,* juvenile (p. 320).

PLATE 10.23 Desert Night Lizard, *Xantusia vigilis* (p. 322).

PLATE 10.24 Rosy Boa, *Lichanura trivirgata* (p. 324).

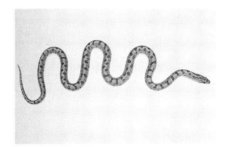

PLATE 10.25 Glossy Snake, *Arizona elegans* (p. 324).

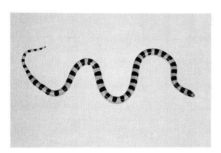

PLATE 10.26 Mojave Shovel-nosed Snake, *Chionactis occipitalis occipitalis* (p. 326).

PLATE 10.27 Nevada Shovel-nosed Snake, *Chionactis occipitalis talpina* (p. 326).

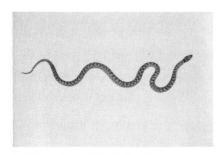

PLATE 10.28 Night Snake, *Hypsiglena torquata* (p. 326).

PLATE 10.29 Common Kingsnake, *Lampropeltis getula* (p. 327).

PLATE 10.30   Coachwhip,
Masticophis flagellum (p. 328).

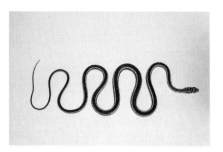

PLATE 10.31   Striped Whipsnake,
Masticophis taeniatus (p. 330).

PLATE 10.32   Spotted Leaf-nosed Snake,
Phyllorhynchus decurtatus (p. 330).

PLATE 10.33   Gopher Snake,
Pituophis catenifer (p. 332).

PLATE 10.34   Long-nosed Snake,
Rhinocheilus lecontei (p. 332).

PLATE 10.35   Western Patch-nosed Snake,
Salvadora hexalepis (p. 334).

PLATE 10.36   Ground Snake,
Sonora semiannulata (p. 334).

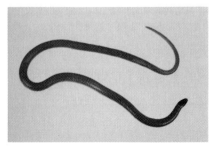

PLATE 10.37   Southwestern Black-headed
Snake, *Tantilla hobartsmithi* (p. 336).

PLATE 10.38 Sierra Garter Snake, *Thamnophis couchii* (p. 336).

PLATE 10.39 Western Terrestrial Garter Snake, *Thamnophis elegans vagrans* (p. 338).

PLATE 10.40 Lyre Snake, *Trimorphodon biscutatus* (p. 338).

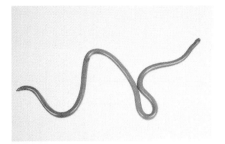

PLATE 10.41 Western Blind Snake, *Leptotyphlops humilis* (p. 339).

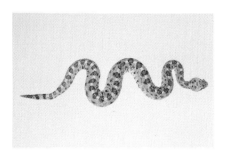

PLATE 10.42 Sidewinder, *Crotalus cerastes* (p. 340).

PLATE 10.43 Speckled Rattlesnake, *Crotalus mitchellii* (p. 342).

PLATE 10.44 Western Rattlesnake, *Crotalus viridis* (p. 343).

PLATE 11.1 Summer visitors to the foothill sagebrush community. Upper left, Mourning Doves (p. 372); upper right, Northern Flicker (p. 380); left center, Say's Phoebe (p. 385); lower left, Brown-headed Cowbird (p. 427); lower right, Brewer's Blackbird (p. 427).

PLATE 11.2   Owl mobbing scene in the Pinyon Woodland. Upper left, Black-throated Gray Warbler (p. 411); upper right, Clark's Nutcracker (p. 390); middle left, White-breasted Nuthatch (p. 395); lower right, Long-eared Owl (p. 374); lower left, Mountain Bluebird (p. 403).

PLATE 11.3 Bird species of canyon cliffs and boulder slides. Upper left, Violet-green Swallow (p. 387); upper right, White-throated Swift (p. 378); lower left, Rock Wren (p. 397); lower right, Canyon Wren (p. 398).

PLATE 11.4   Diverse birds of the Quaking Aspen–Bristlecone Pine association. Upper left, Mountain Chickadee (p. 392); upper right, Pygmy Nuthatch (p. 396); middle left, Western Tanager (p. 413); middle right, Red-naped Sapsucker (p. 379); lower left, Yellow-rumped Warbler (p. 411); lower right, Hermit Thrush (p. 403).

13

Native Land Use:
Archaeology and Anthropology

Robert L. Bettinger

When in 1834 the trapping party of Joseph Reddeford Walker trekked east across the Sierra Nevada and entered Owens Valley, becoming the first white men ever to set eyes on the White Mountains, the range was already well used—tracked with the paths, dotted with the camps, and littered with the debris of 10,000 years of human occupancy. The native groups in residence on Walker's arrival were only the area's most recent occupants, followers of a long procession of earlier cultures. Tragically, they were to be the last in that procession. Their existence was terminated by forces set in motion with the coming of the Walker party, who gave them little notice and squandered the singular opportunity to observe this native eastern California culture in its pristine form.

It is unfortunate that we know so little about the peoples the Walker party passed amidst during the trip north though Owens Valley in 1834–1835. A complete record would have provided key information to aid in understanding the entire history of native land use in this region. However, Walker and his men, conditioned by constant skirmishes with mounted natives during their trapping expeditions in the Rocky Mountains, regarded the American Indian with ignorance and suspicion. Indeed, this very same party had already slain some 40 members of a large group of Northern Paiute assembled on the lower Humboldt Sink. It was an unprovoked—though in their eyes justified—preemptive strike, a single volley that set the tone for all subsequent relations between whites and native inhabitants of the Great Basin.

It comes as no surprise, therefore, that the written account of the native peoples of eastern California met by the Walker party, set down by one of its members, Zenas Leonard, is brief and biased. Subsequent descriptions, which increase in number as Owens Valley and surrounding areas were settled in the early 1860s, are written in the perspective of those with vested interest in justifying the displacement of native groups from lands to which their claim by traditional possession was beyond dispute. The view they present is colored accordingly, and it is commonly difficult to distinguish fact from folklore.

It was not until the 1920s that a deliberate attempt was made by trained anthropologists to investigate and document the culture of the various aboriginal groups that lived at the foot of the White Mountains. However, by this time the pathetic battles had all been fought, the diseases had run their course, the major villages had been abandoned, and native lifeways existed only in the memories of the few aged individuals born long before the first white settlement was built in Owens Valley.

Whatever their flaws, the early anecdotal accounts and the systematic records made much later by trained observers can be pieced into a picture of aboriginal culture in and around the White Mountains on the eve of the Walker expedition. Archaeological evidence makes it possible to extend this view several thousand years into the past, to the first entry of people to eastern California.

It is fortunate, given the purpose of this volume, that the pattern of life of these pedestrian hunter-gatherers, without metal tools or benefit of domesticated plants, is best understood in terms of the exigencies of making a living by the judicious use of native plants and animals. The greater part of the activities and movements of these peoples were dictated by the rhythm of seasons and by the life cycles of native flora and fauna. This is by no means all there is to native culture, but it is the part that is best known and that is emphasized here.

THE PAIUTE

In ethnographic times, that period for which first-hand observations exist, the White Mountains were regarded as the territory of three different aboriginal groups, each of which resided most of the year in the lowlands below this range (Fig. 13.1). By convention, all three groups are designated *Paiute*, although they referred to themselves simply as *Numu*, "the people," and their neighbors knew them by different names according to their own tongues.

The entire western drainage of the White Mountains was traditionally used by the Owens Valley Paiute, the eastern drainage by the Fish Lake Valley Paiute, and the southern drainage—that part emptying into Deep Springs Valley—by the Deep Springs Valley Paiute. All three groups spoke varying dialects of a language known as Mono, one of six languages in the larger Numic language group. The collective speakers of the Numic language account for virtually all of the native peoples living in the Great Basin—from the Sierra Nevada in the west to the Wasatch Mountains of Utah in the east, and from Death Valley in the south to the Snake River Plains, Idaho, in the north.

There were distinguishable differences among the Owens Valley, Fish Lake Valley, and Deep Springs Valley Paiute, but in a broad sense they made use of the same technology and their adaptations were of similar kind, especially with respect to the use of the natural resources of the White Mountains, which is of principal concern here.

TECHNOLOGY

Technology—the tools, implements, and facilities used to gather plants, take game, make tools, and provide shelter from the elements—was relatively simple, though not unsophisticated.

The more substantial dwellings were built at important, long-term settlements. In the lowlands these were circular, domed willow pole frameworks thatched with

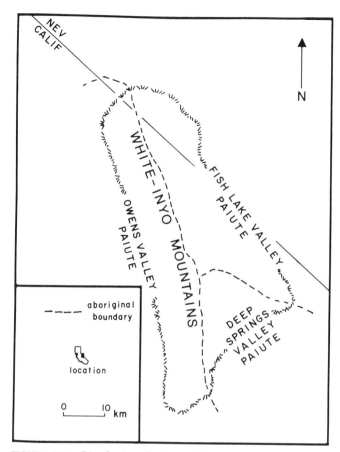

FIGURE 13.1   Distribution of ethnographic groups using the White-Inyo Range at the time of Euro-American contact.

Tule or Bulrush (*Scirpus* spp.) or grasses (esp. *Elymus* spp.) (Fig. 13.2). In the White Mountains, with the different materials at hand, houses were conical or oblong gabled affairs (Fig. 13.3) made with Pinyon Pine (*Pinus monophylla*) or Utah Juniper (*Juniperus osteosperma*) limbs and covered with fresh pine boughs or pine duff.

Both lowland and upland houses were furnished with fireplaces, principally for warmth. Most cooking was done outside or in a structure similar in construction to dwellings and built especially for that purpose.

Settlements used for shorter periods, less than a month or so, were generally furnished only with low, circular brush enclosures or windbreaks. There might be one for each family—each with its own hearth—or a single, large one for several families, within which each family used and maintained a separate fireplace for cooking and heating. Such brush "surrounds" where also built at more permanent settlements, for cooking or sleeping in warm weather.

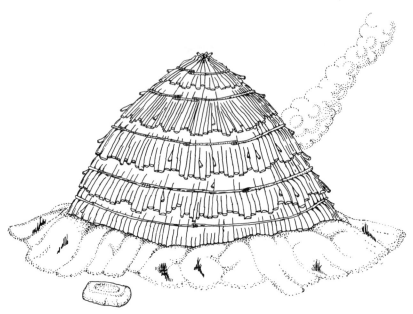

FIGURE 13.2 Tule-thatched house used in the lowlands. Here smoke exits from doorway on opposite side. Houses of this type were between 5 and 7 m in diameter.

FIGURE 13.3 Cutaway view showing interior of gabled log house used in the Pinyon Woodland. Such houses were between 4 and 8 m in length.

Hunters unable to return to their base camps at night often built little or no shelter and kept themselves warm by means of a small fire built in the open, although they might seek the cover of rock ledges or cave mouths in inclement weather.

Virtually all containers were of basketry, which in both durability and weight suited the needs of peoples often on the move. Among the most important of these wares (Fig. 13.4) were the large, conical carrying baskets fitted with tumplines, pitch-covered or lined water jugs, storage baskets, plaque-like serving trays, and cooking vessels, the contents of which were heated by means of hot rocks. Small quantities of pottery vessels (Fig. 13.5), made of clay from weathered granitic outcrops and fashioned in coils laid one atop another and then scraped smooth, were also used

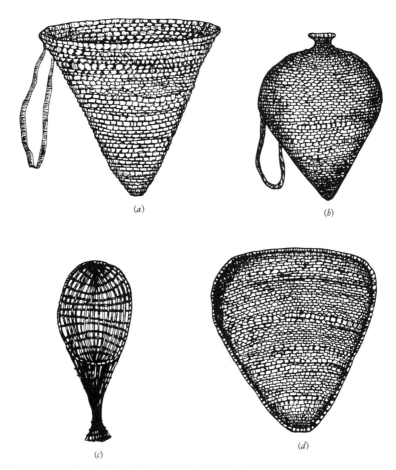

(a)

(b)

(c)

(d)

FIGURE 13.4   Various basket forms used as utensils. (a) Conical carrying basketry with tumpline. (b) Pitch-lined water jug with carrying strap. (c) Seed beater. (d) Triangular winnowing tray.

FIGURE 13.5   Conical ceramic
cooking vessel.

as cooking vessels. An advantage of such vessels was that their contents—generally mixed stews of seed mush and meat—could be cooked directly over a fire.

The stone *mano* (Fig. 13.6*a*), a small bun-shaped implement with a flat or rounded grinding face, was held by hand (hence its name, the Spanish word for "hand") and worked over a large millingstone (*metate*, Fig. 13.6*b*). The flat or basin-shaped surface of the *metate* served to render seeds into flour, which could be eaten as paste or cooked into mush.

Subsistence

With the exception of a few resources that were taken cooperatively, the procurement of plants and animals was performed by individuals working entirely in isolation, or singly but in the company of a few others engaged in the same task, and was

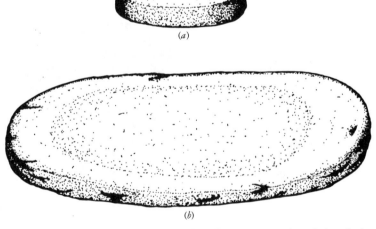

FIGURE 13.6   Stone grinding implements used in the preparation of plant foods.
(*a*) Handstone or *mano*. (*b*) Millingstone or *metate*.

more or less strictly divided along the lines of sex: plant collection was generally the responsibility of women, animal procurement the responsibility of men. The gear used by men and women differed accordingly.

Plant procurement. Many plant foods could simply be picked by hand: succulent sprouts and shoots, leafy greens, and some berries and seeds. The bulk of plant collection, however, entailed the use of two tools: the seed beater, generally used in conjunction with a collecting tray, and the digging stick. The basketry seed beater (see Fig. 13.4c), similar in construction to but slightly smaller than a tennis racquet, was used to strike ripened seeds from their stalks directly into the conical carrying basket or into a shallow, triangular collecting tray (see Fig. 13.4d). The latter also served in the winnowing and parching of seeds. The digging stick, generally about a meter long, sharpened and fire-hardened at one end, was used primarily to excavate roots and bulbs, but it also served to probe for and expose caches to roots and seeds stored by rodents.

When traveling in the field, women commonly carried with them basketry repair kits — foreshortened versions of more elaborate gear used at home — which included a cactus spine awl, willow splints for material, and a small, sharp flake of stone to cut and shape the willow splints. A woman also might equip herself with a stone knife hafted in wood (Fig. 13.7a), which both at home and in the field was used as a general-purpose tool for cutting, sawing, and scraping wood, fiber, hide, meat, and a variety of other materials.

Plant collecting expeditions were generally conducted within a two-hour walk of the base settlement, either a permanent village or short-term collecting camp. Operation within this restricted area permitted individuals the time to locate promising collecting areas and work them thoroughly and still return to the base camp before nightfall.

Plants were the center of the Paiute adaptation. They furnished fully 70% of the annual dietary intake, and their collection and preparation constantly occupied womenfolk. It was the gathering of plants, not the hunting of animals, that dictated the seasonal movements and the location of settlements for these peoples.

Animal Procurement. The major implements used by men were those of the hunt. These included the sinew-backed bow and arrow. The arrow was compound — fletched

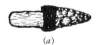

(a)

(b)

FIGURE 13.7 Common implements. (a) Hafted stone knife. (b) Composite arrow with stone point, Greasewood foreshaft, and *Phragmites* mainshaft.

and constructed with a reed (*Phragmites communis*) mainshaft, at the front of which was inserted a hardwood foreshaft, generally of Greasewood (*Sarcobatus vermiculatus*) (Fig. 13.7*b*). The foreshaft might be further modified by the attachment of: (1) a stone point for large game, including deer (*Odocoileus hemionus*) and Mountain Sheep (*Ovis canadensis* spp.); (2) a thick collar of sinew that caused the arrow to bounce along the water, for ducks and geese; (3) a set of four sticks lashed perpendicular to the foreshaft, for such upland birds as quail; or (4) nothing at all, leaving a simple hardened foreshaft for use on small game such as rabbits (*Sylvilagus audubonii*).

In addition, hunters generally carried a stone knife for skinning and cutting and an emergency repair kit with replacement stone points and wooden foreshafts. They were also commonly equipped with an antler flaker to resharpen broken points and stone knives dulled through use, and to fashion other implements made of stone for use by both men and women. Production of the latter kind was always done at base camps rather than in the field, where time was limited and attention was on the hunt.

Depending on the kind of expedition being undertaken, men might also carry the trigger mechanisms and trip cords meeded to fashion snares or deadfalls in the field, the intended prey generally being small birds and rodents to supply the hunter with food. Larger snares, however, were also used to immobilize deer or sheep long enough to be dispatched by hunters lying in wait.

Most Paiute hunting excursions were conducted out of the family base camp, with one or two individuals traveling to specific locations where game was known to be present and particularly susceptible to ambush at a given time of day. Because in this kind of hunting the stalk and chase are quickly done, hunters were able to make longer daily trips than women engaged in seed collection. A kill late in the day or the prospect of success at the following daybreak, however, occasionally meant spending the night far from the main camp.

Communal hunts—large, fire-aided deer drives undertaken by as many as 100 assembled men, and fall antelope and jackrabbit drives engaging the combined efforts of men, women, and children—were alternative forms of animal capture, but they were periodic in occurrence and a substantial departure from the daily pattern. Overall, hunting provided no more than about 30% of annual dietary intake, and the gopher, mouse, wood rat, and rabbit were more common on the menu than the deer, Mountain Sheep, and antelope.

Pinyon procurement. All of the subsistence activities described so far, whether pertaining to plants or to animals, are generalized in the sense that they embrace broad classes of resources rather than one species. The seed beater could be used for no less than 50 individual species of grasses and berries, the bow and arrow for perhaps half as many animals. This offered both hunter and gatherer a wide range of resources of which only the most choice would be sought on any given foray. This wide selection is a reflection that none of these resources was productive and reliable enough to merit special attention.

The nut of the Pinyon Pine (*Pinus monophylla*) stands in marked contrast to all other resources, for it was available in large quantities with some degree of frequency. As a result, a specialized procurement system developed around this one plant. Because there are extensive Pinyon Pine groves in the White Mountains, a substantial proportion of aboriginal activity in this range, prehistoric and historic, centered around this specialized system, which is worth describing in some detail.

The nut of the Pinyon Pine was the single most important food resource in the dietary regimen of the Paiute of Deep Springs, Fish Lake, and Owens valleys. For all three, the major groves were in the White Mountains at elevations between 6560 ft (2,000 m) and 8,528 ft (2,600 m). In the event these groves failed, which was common, there were alternative groves in the Silver Peak Range, east of Fish Lake Valley; in the Benton Range and Glass Mountain Ridge, north of Owens Valley; in the Inyo Mountains, south of the White Mountains; and in the Sierra Nevada, west of Owens Valley.

Pine cones develop and mature over a two-year period, during which they may be lost to drought, wind, frost, or insect infestation. This fragility stretched over a two-year span explains the frequent failure of individual groves to produce any crop at all, which in turn was responsible for much aboriginal movement, commonly over long distances, to find productive groves.

The nut enclosed within the cone ripens by early fall, when the cone is still green and thickly covered with pitch. It was at this time that native groups, commonly entire bands or villages, would move from the lowland summer camps or villages to the lower margin of the Pinyon Woodland. Here they established base camps for the Pinyon Pine harvest, generally on ridges and saddles, where the ground was relatively flat. The size of the crop was readily evident even by casual inspection. If it were large, gabled or conical long dwellings—usually one to a family with a separate cookhouse—were constructed in anticipation of winter residence in these locations. If the crop were judged too small to sustain extended winter occupation, only temporary shelters were made, and with the close of the harvest the site was vacated in favor of a lowland village. Upon departure, that part of the crop that could be transported was taken along and the balance cached for a later trip.

Owing to its importance in the winter diet, all possible measures were taken to maximize the nut harvest. The most crucial step in this regard was the initiation of the harvest while the cones were still green, pitch-covered, tightly closed, and, therefore, relatively inaccessible to the birds and rodents that competed for them. Cones left on the tree until brown and dry are more easily handled and their nuts more easily freed, but this shortens the harvest and brings heavy losses through animal depredation. The Paiute, who were so dependent on the pine nut, therefore undertook the more arduous green cone harvest.

The basic gathering party was the nuclear family. The father, equipped with a long, hooked pole, shook cones loose from the higher limbs. The mother worked the lower limbs by hand or hook, and the children gathered fallen cones and climbed through the lower limbs to shake out the more tenacious ones. The gathering occupied the first half of the day. The second half was devoted to roasting the green cones. A nest of brush was set afire and its smoldering embers heaped over the cones. This burned away most of the pitch, dried the cones, and caused the cone scales to open, duplicating the natural aging that occurs in cones left to brown on the tree. Roasted cones were raked from the embers and, while still hot, struck with a stone hammer on a stone anvil. The nuts were then shaken and pried from the cones. The nuts were then parched with coals on a basketry tray, shelled with the *mano* and *metate*, parched (toasted) again, and then ground into meal.

During the best years, when the slow roasting and shelling process could not keep pace with the flow of the harvest, green cones were stored in grass-lined pits and covered with grass, boughs, and stones. Free nuts were stored similarly.

The Pinyon Pine harvest was a microcosm of Paiute subsistence in two respects. First, it illustrates the complex, time-consuming, and difficult processing attached to the collection, preparation, and storage of nearly all plant foods, which were the mainstays of subsistence. Second, and perhaps less obvious, the heavy investment of time in the Pinyon Pine harvest was primarily a consequence of the importance of the pine nut in the Paiute diet. Lesser reliance on pine nuts would have enabled the Paiute to collect only the ripe, brown cones and forgo the extra effort involved in roasting the green cones. At work here is the general principle of diminishing returns: the greater the quantity exploited, the greater the cost per individual item (cone, root, seed, or animal). Take the familiar activity of apple picking, for example. One or two apples (say, to snack on) can be obtained quickly and effortlessly from the lower branches of a tree. If, on the other hand, one required two or three lugs (boxes) of apples (say, for canning) from that same tree, the average time spent obtaining each individual fruit would almost certainly go up because apples from higher, less accessible branches would be needed to fill the boxes, and it would take more time and effort to get them. One might even be forced to pick smaller apples, and this too would increase the amount of time needed to fill the boxes. To obtain 10 lugs of apples from the tree would doubtless require an even greater average expenditure of time and effort per individual fruit. It might, for instance, demand that a ladder be made, the cost and effort of which would have to be added to the cost directly associated with the job of apple picking.

In the case of the Paiute, the cost per kilo of pine nuts was high because it was important in the diet and exploited in large quantities. In a broader sense, the difficult and time-consuming labor associated with the procurement of nearly all of the plants and animals used by the Paiute is a reflection that, relative to the resources available, the population had by late prehistoric times grown quite large. This is a point that figures prominently in the prehistory of the White Mountains.

The Annual Round

The preceding discussion centers on the various parts of aboriginal Paiute life: the technology, the resources exploited by means of that technology, and the tactics of that exploitation. Underlying these, however, was a general strategy that linked all these parts into a coherent whole, balancing resources and activities to maximize the economic return for the labor expended, and distributing people over the landscape in a way that made this mix possible.

This strategy is termed the *annual round*, and its fundamental basis was the distribution and seasonal availability of various plant and animal resources. Much more than this was involved, however, because out of the more than 100 plant and animal species exploited, several were generally available at the same time, commonly in different places. Choices had to be made, therefore, as to which should be taken and which ignored. Time and location were critical considerations. Many summer grasses, for example, ripen and disperse their seeds within a very narrow "window" of time—often as little as a week. Even a day's tardiness in reaching such plants could reduce the potential harvest by as much as one-third. There was, too, the element of location. Between two resources, exploiting the most productive one might leave a group poorly positioned for subsequent resource collection whereas pursuing the less productive one might fit better with the larger pattern of movements and, in the long run, represent the more economical option.

Complexities inherent in these decisions were exacerbated by circumstances of the moment: a chance thunderstorm that filled a dry basin with a shallow lake teeming with Fairy Shrimp, or a rocky cleft with sufficient water to supply a collecting expedition in an area normally too far from water to be exploited; an unusual concentration of edible insects; an abundance of bulb-bearing plants; or a windstorm that scattered seeds that would normally have been gathered.

All of these conditions defied solution according to rigid timetables and unvarying schedules and yielded only to a flexible pattern in which the general structure—the annual round—was determined but the details varied from year to year, season to season, and moment to moment. Two basic rules prevailed: (1) Seasonal resources were exploited in preference to nonseasonal resources. (2) Plant foods rather than animal foods dictated movements and activities.

It is only in reference to this larger context that aboriginal land use of the White Mountains can be properly understood. The White Mountains were but one small aspect of the Paiute annual round, and the decision to use their resources was always balanced against what was available elsewhere—especially in the lowlands, where travel was easier and, as a consequence, most activities tended to concentrate.

A brief sketch of the Paiute annual round, therefore, begins with the observation that most of the year was spent in the lowlands below the White Mountains. The gathering year began with the appearance of edible roots and greens, the first fresh food after a winter of stored food. Because spring comes earlier at low elevations, most groups worked the valley floors at this time, moving there from upland villages if they had spent the winter in the mountains. By late spring, attention turned to seed plants, which reached peak abundance both in number of species and quantity of crop in midsummer. Because plants in dry habitats generally ripen earlier than those in wet ones, summer resource exploitation required a balance between availability of food resources and access to water. Because stored summer plants were an essential part of the winter diet, the prospective location of winter camps, from which food caches had to be accessible, also figured prominently in the location of summer plant procurement.

In the late summer and early fall, attention turned first to wetland plants and then to the critical fall Pinyon Pine harvest. It was also in this season that annual festivals were held, generally in conjunction with antelope or rabbit drives, which could sustain a large group without unduly straining the winter stores of the host band or village. At this time of maximum social aggregation, new social ties were established and old ones strengthened. Plans for the future were made and publicized. It would be easy to mistake this socializing as nothing more than indulgence in the pleasure of company, but it had a more serious aspect: It was an essential ingredient of efficient resource exploitation that reduced the possibility of two families by chance disrupting each other's collecting round by targeting the same set of resources in the same general area. Further, it facilitated the planning of undertakings that required the cooperation of more than one family. Following the festival, groups returned to their winter camp—in the Pinyon Woodland if the nut crop had been large, or in the lowlands if it had been small. In these camps the winter was waited out, the time filled with the repair and manufacture of equipment and the recounting of ancient story cycles that explained the origin of the world and described the role of the Paiute in the deeper scheme of things.

We can underscore the relationship of the White Mountains to the Paiute annual round by noting that only two resources present in this range figured prominently in that system: the pine nut and large game—Mountain Sheep, deer, and possibly antelope. Stated another way, in terms of food return for unit of labor expended, out of all the natural resources potentially available in these uplands, only the pine nut and large game compared favorably with the lowland resources routinely exploited by the Paiute.

Hunters worked into the lower parts of the White Mountains on a daily basis when their family camps were located sufficiently nearby and game was in residence there—principally in the summer, when most herds grazed at elevations well above their low winter rangelands. The most intensive activity, however, was in the fall, when the Owens Valley Paiute, Deep Springs Valley Paiute, and Fish Lake Valley Paiute gathered, processed, and stored pine nuts in the extensive Pinyon Pine groves of this range, commonly remaining there until the following spring, provided the pine nut take was sufficiently large. Hunters also worked out of these fall and winter Pinyon camps, although they were far more successful in the fall, when herds, fat from summer grazing and their coats in peak condition, funneled out of the highlands along established migration routes. Later in winter, travel was more difficult for hunting parties and game was in poorer condition owing to lack of feed.

NATIVE LAND USE BEFORE HISTORY

It bears repeating that the foregoing view of Paiute culture derives entirely from accounts written by those who saw it first-hand or transcribed from the recollections of those who lived it. As such they are all subject to the same basic limitation: They refer only to the most recent periods of human occupancy of the White Mountains, beginning no earlier than about 1820. Because there is good reason to believe that eastern California has been continuously populated for the last 10,000 years, exclusive reliance on written records as a basis of inference about native land use would leave about 9,800 years—98% of the entire period—unspoken for.

Our only access to this earlier period of land use is through the study of the material residues resulting from that use, which is the concern of archaeology. Archaeological interpretation is in some respects more difficult than ethnographic interpretation because direct observation is limited to the physical remains left by an activity and from which the activity itself must be inferred; and if these activities can be inferred at all, it still remains to interpret the more general patterns they represent, just as piecemeal historical accounts and narratives must be organized into a coherent interpretation of native lifeways. The aims of archaeology and enthnography are similar, but the data of archaeology are more remote, the techniques and inferences are more complicated, and the interpretations are generally less precise and apply to broader periods of time.

It is an advantage of archaeology, however, that its data are not—as historical accounts and transcribed recollections are—subject to cultural preference and bias. The historical record is entirely blank on several aspects of the native life now considered central to the interpretation of aboriginal adaption, simply because neither early observers nor native participants saw them as particularly worthy of remark. Archaeology, then, offers the opportunity to examine these unrecorded aspects of native culture even in periods documented by written accounts. In the case of native land use in the White Mountains, however, the greatest potential application of archaeology is clearly in the area of prehistory, where there is no written record at all.

Like the most painstaking detective, the modern archaeologist takes it as given that, within certain limits, every human act leaves some form of evidence. In the simplest case, an object modified by a human—an *artifact*—can be recognized by its unnatural shape or the presence of unnatural markings; an unpeeled willow twig whittled to a point at one end is a good example. In a slightly different sense, plant and animal remains found in association with other evidence of human activity are termed *ecofacts*, which reflects their importance in reconstructing prehistoric diet and environment (i.e., the prehistoric ecosystem). At a more complex level of interpretation, any group of objects placed in such a way that the resulting pattern is recognizably unnatural is termed a *feature*; the remains of structures, firepits, food caches, and refuse dumps, to name a few, are features. At a still more complex level, a concentration of artifacts or features or both in one location is termed a *site*. Sites are generally taken to represent a focal point for one or more activities, which may be something as simple as the spot where an animal was killed and butchered or as complex as a permanent village. In addition to its archaeological assemblage, the location of a site with respect to the surrounding terrain and access to resources provides a major clue to the activities that were performed at the site.

A group of sites that exhibit similar kinds of artifacts, ecofacts, and features and occur in similar natural settings—suggesting use for the same purposes, in the same seasons, by groups of similar size and social composition (e.g., by families)—are said to constitute a *settlement category*. The remains of the different Pinyon camps occupied in the fall and winter by the historic Paiute would in this sense be considered a settlement category.

Finally, at the most complex level, all of the settlement categories used by one prehistoric group are collectively defined as its *settlement system*. By analogy, all of the various camps, villages, and temporary work stations used by the historic Paiute may be said to constitute the Paiute settlement system. Most of the following discussion of prehistoric land use in the White Mountains refers to the different kinds of settlement categories represented in this range and their relationship to the settlement systems of which they are a part.

Dating

Dating—the placement of cultural objects in time—is central to the study of pre-historic land use in the White Mountains. It is necessary as a basis for establishing contemporaneity between sites and settlement categories, which is critical to the in-terpretation of the full spectrum of aboriginal activities at any one time and for the examination of changes in these activities through time.

Three dating techniques have been particularly useful in establishing a chronolog-ical framework for the White Mountains. Of these, the most accurate is *radiocarbon*, which determines the age of organic matter—in archaeology, principally charcoal and bone—by the content of ^{14}C, an unstable isotope of elemental carbon that decays with age; the less ^{14}C in a sample, the older it is. Radiocarbon provides dates in calendar years, partly on the basis of precise correlations obtained by the radiocarbon dating of Bristlecone Pine samples from the White Mountains that have been dated independently by dendrochronology (tree-ring dating).

A second commonly used dating technique is *obsidian hydration*. Less accurate than those provided by radiocarbon, obsidian hydration dates are obtained by microscopic examination of small slices of obsidian—a natural volcanic glass widely used for tools by native groups—to determine the amount of moisture absorbed since the glass was first exposed to the atmosphere. Slices taken from artifacts made of this glass indicate when the tool was fashioned, this being the point at which the tool surface was first exposed to atmospheric moisture. Obsidian hydration also provides dates in calendar years.

The third, and by far the most common, method for dating sites in the White Mountains is by the presence of certain artifact forms known to have been popular only during limited periods of time, thus identifying the assemblages with which they are found as belonging to that period. Projectile points— the broader term that subsumes both the smaller arrow points and the larger points used on darts cast by means of a spear thrower (*atlatl*)—are the most important of these time-sensitive artifacts. Projectile points distinctive of specific periods of prehistory in the White Mountains are illustrated in Fig. 13.8. In this figure, the appearance of the bow and arrow at about A.D. 600 is reflected by the shift to smaller projectile points

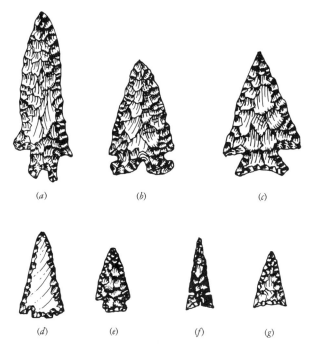

FIGURE 13.8 Projectile points representing different periods of aboriginal occupation in the White-Inyo Range. (*a*) 2500 B.C.–1200 B.C. (*b*), (*c*) 1200 B.C.–A.D. 600. (*d*), (*e*) A.D. 600–A.D. 1300. (*f*), (*g*) A.D. 1300–Euro-American contact. (*a*)–(*c*) Dart points. (*d*)–(*g*) Arrow points.

(arrowheads). Prior to this time the major hunting implement was the *atlatl*, or spear thrower, which cast a heavier dart, tipped by a heavier point (Fig. 13.9).

Archaeological Settlements in the White Mountains

Archaeological research in the White Mountains is still in its infancy, but the work that has been done is sufficient to indicate the broad outline of prehistoric land use and to define the major kinds of sites that are present. We currently divide these sites into three major categories: Pinyon camps, hunting stations, and alpine villages. Pinyon camps are already familiar to us from the discussion of the Paiute. The other two are not.

Pinyon camps. As the name indicates, Pinyon camps are the archaeological equivalents of the camps occupied by the historic Paiute for the fall Pinyon harvest and for winter residence in the mountains near nut caches when the nut crop was large. Excavation at such sites has revealed the charred stubs of structural beams set in circles, reflecting the presence of conical houses, and in ovals, reflecting gabled houses. Simple firepits, generally set to one side of the doorway—which probably served also as a

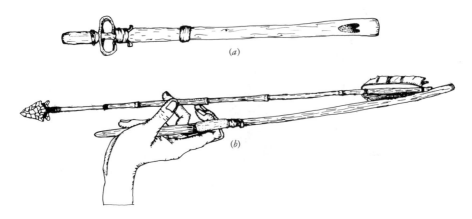

FIGURE 13.9 *Atlatl.* (*a*) Top view. (*b*) With dart, showing manner of use.

smokehole—characterize both kinds of houses. The remains of cone roasting hearths, full of burnt cones and pine nut hulls, are common, many placed in the depressions of abandoned houses. Circular alignments of stones—rock rings—between 2 and 4 m in diameter are very common at these sites; excavation has shown them to be essentially barren of artifacts and without firepits, all of which suggests they are the remains of pinecone caches. Other features regularly encountered at these sites are large, dug out basins and rock dams thrown across small, well-shaded ravines. Evidently these were built as places in which to store snow for use as drinking water—a reminder that most of these camps are far from the nearest water source and that their prolonged occupation was generally possible only after the first major snowfall of the season.

Artifacts found at Pinyon camps include projectile points, knives, scrapers of various sizes, point and knife blanks, and *manos* and *metates*. The points and knives indicate the use of these sites as bases for hunting operations, the scrapers (most of them probably for woodworking) and, again, the knives indicate the manufacture of wooden implements and basketry, and the milling equipment indicates both the processing of pine nuts and the preparation of food. The roasting hearths and cone caches are further evidence of Pinyon exploitation.

In sum, archaeological Pinyon camps contain a range of features and artifacts that corresponds almost exactly to what would have been left behind at a Pinyon camp occupied by the Paiute. On this basis, it is believed that these sites were occupied in the fall for the Pinyon harvest and in the winter when the nut crop was suitably large. Both the numbers of dwellings present at these sites and historic records of Paiute Pinyon camps suggest that the resident group consisted of perhaps 1 to 10 families, each living in a separate structure.

Because archaeological Pinyon camps are presumed to be equivalent to Paiute Pinyon camps, being used in the same seasons and for the same purposes, and since Paiute use of the White Mountains was of a sort that would leave only Pinyon camps as recognizable archaeological remains (the brief trips by Paiute hunters during the summer would produce little visible evidence), it follows that to date Pinyon camps in the White Mountains is to date the antiquity of this aspect of Paiute land use in this range. Radiocarbon dates on house beams, obsidian hydration dates on stone tools, and time-sensitive projectile points all suggest that the use of these Pinyon camps began around A.D. 600. Thus, the fall-winter use of White Mountain Pinyon Pine zone by the Paiute was part of a pattern that began some 1,400 years ago and ended only with the collapse of Paiute culture at the hands of Euro-Americans.

The remaining two settlement categories that have been found in the White Mountains have no analogue in the Paiute annual round and thus reflect patterns distinct from the Paiute adaptation as we know it from historic accounts.

Hunting stations.   Hunting stations are perhaps the most widespread and numerous archaeological sites found in the White Mountains. They occur in all major biotic communities within the range, extending from the lower skirts of the Pinyon Pine Woodland to the highest reaches of the Alpine Tundra. The lack of association with any specific plant resource or with locations that provide special access to plants is an important clue to their function and suggests they were intended for some purpose other than plant procurement. Additional evidence provided by the locations of these sites is their consistent association with certain landforms. Many of them are found on saddles, along ridgetops, on hillsides or in rocky outcrops overlooking springs and meadows, and at narrow defiles where two drainage channels join together. Common to all these and other locations in which hunting stations are found is the opportunity for concealment in an area frequented by mountain ungulates—deer and Mountain Sheep.

From their locations alone, then, we might surmise that the primary connection of these sites is with hunting. Their assemblages support this notion. The only constructions of any sort are hunting blinds, low breastworks of stone just large enough to conceal a hunter. Commonly, these are not positioned directly on the paths traveled by game but along the routes they would have used for escape. This implies hunting by teams, with one hunter assigned the task of ambush and one or more others the task of lying in wait along flight paths. This effective tactic takes advantage of the tendency displayed by both sheep and deer to pause after initial flight, commonly in predictable locations, and glance back toward the point where they were surprised. At just this moment, their attention directed elsewhere, they are particularly vulnerable to a well-cast dart or arrow.

Individual hunting stations commonly consist of several hunting blinds, scattered among which is the artifactural debris from past hunts. Projectile points—many of them broken, but surprisingly many still complete and evidently usable—are present, as are broken and worn butchering tools. Large quartz crystals, probably hunting talismans, are also occasionally found.

Unlike Pinyon camps, hunting camps exhibit no evidence of attempts to construct shelter and little suggestion of activities other than those directly related to hunting and butchering. There is, for instance, no indication of tools for food preparation nor any appreciable workshop debris to document the manufacture of wood or stone tools. Stonework seems to have been limited to resharpening of butchering tools that had broken or become dull.

To date, what limited excavation has been done at these sites has not added to the preceding interpretation; subsurface remains duplicate those found on the surface, consisting mostly of points, knives, and debris from tool resharpening.

That these sites were used exclusively for hunting and butchering, then, seems clear. The form of this hunting, however, appears to differ on several counts from that documented for the Paiute in the White Mountains. First, only the lowermost of these locales—those in the Pinyon Woodland—would be close enough to valley floor base camps and Pinyon camps to permit trips to and from them daily, which is the common manner of Paiute hunting. Those above the upper Sagebrush Scrub plant community are too remote to permit this; to use them would require overnight camps, which is not typical of Paiute hunting. Second, the carefully constructed hunting blinds and artifact litter show that such trips were regularly undertaken by organized hunting parties. This is difficult to reconcile with the Paiute annual round, in which families camped and circulated independently, making it difficult to undertake cooperative ventures, especially since movement centered around the demands of plant procurement.

This implies that these hunting camps were elements of an adaptive system different from that of the Paiute—one in which hunting was more important, at least enough to justify long trips for upland game and to adjust plant collecting to allow several families to join this activity.

Despite its increased importance, this upland hunting was never a lengthy affair. Had these trips lasted very long, it is unlikely that so many complete points would be found at these sites. Given enough time, hunters would no doubt have retrieved these pieces and reworked them to replace those lost or broken. Their presence suggests brief forays during which time was too short to be wasted on tool repair or an extensive search for lost pieces. In all likelihood, hunters carried enough ready-made darts and points to serve their needs, and when one was lost or smashed on a rock, it was simply replaced with another.

The brevity of these trips is understandable since these fast-traveling hunters, anticipating a return trip packing meat, carried few items to make their stay more comfortable or to afford protection from the incessant winds and nightly chill of the highlands. The lack of oxygen and difficulty of exertion that especially afflict newcomers to altitude would have compounded the discomfort of these lowland peoples and added incentive to finish their business with dispatch.

The points that these hunters so considerately left behind for the archaeologist provide the primary means for dating these stations. Only a few obsidian hydration dates are available. The points indicate that these sites were in use by at least 2500 B.C.; they ceased to be used by A.D. 600. Suspicions about the differences between the hunting pattern reflected by these sites and the one noted in ethnographic accounts of the Paiute are confirmed by the absence at these sites of the point styles known to have been used by the Paiute.

The differences in timespan between Pinyon camps and hunting stations suggest a major shift in land use patterns in the White Mountains and, by extension, throughout central eastern California. Before A.D. 600, large game was more important and plant foods—both those of the lowlands and the pine nut—were less important than in later times. There is further the suggestion in the nature of earlier hunting patterns that social fragmentation—the division into independent families—was less pronounced, which made it possible to mount cooperative hunting ventures on a regular basis. This adaptive shift is underscored by the third major category of archaeological sites found in the White Mountains, the alpine village, which ranks as the most unusual and unexpected of all the sites in this range.

Alpine villages. Until relatively recently, the prevailing view was that aboriginal land use above the Pinyon Woodland was limited to hunting. The basis for this inference was both empirical (there was no evidence of other kinds of activities) and logical (resources other than animals are limited in number and kind, and living conditions are rigorous). Additionally, these uplands are far removed from the lowlands, preventing the use of that much more productive area. For all these reasons, the possibility of aboriginal villages at high altitudes had been given no serious consideration among archaeologists working in western North America. It came as a major surprise, therefore, when such sites were found—not just one but several, and in two different mountain ranges within the Great Basin: the Toquima Range, in central Nevada, and the White Mountains. The White Mountains exhibit this pattern best, and it is the sites in this range with which we shall deal exclusively.

So far 11 alpine villages have been found at elevations between 10,400 ft (3,170 m) and 12,640 ft (3,850 m) in the White Mountains. The specific locations of these sites are of little importance; their general location, however, near permanent water sources and on the edges of wet meadows, is of some significance in its implications of prolonged use, for which water is essential, and exploitation of highland plants growing in these meadows.

The assemblages found at these sites are quite different from those of hunting stations. Each village exhibits one to eight dwellings. Excavations suggest these are semisubterranean pit houses with low rock walls and limb and bough roofs supported by four or more upright beams set inside the wall, joined by horizontal stringers or rafters (Fig. 13.10). The roofing limbs are thought to have leaned inward from the low wall to these rafters. The houses exhibit large central firepits lined with stone—probably to conserve fuel, as the rocks would continue to radiate heat long after a fire built within them had gone out.

In contrast to houses at Pinyon camps and at villages on the valley floor, which were primarily used as sleeping quarters, the alpine village dwellings contain evidence of many activities, including stone working. Evidently much work was done indoors to escape the wind and the cold. Points attest to hunting—which, as at Pinyon camps, was carried out from these settlements, and not from separate hunting camps. Knives, drills, and blanks for making points and knives suggest a wide range of specific activities, including butchering, tool repair, and tool replacement. Broken points discarded in these structures commonly show abortive attempts at resharpening. This attests to extended periods of use during which the inhabitants were unable to obtain fresh supplies of raw materials and were forced to use what they had brought to the

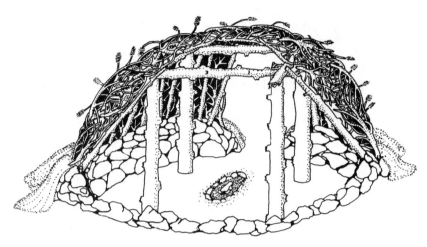

FIGURE 13.10   Cutaway of house form used in alpine villages in the White Mountains. Houses of this type were between 4 and 6 m in diameter.

fullest, scavenging the hillsides in search of lost pieces that might be repaired. This is in marked contrast to the more casual pattern of discard noted at hunting stations, the occupants of which invested most of their time in hunting, not tool repair.

Perhaps the most remarkable aspect of these alpine village assemblages, however, is the presence of grinding tools. There are far more of these than would be needed to prepare what little plant food could have been brought to these sites from camps below. The numbers in which they are found ensures they were used to process local plant foods, most notably roots—charred specimens of which have been recovered from the central hearths of the dwellings; these have been tentatively identified as Bitterroot (*Lewisia pygmaea*). Pine nuts, principally of Limber Pine (*P. flexilis*), which is available within a short distance of these sites, and, in smaller quantity, Pinyon Pine (which must have been imported), have also been recovered from these hearths. It is likely that local grasses and berries were also collected, but work so far has not revealed them.

The intensity of plant collecting is underscored by vast quantities of broken and battered cobble tools with steep working edges, thought to have been used to shred and pulp rootstalks prior to final grinding. These battered cobbles litter the surfaces of alpine villages in great profusion.

Such evidence of plant procurement is a major discovery given the long-standing belief that the harshness of the alpine climate and scarcity of alpine plants would preclude such an exploitative pattern—a view, incidentally, supported by ethnographic accounts, which make no mention of it.

On the basis of these various lines of evidence, we now believe that these alpine villages were occupied by groups of families, probably three to five of them, for extended periods beginning about mid-June and ending sometime in late August or early September. This is the only period during which plant resources are present in any quantity and the weather—though still uncomfortable—is relatively tolerable.

Both plant and animal procurement were intensively pursued. The plants were readily available in the meadows near the villages. Since these habitats are spacially restricted and isolated from each other, it is likely that women engaged in root or seed collection stayed relatively close to home. It may well be that they devoted as much time to the pounding, parching, and grinding of plant foods as to their collection.

Hunting was another matter. The placement of the alpine villages in meadows that had formerly been frequented by sheep and deer no doubt disrupted the movements and distribution of these species, causing them to seek refuge in more inaccessible places and perhaps to move around more to find new rangelands to replace those lost with the establishment of the alpine villages. Because of this, hunters would have had to travel to be successful. Very likely, they worked alone and—rather than hunt by ambush from blinds—kept on the move in order to locate herds, the daily whereabouts of which had become less predictable with their dislocation from traditional feeding grounds. This pattern stands in sharp contrast to earlier hunting patterns, in which groups of hunters stationed themselves along traditional game trails and waited for the game to come to them. Because the alpine villages afforded shelter and other conveniences and were relatively close at hand, it is likely that hunters returned to them nightly, carrying with them the take of that day—unbutchered or perhaps gutted and field-dressed. Marmots, ground squirrels, and White-tailed Jackrabbits may have been occasionally taken as secondary targets by hunters not fortunate enough to capture a sheep or deer; more of these smaller prey, however, were probably taken by snares set near the village and checked daily by those returning from hunts or by children or women who stayed near the village and counted the maintenance of a trap line as a normal part of camp chores.

Alpine hunting ceases to be productive with the first major storm in the fall, which, whether it brings snow or not, drives animals from their summer range along migration routes to the lower winter rangeland. By the time this occurs, nearly all alpine plants are past the point where their exploitation is worthwhile. It seems unlikely, therefore, that alpine villages where inhabited later than this. The occupants of these sites probably remained until Limber Pine nuts could be harvested in late summer and, this done, simply moved downslope into the Pinyon Woodland to undertake the fall Pinyon Pine harvest.

The alpine villages, as suggested by the time-sensitive artifacts form they contain, are dated between A.D. 600 and historic times. That the use of these sites persisted into early historic times is shown by the presence of historic glass beads at several sites. It is curious, therefore, that there is no mention of such villages in historic accounts. The most reasonable explanation is that, unlike Pinyon Pine camps in the White Mountains and lowland villages such as those that existed near the modern towns of Bishop and Big Pine, alpine villages ceased to be used almost immediately after contact. This idea is consistent with our present interpretation of the alpine village pattern and of its implications for late prehistoric human ecology in the White Mountains.

Fundamental to this interpretation is the observation that the alpine environment has always been marginal as a habitat for human use. Its best resources are game, and even they are difficult to exploit here. Plant resources are very sparse in comparison to those at lower elevations, and their exploitation under the best of circumstances could never have been much more than a "break-even" proposition; that is, the best that could be expected was to collect enough plants to supply daily needs, with a little left over to be set aside for winter use. In addition to this, the living conditions are miserable at these altitudes: it is cold and windy, there are violent hailstorms—even snowstorms—throughout the summer, and above 11,000 ft (3,350 m) there is little firewood. In addition to this, the lack of oxygen makes normal exertion difficult and causes various other physiological maladies. All these characteristics would seem to make the alpine environment less desirable as a base for summertime activity than the lowlands, where—although game is scarce in this season—plants are available in comparative profusion, oxygen, of course, is in good supply, and warm temperatures mean that only a little shade is needed to make life comfortable.

With so many apparently undesirable qualities in terms of resources available, the difficulty of their procurement, and the elaborate facilities needed as shelter if they were to be procured, the question naturally arises as to why alpine villages were used at all. It seems that the logical choice for aboriginal groups would have been to remain in the lowlands and gather plants there. Our current solution to this puzzle is that the appearance of alpine villages around A.D. 600 marks the point at which native populations had grown so large and had so pressured the resources available in the lowlands that groups could expect to do as well in the Alpine Zone, where they could hunt and gather in relative isolation, as they could in the lowlands, where they would have to compete with many other families for a dwindling set of plants and animals.

The White Mountains, then, are a sort of resource "pressure gauge." When, in central eastern California, aboriginal populations were relatively sparse and pressure on resources relatively low, only the best of the alpine resources—the large game— were exploited, and this exploitation was relatively brief, confined to short hunting trips. This is the early hunting pattern evident at hunting stations occupied between about 2500 B.C. and A.D. 600. When, on the other hand, the population was large, the pressure on resources was relatively high, and, as a consequence, alpine resources were used intensively; this use extended not only to the best resources (game) but also included less desirable ones that took longer to gather and process (roots and seeds). At the same time, the duration of this exploitation increased from a few days to several weeks.

This interpretation can be made more general in two senses. First, because we know from other evidence that humans have been in eastern California for about 10,000 years, the fact that there is no evidence of alpine land use until 2500 B.C. suggests that before then populations must have been at even lower resource levels—low enough that there was no need to track sheep and deer into their rugged summer rangelands, and certainly no need to contemplate the exploitation of plants in these habitats. The appearance of hunting stations in the White Mountains at 2500 B.C., then, is the first indication of any sort of resource pressure in central eastern California. If this line of reasoning is valid, populations must have continued to grow between 2500 B.C. and A.D. 600, for at the latter date two new settlement types appeared, each connected with upland plant resources: the Pinyon camp and the alpine village. The more intensive use of the uplands evident at these sites must reflect pressure on lowland resources that until then had been used to the exclusion of these mountain plants.

The second implication of this explanation is that around 1850, when the alpine villages were abandoned, something must have relieved the pressure on lowland resources. There is hardly any need to speculate what the source of that "relief" was.

Joseph Reddeford Walker entered Owens Valley in 1834. By 1861, the first permanent white settlement was established in Owens Valley. Disease and warfare followed, each taking its toll on the native population. At the same time, with the establishment of farms and ranches, alternative opportunities for native employment drew many from traditional hunting and gathering, further reducing pressure on natural resources. Thus, the abandonment of the alpine villages shortly after contact bears undeniable testimony to the disruption of the native system by forces outside that system. It may be that life in the alpine village was so unpalatable that they were abandoned without regret. Yet, whatever their hardships, in the broader context their abandonment meant the end of the native system in its entirety. It can hardly be argued that this colossal forfeiture was reasonably compensated simply because it carried the opportunity to spend the summer where it was warm rather than where it was cold.

REFERENCES

Bettinger, Robert L. 1975. The surface archaeology of Owens Valley, eastern California: Prehistoric man-land relationships in the great Basin. Ph.D. dissertation, University of California, Riverside.

Bettinger, Robert L. 1976. The development of pinyon exploitation in central eastern California. *Journal of California Anthropology* 3(1):81–95.

Bettinger, Robert L. 1977. Aboriginal human ecology in Owens Valley, eastern California: Prehistoric change in the Great Basin. *American Antiquity* 43(1):3–17.

Bettinger, Robert L. 1980. Obsidian hydration dates for Owens Valley settlement categories. *Journal of California and Great Basin Anthropology* 2(2):286–292.

Chalfant, W. A. 1933. *The story of Inyo*, 2d ed. Piñon Bookstore, Bishop, Calif.

Harrington, M. R. 1957. *A Pinto site at Little Lake, California.* Southwest Museum Papers, no. 17, Los Angeles.

Lanning, E. P. 1963. Archaeology of the Rose Spring site, Iny-372. *University of California Publications in American Archaeology and Ethnology* 49:237–336.

Leonard, Zenas. 1839. *Narrative of the adventures of Zenas Leonard, a native of Clearfield County, Pa., who spent five years in trapping for furs, trading with the Indians, & C., & C., of the Rocky Mountains.* D. W. Moore, Clearfield, Pa.

Meighan, C. W. 1955. Notes on the archaeology of Mono County, California. *University of California Archaeological Survey Reports* 28:6–28.

Riddell, H. 1951. Archaeology of a Paiute village site in Owens Valley. *University of California Archaeological Survey Reports* 12:14–28.

Steward, Julian H. 1933. Ethnography of the Owens Valley Paiute. *University of California Publications in American Archaeology and Ethnology* 33(3):233–350.

Steward, Julian H. 1934. Two Paiute autobiographies. *University of California Publications in American Archaeology and Ethnology* 33(5):423–438.

Glossary

aboriginal. Referring to the native inhabitants of any region.

accretion. Outbuilding of continental crust.

actinolite. A mineral, monoclinic amphibole similar to the mineral tremolite but iron-bearing; a typical formula is $Ca_2(MgFe)_5Si_8O_{22}(OH_2)$.

acuminate. Tapering to the apex, the sides more or less pinched in before reaching the tip. Compare *acute*.

acute. Tapering to the apex, with the sides straight or nearly so; usually less tapering than acuminate.

adiabatic. An atmospheric process in which descending air is compressed and warmed and ascending air expands and is cooled.

aeolian. Pertaining to the wind; especially said of such deposits as loess (windblown dust of Pleistocene age) and dune sand, of sedimentary structures such as wind-formed ripple marks, or of erosion and deposition accomplished by the wind.

aggregation. The collection of units or parts into a mass or whole.

akene. A small, dry, hard, one-seeded fruit that remains closed at maturity.

albite. Triclinic mineral of feldspar group, $NaAlSi_3O_8$, a variety of the mineral plagioclase.

alkali dust. Fine particles (salts) in desert soils that are concentrated on dry lake beds.

alkaline. Pertaining to substances with a pH greater than 7; basic.

allopatric. Occurring in different geographic regions.

alluvial deposits. Poorly consolidated sand, gravel, silt, and clay.

alluvial fan. An outspread, gently sloping mass of alluvium deposited by a stream, especially in an arid or semiarid region where a stream issues from a narrow canyon onto a plain or valley floor. Viewed from above, it has the shape of an open fan, with the apex at the valley mouth.

alluvial soil. A soil formed from materials deposited by moving water, as along a river bed.

alluvium. A general term for clay, silt, sand, gravel, or similar unconsolidated detrital material deposited by running water.

Alpine Fell-fields. The plant community at elevations above treeline, composed of cushion plants and other low perennials interspersed between large rock surfaces and presenting little exposure to the elements.

Alpine Steppe. Arid plant community above treeline.

alpine Tundra. See *Alpine Fell-fields*.

altocumulus. A principal cloud type that appears in many forms but is always considered a cloud of median height above the terrain, as opposed to a low (cumulus or stratus) or high (cirrus) cloud.

Amphisbaenia. An order of limbless, burrowing reptiles.

anaerobic. Lacking available free oxygen for processes such as respiration and metabolism.

anal fin. The median ventral fin located just posterior to the anus.

andalusite. Varicolored orthorhombic mineral (i.e., crystal system with three axes of symmetry that are mutually perpendicular), Al_2SiO_5. Metamorphic mineral formed at medium pressures and temperatures.

annealing. Recrystallization involving grain coarsening due to the long-term attendance of relatively high metamorphic temperatures.

anomaly. A deviation from the normal value for the same region (usually) in temperature or precipitation over a specified period.

antenna. Flexible appendage on head of arthropods, used for touching and smelling.

anther. The pollen-bearing part of the stamen. (See Fig. 6.1).

anthesis. The action or period of opening of a flower.

anticline, anticlinal. A fold, generally convex upward, whose core contains stratigraphically older rocks.

anticlinorium. A composite anticlinal structure of trough- and arch-shaped folds.

anticyclone. A large-scale atmospheric circulation in which the airflow is clockwise as viewed from above—the opposite direction to that of a cyclone.

apposite. Proceeding from opposite sides of a stem, as opposite leaves. (See Fig. 6.1).

appressed. Pressed flat against another organ or surface.

arachnid. A member of the Class Arachnida, characterized by the presence of one pair of preoral appendages with two or three joints (e.g., spiders, scorpions, mites, and ticks).

arc. Islands or mountains arranged in a great curve.

archaeology. The study of human lifeways by means of material remains.

arête. A rocky, sharp-edged ridge or spur, commonly present above the snowline in rugged mountains sculptured by glaciers, and resulting from the continued backward growth of the walls of adjoining cirques.

arthropods. Segmented invertebrates having jointed legs, such as insects and spiders.

artifact. Portable object modified by human agency.

assemblage. Relatively homogeneous group of fossils that recur at the same stratigraphic level.

atlatl. Spear thrower; an implement used to propel an arrowlike projectile or "dart."

attenuation. A reduction in the amplitude of a signal, seismic wave, or rock fold.

auditory. Pertaining to hearing.

aureole. A zone surrounding an igneous intrusion in which the country rock shows the effects of contact metamorphism.

avifauna. The species of breeding birds that inhabit a region; all species of birds generally present in a region at any season.

awl. A sharp, pointed bone or wood tool used in basket making.

axil. Upper angle formed by a leaf branch with the stem. (See Fig. 6.1.)

banner. Upper petal of a pealike flower. (See Fig. 6.1.)

basalt. A general term for a dark-colored igneous rock, commonly extrusive but locally as intrusive dikes (tubular igneous intrusions).

Basin and Range. Geomorphic province in eastern California and western Nevada; topography or landscape characterized by a series of tilted fault blocks.

biomass. The total mass or amount of living organisms in a particular area or volume.

biotite. Widely distributed rock-forming mineral of the mica group; layer-structure silicate containing essential potash, iron, magnesia, alumina, and H_2O in addition to silica; a typical formula is $K(Mg, Fe^{+2})_3(Al, Fe^{+3})Si_3O_{10}(OH)_2$.

bioturbated. Refers to sedimentary rocks that have been churned and stirred by organisms.

bipedal. Using two legs for locomotion.

boss. A swollen bump on the heads of certain toads.

bract. A reduced leaf subtending a flower, usually associated with an inflorescence.

breastwork. A small, curved rock wall, commonly used as a hunting blind.

buff. Medium to dark tan.

burred phrases. A trilled sequence of rough or gutteral sounds.

bursa. A small outpocketing or sac near the end of the digestive tube in a young bird.

caecilian. An order of limbless, burrowing amphibians occurring in the New and Old World tropics.

calcareous. Refers to limestone or soil impregnated with calcium.

calcic. Said of minerals and igneous rocks containing a high proportion of calcium.

caldera. A large, basin-shaped depression at the site of a volcano (e.g., Crater Lake, Oregon).

callosity, callosites. A hardened thickening.

calyx. The external, usually green, whorl of a flower, contrasted with the inner, showy corolla.

campanulate. Bell-shaped.

canescent. Covered with grayish-white or hoary fine hairs.

cap cloud. An apparently stationary cloud enveloping a peak or mountain range. It is formed by the cooling and condensation of humid air forced up the windward side of the mountain.

Carbon-14, ^{14}C. A heavy radioactive isotope of carbon produced in nature by the reaction of atmospheric nitrogen with cosmic rays. Incorporated into green plants with photosynthesis as $C^{14}O_2$, it decays at an approximately known rate, known as its half-life (which is 5,568 years) when the system is closed (i.e., the plant dies), allowing organic material to be dated.

carbonate. A mineral rich in CO_3^{-2} or sediment formed by the organic or inorganic precipitation of carbonate-rich compounds (e.g., limestone, dolomite).

carpel. One of the foliar units of a compound pistil or ovary; a simple pistil has one carpel. A foliar, usually ovule-bearing unit of a simple ovary.

carpellate. Pertaining to a flower with one or more carpels but no functional stamens; possessing or composed of carpels.

catkins. Hanging clusters of tiny flowers or bracts of willows, alders, and other plants.

centipede. Member of the Class Chilopoda. Centipedes usually have one pair of legs on each body segment.

cephalothorax. The part of the arachnid body that includes the head and the legs.

cercus (pl. cerci). Appendage located on the anal segment ("tail") of cockroaches and other insects.

Cheatgrass. Annual grass of the Genus *Bromus*.

chlorite. A layer-structure silicate mineral consisting of essential amounts of alumina, magnesia, iron, and H_2O, in addition to silica; its formula is approximately $(MgFe^{+2})_5Al_2Si_3O_{10}(OH)_8$.

cinder cone. A conical hill formed by the accumulation of volcanic cinders.

cirque. A deep, steep-walled recess or hollow, horseshoe-shaped or semicircular in plan view, situated high on the sides of a mountain and produced by the erosive activity of a mountain glacier.

cirrus. A principal type of cloud composed of ice crystals; usually the highest form of cloud observed.

clones. A population of cells or individuals derived by asexual division from a single cell or individual. (See also *vegetative reproduction*.)

cloud fall. The extension of the cap cloud down the leeward slope of a mountain range to the level where warming of the air causes the cloud particles to evaporate.

coalesced family groups. Several joined families.

col. A high, sharp-edged pass or saddle-like depression in a mountain range, especially one formed by the headward erosion of two cirque glaciers.

coleopteran. A member of the Order Coleoptera, beetles.

colluvial. Pertaining to loose and incoherent deposits, usually at the foot of a slope or cliff, brought there chiefly by gravity; clasts commonly angular in shape, with deposit poorly sorted.

compound eye. An eye composed of hundreds to thousands of tiny individual "eyes," occurring on insects and some other arthropods.

compound-fletched arrow. An arrow consisting of multiple, fitted segments to which feather vanes are affixed to promote stability in flight.

cone. The dry, compound fruit of pine, spruce, and other trees, consisting of overlapping scales (same as strobilus).

congener. A species in the same genus; closely related species.

conglomerate. A coarse-grained sedimentary rock composed of rounded to subangular fragments or rounded clasts.

conifer. A cone-bearing tree.

cordate. Of a conventional heart shape, the point apical.

cordierite. A blue orthorhombic (see *andalusite*) mineral, $(Mg_1 = e^{+2})_2Al_4Si_5$, commonly a low-pressure metamorphic mineral.

corm. A short, solid, bulblike underground stem, such as the "bulb" of Gladiolus.

cornice. An overhanging mass of snow above a steep leeward mountain slope.

corolla. The inner whorl of a flower, composed of colored petals that may be almost wholly united.

corymbose. Descriptive of a flat-topped flower cluster (corymb).

cotyledon. The primary leaf or leaves of a plant embryo.

covey. A flock or group, as applied to quail.

coxa. The leg segment closest to the body (See Fig. 7.3).

crenate. Toothed, with teeth rounded at apex.

Creosote Bush Scrub. Low-elevation Mojave Desert vegetation type, with Creosote Bush *(Larrea tridentata)* as the dominant species.

cross-bedding. Cross-stratification.

crustacean. A member of the Class Crustacea; any arthropod belonging to the Superclass Crustacea, characterized by the presence of two pairs of antennae on the head.

crustal compression/extension. Outermost layer or shell of the earth undergoing compression or extension.

cryoplanation surface. A relatively flat surface reduced by processes associated with intensive frost action supplemented by the actions of running water, moving ice, and other agents.

culm. The specialized stem of grasses, sedges, and rushes.

cumuliform. Like cumulus clouds, that is, dome- or tower-shaped as opposed to horizontal (stratiform).

cumulonimbus. Cumulus cloud commonly spread out in the shape of an anvil.

cuneate. Wedge-shaped; rather narrowly triangular, the acute angle downward.

cyclone. A large-scale atmospheric circulation in which the airflow is counterclockwise as viewed from above.

cyme. A flat-topped or convex paniculate flower cluster with central flowers opening first.

deadfall. A trap in which the prey (usually small) is killed by a falling stone or log.

debris flow. A moving mass of rock fragments, soil, and water, more than half of the particles larger than sand size, often the result of an intense thunderstorm and accompanying flash-flooding.

deciduous. Falling off at a certain season or stage of growth (e.g., plants with deciduous leaves as opposed to evergreens).

decoy. To attract by means of imitated sounds or models.

decurved. Curved downward or bent down.

defile. Narrow natural passages often favored as hunting locations.

deflexed. Turned abruptly downward (same as reflexed). (See Fig. 6.1.)

deltoid. Triangular leaf, attached at the center of one side.

demographics. Phenomena related to populations.

dendrochronologists. Scientists who study the record of information provided by trees and other woody plants in their ring structure or series.

dendrochronology. A dating method in which distinctive sequences of tree-ring widths are used to establish age.

dentate. Toothed, with the teeth directed outward; loosely used for any large teeth.

diapause. A period, usually longer than one month, in the life cycle of an organism during which the organism is quiescent.

dihedral. Having wings set off from the body at a distinct angle from the horizontal.

dimorphism. The existence of two size or color categories within a species, especially as occurs between the sexes.

dioecious. Flowers unisexual, having the male and female (or staminate and ovulate) elements on different individuals.

diopside. A mineral of the clinopyroxene group, $CaMg(SiO_3)_2$. Occurs as a mineral in contact metamorphism.

dipteran. A member of the Order Diptera, a two-winged fly.

discordant. Lack of parallelism between adjacent strata.

disjunct. Discontinuous, widely separated.

diurnal. Active during the day.

dolomite. 1. A common rock-forming mineral, $CaMg(CO_3)_2$. Part of the magnesium may be replaced by ferrous iron. Dolomite is white to light-colored and has perfect rhombohedral cleavage. 2. A sedimentary rock commonly interbedded with limestone.

dolomite barrens. Areas of dolomite that from a distance appear devoid of vegetation.

dorsal. Refers to the "back" or upper side of an organism.

duff. Organic material (predominantly needles and leaves) that accumulates beneath trees.

echolocation. A system bats use to locate flying prey by monitoring the patterns of high-frequency sound waves emitted by the bat.

ecofacts. Natural materials (e.g., stones, bones, seeds) used or transported but not physically modified by humans.

ecosystem. The system of ecological relationships on which a particular organism or group of organisms depends for existence. It may include such factors as weather, water, food, and predators.

edaphic. Pertaining to ecologic formations or effects resulting from or influenced by local conditions of the soil or substrate.

ejecta (volcanic tuff). Material thrown out from a volcano.

elytra. Hardened forewings of a beetle, covering the membranous hindwings.

emplacement. A term used to refer to the process of intrusion (e.g., emplacement of granitic rocks).

en echelon. In apparent formation or in rows oriented in about the same direction.

endangered. As defined in the Endangered Species Act of 1973, refers to any species or subspecies in danger of extinction throughout all or a significant portion of its range.

endemic. Restricted to a locality or region.

epidote. A green mineral, $Ca_2(Al, Fe^{+3})_3Si_3O_{12}(OH)$. Occurs in low-grade metamorphic rocks.

epiphenomena. A superficial or secondary phenomenon accompanying another and caused by it.

equitant. Two-ranked leaves, flattened, with edges toward and away from the axis; astride, as the leaves of an *Iris*; overlapping or "horseback" leaves.

erratic. A rock fragment transported by a glacier and deposited at some distance from where it was derived; generally, resting on bedrock of different lithology.

escarpment. A long, more or less continuous cliff or relatively steep slope produced by erosion or faulting.

ethnographic. Pertaining to aboriginal lifeways observed firsthand rather than reconstructed through archaeology.

exserted. Protruding, as stamens projecting beyond the corolla; not included, i.e., not protruded. (See Fig. 6.1.)

fanglomerates. Sedimentary rocks of heterogeneous materials that were originally deposited in an alluvial fan and have since become cemented (by carbonates or silica) into solid rock.

farinose. Covered with a meal-like powder.

fascicle. A bundle of pine leaves or other needle-like leaves of gymnosperms.

fault. A fracture or a zone of fractures along which there has been displacement of the sides relative to one another.

fauna. An entire animal population.

feature. A group of objects whose positioning relative to each other is due to human activity.

fell-field. Habitats above treeline supporting only low-growing, commonly sparse vegetation.

felsenmeer. An expanse of large blocks of rock produced by block separation along joints and shattering by frost action at high altitudes.

femur. A segment of an arthropod leg between the coxa and the tibia. (See Fig. 7.3.)

filiform. Threadlike; long, slender, and tapering at both ends.

flexuous. Gently zigzagging.

fluorite. A transparent to translucent varicolored mineral, CaF_2.

fluvial. Of or pertaining to rivers; produced by the action of a stream or river.

foehn. A warm, dry wind blowing down the side of a mountain.

foehn wall. The steep leeward boundary of clouds over a mountain range during foehn conditions; generally, the cap cloud and cloud fall considered together.

foliaceous. Leaflike, said especially of sepals or bracts that resemble leaves in texture or appearance.

forb. An herb or annual flowering plant, other than grass (e.g., small broad-leaved plants).

formation. A body of rock that is mappable and is continuous over a region.

galea. The helmetlike upper lip in certain two-lipped corollas, such as *Castilleja* sp. (Indian Paintbrush). (See Fig. 6.1.)

garnet. A complex group of minerals (e.g., almandine, andradite, grossular, pyrope) commonly present in metamorphic rocks.

garrulous. Noisy and active behavior that characterizes flocks of some birds.

gelifluction lobe. A tonguelike mass of debris, usually associated with periglacial conditions, where soil saturation occurs because frozen ground prevents the downward percolation of water. The melting of ice and snow saturates the surface zone, and soil flowage results.

geologic time scale. An arbitrary or relative chronologic arrangement of geologic events, commonly presented in chart form with the oldest event and time unit at the bottom and the youngest at the top.

geosyncline. A mobile downwarping of the crust of Earth.

glabrous. No hairs present at all; also used for *smooth.*

glacial till. Dominantly unsorted and unstratified drift, deposited directly by and underneath a glacier without reworking by meltwater.

glandular. Secreting sticky fluid; bearing glands, commonly on hairs.

glandular-hairy. A surface bearing both glands and hairs, the hairs commonly tipped with glandular secretion.

glaucous. Covered with a whitish or bluish waxy covering; loosely applied to any whitish surface.

gleaning. Picking from the surface of a plant or object.

glochids. A barbed hair or bristle, such as the minute bristles of Beavertail Cactus (*Opuntia* sp.).

glomerules. A dense cluster of flowers, usually small.

gonad cycle. The annual cycle of activity and inactivity of bird reproduction.

granite. 1. A plutonic or deep-seated rock in which quartz makes up 10 to 50% of the felsic (igneous rock having abundant light-colored minerals in its mode) components, and the alkali feldspar/total feldspar ratio is 65 to 90%. 2. Broadly applied, any holocrystalline quartz-bearing plutonic rock.

granitic soils/substrate. Soil derived from granitic rocks.

granodiorite. A group of coarse-grained plutonic rocks intermediate in composition between quartz diorite and quartz monzonite, containing quartz, oligocase or andesine, and potassium feldspar, with biotite and hornblende. It is the approximate equivalent of the intrusive rock rhyodacite.

graupel. Snow pellets, a form of frozen precipitation.

greenschist facies. A set of physical conditions attending the production of metamorphic rocks rich in the minerals albite, epidote, chlorite, and tremolite-actinolite (and rarely biotite).

grubs. Soft, thick, wormlike larvae of certain insects.

hafted. An object such as a stone knife blade that has been affixed to a handle to make it more serviceable.

halteres. Modified hindwings of a dipteran, used as balance organs during flight.

hemipteran. Member of the Order Hemiptera, true bugs that have mouthparts adapted for piercing and sucking and usually two pairs of wings during life cycle.

herb. A plant with no persistent woody stem aboveground.

herbaceous. Pertaining to an herb, opposed to woody; having the texture or color of a leaf; dying to the ground each year.

herpetologist. A person who studies amphibians and reptiles.

homopteran. Member of the Order or Suborder Homoptera, insects with sucking mouthparts (e.g., aphids).

horn sheath. Outer horn material, analagous in composition and origin to fingernail, that grows over a horn core made of bone. In contrast, an antler is entirely bone.

hybridize. To interbreed or cross two different races.

hymenopteran, hymenopteron. Member of the Order Hymenoptera, highly specialized insects with complete metamorphosis, including bees and ants.

hypersaline. High in salt content.

igneous. Said of a rock or mineral solidified from molten or partly molten material (a magma).

incisor. One of a set of cutting-adapted teeth at the front of the jaw.

inflected. Refers to songs or calls of birds characterized by a change in pitch or loudness.

inflected slurs. Bird calls or songs that smoothly change in pitch.

inflorescence. The disposition of flowers on an axis; the flower arrangement on a plant. (See Fig. 6.1.)

insectivorous. Insect-eating.

inselberg. An isolated residual knob or hill rising abruptly from a lowland erosion surface, especially in desert regions. It is characteristic of a late stage of the erosion cycle.

instar. The stage between moults of a larval or nymphal insect.

interfluve. The relatively undissected upland or ridge between adjacent streams flowing in the same general direction.

internasal scales. Scales between the nostrils.

internode. The portion of a stem between nodes. (See Fig. 6.1.)

introduced. Refers to a plant or animal brought in deliberately by man and growing in the area without cultivation. For example, an introduced fish may be "exotic" (from a foreign land) or "transplanted" (outside its native range but still within the country of origin).

intrusive. Pertaining to an intrusion (emplacement of magma in preexisting rock).

involucre. A whorl of bracts subtending a flower cluster, as in the heads of sunflowers. (See Fig. 6.1.)

isotope. One or more species of the same chemical element that vary in the number of neutrons in the nucleus.

keeled. Possessing a prominent ridge; also refers to the two lower and united petals of a pealike flower. (See Fig. 6.1.) In reptiles, refers to scales with a raised line down the middle.

lamina. The blade or expanded part of a petal or leaf.

lance-elliptic. Descriptive of a leaf shape that falls between lance-shaped and elliptic.

lanceolate. Lance-shaped; several times longer than wide, broadest toward the base and tapering to the apex.

languid. A leisurely or relaxed pace.

lapilli. Pyroclastic rock (volcanic ejecta) in the general size range of 2 to 64 mm.

lapse rate. The decrease of air temperature with height.

larva(e). A juvenile insect; usually does not look like the adult.

legume The fruit of a pealike flower; members of the Family or Superfamily Leguminosae.

leks. Tightly clumped assemblies of courting males to which females are attracted for mating.

lepidopteran. A member of the Order Lepidoptera, comprising the butterflies and moths, which possess wings covered with scales.

ligule. Strap-shaped or tongue-shaped; the straight-sided part of a flower ("petal") in the Chicory Tribe of the Aster (Sunflower) Family.

limestone. Rock composed chiefly of calcium carbonate; soils derived from those rocks.

lithospheric plate. A layer of the Earth that includes the crust and part of the upper mantle, approximately 100 km thick.

loam. An easily crumbled mixture of clay, silt, and sand; said of soil; usually favorable for plant growth.

macrofossils. A fossil large enough to be studied without the aid of a microscope or hand lens.

maggotlike. Refers to a wormlike larva with no legs or visible jaws.

magma. Naturally occurring hot mobile rock material, generated within the Earth.

magmatic stoping. Magmatic emplacement on intrusion that involves detaching and engulfing pieces of the country rock.

magnetite. A black, strongly magnetic, opaque mineral of the spinel group, $(Fe, Mg)Fe_2O_4$.

mandibles. The jaws of an insect.

mano. Small, hand-held stone used in seed grinding.

maxilla. An appendage on the insect head used for manipulating food, located behind the mandibles.

meloid. A member of the Family Meloidae, comprising beetles variable in form, head turned down, with leathery wing covers (e.g., Blister Beetle).

mesa. A plateau or tableland with steep sides.

mesic. Refers to an environment with an average or adequate supply of moisture for plant growth.

mesophyll. The ground tissue of a leaf, located between the layers of epidermis; mesophyll cells generally contain chloroplasts (plastids that contain chlorophyll).

mesoscale. Having to do with airflow patterns and atmospheric features with dimensions in the range of 1 to 100 mi or 1 to 150 km.

metabolic rate. The rate at which an animal oxidizes chemical products of food digestion and stored fats to produce energy.

metamorphism. A mineralogical, chemical, and structural adjustment of solid rocks to physical and chemical conditions imposed at depth.

metate. Flat or basin-shaped stone that serves as a platform in seed grinding.

metavolcanic. Volcanic rocks that show evidence of having been subjected to metamorphism.

mica. A complex group of phyllosilicate minerals, characterized by low hardness, and readily split into their plastic laminae.

microcline. A varicolored mineral of the alkali feldspar group, $KAISi_3O_8$, common in igneous rocks.

middens. Any organic debris deposited by an animal.

midrib. The central rib of a leaf. (See Fig. 6.1.)

millibar. Abbreviated mb, a unit used in reporting atmospheric pressure. For example, average sea-level pressure is 1,013.2 mb, 700 mb is near 10,000 ft, and 500 mb is usually between 18,000 and 19,000 ft.

millipede. A member of the Class Diplopoda, with cylindrical, segmented body, and two pairs of legs on most segments.

molt. The orderly replacement of feathers, hair, or scales.

monadnock. A hill rising conspicuously above the general level of the landscape, representing an isolated erosional remnant in an area that has been largely beveled to a flat plain or plateau.

monocot plant. Plant with parallel-veined leaves (e.g., lily, *Iris*).

monoecious. Having staminate and pistillate flowers on the same plant but not both in the same flower.

monsoon. A seasonal wind generally blowing from ocean to land in summer and in the opposite direction in winter.

montane. Pertaining to mountains.

moraine. A mound or ridge of unstratified glacial drift, chiefly glacial till, deposited by the direct action of glacier ice.

moult. The process in which an arthropod sheds its old skin and hardens the new one underneath.

natal. Pertaining to an animal's birth.

nectary. An organ that secretes or contains nectar.

nocturnal. Active at night.

normal fault. A fault in which the hanging wall (rocks above the fault plane) have moved downward relative to the footwall (rocks below the fault plane).

numu. Word meaning "the people," used by Numic speakers referring to themselves as a group.

nunatak. An isolated knob or peak of bedrock that projects prominently above the surface of a glacier and is surrounded by glacier ice; sculpted by periglacial processes.

nymph. A juvenile insect, usually somewhat resembling the adult of the species.

nymphalid. A member of the Family Nymphalidae, medium-sized butterflies (e.g., Monarch Butterfly, Mourning Cloak, Buckeye, Red Admiral).

oblanceolate. Inversely lanceolate.

obovate. Reverse of ovate, the terminal half broader. (See Fig. 6.1.)

obsidian. A naturally occurring glass of volcanic origin.

obsidian hydration. Dating method in which the thickness of a microscopic "hydration" layer is used to determine the age of a piece of obsidian.

opportunistic. Taking advantage of what is available.

order of magnitude. Refers to a hierarchy of relative size, with each class about 10 times the size of the next smaller class. Features that have characteristic dimensions such as 10, 100, 1,000 and 10,000 mi are said to be of different orders of magnitude.

orogeny. Process of formation of mountains.

orographic. Pertaining to or caused by mountains.

orthopteran. A member of the Order Orthoptera, insects with biting mouthparts, two pairs of wings or none (e.g., crickets and grasshoppers).

ovary. The part of the pistil that contains the ovules. (See Fig. 6.1.)

ovate. The shape of an outline of a hen's egg, the broader end downward.

ovipositor. A pointed organ located on the anal segment ("tail") of an arthropod, used for laying eggs.

ovoid. Solid ovate or solid oval.

oxidation. A biochemical reaction in which a molecule loses an electron, commonly through addition of an oxygen atom, and during which energy is released.

Paiute. A term loosely applied to certain native Numic-speaking peoples. Also spelled Piute. The native Owens Valley peoples are more properly called Mono.

palmate. Describes a leaf with lobes or divisions attached or running down toward one place at the base.

palp. Short appendage located on the head and mouthparts of an arthropod.

panicle. A compound racemose inflorescence.

pappus. A crown of bristles (hairlike) or scales on the summit of the akene in the Aster (Sunflower) Family. Some forms have only a shallow crown. (See Fig. 6.1.)

parching. A step in seed preparation in which seeds are made more edible and susceptible to grinding by heating them with live embers.

parotid gland. Large, swollen glandular area lying behind the head.

parthenogenic. Bearing young from unfertilized eggs.

passerines. Species of the Order Passeriformes, the perching birds (e.g., pigeons).

pedicel. The stalk of a single flower.

peduncle. The stalk of a flower or cluster of flowers.

peirid. A member of the Family Pieridae, butterflies, mostly medium-sized (e.g., Cabbage Butterfly, Dogface, "sulphurs").

pelage. Fur coat.

perched alluvial fan. See *alluvial fan;* section of fan, usually uplifted above surface of contemporary stream.

perennial. Lasting from year to year.

perianth. The petals and sepals taken together. Used particularly when the outer and inner portions of the floral envelope cannot be distinguished.

periglacial. 1. Said of the processes, conditions, areas, climate, and topographic features at the immediate margins of glacier ice sheets and influenced by the cold temperature of the ice. 2. By extension, said of an environment in which frost action is an important factor or of phenomena induced by a periglacial climate beyond the periphery of the ice.

petiole. A leaf stalk. (See Fig. 6.1.)

phyllaries. Individual bracts of the involucre of a flower head in the Aster Family. (See Fig. 6.1.)

physiognomy. The physical structure of the plant community; growth forms of plants composing the vegetation.

pinnate. Describes a compound leaf having leaflets arranged on each side of a common petiole or leaf stalk.

Pinyon Woodland. Lower-elevation montane plant community dominated by an overstory of Pinyon Pine (*Pinus monophylla*).

Pinyon-juniper Woodland. A mid-elevation desert habitat.

pistil. The ovule-bearing organ of a flower, consisting of a stigma, style (elongated part of pistil), and ovary.

pistillate. Provided with pistils and without stamens; female.

plagioclase. A complex mineral group, $(Na, Ca)Al(Si, Al)SiO_2$, including the rock-forming minerals albite, oligoclase, andesine, labradorite, and anorthite.

planation surface. A fundamentally flat or level surface created by processes of erosion.

planted. A general term used to describe the introduction of fish into a body of water, usually from a fish hatchery.

plate rifting. The process in which two of the Earth's plates spread apart and new crust is created between them.

Pleistocene. An epoch of the Quaternary Period, following the Pliocene Epoch of the Tertiary Period and before the Holocene. It began about 1.7 million years ago and lasted until the start of the Holocene, some 10,000 years ago.

plumose antennae. Featherlike antennae.

polygamous. Bearing unisexual and bisexual flowers on the same plant.

polyploidy. An animal possessing more than two sets of chromosomes.

Precambrian. Geologic time and time-rock term, before the beginning of the Paleozoic Era (ca. 570 million years ago); includes about 90% of geologic time.

proleg. A leglike appendage on an insect larva, not jointed like a true arthropod leg.

pro-talus rampart. An arcuate ridge of angular rocks originating from a cliff or steep rocky slope above and marking the downslope edge of an existing or melted snowbank. The rocks accumulate at the edge of the snowbank, some distance beyond any talus near the base of the cliff.

puberulent. Minutely pubescent.

pubescent. Covered with soft hairs; downy.

pumice. A light-colored, glassy rock.

quadrant. The area within a 90° arc; for example, the southwest quadrant encompasses the area between south and west.

quadrupedal. Using four legs for locomotion.

quartzite. A metamorphic rock consisting mainly of quartz, formed by recrystallization of sandstone by regional or thermal metamorphism; a metaquartzite or metamorphosed quartzite is referred to as an orthoquartzite.

Quaternary. Period of the Cenozoic Era of relative geologic time, following the Tertiary Period; also, the corresponding system of rocks. It began 1.7 million years ago and extends to the present. It consists of two epochs: the Pleistocene and the Holocene, or Recent.

raceme. A simple, elongated inflorescence with each flower about equally pedicelled. (See Fig. 6.1.)

racemose. Of the nature of a raceme or in racemes.

rachis. The axil of a spike or raceme or of a compound leaf. (See Fig. 6.1.)

radiocarbon. See *carbon-14.*

radiometric dating. Calculating an age in years for geologic materials by measuring the presence of a short-life radioactive element (e.g., carbon-14 or potassium/argon–40).

raptor. A bird of prey, such as an eagle, hawk, falcon, or owl.

rawinsonde. A device attached to a helium-filled balloon that, as it ascends, relays radio signals of atmospheric pressure, temperature, and humidity readings while it is being tracked by radar to determine wind velocity at various levels.

reflexed. Abruptly bent downward; deflexed. (See Fig. 6.1.)

regenerated tail. A broken tail that has regrown.

regime. A predominant or characteristic spatial or temporal (seasonal) pattern, as in rainfall.

regolith. A general term for the layer of unconsolidated rock material or debris that forms the surface of the land and overlies bedrock.

relict. An individual or group remaining on the site of a once-larger population; may pertain to plants or animals, or even soils and other geologic features.

resinous. Containing resin or having the shining appearance of being resin-coated.

resonance. The phenomenon of amplification of an atmospheric wave by a forced wave imposed by a boundary condition such as the shape of the terrain profile in the form of parallel mountain ranges.

reticulate. A color pattern consisting of linear markings resembling the meshes of a net.

reverse fault. An inclined fault in which the rocks above the hanging wall (above the fault plane) have moved up relative to those below the foot wall (below the fault plane).

rhizome. An underground stem or rootstock that roots as it progresses, commonly described as running rootstock; a type of rootstock with scales at the nodes that become leafy shoots above.

ridge. An anticyclonic (clockwise) bend in the horizontal airflow pattern in the synoptic (weather map) scale.

rime icing. An opaque formation of ice formed by the rapid freezing of supercooled water drops as they impinge upon a solid object.

riparian. Descriptive of plants located on watercourses or along bodies of water.

roche moutonée. A glacially sculpted knob of bedrock with its long axis oriented in the direction of ice movement; the upstream side is gently inclined, rounded, and striated, with the downstream side steeper and fragmented by plucking. Mountains shaped like sheep (French).

roll cloud. The turbulent cumuliform cloud in the crest of a lee wave; generally forms near or somewhat above mountaintop level.

root crown. An enlarged, commonly woody structure formed at the junction of the root and the stem.

rostral scale. The scale at the tip of the snout.

runway. Pathway used repeatedly by some small rodents.

saline. Salty; pertaining to soil or water rich in soluble salts.

salverform. A corolla with a slender tube abruptly expanding into a flat border, as in phlox. (See Fig. 6.1.)

samara. Simple, dry, one-seeded or two-seeded winged fruit.

sandstone. A cemented or otherwise compacted sedimentary rock, commonly composed of quartz grains of sand size (0.6–2 mm).

sapsucker borings. Sap-producing holes drilled in trees by woodpeckers of the Genus *Sphyrapicus.*

scapolite. A complex group of aluminum-silicate minerals, commonly in calcium-rich metamorphic rocks.

scorpioid. A one-sided inflorescence gently coiled at the end like the tail of a scorpion. (See Fig. 6.1.)

scurfy. Clothed with small, branlike scales.

sedentary. Tending to stay quietly in one place.

sedges. A group of plants resembling grasses; solid stems; grasses with hollow stems.

sedimentary. Pertaining to or containing sediment (e.g., sedimentary rock).

seleniferous soil. Soil containing the element selenium.

semiserotinous. Refers to cones that open slowly, releasing seeds over a prolonged time period. Seed shed may be induced by fire.

sepal. A segment of the calyx; the outer whorl of a flower. (See Fig. 6.1.)

sequence. A succession of geologic events, processes, or rocks arranged in chronologic order to show their relative positions.

serrulate. Serrate with small teeth.

serviceberry. Tree or shrub of the Genus *Amelanchier* (Family Rosaceae).

sessile. Attached directly at the base, not stalked, as a leaf without a petiole.

setpoint. A point (e.g., temperature) at which a feedback system attempts to maintain itself, such as the temperature setting on a home heating system.

settlement category. Class of settlement used by aboriginal peoples. Base camps and Pinyon camps are two of many categories of settlement used by the aboriginal peoples of eastern California.

settlement system. An organized pattern of aboriginal land use that incorporates one or more settlement categories.

shadscale. Common name for *Atriplex confertifolia,* a common desert shrub in the Chenopodiaceae.

Shadscale Zone. Semidesert community grown to saltbush or shadscale (Genus *Atriplex*).

shale. A fine-grained, detrital, sedimentary rock formed by the compaction of clay, silt, or mud. It is finely laminated and splits readily. Shale is well indurated but not as hard as argillite or slate. It may be red, brown, black, or gray.

silicle. A short silique, not much longer than wide.

silique. A narrow, many-seeded capsule, much longer than wide, usually in the Mustard Family.

sillimanite. An orthorhombic (see *andalusite*) mineral, Al_2SiO_5; forms at the highest temperatures and pressures of a regionally metamorphosed sequence.

siltstone. Sedimentary rock composed of silt, having the texture of shale but lacking fine laminations.

site. Literally, any place used by humans for activity as reflected by the presence of artifacts and features (see *artifact, feature*).

slate. A compact, fine-grained metamorphic rock that can be split into slabs.

solifluction. The slow downslope movement of waterlogged soil; includes the flow occurring at high elevations in regions underlain by frozen ground acting as a downward barrier to water percolation; initiated by frost action and augmented by meltwater resulting from alternate freezing and thawing of snow and ground ice. (See also *gelifluction lobe.*)

spathelike. Having the appearance of a broad, sheathing bract, as in the Calla Lily.

spatulate. Spatula-shaped; rounded above and gradually narrowing to the base, broader in the upper half. (See Fig. 6.1.)

spinescent. More or less spiny.

spur. A slender projection from a petal or sepal.

squamate. Covered with scales.

stamen. The part of the flower producing the pollen, composed (usually) of anther and filament.

staminate. Having stamens but not pistils, said of a male flower or plant (hence not seed-bearing).

stellate-pubescent. Having a coat of fine, star-shaped, branched hairs.

stigma. The receptive part of the pistil, on which the pollen germinates.

stipe. The stalk beneath an ovary.

stoloniferous. Having stolons, that is, modified stems that bend over and root at the nodes.

stomate. A small opening on the surface of a leaf through which gaseous exchange takes place.

stoops. Long dives by birds (e.g., raptors) either in combat, in courtship, or in pursuit of prey.

strap-shaped. In the form of a narrow, flat strip with straight sides.

strata. Plural of *stratum,* which is a tubular or sheetlike body or layer.

stratigraphic. Refers to layered rocks.

stratocumulus. A common low cloud type that is predominantly horizontal with cumuliform lumps.

stratus. A principal low cloud type that is nearly horizontal, commonly obscures higher terrain, and consists of water droplets.

striate. Marked with fine, longitudinal lines or furrows.

stridulation. Buzzing, trilling, or scratching sound.

strip-bark growth. Concentration of the living cambium and bark along one upright section of the tree trunk, with wood exposed along the remainder of the trunk; characteristic of conifers living in the Subalpine Zone.

subduction. The process of one lithospheric plate (crustal layer) descending beneath another.

subglabrous. With almost no hairs present or almost smooth; usually pertains to leaf surface.

subspecies. A group of organisms ranked below a species.

substrate. The surface an animal clings to or walks on; the substance, base, or nutrient on which, or the medium in which, an organism lives and grows, or the surface to which a fixed organism is attached (e.g., soil, rocks, leaves).

subtended. Below and close to.

subterminal. Almost terminal in position.

succession. A series of strata that succeed one another in chronologic order.

succulent. Juicy, fleshy, somewhat soft.

supercooled. Refers to cloud particles that remain in liquid form at temperatures below freezing (i.e., lower than 32°F or 0°C).

supraocular scales. Scales above the eyes.

symbiotic. Refers to organisms that live in continuous beneficial contact with one another.

sympatric. Occurring together in one locality or region.

synclinal. A fold the core of which contains the stratigraphically younger rocks.

synoptic. Pertaining to an overall view at a given instant; in meteorology, it usually refers to weather maps resulting from analyses of observations and measurements made at the same time at many locations.

Tahoe event. A period of glaciation in the Sierra Nevada, occurring at the same time as the Perry Aiken glaciation in the White Mountains, approximately 18,000–140,000 years before the present. Questionably correlated with the midcontinental Illinoian glaciation.

talisman. Object believed to possess supernatural or magical properties.

talus. Accumulations of unstable rock fragments below steep slopes or cliffs.

taproot. A primary stout, vertical root that gives off small laterals but does not divide.

tarsus. The segment at the tip of the arthropod leg. (See Fig. 7.3.)

taxonomic rearrangement. An alternative classification scheme of a group of animals or plants.

tectonic. Pertaining to the rock structure and external forms resulting from the deformation of the Earth's crust.

tepals. Petal-like sepals, as in the buckwheats.

tephra. A collective term for all clastic materials ejected from a volcano and transported through the air, including volcanic dust, ash, cinders, lapilli, scoria, pumice, bombs, and blocks.

terete. Circular in cross section and more or less elongated; cylinder shape may be slightly tapering.

ternate. Arranged in threes.

terrigenous. Derived from the land or continent.

thorax. The section of the arthropod body to which the legs are attached. (See Fig. 7.3.)

threatened. As defined in the Endangered Species Act of 1973, refers to any species or subspecies likely to become endangered within the foreseeable future throughout all or a significant part of its range.

thrust (fault). A reverse fault in which the inclination to the horizontal is $45°$ or less.

tibia. A leg segment between the femur and the tarsus. (See Fig. 7.3.)

Tioga event. The most recent glaciation of the Sierra Nevada, occurring the same time as the Middle Creek glaciation of the White Mountains, approximately 24,000–12,000 years before the present. Equivalent to the late Wisconsin glaciation of the midcontinent.

toposcale. Refers to phenomena that are closely related to topographic influences and are intermediate in size between mesoscale and microscale.

tor. A high, isolated crag, pinnacle, or rocky peak; commonly formed through periglacial processes.

torpor. Physiological dormancy in warm-blooded animals through lowered body temperature.

tourmaline. A complex group of silicate minerals; commonly associated in igneous rocks and occurring as three-, six-, or nine-sided prisms.

transcurrent fault. A large-scale, strike-slip fault (movement parallel to trend of fault).

tremolite. A monoclinic (i.e., crystal system characterized by either a single or twofold axis of symmetry) mineral of the amphibole group, $Ca_2Mg_5Si_8O_{22}(OH)_2$.

trend. The general term for the direction or bearing of a geological feature.

tribe. The division of a plant family. The large families are commonly divided into tribes.

tridentate. Having three teeth at the apex.

trilobite. An extinct marine arthropod belonging to the Class Trilobita, characterized by a three-lobed (head, middle body, and posterior, or tail) ovoid exoskeleton.

trimodal maximum. Having three nearly equal temporal peaks in the annual distribution of quantity, as for precipitation.

trough. A cyclonic (counterclockwise) bend in the horizontal airflow pattern in the synoptic (weather map) scale.

truncate. Squared at the tip or base as if cut off with a straight blade.

tumpline. Beltlike strap fitted to the head to aid in carrying heavy objects or to permit the free use of hands.

turbinate. Top-shaped, inversely conical.

turfy. Descriptive of a piece of soil bound by roots into a thick mat.

umbel. A flower cluster in which the pedicels come from a common point, like the rays of an umbrella. (See Fig. 6.1.)

understory. Plants beneath the tree canopy in woodland or forest, commonly composed of shrubs, herbs, and juvenile trees.

ungulate. A hooved grazing animal.

uplift. A structurally high area in the crust, produced by positive movements that raise or thrust the rocks upward.

uranium fission. A geological dating method in which the splitting of the nucleus of a uranium atom results in the emission of energy and physical damage to the mineral structure. The number of fission tracks (damaged paths) is indicative of time.

vagrant. An animal occurring outside of its normal distribution.

valve. One of the segments into which a capsule or pod separates, as in the Pea and Mustard families.

vascular. The higher plants, having specialized conducting systems that include xylem (inner two wood elements) and phloem (outer of two tissues).

vegetative reproduction. In seed plants, reproduction by means other than seeds. In other organisms, reproduction by vegetative spores, fragmentation, or division of the somatic cells (cells of the body that compose tissues, organs, and other parts of the individual). Unless a mutation occurs, each daughter cell or individual is genetically identical with its parent. (See also *clones.*)

ventral. Pertains to the underside, or belly, of an organism.

ventral (pelvic) fins. Paired fins located ventrally anterior to the anus.

vermiculations. Wavy, wormlike markings on the back of Eastern Brook Trout (char).

vermiform. Worm-shaped or wormlike.

volcanic tuff. Fine detritus of volcanic rock fused by heat.

voracious. Having a very large appetite.

wall rock. The rock mass making up the wall of a fault or the rock forming the walls of a vein or mineral deposit.

whorl. A ring of similar organs radiating from a node, as a whorl of leaves.

wind shear. Abrupt change in wind velocity (direction and speed) with height or horizontal distance.

wing. A thin, usually transparent or papery extension bordering an organ, as a winged seed; also, a lateral petal of a pealike flower, e.g., Family Fabaceae.

winnowing. A step in seed processing in which wind and/or gravity are used to separate seeds from unwanted plant material, such as chaff.

xeric. Arid-adapted.

xerophytic. Having to do with xerophytes, plants that lose very little water and can grow in deserts or in very dry conditions.

Index